McGraw-Hill Ryerson

ON Science 9

Authors

Leesa Blake
B.Sc., B.Ed., M.A.
Toronto District School Board

Michael Mazza
B.Sc.
Science Writer and Consultant

Alex Mills
B.Sc., M.Sc., LL.B., Ph.D.
Science Consultant and Writer

Frank Mustoe
B.Sc., B.Ed., M.Ed., Ph.D.
Former Science Coordinator
University of Toronto Schools

Jim Ross
B.Sc., B.Ed., M.Ed.
Science Writer and Consultant

Thomas Stiff
B.Sc., M.Sc., Ph.D.
Lakehead University, Orillia Campus

Contributing Authors

Katherine Hamilton
B.Sc., Ph.D.
Science Writer

Natasha Marko
B.Sc., M.Sc., M.A.
Science Writer

Jennifer Parrington
B.Sc., B.Ed.
York Region District School Board

Betty R. Robinson
Science Writer

Program Consultant

Steve Bibla
B.Sc., B.Ed.
Toronto District School Board

Curriculum and Pedagogical Consultant

Tigist Amdemichael
B.Sc., B.A., B.Ed., M.Ed.
Toronto District School Board

Assessment Consultant

Anu Arora
B.Sc. (Hons.), M.Sc., B.Ed.
Peel District School Board

Literacy and Environmental Education Consultant

Steve Bibla
B.Sc., B.Ed.
Toronto District School Board

Consultant

Trudy L. Rising

Aboriginal Consultants

Chris Craig
South Nation Conservation Authority
Member of the Algonquins of
Pikwakanagan

Francis McDermott
Shabot Obaadjiwan Algonquin First Nation
Nibina Forestry

Differentiated Instruction Consultant

Jennifer Parrington
B.Sc., B.Ed.
York Region District School Board

ELL Consultants

Maureen Innes
B.A.
Nipissing University

Wendy Campbell
B.A., B.Ed.
Waterloo Region District School Board

Al Tordjman
B.A., B.Ed.
Waterloo Region District School Board

Advisors

Anjuli Ahooja
B.Sc. (Hons.), M.Sc., Ph.D.
Curriculum Chair, Science and Technology
Appleby College

J. Randy Attwood
B.Sc. (Physics)
Science Writer, Astronomy and Space
Education Specialist, and Consultant

Christina Clancy
B.Sc. (Hons.), M.Sc., B.Ed.
Dufferin-Peel Catholic District School Board

Lea Francis
B.Sc.F., Dip.RM., B.Ed.
York Region District School Board

Craig Jackson
B.Sc., B.Ed., D.Met.
Independent Learning Centre, TVO
Formerly of Kapuskasing District High School

Frank Mustoe
B.Sc., B.Ed., M.Ed., Ph.D.
Former Science Coordinator
University of Toronto Schools

Paul Passafiume
B.A.Sc., B.Ed.
York Region District School Board

Rob Smythe
B.Sc., B.Ed., M.Sc.(T)
Halton District School Board

McGraw-Hill Ryerson

Toronto Montréal Boston Burr Ridge, IL Dubuque, IA Madison, WI New York San Francisco
St. Louis Bangkok Bogotá Caracas Kuala Lumpur Lisbon London Madrid Mexico City
Milan New Delhi Santiago Seoul Singapore Sydney Taipei

McGraw-Hill Ryerson

ON Science 9

ISBN-13: 978-0-07-072689-5
ISBN-10: 0-07-072689-2

4 5 6 7 8 9 TCP 1 9 8 7 6 5 4 3 2

Printed and bound in Canada

PUBLISHER: Diane Wyman
PROJECT MANAGER: Pronk & Associates (Jane McNulty)
DEVELOPMENTAL EDITORS: Pronk & Associates (Michelle Anderson, Kathy Hamilton, Betty Robinson, Gary Von Euer)
MANAGING EDITOR: Crystal Shortt
COPY EDITORS: Linda Jenkins, Paula Pettitt-Townsend
PHOTO RESEARCH/PERMISSIONS: Pronk&Associates
ART BUYING: Pronk&Associates
REVIEW COORDINATOR: Jennifer Keay
EDITORIAL ASSISTANT: Michelle Malda
MANAGER, PRODUCTION SERVICES: Yolanda Pigden
PRODUCTION COORDINATOR: Sheryl MacAdam
SET-UP PHOTOGRAPHY: Dave Starrett
COVER/INTERIOR DESIGN: Pronk&Associates
ELECTRONIC PAGE MAKE-UP: Pronk&Associates

Acknowledgements

Pedagogical Reviewers

Dave Black
Upper Canada District School Board
Brockville, Ontario

Susan Bouwer
Grand Erie District School Board
Brantford, Ontario

Nadia Camara
York Region District School Board
Richmond Hill, Ontario

Erin Connelly
Ottawa Catholic School Board
Kanata, Ontario

Cynthia M. de Souza
York Catholic District School Board
Aurora, Ontario

Katy Farrow
Thames Valley District School Board
London, Ontario

Monica Franciosa
York Catholic District School Board
Richmond Hill, Ontario

Patricia Gaspar
York Region District School Board
King City, Ontario

Vijay Gulati
Toronto District School Board
Toronto, Ontario

John Hallett
Peel District School Board
Caledon, Ontario

Stephen Jacobs
Dufferin-Peel Catholic District
  School Board
Mississauga, Ontario

Michele Laframboise
London District Catholic School Board
St. Thomas, Ontario

Benjamin Law
York Region District School Board
Unionville, Ontario

Beth Lisser
Peel District School Board
  (North Field Office)
Brampton, Ontario

Sharon MacLachlan
Ottawa Catholic School Board
Kanata, Ontario

Annette Nelson-Szpak
Greater Essex County District
  School Board
Windsor, Ontario

Robert J. Noble
Toronto Catholic District School Board
Toronto, Ontario

Kamla Kerry-Ann Reid
York Region District School Board
Unionville, Ontario

Bob Roddie
Hamilton-Wentworth Catholic District
  School Board
Hamilton, Ontario

Julie Silvestri
Hamilton-Wentworth Catholic District
  School Board
Hamilton, Ontario

Frank Villella
Hamilton-Wentworth Catholic District
  School Board
Hamillton, Ontario

Nathan Volkmann
London District Catholic School Board
St. Thomas, Ontario

Accuracy Reviewers

Jenna Dunlop (Unit 1)
Ph.D., M.B.A.
Science Writer
Toronto, Ontario

R. Tom Baker (Unit 2)
B.Sc., (Hons.), Ph.D.
Canada Research Chair in Catalysis
  Science for Energy Applications
Director, Centre for Catalysis Research
  and Innovation
University of Ottawa
Ottawa, Ontario

Paul Delaney (Unit 3)
B.Sc. (Hons.), M.Sc.
Senior Lecturer, Dept. of Physics
  and Astronomy
Director, Division of Natural Science
York University
Toronto, Ontario

Doug Roberts (Unit 4)
Ed.D., Ph.D. (Hon.)
Professor Emeritus, University of Calgary
Calgary, Alberta

T.J. Elgin Wolfe (Unit 4)
M.Ed.
Professor, Ontario Institute for Studies
  in Education
University of Toronto
Toronto, Ontario

Safety Reviewer

Jim Agban
Past Chair, STAO Safety Committee
Mississauga, Ontario

Lab Testers

Lea Francis
York Region District School Board
King City, Ontario

Benjamin Law
York Region District School Board
Unionville, Ontario

Renee Platt
Toronto Catholic District School Board
Toronto, Ontario

Julie Silvestri
Hamilton Wentworth Catholic District
 School Board
Hamilton, Ontario

Bias Reviewer

Nancy Christoffer
Scarborough, Ontario

Literacy Reviewer

Joanie McCormick
Upper Grand District School Board
Fergus, Ontario

**Special Features and
Toolkit Writers**

J. Randy Attwood

Nancy Christoffer

Jenna Dunlop

Laura Edlund

Patricia Gaspar

Eric Jandciu

Natasha Marko

Paul McNulty

Craig Saunders

Study Toolkit Writer

Kelly Stern

Unit Project Writers

Christina Clancy

Alex Mills

Mary Kay Winter

Student Advisory Panel

The authors, editors, and publisher of
ON Science 9 extend special thanks
to the students of Sinclair Secondary
School in the Durham District School
Board and St. Aloysius Gonzaga
Secondary School in the Dufferin Peel
Catholic School Board for their guidance
in the development of this learning
resource.

Set-up Photography

We are very grateful to Lea Francis of
King City Secondary School for her
assistance in facilitating the set-up
photography session.

Contents

Exploring *ON Science 9*. xii
Safety in your Science Classroom. xiv

Unit 1 Sustainable Ecosystems. xviii
Get Ready for Unit 1. 2

Chapter 1 Nutrient Cycles and Energy Flow. 4
1.1 Sustainability. 7
1.2 The Biosphere and Energy. 21
1.3 Extracting Energy from Biomass. 28
Chapter 1 Summary. 43
Chapter 1 Review. 44

Chapter 2 Populations and Sustainable Ecosystems. 46
2.1 Populations and Resources. 49
2.2 Interactions Among Species. 56
2.3 Human Niches and Population. 65
2.4 Ecosystem Services. 69
Chapter 2 Summary. 83
Chapter 2 Review. 84

Chapter 3 Biodiversity. 86
3.1 Measuring Biodiversity. 89
3.2 Communities. 95
3.3 Threats to Biodiversity. 100
3.4 Restoration Ecology. 110
Chapter 3 Summary. 121
Chapter 3 Review. 122

Unit 1 Science at Work. 124
Unit 1 Projects. 126
Unit 1 Review. 128

Unit 2 Atoms, Elements, and Compounds.........132
Get Ready for Unit 2 134

Chapter 4 Properties of Elements and Compounds 136
4.1 Studying Matter................................139
4.2 Physical Properties............................149
4.3 Chemical Properties............................160
Chapter 4 Summary 173
Chapter 4 Review 174

Chapter 5 Understanding the Properties of Elements 176
5.1 Evolution of the Atomic Model 179
5.2 The Structure of the Atom.....................187
5.3 The Periodic Table 194
5.4 Trends in the Periodic Table 207
Chapter 5 Summary 215
Chapter 5 Review 216

Chapter 6 Understanding the Properties of Compounds.......218
6.1 Ionic Compounds 221
6.2 Molecular Compounds..........................232
6.3 Modelling Compounds 242
Chapter 6 Summary 253
Chapter 6 Review 254

Unit 2 Science at Work 256
Unit 2 Projects..................................258
Unit 2 Review 260

Unit 3 The Study of the Universe 264

Get Ready for Unit 3 266

Chapter 7 The Night Sky 268

7.1   Ancient Astronomy 271
7.2   The Constellations 277
7.3   Movements of Earth and the Moon 283
7.4   Meet Your Solar System 291
7.5   Other Objects in the Solar System 297
Chapter 7 Summary 311
Chapter 7 Review 312

Chapter 8 Exploring Our Stellar Neighbourhood 314

8.1   Exploring Space 317
8.2   Exploring the Sun 333
8.3   Exploring Other Stars 341
Chapter 8 Summary 355
Chapter 8 Review 356

Chapter 9 The Mysterious Universe 358

9.1   Galaxies 361
9.2   The Universe 368
9.3   Unsolved Mysteries 377
Chapter 9 Summary 385
Chapter 9 Review 386

Unit 3 Science at Work 388
Unit 3 Projects 390
Unit 3 Review 392

Unit 4 The Characteristics of Electricity 396

Get Ready for Unit 4 398

Chapter 10 Static Charges and Energy 400
10.1 Exploring Static Charges 403
10.2 Charging by Contact and by Induction 411
10.3 Charges at Work 418
Chapter 10 Summary 431
Chapter 10 Review 432

Chapter 11 Electric Circuits 434
11.1 Cells and Batteries 437
11.2 Electric Circuits: Analogies and Characteristics 446
11.3 Measuring the Properties of Simple Circuits 455
11.4 Measuring Electrical Resistance 462
11.5 Series and Parallel Circuits 468
Chapter 11 Summary 479
Chapter 11 Review 480

Chapter 12 Generating and Using Electricity 482
12.1 Electricity at Home 485
12.2 Using Electrical Energy Wisely 492
12.3 Meeting the Demand for Electricity 501
12.4 Sustainable Sources of Electricity 506
Chapter 12 Summary 517
Chapter 12 Review 518

Unit 4 Science at Work 520
Unit 4 Projects 522
Unit 4 Review 524

Guide to the Toolkits and Appendices 528

Science Skills Toolkits 529

Math Skills Toolkits 554

Study Toolkits 561

Appendix A: Properties of Common Substances 568

Appendix B: Using Star Maps 570

Appendix C: Chemistry References 572

**Appendix D: Numerical Answers and
                Answers to Practice Problems** 573

Glossary 574

Index 582

Credits 588

Periodic Table 590

Activities, Investigations, and Features

Activities

1-1 How Disturbed Is Too Disturbed?. 5
1-2 What Symbol Would You Choose? 11
1-3 Recycling in Ontario. 32
2-1 Reducing Wildlife Mortality with Fences. 47
2-2 Graphing Population Change. 52
2-3 What Was for Dinner? 60
2-4 Ecotourism and Monarch Butterflies. 76
3-1 Biodiversity in Canada 87
3-2 Biodiversity Index 93
3-3 Alien Invasion 104
3-4 Plants at Risk. 108
3-5 The Common Good. 113
4-1 Raising Underwater Artifacts 137
4-2 Safety First! 141
4-3 Element, Compound, or Mixture? 145
4-4 What's So Special about Paper Clips? 150
4-5 Slow as Molasses 151
4-6 Hard as Nails 155
4-7 What's New? 162
5-1 The Atomic "Black Box". 177
5-2 How Small Is Too Small? 180
5-3 Atomic Model Time Line 185
5-4 What's Your Number? 189
5-5 Make Your Own Atom 191
5-6 What's in Blackbock's Lake? 195
5-7 The Bohr-Rutherford Periodic Table 208
6-1 Bouncing Glue. 219
6-2 Making Ice Cream 229
6-3 Cornstarch Armour. 240
6-4 Representing Compounds Using
Bohr-Rutherford Models. 244
6-5 Ball-and-Stick Models 246
7-1 Create Your Own Constellation. 269
7-2 Angle of Sunlight 285
7-3 Modelling the Solar System. 293
7-4 Making Craters 303
8-1 Preparing for a Trip to the Moon 315
8-2 An Astronomer's View. 318
9-1 Matter in Motion. 359
9-2 How Big Is the Milky Way Galaxy? 365
9-3 Counting Galaxies by Sampling 366
10-1 Lightning in a Glow Tube 401
10-2 Detecting Static Charge Using an Electroscope. . 412
10-3 Drawing Charges You Cannot See 416
10-4 A Static Spice Separator 426
11-1 Shed Light On It 435
11-2 Make a CELLection. 441
11-3 Charged Cereal and Moving Marbles. 449
11-4 Measuring Current and Potential
Difference in a Series Circuit. 459
12-1 Generating an Electric Current 483

Investigations

1-A Fertilizers and Algae Growth. 37
1-B The Chemistry of Photosynthesis 38
1-C Soil-water Acidity and Plant Growth. 40
1-D Can a Plant Have Too Much Fertilizer? 42
2-A Is the Winter Skate Endangered in Nova Scotia? . . 79
2-B What Happens When Food Is Limited? 80
2-C Putting Your Foot in Your Mouth 82
3-A Zebra Mussels in Lake Ontario 117
3-B Balancing Populations and the Environment 118
4-A Testing Physical Properties of Substances. 166
4-B Chemical Properties of Common Gases 168
4-C Properties of Common Substances 170
4-D CFC Production and Canada's Ozone Layer 172
5-A The Bohr-Rutherford Model of the Atom. 212
5-B Physical Properties of Metals and Non-metals. . . 213
5-C Reactivity Trends in the Periodic Table 214
6-A What Causes Rusting of Iron Nails? 249
6-B Properties of Ionic and Molecular Compounds . . 250

6-C Classification of Household Substances **252**

7-A Modelling the Moon's Movement **307**

7-B The Changing View of the Night Sky **308**

7-C Gravity on Other Planets **310**

8-A The Brightness of Stars **350**

8-B Using Spectral Analysis to Identify
Star Composition **352**

8-C Building an H-R Diagram **354**

9-A Estimating the Age of the Universe **382**

9-B Modelling the Expanding Universe **384**

10-A Comparing Conductivity **429**

10-B Be a Charge Detective. **430**

11-A Constructing and Comparing Voltaic Cells **472**

11-B Loads in Series **474**

11-C Loads in Parallel **476**

11-D Testing Ohm's Law. **478**

12-A Designing a Staircase Circuit. **513**

12-B An Electrical Energy Audit **514**

12-C A "Dry" Investigation **515**

12-D A Plan of Action **516**

Case Studies

The Disappearing Eel **8**

Why Are Honeybees Disappearing? **72**

Saving Dolly Varden. **106**

What Is the Cost of Our Products? **146**

Diamond Mining: Beyond the Sparkle **202**

Taking a Stand on Plastic Bags. **238**

Can We Prevent the Next Big Impact? **304**

Space Junk **330**

Space Exploration Spinoffs **370**

E-waste. **422**

Electric Avenue. **442**

Off the Grid and Living Green **508**

Making a Difference

Yvonne Su. **11**

Allyson Parker **77**

Severn Cullis-Suzuki **101**

Meghana Saincher **147**

Patrick Bowman **204**

Dayna Corelli **240**

Shelby Mielhausen. **280**

Roberta Bondar. **328**

Joel Zylberger **379**

Katie Pietrzakowski. **427**

Corey Centen and Nilesh Patel **444**

Pinky Langat and Chris Palmer. **511**

National Geographic Features

Visualizing the Carbon Cycle. **15**

Visualizing Metals **201**

Visualizing the Kuiper Belt **298**

Visualizing Lightning. **419**

Exploring *ON Science 9*

Solve a Puzzle, Find a Quote

Use the puzzle clues on these two pages to begin your journey through *ON Science 9*. (Do not write in this textbook.) When you are finished, the circled and numbered letters will help you discover a powerful quote by Albert Einstein.

Driven by curiosity and hard work, Albert Einstein developed theories that revolutionized our understanding of space, matter, and time.
What other factor helped Einstein achieve such success in science?

| 1 | 2 | 3 | 4 | 5 | 6 | 7 | 8 | 9 | 10 | 11 | 12 | 13 | 14 | 15 | 16 | 17 | 18 | 19 | 20 | 21 | 22 | 23 |

—Albert Einstein

What does this quote reveal about Einstein's approach to science?
How can you apply this approach to your studies in science?

Engage—Learning Science

What are the four units you will study in *ON Science 9*?

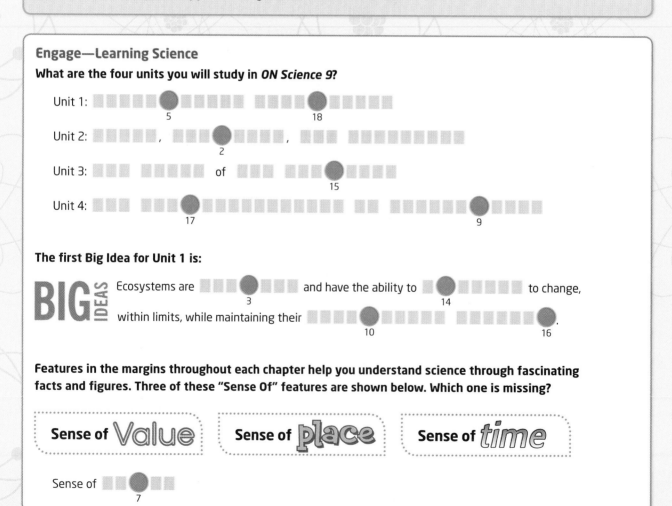

Unit 1: ⬜⬜⬜●⬜⬜⬜⬜ ⬜⬜⬜●⬜⬜⬜⬜
5 18

Unit 2: ⬜⬜⬜⬜⬜ , ⬜⬜⬜●⬜⬜⬜ , ⬜⬜⬜ ⬜⬜⬜⬜⬜⬜⬜
2

Unit 3: ⬜⬜⬜ ⬜⬜⬜⬜⬜ of ⬜⬜⬜ ⬜⬜⬜●⬜⬜
15

Unit 4: ⬜⬜⬜ ⬜⬜⬜●⬜⬜⬜⬜⬜⬜⬜⬜ ⬜⬜ ⬜⬜⬜⬜⬜●⬜⬜⬜
17 9

The first Big Idea for Unit 1 is:

BIG IDEAS Ecosystems are ⬜⬜⬜●⬜⬜⬜ and have the ability to ⬜●⬜⬜⬜⬜⬜ to change,
3 14
within limits, while maintaining their ⬜⬜⬜●⬜⬜⬜⬜⬜⬜⬜⬜●.
10 16

Features in the margins throughout each chapter help you understand science through fascinating facts and figures. Three of these "Sense Of" features are shown below. Which one is missing?

Sense of Value   Sense of place   Sense of time

Sense of ⬜⬜●⬜⬜
7

Explore—Doing Science

What piece of safety equipment does this icon represent?

▢▢▢▢▢▢ ▢▢▢◯▢▢▢
23

The Activities and Investigations in your textbook will help you explore and investigate questions about your world using the skills of scientific inquiry. **Which is the missing skill in the Skill Check below?**

Skill Check
✓ Performing and Recording
✓ Analyzing and Interpreting
✓ Communicating

▢▢▢◯▢▢▢▢▢▢ and ▢▢▢▢▢▢▢▢
19

Where would you look in this textbook to find out how to make a scientific drawing?

▢▢▢▢▢▢▢ ▢▢◯▢▢▢ Toolkit 6
1

Explain—Understanding Science

National Geographic features help you understand science through images. **What is the title of the National Geographic feature in Unit 4?**

Visualizing ▢▢▢▢▢▢▢▢◯
4

Learning how to understand and use science vocabulary is an important communication skill. **What colour is used to highlight key terms and their definitions in the margin?**

▢▢▢▢◯
6

Suppose you are reviewing terms and definitions to study for a test. **What part of this textbook can help you?**

▢▢▢◯▢▢▢▢
13

Extend—Applying Science

Every chapter has a feature that explores a specific real-world scientific topic or issue that relates to that chapter. Questions at the end of the feature challenge you to find out more about the topic. The feature runs along the bottom of two pages. **What is the feature called?**

▢▢▢▢ ▢◯▢▢▢
8

In each chapter you will have the opportunity to read about young Canadians, most of them high school students, who have used the tools of scientific inquiry to positively influence their community, the environment, or some other facet of their lives. **What is the name of this feature?**

▢▢▢▢▢▢ ▢ ▢▢▢▢▢▢▢▢◯▢▢
11

What feature focusses on careers in science?

▢▢◯▢▢▢▢ ▢▢ ▢▢▢▢
12

Evaluate—Studying Science

What feature, at the beginning of each chapter, provides three strategies to help you learn the material in your science textbook?

▢▢▢▢▢ ▢▢▢▢▢◯▢
21

Section Review questions, Chapter Review questions, and Unit Review questions all help you check your understanding. **What question category helps you test your understanding as you read through a section?**

▢▢▢▢▢▢▢▢ ▢◯▢▢▢
20

Answers to some of the review questions are included in this textbook. **Where are they?**

▢▢▢▢◯▢▢▢ ▢
22

Safety in your Science Classroom

Become familiar with the following safety rules and procedures. It is up to you to use them and your teacher's instructions to make your activities and investigations in *ON Science 9* safe and enjoyable. Your teacher will give you specific information about any other special safety rules that need to be used in your school.

1. Working with your teacher …

- Listen carefully to any instructions your teacher gives you.
- Inform your teacher if you have any allergies, medical conditions, or other physical problems that could affect your work in the science classroom. Tell your teacher if you wear contact lenses or a hearing aid.
- Obtain your teacher's approval before beginning any activity you have designed for yourself.
- Know the location and proper use of the nearest fire extinguisher, fire blanket, first-aid kit, and fire alarm.

2. Starting an activity or investigation …

- Before starting an activity or investigation, read all of it. If you do not understand how to do a step, ask your teacher for help.
- Be sure you have checked the safety icons and have read and understood the safety precautions.
- Begin an activity or investigation only after your teacher tells you to start.

3. Wearing protective clothing …

- When you are directed to do so, wear protective clothing, such as a lab apron and safety goggles. Always wear protective clothing when you are using materials that could pose a safety problem, such as unidentified substances, or when you are heating anything.
- Tie back long hair, and avoid wearing scarves, ties, or long necklaces.

4. Acting responsibly …

- Work carefully with a partner and make sure your work area is clear.
- Handle equipment and materials carefully.
- Make sure stools and chairs are resting securely on the floor.
- If other students are doing something that you consider dangerous, report it to your teacher.

5. Handling edible substances …

- Do not chew gum, eat, or drink in your science classroom.
- Do not taste any substances or draw any material into a tube with your mouth.

6. Working in a science classroom …

- Make sure you understand all safety labels on school materials or those you bring from home. Familiarize yourself, as well, with the WHMIS symbols and the special safety symbols used in this book, found on page xvii.

- When carrying equipment for an activity or investigation, hold it carefully. Carry only one object or container at a time.

- Be aware of others during activities and investigations. Make room for students who may be carrying equipment to their work stations.

7. Working with sharp objects …

- Always cut away from yourself and others when using a knife or razor blade.

- Always keep the pointed end of scissors or any pointed object facing away from yourself and others if you have to walk with such objects.

- If you notice sharp or jagged edges on any equipment, take special care with it and report it to your teacher.

- Dispose of broken glass as your teacher directs.

8. Working with electrical equipment …

- Make sure your hands are dry when touching electrical cords, plugs, or sockets.

- Pull the plug, not the cord, when unplugging electrical equipment.

- Report damaged equipment or frayed cords to your teacher.

- Place electrical cords where people will not trip over them.

9. Working with heat …

- When heating an item, wear safety goggles and any other safety equipment that the text or your teacher advises.

- Always use heatproof containers.

- Point the open end of a container that is being heated away from yourself and others.

- Do not allow a container to boil dry.

- Handle hot objects carefully. Be especially careful with a hot plate that looks as though it has cooled down.

- If you use a Bunsen burner, make sure you understand fully how to light and use it safely.

- If you do receive a burn, inform you teacher, and apply cold water to the burned area immediately.

10. Working with various chemicals …

- If any part of your body comes in contact with a substance, wash the area immediately and thoroughly with water. If you get anything in your eyes, do not touch them. Wash them immediately and continuously for 15 min, and inform your teacher.

- Always handle substances carefully. If you are asked to smell a substance, never smell it directly. Hold the container slightly in front of and beneath your nose, and waft the fumes toward your nostrils.

- Hold containers away from your face when pouring liquids.

11. Working with living things …

On a field trip:

- Try not to disturb the area any more than is absolutely necessary.

- If you move something, do it carefully, and always replace it carefully.

- If you are asked to remove plant material, remove it gently, and take as little as possible.

In the classroom:

- Make sure that living creatures receive humane treatment while they are in your care.

- If possible, return living creatures to their natural environment when your work is complete.

12. Cleaning up in the science classroom …

- Clean up any spills, according to you teacher's instructions.

- Clean equipment before you put it away.

- Wash your hands thoroughly after doing an activity or an investigation.

- Dispose of materials as directed by your teacher. Never discard materials in the sink unless your teacher requests it.

13. Designing and building …

- Use tools safely to cut, join, and shape objects.

- Handle modelling clay correctly. Wash your hands after using modelling clay.

- Follow proper procedures when using mechanical systems and studying their operations.

- Use special care when observing and working with objects in motion.

- Do not use power equipment such as drills, sanders, saws, and lathes unless you have specialized training in handling such tools.

Safety Symbols

ON Science 9 Safety Symbols

The following safety symbols are used in *ON Science 9* to alert you to possible dangers. Be sure you understand each symbol used in an activity or investigation before you begin.

 Disposal Alert
This symbol appears when care must be taken to dispose of materials properly.

 Thermal Safety
This symbol appears as a reminder to use caution when handling hot objects.

 Sharp Object Safety
This symbol appears when a danger of cuts or punctures caused by the use of sharp objects exists.

 Electrical Safety
This symbol appears when care should be taken when using electrical equipment.

 Skin Protection Safety
This symbol appears when use of caustic chemicals might irritate the skin or when contact with micro-organisms might transmit infection.

 Clothing Protection Safety
A lab apron should be worn when this symbol appears.

 Fire Safety
This symbol appears when care should be taken around open flames.

 Eye Safety
This symbol appears when a danger to the eyes exists. Safety goggles should be worn when this symbol appears.

Instant Practice—Safety Symbols

Find four of the *ON Science 9* safety symbols in activities or investigations in this textbook. For each symbol, identify the possible dangers in the activity or investigation that the symbol refers to.

WHMIS Symbols

Look carefully at the WHMIS (Workplace Hazardous Materials Information System) safety symbols shown here. The WHMIS symbols are used throughout Canada to identify dangerous materials. Make certain you understand what these symbols mean. When you see these symbols on containers, use safety precautions.

 Compressed Gas

 Flammable and Combustible Material

 Oxidizing Material

 Corrosive Material

 Poisonous and Infectious Material Causing Immediate and Serious Toxic Effects

 Poisonous and Infectious Material Causing Other Toxic Effects

 Biohazardous Infectious Material

 Dangerously Reactive Material

Instant Practice—Safety Symbols

Hydrogen gas is stored in containers under pressure. This gas is highly flammable.

1. What two symbols would you expect to see on a label for hydrogen gas?

2. Describe the following.
   a. the risks illustrated by the two symbols
   b. precautions someone would need to take when working with the gas
   c. where it could be safely stored
   d. first aid or emergency treatment

3. If you did not know the answer to part d., where would you find this information?

BIG IDEAS

- People have the responsibility to regulate their impact on the sustainability of ecosystems in order to preserve them for future generations.

- Ecosystems are dynamic and have the ability to respond to change, within limits, while maintaining their ecological balance.

Roads provide pathways for many human journeys. Roads also divide habitats, forcing animals to face dangers from fast-moving vehicles when the animals migrate or travel within their habitat. Posting warning signs to remind drivers to slow down and watch for animals is one way to reduce collisions and wildlife deaths on our roads.

A road dividing a habitat is an example of human activity that has disturbed an ecosystem. An ecosystem can respond to disturbances—but only within limits. Beyond those limits, the ecosystem cannot recover its ecological balance.

In this unit, you will learn about why sustainable ecosystems are crucial to life on Earth and what people can do to help protect them.

Why does it matter if an animal's habitat is divided?

Chapter 1
Nutrient Cycles and Energy Flow

Chapter 2
Populations and Sustainable Ecosystems

Chapter 3
Biodiversity

Get Ready for Unit 1

Concept Check

1. Examine the forest ecosystem shown in the illustration below. Make a table with the headings "Biotic" and "Abiotic". Give your table a title. Under each heading, list the components of the forest ecosystem that belong to that category.

Biotic	Abiotic

2. Complete each of the following sentences, using one of the organisms from the forest ecosystem shown below to fill in the blanks. (Do not write in this textbook.) The first sentence is completed for you.

   a. A puffball mushroom is a decomposer because it breaks down the remains of dead animals and plants.

   b. A _____ is a *scavenger* because...

   c. A _____ is a *producer* because...

   d. A _____ is a *consumer* because...

   e. A _____ is a *herbivore* because...

   f. A _____ is a *carnivore* because...

   g. A _____ is an *omnivore* because...

3. The food chain shown below is just one of many food chains in a forest ecosystem. Using the organisms shown in the forest ecosystem illustration, draw a different food chain.

4. Use the words below to write a brief explanation of why trees are important to forest ecosystems.

producers	food	shade
oxygen	leaves	plants
habitat	decompose	photosynthesis

5. Choose one of the following events. Make a flowchart to show how the event might affect a forest ecosystem.

   a. A forest fire rages through the forest.

   b. A logging company clear-cuts the trees in the forest.

   c. A beaver builds a dam that results in a stream drying up.

   d. Hunters kill all of the wolves in the area.

   e. A species of beetle kills all of the pine trees in the area.

A Forest Food Chain

A Forest Ecosystem

Inquiry Check

The Ontario Ministry of Transport has taken several steps to try to prevent vehicle collisions with deer, moose, and bears. Researchers found out that most of these collisions happened in May, June, October, November, and December.

6. Analyze In which two seasons do most collisions with deer, moose, and bears occur? Why do you think this is the case? Explain your answer.

7. Predict Which of the government strategies for reducing collisions listed below might be the most effective? Explain your answer.

   a. Installing fencing along major highways

   b. Draining salty ponds near highways

   c. Posting warning signs

   d. Adding highway lighting to improve night visibility

   e. Removing roadside brush so drivers can see the road better

8. Plan You are a scientist hired by the ministry to investigate its anti-collision strategies. Choose one of the five strategies above. Outline a procedure to test how well the strategy works.

Numeracy and Literacy Check

The five areas of Ontario with the highest number of reported vehicle collisions with wildlife are shown below. They are listed in alphabetical order.

Ontario's Highest Number of Reported Wildlife Collisions

Area	Human populatlion	Number of incidents per year in 1997
Kenora	15 177	521
Lanark County	62 495	481
Ottawa	774 072	886
Simcoe County	266 100	656
Thunder Bay	109 140	463

9. Ranking List the areas in order from highest to lowest number of incidents.

10. Graphing Choose an appropriate style of graph and construct a graph to display the information shown in the table. Include a title and labels.

11. Writing Suppose you are a speechwriter for the Mayor of Simcoe County. Write a brief radio message aimed at informing people about the dangers of collisions with wildlife on the roads and suggesting ways to avoid them.

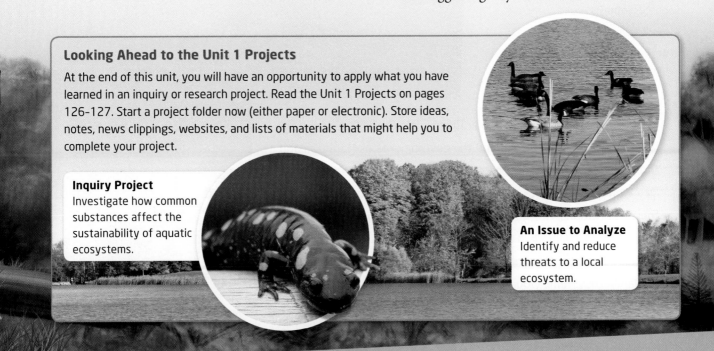

Looking Ahead to the Unit 1 Projects

At the end of this unit, you will have an opportunity to apply what you have learned in an inquiry or research project. Read the Unit 1 Projects on pages 126–127. Start a project folder now (either paper or electronic). Store ideas, notes, news clippings, websites, and lists of materials that might help you to complete your project.

Inquiry Project
Investigate how common substances affect the sustainability of aquatic ecosystems.

An Issue to Analyze
Identify and reduce threats to a local ecosystem.

Chapter 1   Nutrient Cycles and Energy Flow

What You Will Learn

In this chapter, you will learn how to...

- **explain** that life depends on recycled matter
- **describe** the processes of photosynthesis and cellular respiration
- **explain** how humans can affect the cycles of matter and energy flow in ecosystems

Why It Matters

All living things, including humans, rely on the cycles of matter and energy on Earth. When a natural process or human activity affects one of these cycles, the balance of an ecosystem can be thrown off. This imbalance can affect all the organisms in the ecosystem.

Skills You Will Use

In this chapter, you will learn how to...

- **assess** the impact of fertilizers on aquatic ecosystems
- **observe** the chemistry of photosynthesis
- **model** acid precipitation
- **determine** the impact of excess fertilizers on plants

In 2007, four First Nations–Poplar River, Little Grand Rapids, Paunigassi, and Pikangikum–and the governments of Manitoba and Ontario began the process required to designate an area of Canada as a World Heritage Site. The area includes the territories of the four First Nations, Atikaki Provincial Park in Manitoba, and Woodland Caribou Provincial Park in Ontario, shown above. As a World Heritage Site, the sustainability of the area's forest, lake, and wetland ecosystems would be protected.

Activity 1-1

How Disturbed Is Too Disturbed?

Many different types of disturbances can affect an ecosystem. Some disturbances, such as a volcanic eruption or a flood, are natural. Other disturbances, such as water pollution or air pollution, can result from human activities. In this activity, you will model how disturbances can affect the balance of an ecosystem.

Materials
- 27 smooth building blocks, labelled with environmental disturbances

How much instability can your tower take?

Procedure

1. Work in groups of four. Build a tower with nine layers, using three blocks per layer. Place each layer at right angles to the layer below it.

2. Take turns removing blocks from the lower levels of the tower and using these blocks to make new three-block layers on top. Keep track of how many blocks you move.

3. Continue moving blocks until the tower collapses.

Questions

1. What did the tower represent in this model? What did the moved blocks represent?

2. What happened to the tower as more blocks were removed from lower levels and placed on top?

3. How does this activity model how different disturbances can affect an ecosystem?

4. How does what happened to the model in this activity differ from what could happen in a real ecosystem?

Study Toolkit

These strategies will help you use this textbook to develop your understanding of science concepts and skills. To find out more about these and other strategies, refer to the Study Toolkit Overview, which begins on page 561.

To find out more about these and other strategies, refer to the Study Toolkit Overview, which begins on page 561.

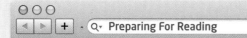 Preparing For Reading

Previewing Text Features

Before reading nonfiction text, a good strategy is to preview the *features* of the text. Text features give readers clues about the main ideas in the text and show how the writer has organized these ideas.

Look at some text features on the next page. The section heading, **1.1 Sustainability**, is a different size and colour from the body text. This heading tells you the main idea of the section. The two subheadings, **The Mystery of Easter Island** and **The Need for Sustainable Ecosystems**, are specific and signal details related to the main idea.

Use the Strategy

1. Browse through Chapter 1, paying attention to the section headings and subheadings. Predict what the main ideas in Chapter 1 will be. Record your predictions and confirm or revise them as you read the chapter.

2. Describe two ways in which colour is used in the chapter to help you navigate.

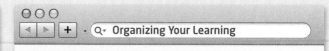 Organizing Your Learning

Comparing and Contrasting

Comparing and contrasting helps you identify how concepts are similar and how they are different. A **Venn diagram** can help you organize this information graphically. For example, the Venn diagram below shows some similarities and differences between "biotic" and "abiotic" characteristics of the environment.

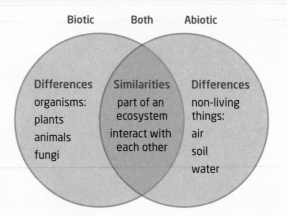

Biotic Both Abiotic

Differences
organisms:
plants
animals
fungi

Similarities
part of an ecosystem
interact with each other

Differences
non-living things:
air
soil
water

Use the Strategy

1. Choose two animals, such as an owl and a turtle.

2. Make a Venn diagram to show the similarities and differences between the two animals in terms of their survival needs.

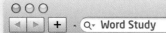 Word Study

Word Families

Drawing a word family web can help you figure out unfamiliar words. The web on the right shows words that all have the prefix *bio*, from the Greek word meaning life. *Biology*, for example, means the study of life.

Use the Strategy

1. Predict and record what you think the other words in the web mean.

2. Check your predictions as you read Chapter 1 or use the Glossary at the end of this textbook.

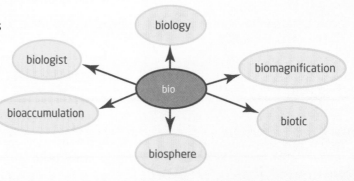

biology

biologist

biomagnification

bio

bioaccumulation

biotic

biosphere

1.1 Sustainability

On Easter day in 1722, a Dutch ship landed on a small treeless island in the South Pacific. A small population of people lived on the island. Along the coast, there were many giant rock statues of human forms, shown in **Figure 1.1**. Some of these statues were as tall as 10 m. How could so few people put together so many large statues?

The Mystery of Easter Island

Many scientists theorize that there was once a thriving population of people on Easter Island, as well as thick forests. The people had come from other islands in the South Pacific, thousands of kilometres away. They built houses, planted crops, and raised the animals they had brought with them. They also built the giant rock statues.

To move the statues from the rock quarry to the coast, they cut down trees and made wooden frames. In addition, the islanders cut down trees to clear the land for their crops and to burn the wood for warmth. Eventually, the last tree was cut down. The loss of trees led to erosion, a loss of plants for food, and no materials for making boats for fishing—or escape. Without the supporting forest, the island could no longer sustain the human population. Their standard of living declined, and their society began to die off. The disappearance of the forests also led to the disappearance of other island residents, such as birds.

The Need for Sustainable Ecosystems

The forests that once grew on Easter Island are an example of an ecosystem. An **ecosystem** includes all the interacting parts of a biological community and its environment. The prefix *eco-* is from the ancient Greek word for home. This is a fitting prefix, since ecosystems are the natural homes of the many organisms that live in them. When the term **sustainable ecosystem** is used, the word *sustain* has two meanings: to endure and to support.

> **Figure 1.1** The cost of erecting these massive statues was the destruction of the sustaining forests on Easter Island.

Key Terms

ecosystem
sustainable ecosystem
biotic
abiotic
lithosphere
hydrosphere
atmosphere
biosphere
nutrients
aquatic ecosystem
terrestrial ecosystem
eutrophication

ecosystem all the interacting parts of a biological community and its environment

sustainable ecosystem an ecosystem that is capable of withstanding pressure and giving support to a variety of organisms

Ecosystems and Survival

"To endure" means to continue in the same state. Sustainable ecosystems endure, but they also support a wide variety of organisms. The Easter Islanders' use of their forest ecosystem was unsustainable. Under the pressure of the tree cutting, the ecosystem could not endure, nor could it support many of the organisms, including humans, on the island.

All organisms require sustainable ecosystems for survival. Many organisms depend on more than one ecosystem to survive. Ruby-throated hummingbirds, shown in **Figure 1.2**, spend the summer in gardens and along the edges of forests of eastern Canada. In the fall, they fly thousands of kilometres to spend the winter in the tropical forests of Central America. In the spring, they begin the long flight back to Canada. Along the way, they stop to drink water, eat nectar and insects, and rest. Because these birds, and many others, migrate long distances every year, they are dependent on the many ecosystems along their migratory route for food and shelter.

- summer
- winter
- migration

Figure 1.2 Ruby-throated hummingbirds fly north from Mexico each spring. Along the way, they need resources from sustainable ecosystems to survive.

STSE Case Study

The Disappearing Eel

The American eel, shown on the right, was once one of the most abundant fish in the St. Lawrence River. The species was so plentiful that there are accounts from the mid-1600s of a person catching 1000 eels in one night with just a spear! Today, the situation has changed. The estimated number of American eels in the St. Lawrence and Great Lakes has decreased by more than 90 percent.

American eels found in the Great Lakes are long, snake-like fish. They are a native species and have an important role in the Great Lakes ecosystem. Eels eat insects, crustaceans, fish, frogs, and dead animals. They are prey for other fish, birds, and mammals.

American eels migrate great distances and change dramatically during their life cycles, as shown on the next page. Eels are catadromous: they spend most of their lives in fresh water, but return to the sea to lay eggs. Both saltwater and freshwater species and their ecosystems are affected by a decrease in the eel population.

Because the eel's life cycle is so long and covers so much distance, the species encounters many threats. Many mature eels do not complete their journey down the St. Lawrence River and back to the Sargasso Sea.

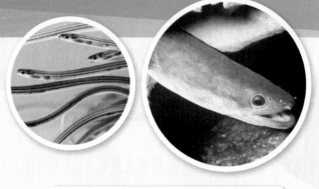

The appearance of an American eel changes many times as it makes its long journey from the Sargasso Sea to the Great Lakes.

About 40 percent of these eels are shredded and killed in dam turbines in the river. Dams also block young eels migrating upstream toward the Great Lakes.

Overfishing has contributed to the decline of American eels. Ontario cancelled its eel fishery in 2004, but eel fishing takes place elsewhere. Overharvesting of seaweed, which makes up the spawning habitat for eels, could also be contributing to a decrease in eels. Chemical contaminants may be affecting eel fertility. Governments, industry, and scientists are working together to decrease the threats that eels face at different points in their life cycles.

Parts of an Ecosystem

Ecosystems can cover large areas of land or water, such as the boreal forest system in Ontario. Ecosystems can also be small, such as a rotting log or a pool of water. Every ecosystem has biotic and abiotic parts. **Biotic** refers to the living parts of an ecosystem. The biotic parts of an ecosystem include plants, animals, and micro-organisms. **Abiotic** refers to the non-living parts of an ecosystem. The abiotic parts of an ecosystem include water, oxygen, light, nutrients, and soil.

biotic the living parts of an ecosystem

abiotic the non-living parts of an ecosystem

Learning Check

1. Describe the ways in which the people's use of trees on Easter Island was unsustainable.

2. What is the two-part meaning of the word *sustain*?

3. Use the map in **Figure 1.2** to explain how ruby-throated hummingbirds are dependent on more than one ecosystem.

4. List some biotic parts of the ecosystem in which you live.

American eels hatch in the Sargasso Sea in the Atlantic Ocean. The larvae migrate to the St. Lawrence River and the Great Lakes. Mature eels often spend 10 to 15 years in the Great Lakes before returning to the Sargasso Sea to reproduce and die.

How Can We Help the American Eel?

- Commercial fishers are helping scientists capture and tag large eels.
- Ontario Power Generation is shipping eels down the St. Lawrence and releasing them in Lac St. Pierre in Québec, so that the eels do not have to pass through dam turbines.
- The First Nations along the St. Lawrence River have agreed to stop all harvesting and work with the Department of Fisheries and Oceans and other agencies to ensure this species is protected.
- Hydro Québec, New York Power Authority, and Ontario Power Generation have built eel ladders at their St. Lawrence River dams to help eels migrate upstream.

Your Turn

1. Why is the American eel an important part of the ecosystem of the St. Lawrence River and Great Lakes?

2. Identify different stakeholders affected by the decline of the American eel (for example, commercial fishers, Aboriginal peoples, workers in the power industry). Write a short paragraph to describe the issue from the point of view of one of the stakeholders.

3. Create a poster for a campaign to raise public awareness about the American eel. Your poster should highlight the importance of the eel to the health of the Great Lakes ecosystem and the historical significance of the American eel to Aboriginal peoples and Ontario's fishing industry.

Biotic Characteristics of an Ecosystem

The biotic characteristics of an ecosystem include all the living things, such as plants, animals, fungi, bacteria, and protists, in an ecosystem. They also include all the interactions among the living things in the ecosystem. Examples of such interactions, shown in **Table 1.1**, include *symbiosis*, *predation*, and *competition*.

Table 1.1 Biotic Interactions

Biotic Interaction	How It Works
Symbiosis 	Symbiosis is the interaction between members of two different species that live together in a close association. Although you cannot see any interaction from the surface, the mushrooms in the photograph help the nearby trees absorb water and nutrients from the soil. Masses of mushroom tissue surround the roots of the trees, increasing the area that the roots cover and thus increasing their absorption. The mushroom tissue also helps to prevent the roots from drying out. The mushrooms benefit as well. The mushrooms get food, in the form of sugar, produced by the trees.
Predation 	Predation occurs when one organism consumes another organism for food. The organism that is consumed is called the prey. The organism that eats the prey is called the predator. The river otter shown in the photograph is a predator. Its prey includes fish, crabs, frogs, and turtles. The river otter is also prey for other predators, such as coyotes. In this way, organisms are linked together through the food chain. The relationship between predators and their prey can influence the population of both the predator and the prey, as well as affect the entire ecosystem in which they live. You will read more about predation later in this chapter and in Chapter 2.
Competition	Competition occurs when two or more organisms compete for the same resource, such as food, in the same location at the same time. The dandelions in the photograph compete with the grass for the same resources. The dandelions may block out light that the grass needs to survive. They may also soak up more water or nutrients from the soil, leaving less for the grass. Competing for resources takes energy. Energy expended on competition is energy that is taken away from other important life processes, such as growth and reproduction. Competition can influence the population size and success of a group of organisms. Sometimes, one group of organisms is outcompeted by another group. You will read more about competition and how it influences populations in Chapter 2.

Activity 1-2

What Symbol Would You Choose?

The statues on Easter Island have probably become one of the best-known symbols for the idea that cultural short-sightedness can lead to unsustainable ecosystems. Sometimes symbols can be biotic factors. For example, the polar bear has recently been used as a symbol to alert people to the consequences of global warming. Other times, a symbol may represent an abiotic factor, such as water or space. What symbol would you choose to represent an environmental issue occurring right now?

Materials
- construction paper
- coloured markers
- scissors
- tape or glue
- Internet access
- computer lab

Procedure
1. Design a symbol or an image to represent the world's current environmental problems.

2. Design another symbol or image to represent a future of increased environmental awareness.

3. Share your designs with your classmates.

Questions
1. How did your designs differ from your classmates' designs?

2. What symbol from our society would you choose to represent our current relationship with the environment? Explain your choice.

Making a Difference

In Grade 9, Yvonne Su discovered that her Newmarket school was not recycling because it lacked the resources. Yvonne felt a responsibility to do something. She and her friends, with the help of some teachers, decided to tackle the recycling themselves, so they started a recycling and environmental club. Yvonne has been involved in environmental activities ever since.

"As Grade 9s, my friends and I didn't know where to turn to learn more about our planet. After speaking to some teachers, we found out that our greatest resources were right in front of us—our science classes."

The more Yvonne and her friends learned, the more they wanted to share their knowledge. They organized campaigns about environmental issues at their school. Then they took their campaigns to schools across Canada. Yvonne was named one of Canada's Top 20 Under 20 in 2007. She is now studying environmental science at the University of Guelph.

What changes would you suggest making at your school to help the environment?

Abiotic Characteristics of an Ecosystem

The abiotic characteristics of an ecosystem, described in **Table 1.2**, are as important as the biotic characteristics. The abiotic characteristics are the factors that living things need to survive.

Table 1.2 Abiotic Characteristics of an Ecosystem

Abiotic Characteristic	Why It Is Important	Effects on Sustainability
Water 	All organisms need water to survive. Plants take up water through their roots. Some animals need water to help regulate their body temperature. Animals also use water to get rid of wastes. Many organisms live in freshwater and saltwater ecosystems.	Both natural processes and human activities can affect the amount and quality of water in an ecosystem. Water sources can dry out during long, hot periods with no rain. Chemicals from industries and agriculture can contaminate water.
Oxygen 	Many organisms, including plants and animals, need oxygen for their life processes. Aquatic organisms get oxygen from water.	Sometimes, as a result of human activities, oxygen levels in water can get so low that fish and other organisms cannot survive.
Light 	Plants and other organisms such as algae need light for photosynthesis, a life process in which organisms produce their own food.	The amount of light that an ecosystem receives can vary. Plants near the floor of a forest may be shaded by taller trees. Light in an aquatic ecosystem can be affected by the amount of sediment in run-off.
Nutrients 	All organisms need nutrients to grow. For example, plants and animals need nitrogen and phosphorus.	Nutrient levels in an ecosystem can become unbalanced as a result of human activities.
Soil 	Soil provides nutrients for plants and a habitat for many micro-organisms.	Top layers of soil, which contain the most nutrients, can be washed away if there is heavy rain or if too many trees have been cut down.

Cycling of Matter and Earth's Spheres

Hummingbirds consume water, insects, and nectar to survive. The water, insects, and nectar, as well as the hummingbird itself, are different forms of living and non-living matter. The hummingbird uses the matter it consumes to fly, build muscle, reproduce, and carry out other life processes. Ecological processes move matter from the biotic and abiotic parts of an ecosystem, and back again, in continuous cycles.

At any time, matter can occupy one of the four spheres that make up Earth. The hard part of Earth's surface is the **lithosphere**, from the Greek word for stone. The salt water in the oceans and the fresh water on the continents form the **hydrosphere**. The Greek word *hydro-* means water. The layer of air above Earth's surface is the **atmosphere**, from the Greek word *atmos-*, which means vapour.

Figure 1.3 shows the lithosphere, hydrosphere, and atmosphere. In this image of North Africa and Europe, the lithosphere is best represented by Earth's largest desert, the Sahara. The North Atlantic Ocean and the Mediterranean Sea represent the hydrosphere, and the light from the Sun shows the thin layer of gases that make up the atmosphere.

Earth's Biosphere

The lithosphere, hydrosphere, and atmosphere are abiotic spheres that are found on other planets, as well as Earth. Mars has all three spheres, although its hydrosphere is mostly ice and its atmosphere has very little oxygen. There is a fourth sphere at Earth's surface, however, that no other planet in the solar system is known to have—a biosphere.

The **biosphere** is the living surface of Earth, but it is not separate from the abiotic spheres. After all, many life forms are found underground, in both fresh water and salt water, and in the atmosphere as well.

lithosphere the hard part of Earth's surface

hydrosphere all the water found on Earth, including lakes, oceans, and ground water

atmosphere the layer of gases above Earth's surface

biosphere the regions of Earth where living organisms exist

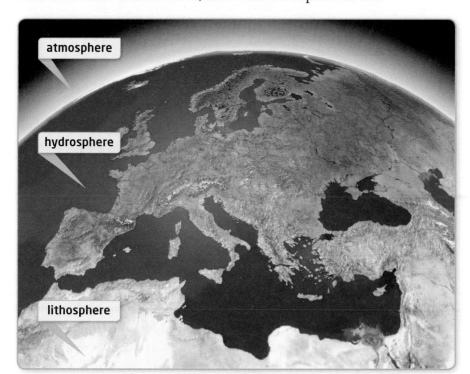

atmosphere

hydrosphere

lithosphere

Figure 1.3 In this image of Earth, all four spheres are visible. The biosphere is all around us. It exists everywhere you can see in the photograph (except in space). Through ecological processes, matter moves among the spheres.

Nutrient Cycles

nutrient a chemical that is essential to living things and is cycled through ecosystems

Ecosystems provide living things with the matter they need, including nutrients. **Nutrients** are chemicals that are needed by living things and are continually cycled through ecosystems. Examples of nutrients include water, carbon, nitrogen, and phosphorus.

The Water Cycle

Perhaps the biosphere's most vital abiotic cycle is the water cycle. **Figure 1.4** shows how water moves between the hydrosphere and the atmosphere as the Sun's rays evaporate huge amounts from oceans and other bodies of water at Earth's surface. As the water vapour rises in the atmosphere, it cools and condenses. Clouds form from condensed water droplets. Eventually, the water falls back to the lithosphere as precipitation (rain or snow, for example). As the water returns to the oceans through river systems and the ground, it erodes rocks and picks up other materials. It is also absorbed by plants and other organisms, or consumed by animals. In this way, it enters the biosphere. The movement of water among Earth's spheres is critical to the operation of sustainable ecosystems.

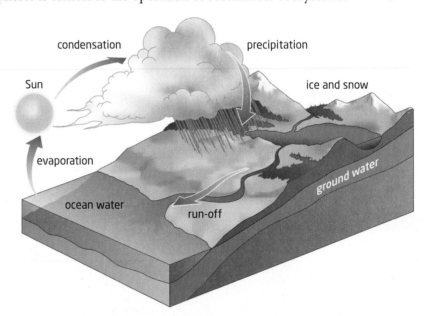

Figure 1.4 Water continually cycles through the hydrosphere, atmosphere, lithosphere, and biosphere through the processes of evaporation, condensation, and precipitation.

The Carbon Cycle

Carbon is another essential nutrient for all living things. **Figure 1.5** shows the carbon cycle. Like water, carbon moves through Earth's spheres as it is cycled through ecosystems. Carbon dioxide, a gas, moves from the atmosphere into the biosphere and back again. Carbon dioxide also moves back into the atmosphere when organisms die and their bodies decompose. Carbon enters the lithosphere when the remains of organisms are trapped underground. After millions of years, these remains are converted into fossil fuels, such as coal, oil, and natural gas. Carbon dioxide is returned to the atmosphere when humans burn the fossil fuels for energy.

Figure 1.5

Carbon–in the form of different kinds of carbon-containing molecules– moves through an endless cycle. The diagram below shows several stages of the carbon cycle. It begins when plants and algae remove carbon from the environment during photosynthesis. This carbon returns to the atmosphere via several carbon-cycle pathways.

A Air contains carbon in the form of carbon dioxide gas. Plants and algae use carbon dioxide to make sugars, which are energy-rich, carbon-containing compounds.

B Organisms break down sugar molecules made by plants and algae to obtain energy for life and growth. Carbon dioxide is released as a waste.

C Burning fossil fuels and wood releases carbon dioxide into the atmosphere.

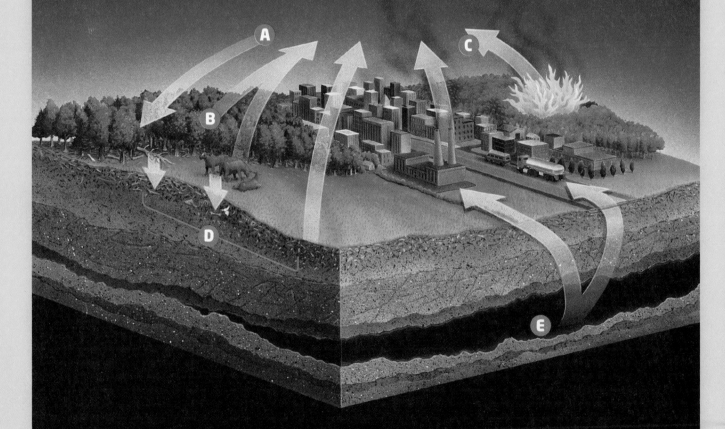

D When organisms die, their carbon-containing molecules become part of the soil. These molecules are broken down by fungi, bacteria, and other decomposers. During this decay process, carbon dioxide is released into the air.

E Under certain conditions, the remains of some dead organisms may gradually be changed into fossil fuels, such as coal, gas, and oil. These carbon compounds are energy rich.

The Nitrogen Cycle

Earth's atmosphere is 78 percent nitrogen (N_2). But most organisms cannot use nitrogen in the form in which it exists in the atmosphere. Therefore, as shown in **Figure 1.6**, an important part of the nitrogen cycle involves processes that convert the nitrogen into usable forms.

For example, in **terrestrial ecosystems**, some soil bacteria convert nitrogen into ammonium. Other types of soil bacteria convert the ammonium into nitrate. Plants absorb both forms of nitrogen through their roots, but most of the nitrogen absorbed is in the form of nitrate. Nitrogen is passed from one level of the food chain to the next as organisms eat and then use nitrogen in their bodies.

In **aquatic ecosystems**, cyanobacteria convert nitrogen into ammonium, which is then absorbed by plants. Nitrogen, in the form of ammonium and nitrate, can also enter both aquatic and terrestrial ecosystems when humans fertilize soil. Bacteria, found on land and in water, convert nitrate back into nitrogen gas, returning it to the atmosphere. As well, nitrogen is returned to the atmosphere as ammonia during volcanic eruptions and when fossil fuels are burned.

In a sustainable ecosystem, the amount of nitrogen converted into usable forms is equal to the amount of nitrogen returned to the atmosphere. Excess nitrate and ammonium eventually enter the lithosphere, becoming part of rocks. This nitrogen returns to the atmosphere only after many centuries, when rocks are broken down into smaller pieces.

terrestrial ecosystem an ecosystem that is land-based

aquatic ecosystem an ecosystem that is water-based, either fresh water or salt water

Figure 1.6 Nitrogen, a nutrient important to living things, moves through the atmosphere, hydrosphere, biosphere, and lithosphere in the nitrogen cycle.

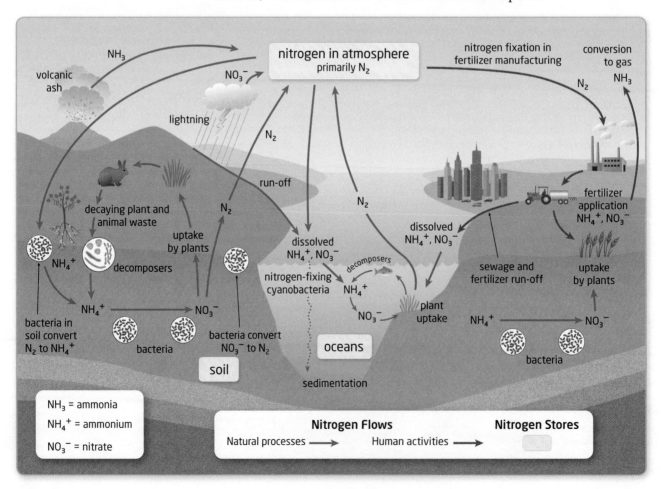

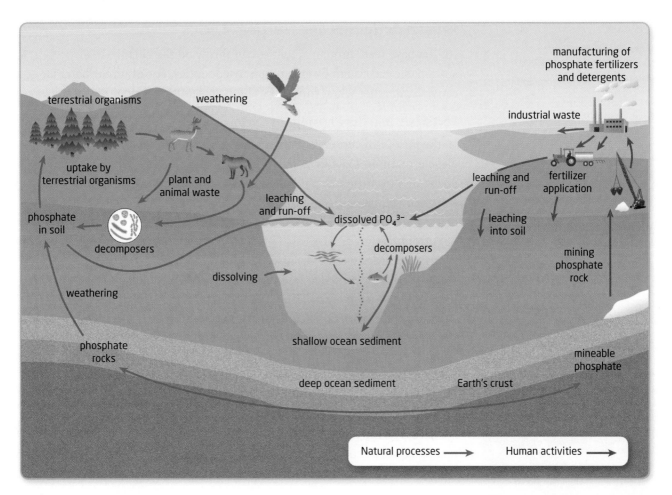

The Phosphorus Cycle

Unlike carbon and nitrogen, which both exist as gases in the atmosphere, phosphorus is stored in the lithosphere. As shown in **Figure 1.7**, phosphorus is stored in rocks and in sediment on the ocean floor. When rocks are broken down into smaller pieces through the natural process of weathering, phosphorus, in the form of phosphate (PO_4^{3-}), is released into the soil. As well, humans mine Earth's surface for phosphate rock. The phosphate rock is used to make fertilizers and detergents, which also release phosphate into the soil. Once in the soil, the phosphate is absorbed by plants through their roots. The phosphate continues to move through the biosphere as animals eat the plants and other animals. As decomposers, bacteria break down dead organisms and animal waste, releasing the phosphate back into the soil. Thus, bacteria ensure that phosphorus is continually recycled within the biosphere.

Phosphate enters aquatic ecosystems through leaching and run-off from land. The rest of the cycle is similar to what occurs on land. Aquatic plants absorb the phosphate and are later consumed by animals. Bacteria then return the phosphate to the water when they break down organic matter.

Some of the phosphate that enters aquatic ecosystems in run-off settles to the bottoms of rivers, lakes, and oceans. As in the nitrogen cycle, phosphate that becomes part of the sediment is not usually returned to the biosphere for many centuries.

Figure 1.7 Phosphorus moves through the hydrosphere, biosphere, and lithosphere in the phosphorus cycle.

Suggested Investigation

Plan Your Own Investigation
1-A, Fertilizers and Algae
Growth, on page 37

eutrophication a process in which nutrient levels in aquatic ecosystems increase, leading to an increase in the populations of primary producers

Human Activities and Nutrient Cycles

As you have read, human activities can throw off the balance in a sustainable ecosystem by affecting nutrient cycles. For example, aquatic ecosystems suffer when run-off has high amounts of agricultural fertilizers.

Fertilizers and the Phosphorus Cycle

In the mid-20th century, many aquatic ecosystems developed excessive algae growth. In Lake Erie, the amount of algae increased by as much as 30 times, upsetting natural balances. The process of **eutrophication** [pronounced u-tro-fi-KAY-shun], in which deposits of excess nutrients cause an overgrowth of algae, is very slow when natural. The alarming rate of eutrophication during the mid-20th century suggested, however, that human activities were the cause.

In 1968, 58 of Ontario's thousands of lakes were chosen to be the Experimental Lakes Area (ELA). Government and university researchers from around the world used this area for experiments to understand more about lake ecology. Ecologists added large volumes of different nutrient combinations. They found that when excess phosphorus was added to the water, the result was eutrophication, as shown in **Figure 1.8**.

How does excess phosphorus end up in bodies of water? Not all the fertilizers that are applied to farmlands are taken up by the crop plants. So, excess fertilizers enter the ground and are transported by water to nearby aquatic ecosystems. **Figure 1.9** illustrates the steps involved in eutrophication, as well as its consequences.

Figure 1.8 Ontario's Experimental Lakes Area was used to learn more about the causes of eutrophication.

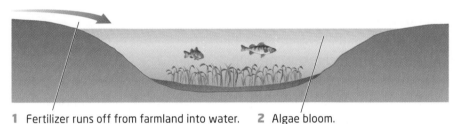

1 Fertilizer runs off from farmland into water.   **2** Algae bloom.

3 Submerged plants die due to reduced light.   **4** Algae and other plants die.

5 Bacteria use oxygen during decomposition.   **6** Oxygen levels in the water drop too low for fish to survive.

Figure 1.9 When nutrients that are normally limited are added in excess amounts, the balance in an aquatic ecosystem is upset by eutrophication.

Learning Check

5. What is eutrophication?

6. Which nutrient was found to be the main cause of eutrophication in northern Ontario lakes?

7. What is one possible source of excess phosphorus in aquatic ecosystems?

8. Suppose that you have a small fishpond in your backyard. You work hard to get your lawn looking thick and green. By the end of the summer, your lawn looks great, but the water in your fishpond is green and the fish are dead. Infer what happened.

Suggested Investigation

Plan Your Own Investigation 1-D, Can a Plant Have Too Much Fertilizer?, on page 42

Science and Social Policy

As a result of the work of the ecologists at Ontario's ELA, a multibillion-dollar phosphorus control program was established for the Great Lakes and St. Lawrence River region. In 1972, both Canada and the United States signed the Great Lakes Water Quality Agreement. In accordance with this agreement, both countries worked "to restore and maintain the chemical, physical, and biological integrity of the waters of the Great Lakes Basin Ecosystem." Although Lake Erie still suffers from pollution and algal blooms, like the one shown in **Figure 1.10**, the amount of phosphorus in the lake has decreased by more than 50 percent.

Environmental Farm Plans

Another way that the impacts of phosphorus have been reduced is through *environmental farm plans*. Farmers volunteer to be part of a program in which particular environmental impacts of a family's farm are examined. Then a plan to reduce some of these impacts is developed. Since 1993, over 27 000 farmers have participated in the program. In Ontario, the Ontario Farm Environmental Coalition manages the program.

Pesticides and By-Laws

Most scientific research is not meant merely to satisfy curiosity. It is meant to provide crucial information for modern societies, where it is used by citizens, governments, business, and even courts. For example, in 1991, the town of Hudson, Québec, passed a by-law banning the use of non-essential pesticides by home-owners and businesses. Two lawn-care companies challenged the by-law in court. The case went all the way to the Supreme Court of Canada. In 2001, the Supreme Court ruled to uphold the anti-pesticide by-law. A similar situation occurred in 2005, after the city of Toronto passed a by-law modelled after Hudson's. Manufacturers of pesticides challenged the by-law in court. Once again, the Supreme Court of Canada ruled to uphold the by-law.

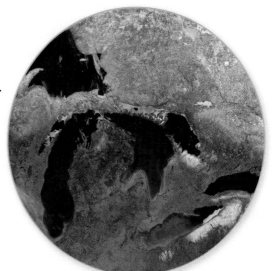

Figure 1.10 This satellite image shows an algal bloom in the western basin of Lake Erie in September, 2008.

Go to **scienceontario** to find out more

Section Summary

- Sustainable ecosystems endure, and they sustain the organisms that live within them.
- Matter, including nutrients such as nitrogen, constantly moves through Earth's spheres.

- Human activities that increase the amount of nutrients reaching a terrestrial or aquatic ecosystem can upset the nutrient balance in the ecosystem.
- Decisions and actions that are taken to protect the health of ecosystems may involve international agreements and court decisions.

Review Questions

K/U **1.** What is a sustainable ecosystem?

C **2.** Draw a flowchart to show how the collapse of the forest ecosystem on Easter Island affected the human population that lived there.

K/U **3.** Identify and describe three abiotic characteristics of ecosystems. Give an example of how each characteristic could be affected by a human activity.

C **4.** Draw the nitrogen cycle. Explain the role that bacteria play in this cycle.

C **5.** The phosphorus cycle is an important part of sustainable ecosystems.

   a. How can human activities affect the phosphorus cycle?

   b. Suggest a way that eutrophication due to human activities can be avoided.

T/I **6.** How can scientific research influence society to push for change? Include specific examples in your answer.

A **7.** Farmers, fertilizer companies, governments, and consumers all play a role in helping to reduce nutrient pollution of aquatic ecosystems. List positive actions that each group could take.

A **8.** Use the data in the graph on the right to describe how phosphorus levels in the Central Basin of Lake Erie have changed over the last 30 years.

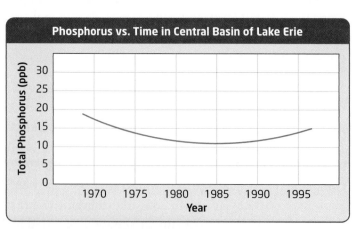

The graph shows the average amount of phosphorus during the months of June, July, and August in the Central Basin of Lake Erie for a 30-year period.

1.2 The Biosphere and Energy

All activities require a source of energy—a fuel. For example, to sustain a campfire, you need to keep it supplied with wood. To reach a destination by car, you need to have enough gas in the tank. To migrate successfully, hummingbirds need to burn the fat that is stored in their tissues.

In each of these examples, the fuel is different—wood for the campfire, gasoline for the car, and nectar stored as fat for the hummingbirds. In a different sense, however, the three fuels are the same. They all come from the same source—solar energy that has been converted to and stored as chemical energy. Solar energy is energy from the Sun, as shown in **Figure 1.11**. This energy is given off by nuclear reactions in the Sun. Some organisms in the biosphere trap solar energy and use it to make food, which is then used by all organisms to fuel activity and growth.

Photosynthesis and the Sun's Energy

An enormous amount of energy reaches Earth from the Sun. At the same time, there is a never-ending loss of energy from Earth. The energy is lost as heat when it spreads back out from Earth's surface, beyond Earth's atmosphere. Earth's atmosphere is able to trap some of the heat, warming the atmosphere and making Earth habitable.

Matter is used over and over as it moves through Earth's four spheres. The nutrient cycles you read about in Section 1.1 show this concept. The nutrients may change form or take millions of years to complete their cycle, but no matter is lost as they move through Earth's four spheres.

Chlorophyll and Photosynthesis

The conversion of solar energy to chemical energy, in the form of food, is important to life for two reasons. First, the Sun will continue to supply Earth with energy for billions of years. Second, many organisms on Earth, including plants, algae, and some bacteria, contain chlorophyll, which allows the biosphere to harvest some of this reliable solar energy.

Chlorophyll is the central player in **photosynthesis**, a process that is crucial to life on Earth. The terms "chlorophyll" and "photosynthesis" are both built from ancient Greek words. *Chloros* means green, and *phyllon* means leaf. Chlorophyll is a pigment that gives leaves their green colour. *Photo* means light, and *synthesis* means putting together. Photosynthesis refers to putting something together using light. What does photosynthesis put together using chlorophyll and light? Photosynthesis puts together carbon, hydrogen, and oxygen to make life's universal energy supply— sugar. You may already know that there are different types of sugars. Photosynthesis produces one specific type of sugar, called glucose.

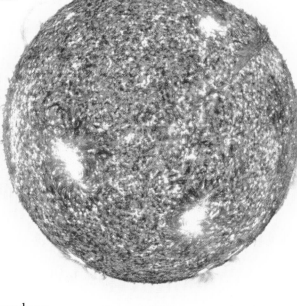

Figure 1.11 Nuclear reactions in the Sun are the energy source for almost all life on Earth. Although only a small fraction of the Sun's energy reaches Earth's surface, this is enough to sustain the biosphere.

photosynthesis a process that changes solar energy into chemical energy

Suggested Investigation

Inquiry Investigation 1-B, The Chemistry of Photosynthesis, on pages 38-39

What Happens During Photosynthesis?

Sugars, including glucose, are in a class of molecules called carbohydrates. Carbohydrates are made from carbon, oxygen, and hydrogen. Thus, to make glucose, plants need ready supplies of these three elements. They get the hydrogen from water, mostly through their roots. They get the carbon and oxygen from carbon dioxide gas, through tiny pores in their leaves called stomata (singular, stoma or stomate), as shown in **Figure 1.12**.

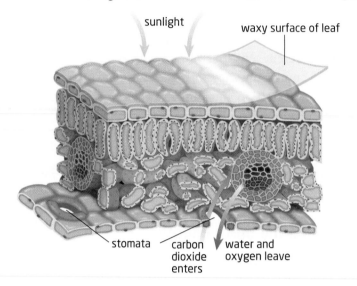

Figure 1.12 Plants take in carbon dioxide and release oxygen through small pores in their leaves called stomata.

In the process of photosynthesis, shown in **Figure 1.13**, the chlorophyll in plant leaves uses solar energy to assemble glucose molecules from water and carbon dioxide. Oxygen is also produced by photosynthesis. The chemical formula for photosynthesis is shown below.

$$6CO_2 \quad + \quad 6H_2O \quad \xrightarrow{\text{light energy}} \quad C_6H_{12}O_6 \quad + \quad 6O_2$$

carbon dioxide   **water**   **glucose**   **oxygen**

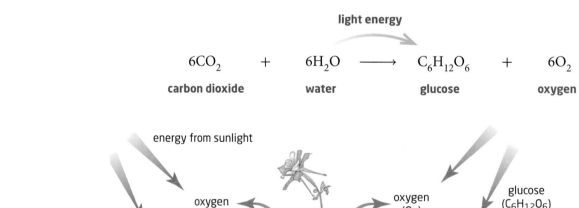

Figure 1.13 Without light energy, photosynthesis cannot occur.

Sources of Oxygen

Photosynthesis is vital for the biosphere. Photosynthesis produces glucose, an energy supply that plants, and the organisms that eat them, require for all of life's essential activities. As well, photosynthesis continuously adds oxygen to the atmosphere, which many organisms breathe. Finally, photosynthesis continuously removes carbon dioxide from the atmosphere.

Wherever there are chlorophyll-containing organisms, oxygen is generated. Not all parts of the biosphere produce oxygen at the same rate, however. **Figure 1.14A** shows that two ecosystems are particularly important. One of these ecosystems is tropical forests. Even though they cover only about 5 percent of Earth's surface, tropical forests are responsible for about 30 percent of Earth's photosynthesis. The second ecosystem is the world's oceans, which are also responsible for about 30 percent of Earth's photosynthesis. In aquatic ecosystems, photosynthesis is mainly performed by algae and chlorophyll-containing microscopic organisms, known as phytoplankton. Phytoplankton are shown in **Figure 1.14B**.

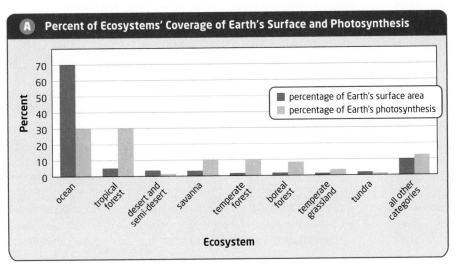

Sense of scale

Photosynthesis produces the equivalent of 100 to 200 billion tonnes of sugar each year. This amount of sugar is enough to make about 3.0×10^{17} sugar cubes!

A Percent of Ecosystems' Coverage of Earth's Surface and Photosynthesis

- percentage of Earth's surface area
- percentage of Earth's photosynthesis

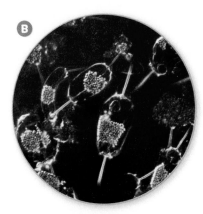

phytoplankton

Figure 1.14 In **A**, the dark blue bars represent the percentage of Earth's surface area that each ecosystem covers. For example, the oceans cover about 70 percent of Earth. The light blue bars represent the percentage of photosynthesis in each ecosystem. **B** shows phytoplankton, which carry out photosynthesis in aquatic ecosystems.

Learning Check

1. What is chlorophyll?

2. Write the word equation for photosynthesis. Indicate the source of each material.

3. Draw a diagram of a leaf, and label the stomata. If the stomata of a leaf are damaged, what are some possible effects?

4. In the winter, very little photosynthesis occurs in Canada. Explain how, on a January day, you may directly benefit from tropical forests.

Trophic Levels

Matter and energy are transferred between trophic levels within the biosphere. A **trophic level** is a category of organisms that is defined by how the organisms gain energy. Examples of trophic levels include primary producers and consumers. *Primary producers* are organisms that can make their own food, such as plants. *Consumers* are organisms that cannot make their own food. Consumers must eat other organisms to get the matter and energy they need to survive.

Study **Figure 1.15**, which shows a sample food chain. Notice that there are four trophic levels in this food chain. The primary producers are at the first trophic level. The grasshopper is the primary consumer, at the second trophic level. The barn swallow is the secondary consumer, at the third trophic level. Secondary consumers eat primary consumers to obtain energy. The hawk, a tertiary consumer, is at the fourth trophic level. Tertiary consumers feed on secondary consumers to obtain energy.

Since the grasshopper only eats plants, it is called a herbivore. Consumers that only eat other animals, such as the barn swallow and the hawk, are called carnivores. Consumers that eat both plants and other animals are called omnivores. Both energy and matter, including nutrients, move through the trophic levels of this food chain.

Notice that all the levels of this food chain are linked to decomposers. Ultimately, decomposers move the nutrients in the decaying bodies and wastes of producers and consumers back to the abiotic parts of the ecosystem as they take in the nutrients they need to survive.

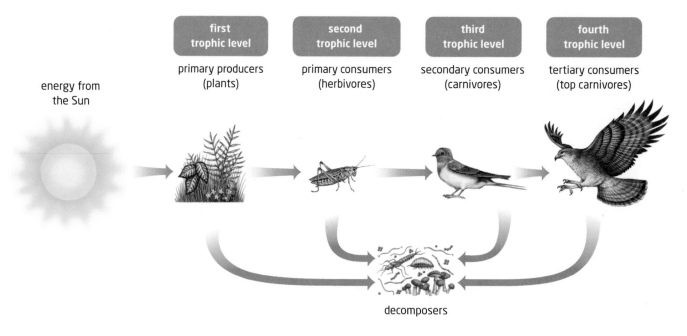

Figure 1.15 Matter moves through the biosphere by travelling from one trophic level to the next in a cycle.

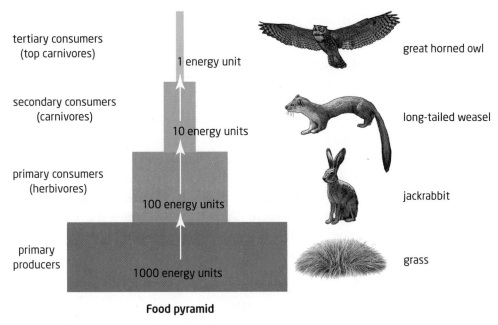

tertiary consumers
(top carnivores)

1 energy unit

great horned owl

secondary consumers
(carnivores)

10 energy units

long-tailed weasel

primary consumers
(herbivores)

100 energy units

jackrabbit

primary
producers

1000 energy units

grass

Food pyramid

Figure 1.16 Energy that is stored in biomass at one trophic level moves to the next trophic level through a food chain.

Trophic Efficiency

Biomass is the mass of living cells and tissues that has been assembled by organisms using solar energy. Leaves, stems, wood, roots, and flower nectar are all packed with chemical energy that has been converted from solar energy. Animals indirectly rely on solar energy too, by eating plants or other animals that eat plants.

Trophic efficiency is a measure of how much of the energy in organisms at one trophic level is transferred to the next higher trophic level. This percentage is always less than 100 percent because organisms use much of the energy from the biomass they consume for their life functions, and they produce wastes as well. In fact, trophic efficiencies are usually quite inefficient—only about 10 percent.

Figure 1.16 shows a sample food chain from a primary producer, grass, to a tertiary consumer, the great horned owl. Suppose that the grass biomass contains 1000 units of energy. If only 10 percent of this energy is transferred to the jackrabbit, only 100 units of energy will reach the jackrabbit. Of these 100 units, only 10 will be transferred from the jackrabbit to the long-tailed weasel. Of the 10 units that reach the weasel, only 1 unit of energy will reach the great horned owl.

There are several reasons why biomass decreases from one trophic level to the next. Herbivores may not eat all the parts of a plant; for example, they may eat only the tops of the plants and leave the roots. Not everything that is eaten is digested; for example, fur may not be digested. Also, at every level, energy is lost as heat from the bodies of organisms. Because of the inefficiency of energy transfer among trophic levels, there are usually fewer carnivores than herbivores, and fewer herbivores than plants.

biomass the total mass of living organisms in a defined group or area

trophic efficiency a measure of the amount of energy or biomass transferred from one trophic level to the next higher trophic level

Water Pollution and Bioaccumulation

The monarch butterfly is poisonous to eat. It does not make its own poison, however. As a caterpillar, it feeds on a plant called milkweed. It ingests toxins, or poisonous substances, from the milkweed. The toxins are stored in the butterfly, in tissues where they do not harm it. The ingestion of toxins at a rate faster than they are eliminated is called **bioaccumulation**.

In this example, bioaccumulation works to the advantage of the species. If fewer individuals of the species are eaten because they are poisonous, more individuals will survive to reproduce. In contrast, the bioaccumulation of toxins from human-made pollution can be devastating to a species. These toxins can cause health problems or death. *Biomagnification* is a process that is related to bioaccumulation. Biomagnification is the increase in the concentration of a toxin as it moves from one trophic level to the next.

bioaccumulation a process in which materials, especially toxins, are ingested by an organism at a rate greater than they are eliminated

DDT

DDT (**d**ichloro-**d**iphenyl-**t**richloroethane) is an agricultural insecticide that was once used in North America. When DDT entered the environment in run-off from land, it was absorbed by algae in the water. Microscopic animals ate the algae, and small fish ate the microscopic animals. At each trophic level in the food chain, the concentration of DDT in the tissues of the organisms increased. At high concentrations, the DDT affected reproduction in fish-eating birds. Following the ban on DDT in the 1970s, populations of DDT-vulnerable birds slowly increased in numbers in Canada.

PCBs

PCBs (**p**oly**c**hlorinated **b**iphenyls) were previously used by industries. PCBs entered water, air, and soil while they were being used and disposed of. **Figure 1.17** shows how the concentration of PCBs, given in parts per million (ppm), is biomagnified in higher-level consumers in the Great Lakes. Peregrine falcons were affected by both DDT and PCBs. Exposure to PCBs also affected reproduction in these birds. After PCBs were banned, peregrine falcons were brought back from the brink of extinction by having captive birds produce young, which were then raised by humans in boxes on nesting cliffs or tall downtown buildings.

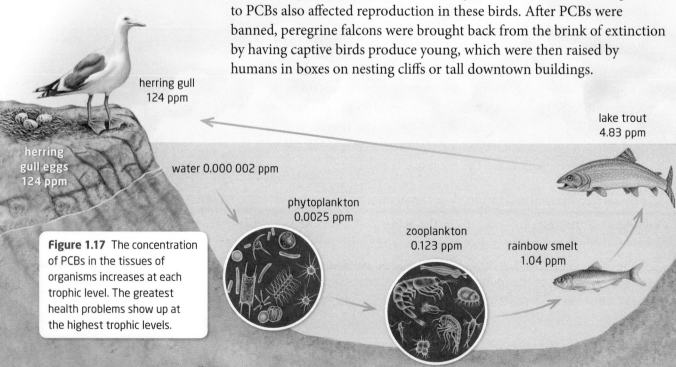

herring gull
124 ppm

lake trout
4.83 ppm

herring gull eggs
124 ppm

water 0.000 002 ppm

phytoplankton
0.0025 ppm

zooplankton
0.123 ppm

rainbow smelt
1.04 ppm

Figure 1.17 The concentration of PCBs in the tissues of organisms increases at each trophic level. The greatest health problems show up at the highest trophic levels.

Section Summary

- The biosphere relies on a constant source of solar energy.
- Chlorophyll in primary producers converts solar energy to chemical energy through photosynthesis.
- Most of the stored energy in one trophic level does not move to the next trophic level.
- Bioaccumulation and biomagnification can result in unhealthy levels of pollutants in organisms.

Review Questions

K/U **1.** Explain the process of photosynthesis.

K/U **2.** What three chemical elements are the building blocks of carbohydrates?

C **3.** Should photosynthesis win the "Most Important Chemical Reaction on Earth" award? Explain your answer.

K/U **4.** What is the difference between a producer and a consumer?

A **5.** Calculate the units of energy at each trophic level in the food chain below, assuming that the trophic efficiency at each level is 10 percent.

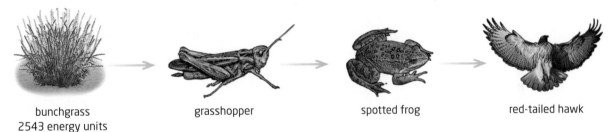

bunchgrass   grasshopper   spotted frog   red-tailed hawk
2543 energy units

K/U **6.** Trophic efficiency is usually only 10 percent. What happens to the energy that does not move up to the next trophic level?

C **7.** Use a Venn diagram to compare and contrast bioaccumulation and biomagnification. Give one example of each.

T/I **8.** Refer to **Figure 1.17**. Suppose that a lake is located beside an abandoned manufacturing plant. Someone discovers that the plant is leaking chemicals into the lake. The chemicals are absorbed by phytoplankton, which are consumed by zooplankton. Which size of fish would you expect to have higher levels of chemicals in their tissues: smaller fish that eat zooplankton or larger fish that eat the smaller fish? Explain your answer.

cellular respiration a process that releases energy from organic molecules, especially carbohydrates, in the presence of oxygen

fermentation a process that releases energy from organic molecules, especially carbohydrates, in the absence of oxygen

1.3 Extracting Energy from Biomass

Photosynthesis produces glucose, removes carbon dioxide from the atmosphere, and supplies the atmosphere with oxygen. Although not all organisms undergo photosynthesis, all organisms, from single-celled bacteria to complex many-celled life forms such as humans, get energy from glucose. For organisms to release and use the energy, however, the glucose has to be broken down. Once this has happened, cells can extract the energy to complete the processes that are essential to life, such as nursing offspring, as shown in **Figure 1.18**. There are two main processes through which organisms extract the energy from glucose: cellular respiration and fermentation. **Cellular respiration** occurs when oxygen is present, or under aerobic conditions. **Fermentation** occurs when oxygen is absent, or under anaerobic conditions. Organisms such as bacteria and some fungi use fermentation to release the energy in glucose.

Cellular Respiration

The most common and efficient method for extracting the energy from glucose is cellular respiration. Plants, animals, fungi, and other organisms use cellular respiration to do this.

In cellular respiration, as in fermentation, the glucose that was originally assembled by photosynthesis is broken down to make the energy available to body cells. The energy you use when you blink your eyes as you read comes from cellular respiration. In contrast to photosynthesis, cellular respiration *consumes* oxygen and *produces* carbon dioxide. The chemical equation for cellular respiration is shown below.

$$C_6H_{12}O_6 \quad + \quad 6O_2 \quad \longrightarrow \quad 6CO_2 \quad + \quad 6H_2O + \text{energy}$$

glucose   oxygen   carbon dioxide   water

Figure 1.18 By eating grass, the cow obtains the glucose produced by photosynthesis. The cow's digestive system breaks down the glucose to release the energy. The energy is used to complete life processes, such as reproducing and nursing young.

Extracting Energy from Food

In cellular respiration, organisms take in oxygen, which reacts with the glucose in cells to produce carbon dioxide, water, and energy. All organisms undergo some type of process to extract energy from biomass, whether in the presence of oxygen or not. Most organisms, including animals and plants, extract energy through the process of cellular respiration. So, even though plants produce their own food through photosynthesis, they still have to break down the glucose to get energy from it. Plants break down the glucose through cellular respiration. **Figure 1.19** shows how a plant uses both carbon dioxide and oxygen to carry out life processes.

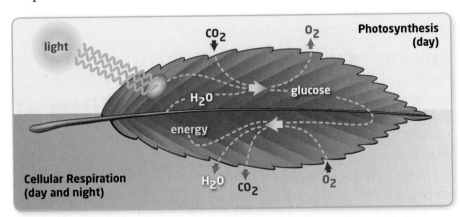

Figure 1.19 Plants and algae undergo both photosynthesis and cellular respiration. Cellular respiration makes energy available to cells by consuming oxygen and producing water and carbon dioxide.

Carbon Dioxide and Other Greenhouse Gases

Greenhouse gases are atmospheric gases that prevent heat from leaving the atmosphere, thus increasing the temperature of the atmosphere. Examples of greenhouse gases include water vapour, carbon dioxide, and methane. Without greenhouse gases, Earth's temperatures would average less than 0°C. This natural insulating capacity of greenhouse gases, shown in **Figure 1.20**, is known as the **greenhouse effect**.

greenhouse gases atmospheric gases that prevent heat from leaving the atmosphere, thus increasing the temperature of the atmosphere

greenhouse effect the warming of Earth as a result of greenhouse gases, which trap some of the energy that would otherwise leave Earth

Figure 1.20 Greenhouse gases trap heat within Earth's atmosphere, similar to the way that glass traps heat within a greenhouse.

Biomass and Fossil Fuels

Based on fossil evidence, scientists have concluded that single-celled organisms used photosynthesis to generate biomass more than 3 billion years ago. Most of the matter in this biomass has been cycled through the biosphere countless times. Small amounts, however, escaped the biosphere's cycling system when the remains of organisms settled in places where there was not enough oxygen to decompose them. Over time, with pressure and heat, the biomass changed into fossil fuels such as coal, petroleum, and natural gas. Because fossil fuels come from biomass that was produced by photosynthesis millions of years ago, it is not surprising that burning them has an effect that is very similar to cellular respiration. Both processes are chemical reactions that consume oxygen, release energy, and produce carbon dioxide.

Enhanced Greenhouse Effect

Fossil fuels have been accumulating for many millions of years. However, significant portions of Earth's reserves have been burned by humans in the span of only a few centuries. Because humans have "suddenly" released much of the carbon dioxide that was converted to biomass by ancient plants, the net result for the atmosphere is added carbon dioxide.

Figure 1.21A shows that since the Industrial Revolution, which began in the late 1700s, the concentration of carbon dioxide in the atmosphere has increased. The Industrial Revolution marked the start of increased and widespread burning of fossil fuels as a source of energy for many countries around the world. Many scientists hypothesize that the increased concentration of carbon dioxide in the atmosphere, along with an increase in other greenhouse gases, such as methane, is the cause of global warming.

Global warming is the increase in Earth's average surface temperature. **Figure 1.21B** shows that as the amount of carbon dioxide in the atmosphere has increased, so has Earth's average surface temperature.

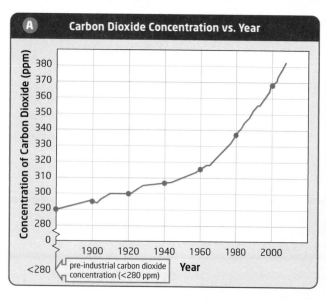

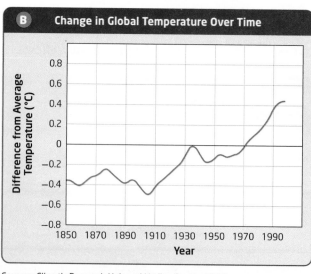

Sources: Climatic Research Unit and Hadley Centre, 2008

Figure 1.21 A Since the Industrial Revolution, carbon dioxide levels have risen steadily. **B** Earth's average surface temperature has also increased by about 0.74°C.

Reducing Carbon Dioxide in the Atmosphere

There are many ways to reduce the amount of carbon dioxide being released into the atmosphere. These include international initiatives by governments from around the world, initiatives by the federal, provincial, and local governments of Canada, and efforts by individuals. **Table 1.3** presents three examples of efforts to reduce carbon dioxide.

Table 1.3 Reducing Carbon Dioxide in the Atmosphere

Action	Description	
Kyoto Protocol	The Kyoto Protocol is an international agreement to reduce greenhouse gas emissions, which was signed by over 180 countries. To meet the terms of the Protocol, countries can reduce emissions or get credits for removing carbon dioxide from the atmosphere by planting trees in non-forested areas. Since plants remove carbon dioxide from the atmosphere, large areas of trees and other plants, such as forests, are known as carbon sinks.	
Protecting existing forests	In July 2008, Ontario announced that roughly half of its boreal forests will be protected. The protected forests will only be used for tourism and traditional Aboriginal purposes. About 225 000 km² of forests will be protected from logging, mining, and oil and natural gas exploration. Like other forests, the boreal forest in Ontario is a carbon sink, absorbing about 12 million tonnes of carbon dioxide per year.	
Recycling programs	Recycling helps to reduce carbon dioxide emissions because, in most cases, less energy is needed to make something from recycled materials than from new materials. For example, energy input is reduced by 95 percent when an aluminum product is made from recycled aluminum, rather than a raw material. In 1978, the Recycling Council of Ontario was established in Toronto, Ontario. Through its programs, more than 2.3 million tonnes of waste are recycled or composted each year.	

Learning Check

1. Explain the process of cellular respiration.

2. Describe the greenhouse effect.

3. Make a list of actions you could take to reduce the amount of carbon dioxide being released by the burning of fossil fuels.

4. As you write your answers to questions, using either a pen or a keyboard, you are using energy. Draw a flowchart that traces this energy back to the Sun.

Recycling in Ontario

Recycling helps to reduce the amount of carbon dioxide released into the atmosphere and the amount of waste placed in landfills. The table below contains data from Statistics Canada. Electronic waste consists of materials such as computers, printers, and cellphones.

Amounts of Materials Recycled in Ontario in 2002, 2004, and 2006 (t)

Material Recycled	2002	2004	2006
Newspapers	479 473	410 496	380 281
Cardboard	357 881	467 476	474 211
Glass	152 484	189 804	179 341
Aluminum and copper	17 265	21 327	21 290
Plastic	37 396	52 935	60 195
Tires	no data	6 441	4 948
Electronic waste	no data	5 259	4 251

Materials

- graph paper
- ruler
- coloured pencils

Procedure

1. Construct a bar graph with "Year" on the *x*-axis and "Tonnes of Recycled Materials" on the *y*-axis. Plot the data for newspapers, cardboard, and glass for each year. Use a different-coloured pencil to represent each material.

2. Construct a second bar graph to plot the data for the remaining materials listed in the table.

Questions

1. Describe the trend in recycling for each material in your graphs.

2. What factors may be affecting the amounts of materials that are being recycled in Ontario?

3. Some people, such as those who live in rural areas or apartment buildings, may not be included in curb-side recycling programs. Describe an action that could be taken by the Government of Ontario or by an environmental group to ensure that recycling programs reach these people.

Fermentation, Methane, and Landfills

Landfill sites are not as attractive as tropical rainforests, but the gulls, raccoons, and other animals that visit them confirm they are ecosystems. The presence of these animals is usually obvious. Either the animals themselves or the evidence of their visits can be seen. There are, however, other organisms in a landfill ecosystem—organisms that are not as easily seen. Within the landfill are organic wastes, such as food scraps and yard waste, which contain countless energy-storing molecules, especially glucose from photosynthesis. Here, many trillions of bacteria are at work.

Figure 1.22 Methane from a landfill site can be processed, and then transported to a nearby power generating plant, where it can be burned to produce electricity.

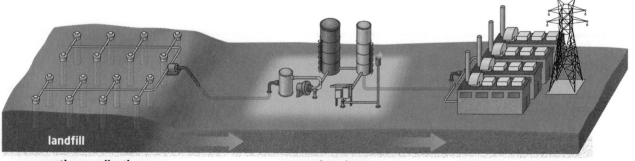

landfill

methane collection processing plant power generating plant

Fuel from Waste

Since there is almost no oxygen in a landfill ecosystem, the bacteria break down the glucose in the waste using fermentation. This process allows them to use some of the energy that is stored in the glucose molecules. But they cannot extract all the energy. The energy they cannot extract gets re-assembled into a gas called methane (CH_4). The bacteria then release this gas, which moves through the landfill.

Methane gas is a fuel. Recognizing that fermentation in landfills produces large quantities of methane, Ontario has introduced a law requiring all large landfill sites to install pipes to collect the gas. **Figure 1.22** shows how methane gas is collected from a landfill and burned to produce electricity. Many homes in Canada run on electricity that is at least partly generated from bacteria at a local landfill site! In Sudbury, Ontario, methane gas from a landfill site is used to produce about 1.6 MW (megawatts) of electricity per year. This is enough energy to power about 1200 homes.

Go to **scienceontario** to find out more

Acid Precipitation

Since fossil fuels come from ancient organisms, they contain the same nutrients that are found in living things. Although these nutrients are vital for the health of living things, they can be released in undesirable forms when fossil fuels are burned. **Figure 1.23** shows how nitrogen oxides and sulfur dioxide are produced when fossil fuels are burned. When these gases combine with water in the atmosphere, nitric acid and sulfuric acid are produced. These acids can travel great distances in the wind, eventually descending to Earth's surface in rain, sleet, or snow. As a result, the precipitation becomes acidic. This phenomenon is called **acid precipitation**.

acid precipitation rain, snow, or fog that is unnaturally acidic due to gases in the atmosphere that react with water to form acids

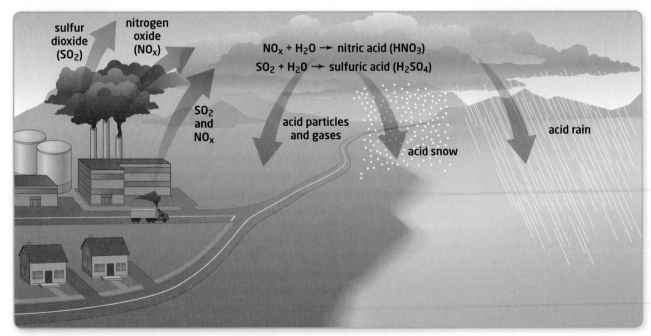

Figure 1.23 Acids from burning fossil fuels combine with water in the atmosphere to form acid precipitation. Acid precipitation may fall locally or hundreds of kilometres downwind, far from the source.

Measuring pH

Suggested Investigation

Inquiry Investigation 1-C, Soil-water Acidity and Plant Growth, on pages 40-41

Like the pH of other substances, the pH of precipitation can be measured. A pH scale is shown in **Figure 1.24**. A substance that has a pH of 7, such as pure water, is considered neutral. A substance that has a pH higher than 7 is considered basic. A substance that has a pH below 7 is considered acidic. The closer the pH is to 0, the stronger the acid is. The pH of rainwater that has not been affected by pollution is about 5.6. The pH of acid precipitation can be as low as 4.2.

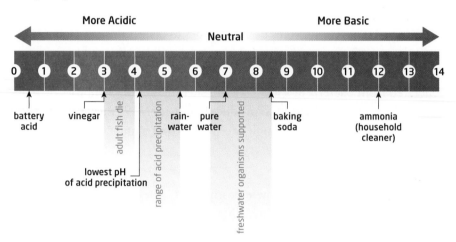

Figure 1.24 The pH scale identifies a substance as acidic, neutral, or basic.

Effects of Acid Precipitation

Continued exposure to acid precipitation causes forest soils to lose valuable nutrients, such as calcium. Although calcium does not dissolve in water, it does dissolve in acids, so it can be washed away. On the other hand, acid precipitation increases the amount of aluminum in soil, which interferes with the uptake of nutrients by trees. Some trees, such as those shown in **Figure 1.25**, cannot survive the changes to their ecosystem caused by acid precipitation.

Acid precipitation can be even more devastating to aquatic ecosystems, because it can lower the pH of the water, causing problems for fish, amphibians, and other organisms that live in the water. Many aquatic organisms cannot survive if the pH of the water begins to drop. **Figure 1.26** shows the tolerance level of certain aquatic organisms to pH changes in the water. Some organisms, such as clams and snails, are very sensitive to a drop in pH. Other organisms, such as frogs, have a higher tolerance for changes. However, if the food that the organisms consume, such as the mayflies that frogs consume, cannot survive, then the organisms will face a reduced food supply.

Ecologists at the Experimental Lakes Area demonstrated many negative effects of acidification when they modelled acid precipitation by adding acids to the experimental lakes. Because the ecologists were required to return the lakes to a natural state following their experiments, they also studied how lakes can recover from acid damage.

Figure 1.25 Trees in this forest could not survive changes to the environment as a result of acid rain.

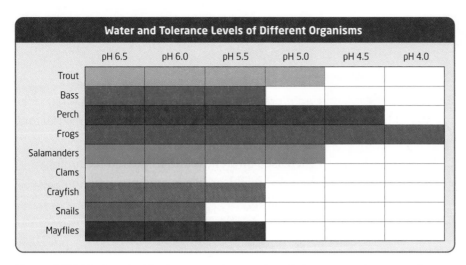

Figure 1.26 The bars in this chart extend out to the pH that an organism can no longer tolerate. For example, trout cannot survive if the pH of the water drops below 5.

Reducing Acid Precipitation

In the 1980s, by studying wind patterns, precipitation, and sources of pollution, scientists discovered that more than half of the acid precipitation in eastern Canada came from pollution sources in the United States, including states that border the Great Lakes. Negotiations between the two countries led to agreements and laws that reduced emissions in both countries. The graph in **Figure 1.27** shows the extent to which Canada has reduced its emissions of sulfur dioxide and nitrogen oxides since 1990.

Like eutrophication, however, acid precipitation has not disappeared. But improved technologies, such as scrubbers to remove undesirable gases from industrial emissions, as well as higher standards for motor-vehicle emissions, have reduced the acidity of precipitation since the 1980s.

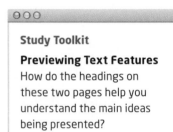

Study Toolkit

Previewing Text Features
How do the headings on these two pages help you understand the main ideas being presented?

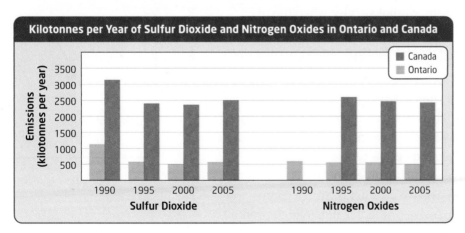

Figure 1.27 Canada has made progress in reducing its emissions of sulfur dioxide and nitrogen oxides.

Section 1.3 Review

Section Summary

- Organisms use cellular respiration and fermentation to extract the energy stored in the glucose produced by photosynthesis.

- Burning fossil fuels has dramatically increased the concentration of carbon dioxide, a greenhouse gas, in the atmosphere.

- Acid precipitation is caused by burning fossil fuels. It can have negative effects on terrestrial and aquatic ecosystems.

- Increased awareness and improved technology have led to a decrease in acid precipitation since the 1980s.

Review Questions

K/U **1.** Identify two processes that organisms use to extract the energy stored in the glucose produced by photosynthesis.

K/U **2.** What gas must be present for the aerobic breakdown of glucose to occur?

C **3.** Draw a flowchart to show how methane gas can be collected from a landfill site and used to produce electricity.

K/U **4.** Write two or three sentences to explain the following statement: "In the last 200 years, humans have 'suddenly' released previously stored carbon dioxide."

K/U **5.** What substances that are responsible for acid precipitation are released into the atmosphere from burning fossil fuels?

T/I **6.** Certain types of aquatic organisms, such as clams and crayfish, are negatively affected when the pH of the water drops below 5.5. Some fish, such as trout, cannot survive when the pH of the water drops below 5.0. Use the graph on the right to determine whether any of these organisms can survive if a lake becomes acidic.

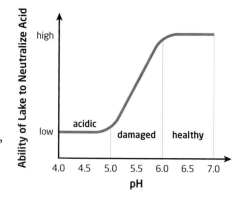

Acid Neutralization and the pH of Lake Water

T/I **7.** Suppose that you have a choice between two products of equal quality. You look at the labels of the two products to see where they were made. You have a list of countries that are committed, under an international agreement, to requiring industries to become more efficient by reducing greenhouse gas emissions. You see that the more expensive product is from a country on your list, but the less expensive product is not. Which product would you buy? Explain your choice.

A **8.** Many Ontario residents commute thousands of kilometres each year by car between home and work. How may their commuting be connected to the death of trees?

Skill Check

✓ Initiating and Planning

✓ Performing and Recording

✓ Analyzing and Interpreting

✓ Communicating

Safety Precautions

- To avoid skin irritation, use rubber gloves when handling the fertilizer.
- Follow your teacher's directions when disposing of the fertilizer.
- Clean any spills immediately, and inform your teacher.

Suggested Materials

- balance
- scoop
- 50 mL graduated cylinder
- small funnel
- five 250 mL beakers
- liquid fertilizer that contains nitrogen and phosphorus
- algae culture
- distilled water
- adhesive labels
- marker

Algae need light to grow. Put your beakers in a sunny place.

Fertilizers and Algae Growth

Fertilizers in run-off from agriculture can add extra nutrients to aquatic ecosystems. In this investigation, you will model what happens when fertilizer in run-off enters aquatic ecosystems.

Question

How does fertilizer affect algae growth?

Plan and Conduct

1. Brainstorm how you could test the effects of fertilizer on algae growth.

2. Determine what your independent variable will be. What will your dependent variable be? Will you have a control group?

3. Make a table for recording your data. How often will you make observations?

4. Ask your teacher to approve your investigation procedure, data table, and safety precautions.

5. Carry out your investigation.

Analyze and Interpret

1. What was your independent variable? What was your dependent variable?

2. Describe the changes you observed in the dependent variable, and propose an explanation.

Conclude and Communicate

3. Suppose that a large quantity of fertilizer was added to a lake ecosystem. Suggest what might happen to the populations of

   a. producers   **b.** consumers   **c.** decomposers

4. Think about the tools, techniques, and processes that you used to gather evidence. What improvements could you make?

Extend Your Inquiry and Research Skills

5. **Research** Most fertilizers are described by three numbers, which give the ratio of nitrogen (N) to phosphorus (P) to potassium (K). Research why potassium is added to fertilizers.

Inquiry Investigation 1-B

Safety Precautions

- Follow your teacher's directions for safe conduct.
- Wear appropriate safety equipment in the laboratory.
- Never taste or eat any materials in the laboratory.
- Clean any spills immediately.

Materials

- 250 mL beaker
- water
- bromothymol solution
- drinking straw
- 2 test tubes with stoppers
- test-tube rack
- 2 freshwater plant sprigs (*Elodea* or a similar species)
- black paper
- masking tape

Science Skills

Go to **Science Skills Toolkit 12** for information about conducting research.

The Chemistry of Photosynthesis

You have already read that plants take in carbon dioxide from the atmosphere for the process of photosynthesis. Unfortunately, the gas exchange between a plant and the surrounding air is not something you can observe by just looking at a plant. When carbon dioxide gas dissolves in water, however, it forms a weak solution of carbonic acid. You can measure the acidity of the water using a chemical indicator, such as bromothymol blue, whose colour is dependent on acidity.

Question

How can you demonstrate that plants absorb carbon dioxide?

The contents of both test tubes are the same. What variable does the black paper control?

Procedure

1. Fill the beaker with 200 mL of water. Then add three drops of bromothymol blue. This indicator is blue when the pH of a solution is 7 or higher (basic) and yellow when the pH of a solution is less than 7 (acidic).

2. Use the drinking straw to gently blow into the solution until the indicator changes colour. CAUTION: Ensure that you blow gently and are wearing safety goggles.

3. Pour the solution into two test tubes until the test tubes are three quarters full.

4. Add a sprig of the plant to each test tube. Seal each test tube with a stopper.

5. Tape a piece of black paper around one of the test tubes so that no light can enter.

6. Place both test tubes back in the test-tube rack. Place the test-tube rack in bright sunlight for several hours.

7. Remove the paper from the test tube. Record your observations of both test tubes.

Analyze and Interpret

1. What gas did you add to the solution using the straw?

2. Why did this gas produce a colour change in the indicator?

3. Describe what colour change you observed in each test tube.

4. Explain your observations, with reference to the equation for photosynthesis in Section 1.2.

Conclude and Communicate

5. Did this investigation have a control? If so, identify the control. If not, suggest what control you would set up, and explain why.

6. How does this investigation demonstrate the stages of the carbon cycle? To answer, make a simple sketch that shows the flow of carbon you observed.

Extend Your Inquiry and Research Skills

7. **Inquiry** Think of another question you would like to investigate about photosynthesis. How would you design an experiment to help you find the answer?

8. **Research** Write a brief report about the contributions of one of the following scientists to our understanding of photosynthesis:
   - Jan Baptista van Helmont (1577–1644)
   - Jan Ingenhousz (1730–1799)
   - Joseph Priestley (1733–1804)
   - Jean Senebier (1742–1809)
   - Nicolas de Saussure (1767–1845)
   - Julius von Sachs (1832–1897)

Inquiry Investigation 1-C

Skill Check

✓ **Initiating and Planning**

✓ **Performing and Recording**

✓ **Analyzing and Interpreting**

✓ **Communicating**

Safety Precautions

- You will be working with liquids of different acidities. Avoid getting these liquids on your skin and clothing.
- If you spill a liquid on your skin or clothing, rinse with plenty of water.
- Inform your teacher of any spills, and follow his or her directions for safe clean-up.

Materials

- 5 small plastic or paper cups
- pencil
- marker
- tray
- potting soil
- seeds (such as beans, radish, or Brassica)
- 50 mL graduated cylinder
- 5 stoppered Erlenmeyer flasks, containing solutions with pH levels of 3, 4, 5, 6, and 7
- ruler
- grow light (optional)

Math Skills
Go to **Math Skills Toolkit 3** for information about constructing graphs.

Soil-water Acidity and Plant Growth

Certain types of air pollution can make rainwater more acidic. Rainwater is absorbed into the ground and the soil, and then taken up by plants. In this investigation, you will compare plant growth in soils that have absorbed water of different acidity levels. Remember that the lower the pH, the higher the acidity is.

Question

How does the acidity of rainwater influence the fertility of soil?

Hypothesis

Make a hypothesis about how the plants will respond to increasing levels of acidity in the soil and water.

How are plants affected by acid rain?

Procedure

1. With a pencil tip, poke a hole in the bottom of each cup for drainage.

2. Label each cup with your name(s) and the level of pH (pH 3, pH 4, pH 5, pH 6, pH 7, respectively).

3. Place the cups on the tray.

4. Add soil to each cup until the cup is three quarters full.

5. Place a bean, or another seed, about 3 cm below the surface of the soil in each cup. Cover the seed with soil.

6. Using the graduated cylinder, water the seed in each numbered cup with 10 mL of water from the Erlenmeyer flask with the matching pH number. Be sure to rinse the graduated cylinder after you water each seed.

7. Place the tray in the sunlight or under a grow light, if possible.

8. Water each seed daily with 10 mL of water if the tray is in the sunlight or under a grow light. Otherwise, use 5 mL of water per day. Pour the water directly into the soil, not on any leaves.

9. Make a table like the one shown below. Give your table a title.

Day	Water pH	Plant Height (cm)	Number of Leaves	Leaf Colour
Day 1	pH 3			
	pH 4			
	pH 5			
	pH 6			
	pH 7			
Day 2	pH 3			
	pH 4			
	pH 5			
	pH 6			
	pH 7			

10. Make and record your observations about the height of each plant, the number of leaves, and the leaf colour every day for two weeks.

Analyze and Interpret

1. Construct and plot a graph for each plant with "Time (days)" on the x-axis and "Plant Height (cm)" on the y-axis.

2. Which pH level supported the greatest rate of growth? Which pH level produced the least growth?

Conclude and Communicate

3. Based on your analysis, write a general statement about the effect of rainwater pH on the soils in which plants are growing.

4. Was your hypothesis supported by your results? Explain why or why not.

Extend Your Inquiry and Research Skills

5. **Inquiry** How acidic is the rain in your area? Design an investigation in which you use pH paper and clean containers to test the rainwater in your area and compare it with rainwater in other parts of the province.

6. **Inquiry** The effects of acid precipitation on soil pH vary with the type of underlying bedrock. Design an investigation to identify the types of rock that are good at neutralizing acidic conditions.

Plan Your Own Investigation 1-D

Skill Check

✓ Initiating and Planning

✓ Performing and Recording

✓ Analyzing and Interpreting

✓ Communicating

Safety Precautions

- To avoid skin irritation, use rubber gloves when handling the fertilizer.
- Follow your teacher's directions when disposing of fertilizers.
- Clean any spills immediately, and inform your teacher.

Suggested Materials

- green pea seeds
- large cups
- soil
- garden trawl
- marker
- water
- fertilizer that contains nitrogen
- soil test kits for nitrogen

Fertilizer is beneficial to plants, but how much is too much?

Can a Plant Have Too Much Fertilizer?

A fertilizer can include a human-made chemical or compost from animals and other organic wastes. If a small amount of fertilizer produces healthy plants with a lot of tomatoes, will a lot of fertilizer produce larger plants with more or larger tomatoes? Can a plant have too much fertilizer? In this investigation, you will monitor the effects of fertilizer and the nitrogen content of soil on the growth of plants.

Hypothesis

Make a hypothesis about how the pea plants will respond to different amounts of fertilizer.

Plan and Conduct

1. Brainstorm how you could test the effects of fertilizer on plant growth. Write a question to focus your investigation.

2. Determine what your independent variable will be. What will your dependent variable be? Will you have a control group? How will you measure the effects of the fertilizer?

3. Make a table for recording your data. How often will you make observations?

4. Ask your teacher to approve your investigation procedure, data table, and safety precautions.

5. Carry out your investigation.

Analyze and Interpret

1. From your observations, write a general statement about the effects of fertilizer on pea plant growth.

Conclude and Communicate

2. Why is it important to know how much fertilizer to add to a garden or an agricultural field?

3. Suppose that a large quantity of fertilizer was added to an agricultural field. How might the run-off affect trees in a nearby forest?

Extend Your Inquiry and Research Skills

4. **Inquiry** Design an experiment to test how the addition of compost to the soil affects plant growth. How could you test the effectiveness of compost made from different sources, such as animal manure, grass clippings and leaves, and leftover food?

Chapter 1 Summary

1.1 Sustainability

Key Concepts

- Sustainable ecosystems endure, and they sustain the organisms that live within them.

- Matter, including nutrients such as nitrogen, are constantly moving through Earth's spheres.

- Human activities that increase the influx of nutrients into a terrestrial or aquatic ecosystem can upset the nutrient balance in the ecosystem.

- Decisions and actions that are taken to protect the health of ecosystems may involve international agreements and court decisions.

1.2 The Biosphere and Energy

Key Concepts

- The biosphere relies on a constant stream of solar energy.

- Chlorophyll in primary producers converts solar energy to chemical energy through photosynthesis.

- Most of the stored energy in one trophic level does not move to the next trophic level.

- Bioaccumulation and biomagnification can result in unhealthy levels of pollutants in organisms.

1.3 Extracting Energy from Biomass

Key Concepts

- Organisms use cellular respiration and fermentation to extract the energy stored in the glucose produced by photosynthesis.

- Burning fossil fuels has dramatically increased the concentration of carbon dioxide, a greenhouse gas, in the atmosphere.

- Acid precipitation is caused by burning fossil fuels. It can have negative effects on terrestrial and aquatic ecosystems.

- Increased awareness and improved technology have led to a decrease in acid precipitation since the 1980s.

Make Your Own Summary

Summarize the key concepts of this chapter using a graphic organizer. The Chapter Summary on the previous page will help you identify the key concepts. Refer to Study Toolkit 4 on pages 566–567 to help you decide which graphic organizer to use.

Reviewing Key Terms

1. The regions of Earth where living organisms exist is called the _____. (1.1)

2. _____ is a process in which nutrient levels in aquatic ecosystems increase, leading to an increase in the populations of primary producers. (1.1)

3. An _____ includes all the interacting parts of a biological community and its environment. (1.1)

4. The chemical reaction that changes solar energy into chemical energy is _____. (1.2)

5. A category of living things that is defined by how they gain energy is called a _____. (1.2)

6. _____ is a process that derives energy from organic molecules in the presence of oxygen (1.3)

7. The warming of Earth caused by greenhouse gases trapping some of the energy that would otherwise leave Earth is called the _____. (1.3)

Knowledge and Understanding K/U

8. Explain the meaning of the word "ecosystem."

9. Sustainable ecosystems "endure and support." Clarify what this means.

10. Explain why keeping aquatic ecosystems sustainable is important to organisms that live in terrestrial ecosystems.

11. What organisms are considered primary producers? What important function do they perform in the biosphere?

12. Copy the following diagram into your notebook. Use arrows to indicate the direction of the movement of water in the diagram. Then identify and explain the process that occurs at each numbered step.

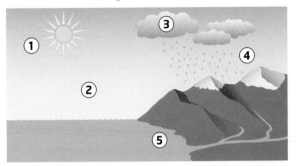

13. What is one possible cause of the increase in carbon dioxide in the atmosphere since the mid-19th century?

14. Explain the connection between fossil fuels and photosynthesis.

15. Identify the key difference between cellular respiration and fermentation.

16. Greenhouse gases are in Earth's atmosphere.

    a. List three examples of greenhouse gases.

    b. How have greenhouse gases affected the biosphere?

17. Countries around the world are monitoring carbon dioxide emissions.

    a. What is the Kyoto Protocol?

    b. How can countries reduce the amount of carbon dioxide that they are releasing into the atmosphere?

Thinking and Investigation T/I

18. Research information about a local landfill site. Find the answers to the following questions:

    a. Is methane extracted at this landfill site?

    b. Is this landfill site working on a plan to conform with the Ontario legislation to collect methane gas?

    c. Does this landfill site have a plan to use the collected methane?

d. Although the methane can be simply burned off, the Ontario legislation requires landfills to collect methane. Why?

19. Make a list of the ways in which you use fossils fuels (directly or indirectly) in a typical day. Consider which two events or activities would be easiest for you to change to reduce your consumption of fossil fuels.

20. Canada has made progress in reducing its emissions of sulfur dioxide and nitrogen oxides, the two substances that acidify precipitation. What are some contributions that individuals can make to reduce these emissions?

Communication C

21. **BIG IDEAS** Ecosystems are dynamic and have the ability to respond to change, within limits, while maintaining their ecological balance. Draw a diagram to show what happens to excess nitrogen in an ecosystem. Label the pathway of nitrogen from its gas form in the atmosphere, to the lithosphere, and back to the atmosphere again. Identify clearly on your diagram some human factors that could alter the balance in this pathway. Show and explain, why, within limits, excess nitrogen does not upset the balance of that ecosystem.

22. **BIG IDEAS** People have the responsibility to regulate their impact on the sustainability of ecosystems in order to preserve them for future generations. Write an e-mail to a friend, explaining why it is important for governments to protect areas of existing forest.

23. Suppose that you are a science teacher. Your class of Grade 5 students is studying trophic levels. Prepare an explanation that will help the students identify the trophic level of each organism in the following food chain in an aquatic ecosystem:

    Zooplankton are microscopic animals that eat phytoplankton. Zooplankton are eaten by crabs. Sea otters eat crabs.

24. Draw a diagram that represents the position and interaction of Earth's four spheres (lithosphere, hydrosphere, atmosphere, and biosphere).

25. Copy the following table into your notebook. Complete the table to compare photosynthesis and cellular respiration.

Reaction	Photosynthesis	Cellular respiration
Organism in Which Reaction Occurs		
Reactants		
Products		
Is Energy Absorbed or Released?		

26. In the past, one response to concerns about industrial pollution was to build taller smokestacks, so that pollution from the burning fossil fuels was released higher into the atmosphere. Write two or three sentences that make an argument against building taller smokestacks at industrial sites as a long-term solution to pollution.

27. Write a short paragraph that explains the difference between the greenhouse effect and the enhanced greenhouse effect.

Application A

28. Describe a sample scenario to explain how an animal living hundreds of kilometres from an area sprayed with DDT might get DDT in its body.

29. DDT is stored in the body fat of organisms and remains toxic for many years. Explain why these two characteristics are undesirable in a pesticide. What characteristics would you want in a pesticide to make it less harmful to non-pest organisms?

30. If you eat a plate of rice with vegetables for lunch, at what trophic level are you? If you eat a hamburger for lunch, at what trophic level are you? Explain.

Chapter 2 Populations and Sustainable Ecosystems

What You Will Learn

In this chapter, you will learn how to...

- **explain** that populations tend to increase until they reach a natural limit
- **explain** how factors affect the carrying capacity of an ecosystem
- **describe** how no two species have exactly the same function in an ecosystem
- **explain** the value of ecological processes, known as ecosystem services

Why It Matters

For any given species, the number of organisms that an ecosystem can support is limited. Human populations are not exempt from this limiting principle. As the human population continues to increase, issues related to sustainability must be considered.

Skills You Will Use

In this chapter, you will learn how to...

- **monitor** and **manipulate** the growth of populations of organisms
- **analyze** the effect of human activity on the population of fish by interpreting data and generating graphs
- **assess** your own impact on the ecosystems that sustain you

The way each species occupies a particular place in an ecosystem makes it a unique contributor to the biosphere. It provides services for other species, including humans. For example, the great grey owl lives in boreal forests throughout Canada. During the winter, the great grey owl eats large numbers of meadow voles, a rodent that can be a farm pest when its population grows too big.

Activity 2-1

Reducing Wildlife Mortality with Fences

As humans build more roads, the number of wildlife deaths due to vehicle collisions is increasing. These deaths can have a major influence on the population and status of a species. Some species that have been affected by deaths from vehicle collisions include the painted turtle, the white-tailed deer, and the black bear. The graph below shows the mortality rates of animals along sections of the Trans-Canada Highway (TCH).

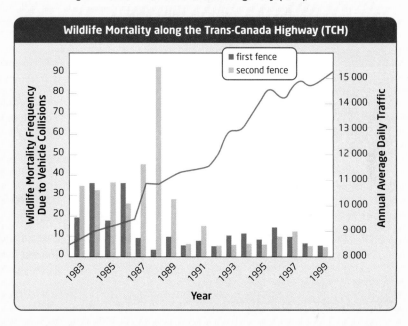

Wildlife Mortality along the Trans-Canada Highway (TCH)

Procedure

1. Study the graph above. The data were collected as part of an attempt to reduce animal deaths from vehicle collisions. Fencing was installed along sections of the TCH. Scientists collected data on the mortality rates of animals, as well as the amount of daily traffic along the fenced sections.

Questions

1. What wildlife mortality patterns does the graph show?

2. What happened to the amount of daily traffic between 1983 and 1999?

3. Did the fencing succeed in reducing wildlife mortality due to vehicle collisions? Explain your answer using data from the graph.

4. Why do you think it is important to monitor wildlife mortality due to vehicle collisions?

Study Toolkit

These strategies will help you use this textbook to develop your understanding of science concepts and skills. To find out more about these and other strategies, refer to the Study Toolkit Overview, which begins on page 561.

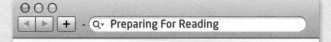

Making Connections to Visuals

Textbook writers include visuals to clarify or expand on information in the text. Making connections to visuals will help you understand their purpose and meaning. When you look at a visual in a textbook, first read the caption. Then think about the answers to these questions:

1. What personal connections can I make to the photograph, based on my prior knowledge?
2. What do the accompanying text and the caption tell me about the photograph?
3. What else might be in the scene that the photograph does *not* show?
4. What questions do I have about the photograph that the text and caption do not answer?

Use the Strategy

With a partner, examine **Figure 2.1** on the opposite page. Discuss answers to the four questions above.

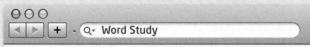

Base Words

One strategy to figure out the meaning of a new word is to cut it down to its *base*. For example, follow these steps to figure out the meaning of *intensification*.

1. Cut the word down to *intensify*.
2. Cut *intensify* down to its base: *intense*. This means *strong* or *powerful*.
3. Now build the word back up from the base. Adding *-ify* changes the meaning to *become or make more intense*.
4. Adding *-ation* indicates a state of being or a process, so now you can figure out that *intensification* means *the process of becoming more intense*.

Use the Strategy

Follow the steps above to predict the meaning of *desertification*. Check your prediction as you read Chapter 2, or consult the Glossary at the back of this book.

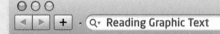

Interpreting Line Graphs

Line graphs are diagrams that show relationships between two sets of numbers. Before interpreting a line graph, first read its title, the labels on the *x*-axis and the *y*-axis, and the caption. Note metric units and how the sets of numbers are scaled.

To interpret a line graph, look for and describe patterns in the shape of the graph. For example, the graph on the right shows a steady decline in the number of eggs laid by female sparrows as the number of females increases. This pattern can be used to predict that the number of eggs laid will continue to decline as the number of female sparrows increases.

Use the Strategy

Examine the line graph in **Figure 2.5** on page 51.

1. Read the graph's title, axis labels, and caption.
2. Identify any patterns that define the relationship between the two sets of data.
3. Write a description of the pattern.
4. Use the pattern to make predictions about the future.

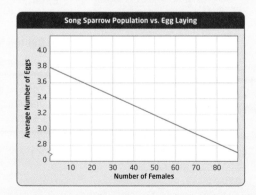

2.1 Populations and Resources

A **population** is a group of organisms of one species that lives in the same place, at the same time, and can successfully reproduce. All populations tend to increase when individuals reproduce at rates that are greater than what is needed to replace individuals that have left the area or died. This is even true for organisms that reproduce slowly, such as elephants. Elephants only produce about six offspring in a 100-year life span. In theory, the descendants of a single pair of elephants could number 19 million after 750 years!

Exponential Growth

Population growth that occurs like this is called exponential growth. Usually, **exponential growth** of a population only occurs under certain conditions and for a short time in nature. In some cases, it is seen when an organism comes to a new habitat that has a lot of resources, such as the first time that algae grows in a newly formed pond. In other cases, it occurs when other pressures on a population are removed. In South Africa's Kruger National Park, elephants became protected after many years of being hunted to obtain ivory from their tusks. The graph in **Figure 2.1** shows that population numbers were low until about 1960, when the elephants became protected. After 1960, the population grew exponentially.

Key Terms

population
exponential growth
limiting factors
carrying capacity
equilibrium
urban sprawl

population all the individuals of a species that occupy a particular geographic area at a certain time

exponential growth accelerating growth that produces a J-shaped curve when the population is graphed against time

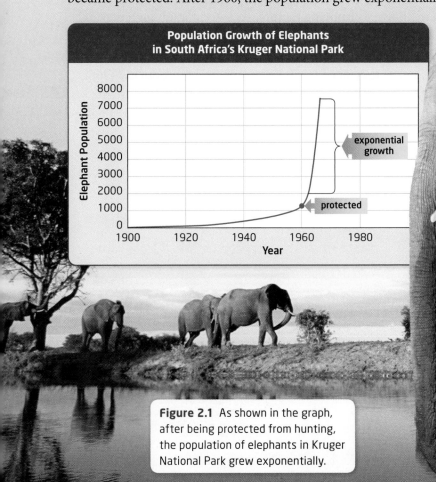

Figure 2.1 As shown in the graph, after being protected from hunting, the population of elephants in Kruger National Park grew exponentially.

Re-introduced Species and Exponential Growth

Among the wildlife that European settlers found plentiful in parts of Ontario was the wild turkey. During the 19th century, the removal of forests and hunting were so severe that all the Canadian populations of wild turkeys had disappeared by 1909. Some American populations survived, however.

In the 1980s, with many parts of southern Ontario reforested and a hunting community that supported careful management of hunted species, the Ontario Ministry of Natural Resources decided to re-introduce the wild turkey to the province.

Over the next two decades, about 4400 turkeys were released in various parts of the province. The turkeys, shown in **Figure 2.2**, found the resources they needed here. By 2001, there were about 30 000 turkeys. By 2008, the number had reached 70 000. This exponential growth occurred even though hunting began to be permitted in the late 1990s. In addition, some turkeys have been sent to Québec as part of a re-introduction program there.

Limiting Factors and Exponential Growth

Exponential growth cannot be sustained in nature. A female Ontario yellow perch, shown in **Figure 2.3**, can produce about 23 000 eggs per year. Even though female yellow perch do not breed until their fourth year, that one female and her daughters, if they all lived, would produce almost a trillion offspring in just five years!

This kind of growth cannot continue for long because no ecosystem has an unlimited supply of the things that organisms need. These restrictions are known as **limiting factors**. As a population increases in size, each individual has access to fewer resources, limiting the growth of the population. The young perch, for example, require food for the nutrients and energy they need to survive, grow, and reproduce. Abiotic factors require the perch to live in parts of lakes and rivers that are the right temperature and pH for growth and activity. The habitat must have enough dissolved oxygen, light, and hiding places, as well. In natural ecosystems, there are simply not enough places where a trillion or more yellow perch can have these needs satisfied. Additional biotic factors can also regulate population growth, as you will read in Section 2.2.

Figure 2.2 When the wild turkey was re-introduced to Ontario after decades of absence, its population increased exponentially.

limiting factor a factor that limits the growth, distribution, or amount of a population in an ecosystem

Figure 2.3 If there were no factors limiting the exponential growth of yellow perch, a single female and her daughters could reach almost a trillion individuals in five years.

Learning Check

1. When do populations tend to increase?

2. Why did the re-introduced turkey population in Ontario grow exponentially?

3. List three examples of limiting factors.

4. Occasionally, humans are put in situations in which their resources are limited. In the summer of 2003, eastern North America experienced a sustained power failure. What resources do you think became quickly limited?

Carrying Capacity

Carrying capacity is the size of a population that can be supported indefinitely by the resources and services of a given ecosystem. Beyond this carrying capacity, no additional individuals can be supported, at least not for long. When a population is maintained at its carrying capacity, the size of the population is at an **equilibrium**, or balance. In a given time period, there is a balance between the number of individuals that are added to the population and the number of individuals that leave or die.

When one of the necessary resources is being used at a rate that exceeds the carrying capacity of the ecosystem, the population will drop to a natural equilibrium. The limiting resource might be food, but it could also be an abiotic factor. For example, polar bears need pack ice on which to hunt, lake trout need rocky lake bottoms on which to lay eggs, and the flying squirrels in **Figure 2.4** need holes in trees as a place to roost.

The impact of limiting factors on exponential growth has been seen with the population of the northern fur seal. In the 1800s, the fur trade led to a drastic reduction in the northern fur seal population. This decline prompted the first international treaty ever designed to conserve wildlife, which was signed in 1911. As shown in the graph in **Figure 2.5**, the fur seal population underwent exponential growth following protection, but eventually levelled out at the ecosystem's carrying capacity.

carrying capacity the size of a population that can be supported indefinitely by the available resources and services of an ecosystem

equilibrium the balance between opposing forces

Figure 2.4 Flying squirrels are common in Ontario forests. They depend on the holes in dead trees for roosting. Local populations are affected if the removal of dead timber significantly reduces the number of holes.

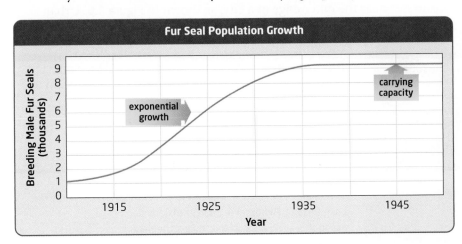

Fur Seal Population Growth

Breeding Male Fur Seals (thousands)

exponential growth

carrying capacity

Year

Figure 2.5 The fur seal population underwent exponential growth, then reached its carrying capacity.

Activity 2-2

Graphing Population Change

How have bird populations changed over the years? To make sure that a population is sustainable, wildlife managers and sometimes citizens do surveys to find out if the population is in equilibrium, growing, or declining. In this activity, you will graph and analyze the results of surveys for three species.

Barrie, Ontario Bird Count: 1983 to 2007

Year	Downy Woodpecker	Mourning Dove	Ruffed Grouse
1983	26	14	13
1985	27	119	14
1987	37	124	11
1989	35	211	11
1991	40	247	5
1993	29	242	2
1995	29	325	4
1997	50	190	3
1999	29	264	6
2001	24	402	5
2003	16	182	4
2005	38	416	2
2007	36	226	9

Materials

- 3 pieces of graph paper
- ruler

Procedure

1. Plot the data for the survey results on three pieces of graph paper (one per species). Determine the proper scale for each graph.

2. Draw a line of best fit to estimate the pattern of the data.

3. Using the line of best fit, extrapolate to the year 2020.

Questions

1. Describe the population growth of each species using the terms "increasing," "decreasing," and "equilibrium."

2. Identify two factors that could affect the declining species in this area.

3. Identify two factors that could affect the increasing species in this area.

4. In the 2006 Canadian census, Barrie was found to be the fastest-growing city in Canada. Does this information change the answers you gave for questions 2 and 3? Explain.

5. Is extrapolation using a straight line likely to be reliable for many decades in the future? Why or why not?

Human Activities and Carrying Capacity

urban sprawl the growth of relatively low-density development on the edges of urban areas

As humans alter natural ecosystems to suit their needs, the carrying capacities of these ecosystems change. The carrying capacity may increase for species that occupy human-altered landscapes, but often it decreases.

Urban sprawl is a term that is used to describe a city's growth as its population increases. In urban sprawl, people build new homes and new businesses near the outer edge of a city, as shown in **Figure 2.6**. Urban sprawl is one form of development that reduces the carrying capacity for many species. Negative effects from urban sprawl include more dependence on automobiles, decreased farmland as roads are built, and reduced carrying capacities for native organisms.

Figure 2.6 The Golden Horseshoe is the name of the highly developed area at the west end of Lake Ontario. Almost one quarter of Canadians live in this small area. In this image, the dark pink areas are high-density population areas.

The Story of the Redside Dace

Most of the people in Ontario live in the Golden Horseshoe, shown in **Figure 2.6.** The Golden Horseshoe is the land around the west end of Lake Ontario. Urban sprawl, resulting from over 200 years of development and industrialization, has greatly altered the ecosystems in this area.

The redside dace, shown in **Figure 2.7**, looks like an aquarium fish—colourful and about 10 cm long. Because this species needs cool water to survive, it inhabits areas of streams that are shaded from overhanging vegetation. In Canada, the range of these fish is small. Most inhabit streams in the Golden Horseshoe that flow into Lake Ontario.

As urban sprawl in the Greater Toronto Area increased during the 20th century, development led to changes in the abiotic and biotic factors in the streams inhabited by these fish. Two abiotic factors, in particular, were affected. As trees were cut down to make room for human structures, the amount of shade cover around streams decreased. Many streams also experienced an increase in drainage from surrounding areas. These changes led to a reduced carrying capacity for the redside dace. Many populations disappeared. Today, the remaining populations are found in the upper reaches of streams in an area that is known as the Oak Ridges Moraine, shown in purple on the map in **Figure 2.7**. Here, there is some residential and agricultural development, but the development is not nearly as intensive as it is in the urban areas downstream. Since the lower reaches of the streams are no longer suitable for dace, however, the remaining populations are isolated from each other.

Suggested Investigation

Data Analysis Investigation 2-A, Is the Winter Skate Endangered in Nova Scotia? on page 79

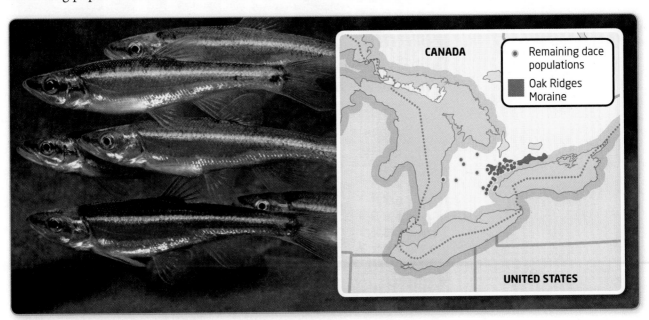

Figure 2.7 The redside dace is a native species that is found in several Ontario river systems (see the red dots on the map). Unlike most minnows, it jumps out of the water to capture small insects that fly just above the surface.

Intensification

The human population of the Golden Horseshoe is expected to increase by about 3.7 million between 2005 and 2031. This poses a tremendous challenge for the people who plan and manage cities. How can urban planners make room for so many additional people and, at the same time, ensure that the ecosystems in the area remain sustainable? How can the remaining carrying capacity for redside dace be protected?

One policy that Ontario has adopted to reduce urban sprawl is called *intensification*. The intensification policy requires that a large percentage of new development must occur on land *within* the boundary of the city. For example, **Figure 2.8** shows how more space can be added by building additional floors on top of an existing building, instead of building a new building. Also, the province has passed a law called the Oak Ridges Moraine Conservation Act, which was designed to place strict controls on development. Although this law does not use the word "sustainable," one objective is to ensure "that the Oak Ridges Moraine Area is maintained as a continuous natural landform and environment for the benefit of present and future generations." Perhaps these measures will prevent further reduction of the carrying capacity for redside dace in this area.

Figure 2.8 Intensification counteracts urban sprawl by requiring a large percentage of new development to be within existing urban boundaries. This increases population density, but it reduces pressure on natural areas and farmland.

Section Summary

- Populations tend to increase exponentially when there are available resources.
- When resources that are needed by populations become limited, the carrying capacity of an ecosystem has been reached.
- Human alterations of an ecosystem, such as through urban sprawl, often reduce the carrying capacity of the ecosystem for other species.

Review Questions

K/U **1.** Explain why exponential growth is not sustainable in nature.

K/U **2.** How would the removal of dead timber from an area affect the carrying capacity for flying squirrels?

K/U **3.** Identify two factors that limited the growth of the redside dace, and describe how they limited its growth. Then identify one other factor, not mentioned in the section, and describe how it could limit the growth of this species.

T/I **4.** The graph on the right shows how a population of water fleas changed over time. The data were collected in a laboratory situation. Explain how the population changed, using the terms "carrying capacity," "equilibrium," "exponential growth," and "limiting factors."

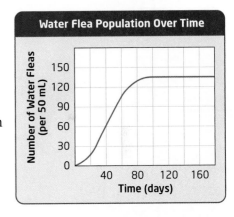

A **5.** One of the objectives of the Oak Ridges Moraine Conservation Act is to "ensure that only land and resource uses that maintain, improve or restore the ecological and hydrological functions of the Oak Ridges Moraine Area are permitted." Explain how this objective could help to maintain or increase the carrying capacity of the area.

K/U **6.** Explain the concept of intensification.

C **7.** Answer the following questions about your own community.

   a. Is there new construction in your community? If so, how do you think this construction might impact an ecosystem near the area?

   b. Pick a species that lives in your community and list what limiting factors regulate the population of this species.

Key Terms

ecological niche
bog
predator
prey
mutualism
parasite

ecological niche the way that an organism occupies a position in an ecosystem, including all the necessary biotic and abiotic factors

2.2 Interactions Among Species

Resource needs and abiotic factors are not the only influences on population growth and size. All organisms interact with other species in multiple ways, and these interactions can have positive and negative effects on a population. Recall, from Chapter 1, that predation, competition, and symbiosis are the major types of interactions among species. These interactions, along with the limiting factors introduced in the previous section, restrict populations to particular places, roles, and sizes in the ecosystems they occupy.

A Species' Ecological Niche

Species spend most of their time doing two things: surviving and reproducing. They do not have "jobs" in the familiar sense—having obligations or responsibilities to their ecosystem. As they pursue their daily activities, however, they consume food and interact with other species. Thus, they have jobs in the sense of providing benefits to their ecosystem. The resources that are used by an organism, the abiotic limiting factors that restrict how it can survive, as well as the biotic relationships that it has with other species all make up an organism's **ecological niche**. For the big brown bat shown in **Figure 2.9**, the biotic niche factors include all the insects that it eats, its competitors, such as the common nighthawk, and its predators. The abiotic niche factors include the places it uses for roosting and hibernation, the time of night it hunts for food, the airspace it flies through when hunting, and the temperature range it can tolerate.

Different species provide many different services to their ecosystems by occupying their ecological niches. These services may include the regulation of population sizes of other organisms, as well as specific services related to matter cycling or energy flow. For example, one likely ecological service provided by the big brown bat is the regulation of insect populations. Cave-dwelling bats also regulate insect populations, but another service they provide is to support many cave-dwelling organisms. The food webs that support these organisms are dependent on nutrients that are brought into the caves through bat droppings.

No two species can occupy the exact same ecological niche or provide the exact same services to their ecosystem, because no two species live in exactly the same way.

Figure 2.9 The space this brown bat takes up while sleeping in the cave is part of its ecological niche.

Occupying Ecological Niches

There are millions of species on Earth. Thus, there are millions of niches, all with particular services to provide. One common Canadian ecosystem with many niches is a type of wetland known as a **bog**. If you have ever seen a bog, you may have thought that it looked like a great place for plants to grow. Bogs have a lot of water and sunlight, which are two things that plants need. The water and soil, however, are acidic and deprived of nutrients, such as nitrogen, due to poor water flow. As a result, most bog plants are adapted to occupy niches that are limited by these conditions.

Most plants get nutrients by absorbing them from the soil and water through their roots. If the soil and water in bogs are nutrient-poor, bog plants must have another way to get nutrients for survival. How can bog plants import nutrients into a nutrient-poor environment? They are carnivorous. By consuming insects, bog plants are able to get the nutrients they need to survive. **Figure 2.10** shows some of the different ways that carnivorous bog plants trap insects, including drowning them in pitcher-shaped leaves filled with water and trapping them on sticky leaves.

By consuming insects, bog plants are meeting their survival needs. In the process of doing this, they are also bringing relatively rare nutrients into their ecosystem by digesting the insects. The niches of carnivorous plants are very particular, and carnivorous plants are well adapted to live in these niches. Carnivorous plants do well as bog specialists, but they could not thrive in other environments.

> **bog** a type of wetland in which the water is acidic and low in nutrients

Sense of Value

The pitcher plant *Sarracenia purpurea* is found throughout Newfoundland and Labrador, and is its official flower. In 1954, the pitcher plant was chosen as a symbol of this province's natural beauty, and of its people's strength of character.

Figure 2.10 A The pitcher plant has a tubular leaf that holds water. The moth will be broken down by digestive juices in the water.
B The sundew leaf is sticky and can curl over a trapped insect.

Predation and Population Size

predator an organism that kills and consumes other organisms

prey an organism that is eaten as food by a predator

In a sense, the carnivorous plants in bogs are **predators** because they capture and consume **prey**—the insects they eat to survive. You may be more familiar with examples of animal predators, such as lions, sharks, and owls. In fact, most predators are animals.

Bottom-Up Population Regulation

Predators and their prey influence one another, especially in terms of population size. There are two ways that predator-prey interactions can influence, or regulate, population size. Think about the following example. A plant-eating species, such as a grasshopper, is the prey for a predatory carnivore, such as a shrew. If the grasshoppers consume too many of the plants they eat for food, their numbers may eventually decline due to lack of food to support the population. If the population size of the grasshoppers decreases, there will be less food for the shrews. As the food that the shrews eat decreases, the number of shrews will eventually decrease too. What happens in this example is known as *bottom-up population regulation*. A shortage in the plant resource at the base of the food chain causes declines in the animals in the higher trophic levels.

Top-Down Population Regulation

Now consider another example. A population of prey, such as rabbits, increases in number. With more rabbits to eat, the population of predators, such as coyotes, will also increase in size. As the coyote population increases, the coyotes consume more rabbits, leading to a decrease in the rabbit population. This situation is known as *top-down population regulation*. Eventually, the number of coyotes will decrease as well.

The graph in **Figure 2.11** shows how the population sizes of lynx and snowshoe hares are influenced by their predator-prey relationship. Lynx prey on snowshoe hares. Notice that the rise and fall of both populations occurs about every 10 years. Scientists have found that a combination of factors affects this repeating cycle. These factors include the availability of food for the hares and the interactions between the hares and other predators, such as foxes, coyotes, and wolves.

Figure 2.11 As the number of hares increases, the number of lynx increases. When the number of hares decreases, the population of lynx also decreases.

Do Wolves Affect Moose Numbers?

In Canada's boreal forest, the largest herbivore is the moose, and the top predator is the wolf. Wolves eat moose, as shown in **Figure 2.12**. The predator-prey relationship between moose and wolves has been extensively studied. Some research projects have been relatively simple, focussing on moose as the only large prey and wolves as the only predator. Other research projects have been more complex, also studying other large prey, such as caribou, and other predators, such as bears or humans that hunt.

Although the research does not point to one simple conclusion, the number of moose seems to be regulated more by other factors than by the number of wolves. The number of wolves, however, is significantly influenced by the number of moose. On Isle Royale, an island in Lake Superior, the predator-prey relationship between moose and wolves has been studied since 1958. The graph in **Figure 2.12** shows that sometimes predation by wolves affects the moose population, but exceptionally cold winters and tick infestations, which can affect the health of the moose, may also be factors that lead to periodic moose population declines.

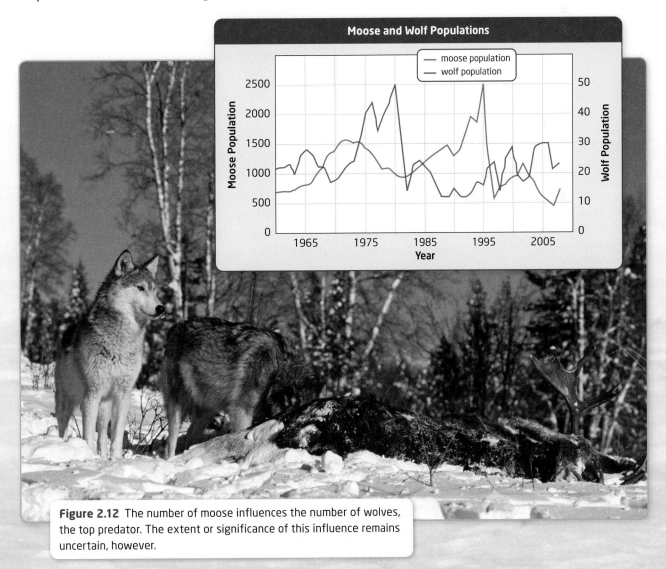

Figure 2.12 The number of moose influences the number of wolves, the top predator. The extent or significance of this influence remains uncertain, however.

Activity 2-3

What Was for Dinner?

Owl pellets are regurgitated clumps of the indigestible parts of the prey—mostly bones, feathers, and fur. What can you find out about an owl's niche by examining a pellet?

Safety Precautions

- Wash your hands when you have completed this activity.

Materials

- owl pellet
- paper towel
- forceps, tweezers, or probe
- magnifying glass
- identification key

Procedure

1. Place the owl pellet on a paper towel. Using forceps, tweezers, or a probe, carefully break apart the pellet. Then separate out all the smaller pieces.

2. Use the identification key to identify and describe each item you were able to separate out from the pellet. Be as specific as possible.

3. Clean up as your teacher directs, then wash your hands.

Questions

1. List the prey of an owl. What inferences can you make about the ecological niche of an owl based on its prey?

2. What is the most common prey identified in the class? Infer why this prey is the most common in the owls' diet.

3. In southern Ontario, screech owls catch fish. What would you expect to find in a screech owl's pellet that would reflect this?

Competition

Figure 2.13 As competition for food increased due to increased population, the average number of eggs laid by female song sparrows decreased.

Recall, from Chapter 1, that competition occurs when two or more organisms compete for the same resource, such as food or space, in the same place at the same time. Competition can limit the size of a population. The more energy an organism spends competing, the less energy it has for growth and reproduction. Competition can also influence the ecological niche of an organism.

As the population of a species increases, the competition for resources also increases. The result can be a decrease in the birth rate of the population. For example, consider the graph in **Figure 2.13**. As the size of a population of female song sparrows increases, the average number of eggs laid decreases. Scientists performed an experiment to test the hypothesis that competition for food leads to a decline in the reproductive output in these birds. In the experiment, female song sparrows living among an increased population of birds were given extra food. These birds did not show a decrease in the number of eggs laid.

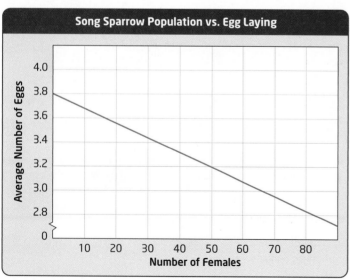

Song Sparrow Population vs. Egg Laying

Average Number of Eggs: 4.0, 3.8, 3.6, 3.4, 3.2, 3.0, 2.8

Number of Females: 10, 20, 30, 40, 50, 60, 70, 80

Competition and Stickleback Fish

An example of how competition influences an organism's ecological niche can be seen in the stickleback fish that live in northern Ontario lakes. The stickleback is a small freshwater fish with spines along its back. The male stickleback uses vegetation to build an underwater nest in which the female lays her eggs. The male then protects the nest. Some northern Ontario lakes have brook sticklebacks, while others have both brook sticklebacks and nine-spine sticklebacks. Both species favour shoreline habitats, where they consume a variety of invertebrates, including larval insects.

Careful studies have shown that the areas of a lake in which brook sticklebacks look for food vary, depending on whether the second species is also present in the lake. In a lake with just brook sticklebacks, they can be found feeding along the bottom, among the vegetation growing from the bottom, and in the shoreline waters above the vegetation. When they share a lake with the nine-spine sticklebacks, however, they are only found on the bottom, as shown in **Figure 2.14**. The nine-spines are found in the water above the vegetation.

Patterns like this, in which species that compete for a resource divide the resource into two parts, have been reported for many organisms. The best explanation is that when there is no competition, a species can occupy a broad niche. When there is competition, however, the same species is forced into a narrower niche. These patterns demonstrate that resource competition can influence the niches and populations of competing species.

Suggested Investigation
Inquiry Investigation 2-B, What Happens When Food Is Limited?, on page 80

Figure 2.14 The niche of the brook stickleback depends on whether it shares a lake with the nine-spine stickleback.

brook stickleback

nine-spine stickleback

Learning Check

1. What is an ecological niche?

2. What factors influence the populations of moose and wolves on Isle Royale?

3. What would be the advantage of studying an island ecosystem in which the only large herbivore was the moose and the only large predator was the wolf? What would be the disadvantage?

4. Imagine an island with maple trees and pine trees, and only one species of insect-eating bird. On another island with maple trees and pine trees, there are two species of insect-eating birds. In terms of where the birds look for food, what kinds of patterns might exist on the two islands?

Symbiosis

As you learned in Chapter 1, symbiosis is the interaction between members of two different species that live together in a close association. Two types of symbiosis are mutualism and parasitism.

Mutualism

Mutualism is the symbiotic relationship between two species in which both species benefit from the relationship. Canada's oceans are home to corals, but the world's best-known and most colourful coral reef systems are tropical. Special photosynthetic algae live inside the tissues of most tropical reef-building corals, as shown in **Figure 2.15A**. The algae provide the coral *host* with up to 90 percent of the coral's energy requirements. The coral provides the algae with protection, nutrients, and a constant supply of carbon dioxide for photosynthesis.

In 1998, about 16 percent of the world's tropical coral reefs were destroyed when the corals within them turned white, as shown in **Figure 2.15B**. This is known as bleaching. Bleaching occurs because of a breakdown in the mutualistic relationship between the coral animal and its photosynthetic algal partner. The algae contribute most of the colour to the coral. When the algae leave, so does the coral's vibrant colouration. Although not fully understood, scientists hypothesize that higher than normal temperatures cause the coral to lose the algae, which leads to bleaching. Elevated sea temperatures that last as little as six weeks can lead to coral death.

Coral reef bleaching demonstrates that the niches of organisms are defined by both abiotic and biotic factors. For corals, an essential biotic factor is their symbiotic algal partner. An essential abiotic factor is sea temperatures that do not become excessively warm. Scientists use satellite images, such as the one shown in **Figure 2.15C**, to monitor sea surface temperatures.

Figure 2.15 A The rich colours of healthy corals are partly due to the relationship between the coral animal and a photosynthetic species of algae. **B** Sea-temperature increases of as little as 2°C for six weeks can trigger coral bleaching. Death follows if the temperatures remain high. **C** Satellite images can be used to determine sea surface temperatures to monitor risk to the coral reefs. In this image, red represents the warmest temperatures.

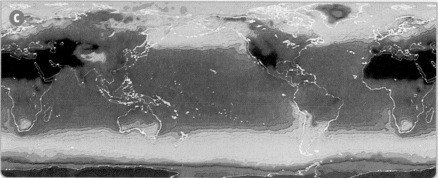

Parasitism

A **parasite** is an organism whose niche is dependent on a close association with a larger host organism. The brainworm, for example, is a common parasite of white-tailed deer. **Figure 2.16** shows how eggs that are laid in the blood vessels of a deer's brain travel through the circulatory system to the deer's lungs, where they hatch. Eventually, the larval worms are excreted. The larval worms then live inside snails and slugs, which are consumed by other deer as they browse on vegetation.

Parasites usually harm their hosts to some extent, but white-tailed deer appear to be little affected by the brainworm. In fact, the minimal impact of the brainworm on its host allows the brainworm to complete its life cycle successfully. Other members of the deer family that are not the usual hosts, however, are very vulnerable. For example, when a brainworm infects a moose, the moose suffers from *moose disease*. This is a degenerative condition that is characterized by stumbling movements and apparent confusion, often leading to death. As for the brainworm, it is unlikely to complete its life cycle in the moose.

Brainworms and white-tailed deer probably have an ancient relationship. This may be why deer are relatively immune to the damage. As deer have moved north into the range of the moose, however, they have brought brainworms with them. Thus, the damaging moose-brainworm relationship is probably relatively recent. Even though wolves seem to have relatively little impact on moose populations, the deer-brainworm team can have a severe impact.

parasite an organism whose niche is dependent on a close association with a larger host organism

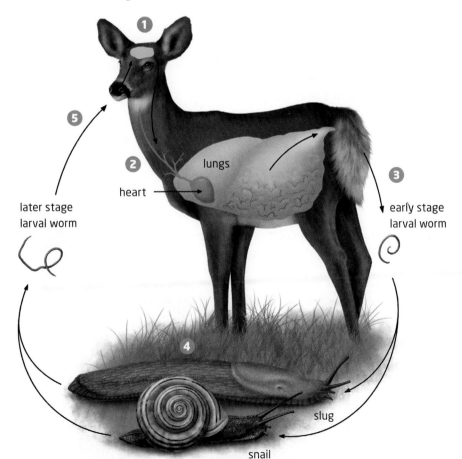

Figure 2.16 White-tailed deer can tolerate brainworm parasites, but other members of the deer family, such as moose, cannot.

1. The worm lays eggs in the blood vessels that cover a deer's brain.
2. The eggs travel through blood vessels to the lungs, where they hatch.
3. Eventually larval worms are excreted.
4. The worms are consumed by and then live inside snails and slugs.
5. The worm enters the deer's body when the deer consumes plants on which snails and slugs are attached.

Section Summary

- Each species occupies an ecological niche, which has biotic and abiotic components.
- Many species, such as bog plants, occupy narrow niches for which they are well adapted.
- Predation, competition, mutualism, and parasitism are four major kinds of relationships between species.
- These relationships help to define a species' niche and influence the distribution and abundance of the species.

Review Questions

K/U **1.** Use a Venn diagram to compare and contrast an ecological niche and a job.

T/I **2.** Analyze what would happen to a niche if the resources and energy in the ecosystem were not sustainable.

K/U **3.** What adaptation allows bog plants to live in a bog? Why do they need this adaptation to live in a bog?

A **4.** Name two different types of organisms that are responsible for inputting nutrients into nutrient-deprived ecosystems.

A **5.** Suppose that you are in charge of a plan to restock elk in Ontario. What factors would you consider if you wanted to have success?

C **6.** Consider an ecosystem with snowshoe hares and lynx, as well as shrubs that are food for the snowshoe hares. Over many years, you notice that the shrubs are never in short supply. You also notice that the populations go up and down over the years.

- First, the hares increase.
- Then lynx increase.
- The hares decrease once the lynx become common.
- Then the lynx decrease.
- Then the pattern starts over again.

Distinguish between top-down and bottom-up regulation, and argue why you think one or the other is operating in this ecosystem.

A **7.** In many species of birds of prey, such as the osprey shown on the right, the female is considerably larger than the male, so much so that males and females capture different types of food. What would be a good explanation for this pattern? Refer to carrying capacity or competition in your explanation.

Ospreys are birds of prey that feed on fish.

K/U **8.** Describe the symbiotic relationship between corals and algae. What causes the colour loss associated with bleaching?

2.3 Human Niches and Population

Key Terms

sustainable use
doubling time
ecological footprint
unsustainable
sustainability

Recall, from Section 2.2, that carnivorous plants are well-adapted for living in a bog. If they were moved to a habitat with different conditions, they might not survive. The fact that most organisms are limited to particular niches is partly why different species are only found in particular types of ecosystems in particular parts of the world. But what about the human ecological niche?

The Human Niche

Humans cannot run as fast as pronghorn antelopes or move through water as efficiently as dolphins. Humans do not have big teeth or big claws, like those of the black bear shown in **Figure 2.17**, or the poisonous venom of a snake. What humans do have is a brain that has allowed us to move out of the narrow niche that was inhabited by our ancient ancestors. By building complex tools, controlling external forms of energy, and expanding our use of resources, humans have been able to live successfully in many different ecosystems, including desert and arctic ecosystems. Unlike other organisms, we have constructed our own niche.

For humans to continue to occupy such a broad niche, we must use the ecosystems we inhabit and the resources they contain in a sustainable way. **Sustainable use** of a resource is use that does not cause long-term depletion of the resource or affect the diversity of the ecosystem from which the resource is obtained. Sustainable use of a resource, whether it is water or an entire ecosystem, allows the resource to meet the needs of present and future generations. If humans do not use resources in a sustainable way, our niche may shrink again over time.

sustainable use use that does not lead to long-term depletion of a resource or affect the diversity of the ecosystem from which the resource is obtained

Cat Brain

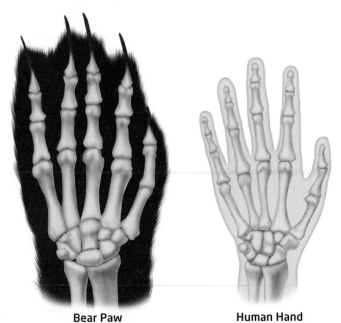

Bear Paw   **Human Hand**

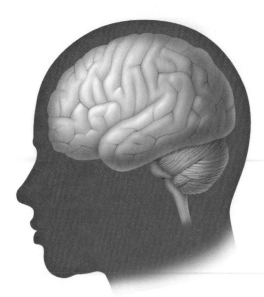

Human Brain

Figure 2.17 Unlike other organisms, the human brain has allowed us to construct our own niche and live successfully in many different ecosystems.

Humans and Carrying Capacity

The populations of most species are regulated by the carrying capacity of the ecosystems that the species occupy. Early humans were regulated by the carrying capacity of their ecosystems. More recently, however, the intellectual abilities of humans have allowed us to create our own niche, as well as increase the carrying capacity of the biosphere for our population. From early developments, such as using fire and making simple tools and weapons, humans have progressed to exploiting huge amounts of energy and resources to run complex, modern societies.

Recall that the populations of all species, including humans, tend to increase exponentially until their carrying capacity is reached. Human exploitation of natural resources has produced improvements in public health, education, agriculture, medicine, and technology. Because these improvements have increased the carrying capacity for humans, the human population has increased, as shown in **Figure 2.18**.

Until about 400 years ago, human population growth had been steady but not explosive. At that time, the population was about half a billion people. It had taken about 650 years for the population to double from a quarter-billion. In the early 1800s, the human population reached one billion—a **doubling time** of only 200 years. The present doubling time is about 60 years.

Earth's human population currently stands at more than 6.7 billion. No one knows what the sustainable carrying capacity is for humans, but it is closely linked to energy. This is because highly productive agriculture requires large expenditures of energy. Many scientists believe that the biosphere's carrying capacity is unlikely to be able to sustain the 9 or 10 billion people expected by the end of the century.

Go to **scienceontario** to find out more

doubling time the period of time that is required for a population to double in size

○○○

Study Toolkit

Interpreting Graphs
How does the graph in **Figure 2.18** help you understand how the human population has grown?

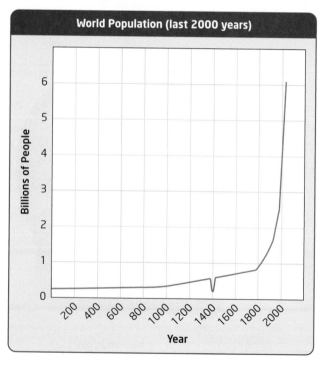

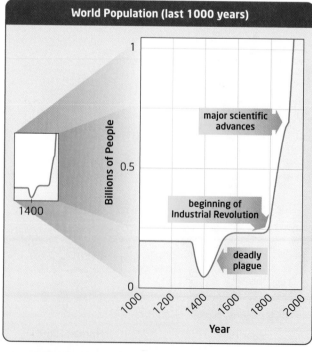

Figure 2.18 Earth's human population has been slowly growing for thousands of years. Since the Industrial Revolution, however, the rate of growth has increased dramatically.

Learning Check

1. How have humans been able to occupy a broad niche?

2. What is sustainable use?

3. What is the current doubling time of the human population?

4. What is the sustainable carrying capacity for humans?

Ecological Footprints and Carrying Capacity

Altering an ecosystem so that more energy and resources can be consumed is only one way to increase the carrying capacity of the ecosystem. The second way to increase its carrying capacity involves altering behaviour, rather than the ecosystem itself.

An **ecological footprint** is a measure of the impact of an individual or a population on the environment. Data used to measure an ecological footprint include energy consumption, land use, and waste production. An ecological footprint reflects the behaviour of individuals and the communities they live in. It is a measure of the productive land and water that are needed to support an individual's standard of living forever.

The average person in developed countries, which includes Canada, has one of the largest ecological footprints in the world, as shown in **Figure 2.19**. Ecological footprints this large in a world that has finite resources and is dependent on non-renewable fossil fuels are likely to be **unsustainable**. The increasing world population is putting stresses on ecological support systems. As the ecological footprints of people in developing nations also increase in size, these stresses will be multiplied. Modern societies must seek to establish ecological footprints that reflect the principles of **sustainability**—use of Earth's land and water at levels that can continue forever. Ways that individuals can reduce their ecological footprint include consuming fewer resources or using existing resources more efficiently through technological innovation, energy efficiency, and recycling.

ecological footprint a measure of the impact of an individual or a population on the environment in terms of energy consumption, land use, and waste production

unsustainable a pattern of activity that leads to a decline in the function of an ecosystem

sustainability use of Earth's resources, including land and water, at levels that can continue forever

Suggested Investigation
Data Analysis Investigation 2-C, Putting Your Foot in Your Mouth, on page 82

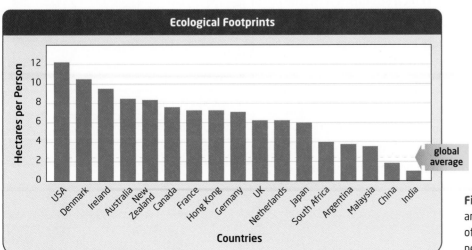

Figure 2.19 Ecological footprints are often measured by the amount of land that is required annually per citizen.

Section Summary

- The ecological niche of humans has been broadened by our intellectual abilities and the development of technology.

- Humans have altered the ecosystems that support us, so our carrying capacity is high.

- Modern human societies are still subject to the ecological principle of carrying capacity.

- Human growth has rapidly accelerated over the past 400 years, with a current doubling time of less than one human lifetime.

- An ecological footprint is used to describe the impact of a person's or population's consumption habits on the supporting ecosystems.

Review Questions

K/U **1.** What has the human brain allowed us to do to our ancestral niche and to our original carrying capacity?

C **2.** Sketch what you consider to be your own personal niche.

K/U **3.** What are the two ways that carrying capacity can be increased?

K/U **4.** List several specific ways that humans have been able to increase their carrying capacity.

C **5.** Draw a footprint in your notebook. At each toe, write one thing you do that reduces your ecological footprint. At the heel of your footprint, write the one thing you do (or don't do) that causes your greatest ecological impact. Across the middle of your footprint, write the one thing you would find most difficult to change to shrink your ecological footprint.

T/I **6.** The table on the right contains data about the ecological footprints of different countries.

    a. Construct a bar graph of the data in the table.

    b. Which countries have the largest ecological footprint per person? Which countries have the smallest ecological footprint per person?

    c. Why do you think there are such large differences in the footprints of these countries?

A **7.** According to one source, the ecological footprint of Canada (in hectares per person) is 7.7. The global average footprint is about 2.2. Why do you think Canadians have such a large ecological footprint? Consider Canada's history and geography when answering this question.

Ecological Footprints

Country	Ecological Footprint (hectares per person)
Afghanistan	0.1
Brazil	2.1
Ethiopia	0.8
Japan	5.9
Russia	4.4
United Arab Emirates	11.9
United Kingdom	6.3
United States	12.3

2.4 Ecosystem Services

Key Terms

ecosystem services

desertification

watershed

connectivity

ecotourism

The concepts of *niche* and *carrying capacity* include the idea of services. **Ecosystem services** are the benefits experienced by organisms, including humans, that are provided by sustainable ecosystems. Ecosystem services are the natural result of all the activities that occur in the biosphere. They include

- the provision of food and clean water
- the cycling of nutrients
- the conversion of atmospheric carbon into biomass (which influences climate and weather)
- the pollination of crops and natural vegetation
- the balance of processes such as growth and decomposition
- the provision of beauty and spirituality

Ecosystem services allow ecosystems to function, which is a requirement of sustainability.

ecosystem services the benefits experienced by organisms, including humans, that are provided by sustainable ecosystems

The Ecosystem Services Provided by Forests

In the past, the value of a forest was measured in dollars, based on the value of the trees that could be harvested for building or paper products. This value is still important. The forest industry in Canada is responsible for billions of dollars' worth of economic activities each year from logging operations and the manufacture of wood and paper products. The forest industry is particularly important in northern Ontario, where many communities are economically dependent on logging. A supply of trees, harvested in a sustainable manner, is needed to maintain the economic activities of these communities. Forests also perform many other ecosystems services, such as influencing climate—shown in **Figure 2.20**—reducing erosion in watersheds, and providing a habitat for thousands of species. In Chapter 3, you will read that tropical rainforests, in particular, are home to millions of species of insects, birds, plants, and other organisms.

Figure 2.20 Rain clouds form over forests, which help keep the climate cooler and wetter than it would be without the forest.

The Influence of Forests on Climate

Trees extract huge amounts of water from the soil. On hot days, much of this water escapes through the stomata, adding water vapour to the atmosphere. This helps to reduce temperatures and form rain clouds, as shown in **Figure 2.20**. More than half of the moisture above tropical forests comes from the trees.

When large forested areas are cleared, the local annual precipitation drops and the climate gets hotter and drier. The clearing of large forested areas is one factor that can lead to the desertification of an area. **Desertification** is the change of non-desert land into a desert.

Areas of Ontario have suffered from desertification in the past. When European settlers came to Norfolk County in southern Ontario, they cut down trees for lumber and cleared the land for agriculture. This led to desert-like conditions. Severe droughts and erosion forced the settlers to abandon their farms. In 1908, the St. Williams Forestry Station was created and more than 300 000 trees were planted. The area is now reforested and has become a model for restoring forests.

Forests and Watersheds

Forests can also benefit local watersheds. A **watershed** is an area of land that run-off drains over, into a body of water. Studies have compared run-off over watersheds that have been cleared of trees with run-off over watersheds that still have trees. These studies have shown that run-off increases by 30 to 40 percent in cleared areas. This means that soils in cut areas are less likely to retain rainwater and meltwater, and that the amount of erosion increases. In cleared areas, there is also an increased loss of nutrients, such as nitrogen, that are in limited supply.

The graph in **Figure 2.21** shows that the amount of nitrogen in run-off from a cleared watershed was 60 percent higher than the amount of nitrogen in run-off from an uncut watershed. Recall, from Chapter 1, that an excess of nutrients in water, or eutrophication, can lead to an overgrowth of algae that can affect an entire ecosystem.

desertification the change of non-desert land into a desert; desertification may result from climate change and unsustainable farming or water use

watershed an area of land over which the run-off drains into a body of water

Sense of Value

Other ecosystem services of forests include producing oxygen and removing pollutants from the air. In 50 years, a single tree can produce about $30 000 worth of oxygen and remove pollutants that would cost about $60 000 if humans were to try to remove them from the air.

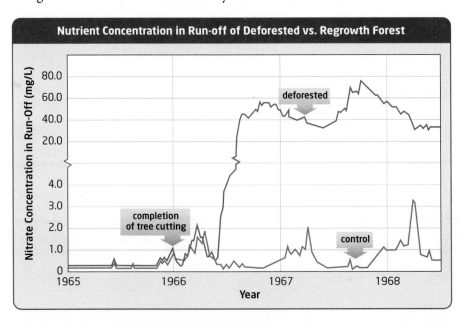

Figure 2.21 This graph compares the amount of nitrogen in run-off from a watershed that has been cleared to a watershed that is forested.

> **Learning Check**
>
> 1. What are ecosystem services?
>
> 2. Briefly describe how forests can influence climate.
>
> 3. What are two negative outcomes of cutting down a forest?
>
> 4. Using data from **Figure 2.21**, explain one effect that cutting a forest has on a watershed.

Figure 2.22 Not all pollination is brought about by insects. Some plants rely on birds, bats, and other mammals to transfer pollen from one flower to another.

Insects and Ecosystem Services

Like many organisms, most plants reproduce through sexual reproduction. Male pollen from one flower fertilizes the female ovary in another flower of the same species in a process known as *cross-pollination*. The majority of plants rely on animals to move pollen from one flower to another. The most common pollinators are insects such as bees and beetles. Other organisms, such as the bat shown in **Figure 2.22**, are also important pollinators. Cross-pollination can also occur when pollen is transferred from one flower to another by wind. Sometimes pollination occurs through *self-pollination,* in which flowers can pollinate themselves or another flower from the same plant.

Pollination and the World's Vegetation

Many studies have confirmed that, for most plants, productivity is much greater when flowers are visited by pollinators. In wild species such as blueberries and raspberries, as well as in agricultural plants such as vegetables, livestock crops, and spices, fruit and seed production are much higher when plants are pollinated by insects. The graphs in **Figure 2.23** show two examples of plants that produced more seeds when they were cross-pollinated than when they self-pollinated. Cross-pollination by insects deserves the credit for perhaps one third of our food, a service that has been estimated at about $250 billion per year worldwide.

The best-known pollinators are honeybees. A recent phenomenon coined *colony collapse disorder* has concerned ecologists. The case study on the next page describes colony collapse disorder and its possible causes.

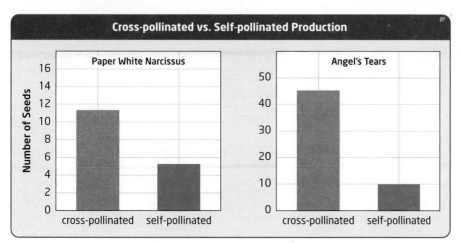

Figure 2.23 Laboratory studies show that plants that are cross-pollinated are more successful in producing fruit and seeds. In nature, cross-pollination usually occurs when animals move pollen from one flower to another.

Insects and Decomposition

Section 2.2 reviewed four important relationships among living organisms: predation, competition, mutualism, and parasitism. Decomposition is a fifth important ecological relationship. It is also an ecosystem service. Decomposition is the breakdown of organic wastes and dead organisms. It differs from the other relationships in one important way: it occurs between a living organism and a dead organism. All living things die eventually. Locked up in their dead bodies are nutrients and energy that must be recycled.

Insects are one of three main groups of organisms that serve as decomposers in ecosystems. The other two groups are bacteria and fungi. Decomposer insects, such as beetles, flies, wasps, and ants, feed off dead plants, animals, or animal feces. The burying beetles in **Figure 2.24** are one example of an insect that is a decomposer. Decomposition is an important part of the nutrient cycles discussed in Chapter 1. Nutrients are returned to the soil, water, and air as dead organisms decay.

STSE Case Study

Why Are Honeybees Disappearing?

Why are honeybees mysteriously disappearing from North American beehives? Beekeepers are finding that many of their hives are empty or contain only frail young worker bees and the queen. Mature worker bees have left the hives and disappeared. The bees that remain cannot maintain the hives alone. This is known as colony collapse disorder.

About 15 percent of the commercial bee colonies in Canada are lost each winter. In the winter of 2008, 35 percent of the colonies were lost. Honeybees and other pollinators are critical for many fruit and vegetable crops. The value of crop pollination services is estimated to be at least $1.2 billion per year in Canada.

Many scientists and beekeepers think that the decline of honeybees is due to a combination of factors, including parasites, pesticide use, and beekeeping practices. More research is needed to determine why honeybees are disappearing and to save these important pollinators.

In a healthy beehive, worker bees cover most of the combs. As a result of colony collapse disorder, only a few weak worker bees remain in the unhealthy hive.

When burying beetles find the body of a small animal, such as a mouse, they quickly dig soil out from under the body.

The body sinks below the surface and the beetles then cover the body to help prevent flies from laying eggs.

The adult beetles lay eggs on the decaying body, then use it to feed their growing larvae.

Figure 2.24 Burying beetles are among the countless organisms whose niches bring about the decomposition of dead bodies and other waste.

What Happened to the Bees?

Scientists hypothesize that one or several factors may be to blame:

- Pesticides may affect the ability of honeybees to find their way back to their hives. As a result, the bees leave their hives and never return.

- Radiation from cellphones may interfere with the ability of honeybees to navigate. In one study, researchers found that when cellphones were placed near hives, the bees stayed away.

- A parasite called the *Varroa destructor* mite attaches itself to the outside of honeybees and feeds off their fluids. Another mite, called the honeybee tracheal mite, attaches to the tracheas of honeybees and suffocates them.

- Transportation of colonies over long distances can affect honeybees. Confinement or the temperature and vibrations on trucks may disrupt the bees' life cycle.

Varroa destructor mites attach to the outside of honeybee larvae. They feed on body fluids from the bees and weaken the bees as they mature into adults.

Your Turn

1. What two parasites are named in the case study as being potential factors in the decline of honeybees? Conduct research to find out how one of these parasites was introduced to North America. Write a brief explanation. What attempts have been made to eliminate this mite?

2. Honeybees were introduced to North America by European settlers. Identify one species, native to Canada, whose pollination of plants is important. Identify the plant species it pollinates. Write a short paragraph about the ecosystem in which the species lives.

3. Some taxpayers are concerned that the Ontario government is compensating beekeepers for their losses and providing them with funds to help them rebuild their colonies. Write a letter to the editor of your local newspaper, explaining why honeybees are important in Ontario and why the government should continue to support beekeepers.

The Role of Migratory Birds

Some insects are considered to be pests of crops and forests. Other insects, such as mosquitoes, can carry and spread disease. The complete elimination of these species would have very negative consequences for ecosystems, but the regulation of their numbers is desirable.

Some organisms, known as *aerial insectivores*, consume flying insects. Unfortunately, the populations of many aerial insectivore birds that breed in Canada have declined since the 1980s, as shown in **Figure 2.25**. As in the case of honeybees, there are many ideas about the cause of their decline, but no firm answers. A complication is that all aerial insectivores leave Canada for the winter. Scientists are uncertain whether the challenges that the birds are experiencing exist here in the spring or summer or elsewhere at other times of year. The use of distant parts of Earth by many migratory species underscores the importance of having sustainable practices everywhere. Habitat destruction or poorly regulated insecticide use in the tropics, thousands of kilometres away, could be contributing to the losses of aerial insectivores here.

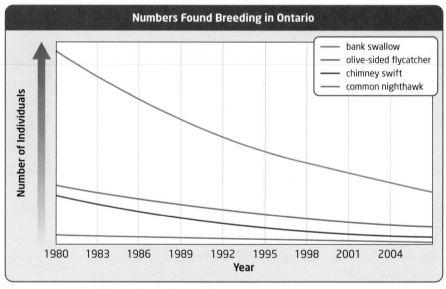

Figure 2.25 Species of birds that eat flying insects have generally been declining in Canada since 1980. These four species, from four different bird families, all spend the winter in South America.

Learning Check

5. What are two ecosystem services that insects provide?

6. List three possible causes of colony collapse disorder.

7. What ecosystem service do aerial insectivores provide?

8. Describe what the graph in **Figure 2.25** shows.

Coffee Plantations and Canadian Birds

Many songbirds that occupy Canadian woodlands during the summer seek out forest habitats in the tropics during the winter. One tropical ecosystem that many Canadian songbirds find sustaining during the winter is an ecosystem in which coffee is grown.

Coffee can be grown in sunlight or in shade, as shown in **Figure 2.26**. Most mass-marketed coffee is grown in an unsustainable way. Forests are cleared, pesticides and fertilizers are applied, and a sun-tolerant coffee plant is grown in a monoculture. A monoculture is an area of land in which the plants are all the same species. A smaller percentage of coffee is shade-grown coffee. Shade-grown coffee has lower yields than sun-tolerant coffee, but it is grown in natural landscapes that include the shade of overhanging trees.

These shade-grown operations, often managed by indigenous peoples, provide sustainable ecosystems for many Canadian songbirds during the winter. This is sustainable use because it serves human needs—the growth of coffee beans—as well as the requirements of the songbirds. For shade-grown operations to succeed commercially, coffee consumers need to know the difference and to demand shade-grown brands.

Study Toolkit

Making Connections to Visuals How do the photographs in **Figure 2.26** help you understand the difference between sun-grown coffee and shade-grown coffee?

Go to **scienceontario** to find out more

Figure 2.26 A When coffee is grown in sunlight, it becomes a monoculture. The diversity of living things decreases. **B** When coffee is grown naturally in shade, it is part of an ecosystem that supports many other species of plants and animals.

International Co-operation for Ecological Connectivity

The concept of linked ecosystems, which have to be sustainable together, is known as **connectivity**. In 1916, Canada and the United States recognized this concept when they negotiated a formal agreement designed to protect birds that moved across their shared border. More recently, conservation initiatives have spread farther. Biologists at Bird Studies Canada, an organization dedicated to the welfare of Canadian birds, have developed an international program that uses financial resources and expertise to foster stewardship and bird research in tropical regions of North and South America.

Recreational Opportunities as Ecosystem Services

Ecotourism is a nature-based, sustainable form of tourism that is now a multibillion-dollar industry worldwide. Some tourists plan coastal holidays that include boat trips to view whales, dolphins, and sea birds. Other tourists plan holidays and weekend events to watch birds fly back and forth annually between breeding grounds in Canada and wintering grounds farther south. There are many other ways in which Canadians and visitors to Canada can get recreational enjoyment from sustainable ecosystems. Hiking, snowshoeing, shown in **Figure 2.27**, fishing, and kayaking are just a few examples.

connectivity the collection of links and relationships between ecosystems that are separated geographically

ecotourism a form of tourism that is sensitive to the health of an ecosystem and involves recreational activities provided by sustainable ecosystems

Figure 2.27 Snowshoeing is one of many outdoor activities people participate in as ecotourists.

Activity 2-4

Ecotourism and Monarch Butterflies

Every year, millions of monarch butterflies migrate over 3000 km from Canada and the United States to spend the winter in central Mexico. These butterflies stay in fir-tree forests at high altitudes in the mountains of the Mexican states of Michoacan and Mexico. Recently, the Mexican government has encouraged ecotourism to this area.

Procedure

Use the Internet to research monarch butterflies and ecotourism to this area. Find answers to the following questions:

a. How many people visit this area each year?

b. What has the Mexican government done to encourage ecotourism in this area?

c. How could illegal logging in the fir-tree forests affect ecotourism in this area?

Questions

1. Why is it important to ecosystems in Canada that the butterflies have a sustainable ecosystem in which to spend the winter?

2. List some possible ways that ecotourism could negatively affect the butterflies.

3. Make a pamphlet that promotes ecotourism to this area of the world.

Beauty and Spirituality in Sustainable Ecosystems

Canada's indigenous peoples have had a long, rich, and complex spirituality tied closely to the ecosystems they occupy. In the Queen Charlotte Islands on Canada's west coast, for example, the Haida people used tall rainforest trees to construct totem poles, which were both artistic and sacred. Many Aboriginal peoples continue these spiritual traditions that are connected to nature.

Many other Canadians also find ecosystems sustaining, not only in the sense of the services they provide but also in a spiritual sense. The rugged and wild north inspired the artists in Canada's renowned Group of Seven. One of their paintings is shown in **Figure 2.28**. It is vital that we study ecosystems scientifically, but artistic expressions of ecosystems provide another perspective that is also meaningful.

Figure 2.28 Lawren Harris' *Above Lake Superior* is one example of art inspired by the landscape.

Making a Difference

Allyson Parker got her first pair of binoculars when she was 8 and has been bird-watching ever since. She has volunteered as an interpreter at Presqu'ile Provincial Park Waterfowl Festival, educating the public about waterfowl species, since she was 11. She also volunteers as a bird bander at the Prince Edward Point Bird Observatory.

Allyson's interests also include other wildlife and conservation issues. At her Cobourg high school, Allyson was president of the environment club, which introduced recycling programs and participated in the Great Canadian Shoreline Clean Up. In 2006, Allyson travelled to Antarctica after winning the Canadian Geographic Polar Bound Contest. After her trip, she shared her experience with other students.

Allyson's passion for birds has helped her make a difference. She believes that teaching and helping others feel passionate about nature is the best way to help the environment. Allyson is studying wildlife biology at the University of Guelph.

How could you help others in your community learn about wildlife?

Section Summary

- When a species occupies its niche, it provides ecosystem services for other organisms.
- Forests influence climate and play a vital role in the regulation of watersheds.
- Insects provide many ecosystem services, including pollination and decomposition.
- The health of migratory bird populations is dependent on the health of the ecosystems they visit during their migration.
- Ecological connectivity means that international co-operation is necessary to keep ecosystems sustainable.
- Visual beauty and spiritual appreciation are two services that ecosystems provide for humans.

Review Questions

K/U **1.** Identify the ecosystem services that are provided by forests.

C **2.** 2006 was the International Year of Deserts and Desertification. Write two or three sentences explaining why it is important to focus attention on desertification.

K/U **3.** Explain the process of pollination. Give three examples of pollinators.

C **4.** Make a mini-poster that explains colony collapse disorder and its possible causes.

A **5.** The olive-sided flycatcher is an aerial insectivore whose population numbers have decreased in Canada since the 1980s. The map on the right shows the range of this species. What are some possible reasons for the decline in its population?

T/I **6.** Describe the results shown in the graph in **Figure 2.21**. Explain the impact of deforestation on the amount of nitrate retained in the soil.

A **7.** Do you think governments should manage ecological health by considering connectivity? What steps should governments take to recognize connectivity?

K/U **8.** Briefly describe one way that the Haida people expressed their reverence for the forest and sustainable ecosystems.

- year-round
- summer (breeding)
- winter
- migration

Data Analysis Investigation 2-A

Materials

• graph paper

Biomass of Winter Skate (1975-2004)

Year	Biomass
1975	59
1976	70
1977	34
1978	54
1979	47
1980	57
1981	54
1982	47
1983	27
1984	25
1985	25
1986	26
1987	43
1988	40
1989	47
1990	32
1991	48
1992	40
1993	30
1994	14
1995	16
1996	20
1997	20
1998	18
1999	15
2000	13
2001	8
2002	5
2003	7
2004	8

Is the Winter Skate Endangered in Nova Scotia?

Skates are flat-bodied fish that are related to sharks. In Atlantic Canada, there is a small winter skate fishery. Also, many skates are unintentionally caught in fisheries aimed at catching groundfish, a commercially important species that feeds and dwells near the bottom. In this investigation, you will graph and analyze population data for winter skates off Nova Scotia.

Question

Should the winter skate be listed under Canada's Species at Risk Act?

Organize the Data

1. Examine the table, which lists the biomasses of winter skates captured in summer samples taken off Nova Scotia.

2. Graph the data in the table. For each year, you should have one point on the graph. This type of graph is called a scatter plot.

Analyze and Interpret

1. To show the overall trend, estimate a *line of best fit*. To do this, carefully look at the points and draw a single straight line that you think best estimates the population trend.

2. Describe the pattern over time shown on your graph.

Conclude and Communicate

3. Predict the biomass for 2010. Consider using extrapolation. Is there more than one justifiable estimate for this biomass?

4. According to the Species at Risk Act, a species is *endangered* if it is likely to become extinct in Canada in the near future. Endangered species are entitled to special protection. Would you recommend to Environment Canada that the winter skate population off Nova Scotia be listed as endangered?

5. What if listing the winter skate population as endangered would restrict the groundfish industry? Groundfish make up about half the total catch in Atlantic Canada. How would this affect your decision?

Extend Your Inquiry and Research Skills

6. **Research** Find out more information about the Species at Risk Act.

   a. What is the history of the Species at Risk Act?

   b. Evaluate the effectiveness of the Species at Risk Act.

Inquiry Investigation 2-B

Skill Check

✓ Initiating and Planning

✓ Performing and Recording

✓ Analyzing and Interpreting

✓ Communicating

Safety Precautions

- Remember proper techniques for using a microscope, including handling the microscope with care.

- If you have a mirror on the microscope, do not direct it toward the Sun.

Materials

- 2 plastic cups with labels
- felt marker
- 50 mL graduated cyclinder
- paramecium culture
- medicine dropper
- yeast culture
- toothpicks
- methyl cellulose
- 6 microscope slides
- scissors
- 30 cm cotton thread
- tweezers
- 6 cover slips
- light microscope
- plastic wrap
- 2 rubber bands
- distilled water

Science Skills

Go to **Science Skills Toolkit 8** for more information on using a microscope.

What Happens When Food Is Limited?

Paramecia (paramecium, singular) are unicellular organisms that are commonly found in freshwater ponds and marshes. They are covered in fine hair-like structures, which they beat to move themselves around and to sweep bacteria and other small food particles into a pore that serves as a mouth. In this investigation, you will study the factors that limit the growth of a paramecium population in a given volume of water over three weeks.

Question

How are population size and growth related to food supply?

Prediction

Make a prediction about the patterns you will see if you graph population size versus time. Make specific predictions about an ecosystem in which food is available and an ecosystem in which food is limited.

Procedure

1. Make two copies of the data table below. Title one "Added Food" and the other "Limited Food."

Day	Number of Paramecia in Sample			Average Number of Paramecia
	Slide 1	Slide 2	Slide 3	
1				
3				
5				

2. Label one cup "added food" and the other cup "limited food." Using the graduated cylinder, carefully measure 10 mL of paramecium culture into each plastic cup.

3. Using the marker, draw a line on each cup to indicate the level of the water.

4. Add one drop of yeast culture into the cup labelled "added food."

5. Using the toothpick, smear a small amount of methyl cellulose in the middle of each of three slides. The methyl cellulose should cover an area that is roughly the size of a cover slip.

6. Cut the thread into 12 pieces, each about 5 mm long.

7. Using the tweezers, place four pieces of cotton thread on each slide. These threads, together with the methyl cellulose, will be obstacles for the paramecia and slow down their movement enough for you to count them. Number each slide.

8. Place one drop of paramecium culture from the cup labelled "added food" on each slide. Put a cover slip over the drop on each slide.

9. Using the low power of the microscope, count the number of paramecia in one field of view on each slide.

10. Record your counts in your data table for added food. Calculate and record the average.

11. Repeat steps 5 to 10 for the culture in the cup labelled "limited food."

12. Cover each cup with plastic wrap, and secure the plastic wrap with a rubber band. Make several small holes in the plastic wrap so that air can enter.

13. Clean your slides and cover slips in preparation for the next samples. Repeat steps 5 to 11 every two days (or more, as your teacher directs). Always wash your hands after completing the procedure.

14. Add distilled water to each cup every few days to keep the water level constant.

15. After three weeks, make a line graph of your data for each culture. Put "Average Number of Paramecia" on the *y*-axis and "Time (days)" on the *x*-axis.

Analyze and Interpret

1. Why did you count three samples for each culture, rather than one sample?

2. Compare the shapes of your graphs. What can you infer about the role of food in limiting population growth?

Conclude and Communicate

3. Predict the effect of doubling the amount of food added to a paramecium culture. Explain your answer.

4. You counted the paramecia in one field of view to estimate changes in the population size over time. Outline a method you could use to estimate the size of the entire population of paramecia in each cup.

Extend Your Inquiry and Research Skills

5. **Inquiry** The following graphs show the results of an experiment with two species of paramecia. This experiment was first carried out by population biologist G. F. Gause. He observed the growth of populations of these two species when each population was grown alone and when the two populations were grown together. Study the two graphs, and answer the following questions.

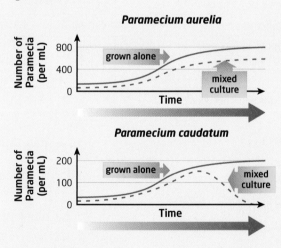

Paramecium aurelia

Paramecium caudatum

a. What is the carrying capacity for each of the two species, *Paramecium aurelia* and *Paramecium caudatum*?

b. What happens to the carrying capacity of each paramecium when the two species are mixed?

c. What can you infer about each species of paramecium's ability to compete?

Skill Check

Initiating and Planning

Performing and Recording

✓ Analyzing and Interpreting

✓ Communicating

Putting Your Foot in Your Mouth

In the table below, various patterns of consumption are expressed as an estimate of the number of hectares that each lifestyle pattern consumes.

Question

What is your ecological footprint?

Ecological Footprint Estimates

Pattern of Consumption	Hectares (per year)							
	0	0.2	0.3	0.6	1.0	1.5	2.1	3.0
Meat per week		never				few times	most days	daily
Processed food	very little		<50%	>50%				
Imported food	very little	about 25%	25 to 50%	>50%				
People in household			>4	4	3	2	1	
Size of home		apartment	small house	medium house	large house			
Renewable energy	yes			no				
Public transport per week		<100 km	>100 km					
Car transport per week		<50 km		50–150 km	150–300 km	300–450 km		
Added consumption for vehicle type	small vehicle or hybrid	medium vehicle	large vehicle					
Flying hours per year			3–5	5–15	16–25	26–40	41–100	>100

Organize the Data

1. For each pattern of consumption, choose the best description for your own situation. Record the number of hectares you require.

2. Calculate your ecological footprint.

Analyze and Interpret

1. What is your greatest area of consumption? What is your least?

Conclude and Communicate

2. Describe two strategies that would allow you to reduce your ecological footprint.

Extend Your Inquiry and Research Skills

3. **Research** Find out more about how an ecological footprint is calculated. What factors are considered in the calculation? Can you think of any factors that should be added to the calculation?

Chapter 2 Summary

2.1 Populations and Resources

Key Concepts

- Populations tend to increase exponentially when there are available resources.
- When resources that are needed by populations become limited, the carrying capacity of an ecosystem has been reached.
- Human alterations of an ecosystem, such as through urban sprawl, often reduce the carrying capacity of the ecosystem for other species.

2.2 Interactions Among Species

Key Concepts

- Each species occupies an ecological niche, which has biotic and abiotic components.
- Many species, such as bog plants, occupy narrow niches for which they are superbly adapted.
- Predation, competition, mutualism, and parasitism are four major kinds of relationships between species.
- These relationships help to define a species' niche and influence the distribution and abundance of the species.

2.3 Human Niches and Population

Key Concepts

- The ecological niche of humans has been broadened by our intellectual abilities and the development of technology.
- Humans have altered the ecosystems that support us, so our carrying capacity is high.
- Modern human societies are still subject to the ecological principle of carrying capacity.
- Human growth has rapidly accelerated over the past 400 years, with a current doubling time of less than one human lifetime.
- An ecological footprint is used to describe the impact of a person's or population's consumption habits on the supporting ecosystems.

2.4 Ecosystem Services

Key Concepts

- When a species occupies its niche, it provides ecosystem services for other organisms.
- Forests influence climate and play a vital role in the regulation of watersheds.
- Insects provide many ecosystem services, including pollination and decomposition.
- The health of migratory bird populations is dependent on the health of the ecosystems they visit during their migration.
- Ecological connectivity means that international co-operation is necessary to keep ecosystems sustainable.
- Visual beauty and spiritual appreciation are two services that ecosystems provide for humans.

Chapter 2 Review

Reviewing Key Terms

Match each key term listed below to its definition.

a. carrying capacity   **e.** mutualism

b. connectivity   **f.** parasite

c. ecological footprint   **g.** population

d. ecological niche

1. [   ] a symbiotic relationship between two species in which both species benefit from the relationship (2.2)

2. [   ] a group of organisms of one species that lives in the same place, at the same time, and can successfully reproduce (2.1)

3. [   ] the biotic and abiotic factors that are necessary for a species to survive (2.2)

4. [   ] the size of population that can be supported indefinitely on the available resources and services of an ecosystem (2.1)

5. [   ] an organism whose niche is dependent on a close association with a larger host organism (2.2)

6. [   ] the measure of the impact of an individual or a population on the environment (2.3)

7. [   ] the links and relationships between ecosystems that are separated geographically (2.4)

Knowledge and Understanding (K/U)

8. Identify a resource, other than nutrients and energy, that is needed by each organism.

a. polar bear   **c.** nesting tree swallow

b. hibernating bat

9. What two factors caused the wild turkey to be eliminated in Ontario during the 19th and early 20th centuries?

10. What is one way to reduce the impact of rapid population growth on natural ecosystems and farmland in the Golden Horseshoe?

11. Explain what happens during coral bleaching. What kind of relationship breaks down?

12. In the 1960s, the doubling time for the human population was about 35 years. What is the approximate doubling time now? What does this mean?

13. At the current rate of population increase, how many days are necessary for Earth's population to increase by 34 million people (the approximate population of Canada).

14. Identify how forestry practices can contribute to desertification.

15. What ecological service do aerial insectivores provide?

Thinking and Investigation (T/I)

16. Most species of songbirds build "cup" nests. A few species, such as the eastern bluebird, are cavity nesters. This means that they only nest in holes. When the European starling was introduced into North America, its population swelled to the tens of millions. At the same time, the populations of some cavity nesters decreased. What is one possible explanation for the decrease?

17. In Activity 2-2, Graphing Population Change, you discovered that the populations of some bird species around Barrie have been changing since the early 1970s. If you wanted to determine whether Barrie's urban sprawl was the cause, what evidence would you look for?

18. Either animals or wind can transport pollen from one flower of a seed plant to another. Which kind of pollination is likely to result in dull, smaller, and non-fragrant flowers? Which kind is likely to result in bright, larger, and fragrant flowers? Explain your answers.

19. The following graph shows the relationship between the number of plantain seeds planted per square metre and the average number of seeds produced per individual.

a. Describe the pattern that is shown in the graph.

b. What is a possible explanation for this pattern?

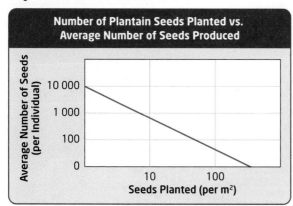

20. Extrapolation involves estimating the pattern of a graph beyond the existing data. In **Figure 2.1**, you examined a graph that shows the growth of an elephant population. If you were extrapolating, would you use a straight line, as suggested by the most recent data? Make sure that you consider **Figure 2.5** before answering.

Communication C

21. **BIG IDEAS** Ecosystems are dynamic and have the ability to respond to change, within limits, while maintaining their ecological balance. What are some potential problems that may occur on Earth when the human population reaches its peak?

22. **BIG IDEAS** People have the responsibility to regulate their impact on the sustainability of ecosystems in order to preserve them for future generations. In Section 2.4, you read about the two ways that coffee is grown. How might what you read influence the type of coffee you would buy? What if shade-grown coffee is more expensive? Would this affect your decision? Explain.

23. Have you ever participated in an activity that you consider ecotourism? Describe your experience. If you have not participated in such an activity, describe and explain an ecotourism activity you would like to participate in.

24. Argue why an animal that is hunted by humans, such as the wild turkey, may never reach an ecosystem's carrying capacity. Do you think this is a problem for the ecosystem or the animal?

25. Every species contributes innumerable services that benefit other species in its ecosystem. Draw a table, that includes visuals, of examples of these services.

Application A

26. When populations get too small, they may become extinct unless the remaining individuals can reproduce with individuals from a nearby population. Why would this solution not work for redside dace populations?

27. Many First Nations cultures believe that humans are the only living things that disregard the laws of carrying capacity. Explain whether you agree or disagree with this statement and why.

28. In developed countries such as Canada, the birth rate and death rate are low. In the transition from developing to developed country, the death rate of a country always drops well before the birth rate, usually about two generations before. What would this mean for population growth during the time between the drop in death rate and the drop in birth rate?

29. In 1901, the famous early American naturalist John Muir made the following comment about some of his favourite places in the American West: "It is a mistake to suppose that the water is the cause of the tree groves being there. On the contrary, the groves are the cause of the water being there." What did he mean?

30. A wildlife biologist observed that an insect-eating migratory bird species was declining summer after summer in Canada. The biologist studied the nesting habits of these birds, but found that they were successfully raising their young. Speculate about what the problem might be.

Chapter 3　Biodiversity

What You Will Learn

In this chapter, you will learn how to...

- **discover** that Earth's biodiversity includes millions of species
- **explain** the role of certain species within a community or ecosystem
- **describe** how human activities can affect biodiversity

Why It Matters

The biosphere is made up of many species, each with a special role. Energy flows and nutrients cycle through millions of species. Understanding the roles of different species and ensuring that they continue to exist and provide ecosystem services will allow the biosphere to remain sustainable for all life.

Skills You Will Use

In this chapter, you will learn how to...

- **interpret** qualitative data
- **communicate** results graphically
- **assess** how invasive species affect an ecosystem
- **explain** why biodiversity is important for the sustainability of ecosystems

As scientists realize how important wetlands are to the sustainability of ecosystems and to maintaining high species diversity, more work is being done to protect them. At 4200 ha (hectares) in size, the Alfred Bog, a type of wetland, is the largest bog in southern Ontario. Rare species, such as the bog elfin butterfly shown on the next page and the white fringed orchid, call this bog home. For over 20 years, environmental groups have worked with the Canadian government to protect the bog from being drained and being mined for peat. Today, over 70 percent of the bog area is protected and managed as a nature reserve.

Activity 3-1

Biodiversity in Canada

The groups involved in protecting the Alfred Bog encourage people to be aware of the variety of plants and animals found there, and the importance of the ecosystem. Suppose that you have been hired to educate people about protecting the diversity of plants and animals across Canada. How could you help them appreciate the number of living things in our country?

The bog elfin butterfly can be found in the Alfred Bog.

Materials
- readily available classroom materials

Procedure

1. Suppose that you are a park naturalist. You have a group of Grade 6 students coming for a lecture. You want to present the data in this table to help them understand more about species diversity in Canada. Spend about 10 min brainstorming a creative way to represent the data.

2. Your model should accurately reflect the proportions of different species in relation to one another. Your model could be two-dimensional or three-dimensional.

3. Spend about 10 min creating your model.

Species Diversity in Canada

Group of Organisms	Number of Known Species
Amphibians	42
Arachnids	3 275
Birds	426
Crustaceans	3 139
Fish	1 100
Fungi	11 800
Insects	18 530
Mammals	194
Molluscs	1 500
Plants	4 934
Reptiles	42

Questions

1. Did any of the numbers of known species surprise you? Explain.

2. Compare your model with another group's model.
   a. Describe any similarities and differences between the two models.
   b. Describe the best features of each model.

3. If you were to redesign your model, how would you change it and why?

Study Toolkit

These strategies will help you use this textbook to develop your understanding of science concepts and skills.
To find out more about these and other strategies, refer to the Study Toolkit Overview, which begins on page 561.

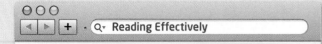

Identifying the Main Idea and Details

The *main* idea of a text is the *most important* idea. Details in the text help support this idea. Here are some strategies for identifying the main idea of a chapter, section, or paragraph.

- Pay attention to titles, headings, and subheadings. Note how type size helps you differentiate among them.
- Skim the text and glance at the visuals to get a general sense of the content.
- Note any terms that are boldfaced or differentiated in another special way.

Use the Strategy

Examine page 93. Apply the strategies above to identify the main idea of the page. Compare your main idea with a classmate's main idea, and discuss how you made your decision.

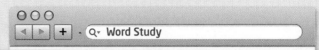

Word Origins

One strategy for learning a new word is to study its origins, or where it came from. For example, to understand the meaning of *entomology,* find this word in a dictionary and look at the entries before and after it. You will probably see an entry like the one below.

entomo- *pref.* Insect: *entomology.*
[Fr. < Gk. *entomon* < neut. of *entomos,* cut (< its segmented body) < *entemnein,* to cut up : *en-,* in; see EN-[2] + *temnein,* to cut; see **tem-***.]

This entry tells you that the prefix *entomo-* means insect and comes from the Greek *entomon,* meaning cut or segmented. This might help you remember that *entomology* means "the study of insects."

Use the Strategy

Look up the word *diversity,* and search the entries before and after it until you find its Latin origin. Explain how the Latin root helps you understand the current meaning of the word.

Interpreting Tables

A table consists of *cells* that are organized in rows and columns. Each cell contains data. Each column and row has a heading to help you interpret each cell. To read a table or to find patterns in a table, move your eyes left and right across the rows, and up and down along the columns. In the table on the right, the number 500 is found in the column labelled "Number of Zebra Mussels (per m^2)" and in the row labelled "1992." This number can be interpreted as "500 zebra mussels per m^2 were found in Lake Ontario in 1992."

Zebra Mussels and Chlorophyll a in Lake Ontario

Year	Number of Zebra Mussels (per m^2)	Chlorophyll a (µg/L)
1990	0	4.4
1991	230	3.3
1992	500	3.4

Use the Strategy

Turn to the table in Activity 3-3 on page 104.

1. Cover the table, and read only the title. Based on the title, explain what kind of information you expect to see in the cells.

2. Read the column and row headings carefully. Explain what they mean.

3. Pick any cell in the table, and interpret its contents by writing a complete sentence.

3.1 Measuring Biodiversity

Every year, a news headline reads, "New species discovered in …." For example, in 2006, scientists discovered 36 new species of fish, corals, and shrimp in the warm ocean waters off the coast of New Guinea. One of these was a shark that "walks" along the bottom of the ocean, shown in **Figure 3.1A**. In 2007, 11 new species of plants and animals were found in the rainforests of Vietnam. These included five species of orchids, one of which is shown in **Figure 3.1B**, a snake, and two butterflies. In 2008, scientists in Fiji found a new iguana. The list goes on.

How many species are there on Earth? So far, scientists have identified about 2 million species. However, estimates of the total number of species on Earth range from 5 million to 100 million. One of the tasks of ecologists is to help document the biodiversity of Earth. **Biodiversity** includes the number and variety of organisms found in a specific region. Part of biodiversity also includes the variety of Earth's ecosystems. In order for biodiversity to remain high, diverse ecosystems need to remain sustainable. Recall that nutrients and energy cycle through ecosystems, and that what happens in one ecosystem can affect cycles in other ecosystems and in Earth's three other spheres. Preserving and **protecting** individual species and the ecosystems they inhabit are critical to maintaining biodiversity on Earth.

biodiversity the number and variety of life forms, including species, found within a specific region as well as all the number and variety of ecosystems within and beyond that region

protect to guard legally from harm a species that is listed as endangered, threatened, or of special concern

Figure 3.1 A This newly discovered shark "walks" along the ocean floor on its fins. **B** Five new species of orchids were discovered in Vietnam in 2007.

How Do Scientists Measure Biodiversity?

Scientists use several methods to measure biodiversity. These include canopy fogging, quadrat sampling, transect sampling, and netting. The method used depends on the types of organisms ecologists are counting and on the habitat. For example, scientists may not be able to use the same method to count insect species living in a tree in a rainforest as they would to count fish species living on a coral reef in an ocean. **Table 3.1** describes different sampling methods in more detail.

○○○

Study Toolkit

Interpreting Tables
How does reading the title of **Table 3.1** help you understand what information the table will contain?

Table 3.1 Methods of Measuring Biodiversity

Method	How It Works	In Action
Canopy fogging	Canopy fogging is an effective way of collecting information about the biodiversity of insects. A low dose of insecticide is sprayed up into the top of a tree. When the insects fall, they are collected on a large screen, shaped like a funnel. Scientists may keep and observe some insects. This helps scientists learn more about the life cycle of these insects.	
Quadrat sampling	A quadrat is a known square area that is marked using a pre-made square of plastic, or stakes and string. Quadrats can range in size from 1 m^2 to 20 m^2, depending on the type of habitat surveyed. Different species and their numbers within the quadrat are counted. Counting is repeated many times in different places throughout the habitat to get an accurate representation of biodiversity.	
Transect sampling	Transect sampling is done using a transect line. A transect line is usually a rope or measuring tape that has been marked at set intervals, such as every metre. The line is unrolled within the habitat. At every interval, the type and number of species along the line are recorded.	
Netting	Fine mesh nets are used to capture birds and bats in terrestrial ecosystems, and fish and other organisms in aquatic ecosystems. Once captured, an organism is identified. In addition, it may be measured, blood may be taken for genetic analysis, and it may be tagged. In many cases, the organism is then released.	

Documenting Biodiversity and Its Distribution

To protect Earth's biodiversity, scientists need a system for recording the identity of each species and where it exists. Museums house many collections of preserved specimens, such as the insects shown in **Figure 3.2**, as a record of Earth's biodiversity. As well as including specimens from recent investigations—such as insects from canopy fogging—they also contain many specimens from early explorations, some hundreds of years old. The Canadian Museum of Nature in Ottawa and the Royal Ontario Museum in Toronto have massive collections of biological specimens from all over the world.

Figure 3.2 Biological collections housed in museums have helped ecologists catalogue Earth's species.

Since most ecosystems are now influenced by human activities, it is helpful for land-use planners to know the locations of different species, especially rare or sensitive ones. Computer databases can handle huge volumes of such records. Biologists at Ontario's Natural Heritage Information Centre manage such a database and provide biodiversity information relevant to land-use planning.

Canada's Biodiversity

Canada, a large country with many aquatic and terrestrial ecosystems, is home to thousands of species, such as the red mulberry tree shown in **Figure 3.3A**. Recall, from the table in Activity 3-1 on page 87, that plants, insects, fungi (such as mushrooms), and small invertebrates (such as spiders) are far more diverse than larger animals. For example, almost 5000 species of plants have been identified in Canada. Some species, such as the Peary caribou shown in **Figure 3.3B**, are only found in certain locations around the world. Peary caribou are only found in the Canadian Arctic and in Greenland, so Canadians have a special responsibility for their welfare.

Go to **scienceontario**
to find out more

Figure 3.3 These two species in Canada need protection. **A** The red mulberry tree is only found in southwestern Ontario. **B** The Peary caribou live mainly in the high arctic islands.

Hotspots of Biodiversity

In analyzing the distribution of the world's biodiversity, ecologists have found that there are "hotspots" of diversity. A **biodiversity hotspot** is a place where there is an exceptionally large number of species in a relatively small area. Hotspots in Canada include Carolinian Canada and the Leitrim Wetlands, both in Ontario. Carolinian Canada, shown in **Figure 3.4**, is an area of deciduous forest in southern Ontario. Although the area makes up only 1 percent of Canada's total landmass, it has a higher number of species than any other ecosystem in Canada. It is estimated to have 2200 plants, including endangered trees and orchids, as well as 40 percent of Canada's breeding bird species. The Leitrim Wetlands, near Ottawa, is home to more than 200 species of plants and 90 species of birds.

In Canada, some of these hotspots have been given special status, which often gives them extra protection from development, such as building houses or industries in the area. For example, Long Point Bay on Lake Erie has been named a World Biosphere Reserve, one of many in an international network of such places that have unique features and a commitment to sustainable development. In the spring and fall, Long Point Bay is home to a rich diversity of wetland species, such as ducks and migrating shorebirds. The Georgian Bay Biosphere Reserve, also shown in **Figure 3.4**, is another Canadian hotspot.

Figure 3.4 Two of Ontario's biodiversity hotspots are the Carolinian Canada and Georgian Bay Biosphere Reserves. **A** Ferns grow on the forest floor of the Carolinian forest in Rouge Park in Toronto. **B** The eastern massasauga rattlesnake, found in the Georgian Bay Biosphere Reserve, is threatened.

MANITOBA

Hudson Bay

QUÉBEC

ONTARIO

Georgian Bay Biosphere Reserve

Carolinian Canada

Learning Check

1. What is biodiversity?

2. Explain one method used to collect data on biodiversity.

3. Why should scientists record information about biodiversity?

4. How does protecting an ecosystem, such as a wetland, help to preserve biodiversity?

Biodiversity in the Tropics

Although biodiversity in some areas of Canada is high, ecologists have shown that most of the biosphere's diversity hotspots are in the tropics of South America, Africa, and Asia. In tropical East Africa, Lake Malawi, shown in **Figure 3.5**, is home to about 1000 species of fish, many of which can be found only in this lake. Lake Malawi has about the same area as Lake Erie, which is home to about 150 fish species. The results of one study led researchers to conclude that 77 percent of the world's species of vertebrate animals can be found in tropical hotspots that cover only 16 percent of Earth's land surface.

Most tropical hotspots are in developing nations. For example, although Colombia (in South America) is only one ninth the size of Canada, it has four times as many bird species. Developing nations are less likely to have a workforce that has the specialists needed to fill the roles of environmental planners. There are many initiatives in developed nations, such as Canada, to assist in the protection of key ecosystems in these regions.

Figure 3.5 Lake Malawi is a biodiversity hotspot.

Activity 3-2

Biodiversity Index

Scientists can calculate the biodiversity index of an ecosystem using a simple formula. The closer the biodiversity index is to 1, the higher the biodiversity of the ecosystem is.

Materials

- model ecosystems provided by your teacher

Procedure

1. Choose one model ecosystem. Each colour of bead represents a different species. Count the number of different species in the ecosystem. Then count the number of individuals of each species. Calculate the total number of organisms in the ecosystem.

2. Record your data in a table like the one below.

3. Calculate the biodiversity index for each ecosystem. Divide the number of species in the ecosystem by the total number of organisms in the ecosystem.

4. Repeat steps 1 to 3 for the remaining ecosystem models.

Questions

1. Which ecosystem had the highest biodiversity? Which had the lowest?

2. What are the strengths of using the biodiversity index as a measure of biodiversity for an ecosystem? What are the weaknesses?

3. Give an example of a change to an abiotic or biotic factor in an ecosystem that could change the biodiversity index.

Biodiversity in Ecosystems

Ecosystem	Number of Species	Number of Individuals in Each Species	Total Number of Organisms	Biodiversity
Boreal forest	3	6 of species A 10 of species B 4 of species C	20	$\frac{3}{20}$ = 0.15

Section Summary

- Biodiversity is the number and variety of organisms found within a specific region.
- Scientists have identified about 2 million species on Earth.
- Scientists measure biodiversity using several different methods.
- There are places on Earth where there is an exceptionally large number of species in a relatively small area.
- Most biodiversity hotspots are in tropical areas.

Review Questions

K/U **1.** Use the terms *biodiversity* and *protect* in a single sentence.

K/U **2.** Use a **Venn diagram** to compare and contrast quadrat sampling and transect sampling.

A **3.** Identify the method that would be used to analyze the biodiversity in the area shown in the photograph on the right.

  a. What are some possible advantages and disadvantages of this method?

  b. If you were an ecologist, which method would you use to analyze the biodiversity of fish in a lake?

C **4.** Argue why scientists should receive funding to record information about biodiversity.

K/U **5.** Refer to **Figure 3.5** to identify and describe a biodiversity hotspot in the tropics.

T/I **6.** Scientists have identified about 2 million species. However, estimates of the total number of species on Earth range from 5 million to 100 million. What are some possible reasons why scientists may not have an accurate count of the number of species on Earth?

T/I **7.** Form a hypothesis to explain why most of the world's biodiversity hotspots are in the tropics.

K/U **8.** Explain why developed countries, such as Canada, have initiatives to help protect ecosystems in other areas of the world.

3.2 Communities

Observing and recording data about the number of species on Earth is an important way for scientists to measure biodiversity. However, ecologists also measure biodiversity at the more complex level of communities. A **community** is all the populations of the different species that interact in a specific area or ecosystem. The fish, corals, and sponges in **Figure 3.6** are all part of the community on this coral reef. Recall, from Chapter 2, that there are many types of relationships among organisms in a community, such as symbiosis, competition, and predation. Because species depend on these interactions, it is important to preserve the biodiversity of communities in order to protect the individual species in that community. As you read further, you will see that the removal of certain species from a community or ecosystem can have serious consequences for the community as a whole.

Important Species in a Community

Certain species can have a greater impact on a community or ecosystem. This can be because they have a high population number or they perform a critical ecosystem service. Sometimes their impact can be seen through food chain interactions. Other times, the species may change the environment physically. Three types of species that affect communities are dominant species, keystone species and ecosystem engineers.

Key Terms
community
dominant species
keystone species
captive breeding
ecosystem engineer
succession

community all the populations of the different species that interact in a specific area or ecosystem

Figure 3.6 Many populations, including different types of fish, corals, and sponges, make up this community.

Dominant Species

Dominant species are so abundant that they have the biggest biomass of any community member. *Biomass* is the total mass of living organisms in an area. In terrestrial ecosystems, dominant species are always primary producers because consumer biomass is always less than producer biomass.

The removal of a dominant species can result in a decrease in biodiversity within an ecosystem. For example, the American chestnut was a dominant tree in eastern North American forests in the early 1900s. By 1950, all American chestnut trees had been killed as a result of a fungus that had been accidentally introduced. Although no birds or mammals were affected by the loss of the chestnuts in the forests, seven species of insects that relied on the trees as a food source became extinct.

Keystone Species

It is easy to see why abundant, dominant species can be very important in a community. However, much less common keystone species can be equally important. A **keystone species** is one that can greatly affect population numbers and the health of an ecosystem. Keystone species are generally not abundant, and they can be plants or animals.

Sea Otters

One example of a keystone species is the sea otter. Sea otters are keystone predators in British Columbia's coastal kelp forests. As shown in **Figure 3.7**, sea otters eat sea urchins, which feed on kelp. During the 20th century, sea otter populations were greatly reduced as otters were trapped for their fur. As their numbers declined, the number of sea urchins increased. More sea urchins began eating the kelp, so the kelp biomass decreased. When this happened, the fish that depend on kelp forests as a habitat also declined in number, as shown in **Figure 3.7**. When sea otters were re-introduced, the kelp forests recovered. Sea otters are a keystone species because they keep the number of sea urchins in check, allowing the kelp to survive.

dominant species species that are so abundant that they have the biggest biomass of any community member

keystone species a species that can greatly affect population numbers and the health of an ecosystem

Sense of Value

The keystone is the brick at the top of an arch. The word *keystone* is used figuratively to refer to the central element of a system. The term *keystone species* is used in this sense, as an organism that provides stability to an ecosystem.

Figure 3.7 When the population of sea otters declines, the number of sea urchins increases, leading to a decrease in kelp biomass.

| Sustainable Sea Otter Population | Unsustainable Sea Otter Population |

Prairie Dogs and Black-footed Ferrets

Another example of a keystone species is the prairie dog, shown in **Figure 3.8**. Prairie dogs build burrows in huge colonies, known as "dog towns." As European settlement spread across the western grasslands of North America, prairie dogs were once thought of as pests, especially because they consumed crops and interfered with ranching. Through poison, trapping, and guns, prairie dog populations were drastically reduced in Canada and the United States. The wild prairie ecosystems suffered when populations of this keystone species were reduced. In places where the prairie dog has persisted, ecologists have discovered that dog towns are important for increasing plant diversity, turning over tonnes of soil, increasing the nitrogen content of the soil, and allowing deeper water penetration of the soil.

Another feature of dog towns that make prairie dogs a keystone species is that many species use the burrow system they establish. Black-footed ferrets are predators that use these burrows, and they eat prairie dogs. As the dog towns disappeared, so did the ferret. The last black-footed ferret in Canada was seen in 1937. The species survived longer in the United States, but it was thought to be completely extinct by 1979. However, in the early 1980s, a small American population was found. When that population dropped to only 18 individuals, wildlife managers captured them.

Captive Breeding Since 1992, the Toronto Zoo has been one of the facilities involved in the black-footed ferret **captive breeding** program, designed to bring these animals back from the brink of extinction. Hundreds of young ferrets have been born in the captive breeding program at the Toronto Zoo. Most, like the ferret shown in **Figure 3.9**, have been released back into the wild, following a program that trains them to capture wild prey and to avoid the natural risks they may encounter in the wild.

So far, the release sites have been in the United States, where the natural population of black-footed ferrets is now in the hundreds. The current plan to re-introduce the species to Canada involves re-establishing a stable population of prairie dogs too, so that the ferrets' ecosystem will be sustainable. The planned release site is Saskatchewan's Grasslands National Park, where a self-sustaining prairie dog population now occupies a large area of protected wild prairie.

Figure 3.8 Prairie dogs live in large colonies in networks of underground tunnels.

captive breeding
the breeding of rare or endangered wildlife in controlled settings to increase the population size

Figure 3.9 This wildlife biologist is releasing a ferret into the wild.

Learning Check

1. Why is it important to protect communities in order to protect particular species?

2. Use **Figure 3.7** to help you define *keystone species* and give an example of a keystone species.

3. What is the purpose of a captive breeding program?

4. Why must the prairie dog population be stable for the black-footed ferret population to survive?

Ecosystem Engineers

Beavers, like the one in **Figure 3.10**, are examples of ecosystem engineers.
Ecosystem engineers are species that cause such dramatic changes to
landscapes that they create a new ecosystem. In a matter of a few weeks,
beavers can convert a small stream in a forest into an aquatic ecosystem
that suits their needs perfectly. By building dams across streams and
creeks, they create ponds that provide them with safety and a food supply
of aquatic plants. Their tree-cutting activities also make small clearings
in the forest. Many species of fish, birds, amphibians, and insects benefit
from a beaver-pond ecosystem. What was once moving water becomes
a calm refuge for juvenile fish, migrating birds, and aquatic insects.
The beaverpond basket-tail dragonfly, shown in **Figure 3.10**, is one of
many animals that benefit from beavers creating ponds. Their larvae live
underwater and the adults hunt insects above the pond's surface.

Succession

By building a dam, a beaver's actions commonly kick start a succession of
different ecosystems. **Succession** is the series of changes in an ecosystem
that occurs over time, following a disturbance. In the case of a beaver pond,
the area changes from forest to a flooded forest, and then to sunny pond,
and ultimately to an abandoned pond that becomes a beaver meadow.

Each of these stages is ideal for different species. Even the final stage,
the beaver meadow, provides important habitat in otherwise forested
ecosystems. Beaver meadows are used by wolf packs.

Figure 3.10 The beaver is
the best-known example of
an ecosystem engineer. The
clearings and ponds it creates
support organisms, such as
the beaverpond basket-tail
dragonfly.

Section 3.2 Review

Section Summary

- Species live in communities where relationships among different species are very important.

- Dominant species are very common primary producers.

- Keystone species are especially significant in maintaining an ecosystem through their relationships with other species.

- Ecosystem engineers alter a landscape in a way that makes it suitable for additional species.

- Succession is the series of changes in an ecosystem that occurs over time, following a disturbance.

Review Questions

K/U **1.** What is the relationship between the terms *community* and *population*?

K/U **2.** Compare and contrast *dominant species* and *keystone species* using a Venn diagram.

C **3.** Debate why the removal of a rare species from an ecosystem may not change the ecosystem very much, but the removal of the dominant species causes a drastic change.

A **4.** The beetle shown on the right lives in the desert in Mexico. The beetle chews on the stems of mesquite shrubs, forcing the shrubs to grow new branches every spring. The trees take up more nutrients from the soil to support the new growth. This means there are fewer nutrients for other plants, such as grasses. Partly due to the action of the beetle, the desert has changed from mostly grasses to mostly mesquite shrubs over the last 150 years. How would you classify this beetle in terms of its role in the ecosystem? Explain your answer.

This beetle chews on the stems of mesquite shrubs.

A **5.** A person with *charisma* attracts attention and admiration. People sometimes use *charismatic species* to help draw attention to an environmental problem. Explain why you would or would not choose the following as charismatic species in a campaign to protect the ecosystems in which they live.

    a. polar bear   **b.** fern   **c.** blue whale   **d.** earthworm

    Do you think that charismatic species at risk deserve to get more attention than other species at risk? Justify your response.

K/U **6.** Explain succession in your own words.

K/U **7.** Look back at **Figure 3.10**. What do beaverpond basket-tail dragonflies and wolves have in common?

A **8.** Complete the following analogy: An ecosystem engineer is like a(n)....

Key Terms

habitat loss
deforestation
alien species
invasive species
overexploitation
extinction
biodiversity crisis

habitat loss the destruction of habitats, which usually results from human activities

deforestation the practice of clearing forests for logging or other human uses, and never replanting them

Figure 3.11 Deforestation results in habitat loss.

3.3 Threats to Biodiversity

For most of modern history, human actions have proceeded without people giving much thought to the sustainability of ecosystems. These actions often include things that drastically alter the conditions in an ecosystem, such as draining wetlands, cutting down trees, and damming rivers. Sometimes, these actions threaten biodiversity within a community or ecosystem and on Earth as a whole. Recall that one measure of biodiversity is the variety of ecosystems on Earth. If human actions lead to the destruction of entire ecosystems, such as wetlands or rainforests, biodiversity on Earth could decrease. As scientists learn more about the effects of human actions on ecosystems, we are paying more attention to decreasing human impact on ecosystems and restoring ecosystems that have already been altered.

Habitat Loss

Habitat loss occurs when events, due to natural disasters or human activities, alter a terrestrial or aquatic ecosystem so drastically that many species can no longer survive there. If the organisms cannot move somewhere else, or if no alternative habitat is available, species may not survive and biodiversity is threatened. Natural sources of habitat destruction are events such as volcanic eruptions, wildfires, droughts, and severe storms, such as hurricanes. Human activities that destroy habitats include **deforestation**, shown in **Figure 3.11**, draining wetlands, and damming rivers.

Deforestation

Deforestation occurs when forests are logged or cleared for human use and never replanted. In some areas of the world, large sections of forests are cut down for timber or cleared for agricultural use. Recall, from Section 3.1, that tropical regions, especially tropical rainforests, often have biodiversity hotspots. Although tropical forests cover only about 7 percent of Earth's land, it is estimated that they contain about half of all the species on Earth. The graph in **Figure 3.12** shows the percent of forest lost in the top 20 countries in which deforestation has occurred.

Canada has a vast boreal plains ecosystem, stretching across Manitoba, Saskatchewan, and Alberta. This ecosystem, which is a mix of plains and boreal forests, is home to more species of breeding birds than any other forest ecosystem in North America. Annual deforestation rates in this area from 1966 to 1994 were almost three times the average rate of deforestation worldwide, with forest cover decreasing by up to 55 percent during that time. Researchers at Environment Canada have found that along one of their survey routes in this ecosystem, the number of bird species declined from a maximum of 105 species in 1987 to only 67 species by 1995.

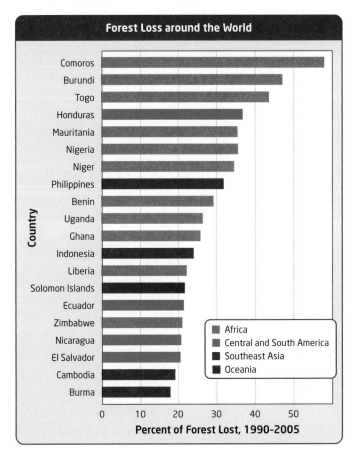

Figure 3.12 Deforestation in tropical rainforests has resulted in the loss of 20 to 50 percent of forests in some countries.

Making a Difference

As a nine-year-old, Severn Cullis-Suzuki witnessed the burning of the Brazilian Amazon rainforest. This experience led her to start the Environmental Children's Organization to help other children learn about environmental issues. Severn and her friends raised enough money to attend the 1992 Rio Earth Summit. At the Summit, Severn, then 12, gave a speech that received international attention. She reminded her audience that decisions they made about the environment would affect future generations. In 2002, Severn attended a UN panel on sustainable development in Johannesburg, South Africa. She brought a pledge from students to be accountable and challenged older generations to lead by example.

Today, Severn is a board member of the David Suzuki Foundation. This foundation was founded by her father, Dr. David Suzuki, who is a geneticist, environmentalist, and well-known broadcaster. It uses science and education to help society achieve sustainability.

What kind of pledge, or commitment, could you make to improve the sustainability of your lifestyle?

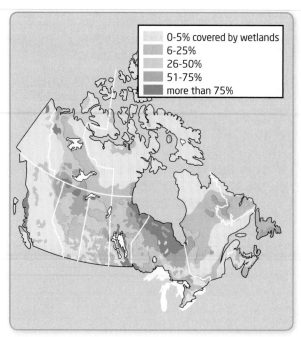

Legend:
- 0-5% covered by wetlands
- 6-25%
- 26-50%
- 51-75%
- more than 75%

Figure 3.13 Wetlands cover about 14 percent of Canada's total land area.

alien species a species that is accidentally or deliberately introduced into a new location

invasive species a species that can take over the habitat of native species

Go to **scienceontario** to find out more

Draining Wetlands

Wetlands, areas of land that are covered by water for part or all of the year, are an important ecosystem for many different species. They cover about 6 percent of Earth's surface. About 24 percent of the world's wetlands are in Canada. **Figure 3.13** shows that most of Canada's wetlands are in Manitoba and Ontario. Plants, turtles, snakes, mink, and thousands of other organisms live in wetlands. For juvenile animals, wetlands are a protected environment in which they can grow and develop. Every spring and fall, migrating birds also use wetlands to feed and rest. About 30 percent of birds in North America stop in wetlands throughout Canada. Besides providing habitat for many organisms, wetlands perform another important ecosystem service—the plants that grow in them filter sediment and pollution from water.

Wetlands are often drained for farming or for building homes and other buildings. Sometimes, they are drained for mosquito control. Up to 90 percent of wetlands along Lake Ontario have been destroyed. As scientists have learned more about the importance of wetland areas, more work is being done to preserve and protect existing wetlands. You will read more about how wetlands can be restored in Section 3.4.

Alien Species

Species introduced to new parts of the biosphere from other parts go by many names—**alien species**, introduced species, non-native species, and exotic species. Alien species may be released on purpose, but usually they arrive by accident in shipments of food and other goods. Most alien species are harmless or beneficial in their new environments.

However, sometimes alien species are also invasive species. An **invasive species** is one that can take over the habitat of native species. A native species is one that naturally inhabits an area. In many cases, invasive species upset the equilibrium of an ecosystem, causing problems for the native species. Many alien species invade aquatic ecosystems by way of cargo ships, particularly in ballast water. In order to increase their stability at sea, departing ships pick up water as ballast and hold it in tanks inside the hull. When they arrive at their destination, perhaps halfway around the world, the ballast water is dumped. Ballast water is like a giant aquarium, including microscopic organisms and fish.

Figure 3.14 Zebra mussels are an invasive species.

Zebra Mussels

Zebra mussels are a species of freshwater mollusc that is native to Asia. They were introduced to the Great Lakes through ballast water in the 1980s. Since then, scientists have been monitoring the impact of this invasive species on the Great Lakes ecosystem. Zebra mussels, shown in **Figure 3.14**, can out-compete native mussels and other native organisms in the lakes. One organism that has declined in number since the arrival of zebra mussels is a small, shrimp-like crustacean that shares the same food source as the zebra mussels. The crustaceans are a food source for many fish, including whitefish and smelt. As the number of these crustaceans has declined, so have the numbers of these fish. Scientists are studying more about the link between the arrival of zebra mussels and the decline of these organisms.

Suggested Investigation
Real World Investigation 3-A, Zebra Mussels in Lake Ontario, on page 117

Round Gobies in the Great Lakes

Until 1990, the Asian round goby, shown in **Figure 3.15**, had not previously been found in North America. They probably arrived in ballast water, and they were soon found breeding around Lake Erie shipwrecks. Their population spread widely and grew exponentially. It is too early to tell how round gobies will change the Great Lakes ecosystems, but they certainly will. Within a decade of arrival, they were found in all five Great Lakes, and their western Lake Erie population is now estimated in the billions!

Figure 3.15 The round goby from Asia now lives in the Great Lakes, where it competes with native fish for spawning areas. The round goby is also known to eat the eggs of native fish.

Learning Check

1. What is habitat loss?

2. List two reasons why wetlands are drained.

3. Give three reasons why alien species often do well when they are released in a new part of the world.

4. Describe why round gobies might function effectively as predators and competitors in the Great Lakes.

Overexploitation

overexploitation the use or extraction of a resource until it is depleted

Biodiversity is threatened when **overexploitation** occurs. Overexploitation is the use or extraction of a resource until it is depleted. Overexploitation can lead to dangerously low population numbers, if not the complete disappearance of a species. For example, the population of passenger pigeons was once about 5 billion. However, partly due to overhunting by early North American settlers, the last passenger pigeon died in the early 1900s. Overfishing of yellowfish tuna and Atlantic cod during the past few decades has reduced the numbers of these species by 90 percent. The graph in **Figure 3.16** shows the reduction in the number of tonnes of Atlantic cod caught off the coast of Newfoundland from 1950 to 1999.

Figure 3.16 The reduced catch of Atlantic cod reflects a decrease in population as a result of overexploitation.

Atlantic Cod Catch

(Graph: Atlantic Cod Catch (thousands of tonnes) vs Year)

- 1950–1959: ~850
- 1960–1969: ~1420
- 1970–1979: ~760
- 1980–1989: ~640
- 1990–1999: ~190

Activity 3-3

Alien Invasions

Purple loosestrife (*Lythrum salicaria*) is an alien invasive species that was introduced to North America in the 1800s. In wetlands, purple loosestrife out-competes the native plant species. Controlling purple loosestrife is important to the sustainability of ecosystems around Ontario.

Procedure

1. Study the chart on the right, which contains information about the best methods for controlling purple loosestrife. Then answer the following questions.

Questions

1. What are the different methods used for controlling purple loosestrife?

2. A conservation officer has discovered some isolated purple loosestrife plants, with a low density, in a park. What methods should be used to help control the spread of the plants?

3. Why do you think several methods are needed to control purple loosestrife?

4. Suppose that you are a conservation officer and you need the public's help to remove all the purple loosestrife plants from a wetland area. It is a small area with a medium density of plants. Outline a design for a community action poster that asks people to help clean up on a Saturday. Include details about why the clean-up is important and what tasks need to be done.

Purple Loosestrife Control Methods

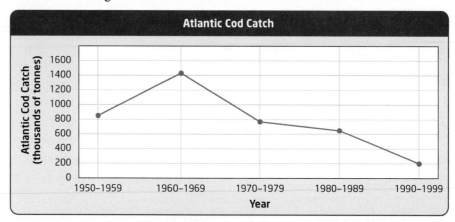

Size of Infested Area	Density of Infested Area		
	Low 1–50 plants (1–25% of area)	Medium 50–1000 plants (25–75% of area)	High 1000+ plants (75–100% of area)
Isolated plants	digging and pulling, chemical control	chemical control, cutting	biological control
Small less than 1 acre (0.1–0.5 ha)	digging and pulling, chemical control	digging and pulling, cutting	biological control, chemical control
Medium up to 4 acres (0.5–2 ha)	digging and pulling, chemical control	biological control, cutting, chemical control	biological control
Large more that 4 acres (more than 2 ha)	cutting, chemical control	biological control	biological control

digging and pulling   chemical control   cutting   biological control

Disrupting Connectivity across Ecosystems

What would you think if you read the headline "Salmon help to keep temperate rainforests of British Columbia healthy"? You might be puzzled. How can salmon, which live in aquatic ecosystems, be connected to terrestrial-dwelling trees in temperate rainforests? Dr. Tom Reimchen of the University of Victoria, in British Columbia, has an explanation.

As shown in **Figure 3.17**, salmon are hatched in freshwater streams throughout the temperate rainforest. They then migrate to the Pacific Ocean and spend their adult lives in the marine ecosystem. Every year, thousands of salmon swim upstream to return to the streams in which they hatched to spawn (reproduce). During this time, bears and other organisms, including wolves, bald eagles, and crows, feed on the salmon. In particular, bears move the salmon from the stream beds far into the forest. When the remains of the salmon decay in the forest, nutrients from their bodies, including nitrogen, enter the soil.

Based on his research, Dr. Reimchen estimates that up to 70 percent of the nitrogen in plants, trees, insects, birds, and bears in the temperate rainforest comes from the Pacific Ocean via the salmon. These nutrients help to increase biodiversity in the forest. He has found that species diversity in areas without salmon is lower than in areas with salmon. Since the 1880s, salmon populations on the west coast of North America have decreased by 80 to 90 percent. This decline in salmon population may result from a number of factors, including overfishing and habitat destruction from logging and dam construction. Studies on the decrease in the salmon population and its effects on the temperate rainforest are ongoing. A reduction in the carrying capacity and in the biodiversity of the temperate rainforest ecosystem are two possible consequences of the decline in the number of salmon.

○○○

Study Toolkit

Identifying the Main Idea and Details How do the heading and visual on this page help you identify the main idea of the text?

Figure 3.17 Several ecosystems are connected as a result of the life cycle of salmon and the feeding habits of bears and other animals in the temperate rain forest.

1. Salmon hatch in freshwater streams in the temperate rainforest.
2. Salmon spend their adult life in the Pacific Ocean, picking up nutrients from the marine ecosystem.
3. Salmon return to their birthplace to spawn.
4. Bears move salmon into the forest. Nutrients released from the salmons' decaying bodies are absorbed by plants in the forest.

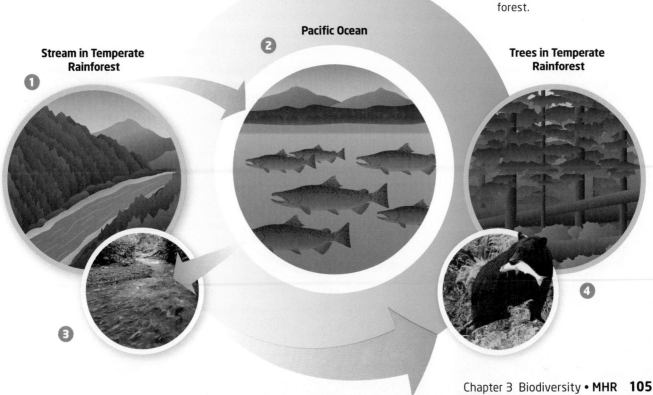

Stream in Temperate Rainforest ❶ ❸

Pacific Ocean ❷

Trees in Temperate Rainforest ❹

Extinction Reduces Biodiversity

Extinction occurs when all the individuals of a species have died. Long before humans existed, many species on Earth existed and became extinct in both terrestrial and aquatic ecosystems.

extinction the death of all the individuals of a species

How Does Extinction Occur?

Extinction occurs when the death rate of a species remains higher than the birth rate for a long period of time. The birth rate is the speed at which new individuals are added to a population, and the death rate is the speed at which individuals are removed from the population by death. Over long periods of time, these two rates have to be equal for a species' population to remain stable.

Even in ecosystems that are unaffected by human activities, things never remain the same forever. Sometimes a significant biotic or abiotic feature of a species' ecosystem changes. For example, an abiotic factor for a plant species could be a decline in rainfall that makes soils more dry. A biotic factor for a plant species could be the arrival of a new insect species whose leaf-feeding habit weakens the plants. Such factors may not cause the extinction of the species directly, but if the change results in the death rate being greater than the birth rate over an extended period of time, extinction eventually occurs.

STSE Case Study

Saving Dolly Varden

In 2006, the Gwich'in Renewable Resource Board saw a problem with the declining population of the Dolly Varden, a species of fish in the Rat River in Canada's North. A ban was placed on commercial and sport fishing in the river during periods of migration and spawning. Unfortunately, the population of Dolly Varden continued to decline and the river was closed to all fishing, including fishing by the Gwich'in for food.

The Gwich'in are one of Canada's most northerly Aboriginal peoples. Scientists can learn a lot about ecosystems and sustainability from Aboriginal peoples. The Gwich'in, for instance, have a unique understanding of the Dolly Varden fish because they have interacted with the species for centuries and their traditional use has not threatened the fish. This understanding is called traditional ecological knowledge.

The Dolly Varden Life Cycle

Dolly Varden spend the bulk of the year in salt water and then migrate in the fall to fresh water to spawn. They travel from the Beaufort Sea to fish holes (parts of a river that do not freeze completely) in tributaries (branches) of the Mackenzie River, including the Rat River.

Because of their speckled, pink appearance, Dolly Varden fish are named after a character in a Charles Dickens' novel. The character, Dorothy Varden, wore dresses with pink polka dots.

Patterns of Natural Extinction

By examining fossil evidence, scientists have described two patterns of extinction in the history of Earth. The difference between these patterns is the speed with which they occur. One pattern, called background extinction, is apparent over long periods of time. As ecosystems gradually change over long periods of time, some existing species become extinct while new species appear through evolution.

The second pattern is mass extinction. Mass extinction is thought to happen when there is a relatively sudden change to Earth's ecosystems, making them both unsustainable and unsustaining. As shown in **Figure 3.18**, this is believed to have occurred five times in Earth's history. The best-known example of mass extinction is the death of the dinosaurs. Many scientists hypothesize that an asteroid hit Earth 65 million years ago, causing huge changes to Earth's climate and thus eliminating the dinosaurs. Earlier, there was an even more devastating mass extinction of sea life. This is thought to have occurred when an extended period of massive volcanic activity in Asia caused significant climate change around the world.

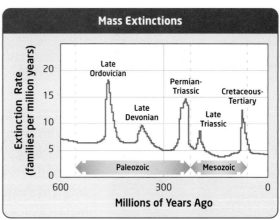

Figure 3.18 Five times in the past there were short periods when many species disappeared. These are known as mass extinctions.

Canadian scientists and members of the Gwich'in community are teaming up to try to save a fish called the Dolly Varden in the Rat River, a tributary of the Mackenzie River.

What is traditional ecological knowledge?
Traditional ecological knowledge is

- collective information held by Aboriginal peoples through their connectedness to the land

- thinking passed down by generations through stories, song, and art

- knowledge that can help to answer complex questions about the environment and sustainability

The Rat River population of Dolly Varden has fallen from about 12 000 in 2002 to only 3500 in 2006. Scientists suspect that the drop in population is due to overfishing, as well as habitat and climate change.

Gwich'in fishers have been hired to catch a small number of the fish for research, but until the population of Dolly Varden begins to increase, the ban on fishing will remain in place.

Your Turn

1. Research the ways in which the Gwich'in have used the Dolly Varden for food and medicine.

2. How would you explain traditional ecological knowledge to a Grade 6 student?

3. Explain why traditional ecological knowledge might be particularly useful in Canada's North.

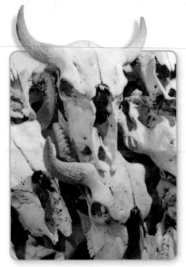

Figure 3.19 The plains bison is not extinct, but its numbers have been dramatically reduced, primarily due to overhunting. In the 1800s, piles of bison skulls were ground into fertilizer.

biodiversity crisis the current accelerated rate of extinctions

Current Extinction Rates

Fossils tell us that for most of Earth's history, changes to ecosystems have occurred slowly enough or on a small enough scale that only background extinction occurs. But they also tell us that, in rare instances, changes are so big that much—even most—of the biosphere's biodiversity becomes extinct.

With ever-increasing technological sophistication and a population approaching 7 billion, humans make heavy demands on ecosystems. One of the costs to ecosystems is the extinction of species. Some ecologists estimate that the current rate of extinction is 100 to 1000 times higher than a normal background rate. In one study that assessed the status of over 40 000 species, 39 percent of those species were found to be at risk of extinction. These included species of trees, amphibians, birds, and mammals, such as the plains bison in **Figure 3.19**. This problem has been called the **biodiversity crisis**. Scientists hypothesize that the biodiversity crisis has resulted from the actions of humans. Activities that lead to deforestation, habitat destruction, and air and water pollution are changing the abiotic and biotic conditions in ecosystems. In some cases, the conditions change so much that organisms are unable to survive.

Activity 3-4

Plants at Risk

There are 77 plant species at risk in Ontario. The bar graph below shows how many species are in each category of concern.

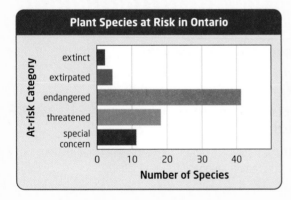

Materials

- calculator
- dictionary

Procedure

1. Research and record the definition of each of the categories shown on the y-axis of the graph.

2. Study the graph, then answer the following questions.

Questions

1. Which category contains the most plant species? Which contains the least plant species?

2. There are approximately 2000 plant species in Ontario. What percent of Ontario's plant species are endangered? What percent are threatened?

3. Deerberry is a small shrub that is threatened. One of the threats to this species is that remaining plants may be trampled by hikers who leave the marked trail in St. Lawrence Islands National Park. Design a one-page flyer to make hikers aware of this issue and persuade them to stay on the marked trail while at the park.

4. Suppose that there are two plant species at risk in your area. One of these species is threatened, and the other is endangered. A local environmental organization has only enough resources to try to save one species. Write a brief persuasive argument for which plant should be saved, based on its status.

Section Summary

- Threats to biodiversity include habitat loss, the introduction of alien species, overexploitation, and breaking the connectivity among ecosystems.
- Deforestation and draining wetlands can result in habitat loss.
- Extinction is a natural event that has occurred throughout Earth's history.
- Current extinction rates may be accelerated due to human activities.

Review Questions

K/U **1.** Give two examples of how human actions can lead to habitat loss.

A **2.** Suppose that you are a member of the town council. A local business has requested permission to expand its buildings onto a nearby wetland. The wetland would be drained and a new hotel would be constructed. The expansion of the business would mean more jobs for the community. How would you vote on this issue? Explain what factors you would consider when making your decision.

T/I **3.** Occasionally, biologists discover that a species has invaded a new area without the assistance of human beings. For instance, the African cattle egret, the wading bird shown on the right, invaded North America when several individual egrets crossed the Atlantic Ocean. Use a T-chart to summarize the advantages and disadvantages of eliminating a naturally invasive species.

The African cattle egret is an invasive species in North America.

K/U **4.** Explain how overexploitation can threaten biodiversity.

C **5.** Write a slogan for a public awareness campaign to identify three human activities that have a negative effect on biodiversity. Share your slogan with your class.

K/U **6.** Use a Venn diagram to compare and contrast the two patterns of natural extinction.

K/U **7.** What do scientists hypothesize as possible causes of mass extinctions?

K/U **8.** What is the biodiversity crisis?

Key Terms

stewardship
restoration ecology
reforestation
biocontrol
bioremediation
bioaugmentation

stewardship the active assumption of responsibility for the welfare of the environment

Sense of *time*

When thinking about environmental stewardship, Aboriginal peoples believe that the current generation should always work to protect the environment for the seven generations that will follow it.

3.4 Restoration Ecology

A *steward* is someone who is responsible for looking after someone else's property. Environmental **stewardship** is the idea that all humans are responsible for looking after a huge piece of property that belongs to all living things—the biosphere. There are both ethical and practical reasons for environmental stewardship. The ethical reasons are based on the idea of what is moral. For whom do we look after the biosphere? We look after the biosphere for other human beings, for future generations, and for other organisms, such as the spotted turtle in **Figure 3.20**. The practical reasons can be summarized using an analogy made by an ecologist.

An Ecosystem Analogy

Suppose that you are in a jet taking off, and you see that one out of hundreds of rivets holding the wings together is missing. You are not too worried. After all, engineers "over-engineer" such structures so that they are much stronger than the stresses placed on them. However, if you see that dozens of rivets are missing, you might begin to worry. The jet might not be "sustaining" or "enduring," meaning that a crash is likely.

Just as rivets hold an airplane wing together, species hold ecosystems together. There are some special "rivets" that ecosystems cannot afford to lose, such as the keystone species you read about in Section 3.2. However, ecosystems tend to be over-engineered with lots of rivets too, especially rivets with high biodiversity. Most ecosystems might remain sustainable with the loss of one or two rivets, but as more rivets are lost, the ecosystems will lose their ability to sustain the remaining species, including humans.

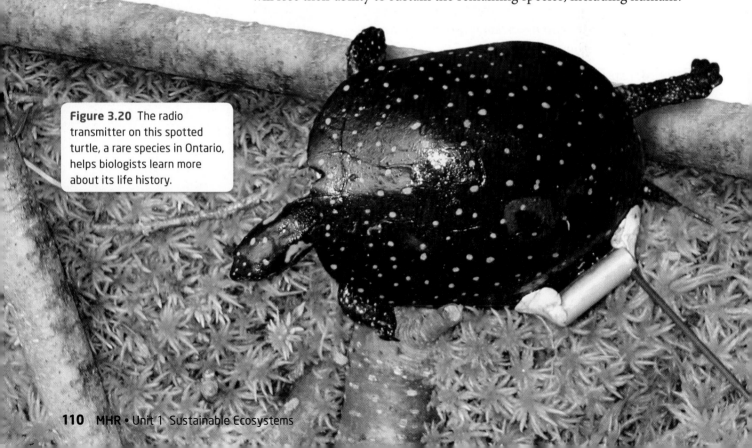

Figure 3.20 The radio transmitter on this spotted turtle, a rare species in Ontario, helps biologists learn more about its life history.

Restoring Altered Ecosystems

For most of modern history, human actions have proceeded without much thought to the sustainability of the ecosystems. As scientists learn more about the effects of human actions on ecosystems, however, more attention is given to decreasing human impact on ecosystems and restoring those that have already been altered. A major goal of restoration ecology is to stimulate natural processes of regeneration to produce a sustainable, if not identical, ecosystem. **Restoration ecology** is the renewal of degraded or destroyed ecosystems through active human intervention.

A Restoration Plan

The Don Valley Brick Works, shown in **Figure 3.21**, was a business that operated for almost a century, at what was once the edge of Toronto. Bricks were made at the site, and rock was mined in a quarry there.

The site was purchased as conservation land in 1990, and the restoration plan was implemented in 1994. The old quarry was filled in, using material excavated from a site in downtown Toronto. In addition, the site was landscaped to create a series of three ponds, using water diverted from Mud Creek, a stream that passes through the site. The first pond captures sediment carried by the current, and plants in the other two ponds filter the water before it flows into Lake Ontario. The ponds are a feature of interest for visitors. They also provide habitat for wildlife, including migrating birds that seek green spaces when they make stops in urban areas. Mud Creek itself, which had been buried underground for decades, was uncovered using a restoration technique known as *daylighting*.

> **restoration ecology** the renewal of degraded or destroyed ecosystems through active human intervention

> **Suggested Investigation**
>
> Inquiry Investigation 3-B, Balancing Populations and the Environment, on pages 118-120

Figure 3.21 Ecological restoration has converted Toronto's Don Valley Brick Works (shown in 1891 and today) into a natural environment and cultural heritage park that includes wetlands, a boardwalk, a wildflower meadow, and restored historic buildings.

1891

Present day

Learning Check

1. What is stewardship?

2. What does *daylighting* mean to a restoration ecologist?

3. How can a series of ponds be used to improve water quality?

4. Connect the terms *stewardship* and *restoration ecology*.

Restoration Methods

Restoration ecologists use many techniques to restore sustainable ecosystems.

Reforestation

Reforestation is the regrowth of a forest, either through natural processes or through the planting of seeds or trees in an area where a forest was cut down. The regrowth of a forest takes many years, but, with proper planning and management, it can be done successfully. In the early 1900s in eastern Canada, red pine trees were planted in some areas that had previously been cleared for agriculture by European settlers. As the rows of red pines matured, the trees provided shade under which the seeds of native trees grew. Natural succession, shown in **Figure 3.22**, in these areas over the past 80 years has yielded the gradual return of native tree species such as the sugar maple, American beech, hickory, and ash.

reforestation the regrowth of a forest, either through natural processes or through the planting of seeds or trees in an area where a forest was cut down

○○○

Study Toolkit

Word Origins How do you think the words *restoration* and *reforestation* are related?

Figure 3.22 Red pines, which were planted to control soil erosion, helped to accelerate natural forest succession. **A** Forest was cut down to use the land for agriculture. **B** Red pine trees were planted to reforest the area. **C** As the red pines grew, they provided shade under which other species grew. **D** After many years, natural succession occurred, and there was a gradual return of native species.

Wetlands Restoration

The story of Alfred Bog, which you read about at the beginning of this chapter, is just one example of how existing wetlands are being protected today. But what happens to wetland areas that were drained and the land used for other purposes? Many government agencies and non-profit organizations across Canada are working to restore some of these areas. Wetland restoration is a process in which a wetland is, to the greatest extent possible, returned to its natural state in terms of soil quality and composition, water coverage, the type of plants that grow there, and the habitat. In southern Ontario, the Ministry of Natural Resources in Norfolk County has begun a Wetlands Drainage Restoration Project. Through this project, potential restoration sites are identified and water is allowed to return to natural levels through the use of water control structures, like the one shown in **Figure 3.23**. Since 1996, efforts related to the project have restored numerous wetlands in Norfolk County.

Figure 3.23 Water control structures are used by wetland conservationists to help restore and maintain water levels.

Controlling Alien Species

Recall, from Section 3.2, that an alien species can upset the equilibrium of an ecosystem. Being able to successfully control the spread of an alien species is an important part of maintaining sustainable ecosystems. Biocontrol and chemicals are two methods that ecologists use to help control alien species.

biocontrol the use of a species to control the population growth or spread of an undesirable species

Biocontrol The European gypsy moth, shown in **Figure 3.24**, escaped from an American lab into the forest ecosystems of eastern North America in the 1800s. The species then began to spread, and it remains a serious forest pest in many areas, including much of Ontario. These moths feed on tree leaves, and, during peak years, they can remove all the leaves on a tree. To battle this pest, a European fly called a parasitoid was introduced, as a form of biocontrol. **Biocontrol** is the use of one species to control the population growth or spread of an undesirable species. The parasitoid was known to lay its eggs inside the gypsy moth caterpillar, eventually killing it.

Although the parasitoid fly probably helps to regulate the European gypsy moth here, it has two traits that make it a problem for the ecosystem. First, it has several generations each summer, whereas the gypsy moth has only one. Second, the fly has to overwinter inside a caterpillar, but gypsy moths overwinter as eggs. Consequently, the fly also must attack native moths. One study showed that 81 percent of robin moths, the largest moth found in Ontario, were attacked by the alien fly.

Figure 3.24 Gypsy moths can eat all the leaves on a tree.

Activity 3-5

The Common Good

Most resources are shared by many organisms. What problems occur when a population shares a limited resource?

Materials
- bingo chips or similar items (100 per group)
- watch or clock

Procedure

1. Arrange your team of about 10 in a circle.

2. Place 100 chips in the centre of each team's circle.

3. Each team will "harvest" chips from its supply for short periods of time (between 30 s and 2 min). Your teacher will signal the start and end of each harvest. Your goal is to obtain the maximum points for your team.

4. Points are obtained as follows:
   - Each student obtains one point for every 10 chips she or he harvests.
   - At the end of each harvest, the supply of chips that remains in the centre of each group will be doubled (up to a maximum of 100 chips).

- The group with the largest supply of chips left in the centre after each harvest will obtain one point for each student in the group.

5. Carry out the first harvest and calculate the total points obtained by each group.

6. Repeat the harvest three more times.

Questions

1. What strategies of harvesting led to the greatest decline in a team's resources (the chips)?

2. What strategy of harvesting led to the highest number of points obtained by a team?

3. Is the strategy that provides maximum points to individuals the same as the strategy that provides maximum points to groups? Explain.

4. Suggest some real-life resources that the chips in the model might represent.

Chemicals Sometimes, chemicals can be used carefully with success. Langara Island, off the coast of northern British Columbia, is home to countless nesting sea birds, including burrowing species. The island suits such birds because it was, originally, relatively predator-free. Then two alien species of rats, Norway rats and black rats, were accidentally introduced by ship. The rats ate birds' eggs and nestlings, causing the island's bird population to decline steadily. For example, the population of ancient murrelets, shown in **Figure 3.25**, was reduced by almost 40 000 individuals after the rats arrived on the island. Trapping failed to eliminate the rat population, but a poisoning campaign succeeded. Bait containing the poison was placed around the island for the rats. Although other animals, such as ravens and shrews, were also affected by the poison, the rats suffered a devastating population decline as a result of the poisoning campaign. By 1996, the rats had been eliminated from Langara Island. Since then, the population of ancient murrelets has rebounded.

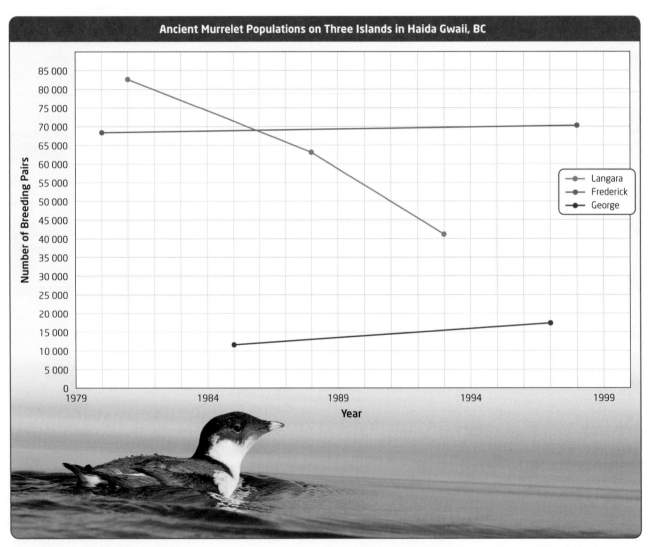

Figure 3.25 Following the accidental introduction of foreign rats around 1981, the colony of ancient murrelets on British Columbia's Langara Island dropped steadily. No rats were introduced to nearby Frederick Island or George Island.

Bioremediation and Bioaugmentation

Bio means life. In **bioremediation**, scientists introduce living plants and fungi to do more than simply revegetate landscapes. Certain plants are grown at toxic sites because they clean soils by collecting the poisons in their tissues. When these plants are harvested, the soil quality is improved. In another example, bacteria have been used with some success to break down oil from oil spills that damage coastline ecosystems.

Bioaugmentation is another restoration tool. **Bioaugmentation** is the use of organisms to add essential nutrients to depleted soil. For example, the clover shown in **Figure 3.26** is often planted to replenish nitrogen levels in soil. Recall that nitrogen is an important nutrient for plants.

The Future of Restoration Ecology

Given population growth and the related widespread alteration of ecosystems, this century will require humans to restore and enhance sustainable ecosystems. Restoration ecology has developed tremendously, but many challenges remain, including the sometimes slow pace of recovery, the restoration of a different type of ecosystem than planned, the requirement of continuous intervention, and projects of very large scale, such as the Alberta Tar Sands, shown in **Figure 3.27**. The extraction of petroleum from the Alberta Tar Sands involves almost total destruction of huge areas of boreal forest, as well as the production of tremendous volumes of *tailings* containing toxic waste. The scale of this project promises to be a major challenge for restoration.

Figure 3.26 Clover is often planted to replenish nitrogen levels in soil.

bioremediation the use of living organisms to clean up contaminated areas naturally

bioaugmentation the use of organisms to add essential nutrients to depleted soils

Figure 3.27 Removal of petroleum from the Alberta Tar Sands leaves the area almost completely devastated.

Section Summary

- Restoration ecology includes reforestation, wetlands restoration, controlling alien species, bioremediation, and bioaugmentation.
- The flow of nutrients through ecosystems can be interrupted by human activities, and restoration techniques can offset those interruptions.
- Alien species are extremely difficult to eradicate in most situations.
- There are many ecosystems that require restoration, and the Alberta tar sands will be a major challenge.

Review Questions

A **1.** Make a list of actions you take that contribute to environmental stewardship.

K/U **2.** What kinds of human activities create the need for restoration ecology?

K/U **3.** Use **Figure 3.21** to help you explain how the restoration of the Don Valley Brick Works is an important example of the support of ecological restoration in cities.

C **4.** Recall, from Chapter 1, that modern societies use fossil fuels at high rates. Extraction of petroleum from the Alberta tar sands requires deforestation and removal of soils, both of which have very significant effects on the environment. Write a short paragraph stating your opinion on this issue. Should petroleum be extracted in this way? Why or why not?

K/U **5.** List some methods that can be used to eliminate alien species.

A **6.** Langara Island is approximately 6 km by 5 km. How successful do you think a poisoning campaign to eliminate non-native rats would be on New Zealand's two main islands, each of which has an area of over 100 000 square km? Explain your answer.

T/I **7.** The Ontario government began dropping tens of thousands of food baits inoculated with a vaccine against rabies, an alien virus, in 1989. The graph on the right shows the number of cases of rabies in Ontario from 1988 to 2000. Based on the data in the graph, do you think the campaign to control the spread of the rabies virus has been successful? Explain your answer.

K/U **8.** How have bacteria been used in restoration ecology?

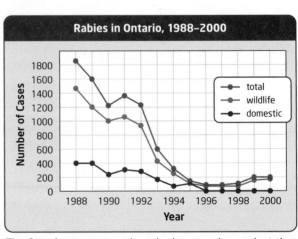

The Ontario government launched a campaign against the spread of rabies.

Skill Check

✓ **Initiating and Planning**

Performing and Recording

✓ **Analyzing and Interpreting**

✓ **Communicating**

Materials

• graph paper
• coloured pencils
• access to the Internet

Zebra Mussels and Chlorophyll a in Lake Ontario

Year	Number of Zebra Mussels (per m²)	Chlorophyll a (μg/L)
1990	0	4.4
1991	230	3.3
1992	500	3.4
1993	800	3.0
1994	1080	3.5
1995	1130	2.3
1996	770	3.6
1997	250	3.5
1998	410	3.3
1999	25	5.6
2000	25	2.8
2001	20	3.3
2002	10	3.6
2003	5	5.9
2004	no data	4.5

Math Skills

Go to **Math Skills Toolkit 3** for information about constructing a graph.

Zebra Mussels in Lake Ontario

Zebra mussels feed on phytoplankton, which are microscopic producers in aquatic ecosystems. The presence and productivity of phytoplankton are often inferred from the amount of chlorophyll a in the water. The table below contains data on the population of zebra mussels and the concentration of chlorophyll a in Lake Ontario from 1990 to 2004.

Question

How do zebra mussels affect the biotic and abiotic conditions in an aquatic ecosystem?

Prediction

Preview the data in the table, and make a prediction about the relationship between the two variables.

Organize the Data

Graph both sets of data on the same graph. Be sure to include a key to indicate what each data line represents.

Analyze and Interpret

1. Explain the relationship between changes in zebra mussel numbers and the concentration of chlorophyll a.

2. Infer how zebra mussels change the biotic conditions in an aquatic ecosystem. How could the changes affect the biodiversity of the ecosystem?

3. When the number of phytoplankton in water decreases, the clarity of the water increases. Light can penetrate deeper into the water as a result. How might this change to abiotic conditions in an aquatic ecosystem affect the biodiversity of the ecosystem?

Conclude and Communicate

4. Write an editorial article for a newspaper explaining why you think it is important for ships to sanitize ballast water before releasing it into the Great Lakes.

Extend Your Inquiry and Research Skills

5. **Research** In 2006, Transport Canada implemented the Ballast Water Control and Management Regulations. Find out more about these regulations. Explain how the regulations are an example of different countries and government agencies working together to protect an ecosystem.

Safety Precautions

- Use caution when working with the sharp pencil to make holes through poster paper.

Materials

- 2 sheets of white poster paper (32 cm × 32 cm each)
- ruler
- sharp pencil
- 32 square green sticky notes (4 cm × 4 cm each)
- bag of 100 checkers or similar objects (50 black and 50 red)
- calculator
- graph paper

Balancing Populations and the Environment

A *commons* is a parcel of land that is shared by multiple users. In this type of arrangement, all individuals share the costs, but only some individuals experience gains. For example, cattle herders may share an area of common grazing land. If one herder puts more animals on the commons, that herder will gain. However, the other herders will experience poorer grazing land for their cattle without receiving any benefit. Therefore, they may be inclined to increase the size of their herds too, with the result that the commons becomes overgrazed.

Parks are modern examples of commons. One goal of a park manager is to maintain the resources of the park for the benefit of all its users over many years. An increase in demand for resources by any species affects all the other users of the park. In this investigation, you will play the role of park manager. Your job is to help maintain the deer population at or near the park's carrying capacity for deer. Recall that the carrying capacity is the maximum number of individuals of a species that an ecosystem can sustain.

Question

What factors might affect the equilibrium of a population, leading it to become out of balance with the carrying capacity of the ecosystem?

Hypothesis

Make a hypothesis about how the population of deer in a park will respond to pressures such as hunting, migration, seasonal changes, and mating.

Procedure

1. Work in a group of four. On one sheet of poster paper, draw a grid of eight squares by eight squares. Each square should be 4 cm by 4 cm. This grid represents a provincial park. Indicate which direction is north, and give your park a name.

2. Prepare a hunting screen from the second sheet of poster paper. Using a sharp pencil, make 10 holes at random in the paper. Push the pencil through, rather than stabbing it through.

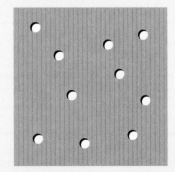

hunting screen

3. The 32 square green sticky notes represent land with sufficient vegetation for deer to graze. Stick all the squares onto your park, within the squares created by the grid lines. Think about how the pattern of squares you create might affect the deer. The 32 uncovered (white) squares represent land that is overgrazed or otherwise unsuitable for deer.

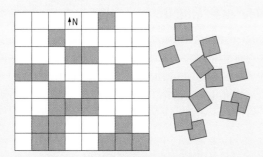

4. The black checkers are male deer (bucks), and the red checkers are female deer (does). To begin, stock your park with 32 deer randomly chosen from the bag. Place one deer on each green square. This population size (32) represents the carrying capacity of the park.

5. You will manage your deer population for five years. At the start of each year, you will establish a wildlife management policy. (For example, you may restrict hunting or supply extra food in the winter). During the rest of the year, the following four factors will affect the number of deer:

- mating season (see Rules of the Game)
- hunting season (see Rules of the Game)
- immigration and emigration (see Rules of the Game)
- seasonal impacts, either human or natural, such as a forest fire or flood, disease, deep snow, and poaching (These are not defined in the rules. It is for you to decide how much any of these impacts might affect the population each year, if at all. For example, a disease may sweep through the population, eliminating 10 percent of the deer. You would then randomly remove these individuals from your grid.)

Rules of the Game

Mating Season Any doe that has sufficient nutrition (is on a green square) and has a buck in an adjacent square mates with him to produce one fawn. The fawn (choose a new checker randomly from the bag) is placed under the doe checker. At the end of each year, the fawns must move from their mother's care into a vacant adjacent square. If no suitable land (a green square) is available, the fawn must move to overgrazed land (a white square). If there is no vacant adjacent square in the park, the fawn dies and is removed from the board.

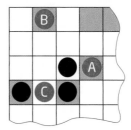

Rules for mating: Doe A can mate. Doe B cannot mate (no adjacent buck). Doe C cannot mate (on a white square).

Hunting Season Place the hunting screen on top of your park. Any deer that can be seen through the holes is shot by hunters and removed from the park–unless your management policy affects the hunting rules for the year. Each year, exchange hunting screens with a different group (or flip the screen to a different orientation).

Immigration and Emigration Any deer on a perimeter white square (overgrazed land) either moves to an empty adjacent green square or leaves the park (emigration). Any unoccupied good land (a green square) on the perimeter of the park is filled by new deer entering the park (immigration). Choose new deer at random from the bag.

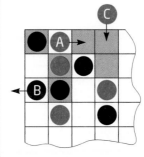

Rules for migration: Doe A moves to adjacent green square. Buck B leaves park (no adjacent vacant green square). Doe C enters park (vacant green square on perimeter).

6. As a class, create a list of events for each of the five years, using all the factors in the order presented in step 5. All the groups will follow the same list, but different parks may get different results.

7. Make a data table, as shown below. After each event, record the number of deer in your data table. At the end of the game, make line graphs to display your data.

Deer Population over Time

Time	Factor	Number of Deer		
		Females	Males	Total
Start				
Year 1	Mating season			
	Hunting season			
	Migration			
	Seasonal impact			

8. Present your results to the class.

Analyze and Interpret

1. Was there a trend in the deer population in your park? Explain.

2. If you experienced a consistent increase or decrease in deer numbers, explain the main reason for this change. How could you achieve a more stable population?

3. Did different parks experience different results? If so, suggest the main cause of the differences.

4. How are the factors that determine the size of a deer population in a park similar to the factors that determine the human population of Canada? How are they different?

5. Over the past two centuries, the numbers and distribution of deer in parts of North America have varied greatly as a result of human activities. How would each of the following activities affect deer numbers?

   a. deforestation   c. removing wolves

   b. reforestation   d. restricting hunting

Conclude and Communicate

6. Local conservation groups want to re-introduce wolves into your park. As park manager, explain why you would agree or disagree with the proposal. List various effects that a population of wolves might produce in your park.

Extend Your Inquiry and Research Skills

7. **Inquiry** Suppose that you need to monitor the population of real deer in a park over a 10-year period. What methods would you use to measure the population? How often would you do a population count? What other data could you track that may affect population numbers?

8. **Research** In this investigation, you used a simulation to examine some of the factors that affect a deer population. Research how simulations are used in the study of ecology.

Chapter 3 Summary

3.1 Measuring Biodiversity

Key Concepts

- Biodiversity is the number and variety of organisms found within a specific region.
- Scientists have identified about 2 million species on Earth.
- Biodiversity is measured using several different methods.
- There are places on Earth where there is an exceptionally large number of species in a relatively small area.
- Most biodiversity hotspots are in tropical areas.

3.2 Communities

Key Concepts

- Species live in communities where relationships among different species are very important.
- Dominant species are very common primary producers.
- Keystone species are especially significant in maintaining an ecosystem through their relationships with other species.
- Ecosystem engineers alter a landscape in a way that makes it suitable for additional different species.
- Succession is the series of changes in an ecosystem that occurs over time, following a disturbance.

3.3 Threats to Biodiversity

Key Concepts

- Threats to biodiversity include habitat loss, the introduction of alien species, overexploitation, and breaking the connectivity among ecosystems.
- Deforestation and draining wetlands can result in habitat loss.
- Extinction is a natural event that has occurred throughout Earth's history.
- Current extinction rates may be accelerated due to human activities.

3.4 Restoration Ecology

Key Concepts

- Restoration ecology includes reforestation, wetlands restoration, controlling alien species, bioremediation, and bioaugmentation.
- The flow of nutrients through ecosystems can be interrupted by human activities, and restoration techniques can offset those interruptions.
- Alien species are extremely difficult to eradicate in most situations.
- There are many ecosystems that require restoration, and the Alberta tar sands will be a major challenge.

Make Your Own Summary

Summarize the key concepts of this chapter using a graphic organizer. The Chapter Summary on the previous page will help you identify the key concepts. Refer to Study Toolkit 4 on pages 566–567 to help you decide which graphic organizer to use.

Reviewing Key Terms

1. The current accelerated rate of extinction is known as _____. (1.3)

2. Human actions that protect and restore ecosystems for future inhabitants of the biosphere are examples of _____. (1.4)

3. The technique that purposely introduces an alien organism into an area to control an undesirable species is an example of _____. (1.4)

4. A series of ecosystem changes in a particular area over time is known as ecological _____. (1.2)

5. _____ is a technique used to remove soil toxins at sites that have been environmentally damaged by human activities. (1.4)

6. Taking individuals of threatened or endangered species into a breeding facility to increase their population sizes is known as _____. (1.2)

7. The number and variety of organisms found within a specific region is _____. (1.1)

Knowledge and Understanding K/U

8. Why is maintaining biodiversity on Earth important?

9. List and describe three methods that scientists use to measure biodiversity.

10. What is a biodiversity hotspot? Where are the most significant biodiversity hotspots found?

11. Explain how the birth rate and death rate of a species are relevant to the issue of extinction.

12. When was the most recent mass extinction, according to the fossil record? What organisms especially suffered at that time?

13. The dinosaur extinction has been linked to evidence that an asteroid hit Earth, causing climate change. What do scientists think caused the greatest mass extinction of all time?

14. Is it possible to protect a species in trouble without regard to the community that it belongs to? Explain your answer.

15. Why is a place like Langara Island suitable for nesting sea birds, and why did their populations suffer losses?

16. Why is deforestation a threat to biodiversity?

Thinking and Investigation T/I

17. The circle graph below shows the proportion of animal species with backbones in Canada. Which group has the greatest biodiversity?

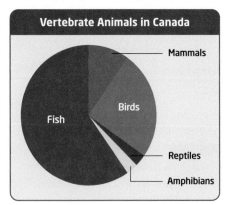

18. Elk eat aspen trees and other vegetation. Wolves eat elk (and other animals). Imagine a situation in which the wolves were eliminated long ago.

   a. What impact might this have on the growth of new aspen trees that are needed to replace the old aspen trees?

   b. What affect do you predict the re-introduction of wolves might have on aspen trees?

19. Imagine the same situation as in question 18. Prior to the re-introduction of the wolves, the number of beavers in this ecosystem dropped to zero. Beavers also eat aspen trees. Once the wolves were re-introduced, beavers started appearing in the area. Explain why the number of beavers increased after the wolves were re-introduced.

20. Should biocontrol methods that increase the numbers of predators or parasites in ecosystems be used against native species?

21. How could wildfires in forests have an effect on an ecosystem similar to the effects of organisms that are ecosystem engineers?

Communication C

22. **BIG** IDEAS Ecosystems are dynamic and have the ability to respond to change, within limits, while maintaining their ecological balance. Through the process of evolution, species change over long periods of time, and the communities and niches that they occupy must also change. Assume that no more alien species will be introduced into a particular ecosystem. Predict what might happen to the alien species already in this ecosystem over a long period of time.

23. **BIG** IDEAS People have the responsibility to regulate their impact on the sustainability of ecosystems in order to preserve the ecosystems for future generations. Choose an ecosystem or species that you like or value. What might you be willing to do as steward for this ecosystem or species?

24. The province is considering closing the Natural Heritage Information Centre, which maintains a database of the distribution and status of Ontario's biodiversity. As a concerned environmentalist, take a stand against this action. Identify three reasons why the centre should not be closed.

25. How would you make an argument for stewardship, based on ethics?

26. How would you make an argument for stewardship, based on practical issues?

27. By making reference to the trophic pyramid from Chapter 1, explain why dominant species have to be primary producers.

28. The rivet analogy is used to explain why humans should be concerned about losing biodiversity. Provide another analogy to explain this concept.

Application A

29. Captive breeding programs are expensive. Are they worth it, in your opinion? Explain why or why not.

30. Where on the graph below would you argue that a keystone species fits: location A, B, or C? Explain your answer.

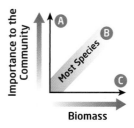

31. Biocontrol of purple loosestrife involves releasing several types of beetles that eat the leaves and new growth of the plants, destroy the roots, or interfere with seed production. Scientists believe that biocontrol can reduce the amount of purple loosestrife by 80 percent, but this takes 10 to 20 years. In cases where there is a high density of purple loosestrife covering a large area, biocontrol is the only option for removing the plants. Why do you think it is the only option?

32. Ships use ballast to adjust how they sit in the water. If you were involved in reducing the problems associated with unintentional introductions of alien species by ballast water, what would you propose?

Science at Work

Canadians in Science

Dr. Bridget Stutchbury loved exploring nature and the outdoors as a child. She decided to turn her love of nature into a rewarding career. Today, she is a professor of biology at York University in Toronto and an expert on migratory birds. Dr. Stutchbury is trying to find out why bird populations in the western hemisphere are declining. She has written a book titled *Silence of the Songbirds*. In her book, she suggests that toxic pesticides and the loss of forests are the main causes of the dwindling number of songbirds.

Dr. Bridget Stutchbury is a biology professor at York University. Her research focuses on finding causes for why bird populations in the western hemisphere are declining.

In Dr. Bridget Stutchbury's Words

The threats to migratory birds point to greater challenges for human society and for the environment. From the point of view of ecology, how we live today is not sustainable. Natural resources are not limitless. We need to develop better ways to manage the resources that we depend on.

This is an exciting time for students who are interested in ecology. Society is at the forefront of an environmental revolution. Many people in Canada, including leaders in governments and businesses, agree that we must change how we interact with our natural environment. This opens the doors to many career opportunities connected to ecology. There is a demand not only for solid technical skills, but also for good communication skills. People in science and related fields need to be able to write and speak effectively. We need good communication skills to share information about issues that affect ecosystems and to persuade governments and businesses to make the best decisions.

Studying science is valuable, even if you do not pursue a science career. Knowing about scientific methods will help you understand and evaluate results of research in subjects such as biology, chemistry, and medicine. This will help you to make informed decisions about personal issues, such as health and diet. And it will help you, as a consumer, make choices that will shape the ecology of tomorrow's world.

Researchers often capture and band birds to track their movements.

Ecology at Work

The study of ecology contributes to these careers, as well as many more!

Zookeeper

Zookeepers take care of animals at zoos and aquariums. Their duties, however, include more than just feeding and checking the health of the animals. Zookeepers also help to collect data for research and scientific studies. In addition, they often help to manage breeding programs for rare and endangered species. Zookeepers study biology and zoology at university.

Environmental Lawyer

Environmental lawyers help clients understand and obey laws and regulations that protect the environment. As well, environmental lawyers give advice to companies and other organizations about activities to conserve ecosystems and use natural resources efficiently. In Canada, governments often ask environmental lawyers to make recommendations about policy decisions related to important environmental issues.

Park Naturalist

Park naturalists develop education programs for park visitors of all ages. They often guide visitors on nature hikes. They also monitor the conditions of ecosystems within a park. Park naturalists usually have a university degree in forestry or environmental science.

Go to **scienceontario**
to find out more

Over To You

1. Dr. Stutchbury states that "threats to migratory birds point to greater challenges for human society and for the environment." What do you think she means by this statement? Explain what you think are the main ecological challenges facing Canadians today.

2. Identify three strategies that Canadians could use to manage natural resources better. Share your strategies with a partner. What are the similarities and differences between your strategies and your partner's strategies?

3. Growing scientific evidence suggests that loss of habitat and other major environmental threats are causing many bird populations to decline. How might a decline in a bird population affect an ecosystem?

4. From the list of careers related to ecology, choose one that interests you. Use Internet or print resources to research this career. What you would need to do if you wanted to pursue it? **What essential skills would you need for this career?**

Inquiry Project

Pollutants and Aquatic Ecosystems

Many substances can dissolve in water. This does not mean that they disappear, however. It means that they are reduced to small particles. These particles can move with the water as it travels through the ground or from one ecosystem to another, such as from a stream to a river to a lake. As you have learned, some substances that are produced by humans pollute the aquatic ecosystems of the biosphere.

Inquiry Question

How do common substances affect the sustainability of aquatic ecosystems?

Initiate and Plan

1. Design at least two aquatic ecosystems, or *ecojars*. Use simple containers, such as large jars, modified 2 L soft-drink bottles, or small aquariums.

2. Plan what you will put in your ecojars by making a list of possible abiotic and biotic components.

3. Decide what substance(s) to investigate. Remember to use one of your ecojars as a control.

4. List the materials you will need, the steps in your procedure, and any safety precautions you should take.

5. Decide how you will measure the effects of each substance on the ecosystem.

6. Select an appropriate format, such as a table, to organize and record your data.

7. Formulate predictions about what will happen to the water and to the plants when you add each substance to the ecosystem.

8. Have your teacher approve the design of your investigation.

Perform and Record

9. Set up your ecojars, and conduct your investigation. Record your results.

Analyze and Interpret

1. Describe any patterns or trends you observed in the data you collected.

2. Did the trends in the data you collected match the predictions you made? Provide some possible explanations for any differences you observed.

3. Evaluate the design of your investigation. Were you able to control and identify the effects of variables? Was your measure of the effects of the substances accurate? What changes would you make to your design for future investigations on this topic?

Communicate Your Findings

4. Present your results using both a visual component and a written component, taking into consideration both the purpose and the audience.

Assessment Criteria

Once you complete your project, ask yourself these questions. Did you...

- **K/U** provide an accurate description of the abiotic and biotic characteristics of the ecosystem?

- **T/I** formulate appropriate predictions for the impact of the investigated substance(s)?

- **T/I** control appropriate variables and use equipment and materials safely, accurately, and effectively?

- **T/I** analyze and interpret qualitative and quantitative data to determine whether the evidence supports or contradicts your initial predictions?

- **T/I** identify sources of error that may have influenced the outcome, and suggest improvements to the original design?

- **C** organize and record data appropriately?

- **C** take the purpose and audience into account?

An Issue to Analyze

Protecting Ecosystems

The Oak Ridges Moraine is a valuable ecosystem in Ontario. Diverse natural habitats, such as ancient forests and complex wetlands, provide living space for all kinds of organisms. Much of the water supply for the Greater Toronto Area begins in the ground-water system of the moraine's glacial soils.

To preserve this 1900 km² ecosystem from excessive development, a law was passed that placed strict controls on development. The Oak Ridges Moraine is only one of many special ecosystems in Ontario needing protection.

Issue

What can be done to protect a valuable ecosystem in your area?

Initiate and Plan

1. Choose an ecosystem that needs protection (either a large ecosystem or a small green space near your home).

2. Research and describe the human factors that threaten or could threaten the ecosystem you have chosen. Think of some questions to help you focus your research. To do this, consider what issues are involved and what groups may have a stake in these issues. Consider researching some or all of the following questions:

   • Are there threats from erosion, deforestation, pollution, recreational overuse, wetland drainage, or housing developments?

   • Which threats to the ecosystem will you address?

   • Who will your audience be? Will you communicate directly with those who are posing the threats? Will you communicate with a government (municipal, provincial, or federal)? Will you seek the attention of the public through a newspaper, a media broadcaster, or a widely read blog?

3. Decide how you will conduct and record your research. What sources will you use?

Perform and Record

4. Conduct your research to answer your questions.

Analyze and Interpret

1. Based on your research, identify the threats to the ecosystem and explain the issues involved.

2. Explain the perspective of the people who are posing the threats. How do they justify their activities?

3. Propose one or more practical strategies that people, including you, could take to reduce or eliminate the threats.

Communicate Your Findings

4. Choose an appropriate form of communication for your audience (for example, a newspaper article, a protest sign, or a podcast).

Assessment Criteria

Once you complete your project, ask yourself these questions. Did you...

• **K/U** describe human factors that impact the ecosystem?

• **C** collect information from a variety of sources?

• **C** organize your information appropriately for your intended audience?

• **C** use appropriate scientific vocabulary?

• **A** analyze your information for bias and accuracy?

• **A** analyze your information to identify both the protection strategies and the obstacles?

• **A** propose alternative courses of action that could be taken to improve the status of the ecosystem?

Connect to the BIG IDEAS

Use this bicycle wheel graphic organizer to connect what you have learned in this unit to the Big Ideas, found on page 1. Draw one bicycle wheel for each Big Idea and write the Big Idea in the centre. Between the spokes of the wheel, briefly describe six examples of that Big Idea.

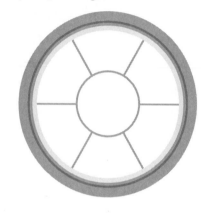

Knowledge and Understanding K/U

For questions 1 through 5, select the best answer.

1. The lithosphere is

  a. the water in oceans on Earth

  b. the non-living components of an ecosystem

  c. the layer of air above Earth's surface

  d. the hard part of Earth's surface

2. Trophic efficiency is a measure of how much energy in organisms can be   from one trophic level to another.

  a. lost   **c.** spent

  b. saved   **d.** transferred

3. The size of a population that can be supported indefinitely by the resources and services of an ecosystem is known as its

  a. carrying capacity

  b. ecological footprint

  c. exponential limit

  d. niche

4. Which situation is an example of biomagnification?

  a. A bear eats a large meal and stores the nutrients as fat.

  b. A frog is poisoned by the nearby use of pesticides and dies soon after.

  c. A hawk eats a fish that has eaten many smaller aquatic animals, which all had toxins in their bodies.

  d. A caterpillar feeds on leaves that contain toxins, and the toxins are stored faster than they are eliminated.

5. A low dose of insecticide is sprayed up, into the top of a tree. The insects that fall out as a result are collected, counted, and analyzed. This method of measuring biodiversity is called

  a. canopy fogging

  b. netting

  c. quadrat sampling

  d. transect sampling

6. Nutrients were added at the Experimental Lakes Area to study eutrophication. Which nutrient had the greatest direct influence on eutrophication?

7. Why has the level of carbon dioxide in the atmosphere been steadily increasing since the mid-19th century?

8. The bird on the giraffe's head in the photograph below is called an oxpecker. The bird searches the hides of large mammals for parasites, which it harvests and eats. Identify whether the relationship between the bird and the mammal is an example of predation, competition, mutualism, or parasitism. Explain your answer.

9. In your own words, describe the concept of urban sprawl.

10. What are two factors that have made it difficult for scientists to determine the number of species on Earth?

11. Identify two biodiversity hotspots in Canada.

12. Draw a diagram that shows the relationship between the water cycle and the phosphorous cycle.

13. How are plants used for bioremediation?

14. Explain how driving a car in Ontario could affect ecosystems elsewhere in Canada?

15. What happens to the energy in tertiary consumers when they die?

Thinking and Investigation T/I

16. Use either the monarch butterfly or the ruby-throated hummingbird to explain how ecosystems are connected. Why is it important to maintain connectivity among ecosystems?

17. The graphs below represent the growth patterns of two different bacterial cultures over a period of time.

   a. Analyze each graph. Describe, in words, what is happening in each bacterial culture.

   b. Which graph shows only exponential growth?

   c. Which graph shows a growth pattern that is exponential for part of the time?

   d. Has either of these populations reached its carrying capacity? Explain your answer.

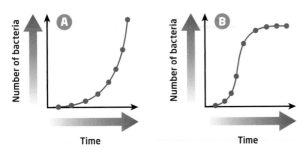

Bacterial Growth over Time

18. Estimate the carrying capacity for the population shown in the graph below. Why do you think the carrying capacity in real-life situations is not a smooth, flat line?

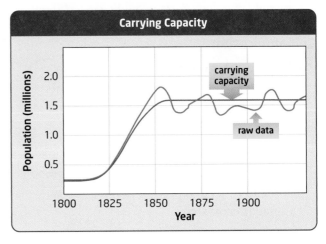

19. Different species provide many different services for their ecosystems by occupying their ecological niches. The red squirrel is a familiar Ontario species. Brainstorm a number of "services" that a red squirrel provides for the ecosystems in which it lives.

20. Explain how acid precipitation could affect biodiversity.

21. Study the following table. Identify two factors that may help to explain why Canadians have a larger ecological footprint than people in Vietnam.

Resource Use in Canada and Vietnam

Country	Canada	Vietnam
Size (km^2)	9 985 000	330 000
Population (millions)	33	84
Population density (people/km^2)	3.2	251.5
Annual electricity use (billion KW•h)	487	32
Oil consumption (barrels per day)	2 200 000	185 000
Highways (km)	1 408 800	93 300
Wealth generated per person per year ($)	31 500	2 700

22. Imagine that you work as a lake ecologist at the Canadian Centre for Inland Waters. Create a questionnaire that a ship's captain, arriving at inland Canadian ports, would have to fill out.

Communication $\boxed{C}$

23. Prepare a short paragraph that promotes the virtues of the greenhouse effect and its contribution to the development of life on Earth.

24. The maple leaf is a familiar symbol of Canada. Using an outline of a maple leaf, draw symbols at the five tips to represent the richness of Canada's ecosystems.

25. The ecosystem that includes prairie dogs and black-footed ferrets is complex. Create a flowchart that you could use as a visual aid if you were giving an oral presentation about this ecosystem to a Grade 5 class.

Application $\boxed{A}$

26. Suppose that you are a science writer who is working on an article about the effects of the biomagnification of certain chemicals. What questions would you ask a group of scientists who recently created a new pesticide?

27. Many migratory birds travel great distances, living in ecosystems that are thousands of kilometres apart. The Canada warbler, a species in decline, breeds in Canada but spends the winter in several South American countries. Why is designing a plan to stabilize the Canada warbler population more challenging than designing a plan for a Canadian species that does not migrate?

28. Gulls and raccoons are organisms that have benefited from human development, particularly in urban areas. In Canada, black bears have benefited from the landfill sites created by humans.

Choose one of the following organisms, and propose a course of action to deal with their increased population growth. A few suggestions are given for each organism.

- Gulls: poison, disrupt nesting, post fines and prosecute for feeding, use birds of prey
- Raccoons: trap, sterilize, use raccoon-proof garbage containers
- Bears: educate the public, use better fencing, promote spring bear hunting, trap and relocate

29. Suppose that your community is looking for ideas to promote sustainable development. Describe an activity that is sustainable in your community. Contrast this activity with a non-sustainable activity to show how the sustainable activity uses resources more efficiently.

30. Many wetlands have been drained in southern Ontario, but some have been reclaimed through wetland restoration. Prepare a checklist that could be used to determine areas that are suitable for wetland restoration.

31. Both the eastern foxsnake and the queen snake have small Ontario ranges. Most of the world's eastern foxsnakes are found in Ontario, but the queen snake has a large range in the United States. How might this information influence your ideas for a conservation plan to protect snakes, if you have limited funds?

Literacy Test Prep

Read the selection below, and answer the questions that follow it.

People in North America use resources at a greater rate per person, compared with people in many other countries in the world. If everyone on Earth consumed as much as the average person in North America does, three more Earths would be needed to sustain the human population. The following table contains data about resource use.

Resource Use in Canada and the World

Category	Canadian Average	Global Average
CO_2 produced from the consumption of fossil fuels and farm products, and the clearing of land per person, per year	17.0 tonnes	4.1 tonnes
Vehicles driven per 100 people, per year	47	9
Paper used per person, per year	281 kg	52 kg
Gasoline used per person, per year	1389 L	174 L
Fresh water used per person, per year	1494 m³	633 m³

Multiple Choice

In your notebook, record the best or most correct answer.

32. The table above provides information about

- **a.** the amounts of resources used by the average person in North America, compared with the amounts used by the average person globally
- **b.** the amounts of resources used by the average Canadian, compared with the amounts used by the average person globally
- **c.** the amounts of resources used by people in different countries around the world
- **d.** the amounts of resources used by the average person in the United States

33. How much paper is used by the average Canadian?

- **a.** 17.0 tonnes per year
- **b.** 281 kg per year
- **c.** 1389 L per year
- **d.** 1494 m³ per year

34. For which category is use by the average person in the world greater than use by the average Canadian?

- **a.** vehicles driven per 100 people, per year
- **b.** gasoline used per person, per year
- **c.** all of the categories
- **d.** none of the categories

35. How does the data in the table support this statement: "If everyone on Earth consumed as much as the average person in North America does, three more Earths would be needed to sustain the human population?"

- **a.** For every category, the global average consumption is two to eight times higher than the Canadian average.
- **b.** For every category, the Canadian average consumption is two to eight times higher than the global average.
- **c.** The average Canadian uses only 174 L of gasoline per year.
- **d.** The average person in the world uses 1494 m³ of water per year.

Written Answer

36. Make a list of how each resource use in the table affects the sustainability of ecosystems. Then write a paragraph about sustainable practices that might reduce the impact of Canadians on ecosystems.

BIG IDEAS

- The use of elements and compounds has both positive and negative effects on society and the environment.

- Elements and compounds have specific physical and chemical properties that determine their practical uses.

One of the most familiar and essential substances on Earth is water. In Canada, we are lucky to have safe drinking water straight from the tap. But more and more, for convenience or due to safety concerns, people are reaching for bottled water. In 2005, Canadians drank on average 60 L of bottled water per person. Worldwide, people consumed over 189 000 000 000 L of bottled water in 2007.

What is the problem with bottled water? For one thing, resources are used to make the bottles, fill them, and transport them. The bottles then become waste that must either be dumped in a landfill or recycled. There is another option: you could use a refillable container to make your own "bottled water."

In this unit, you will learn how the properties of substances determine how they are used, as well as the risks and benefits of using them.

How do the chemical and physical properties of water and plastic affect their uses and their interaction with the environment?

Chapter 4
Properties of Elements and Compounds

Chapter 5
Understanding the Properties of Elements

Chapter 6
Understanding the Properties of Compounds

Get Ready for Unit 2

Concept Check

1. In two minutes, jot down all the words you can think of that describe matter. Share your list with a partner and exchange words that you did not have on your individual lists.

2. Examine the beach scene shown in the illustration below and write one example of each of the following in your notebook:

   a. matter in its solid state

   b. matter in its liquid state

   c. matter in its gas state

   d. fusion (melting)

   e. evaporation

   f. a reversible physical change

   g. an irreversible chemical change

3. Use the words below to complete each sentence. Write the complete sentences in your notebook.

fruit punch	pure substance	solution
rocky road ice cream	helium	mechanical mixture

   a. _____ is a _____ because it is made up of two or more kinds of particles but appears as one type.

   b. _____ is a _____ because it is made up of two or more kinds of particles that can be seen as separate.

   c. _____ is a _____ because it is made up of only one type of particle.

4. Copy the table below into your notebook. Identify each property as physical or chemical. Find examples of matter in the illustration of the beach scene below that have these properties (you can use the same example more than once).

   ### Examples of Physical and Chemical Properties

Clue	Physical or Chemical Property?	Substance
a. Smells sweet		
b. Does not react with water		
c. Feels rough		
d. Is red		

5. Read each statement below and determine whether it describes the particles that make up air or the particles that make up water. Write your answers in your notebook.

   a. particles are close together

   b. particles are spread far apart

   c. particles move freely about one another

Inquiry Check

An investigation was conducted to demonstrate the effect of temperature on the solubility of salt and sugar. The results are shown in this graph.

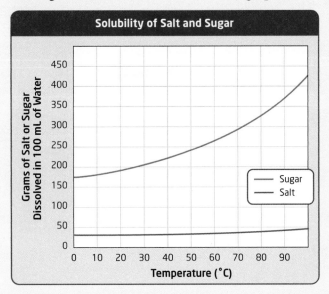

Solubility of Salt and Sugar

Grams of Salt or Sugar Dissolved in 100 mL of Water vs. *Temperature (°C)*

Legend: Sugar, Salt

6. **Analyze** How many grams of (a) sugar and (b) salt will dissolve in water at 50°C?

7. **Interpret** Which substance showed a greater change in solubility as the temperature increased?

Numeracy and Literacy Check

The table below compares the mineral content of bottled water and tap water.

Mineral Content of Bottled Water Compared to Tap Water

Type of Water and Source	Mineral Content (in mg/L)		
	Sodium	**Calcium**	**Magnesium**
Bottled spring water from Guelph, Ontario	33	100	37
Tap water in Toronto, Ontario	12	40	9

8. **Unit Conversions** Mineral concentrations are typically measured in mg/L, but you can convert these measurements to other units if required.

   a. Convert the calcium content in bottled spring water from Guelph, Ontario from mg/L to g/L.

   b. Convert the sodium content in tap water in Toronto from mg/L to mg/mL.

9. **Writing** What criteria do you use when you choose the type of water that you drink? Write a brief article for your school newsletter justifying your choice of bottled water or tap water.

Looking Ahead to the Unit 2 Project

At the end of this unit, you will have an opportunity to apply what you have learned in an inquiry or research project. Read the Unit 2 Projects on pages 258-259. Start a project folder now (either paper or electronic). Store ideas, notes, news clippings, websites, and lists of materials that might help you to complete your project.

Inquiry Project
Investigate how the chemical properties of other materials could prevent iron from rusting.

An Issue to Analyze
Take a position on whether the benefits of metal mining justify the costs.

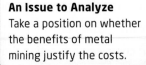

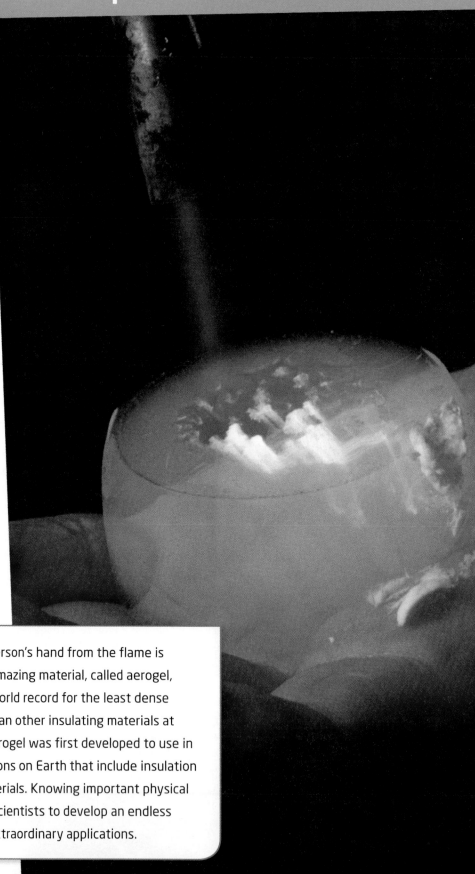

Chapter 4 Properties of Elements and Compounds

What You Will Learn

In this chapter, you will learn how to...

- **identify** elements and compounds
- **describe** important physical and chemical properties of elements and compounds
- **explain** how properties of elements and compounds determine their practical uses

Why It Matters

Everything you eat, breathe, wear, and use is matter. A certain class of matter, called pure substances, is composed of elements and compounds. Understanding the properties of elements and compounds is essential for making good decisions about the products you use.

Skills You Will Use

In this chapter, you will learn how to...

- **investigate** the physical and chemical properties of compounds and elements
- **conduct** tests to identify common gases based on their chemical properties

The only thing protecting this person's hand from the flame is a layer of cloudy material. This amazing material, called aerogel, is 99.8 percent air. It holds the world record for the least dense solid, and it is 39 times better than other insulating materials at protecting objects from heat. Aerogel was first developed to use in space. It now has many applications on Earth that include insulation in winter coats and building materials. Knowing important physical and chemical properties allows scientists to develop an endless number of new materials with extraordinary applications.

Activity 4-1

Raising Underwater Artifacts

When archaeologists recover artifacts from a shipwreck, they use inflatable bags to raise the artifacts to the surface. The inflatable bags help to preserve the artifacts for future study. How can some common household chemicals be used to mimic this?

Safety Precautions

- Wear safety goggles and a lab apron.

Materials

- 50 mL water
- 400 mL beaker
- 100 mL graduated cylinder
- 150 mL vinegar
- 5 raisins
- 25 g baking soda
- electronic balance

Recovering underwater artifacts relies on the properties of substances.

Procedure

1. Make a table like the one below to record your observations. Be sure to include a title for your table.

	+ Vinegar	+ Raisins	+ Baking Soda	1 min	3 min	5 min
Observations						

2. Pour 50 mL of water into the 400 mL beaker.

3. Using the graduated cylinder, measure 150 mL of vinegar. Add the vinegar to the beaker of water. Record your observations.

4. Add the raisins to the beaker. Record your observations.

5. Slowly add 25 g of baking soda to the beaker. Immediately record your observations. Then describe any changes that occur at 1 min, 3 min, and 5 min intervals.

Questions

1. Name the different states of matter that you observed in this activity.

2. How do you think this activity is similar to using inflatable bags to raise underwater artifacts?

Study Toolkit

These strategies will help you use this textbook to develop your understanding of science concepts and skills. To find out more about these and other strategies, refer to the Study Toolkit Overview, which begins on page 561.

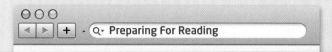

Preparing For Reading

Previewing Text Features

Previewing text features can help you understand how a text is organized and predict its main ideas. Text features also help you distinguish the main body text from other text elements, such as key term definitions, activities, case studies, and sidebars. These elements are often boxed or set off in the margin. They may also have a coloured banner running along the top.

Use the Strategy

Browse through Chapter 4 and identify three different text features. How does each text feature differ from the main body text?

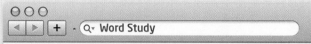

Word Study

Multiple Meanings

Your science textbook contains many words you may have seen before, such as *property*. Sometimes *property* refers to something that is owned by a person, but the word has a different meaning when it appears in text about chemistry. One strategy to help reinforce your understanding of a word's multiple meanings is to draw a **word map**, such as the one below. It shows the meaning of *element* in two different contexts.

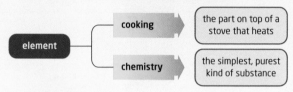

element → cooking → the part on top of a stove that heats

element → chemistry → the simplest, purest kind of substance

Use the Strategy

Think about the word *model*. What does this word mean in these three contexts: a fashion magazine, a car dealership, and a science textbook? Draw a word map to show multiple meanings of the word *model*. Use a dictionary if you wish.

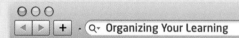

Organizing Your Learning

Summarizing

Often it is helpful to organize your learning in the form of a summary. This means restating the main ideas of a text in your own words. A summary can be in sentence or paragraph form, in point form, or in graphic form. For example, the table below shows how to create a summary of the paragraph on page 136.

Use the Strategy

Read the two paragraphs on page 139. Fill in a table like the one below, writing a summary sentence for each paragraph. Then, combine the two summary sentences into one. Compare your table and sentences with a partner and revise as necessary.

Section of Text	Main Topic	What the Text Says about the Main Topic	Supporting Details
page 136, paragraph	the properties of elements and compounds	1. Aerogel is an example of a substance with interesting properties. 2. Knowing the properties of elements and compounds will help us develop new materials.	1. Aerogel is almost all air, holds the world record for least dense solid, and is one of the best insulators available. 2. Scientists use physical and chemical properties as a basis for developing new materials.
Summary sentence: Knowing more about important properties of elements and compounds supports the development of new products.			

4.1 Studying Matter

Key Terms
matter
pure substance
mixture
element
compound

Look around you. Everything you see is **matter**. This book, your desk, and even your classmates are matter. But you do not have to see something for it to be matter. The air you breathe is also matter. By studying matter in its many forms, scientists can better understand the different properties of materials, which can determine their practical uses. In some cases, knowing about the properties of matter means knowing how hazardous certain materials are and how best to handle them in a safe and effective way. This is especially important when something goes wrong.

matter anything that has mass and occupies space

Knowing how to deal with a hazardous material was a top priority for Toronto's police officers and firefighters when a fire erupted at a propane depot in northwest Toronto on August 10, 2008, as shown in **Figure 4.1**. Huge blasts from exploding propane were heard far away, and fireballs erupted in the sky. Authorities closed major roadways and evacuated thousands of people. Knowing the properties of propane, a highly flammable and explosive gas, enabled emergency personnel to deal with the fire, as well as keep people safe.

Figure 4.1 The damage from a fire at this propane depot in Toronto demonstrates how the properties of some substances can make them hazardous.

How Good Are Your Safety Skills?

Making sure that you know how to handle materials safely in the laboratory is an essential part of studying chemistry. During previous science studies, you have learned and practised safe techniques and procedures. **Figure 4.2** will help to refresh your memory on some of the safety icons and WHMIS symbols that you are likely to see in this unit. The Safety in the Science Classroom section on page xiv has a more complete list of safety icons and WHMIS symbols. Also, as part of the WHMIS system, there are material safety data sheets (MSDS) that are available for each chemical that you will handle in the lab. Once you have reviewed the safety icons and symbols, complete Activity 4-2 to test your ability to apply them to various situations.

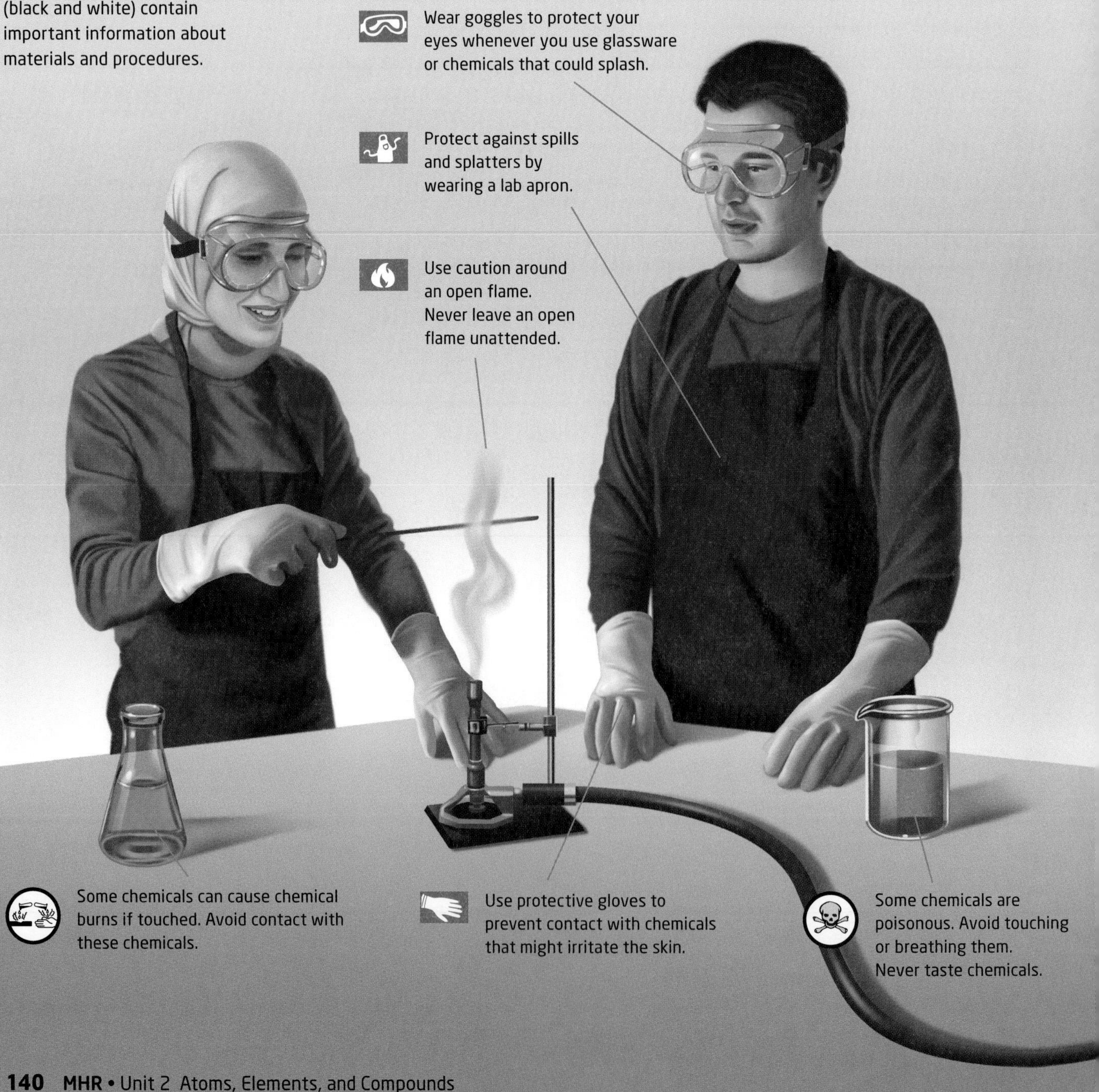

Figure 4.2 Safety icons (red and white) and WHMIS symbols (black and white) contain important information about materials and procedures.

Wear goggles to protect your eyes whenever you use glassware or chemicals that could splash.

Protect against spills and splatters by wearing a lab apron.

Use caution around an open flame. Never leave an open flame unattended.

Some chemicals can cause chemical burns if touched. Avoid contact with these chemicals.

Use protective gloves to prevent contact with chemicals that might irritate the skin.

Some chemicals are poisonous. Avoid touching or breathing them. Never taste chemicals.

Activity 4-2

Safety First!

When performing a chemistry experiment, you must be able to recognize the safety icons and symbols that are used and know the precautions you need to take. Can you easily recognize all the potential hazards associated with the instructions below?

Procedure

1. Read over the list of safety icons and the list of WHMIS symbols in the Safety in the Science Classroom section on page xiv.

2. The instructions below describe eight different lab procedures. As you read the instructions, draw the symbols that apply to each instruction. You should use every icon and symbol at least once in this activity.

Instructions

A. Make sure that your lab station is clear and dry. Then plug in the electric hot plate and turn it on.

B. Do not add water to the sugar before heating the sugar.

C. Light the Bunsen burner. Then heat the test tube gently by holding it above the flame.

D. Let the steel pin cool for 10 min. When the pin has cooled, put it into the container as the teacher has shown.

E. Heat the test tube with a Bunsen burner gently at first, and then more strongly. Do not breathe the irritating ammonia gas that forms.

F. Using a medicine dropper, add the acid, one drop at a time, to the base. Be careful that you do not spill either the acid or the base.

G. Add two drops of the solution. The solution can be absorbed into the skin, so be careful that you do not get any on you.

Questions

1. Which safety icons could be used for almost every laboratory procedure?

2. Write a "**Caution!**" statement for each instruction, to draw attention to one safety hazard. For example, "Caution! Wear safety goggles to protect your eyes."

Classification of Matter

When studying matter, scientists classify or group materials based on different characteristics. The chart in **Figure 4.3** represents one way you have learned to classify matter.

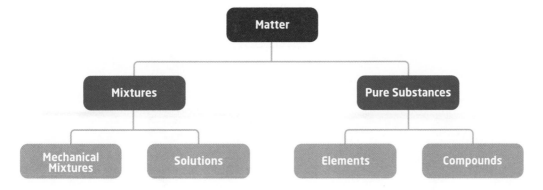

Figure 4.3 Matter can be classified according to whether it is a mixture or a pure substance.

The Particle Theory of Matter

One way that matter can be classified is according to the particle theory of matter.

> **The Particle Theory of Matter**
> - All matter is made up of tiny particles.
> - Each pure substance has its own kind of particle, which is different from the particles of other pure substances.
> - Particles attract each other.
> - Particles are always moving.
> - Particles at a higher temperature move faster, on average, than particles at a lower temperature.

pure substance matter that contains only one kind of particle

mixture matter that contains more than one kind of particle

Based on the particle theory of matter, matter can be classified as either a **pure substance** or a **mixture**. Pure substances contain only one kind of particle. Mixtures contain more than one kind of particle. So, for example, water is a pure substance, but salt water is a mixture of salt dissolved in water. Oxygen gas is a pure substance but the air we breathe is a mixture of gases that includes nitrogen, oxygen, carbon dioxide, and other components. The particle theory of matter is one example of a scientific model. It helps you to visualize the particles that make up matter and how the particles in different types of matter interact.

Pure Substances

Since a pure substance contains only one kind of particle, you may think that pure substances are rare and hard to find. Actually, many are very common. Two examples of pure substances that you may be familiar with are shown in **Figure 4.4**. Notice how the particles of helium look very different from the particles of water. According to the particle theory of matter, these pure substances have different properties because they are composed of different particles. Scientists have classified pure substances into two main groups: elements and compounds.

Figure 4.4 **A** Helium and **B** water are pure substances. The particles of helium are all the same, but they are different from the particles of water.

Elements and Compounds

An **element** is a pure substance that cannot be broken down further by chemical or physical methods. You could try heating, crushing, or grinding an element, but you would not change it into a simpler form.

If you look again at **Figure 4.4A**, you can see that helium consists of only one kind of particle. Helium is an element. This simple substance has many uses. As you may know, helium is used to inflate balloons and blimps. Helium also has many scientific applications that include thermometers, lasers, and superconducting magnets. Since the 1800s, scientists have organized elements into a table based on similar properties. You will learn about this table in Chapter 5.

A **compound** is a pure substance that is made of two or more different elements that are chemically combined. Water, in **Figure 4.4B**, is a compound made of the elements hydrogen and oxygen. Because the elements in a compound are chemically combined, a compound can be broken down into its elements only by chemical methods. For example, to break down water into hydrogen and oxygen, a chemical process called electrolysis must be used.

The scene in **Figure 4.5** illustrates that elements and compounds are not just chemicals in a laboratory. They are part of your daily life.

element a pure substance that cannot be broken down into simpler parts by chemical methods

compound a pure substance made of two or more different elements that are chemically combined

Study Toolkit

Multiple Meanings You have probably heard the word *compound* used in English class to mean a word composed of two or more other words. *Compound* also refers to a mixture of plaster used in home repairs. How are these related to the meaning of *compound* in chemistry? Draw a word map to show these three meanings. Use a dictionary if you wish.

Titanium Oxide a compound in sunscreen

Oxygen an element in air

Aluminium an element in a drink can

Gold an element used in jewellery

Acetic Acid a compound in vinegar

Sodium Chloride also known as table salt

Water a compound essential to life

Silicon an element used to make electronic devices

Figure 4.5 Each day, you interact with and depend on many elements and compounds.

Compounds Versus Mixtures

What if hydrogen and oxygen are placed in a container without being chemically combined? What are they called then? As you have learned, anything that is made of more than one kind of particle is a mixture. Therefore, the gas in the container is a mixture of the elements hydrogen and oxygen. The components of a mixture are physically combined. As a result, a mixture can be separated by physical methods. Examples of methods that can be used to separate the components of a mixture are shown in **Table 4.1**.

Table 4.1 Separating Mixtures

A filter can be used to separate solids from liquids or gases. This filter separates coffee grounds from the brewed coffee that passes through.	
Distillation can be used to separate liquids in a mixture, based on boiling point. This apparatus shows how a liquid, with a lower boiling point than other components in a mixture, is vapourized, condensed, and collected in a beaker.	
A magnet will attract iron and steel objects and leave other objects behind. This machine has been fitted with a magnet to pull out certain objects from this pile of scrap metal.	

Go to **scienceontario** to find out more

Learning Check

1. Which two safety icons are you likely to see in almost every laboratory procedure?

2. According to the particle theory of matter, what is a pure substance?

3. Can a compound be separated into its elements by filtration? Explain.

4. Name an element that is a part of your everyday life, and describe how you use it.

Activity 4-3

Element, Compound, or Mixture?

Elements and compounds are both pure substances, based on the particle theory of matter. What is their relationship to mixtures, and how can they be used to make mixtures?

Materials

- 3 sets of paper clips, each a different colour

Procedure

1. Sort the paper clips into piles, by colour. Each paper clip represents one element. Each colour represents a different element.

2. Link the paper clips to create models of two different compounds with two different elements and three different compounds with three different elements. Where the paper clips have been linked represents where two elements are chemically combined.

3. Identify the elements in your models of compounds.

4. Use your models of elements and compounds to make a mixture.

Questions

1. How many different elements did you have?

2. Describe how you made your mixture in step 4. How did this differ from what you did in step 2? Is it possible to make more than one type of mixture? Explain.

3. How were your paper clip models similar to real-life elements, compounds, and mixtures? How were they different?

Chemistry, Society, and the Environment

In this unit, you will examine the properties of a variety of elements and compounds, as well as some of the social, economic, and environmental effects that these chemicals have—both positive and negative—on society. **Figure 4.6** summarizes some of the important issues related to the use and production of chemicals.

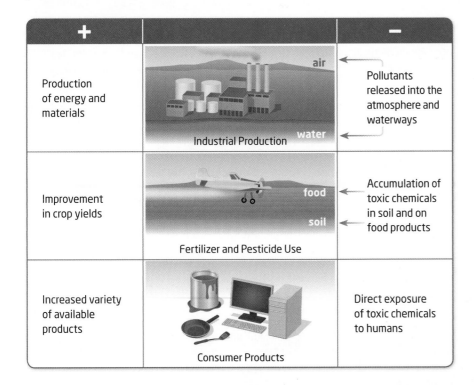

+		−
Production of energy and materials	air — water Industrial Production	Pollutants released into the atmosphere and waterways
Improvement in crop yields	food — soil Fertilizer and Pesticide Use	Accumulation of toxic chemicals in soil and on food products
Increased variety of available products	Consumer Products	Direct exposure of toxic chemicals to humans

Figure 4.6 It is important to find a good balance between the advantages and disadvantages that are associated with the use, production, and disposal of chemicals.

Advantages and Disadvantages

Suggested Investigation

Real World Investigation 4-D, CFC Production and Canada's Ozone Layer, on page 172.

Elements and compounds have many positive effects on society, such as making our lives healthier and safer, and allowing us to accomplish things that were once unimaginable. These accomplishments, however, have resulted in some negative consequences, which must be considered and dealt with. For example, toxic chemicals that are used or produced in the manufacture or isolation of certain elements and compounds can be released into the environment. Once in the environment, they can accumulate or react with other substances and result in harmful by-products. Throughout this unit, you will study specific examples of elements and compounds and learn how their properties can influence their practical uses.

STSE Case Study

What Is the Cost of Our Products?

Think about all the products that are part of your everyday life. For example, think about the clothes you wear, the personal hygiene products you use, and the various plastic-containing products you buy, such as electronic devices and school supplies. Now think about what your day would be like without them. These products are very useful and of economic advantage since many of them are produced in Ontario.

Canada's Chemical Valley

The city of Sarnia and the Aamjiwnaang [pronounced OMM-jew-nong] First Nation lie on the south shore of Lake Huron. They are bordered by one of the most highly industrialized areas in Canada, which is nicknamed Chemical Valley because of the large number of chemical plants.

In the 1960s, most of the world's largest oil and chemical companies built factories in this area. Canada's first commercial oil wells were near Sarnia. Transportation to nearby large markets in the United States and central Canada was easy, especially given Sarnia's deepwater ports. By the 1970s, the average income of people in the Sarnia area was 35 percent higher than the national average—primarily due to industrial development. The area was one of the most successful in Canada.

There is now evidence, however, that suggests the health of many Sarnia area residents may have been harmed by exposure to toxic chemicals from Chemical Valley. In addition to high rates of heart disease and breathing-related illnesses, cancer rates are higher than the provincial average. Each year, there are more pollutants released from Chemical Valley than the provincial totals for Manitoba, New Brunswick, and Saskatchewan. Community groups have come together to take matters into their own hands.

Sample Data Collected by the Bucket Brigade

Toxic Chemical	Measured Level ($\mu g/m^3$)	Acceptable Level ($\mu g/m^3$)
carbon disulfide (CS_2)	41	3-30
chloromethane (CH_3Cl)	130	1.1
benzene (C_6H_6)	9.9	0.25

These are only some of the toxic chemicals that have been detected by the Aamjiwnaang First Nation's bucket brigade. The acceptable levels provided are based on standards in the United States. Canada does not have comparable health-based standards for these chemicals.

Making a Difference

While in Grade 11, Meghana Saincher noticed that wooden pieces from local playgrounds had been replaced with plastic and steel materials. She questioned this change and discovered that it was done because preservatives in the wood were toxic. Meghana decided to find out if there were non-toxic wood preservatives that could be used instead. Upon receiving a research grant to carry out her studies at the University of British Columbia, Meghana showed oregano oil to be an effective and non-toxic wood preservative.

Meghana shared her experience with other students, and started a biotechnology club at her Surrey, BC, high school. Most importantly, she helped motivate her peers to conduct research. In 2006, Meghana was named one of Canada's Top 20 Under 20. She is now studying medicine at the University of Alberta.

Are there toxic chemicals in your community that could be replaced with safer alternatives?

The Bucket Brigade

Since the early 1990s, the Aamjiwnaang First Nation has experienced the lowest rate of male births in the world. As well, health surveys indicate that almost all households have someone with a serious long-term or deadly illness. Believing that these effects are due to pollution, the Aamjiwnaang First Nation Health and Environment Committee decided to take action. Volunteers are using a "bucket brigade" to conduct regular monitoring of the air in the region. The data collected are scientific evidence that residents are being exposed to toxic pollutants. This has prompted more extensive research studies, support of the Environmental Commissioner of Ontario (the province's environmental watchdog), and the installation of a new air-monitoring station in the First Nation community by Ontario's Ministry of the Environment.

Your Turn

1. Ontario's chemical industry produces numerous products. These products include pharmaceuticals, paints, inks, adhesives, petrochemicals, soaps and other personal hygiene products, and chemicals for manufacturing products such as synthetic clothing and plastic containers. To reduce air pollution, what products would you be willing to give up?

2. It has been difficult to prove that pollution from Chemical Valley is the direct cause of certain illnesses in the Sarnia area. Why do you think this is so?

3. Research the toxic chemicals that are listed in this case study. What are some of the effects that long-term exposure to unsafe levels has on people's health?

air sample is pulled into the bag and stored for analysis

How the Bucket Brigade Works

- A simple, portable device is contained within a plain 23 L plastic bucket–the reason for the name "bucket brigade."
- The device can detect almost 90 toxic gases.
- A sample of air is trapped and stored in a sealable bag. Then it is sent to a laboratory for analysis.

Section Summary

- When studying matter, it is important to know the location of safety equipment in your classroom and the meanings of the safety icons and WHMIS symbols.

- Matter can be classified according to its composition, as mixtures or pure substances.

- An element is a pure substance that cannot be broken down into simpler substances through physical or chemical methods.

- A compound is a pure substance that is composed of two or more different elements that are chemically combined. A compound can be broken down into its elements only by chemical methods.

- The production and use of new chemicals can have both negative and positive consequences. Benefits must be weighed against negative consequences.

Review Questions

T/I **1.** What hazards are associated with heating a liquid in a test tube that is tightly closed with a cork?

A **2.** Name an occupation that requires workers to know safety icons and WHMIS symbols.

C **3.** Using a diagram, apply the particle theory to explain why a drop of liquid water tends to be round.

K/U **4.** Name two classes of pure substances and give an example of each.

T/I **5.** Decide whether each of the following is a pure substance. Explain your reasoning.

    a. salt water

    b. gold

    c. a pencil

T/I **6.** Would a pure substance ever settle out and form two distinct layers? Explain your reasoning.

K/U **7.** Describe the relationship between an element and a compound.

T/I **8.** The circles and triangles in the diagram on the right represent two different elements. Use these shapes to draw a compound and a mixture. Is it possible to draw more than one compound? Explain why or why not.

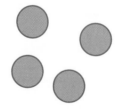

element A

element B

Elements A and B can be used to make compounds and mixtures.

4.2 Physical Properties

Key Terms

physical property
viscosity
melting point
boiling point
solubility
density

How would you describe the work of art in **Figure 4.7**? What physical characteristics would you mention? You could mention the colours and the texture of the surface. You could also describe how shiny or dull the surface is.

You can use a similar approach when describing an element or compound. In chemistry, these physical characteristics are referred to as physical properties. A **physical property** is a characteristic of a substance that you can observe and measure without changing the identity of the substance. The physical properties of elements and compounds play a significant part in determining the practical uses of these substances. Certain characteristics are especially important when scientists observe and describe elements and compounds.

physical property a characteristic of a substance that can be observed and measured without changing the identity of the substance

Figure 4.7 This sculpture at the National Gallery in Ottawa has distinct physical characteristics that can be used to describe it.

Qualitative Physical Properties

A *qualitative* physical property can be observed and described without detailed measurement. Usually, qualitative physical properties are obvious and easy to observe. For example, colour is a qualitative physical property. The colour of the element aluminum is grey. The orange-brown colour of a roof is one clue that the roof is made from the element copper. A greenish-yellow gas could be a warning that chlorine gas is present. How a substance smells is another qualitative physical property. The compound hydrogen sulfide has a very characteristic odour, which resembles the smell of rotten eggs. Another qualitative physical property is the state of a substance. When you look at a sample, you can easily see if it is a solid, a liquid, or a gas. **Table 4.2** lists some of the qualitative physical properties that are often used to describe matter.

Table 4.2 Qualitative Physical Properties

Property	Examples
colour	colourless, red, black
odour	sweet, pungent, mouldy
state	solid, liquid, or gas
texture	rough, smooth, bumpy
lustre	shiny, dull
malleability	soft, pliable, hard

Activity 4-4

What's So Special about Paper Clips?

The metal paper clip was invented over 100 years ago, and it is still used today. How do the physical properties of this handy tool help it to carry out its functions?

Materials

- 2 paper clips

Procedure

1. Your teacher will give you and a partner two paper clips.

2. Spend about 5 min making a list of the qualitative physical properties of your paper clips. Use the list of physical properties in **Table 4.2**.

Questions

1. Describe six qualitative physical properties of your paper clip.

2. What provides your paper clip with many of the properties that you observed?

3. Think of what a paper clip is used for. How are the properties that you listed related to the function of the paper clip?

Quantitative Physical Properties

Although qualitative descriptions of a substance can provide some information, ultimately scientists rely on properties that can be measured. A *quantitative* physical property can be measured and assigned a particular value. For example, the melting point of a compound is a quantitative physical property. Quantitative physical properties are often distinctive, or unique, to a particular element or compound, and recorded values are available for reference. **Table 4.3** lists the quantitative physical properties that are most often studied. Try Activity 4-5 to gain some experience with a physical property called **viscosity**, which is a measure of how easily a fluid flows. The more viscous a fluid is, the slower it flows.

viscosity the measure of a substance's resistance to flow

Table 4.3 Quantitative Physical Properties

Property	Description
viscosity	resistance to flow
melting point	temperature of melting
boiling point	temperature of boiling
solubility	ability to dissolve in another substance
hardness	ability to scratch another material
conductivity	ability to conduct electricity or heat
density	ratio of mass to volume

Activity 4-5

Slow as Molasses

Have you ever heard the phrase "as slow as molasses"? You are about to see, firsthand, what is meant by this expression.

Materials

- 2 beakers of the same size
- 2 scoopulas
- water
- molasses
- medicine droppers
- stopwatch

Procedure

1. Work with a partner. You and your partner should each place your scoopula inside a beaker. Position the scoopula so the wider end is at the top and so it rests against the side of the beaker.

2. One partner adds a drop of water to the wide end of one scoopula. The other partner adds a drop of molasses to the wide end of the other scoopula.

3. At the same time, start the stopwatch. Make sure that you and your partner hold the scoopulas at the same angle. Observe and record the time that it takes for the water and the molasses to run to the bottom of each scoopula.

Questions

1. How long did it take for the water and molasses to run down the scoopulas?

2. What physical property of molasses does the expression "slow as molasses" refer to?

3. What is another way that you could measure the difference between the viscosities of water and molasses?

States of Matter

The specific temperature at which an element or a compound changes state is a characteristic physical property. **Figure 4.8** reviews the different changes of state that matter undergoes. *Melting* is the change of state from solid to liquid. The temperature at which a solid changes into a liquid is called the **melting point**. The melting points of compounds and elements have been used for numerous applications, such as the melting of gold for things like jewellery, shown in **Figure 4.9**. *Solidification* is the opposite of melting, when a substance changes from a liquid to a solid.

Evaporation is the change of state from liquid to a gas. The temperature at which a liquid changes into a gas is called the **boiling point**. As you probably know, the boiling point of water is 100°C. In comparison, the boiling point of helium is –269°C. Because of its low boiling point, helium is used to keep things very cold. When liquid helium is introduced into a system and allowed to boil, it brings the temperature of the system down to its boiling point, which is very near absolute zero. Condensation is the opposite of evaporation and is the change in state from a gas to a liquid.

Some substances have the ability to change directly from a solid to a gas. This process is called *sublimation*. A well-known example of this is solid carbon dioxide—also called dry ice. As you can see in **Figure 4.10**, it is often used in live performances because it creates the effect of fog. When substances change from a gas to a solid, it is called *deposition*.

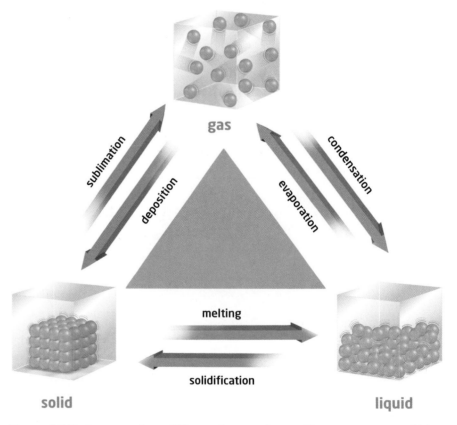

Figure 4.8 Matter can undergo different changes of state. The temperature at which a pure substance undergoes a change of state is an important physical property.

---

melting point
the temperature at which a solid turns into a liquid

boiling point
the temperature at which a liquid turns into a gas

Figure 4.9 Gold is melted and used for products like jewellery.

Figure 4.10 The sublimation of dry ice is often used to mimic fog in stage performances.

Solubility

Another important physical property is **solubility**. The solubility of a substance is recorded as the maximum quantity of a substance that can dissolve in a given amount of solvent at a particular temperature and pressure. The solubility of a substance is expressed as a concentration. Typically, the units are mass of solute per mass of solvent, or mass of solute per volume of solvent. A substance is highly soluble if large amounts of the substance will dissolve in a given amount of solvent. For example, salt easily dissolves in water to produce a salt solution, as shown in **Figure 4.11**. The reported solubility of sodium chloride in water at 25°C and atmospheric pressure is 39.5 g/100 mL. This is a quantitative physical property of sodium chloride. A solution with water as a solvent is called an *aqueous solution*. One of the most important aqueous solutions is blood serum. The serum is the liquid component of blood, which blood cells are suspended in. Numerous chemicals that are essential for life are dissolved in aqueous-based blood serum and are transported throughout the body.

A substance that does not dissolve or has a very low solubility is sometimes described as being insoluble. For example, copper and iron are insoluble in water—which is good. Otherwise, every time it rained, many structures around you would dissolve!

solubility a measure of the ability of a substance to dissolve in another substance

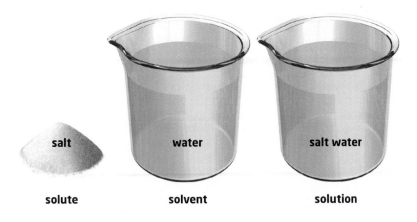

| salt | water | salt water |
| solute | solvent | solution |

Figure 4.11 Salt is a solute that easily dissolves in the solvent water to produce a saltwater solution.

Solubility and the Environment

Solubility in fat is an especially important property for some chemicals, because of bioaccumulation and biomagnification. As discussed in Chapter 1, *bioaccumulation* involves the build-up of toxic substances in the tissues of animals over time. This can lead to *biomagnification*, which involves the accumulation of these toxic substances in progressively higher concentrations toward the top of food chains. Often, these toxic substances are highly soluble in fat and collect in fat deposits in animals.

The chemical **d**ichloro-**d**iphenyl-**t**richloroethane (DDT) is an example of a fat-soluble substance that bioaccumulates and biomagnifies in mammals. DDT is a synthetic pesticide that was used extensively in the 1940s and 1950s to eliminate insect-carrying diseases and increase crop yields throughout the world. For many years, DDT was seen as a huge success. By the 1970s, over a billion kilograms of DDT had been introduced into the environment in North America alone. Since then, however, scientists have learned that DDT does not break down easily, and is stored in the fatty tissue of animals. This has a negative impact on mammals in Canada, such as Arctic polar bears and seals, as shown in **Figure 4.12**. DDT is carried to the Arctic by atmospheric transport and ocean currents. Phytoplankton, which take up the DDT water pollutant, are consumed by snails. Arctic cod thrive on snails and retain all the DDT from every snail they eat. A ringed seal, in turn, can consume large quantities of DDT-contaminated arctic cod. The ringed seal stores the DDT it has consumed. The DDT concentration in the seal can be several hundred times higher than in organisms lower on the food chain. Ultimately, the DTT from the ringed seal is passed to the polar bear that consumes the seal.

Go to **scienceontario** to find out more

Figure 4.12 The concentration of DDT increases at each trophic level of this Arctic food chain. Since DDT is soluble in fat but not in water, organisms do not excrete it in significant amounts. Instead, they store DDT in the fat of their bodies.

DDT

phytoplankton

snails

arctic cod

ringed seal

polar bear

Hardness

The *hardness* of a substance refers to its ability to be scratched. Harder substances can scratch softer substances, but softer substances cannot scratch harder substances. The hardness of a substance is often helpful for determining its practical use. Hardness is usually given as a number between 1 and 10 on a scale called the Mohs scale. For example, your fingernail has a hardness of around 2 on the Mohs scale. Diamond, which is the hardest natural material, has a hardness of 10.

Hardness is one of several properties that make diamonds useful in a variety of applications. High lustre, transparency, and their way of reflecting light make diamonds very valuable as gemstones. Nevertheless, the majority of diamonds are used in industry. Hardness, low reactivity with chemicals, low electrical conductivity, high thermal conductivity, and high density are just a few physical properties that make diamonds useful in industry. The most common industrial applications of diamonds are ones requiring a great deal of durability, such as drilling, cutting, and grinding. For example, drill bits for drills used in drilling oil wells contain diamonds. Each of the cutting tips in **Figure 4.13** has grains of diamond embedded into the end of it.

Figure 4.13 Diamonds have been embedded into the ends of these drill bits to make it easier for the drills to cut through rock.

Activity 4-6

Hard as Nails

The hardness of a material can play a big part in determining what the material is used for. How do some common substances, with very different uses, compare with each other in terms of hardness?

Materials

- piece of talc
- copper penny
- steel nail

Procedure

1. Examine the three materials that your teacher has given you. Rank them from least hard to hardest, by simply observing and touching them.

2. Make a table similar to the one on the right to record your results. List the materials that you are using to scratch in the vertical column and the materials being scratched as the horizontal headings.
   Perform scratch tests on each material, by systematically scratching each material with each of the other materials, as well as with a sample of itself.

3. Use a plus sign (+) to indicate ability to scratch, and use a minus sign (-) to indicate inability to scratch. One box has been filled in for you, indicating that talc cannot scratch a penny.

Scratch Tests

	Talc	Penny	Nail
Talc		(−)	
Penny			
Nail			

Questions

1. Based on your scratch tests, rank the three materials from least hard to hardest. What happened when you scratched two samples of the same material?

2. How did your initial hypothesis about the relative hardness of the materials compare with your experimentally determined rankings?

3. What does the fact that chalk is used to write on a chalkboard tell you about the relative hardness of chalk and chalkboard material?

Learning Check

1. What is the difference between qualitative physical properties and quantitative physical properties?

2. What physical property of DDT contributes to its bioaccumulation in animals?

3. How could knowing the melting points of two pure substances that look alike help you tell the substances apart?

4. Why do people often check to see if a diamond is real by rubbing it against glass?

Sense of Value

Although copper and silver have very similar electrical conductivity properties, silver is over 100 times more expensive than copper. Therefore, it is more economical to use copper in things like wiring.

density the ratio of the mass of a substance to the volume it occupies

Conductivity

The ability of a substance to conduct electricity is another distinguishing physical property. You have probably learned that electrical wires are made from copper. Copper is used because it has a high electrical conductivity. In other words, it conducts electric current very well. Aluminum pans are useful for cooking food because aluminum has a high thermal conductivity—it transfers heat easily. The burner heats the bottom of the pan. The pan then transfers the energy to the food. In comparison, the handles on many pots and pans are made of plastic because plastic has a low thermal conductivity and helps to protect you from burning your hands while cooking.

Density

You have learned that matter is anything that has mass and volume. You can use the mass and volume of a sample to determine an important physical property called density. **Density** is defined as the mass of a substance that occupies a certain unit volume. In other words, for a particular mass of a substance, a certain volume is required.

Density is not just a property of solids. It is also a property of gases and liquids. Liquids that have different densities will separate into distinct layers when added to the same container. The liquid that is the most dense will be the bottom layer, while the liquid that is the least dense will be the top layer. Of course, this only occurs when neither of the liquids are soluble in each other. You may have heard about the *Exxon Valdez* oil spill, shown in **Figure 4.14**. An oil spill can have devastating consequences because oil is insoluble in water and less dense than water. As a result, it floats on the water. Ultimately, a great deal of the oil spreads on the water, until reaching a shoreline.

Figure 4.14 The 1989 *Exxon Valdez* oil spill, which occurred in Prince William Sound off the coast of Alaska, was one of the worst environmental disasters in history. It affected almost 4000 km of shoreline.

Determining Density

Density can be calculated using the formula

$$\text{density} = \frac{\text{mass}}{\text{volume}} \quad \text{or} \quad D = \frac{m}{V}$$

Density is often expressed as grams per cubic centimetre, represented as g/cm^3. When calculating density using these units, make sure that the mass is in grams and the volume is in cubic centimetres.

Sample Problem: Calculating Density

Problem

A sample of silver has a mass of 5.04 g and a volume of $0.480\ cm^3$. What is the density of silver?

Solution

This problem requires you to determine the density.
The values for mass and volume are given:

$m = 5.04$ g and $V = 0.480\ cm^3$

The equation for density is $D = \dfrac{m}{V}$

Substitute the given values into the equation, and solve:

$$D = \frac{5.04\ \text{g}}{0.480\ cm^3}$$

$D = 10.5\ g/cm^3$

The density of silver is $10.5\ g/cm^3$.

Check Your Solution

By rounding the mass to 5 g and the volume to $0.5\ cm^3$, you can see that the mass is about 10 times larger than the volume. An estimate of $10\ g/cm^3$ for the density is close to the calculated value of $10.5\ g/cm^3$.

○○○

Study Toolkit

Previewing Text Features
Notice how the sample problem is presented on this page. How do you think this text feature will help you to learn about calculating density?

GRASP
Go to **Science Skills Toolkit 9** to learn about an alternative problem solving method.

Practice Problems

1. A sample of an unknown metal has a mass of 21.6 g and a volume of $8.00\ cm^3$. Calculate the density of the unknown metal.

2. What is the density of a liquid if $95.5\ cm^3$ has a mass of 101 g?

3. A balloon contains $5470\ cm^3$ of gas and has a mass of 10.24 g. The mass of the empty balloon is 2.42 g. What is the density of the gas?

4. One side of a cube of an unknown metal measures 0.53 cm. If the mass of the cube is 0.92 g, what is the density of the cube?

5. A scientist has developed a new type of material that is supposed to float on water. This material has a mass of 2.0 g for every $3.0\ cm^3$ of volume. Will this material float on water (density = $1.0\ g/cm^3$)? Explain.

Water's Unique Physical Properties

Suggested Investigation

Inquiry Investigation 4-A, Testing Physical Properties of Substances, on page 166

One of the most interesting pure substances is also one of the most common—water. Water is colourless, tasteless, and odourless. The "hidden" properties of water, however, allow it to support life on Earth. Some of the unique physical properties of water that make it so special are summarized in **Figure 4.15**.

Water is the only natural substance that exists in all three phases at the temperatures and pressures experienced on Earth.

Water is called the "universal solvent" because it dissolves more substances than any other liquid. This property allows it to carry a large number of essential nutrients and chemicals in waterways and the human body.

Water is unusual because its solid form, ice, is less dense than its liquid form. This means that ice forms on the surface of lakes. The ice acts as an insulator, preventing the water below it from freezing and allowing wildlife in the water to survive.

Water can absorb a lot of heat before it begins to get hot. This makes it resistant to sudden changes in temperature. As a result, aquatic habitats do not experience the extreme fluctuations in temperature that can happen on land.

Figure 4.15 The physical properties of water allow it to support life on Earth.

Section Summary

- A physical property of an element or a compound can be observed without a change to the substance.
- Qualitative physical properties include colour, odour, state, texture, lustre, and malleability. Quantitative physical properties include viscosity, melting point, boiling point, solubility, hardness, conductivity, and density.
- Density can be calculated by dividing the mass of a substance by its volume. The formula is $D = \dfrac{m}{V}$.

- Diamonds are valuable as gemstones because they have high lustre, are transparent, and refract light brilliantly. Diamonds are useful for industrial applications because they are extremely hard, have very low reactivity with chemicals, and have low electrical conductivity.
- The unique properties of water include a solid state that is less dense than its liquid state, the ability to absorb a large amount of heat, and the ability to dissolve numerous essential chemicals and nutrients.

Review Questions

K/U **1.** Compare qualitative and quantitative physical properties. Use examples of properties listed in **Tables 4.2** and **4.3** as part of your discussion.

K/U **2.** Why is melting point considered a physical property?

C **3.** Using a flowchart, describe why the concentration of DDT in ring seals is much higher than the concentration in arctic cod.

T/I **4.** What property determines the choice of material that is used for the inside of an electrical wire and the material that is used for the outside of the wire?

T/I **5.** When might a large volume of material have little mass?

A **6.** Gold has a density of 19.3 g/cm³. Iron pyrite, commonly known as fool's gold because of its colour, has a density of 5.02 g/cm³. Suppose that you find a golden solid that has a mass of 25.04 g and a volume of 4.99 cm³. Have you found gold or iron pyrite? Show your work.

A **7.** The density of red wine vinegar is 1.01 g/cm³, and the density of olive oil is 0.92 g/cm³. A salad dressing that consisted of these two ingredients was left sitting too long. The ingredients separated in the bottle, as shown on the right. Which ingredient is in which layer? Explain.

T/I **8.** Water is unique because the density of its solid, ice, is less than the density of its liquid. Describe how life would be different if this were not true.

Oil and vinegar will separate into two layers of differing densities.

4.3 Chemical Properties

When people think of chemistry, they usually think of different chemicals reacting with each other to produce something new—often envisioning frothing material or an explosion. How a substance reacts with other substances refers to another type of property, called a chemical property. A **chemical property** describes the ability of a substance to react with another substance and form one or more new substances. In **Figure 4.16**, different compounds are reacting with each other to produce a new substance. This reaction involves the production of energy, which is given off as light in a process called *chemiluminescence*.

The chemical properties of a substance are exhibited during a chemical reaction, or the transformation of a substance to form one or more new substances.

chemical property the ability of a substance to change (react) and form new substances

Figure 4.16 Glow sticks are tubes containing different compounds that, when mixed, undergo a chemical reaction. This produces light. The colour of the glow stick depends on the type of dye in the stick.

Reactivity with Other Substances

A large part of chemistry is based on reactions between substances, namely performing chemical reactions to synthesize new chemicals or products. Some examples of the types of reactions that elements and compounds undergo are summarized in **Table 4.4**. You will learn more about chemical reactions in Grade 10 science.

Table 4.4 Examples of Reactivities

Description	Example
Reactivity with Water Calcium carbide is a compound that reacts with water to generate acetylene gas. The acetylene gas is combustible, which makes it useful for generating light. This type of light source was common before battery-operated and electric lights became available. Many cavers still use this as a light source when they are deep underground.	
Reactivity with Oxygen Aluminum metal is very reactive with oxygen. The reaction causes a layer of aluminum oxide to form on the surface of the aluminum, which protects the metal from weathering. This helps to keep aluminum objects that are always exposed to the environment from corroding.	
Reactivity with Acids Baking soda, or sodium bicarbonate, is a compound that reacts with acids to create carbon dioxide gas. Many recipes for baked goods use baking soda because the bubbles of carbon dioxide that form help to make batter and dough rise.	
Reactivity with Another Pure Substance Knowing how pure substances react with each other provides the basis that enables chemists to develop new products.	

What's New?

Although there are too many different types of reactions to demonstrate all of them, these reactions will give you some idea of the different ways that you can observe chemical properties. Can you see evidence that indicates the formation of new substances?

Safety Precautions

- Wear safety goggles.

Materials

- sodium bicarbonate
- 5% acetic acid
- test-tube rack
- balloon
- test tube
- 5 mL water
- universal indicator
- calcium

Procedure

Part 1: Reaction with Acids

1. Two common substances are sodium bicarbonate (baking soda) and acetic acid. Vinegar is a solution of acetic acid in water. Your teacher has already put the sodium bicarbonate in a balloon and the acetic acid in a test tube.

2. Place the balloon that contains sodium bicarbonate over the test tube that contains acetic acid. The baking soda should fall into the test tube so that it can react with the acid. Watch what happens to the balloon!

Part 2: Reaction with Water

3. Your teacher has prepared a test tube that contains 10 mL of water and a few drops of universal indicator.

4. Your teacher will add a small piece of calcium metal to the test tube. Watch to see what happens to the metal and the solution.

Questions

1. What happened to the balloon? Why do you think this happened?

2. What happened to the solution in the test tube when the calcium was added?

3. Some substances, such as sodium metal, react very violently with water. Why do you think they are stored in oil?

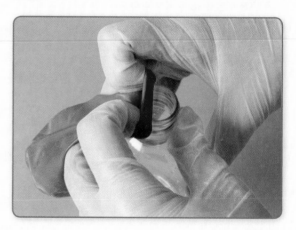

Don't Touch That Dye!

Hydrogen peroxide, also called peroxide, is a common ingredient in many hair dyes. Its chemical properties help to decolorize hair by reacting with the compound melanin, which is responsible for giving hair its colour. Peroxide changes melanin into a colourless compound, and the hair becomes a lighter colour. Peroxide also helps to develop the dyeing compounds that are used to recolour hair. Caution must be taken, however, when using peroxide on hair. Frequent use can damage the outer layer of hair, causing the hair to become brittle and break easily. At low concentrations, peroxide can irritate the eyes or broken skin. At higher concentrations, it can cause bleaching, redness, and even skin blisters.

Combustibility

The ability of an element or compound to burn in air is a chemical property referred to as **combustibility**. For example, the combustibility of propane is an important chemical property that many people take advantage of, as shown in **Figure 4.17**. The reaction of propane with oxygen in the air releases a large amount of heat. Nevertheless, as you saw in the beginning of Section 4.1, the combustibility of propane can be a hazardous property of this compound.

combustibility the ability of a substance to burn in air

Figure 4.17 Propane is combustible, which makes it useful for heating the air in hot-air balloons.

Learning Check

1. Which of the following is a chemical property?
   a. the smell of natural gas
   b. the combustibility of propane
   c. the freezing point of water

2. Is the ability of a substance to reflect light a chemical property? Why or why not?

3. How could the combustibility of a substance influence how the substance is used?

4. Carbonation in soft drinks is due to carbon dioxide. Is the process of carbon dioxide gas leaving a drink as it goes flat a chemical property? Explain.

Suggested Investigation

Inquiry Investigation 4-B, Chemical Properties of Common Gases, on page 168

stability the ability of a substance to remain unchanged

toxicity the ability of a substance to cause harmful effects in plants and animals

Suggested Investigation

Plan Your Own Investigation 4-C, Properties of Common Substances, on page 170

○○○

Study Toolkit

Summarizing Make a table like the one on page 138 to summarize the information on this page. This process of organization will help you to learn the material.

Stability and Toxicity

The **stability** of a substance refers to how easily the substance decomposes or breaks down. The more stable a substance is, the longer it will take to break down. For scientists who focus on trying to synthesize new chemicals, stability is often an issue they must deal with. For a chemical to be useful, it must have enough stability to exist long enough to carry out its required function.

Another chemical property of a substance is toxicity. Generally speaking, **toxicity** refers to the harm that exposure to a substance can cause to animals and plants. Almost all chemicals are poisonous at high enough concentrations. For example, you need oxygen to breathe, but too much will kill you. Therefore, it is important to know how toxic a chemical is. Toxicity is typically reported as a LD_{50} value. This unit of measure refers to the dose required to kill 50 percent of the exposed population.

The tetanus toxin from the bacteria *Clostridium tetani*, shown in **Figure 4.18**, is one of the most poisonous substances to humans. Only 1×10^{-9} g for each kilogram of body mass is needed to kill a person! Other substances may not be as acutely poisonous, but they can cause toxicity due to prolonged exposure over time.

Although the toxicity of a substance is related to its chemical properties, the harm that it does can be related to its stability. Toxicity and stability are often linked together, particularly in discussions of the environmental impact of a chemical. For example, the toxic effects of DDT are made worse by its stability. If DDT easily broke down, then it would not bioaccumulate and biomagnify, and its toxic effects on animals and humans would be lower. You will learn more about stability and toxicity later in this unit, when you explore the impact of certain elements and compounds on the environment.

Figure 4.18 This photo of *Clostridium tetani* was taken using an electron microscope. This organism produces one of the most toxic substances to humans.

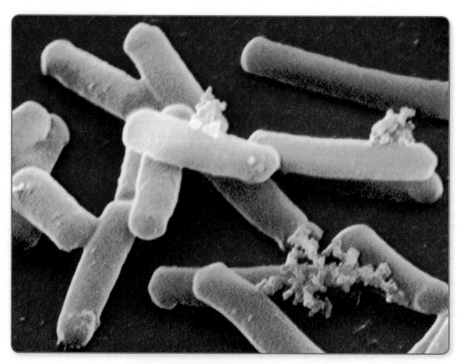

Section Summary

- A chemical property of an element or a compound describes its ability to react with other substances and form new substances.

- Chemical properties of a substance include reactivity with other substances, combustibility, stability, and toxicity.

- The chemical properties of peroxide make it useful in hair dye. Nevertheless, there are hazards associated with its use that include skin and eye irritation.

- The stability and toxicity of a substance may influence its impact on the environment. For example, the toxic effects of DDT are made worse by its high stability.

Review Questions

A **1.** Which property could be a chemical property of hydrogen?

    a. It is a gas.

    b. It is colourless.

    c. It can explode and burn in the presence of air.

K/U **2.** Does the production of a new gas by a substance represent a chemical property? Explain.

A **3.** When objects like this horseshoe are left outside over time, the iron in them will react with oxygen to produce rust. Is this a chemical property of iron? Explain.

C **4.** Write a statement that warns people about the presence of peroxide in hair dyes.

K/U **5.** Name a chemical property of propane.

K/U **6.** Why is the stability of a compound considered a chemical property?

A **7.** Do you think toxicity is a qualitative property or a quantitative property? Explain.

T/I **8.** Explain how stability and toxicity can work together to increase the effects of a chemical on the environment.

Horseshoes are made of iron and, therefore, will rust when left outside.

Inquiry Investigation 4-A

Safety Precautions

- Put on safety goggles and a lab apron.
- Wipe up any spilled materials immediately.

Materials

- aluminum pieces
- carbon (graphite)
- copper(II) sulfate
- magnesium sulfate
- water
- conductivity tester
- scoopula
- five 25 mL test tubes
- test-tube rack
- 50 mL water
- 10 mL graduated cylinder

Testing Physical Properties of Substances

Learning how to perform scientific tests is important when studying chemistry. In this investigation, you will perform scientific tests to determine the physical properties of some common elements and compounds.

Question

What are the physical properties of some common elements and compounds?

Prediction

Before beginning the Procedure, examine the substances carefully. Based on your observations, group substances that seem to have similar physical properties.

Procedure

1. Make a table like the one below to record your observations. Give your table a title.

Element/Compound	Aluminum	Carbon (graphite)	Copper(II) Sulfate	Magnesium Sulfate	Water
State					
Colour					
Lustre					
Odour					
Conductivity					
Melt Test					
Solubility in Water					

Part 1: Visible Properties

2. Indicate the state of each substance in your table.

3. Describe the colour of each substance in your table.

4. Classify the lustre (appearance of the surface) of each substance, according to how dull or shiny it is. Record your observations in your table.

5. To smell each substance, first take a deep breath and hold it. Then, gently waft the air above the sample toward you. Which substances, if any, have an odour? Record your observations in your table.

Part 2: Electrical Conductivity

6. Your teacher will give you a small battery-powered conductivity tester. Touch the two metal probes of the tester to the substance you want to test. The two metal probes should touch the sample. **Make sure that the substance is clean and dry.** If the substance is an electrical conductor, the conductivity tester will light up. Test each substance in turn. Record your observations as yes or no in your table.

Part 3: Melt Test (Teacher Demonstration)

7. Watch while your teacher puts a small amount of each unknown substance on a small aluminum pan and places all the samples on the hot plate.

8. Observe the behaviour of each substance. Record your observations. Indicate whether or not each substance melted.

Part 4: Solubility in Water

9. Put 10 mL of water into each of five 25 mL test tubes. Add a small amount of each solid substance to each test tube. Agitate the test tubes. Observe after 30 s, and record your observations. If some solid is still present, observe after another 30 s.

10. Dispose of all the substances as directed by your teacher.

Analyze and Interpret

1. Which substances, if any, appear to have a similar set of properties?

2. Which substances, if any, have a unique set of properties, not shared by any of the other substances?

3. Which sets of properties often appear together?

Conclude and Communicate

4. How did your results compare with your initial prediction about substances that have similar physical properties? Explain why your prediction and your results were similar or different.

Extend Your Inquiry and Research Skills

5. Inquiry Design a test to help you further distinguish between the different elements and compounds used in this investigation. Use a physical property that was not used in this investigation.

6. Research Assess the usefulness and the hazards associated with one of the substances used in this investigation by conducting research.

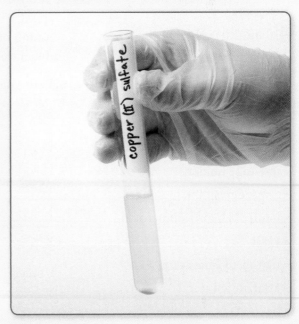

Gently shake each test tube to test the solubility of the materials.

Inquiry Investigation 4-B

Skill Check

Initiating and Planning

✓ **Performing and Recording**

✓ **Analyzing and Interpreting**

✓ **Communicating**

Safety Precautions

- Put on safety goggles and a lab apron.
- Be very cautious when testing for gases.
- Be careful when handling the burning splints. Do not wave them in the air or toward other students in the lab.
- Make sure the splints are properly extinguished immediately after being used.
- If you have long hair, make sure that it is tied back.

Materials

- 10 mL 1.0 mol/L hydrochloric acid
- 4 test tubes
- test-tube rack
- mossy zinc
- rubber stopper
- test-tube holder
- 2 wooden splints
- 5 mL 3% hydrogen peroxide
- yeast
- marble or limestone
- 5 mL limewater
- balloon
- cobalt chloride paper

Chemical Properties of Common Gases

Why is it dangerous to fill balloons and blimps with hydrogen to make them float? In this investigation, you will perform simple tests to better understand the chemical properties of a few common gases.

Question

What tests can you use to identify gases, based on their chemical properties?

Procedure

1. Work with a partner to perform each of the following tests. Record your observations as you complete each step.

2. Be sure to clean up your work station as you complete each part. Place each substance in the appropriate waste container, as directed by your teacher.

Part 1: Test for Hydrogen Gas

3. Obtain 5 mL of hydrochloric acid in a test tube, a piece of mossy zinc, and a wooden splint. Have the wooden splint nearby.

4. One partner holds the test tube at a 45° angle, using a test-tube holder, and then slides the zinc down the side of the test tube into the acid. A reaction should begin. Trap some of the gas in the tube using a rubber stopper.

5. **Test for Hydrogen:** Your teacher will show you how to light the splint. The other partner brings the flaming splint close to the mouth of the test tube. Hydrogen gas will ignite and burn rapidly down the test tube with a "whoop" sound.

6. Extinguish the wooden splint.

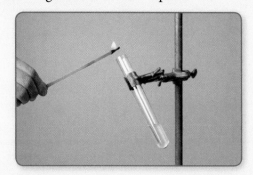

If hydrogen is present, it will ignite rapidly.

Part 2: Test for Oxygen Gas

7. Obtain 5 mL of 3% hydrogen peroxide in a test tube, some yeast, and a wooden splint.

8. One partner adds the yeast to the hydrogen peroxide. A reaction should begin. Trap some of the gas in the tube using a rubber stopper.

9. **Test for Oxygen:** Your teacher will show you how to light the splint and produce a glowing ember. The other partner brings the ember to the mouth of the test tube and inserts the glowing ember into the test tube. If oxygen is present, the glowing ember will burst into a bright flame.

10. Extinguish the wooden splint.

If oxygen is present, a flame will form from the ember.

Part 3: Test for Carbon Dioxide Gas

11. Obtain 5 mL of hydrochloric acid in a test tube, a small piece of marble or limestone, and a second test tube containing 5 mL of limewater.

12. One partner holds the test tube with the acid at a 45° angle, and slides the piece of marble down the side of the tube into the acid. The other partner places the balloon over the top of the test tube. The balloon will inflate with any gas that is produced.

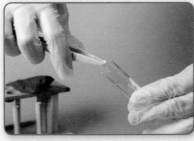

Slide the marble down the side of the test tube.

13. **Test for Carbon Dioxide:** Keep the new gas inside the balloon by twisting the balloon closed. While the balloon is still twisted closed, attach it to the mouth of the test tube containing limewater. Once attached, invert the balloon-covered test tube so the limewater will mix with the gas in the balloon. Then, return the test tube to an upright position. If carbon dioxide is present, the limewater will turn white and milky.

Part 4: Test for Water Vapour

14. Your teacher will give you a fresh piece of dry blue cobalt chloride paper.

15. **Test for Water Vapour:** Hold the cobalt chloride paper close to your mouth. Breathe on it, like you would breathe on a pair of sunglasses before wiping them. Cobalt chloride paper turns from blue to pink in the presence of water.

Analyze and Interpret

1. Could you have used physical properties to identify the gases that you studied in this investigation? Explain.

2. Which chemical properties did you use to identify the different gases?

Conclude and Communicate

3. What advice would you give a person who handles hydrogen and oxygen gas in their workplace?

Extend Your Inquiry and Research Skills

4. **Inquiry** Based on your observations of the gas tests done in this investigation, identify two scientific questions that can be tested through an experiment.

5. **Research** Choose one of the gases tested in this investigation. Identify the chemical and physical properties that make it both useful and hazardous in the workplace.

Plan Your Own Investigation 4-C

Skill Check

✓ Initiating and Planning

✓ Performing and Recording

✓ Analyzing and Interpreting

✓ Communicating

Safety Precautions

- Put on safety goggles and a lab apron.
- Treat all substances as if they are chemicals in a lab. Do not taste them.
- If checking for odour, take a deep breath and keep it while wafting the air above the sample toward you. Do not inhale directly from the sample.
- Clean up all spills immediately, and inform your teacher.

Suggested Materials

- table sugar (sucrose)
- baking soda (sodium bicarbonate)
- aluminum strips
- tin strips
- cooking oil
- vinegar (5% acetic acid in water)
- test tubes
- test-tube rack
- scoopula
- other equipment, as needed, to perform tests

Science Skills

Go to **Science Skills Toolkit 7** for information about creating data tables.

Properties of Common Substances

Substances that you see almost every day and use on a regular basis have characteristic properties. Often, these properties are linked to how the substances are used. In this investigation, you will plan a series of tests to identify important properties of some common substances.

Question

What are the physical and chemical properties of some common substances, and which properties can be used to tell each substance apart?

Plan and Conduct

1. Your teacher will give you six substances to investigate. Plan a procedure to identify four physical properties and two chemical properties of each substance. Choose properties that are listed in the table below. If you cannot remember what a property is or how to determine it, go back to the relevant information in the chapter.

Common Properties

Physical Properties		Chemical Properties
colour	viscosity	reactivity with water
odour	melting point	reactivity with acid
state	boiling point	reactivity with oxygen
texture	solubility in water	reactivity with another pure substance
lustre	conductivity	
malleability	density	

2. Prepare a table to record the results of your tests. Include a title for your table. Make sure that you include enough headings in your table to keep all your observations organized. If you wish, you can include the list of equipment you use in your table.

3. Have your teacher review your procedure, your observations table, and your list of equipment. You must not begin your tests until your teacher has approved your procedure.

4. Perform your tests for the physical and chemical properties of the different substances. Make sure that you complete your tests exactly as you planned them. Do not add additional steps without getting your teacher's approval.

5. Make complete notes for each test. For some tests, you may need to include descriptions (such as colour), or a yes/no answer, or an indication of a rating (such as the hardness of a substance relative to another substance).

6. Share your group's results with your teacher, who will record them in a chart on the board. Add any information that you have not already recorded in your own table.

Analyze and Interpret

1. Examine your observations table. Look for patterns you can use to group the substances, according to common physical and/or chemical properties. What groupings of substances can you make? Explain what these groupings are based on.

2. Analyze your observations to determine if there are certain properties that seem to distinguish one substance from the others. For some substances, it may be one particular property. For other substances, it may be a combination of properties.

Conclude and Communicate

3. Evaluate your tests to determine whether they were useful for distinguishing all the substances from each other, according to their properties. What improvements could you make?

Extend Your Inquiry and Research Skills

4. Inquiry Identify each substance that you studied as either an element, a compound, or a mixture. Did each type of matter share particular properties? If so, which properties?

5. Research Think about how each substance you studied is used. If necessary, use the Internet or a dictionary to help you. How do you think the physical and/or chemical properties of each substance are related to its function?

Real World Investigation 4-D

Skill Check

Initiating and Planning

Performing and Recording

✓ **Analyzing and Interpreting**

✓ **Communicating**

Materials

- graph paper
- ruler

CFC Production and Canada's Ozone Layer

You have been asked to write a blog post about the effects of chlorofluorocarbons, or CFCs, on Canada's ozone layer. CFCs are compounds once used as coolants in refrigerators and as propellants in aerosols. In the 1970s, however, scientists discovered a "hole" in the ozone layer of Earth's stratosphere. CFCs were identified as the main cause of ozone depletion. International agreements have now almost eliminated CFC production. To help write your post, you find a table of data for a main type of CFC, trichlorofluoromethane (CCl_3F).

Effect of CCl_3F on Canada's Ozone Layer

Year	CCl_3F Production (1000 tonnes)	CCl_3F in the Stratosphere (parts per trillion)	Ozone Levels (Dobson units*)
1945	0.4	0	–
1955	26.3	4	366
1965	123	28	363
1975	314	121	364
1985	326	217	352
1995	33	267	340
2005	2	251	332

*A measurement that ozone researchers use to indicate how much ozone is present.

Question

How has the production of CFCs affected Canada's ozone layer?

Organize the Data

1. Draw a line graph for each of the three data sets. Decide on a scale and how to label the *x*-axis and *y*-axis for each graph.

Analyze and Interpret

1. CCl_3F was first produced around 1930. How many years did it take for CCl_3F to enter the stratosphere?

2. In what year did the ozone layer above Canada begin to decline?

3. Once the production of CCl_3F was drastically reduced, how many years did it take for CCl_3F levels to decrease in the stratosphere?

Conclude and Communicate

4. Write a one-page blog entry to explain how the production of CFCs affected, and continues to affect, Canada's ozone layer.

Extend Your Inquiry and Research Skills

5. **Research** Find out how a reduced ozone layer has affected Earth.

Math Skills
Go to **Math Skills Toolkit 3** for information about constructing graphs.

Chapter 4 Summary

4.1 Studying Matter

Key Concepts

- When studying matter, it is important to know the location of safety equipment in your classroom and the meanings of the safety icons and WHMIS symbols.

- Matter can be classified according to its composition, as mixtures or pure substances.

- An element is a pure substance that cannot be broken down into simpler substances through physical or chemical methods.

- A compound is a pure substance that is composed of two or more elements, that are chemically combined. A compound can be broken down into its elements only by chemical methods.

- Elements and compounds are part of your daily life and include such things as water, salt, oxygen, carbon dioxide, and aluminum.

- The production and use of new chemicals can have both negative and positive consequences. Although we may benefit from their applications, potential negative consequences also need to be considered.

4.2 Physical Properties

Key Concepts

- A physical property of an element or a compound can be observed and measured without changing the identity of the substance.

- Qualitative physical properties include colour, odour, state, texture, lustre, and malleability. Quantitative physical properties include viscosity, melting point, boiling point, solubility, hardness, conductivity, and density.

- Density can be calculated by dividing the mass of a substance by its volume $D = \frac{m}{V}$.

- Diamonds are valuable as gemstones because they have high lustre, are transparent, and refract light brilliantly. Diamonds are useful for industrial applications because they are extremely hard, have very low reactivity with chemicals, and have low electrical conductivity.

- Water has many unique properties. It is present on Earth in all three states. It has a solid state that is less dense that its liquid state. It can absorb a large amount of heat. It has the ability to dissolve numerous essential chemicals and nutrients.

4.3 Chemical Properties

Key Concepts

- A chemical property of an element or a compound describes its ability to react with other substances and form new substances.

- Chemical properties of a substance include reactivity with other substances, combustibility, stability, and toxicity.

- The chemical properties of peroxide make it useful in hair dye. Nevertheless, there are hazards associated with its use that include skin and eye irritation.

- The stability and toxicity of a substance may influence its impact on the environment. For example, the toxic effects of DDT are made worse by its high stability.

Chapter 4 Review

Reviewing Key Terms

1. A _____ of a substance can be observed without forming a new substance. (4.2)

2. Dividing the mass of an object by the volume of the object is a way to calculate _____. (4.2)

3. A sample of matter that cannot be broken down into simpler parts by ordinary chemical methods is a(n) _____. (4.1)

4. If there is only one kind of particle in a sample, the sample must be a(n) _____. (4.1)

5. The combustibility of a substance is a _____ property. (4.3)

6. A material that can be broken down by chemical methods is a(n) _____. (4.1)

Knowledge and Understanding (K/U)

7. Identify each of the following properties as physical or chemical.

a. Gallium can melt in your hand.

b. Aluminum is a good conductor of heat and electric current.

c. Kerosene can burn.

d. Limestone bubbles when an acid touches it.

e. A balloon filled with radon gas falls to the floor when released.

f. A metal is easy to bend.

g. Peroxide reacts with melanin in hair.

8. Describe the difference between two elements that form a compound and the same two elements in a mixture.

9. How do the particles in a pure substance compare with each another?

10. The density of pure silver is 10.5 g/cm³. What is the mass of a sample with a volume of 10.0 cm³?

11. Suppose that you have two samples with the same volume, but the mass of sample A is larger than the mass of sample B. Which sample has the higher density? Explain your answer.

12. What property must a substance have if you want to use the substance to make an aqueous solution?

13. Classify each of the following as an element, a compound, or a mixture.

a. aluminum

b. air

c. sugar

d. orange juice

e. DDT

f. tin

14. What chemical property of magnesium is illustrated in the photo below?

15. What type of property of a pure substance describes how that substance might form a new substance?

16. What properties of diamonds make them useful in industrial applications?

17. Calculate the density using the given information. **Hint:** $1\ mL = 1\ cm^3$

  a. A 35.7 g sample occupies 5.01 cm^3.

  b. A 2.56 L balloon contains 3.66 g of gas.

  c. A 45.3 g sample placed in a graduated cylinder causes the water level to rise from 25.0 mL to 41.8 mL.

18. Briefly describe the difference between an element and a compound.

19. How do the chemical properties of peroxide make it suitable for use in hair dyes? What are the hazards associated with its use?

Thinking and Investigation   T/I

20. Suppose that you are comparing several objects. Is it correct to say that the object with the largest volume has the largest mass? Explain your reasoning, and include an example.

21. A chemist working in the lab wants to remove his goggles and apron as soon as he has finished collecting data. He has not yet cleaned up the lab area, however. What would you say to convince him that he needs to keep on his goggles and apron?

22. Use the following data to answer the question below.

Densities of Common Liquids

Substance	Density (g/cm³)
water	1.00
cooking oil	0.894
corn syrup	1.36

The mass of an empty container is measured and found to be 55.75 g. The container is filled to the rim with water. Its mass is measured again and found to be 105.75 g. The container is emptied and dried with a paper towel to remove any traces of water. It is then filled with an unknown liquid. The new mass is 123.75 g. Use calculations to determine if the unknown liquid is cooking oil or corn syrup.

Communication   C

23. **BIG IDEAS** The use of elements and compounds has both positive and negative effects on society and the environment. Make a table that shows the negative and positive effects of DTT use in society.

24. **BIG IDEAS** Elements and compounds have specific physical and chemical properties that determine their practical uses. Write an advertisement for diamonds, emphasizing how their properties make them useful for many applications.

25. Explain why density is more useful for identifying a substance than either mass or volume alone.

Application   A

26. The following graph shows how long it takes two different liquids to flow through a 100 cm length of tubing. Use this graph to determine which fluid is more viscous. Explain your answer.

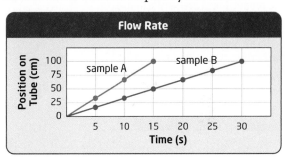

27. Use the particle model of matter to describe what happens when you "see your breath" on a cold day.

28. A facial tissue, a sheet of paper, and a cardboard box are all made from wood fibres. Discuss how the physical properties of each material make it useful for its intended purpose. Name a chemical property that these three materials have in common.

29. How do the properties of water contribute to its use as a coolant in car radiators?

Chapter 5 Understanding the Properties of Elements

What You Will Learn

In this chapter, you will learn how to...

- **explain** how different atomic models evolved over time
- **describe** the current model of the atom
- **explain** the relationship between the atomic structure of an element and the position of the element in the periodic table
- **compare** and **contrast** the physical properties of elements within a group and between groups in the periodic table

Why It Matters

The development of important products depends on understanding the properties of elements. In the periodic table, elements are organized in a way that highlights significant patterns in their properties. This organization reflects the relationship between the atomic structure of each element and the position of the element in the periodic table.

Skills You Will Use

In this chapter, you will learn how to...

- **investigate** the physical and chemical properties of elements and relate these to the elements' positions in the periodic table

What do deodorant and this family's trailer have in common? Both contain the element aluminum! Although aluminum is much less expensive than precious metals like gold, its properties make it extremely valuable. Aluminum is used in thousands of products that range from antacids to airplanes. To better understand what determines the properties of elements like aluminum, the basic structure of an atom needs to be considered.

Activity 5-1

The Atomic "Black Box"

The term "black box" is often used to describe a complex system that cannot be directly studied—like the atom. Indirect observations allow scientists to infer how the "black box" works. Since the atom is so small, scientists who discovered the atom had to do so without ever seeing it. In this activity, you will design experiments to infer what is inside a clay ball. How do you think the clay ball could represent an atom?

This clay ball with an object inside represents a "black box."

Materials

- modelling clay
- thin stir sticks
- simple objects (such as coins, marbles, nuts, bolts, washers, and thimbles)

Procedure

1. In pairs, choose one object and conceal it in modelling clay. Add enough clay to make a smooth ball, about 5 cm in diameter.

2. Form groups of four with another pair of students. The clay ball from the other pair represents the "black box" that you are to analyze.

3. Before starting your analysis, develop a strategy. How will you probe the clay ball with the stir stick to determine what is inside? Keep in mind that you cannot open the ball.

4. Using your planned strategy, probe the clay ball by poking the stir stick through the clay. After 3 to 4 min, you and your partner should make a drawing of what you believe is in the clay ball. The creators of the "black box" will then reveal the object to show if you are correct.

Questions

1. Look up the meaning of the word *inference* in a dictionary. In what ways did you have to make inferences to identify what was inside the clay ball?

2. In what ways do you think identifying the object inside the clay ball represents a model of how scientists have studied the atom?

3. What advice would you give a friend who is going to do this activity?

Study Toolkit

These strategies will help you use this textbook to develop your understanding of science concepts and skills.
To find out more about these and other strategies, refer to the Study Toolkit Overview, which begins on page 561.

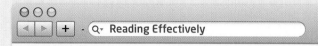

Visualizing

Visualizing means forming an image in your mind based on what you are reading. The table below maps out how a reader might visualize this text from page 180: Dalton referred to the atom as a small, hard, indestructible sphere that is the smallest particle of an element.

Steps	How an Image Forms in My Mind
1. Start with an aspect of the text that is familiar.	"Small, hard, indestructible sphere" makes me think of a marble.
2. Look for details to make your image more accurate.	"The smallest particle of an element" helps me to visualize the marble as being really small.
3. Once you have created an image, make a sketch.	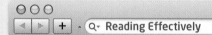

Use the Strategy

While reading about Thomson's atomic model on page 181, visualize how Thomson described the atom.

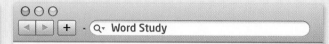

Suffixes

One strategy to figure out the meaning of a new word is to break it down into parts. First, determine the base word. Then check to see if there is a suffix, or an ending after the base word. Some suffixes indicate number or tense, and some change the meaning of the base word. The table below shows some examples.

Suffix and Meaning (in a science context)	Sample Base Word	Base Word + Suffix = New Meaning
-al: of, relating to	environment	*environmental:* relating to the environment
-ic: relating to or characterized by	atom	*atomic:* relating to an atom
-ity: state or quality	reactive	*reactivity:* the quality of being reactive

Use the Strategy

Identify words from Section 5.1 that end with one of the suffixes listed above. Record the base word and predict the definition of the new word. Compare your predictions with those of a partner.

Asking Questions

While reading, stop periodically to ask *who, what, where, why, when,* and *how* questions. Then continue reading to see if your questions are answered by the text. When they are not, check your understanding. This process raises your level of thinking, and helps you make connections beyond the text.

Reread the paragraph on page 176. Here are questions that you might ask while reading:

- *Who* discovered aluminum?
- *What* are its properties?
- *Where* is it found?
- *Why* is it less expensive than gold today?
- *How* can knowing its properties lead to new products?

Use the Strategy

While reading the paragraph on page 179, ask at least three questions. As you read the rest of the section, record any answers you find. Follow up on unanswered questions with a partner.

5.1 Evolution of the Atomic Model

Key Terms
atom
electron
subatomic particle
nucleus
proton
neutron

Studying the **atom** has been a fascination of scientists for hundreds of years. Even Greek philosophers, over 2500 years ago, discussed the idea of there being a smallest piece of matter, which they called the *atomos*. Today, many studies look at particles that are much smaller than the atom. Scientists think that these particles will not only tell us more about the atom, but also help to solve many mysteries about the universe and how it formed. Researchers at the Sudbury Neutrino Observatory, shown in **Figure 5.1**, are studying one of these particles, called the *neutrino*. This particle has almost no mass and has been called the "shy particle" because it has been so difficult to detect—even though neutrinos generated by the Sun are continually bombarding us.

atom the smallest particle of an element that retains the identity of the element

Figure 5.1 The Sudbury Neutrino Observatory uses equipment like this large, highly sensitive detector. The 18-m wide sphere is located 2 km underground, where thick rock shields the detector from other high energy particles that originate in space.

From Particle Theory to Atomic Theory

In Chapter 4, you used the particle theory of matter to describe both elements and compounds in terms of particles. As you know, however, different elements and compounds can have very different properties. In the early 1800s, a British schoolteacher named John Dalton suggested a new way to distinguish between different elements and compounds.

Dalton's Model of the Atom

In the early 1800s, John Dalton experimented with different gases and liquids to study their chemical changes. When he broke down water using an electric current, he observed that the hydrogen and oxygen formed had very different properties from the water. From experimental results like these, Dalton developed a theory that is now called Dalton's atomic theory.

oxygen atom   hydrogen atom

Figure 5.2 Based on his experimental evidence, Dalton stated that different elements are composed of different atoms.

> ### Dalton's Atomic Theory
> - All matter is made up of small particles called atoms.
> - Atoms cannot be created, destroyed, or divided into smaller particles.
> - All atoms of the same element are identical in mass and size. The atoms of one element are different in mass and size from the atoms of other elements.
> - Compounds are created when atoms of different elements link together in definite proportions.

Dalton referred to the atom as a small, hard, indestructible sphere that is the smallest particle of an element. Based on his theory, Dalton developed a model of the atom, shown in **Figure 5.2**.

Dalton's work was an invaluable contribution to the understanding of atoms, elements, and matter. In time, however, new experimental evidence showed that Dalton's model of the atom had to change.

Activity 5-2

How Small Is Too Small?

Atoms are extremely small. The average width of an atom is about 10^{-10} m. Do you think you could cut a piece of paper in half enough times to end up with a piece of paper that is the same width as an atom?

Materials
- round-tipped scissors
- strip of paper (28 cm × 2.5 cm)

Procedure
1. Your teacher will give you a pair of scissors and a piece of paper.

2. Cut the piece of paper in half lengthwise, and discard one half. Then cut the remaining piece of paper in half.

3. Repeat step 2 until the remaining piece of paper can no longer be cut. Keep track of how many times you cut the paper in half.

Questions
1. How many times were you able to cut the paper in half?

2. Estimate the approximate width of the narrowest piece of paper you ended up with.

3. Use your estimate in Question 2 to determine the number of times you would need to cut the paper in half until it became 10^{-10} m wide.

Thomson's Discovery of Electrons

Throughout the 1800s, scientists used gas discharge tubes to study the effects of applying electric currents to gases at low pressure. A more modern version of a gas discharge tube is shown in **Figure 5.3**. At very low gas pressures, scientists determined that a ray was emitted from the negatively charged cathode. The ray then moved toward the positively charged anode. Because the ray began at the negative cathode, scientists inferred that the ray carried a negative charge.

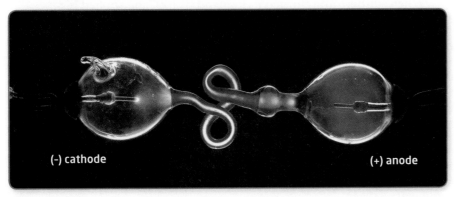

(-) cathode   (+) anode

Figure 5.3 When the cathode and anode of this gas discharge tube are connected to a high-energy source of electricity, an electric current exists in the tube. This current causes the gas inside the tube to glow.

In 1897, a British physicist named Joseph John Thomson demonstrated that the rays were indeed made up of negatively charged particles that are found inside atoms. He predicted that the negative particles would be different for each element and would produce characteristically different results in the cathode ray tube. After trying different materials, Thomson was surprised to find that the same kind of ray was always emitted. Therefore, he had to conclude that the same negatively charged particles are found in all atoms. These particles, which have a very small mass, are now called **electrons**. Electrons were the first **subatomic particles** to be discovered and studied.

electron a negatively charged particle within the atom

subatomic particle a particle that is smaller than the atom

Thomson's New Atomic Model

Thomson knew that an atom did not have an overall charge. He inferred that if every atom contains negative particles, then every atom must also contain positively charged material. From this, Thomson reasoned that Dalton's model of an atom—an atom that could not be divided into smaller particles—must be wrong. Thomson proposed a new model of an atom, based on his experimental evidence. He described the atom as a lump of positively charged material, with negative electrons inserted throughout it, as shown in **Figure 5.4**. This model of the atom is also known as the raisin bun model, with the raisins representing electrons. In 1906, Thomson received the Nobel Prize in physics for his work with electric discharges in gases. Interestingly, his son, G. P. Thomson, earned a Nobel Prize in 1937 for further work on electrons.

Figure 5.4 Experimental evidence led to Thomson's model of the atom, which shows negative electrons inserted throughout a mass of positively charged material.

Although Thomson's model was more accurate than Dalton's model, it was not long before Thomson's model was also revised by one of his students.

Rutherford's Discovery of the Nucleus

Go to **scienceontario** to find out more

Ernest Rutherford, a scientist from New Zealand, was studying under Thomson when Thomson first proposed his atomic model. In 1898, Rutherford moved to Canada to work as a professor at McGill University in Montréal. There, he became involved in studying *radioactive* elements: elements that give off rays of energy as they break down. In 1908, Rutherford was awarded the Nobel Prize in chemistry for the work he did at McGill University.

When Rutherford returned to England in 1907, he applied his knowledge of radiation to an experiment he designed to investigate the structure of the atom. His experiment involved aiming a beam of positively charged particles, called *alpha particles,* at a very thin sheet of gold foil. The source of the alpha particles was a very small amount of the radioactive element radium. Radium was discovered and isolated by the Polish-born physicist Marie Curie. Without Curie's work, Rutherford might not have had the material he needed to perform his experiment. In fact, Marie Curie's contribution to science has been invaluable. She was awarded both a Nobel Prize in physics (1903) and a Nobel Prize in chemistry (1911).

Based on Thomson's model of the atom, Rutherford expected that the particles being shot toward the gold foil would pass through it in a straight line. He expected that only a small number of particles would be slightly deflected from a straight line. As you can see in **Figure 5.5**, his results were very different from what he expected.

Sense of scale

On average, for every 8000 alpha particles that were fired at the gold foil during Rutherford's famous experiment, only one was reflected backward.

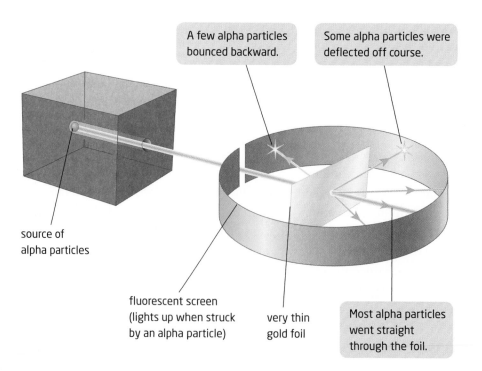

A few alpha particles bounced backward.

Some alpha particles were deflected off course.

source of alpha particles

fluorescent screen (lights up when struck by an alpha particle)

very thin gold foil

Most alpha particles went straight through the foil.

Figure 5.5 Rutherford observed that some of the particles bounced backward, instead of going straight through the foil.

Rutherford's Results

The most surprising observation in Rutherford's experiment was that some of the particles were repelled backward instead of passing right through the foil. This is like shooting a bullet at tissue paper and having it bounce back. Thomson's model of the atom could not provide an explanation for this observation. It could only predict that any particles that were travelling as fast as the alpha particles would simply pass through the spaces between the particles in the foil. As a result, Rutherford had to revise Thomson's model of the atom to fit this observation. Because alpha particles are positively charged, Rutherford inferred that a small region of positive charge in the atoms repelled them. As shown in **Figure 5.6**, he proposed that all the positively charged material in an atom formed a small dense centre, and that the electrons would have to be separated from it. He named this centre the **nucleus** of the atom. He also proposed that the negatively charged electrons revolved around the nucleus. Rutherford's model is sometimes referred to as the planetary model because the motion of the electrons around the nucleus resembles the motion of the planets around the Sun.

Figure 5.6 Rutherford's atomic model includes a dense, positively charged nucleus in the centre.

nucleus in chemistry, the positively charged centre of an atom

Learning Check

1. Using a diagram, explain how Dalton viewed atoms of a single element and how he viewed atoms of different elements.

2. Thomson's experimental evidence indicated that all atoms contain the same negatively charged particles. Describe Thomson's experimental evidence.

3. What was the difference between Thomson's model of the atom and Dalton's model of the atom?

4. Sketch Rutherford's model of the atom.

Bohr's Description of Energy Levels

Although Rutherford's model of the atom explained the existence of a positively charged nucleus, many scientists opposed this model. At the time, it was known that objects with opposite charges attract each other. The question posed by many scientists was, "If Rutherford's model is correct, why don't the negatively charged electrons spiral into the positive nucleus and collide with it?" In 1912, a Danish scientist named Neils Bohr arrived in England to study with Rutherford. It was Bohr who was able to provide an answer to that question.

Electron Energy Levels

Bohr believed that Rutherford's atomic model was fundamentally correct but not quite complete. Bohr was fascinated by what happens when an electric current passes through hydrogen gas: the hydrogen atoms release bands of light in a pattern, and each band of colour corresponds to a specific amount of energy. Bohr wanted his new theory of the atom to be able to explain the evidence that unique bands of light are given off by all the elements. He proposed that electrons could only move within fixed regions or *energy levels,* rather than being able to move anywhere around the nucleus. For an electron to move from one energy level to a higher one, the electron must absorb a specific amount of energy, called a *quantum.* This can be compared to a person on a ladder, as shown in **Figure 5.7**. Someone on a ladder can be only certain distances above the ground because of the positions of the rungs of the ladder. It is not possible for someone to stand between the rungs of a ladder.

This model of the atom, with a central positive nucleus and electrons in energy levels around the nucleus, is often called the *Bohr-Rutherford model.* Although there have been additional changes and refinements to our understanding of the atom, this model is still very useful today. You will learn how to draw the Bohr-Rutherford model in the next section.

Study Toolkit

Asking Questions While reading this page, stop periodically to ask who, what, and why questions related to energy levels. As you read, record your answers in your notebook. If a question is not answered, check to make sure you understand the relevant material.

Figure 5.7 Bohr proposed that electrons could only occupy certain energy levels. This is similar to how a person on a ladder can only be at certain heights, according to the position of each rung.

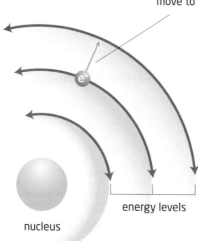

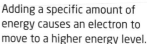

Adding a specific amount of energy causes an electron to move to a higher energy level.

energy levels

nucleus

Learning Check

5. What did Bohr discover about the movement of electrons?

6. Sketch the Bohr-Rutherford model of the atom.

7. How can an electron move from one energy level to a higher energy level?

8. Provide an everyday example that represents how electrons occupy specific energy levels.

The Nucleus

Since before Thomson proposed his model of the atom, scientists knew that atoms must have some type of positive charge. Rutherford's model of the atom showed that this positive charge had to be within the nucleus. Eventually, after many years of work by several scientists, the positive charge was identified and called the **proton**. Scientific evidence indicated, however, that there had to be more to the nucleus than just the protons. For example, Rutherford knew that the mass of a nucleus was more than the mass of the protons alone. From this, he inferred that the nucleus must be composed of two types of particles: the positively charged proton and a neutral particle. Although scientists knew that this neutral particle existed, it was not until 1932 that someone was able to demonstrate this. A British physicist named James Chadwick, who had once worked for Rutherford, was the first person to show experimentally that neutral particles, now called **neutrons**, help to make up the nuclei of most atoms. In 1935, Chadwick was awarded the Nobel Prize in physics for this discovery.

Sense of scale

Suppose that you represented the nucleus of an atom by a loonie placed at centre ice of a hockey rink. The atom itself would be larger than the hockey arena!

proton a positively charged particle that is part of every atomic nucleus

neutron an uncharged particle that is part of almost every atomic nucleus

Activity 5-3

Atomic Model Time Line

The model of the atom, as we know it today, is the combined result of the work of many scientists. In this activity, you will draw a time line to summarize the essential discoveries that contributed to the evolution of the atomic model. Do you see any important connections between the scientists on your time line?

Materials

- graph paper
- coloured pencils

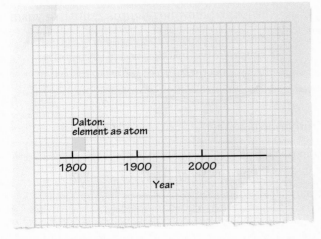

Procedure

1. Place a piece of graph paper in landscape orientation.

2. Draw a line along the bottom of the paper. For the scale on your time line, let each square represent 10 years. Begin the scale at the year 1800, and mark the years 1900 and 2000 along the bottom of the paper, below the line you drew.

3. Draw a coloured line on your grid to represent Dalton's work. The coloured lines that you draw need only represent an estimated time frame, based on the dates provided. Print Dalton's name and one or two of his accomplishments. Include a sketch of his proposed atomic model. Add the names and accomplishments of the other scientists you learned about in this section. If there is some type of relationship between the scientists (for example, if one was a student of another), include the relationship on your time line.

Questions

1. How does your time line show that the development of the model of the atom was dependent on scientists working together and communicating with each other?

2. How do you think improvements in technologies helped to improve the model of the atom?

Section Summary

- John Dalton's atomic theory described elements in terms of atoms, which he believed to be small, indivisible particles that make up all matter. He stated that all the atoms of the same element are identical in mass and size, but different elements are made up of different atoms.

- Joseph John Thomson determined that atoms contain negatively charged particles, which are now called electrons. He developed a model of the atom that shows electrons inserted throughout a mass of positively charged material.

- Ernest Rutherford updated the model of the atom as mostly empty space, with a small, dense, positively charged nucleus in the centre. His continued work, as well as that of others, eventually led to identification of the proton and neutron in the nucleus.

- Neils Bohr revised Rutherford's model of the atom by stating that electrons are stable in specific energy levels around the nucleus.

Review Questions

K/U **1.** According to Dalton's atomic theory, what are elements and what makes one element different from another?

K/U **2.** What did Thomson discover about atoms?

T/I **3.** Why is Rutherford's model of the atom called the planetary model?

C **4.** In your own words, describe Rutherford's experiment, shown in **Figure 5.5**. Sketch what Rutherford expected to observe in his experiment.

K/U **5.** What evidence did Bohr want his model of the atom to explain?

C **6.** Name the particles labelled A, B, and C in the diagram below.

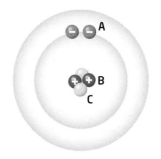

This is a Bohr-Rutherford model of an atom.

K/U **7.** Compare Thomson's model of the atom with Rutherford's model.

T/I **8.** Rutherford used alpha particles in his gold foil experiment. How might the results of his experiment have changed if he had used negative particles instead of positive particles?

5.2 The Structure of the Atom

Key Terms
atomic number
mass number
isotope

The next time you see someone talking on a tiny cellphone, stop and think about atoms. Understanding atoms has helped to make electronic devices smaller and more powerful than they were just a few years ago. **Figure 5.8** shows the change in cellphones over time. In the past, electronic devices relied on circuits made from metal wires and circuit components that were large and bulky. As scientists learned more about atoms, however, they developed ways to build up layers of atoms of different elements on a wafer-thin piece of silicon. This allowed them to build very small circuit components. Thus, scientists have used their understanding of the structure of atoms to create new materials that have helped to make the miniaturization of cellphones possible.

1991

1998

?

2009

Figure 5.8 Due to advances in our knowledge of atoms, today's portable cellphones are much smaller and have many more features than earlier models. Imagine what phones will be like in the future!

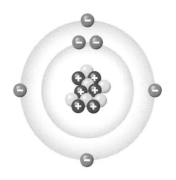

Figure 5.9 This diagram represents an atom of the element carbon.

Inside the Atom

An atom, such as the one drawn in **Figure 5.9**, is the smallest particle of an element that has the same properties of the element. We now know that the atom is composed of many subatomic particles. There are three main types of subatomic particles: protons and neutrons, which make up the nucleus, and electrons, which move in specific regions around the nucleus. Each type of subatomic particle has its own set of properties. Some of these properties are summarized in **Table 5.1**.

Table 5.1 Subatomic Particles

Name	Relative Mass	Electric Charge	Location in the Atom
proton	1836	+	nucleus
neutron	1837	0	nucleus
electron	1	−	energy levels surrounding the nucleus

atomic number the number of protons in the nucleus of an atom

mass number the sum of the number of protons and the number of neutrons in the nucleus of an atom

Protons and Neutrons

Protons and neutrons contribute nearly all the mass of an atom. Neutrons have slightly more mass than protons, but both neutrons and protons have about 1840 times more mass than electrons. This is often referred to as the relative mass of protons and neutrons, compared to electrons. Neutrons have no charge, so they neither attract nor repel protons due to electric charge. Neutrons and protons do attract each other, however, by a force called the *strong force*. This force is the strongest in nature and overcomes the repulsion between positively charged protons. Otherwise, nuclei with more than one proton would never form. Because both protons and neutrons make up the nucleus of an atom, they are often referred to as *nucleons*.

The number of protons in the nucleus of an atom is the **atomic number**. The atomic number identifies an atom as a particular element. For example, there are six protons in the atom shown in **Figure 5.9**, making this atom an element with an atomic number of 6. The element with an atomic number of 6 is carbon. No matter where that atom is in the universe, it will always be carbon. If a proton is added or removed by some type of nuclear reaction, the atom is no longer carbon—it is a completely different element.

The sum of the number of protons and the number of neutrons in an atom is called the **mass number**. The mass number is always a whole number. By knowing the mass number and the atomic number of an atom, you can determine the number of protons, the number of neutrons, and the number of electrons that make up that atom.

> ### Calculating the Number of Subatomic Particles
> atomic number = number of protons
> mass number = number of protons + number of neutrons
> number of neutrons = mass number − atomic number
> number of protons = number of electrons (neutral atom)

Representing Elements

The development of chemical symbols to represent the elements allowed chemists to communicate their findings more easily. Just as it is easier to write "4378" instead of "four thousand three hundred and seventy-eight," it is easier and much less time consuming for chemists to write "Mg" instead of "magnesium." Also, every language has its own way of saying and spelling the names of the elements. The symbols that are used to represent the elements, however, are the same throughout the world—the system is international. So, while a French Canadian scientist may say "hydrogène" and an Italian scientist may say "idrogeno," both use the symbol H to represent hydrogen.

A common notation that scientists use to represent atoms of elements is shown in **Figure 5.10**. This notation, called the *standard atomic notation*, includes the atomic number and mass number of an atom of an element. The mass number is always placed to the top and left of the symbol for the element. The atomic number is always placed to the bottom and left of the symbol. In the next activity, you will practise using symbols to represent elements and you will learn how to use this type of notation properly.

mass number — 11
atomic number — 5
B — symbol for boron

Figure 5.10 This notation provides information about an atom of an element, such as boron.

Activity 5-4

What's Your Number?

Symbols were assigned to the elements as an international way to represent the elements, regardless of language. Standard atomic notation of the elements also provides a universal method of representing atoms of elements. Can you determine some of the rules that are used for assigning symbols to the elements?

Materials

- Appendix A: Properties of Common Substances

Questions

1. The most common elements in your body are oxygen, carbon, hydrogen, and nitrogen. What are the symbols for these elements? Write a rule that might have been used to create these symbols.

2. Calcium is another important element in your body. It is present in your bones, teeth, and blood.

   a. What is the symbol for calcium? Write a rule that might have been used to create this symbol.

   b. What would be the symbol for calcium if you used the rule you wrote in step 1? Why can this not be the symbol for calcium?

3. The Latin names of some metals were used for centuries: *argentum* for silver, *aurum* for gold, *cuprum* for copper, *ferrum* for iron, *hydrargyrum* for mercury, *plumbum* for lead, and *stannum* for tin. Infer possible symbols for these elements. Use Appendix A to check your inferences. Are there exceptions to the rules you wrote in steps 1 and 2 for these symbols? If so, identify them.

4. Copy and complete the table below. Provide a title for your table.

Standard Atomic Notation	Name of Element	Atomic Number	Mass Number	Number of Electrons	Number of Protons	Number of Neutrons
$^{12}_{6}\mathrm{C}$						
$^{65}_{30}\mathrm{Zn}$						
	sulfur	16				16
	calcium		40		20	
	nitrogen	7	14			

Representing Atoms

The Bohr-Rutherford model that was introduced in the previous section is a convenient way of representing the atomic structure of an element. According to this model, electrons occupy specific energy levels, which are sometimes called *shells*. Electrons in levels that are farther from the nucleus have more energy than electrons in levels that are closer to the nucleus. The number of electrons that can occupy each energy level changes as you move outward from the nucleus. You will learn more about the distribution of electrons in energy levels in later science courses. The box below provides a step-by-step description of how to draw Bohr-Rutherford models for atoms with atomic numbers between 1 and 20.

The diagrams in **Figure 5.11** are examples of Bohr-Rutherford models of the atom potassium, which has 19 electrons. Bohr-Rutherford models that you will draw should resemble the diagram on the right.

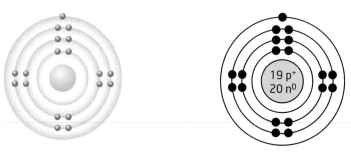

Figure 5.11 Both of these diagrams represent an atom of potassium.

How to Draw Bohr-Rutherford Models

1. Draw a circle that represents the nucleus. Indicate the number of protons and neutrons in the nucleus. You can use the symbols "p^+" to represent protons and "n^0" to represent neutrons.

2. Determine the number of electrons in the atom. Draw the different energy levels using circles around the nucleus.

3. Starting with the energy level nearest the nucleus, put in up to two electrons. Once the first energy level is full, fill the second one with up to eight electrons. Add up to eight electrons to the third energy level, and then the final two electrons to the fourth energy level.

4. Electrons should be placed according to the sequence depicted in the diagram. When filling the first energy level, place the first electron where the 12:00 position is on a clock. Then add the next electron beside it. For the second energy level, begin at the 12:00 position. Then, continue adding electrons at the 3:00 position, then the 6:00 position, and then the 9:00 position. If there are more than four electrons to be added, repeat this pattern. Adding electrons to the third and fourth energy levels is done in the same manner.

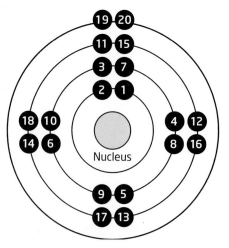

The numbers indicate the sequence to follow when adding the first 20 electrons to Bohr-Rutherford models.

Activity 5-5

Make Your Own Atom

Making a three-dimensional model of an atom can help you remember that atoms are not fixed structures, as they appear to be in diagrams. Electrons move in three-dimensional paths, not simple circles. How accurate can you make your model of an atom?

Suggested Materials

- metal rings (3 different sizes) or wire
- Styrofoam® ball
- clay (3 different colours)
- string

Procedure

1. Work in groups of four. Your teacher will assign your group the atom of an element and tell you the atomic number and mass number of the atom.

2. Determine the number of protons, neutrons, and electrons in the atom.

3. Draw a Bohr-Rutherford model of the atom. Make sure that your teacher has approved your diagram before you proceed to the next step.

4. Build a three-dimensional model of the atom using the materials provided and your diagram as a guide. Use the Styrofoam® ball to represent the nucleus, and use two different colours of clay to represent the protons and neutrons. Use the third colour of clay to represent the electrons. Attach the electrons to the rings made of wire, matching the electron arrangement in your diagram.

5. Make a mobile by hanging your model with string. This will help to hold together the different parts of your model and allow you to manipulate it.

Questions

1. What were some important details you needed to consider when building your three-dimensional model?

2. In what ways is your three-dimensional model a better representation of the atom than the diagram you drew on paper?

3. In what ways do you think your model does not represent an atom accurately?

Isotopes

In **Figure 5.12**, notice that both of the atoms have one proton, but the atom on the right also has a neutron. Even though these atoms are not identical, they are both atoms of the same element, hydrogen, because they have the same number of protons. Atoms of an element that have the same number of protons but a different number of neutrons are called **isotopes** of the element. The atoms shown in **Figure 5.12** are isotopes of hydrogen. Since each isotope has a unique mass number, you can specify an isotope of an element by placing its mass number after the name of the element. For example, the names of these isotopes of hydrogen are hydrogen-1 and hydrogen-2.

> **Suggested Investigation**
>
> Inquiry Investigation 5-A, The Bohr-Rutherford Model of the Atom, on page 212

> **isotope** one of two or more forms of an element that have the same number of protons but a different number of neutrons

hydrogen-1

hydrogen-2

Figure 5.12 These atoms are different isotopes of hydrogen because they have different numbers of neutrons.

Sense of place

The Large Hadron Collider at CERN is the largest particle accelerator in the world. It is used to accelerate subatomic particles and observe what happens when they collide. Here, scientists are hoping to re-create the big bang to better understand the origins of our universe.

A Simple Model of a Complex System

Although models of an atom usually show electrons orbiting around a nucleus, the actual structure of an atom is much more complex. Electrons are thought to exist in cloud-like regions surrounding the nucleus, with different probabilities of finding an electron in a given cloud. In addition, scientists have discovered that protons, neutrons, and electrons are not the only subatomic particles. Since the discovery of the neutron, over 200 other subatomic particles have been identified. Protons and neutrons are actually composed of different types of smaller subatomic particles called quarks.

As scientific technologies continue to improve, the model of the atom will continue to evolve. An exceptional facility that supports this type of research is CERN (Conseil Européen pour la Recherche Nucléaire), shown in **Figure 5.13**. It is the largest laboratory in the world for studying the atom and interactions between subatomic particles. At CERN, thousands of scientists and engineers from more than eight different countries and hundreds of universities work together to uncover even more information about the atom.

Figure 5.13 CERN is located on the border between France and Switzerland. The circle on this photo indicates where the Large Hadron Collider is. This particle accelerator lies about 100 m underground in a tunnel with a circumference of 27 km.

Section Summary

- Atoms are made up of protons, neutrons, and electrons. Protons are positively charged, neutrons have no charge, and electrons are negatively charged.

- The atomic number of an atom is the number of protons in the nucleus. It is always a whole number and identifies the element. The mass number of an atom is the total number of protons and neutrons. Like the atomic number, it is always a whole number.

- Protons and neutrons make up the nucleus and account for most of the mass of the atom. Electrons occupy energy levels outside the nucleus.

- Bohr-Rutherford models are used to depict the atomic structures of elements.

- An element is made up of isotopes, which are atoms that have the same number of protons but different numbers of neutrons.

Review Questions

K/U **1.** What are three types of subatomic particles in the atom? Compare and contrast the properties of these particles, based on information in **Table 5.1**.

K/U **2.** Which particle in the atom has almost no mass?

T/I **3.** If you know the atomic number and the mass number of an isotope of an element, how can you determine the number of protons and neutrons in that atom?

K/U **4.** An istope of oxygen (O) has an atomic number of 8 and a mass number of 16. What is the standard atomic notation for this isotope?

T/I **5.** If an atom has 12 electrons, how many energy levels are occupied?

A **6.** Do the following diagrams show atoms of the same element? Explain.

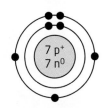 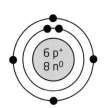

Bohr-Rutherford models provide information that is needed to identify an element.

C **7.** An atom has 8 protons, 9 neutrons, and 8 electrons. Draw a Bohr-Rutherford model of this atom.

T/I **8.** How is a hydrogen-1 atom different from a hydrogen-2 atom? How are they the same?

Key Terms

atomic mass

periodic table

metal

non-metal

metalloid

period

group

5.3 The Periodic Table

Most people have some type of collection, such as a stamp or butterfly collection, or even a sports memorabilia collection, like the one shown in **Figure 5.14**. In order to organize this collection of baseballs, some kind of plan needs to be used. For example, the baseballs could be organized according to the year they were obtained. Alternatively, they could be organized according to the teams that the players who signed them were on. In science, information needs to be organized to help scientists make conclusions or develop new hypotheses.

By the mid-1800s, chemists had discovered more than 50 elements and had determined properties of each. They needed a way to organize all the information, however.

Figure 5.14 When a collection gets too large to be manageable, people often organize the items in some way. How would you organize these baseballs?

Mendeleev's Arrangement of Elements

In the late 1860s, a Russian chemist named Dimitri Mendeleev organized known elements, looking for patterns in the properties. He finally found a pattern when he placed the elements in the order of increasing **atomic mass**. When Mendeleev used atomic mass to organize the elements, he noticed that properties repeated in a pattern that allowed the elements to be organized in a table. Because this organization showed the properties of elements in a pattern of regular intervals, or periodically, Mendeleev's organization of the elements came to be known as the **periodic table**.

Mendeleev left gaps in his table wherever there seemed to be a break in the pattern of the properties. This led to one of the most important features of Mendeleev's table: its usefulness for predicting properties of unknown elements based on the properties of known elements. Mendeleev made several predictions about the properties of unknown elements, which turned out to be correct.

atomic mass the average mass of the naturally occurring isotopes of an element

periodic table a system for organizing the elements into columns and rows, so that elements with similar properties are in the same column

Activity 5-6

What's in Blackbock's Lake?

The water in Blackbock's Lake is very dark and cold, so you cannot see the bottom easily. The people who live near Blackbock's Lake say there are nine different types of fish in the lake. So far, biologists have found only eight types of fish. What might the missing ninth type of fish look like?

Procedure

1. Closely examine the eight fish in the diagram. Look for properties that vary from one fish to another. List the variable properties that you observe.

2. Create a table to organize your observations of the fish. Place similar properties in one row or column. Make your table as organized and consistent as possible.

3. Based on your table, predict the properties of the missing ninth fish.

Questions

1. Which part of this activity took the greatest amount of time and effort? Why?

2. What properties do you think the ninth fish should have? What did you have to assume about the ninth fish?

3. How is this activity similar to what scientists did when organizing the elements into a periodic table?

The Modern Periodic Table

Mendeleev's organization of the elements provided chemists with a valuable tool for studying the elements. Nevertheless, there were a few elements that Mendeleev had to put out of order. This problem was resolved after the discovery of the proton.

Today's periodic table, shown in **Figure 5.15**, is based on arrangement of the elements according to increasing atomic number. Notice how each element has its own box, which contains information about the element. Usually, the name, symbol, atomic number, and atomic mass of the element are included. The legend above the periodic table in **Figure 5.15** shows where this information is located in each box. Note, however, that the periodic table is not in standard atomic notation. The *ion charge* of the element is also included. Some atoms can lose or gain electrons, which makes the atoms become positively or negatively charged. You will look at ionic charges in more detail in Chapter 6, when you study the formation of compounds.

Figure 5.16 on pages 198 and 199 is a pictorial version of the periodic table. For many of the elements, a photograph is provided. What similarities and differences do you see among elements in each row and column?

Synthetic Elements

Go to **scienceontario** to find out more

In the periodic table, most of the elements that have atomic numbers less than 93 are natural—they exist naturally on Earth. The other elements are synthetic—they have been made by scientists. Once the relationships between elements in the periodic table were established, scientists began to predict other elements that could be made. Their predictions were based on what the atomic structure of a synthesized element should be, according to its position in the periodic table. If you look at the names of the synthetic elements, you will see a few that include the names of familiar scientists: for example, curium, mendelevium, rutherfordium, and bohrium.

Today, scientists are still attempting to make new elements. One problem that scientists must always contend with, however, is that new elements are not usually very stable. A new element is often identified based on a single atom that exists for only a small fraction of a second!

Learning Check

1. Why did Mendeleev not consider the number of subatomic particles as a way to organize the elements?

2. How is the modern periodic table organized?

3. Using the periodic table, identify the chemical symbol, atomic number, and atomic mass of the element palladium.

4. Based on what you know about the model of the atom, why do you think new elements can be generated by smashing atoms together?

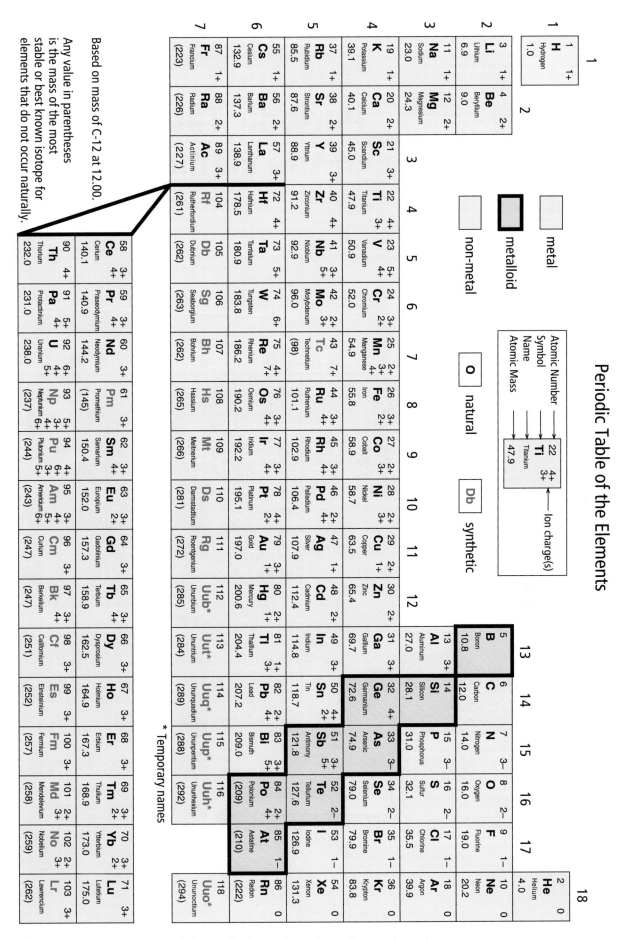

Figure 5.15 Today's periodic table is organized according to increasing atomic number.

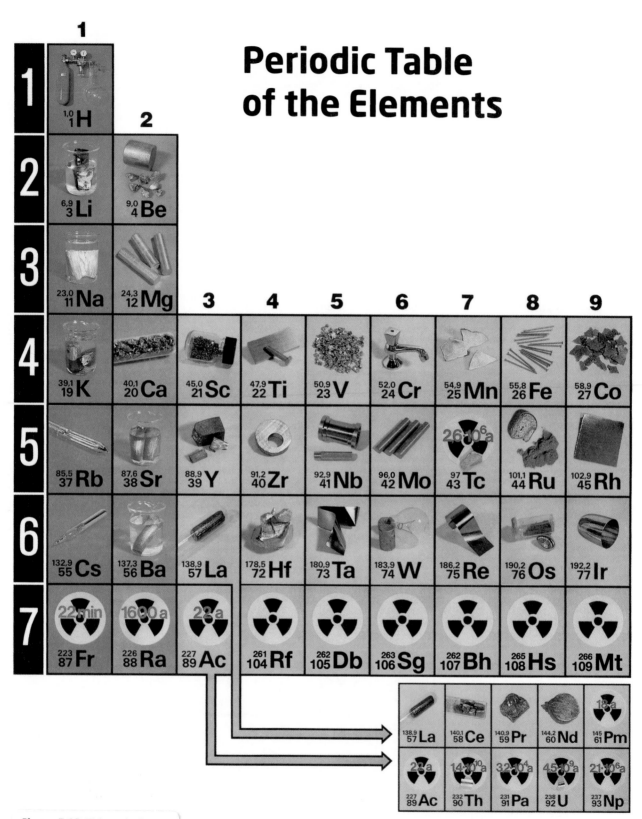

Periodic Table of the Elements

Figure 5.16 This periodic table provides a photographic representation for many of the elements.

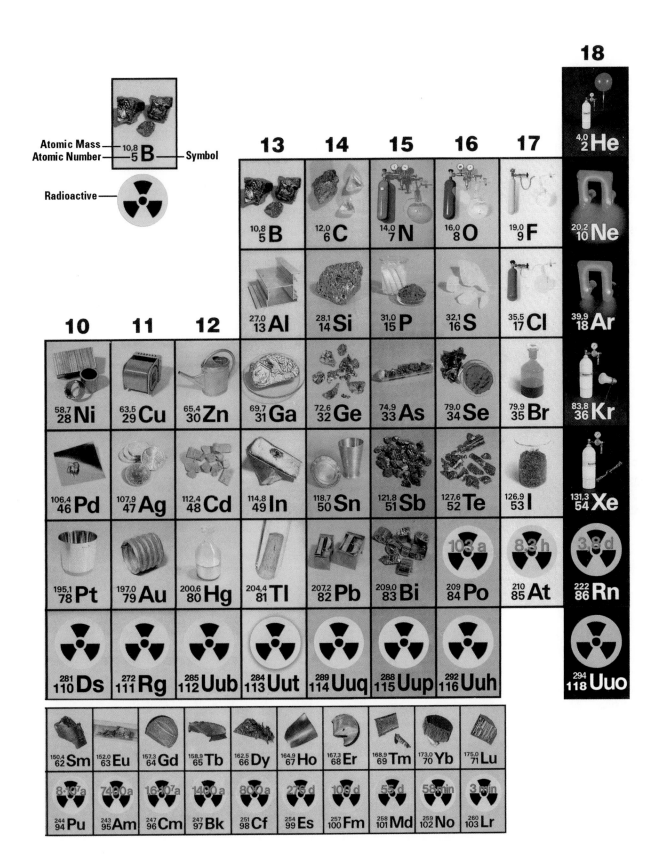

Atomic Mass —10,8
Atomic Number —5 B — Symbol

Radioactive

18

13	14	15	16	17	
					4,0₂He
10,8 5 B	12,0 6 C	14,0 7 N	16,0 8 O	19,0 9 F	20,2 10 Ne
27,0 13 Al	28,1 14 Si	31,0 15 P	32,1 16 S	35,5 17 Cl	39,9 18 Ar

10	11	12						
58,7 28 Ni	63,5 29 Cu	65,4 30 Zn	69,7 31 Ga	72,6 32 Ge	74,9 33 As	79,0 34 Se	79,9 35 Br	83,8 36 Kr
106,4 46 Pd	107,9 47 Ag	112,4 48 Cd	114,8 49 In	118,7 50 Sn	121,8 51 Sb	127,6 52 Te	126,9 53 I	131,3 54 Xe
195,1 78 Pt	197,0 79 Au	200,6 80 Hg	204,4 81 Tl	207,2 82 Pb	209,0 83 Bi	209 84 Po	210 85 At	222 86 Rn
281 110 Ds	272 111 Rg	285 112 Uub	284 113 Uut	289 114 Uuq	288 115 Uup	292 116 Uuh		294 118 Uuo

150,4 62 Sm	152,0 63 Eu	157,3 64 Gd	158,9 65 Tb	162,5 66 Dy	164,9 67 Ho	167,3 68 Er	168,9 69 Tm	173,0 70 Yb	175,0 71 Lu
244 94 Pu	243 95 Am	247 96 Cm	247 97 Bk	251 98 Cf	254 99 Es	257 100 Fm	258 101 Md	259 102 No	260 103 Lr

Classes of Elements in the Periodic Table

metal typically, an element that is hard, shiny, malleable, and ductile, and is a good conductor of heat and electricity

non-metal typically, an element that is not shiny, malleable, or ductile, and is a poor conductor of heat and electricity

metalloid an element that shares some properties with metals and some properties with non-metals

The position of an element, relative to other elements in the periodic table, provides a way to predict the physical and chemical properties of the element.

Most of the elements are classified as either a **metal** or a **non-metal**, according to distinct properties. The shortened form of the periodic table in **Figure 5.17** shows where these two classes of elements appear in the periodic table. The elements on the left side of the periodic table (except hydrogen) are metals. The elements on the right side of the periodic table are non-metals. The properties of metals and non-metals are summarized in **Table 5.2**. Some of the properties of metals and non-metals are also represented in the pictorial periodic table in **Figure 5.16** (previous two pages).

Notice that there are several elements in **Figure 5.17** that fall in a diagonal line between the metals and the non-metals. These elements are called the **metalloids**. As their location in the periodic table suggests, they share some properties with metals (possibly shiny; solid at room temperature) and some properties with non-metals (brittle and not ductile; poor conductors of heat and electricity). **Figure 5.18**, on the page opposite, provides some interesting examples of elements that you probably know about, as well as some applications that you may not know about. If you look for these elements in the periodic table, you will see that they are all examples of metals.

Table 5.2 Physical Properties of Metals and Non-metals

Material	State at Room Temperature (20°C)	Appearance	Conductivity	Malleability and Ductility
Metals	solid (except for mercury, which is a liquid)	shiny	good conductors of heat and electricity	malleable and ductile
Non-metals	some gases and some solids (except bromine, which is a liquid)	not very shiny	poor conductors of heat and electricity	brittle and not ductile

All the metals appear on the left side.

All the non-metals (except hydrogen) appear on the right side.

The metalloids form a diagonal line toward the right side.

1 H								2 He
3 Li	4 Be		5 B	6 C	7 N	8 O	9 F	10 Ne
11 Na	12 Mg		13 Al	14 Si	15 P	16 S	17 Cl	18 Ar
19 K	20 Ca		31 Ga	32 Ge	33 As	34 Se	35 Br	36 Kr
37 Rb	38 Sr		49 In	50 Sn	51 Sb	52 Te	53 I	54 Xe
55 Cs	56 Ba		81 Tl	82 Pb	83 Bi	84 Po	85 At	86 Rn

Figure 5.17 The elements in the blue boxes are metals. The elements in the yellow boxes are non-metals. Metalloids are in the green boxes.

Figure 5.18

Most of us think of gold as a shiny yellow metal used to make jewellery. However, it is an element that is also used in more unexpected ways, such as in spacecraft parts. On the other hand, some less common elements, such as americium (am-uh-REE-see-um), are used in everyday objects. Some elements and their uses are shown here.

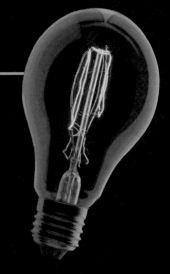

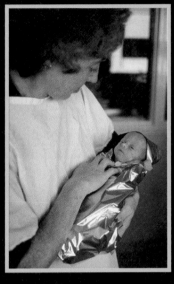

▲ ALUMINUM
Aluminum is an excellent reflector of heat. Here, an aluminum plastic laminate is used to retain the body heat of a newborn baby.

▲ TUNGSTEN
Tungsten has been used as a filament in older models of light bulbs. Due to its high melting point and electrical conductivity, tungsten is used in electrical and electronic industries, as well as in alloys with other metals.

▲ TITANIUM (tie-TAY-nee-um) Parts of the exterior of the Guggenheim Museum in Bilbao, Spain, are made of titanium panels. Strong and lightweight, titanium is also used for body implants.

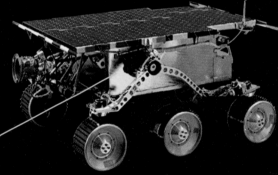

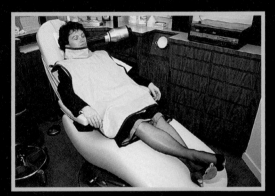

▲ GOLD Gold's resistance to corrosion and its ability to reflect infrared radiation make it an excellent coating for space vehicles. The electronic box on the six-wheel Sojourner Rover, above, part of NASA's Pathfinder 1997 mission to Mars, is coated with gold.

▲ LEAD Because lead has a high density, it is a good barrier to radiation. Dentists drape lead aprons on patients before taking X rays of the patient's teeth to reduce radiation exposure.

◄ AMERICIUM Named after America, where it was first produced, americium is a component of this smoke detector. It is a radioactive metal that must be handled with care to avoid contact.

Mining for Metals

Some elements, such as gold and copper, are precious metals, easy to shape, and found in nature. Because of these properties, Aboriginal peoples have used them to make tools and ornaments for thousands of years. More recently, however, the mining of precious metals has had serious social and environmental impacts.

Today, gold mining relies a great deal on chemistry. The gold is extracted using a cyanide-based chemical to dissolve it. Not only do the mines disrupt the land and potentially harm ecosystems, but there is also a significant risk of the cyanide solution getting into the soil and ground water and contaminating surrounding areas. Cyanide is an extremely toxic substance for humans and wildlife.

Over 85 percent of the gold that is now mined is used for non-essential items, such as jewellery. This fact, combined with the serious environmental concerns associated with gold mining, have prompted many people to buy jewellery made from materials other than gold or to buy only recycled or vintage gold jewellery.

Sense of  place

Bingham Canyon, in Utah, is a mine that produces copper, gold, molybdenum, and silver. It is 4 km across and 1.5 km deep, making it the world's largest open-pit mine. It is so large that it is visible from space.

STSE Case Study

Diamond Mining: Beyond the Sparkle

Canada's diamond mining industry is the third largest in the world, with an annual worth of over $1.5 billion. Although economically successful, diamond mines are located in ecologically sensitive environments that provide essential plant and wildlife resources for local Aboriginal peoples. Many people are asking whether the benefits of diamond mining outweigh the damage done to the environment.

Canada's first diamond mine, the Ekati Diamond Mine, opened in 1998. It is about 300 km from Yellowknife in the Northwest Territories.

Environmental Challenges

Diamond mines can be very disruptive to the surrounding land and waterways. Removal of huge amounts of soil and rock is required. Some diamonds lie beneath lakes, which need to be drained. Roads, airstrips, and power plants that are often built to service the mines can also affect the land. When lakes are drained or water quality changes, fish habitats can be affected. Also, wildlife is often displaced by mines.

Mining can produce large amounts of pollution and waste. Using electricity or fossil fuels, such as diesel, gas, and oil, creates gas emissions that contribute to pollution and climate change.

Meeting the Challenges

Efforts are being made to minimize the social and environmental challenges that are associated with diamond mining. Reclaiming the land that was mined can be done by saving the rock and soil that were removed and putting them back once the mining has stopped. Drained lakes can be refilled with water, and seeds from native plants can be harvested for replanting. The Diavik Diamond Mine monitors caribou, wolverine, grizzly bear, and raptor (bird of prey) activity to ensure minimal impact on local wildlife.

To conserve energy, the Ekati Diamond Mine has established an Energy Smart Program. It includes reducing the use of diesel fuel, recycling waste oil, and promoting energy saving among its employees.

Metals and Health

Metals are not only important economically. They are also part of essential processes in plants and animals. For example, iron is present in blood and is essential for oxygen transport throughout the human body. In fact, iron is present in every body cell, where it is used for important reactions. Other metals that are essential for plants and animals include copper, zinc, magnesium, and calcium.

Metals at too high a level, however, can be harmful. For example, people who must undergo multiple blood transfusions over a period of time can accumulate too much iron, which is present in the transfused blood. This can cause iron to accumulate in the body and severely harm the heart and liver. Exposure to toxic metals in the environment can also occur. Like DDT, which was discussed in Chapter 4, certain metals can bioaccumulate and biomagnify. These metals tend to accumulate in the organs of animals, especially the kidneys and liver. This accumulation can ultimately damage the organs. Some of the toxic metals in the environment include arsenic, aluminum, lead, and mercury.

Suggested Investigation

Inquiry Investigation 5-B, Physical Properties of Metals and Non-metals, on page 213

Sense of

The American eel was once an important food source for Aboriginal peoples in eastern Canada. These eels now show elevated levels of toxins and metals.

1 Ekati Diamond Mine
2 Diavik Diamond Mine
3 Jericho Diamond Mine
4 Snap Lake Diamond Mine
5 Victor Diamond Mine

Diamond Mines and Local Communities

Canada's five diamond mines contribute in many ways to the local communities:

- Some diamond mines are governed by agreements that provide social benefits to the communities, such as training and community programs.

- When possible, local people are hired to work at diamond mines or in support industries, such as maintenance, catering, and transportation.

- Mining companies give donations to local communities and sponsor community events and scholarships.

- Some diamond mines have business venture development programs to encourage the success of local businesses.

Your Turn

1. Make a PMI (plus, minus, interesting) chart for diamond mining in Canada, based on what you have read.

2. BHP Billiton, Rio Tinto, Tahera, and De Beers are companies that own diamond mines in Canada. Research one of these companies. Report what steps, if any, the company is taking to minimize the social and environmental challenges that are associated with diamond mining.

3. Suppose that you are a newspaper reporter who has been assigned to write an article about the social and environmental effects of mining. Choose a metal that is mined in Ontario, such as nickel, gold, silver, or platinum. Research and write an article about the mining industry for the metal you chose. Make sure that you discuss both positive and negative effects of the industry. You can use this case study about diamond mining as a model.

Mercury Pollution of Aboriginal Lands

⊙⊙⊙

Study Toolkit

Visualizing As you read this page, visualize how mercury poisoning can occur in aquatic environments. Use the steps outlined in the table on page 178 for this visualization process.

Although some mercury occurs naturally, most of the mercury in the environment is the result of human activities. These activities include burning waste materials and fossil fuels, such as oil and coal, as well as other industrial operations. Animals do not easily take up mercury when it is present on its own. Some bacteria, however, can convert elemental mercury to a form called methyl mercury, which can be taken up by animals. These bacteria are most active in aquatic environments. This is why waterways are a key source of mercury poisoning.

For centuries, Aboriginal peoples have lived off the land, as shown in **Figure 5.19**. Since the 1970s, however, high levels of mercury have been measured in many of the waterways on Aboriginal lands, particularly in northwestern Ontario. Methyl mercury has contaminated drinking water sources and fish that inhabit the lakes and rivers. This mercury poisoning has been devastating to Aboriginal communities. It has caused severe illnesses in many people, and it has forced communities to stop the important traditional practice of fishing. Fishing represents not only an important source of food for the communities, but also an important source of income through commercial fishing.

Figure 5.19 Fishing has been an important traditional practice for Aboriginal peoples. It has been threatened by the presence of mercury in waterways on Indigenous lands.

Making a Difference

Fluorescent tubes are popular alternatives to conventional light bulbs. The tubes, however, contain mercury, which is toxic to the environment. Many tubes are not recycled and end up in landfills. Hamilton student Patrick Bowman was in Grade 7 when he studied the issue for his science fair project. He learned that up to 1 350 000 mg of mercury from fluorescent tubes enter his city's landfill each year.

To determine the effects these tubes might have on the environment, Patrick made two model landfills using compost. He put broken tubes into one landfill and left the other uncontaminated. He added rainwater to the landfills to model leachate, a liquid produced when precipitation and landfill waste mix. Patrick found that the uncontaminated landfill and leachate supported plant growth and micro-organism life better than the contaminated landfill and leachate. His project "Shedding the Lights from Landfill Sites" won several awards at the 2006 Canada Wide Science Fair.

How could you help raise your community's awareness of the hazards associated with the disposal of fluorescent tubes?

Periods and Groups in the Periodic Table

As you have seen, elements are listed in the periodic table by increasing order of atomic number. You can describe the position of an element in the periodic table by giving its period and group. A horizontal row in the periodic table is a **period**. The periods are numbered from 1 to 7, beginning in the first row of the periodic table and moving downward. A vertical column in the periodic table is a **group**. The groups are numbered from 1 to 18, beginning at the left-hand side of the periodic table and moving across to the right-hand side. A group is also called a family because the elements in a group tend to have very similar physical and chemical properties. If you look back at **Figure 5.15** on page 197, you will see the group and period numbers in the periodic table.

Four well-known groups are the alkali metals, the alkaline-earth metals, the halogens, and the noble gases. **Figure 5.20** shows examples of elements from each of these groups and highlights the important properties of each group.

period a horizontal row of elements in the periodic table

group a vertical column of elements in the periodic table

Figure 5.20 The alkali metals, alkaline-earth metals, halogens, and noble gases have characteristic properties.

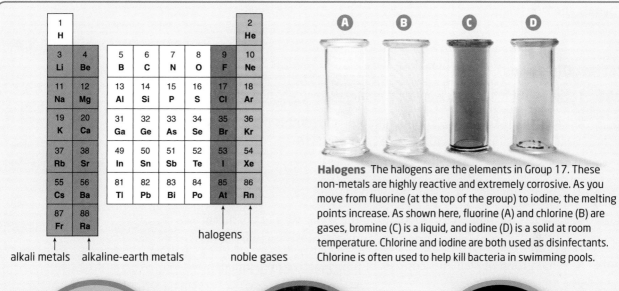

Halogens The halogens are the elements in Group 17. These non-metals are highly reactive and extremely corrosive. As you move from fluorine (at the top of the group) to iodine, the melting points increase. As shown here, fluorine (A) and chlorine (B) are gases, bromine (C) is a liquid, and iodine (D) is a solid at room temperature. Chlorine and iodine are both used as disinfectants. Chlorine is often used to help kill bacteria in swimming pools.

Alkali Metals The alkali metals are the elements in Group 1 (except for hydrogen). These metals have low melting points. Like the freshly cut sodium shown, they are soft enough to be cut with a knife. They are highly reactive. In fact, these metals are usually stored in kerosene or oil to keep water and oxygen away.

Alkaline-Earth Metals The alkaline-earth metals are the elements in Group 2. These metals are highly reactive, but they are less reactive than the alkali metals. If they are heated, they will burn in air. Because they produce bright, colourful flames, the alkaline-earth metals and their compounds are often used in fireworks. Magnesium, shown here, burns with a bright, white light.

Noble Gases The noble gases are the elements in Group 18. These non-metals are all odourless, colourless gases at room temperature. The main property that defines this group, however, is their non-reactivity. The hot metal filament in a light bulb will not react with a noble gas. Therefore, energy-efficient light bulbs, like the one shown here, are filled with argon to extend the life of the filament.

Section 5.3 Review

Section Summary

- The modern periodic table is organized according to the atomic numbers of the elements. When the elements are arranged in order of increasing atomic number, there is a regular repeating pattern in the properties of the elements.

- The three main classes of elements are metals, non-metals, and metalloids. Metals are usually solids at room temperature, shiny, good conductors, malleable, and ductile. Non-metals are usually gases or solids at room temperature, not shiny, poor conductors, brittle, and not ductile. Metalloids share properties of both metals and non-metals.

- Poisoning by metals in the environment is a serious problem. Mercury contamination of fish has severely affected the health and traditional practices of Aboriginal peoples.

- In the periodic table, a period is a horizontal row of elements. A group, or family, is a vertical column of elements. Elements that are in the same group have similar properties. Four major groups of elements in the periodic table are the alkali metals, alkaline-earth metals, halogens, and noble gases.

Review Questions

T/I 1. How did Mendeleev's work help in the discovery of new elements?

K/U 2. Identify the full name, atomic number, and atomic mass of each element, using the periodic table in **Figure 5.15**.

    a. K   **b.** P   **c.** N

K/U 3. What properties are associated with metals?

T/I 4. How has the presence of mercury in the waterways of northern Ontario affected the environment and lives of Aboriginal peoples?

K/U 5. What group of elements consists of non-reactive non-metals?

C 6. A new scam on the Internet involves people selling samples of sodium that they collected from a secret river in the mountains. Write a short statement to explain why this is a scam.

K/U 7. Identify the features of the periodic table on the right, which are indicated by labels A to E.

A 8. What element is at each of the following positions in the periodic table in **Figure 5.15** on page 197? Provide the full name and symbol.

    a. Group 2, Period 3

    b. Group 14, Period 2

    c. Group 18, Period 4

The periodic table is organized into regions with characteristic features.

5.4 Trends in the Periodic Table

Think about all the things that change over time or in a predictable way. For example, the size of the computer has continually decreased over time. You may become more and more excited about a special event as it approaches. There is a definite trend in each of these examples because changes occur gradually at specific intervals. By analyzing the trends, you can make a fairly good prediction about the situation at a certain point in the future.

In a similar way, you can see trends in the properties of elements in the periodic table. As you look across a period or down a group, several properties of elements change in a regular way. The alternate periodic table, shown in **Figure 5.21** is based on a different trend analysis than the standard periodic table that you are used to seeing. The "arms" that stick out from the spiral are the lanthanides and actinides. These are the elements that are in the two rows below the standard periodic table.

Figure 5.21 You might not recognize this chart as a periodic table, but it is. The designer of this table used a spiral format to emphasize certain trends.

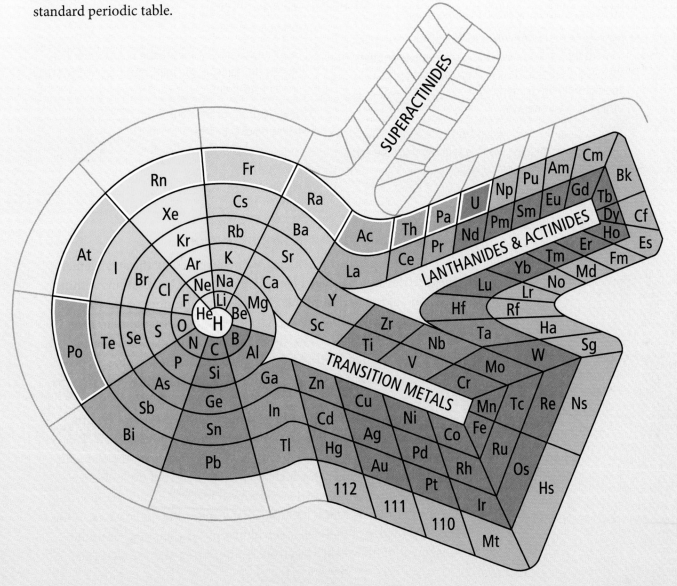

Activity 5-7

The Bohr-Rutherford Periodic Table

To help you understand the structure of the periodic table, you will apply the thinking skills you used in Activity 5-6 to examine the Bohr-Rutherford model cards you made in Investigation 5-A. Can you see any trends in the atomic structures of the first 20 elements?

Materials

- 20 Bohr-Rutherford index cards, which you made in Investigation 5-A

Procedure

1. Arrange the cards that you made in Investigation 5-A so that each Bohr-Rutherford diagram is face up on your desk. Examine each card. In what ways are the cards different? In what ways are they the same?

2. Arrange the cards into rows, so that all the cards in one row are the same in one way but different in another way. Then arrange the cards into columns, so that all the cards in one column are the same in one way but different in another way.

3. Keep moving the cards around until you are satisfied that you have the best possible table, with all the cards arranged in the most logical way.

4. Flip over each card, without moving the card to a different position, so that you can see the name and symbol on the card. Compare your arrangement of the cards with the arrangement of the elements in the periodic table.

5. If your cards do not match the periodic table, turn them over and repeat steps 2 to 4.

6. Once your cards match the periodic table, turn them over again so that you can use the Bohr-Rutherford models to answer the questions below.

Questions

1. Examine Row 2. How are the Bohr-Rutherford models the same across the whole row? How are they different?

2. Examine Column 2. How are the Bohr-Rutherford models the same as you read down the column? How are they different?

3. What features of the Bohr-Rutherford models do not follow an exactly logical pattern?

Reactivity and the Outermost Electrons

Many of the properties of elements are determined by the arrangement of the electrons in the outermost occupied energy level. Atoms within the same group in the periodic table have the same number of electrons in their outer energy level. As a result, elements in a group tend to react in a similar way. The electrons in the outermost occupied energy level of an atom are called **valence electrons**. **Figure 5.22**, on the next page, points out several important trends that occur in the arrangement of electrons in atoms.

In the previous section, **Figure 5.20** highlighted differences among four groups of elements. For example, the elements in Group 18 (the noble gases) are non-reactive non-metals. In comparison, the elements in Group 17 (the halogens), which are just to the left of the noble gases, are the most reactive non-metals. The most reactive metals are in Group 1 (the alkali metals), which are immediately after the noble gases. Why are the reactivities of these elements different? The answer lies in the arrangement of the valence electrons in the atoms of these elements.

valence electron an electron in the outermost occupied energy level of an atom

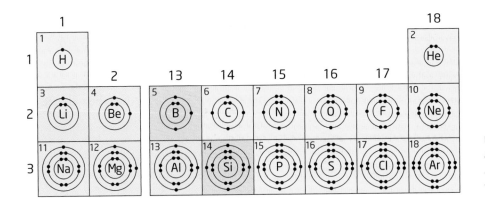

Figure 5.22 Several patterns are visible in the electron arrangements in atoms of the first 18 elements.

Filling the Outer Energy Levels

During a chemical reaction, one atom can join with another atom by gaining, losing, or sharing valence electrons. (You will learn more about these changes in atoms in the next chapter.) The noble gases are non-reactive because their atoms do not gain, lose, or share electrons easily with other atoms. Helium atoms (with two valence electrons) and atoms of the other noble gases (with eight valence electrons) have the maximum number of electrons in their outermost occupied energy level. These atoms are said to have a full set of valence electrons, or a full outer energy level. Having a full outer energy level of electrons provides chemical stability, so these elements do not react easily with other elements.

Atoms of elements other than the noble gases can achieve a full outer energy level, and therefore more stability, by gaining, losing, or sharing electrons. In general, the closer that an element is to the noble gases (either right or left) in the periodic table, the more reactive the element is. By looking at the models in **Figure 5.23** below, you can see why the elements in Groups 1 and 17 are very reactive, as shown in **Figure 5.24**. The atoms of these elements are only one electron away from having a full set of valence electrons. Atoms of the elements in Group 2 (alkaline-earth metals) must lose two electrons to have a full set of valence electrons. So, alkaline-earth metals tend to be less reactive than alkali metals.

Figure 5.24 As you can see in this photo, sodium is highly reactive with water.

Group 17:
very reactive

Noble gas:
non-reactive

Group 1:
very reactive

Figure 5.23 The element to either side of a noble gas on the periodic table is very reactive. This is because they only need to lose or gain one electron to achieve the same electron arrangement as a noble gas atom.

Reactivity and Atom Size

The distance from the centre of the nucleus to the outermost electrons determines the size of an atom. As you move down a group in the periodic table, the elements have valence electrons that occupy higher and higher energy levels. The higher the level is, the farther the valence electrons are from the nucleus and the larger the atom is. **Figure 5.25** shows this trend in atom size in the periodic table.

Figure 5.25 Atomic size increases down a group and across a period, from right to left, in the periodic table. The number under each element symbol is the radius of the atom, in nanometers (nm). A nm is equal to 10^{-9} m.

1	2	3	4	5	6	7	8
H 0.037							He 0.05
Li 0.152	Be 0.111	B 0.088	C 0.077	N 0.070	O 0.066	F 0.064	Ne 0.070
Na 0.186	Mg 0.160	Al 0.143	Si 0.117	P 0.110	S 0.104	Cl 0.099	Ar 0.094
K 0.231	Ca 0.197	Ga 0.122	Ge 0.122	As 0.121	Se 0.117	Br 0.114	Kr 0.109
Rb 0.244	Sr 0.215	In 0.162	Sn 0.140	Sb 0.141	Te 0.137	I 0.133	Xe 0.130
Cs 0.262	Ba 0.217	Ti 0.171	Pb 0.175	Bi 0.146	Po 0.150	At 0.140	Rn 0.140

Suggested Investigation

Inquiry Investigation 5-C, Reactivity Trends in the Periodic Table, on page 214

The farther the valence electrons are from the nucleus, the more easily they can be lost and, therefore, the more reactive the element is. For example, potassium has one valence electron in the fourth energy level, and sodium has one valence electron in the third energy level. A potassium atom loses its valence electron more easily than a sodium atom does, making it more reactive than sodium, as shown in **Figure 5.26**.

Atoms also generally get larger as you move from right to left across a period. All valence electrons for the atoms of elements in a period occupy the same energy level. The change in size results from decreased attraction between the valence electrons and the protons in the nucleus. As you move across a period, the energy levels remain constant but the number of protons decreases. The reduced pull of the electrons toward the nucleus causes an increase in atom size. Therefore, there is also an increase in reactivity of the metals across a period, going from right to left.

Figure 5.26 A potassium atom loses its valence electron more easily than a sodium atom does, so potassium is more reactive than sodium.

sodium

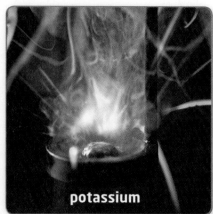
potassium

Section Summary

- There are trends, or regular changes, in the properties of the elements in the periodic table. The arrangement of the electrons in the atoms of the elements influences these trends in properties.

- The electrons in the outer energy level of an atom, called the valence electrons, help to determine many properties of the element. The number of valence electrons in an atom is the same for elements in a group but increases as you move across a period.

- The noble gases are non-reactive because they have a full set of valence electrons. The reactivity of other elements is based on their tendency to gain, lose, or share electrons to achieve a full set of valence electrons.

- The size of an atom increases as you move down a group in the periodic table. The size of an atom also increases as you move from right to left across a period in the periodic table.

Review Questions

T/I **1.** Draw a Bohr-Rutherford model of an atom with one valence electron.

K/U **2.** Examine the diagram on the right. How many valence electrons does an element have that lies one position to the right on the periodic table from this atom?

K/U **3.** Which has more valence electrons: an atom of aluminum or an atom of phosphorus?

T/I **4.** Carbon is the basis of life as we know it. The four valence electrons in carbon atoms allow carbon to react with other elements to form a variety of compounds. What other element shares this property? Explain.

K/U **5.** Explain why halogens are more reactive than noble gases.

K/U **6.** What is the trend in the size of atoms as you move across a period? What is the trend as you move down a group?

T/I **7.** Based on **Figure 5.25**, which is larger: an atom of oxygen or an atom of sulfur? Explain.

T/I **8.** Which is more reactive: magnesium or calcium? Explain.

C **9.** Describe a model that would help someone understand the trends in the sizes of atoms.

K/U **10.** In the example of potassium and sodium, why is the larger atom more reactive? Explain.

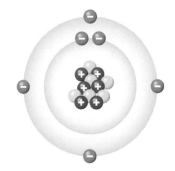

The number of valence electrons in an atom indicates where the element is on the periodic table.

Inquiry Investigation 5-A

Skill Check

Initiating and Planning

✓ Performing and Recording

✓ Analyzing and Interpreting

✓ Communicating

Materials

• 20 blank index cards

Mass Numbers

Atom	Mass Number
H	1
He	4
Li	7
Be	9
B	11
C	12
N	14
O	16
F	19
Ne	20
Na	23
Mg	24
Al	27
Si	28
P	31
S	32
Cl	35
Ar	40
K	39
Ca	40

The Bohr-Rutherford Model of the Atom

The Bohr-Rutherford model is commonly used by scientists to represent the atoms of elements. In this investigation, you will make Bohr-Rutherford models for 20 elements.

Question

How can the atomic structure of an element be represented using the Bohr-Rutherford model?

Procedure

1. Your teacher will give you 20 index cards. On the blank side of each card, write the name, symbol, atomic number, and mass number of one of the 20 element isotopes listed in the table on the left. Note that the atoms in the table are listed according to increasing atomic number, from 1 (H) to 20 (Ca). Use standard atomic notation to represent each atom, as shown for sodium.

2. On the other side of each index card, draw a Bohr-Rutherford model for the atom of the element. Refer to the instructions for drawing Bohr-Rutherford models on page 190.

3. Complete the cards for all 20 atoms in the same way.

Analyze and Interpret

1. As a general rule, how much larger is the mass number than the atomic number?

2. Which elements in the table follow the general rule exactly? Which elements follow the general rule approximately?

Conclude and Communicate

3. Which atoms in the table have no neutrons?

4. Which atoms have an outer energy level of electrons that is full?

5. Which atoms have an outer energy level of electrons that is one electron short of being full?

Extend Your Inquiry and Research Skills

6. **Research** Identify the elements listed in the table that have additional isotopes. Choose two of these elements and draw Bohr-Rutherford models of their isotopes.

Inquiry Investigation 5-B

Skill Check

Initiating and Planning

✓ **Performing and Recording**

✓ **Analyzing and Interpreting**

✓ **Communicating**

Safety Precautions

- Handle all materials with care.
- Wear safety goggles and a lab apron.

Materials

- carbon (charcoal)
- sulfur
- aluminum
- magnesium
- mallet
- conductivity tester

Physical Properties of Metals and Non-metals

In this investigation, you will study four elements and classify each as a metal or a non-metal, based on its physical properties.

Question

How can an element be classified as a metal or a non-metal?

Procedure

1. Design a table like the one below to record your observations. Give your table a title.

	Lustre	Conductivity	Malleability
Carbon			
Sulfur			
Aluminum			
Magnesium			

2. Record the lustre of each element. You can indicate relative shininess in your table using + and – signs.

3. Malleability is the ability to be hammered without cracking. Determine the malleability of each element using the mallet.

4. Test each element for conductivity using the conductivity tester.

5. Clean up your work area. Return all equipment, and dispose of all waste materials according to your teacher's instructions.

Analyze and Interpret

1. Group together the elements with similar properties. Which elements always appeared to have similar properties?

Conclude and Communicate

2. Identify the group of elements that had the properties of metals. What properties appear to be common to metals?

3. Identify the non-metal elements. What properties are common to these elements?

Extend Your Inquiry and Research Skills

4. **Research** Conduct research on one of the metals you studied in this investigation. Identify common uses of this metal that are based on its physical properties.

Inquiry Investigation 5-C

Skill Check

Initiating and Planning

✓ **Performing and Recording**

✓ **Analyzing and Interpreting**

✓ **Communicating**

Safety Precautions

- Wear safety goggles, safety gloves, and a lab apron.
- Be very careful when working with the acid solution. Acid can burn skin. If you spill any of the acid solution on your hands, rinse it off immediately with cold water and inform your teacher.
- Clean up any spills on your work area, and inform your teacher immediately.
- Do not handle the calcium with your bare hands.

Materials

- water
- 3 test tubes
- test-tube rack
- aluminum
- calcium
- magnesium
- 1 mol/L acid solution (HCl)

Science Skills

Go to **Science Skills Toolkit 7** for information about creating data tables.

Reactivity Trends in the Periodic Table

Periodic trends include both physical and chemical properties of elements. In this investigation, find out if (and how) the reactivity of metals relates to their position on the periodic table.

Question

Is there a relationship between the reactivity of a metal and its position in the periodic table?

Procedure

1. Design a table to record your observations.

2. Put 10 mL of water into each of the three test tubes. Add one metal to each test tube. Observe any changes and record the relative reactivity of each metal.

3. When the reactions stop, dispose of the water as directed by your teacher. You will use the magnesium and aluminum metals for the next step.

4. Add 10 mL of HCl to the remaining magnesium and aluminum samples. Record your observations and indicate the relative reactivity of each metal. Clean up your work area and dispose of the materials as directed by your teacher.

Analyze and Interpret

1. Which of the three metals was the most reactive? Which metal was the least reactive?

2. Compare the reactivities of magnesium and calcium. Does the reactivity of metals appear to increase or decrease as you read down a column in the periodic table?

3. Compare the reactivities of magnesium and aluminum. Does the reactivity of metals appear to increase or decrease as you read across a row?

Conclude and Communicate

4. Compare the Bohr-Rutherford models for magnesium, calcium, and aluminum. How might their different atomic structures explain their different reactivities?

Extend Your Inquiry and Research Skills

5. **Research** Infer the reactivities of sodium, potassium, and strontium, compared with each of their neighbours in the periodic table. Check your answers by conducting research.

Chapter 5 Summary

5.1 Evolution of the Atomic Model

Key Concepts

- John Dalton's atomic theory described elements in terms of atoms, which he believed to be small, indivisible particles that make up all matter.

- Joseph John Thomson determined that atoms contain negatively charged particles, which are now called electrons. He developed a model of the atom that shows electrons inserted throughout a mass of positively charged material.

- Ernest Rutherford updated the model of the atom as mostly empty space, with a small, dense, positively charged nucleus in the centre. His continued work, as well as that of others, eventually led to identification of the proton and neutron in the nucleus.

- Neils Bohr revised Rutherford's model of the atom by stating that electrons are stable in specific energy levels around the nucleus.

5.2 The Structure of the Atom

Key Concepts

- Atoms are made up of protons, neutrons, and electrons. Protons are positively charged, neutrons have no charge, and electrons are negatively charged.

- The atomic number of an atom is the number of protons in the nucleus. It is always a whole number and identifies the element. The mass number of an atom is the total number of protons and neutrons. Like the atomic number, it is always a whole number.

- Protons and neutrons make up the nucleus and account for most of the mass of the atom. Electrons occupy energy levels outside the nucleus.

- Bohr-Rutherford models are used to depict the atomic structures of elements.

- An element is made up of isotopes, which are atoms that have the same number of protons but different numbers of neutrons.

5.3 The Periodic Table

Key Concepts

- The modern periodic table is organized according to increasing atomic number, with a regular repeating pattern in the properties of the elements.

- Metals are usually solids at room temperature, shiny, good conductors, malleable, and ductile. Non-metals are usually gases or solids at room temperature, not shiny, poor conductors, brittle, and not ductile. Metalloids share properties of both metals and non-metals.

- Poisoning by metals in the environment is a serious problem. Mercury contamination of fish has severely affected the health and traditional practices of Aboriginal peoples.

- In the periodic table, a period is a horizontal row of elements. A group, or family, is a vertical column of elements. Four major groups of elements in the periodic table are the alkali metals, alkaline-earth metals, halogens, and noble gases.

5.4 Trends in the Periodic Table

Key Concepts

- In the periodic table, there are trends in the properties of elements. These are influenced by the arrangement of electrons in the atoms of the elements.

- Valence electrons help to determine many properties of the element. The number of valence electrons in an atom is the same for elements in a group but increases as you move across a period.

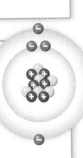

- The noble gases are non-reactive because they have a full set of valence electrons. The reactivity of other elements is based on their tendency to gain, lose, or share electrons to achieve a full set of valence electrons.

- The size of an atom increases as you move down a group in the periodic table. The size of an atom also increases as you move from right to left across a period in the periodic table.

Chapter 5 Review

Reviewing Key Terms

1. An electron in the outermost occupied energy level of an atom is a ▭▭▭▭▭▭. (5.4)

2. A ▭▭▭▭▭▭ is a column in the periodic table. (5.3)

3. An element that is not shiny, malleable, or ductile and is a poor conductor of heat is a ▭▭▭▭▭▭. (5.3)

4. A system for organizing the elements by atomic number is the ▭▭▭▭▭▭. (5.3)

5. The number of protons in an atom is the ▭▭▭▭▭▭. (5.2)

6. The centre of an atom, which is composed of protons and neutrons, is the ▭▭▭▭▭▭. (5.1)

7. The negatively charged particles in an atom are the ▭▭▭▭▭▭. (5.1)

8. The ▭▭▭▭▭▭ of an atom is the sum of the number of protons and the number of neutrons. (5.2)

Knowledge and Understanding K/U

9. What component of the atom did Rutherford identify in his gold foil experiment? Describe the experimental evidence that supported this discovery.

10. Describe the relative masses of a proton, a neutron, and an electron. What charge, if any, does each have?

11. What can you determine from the atomic number of an atom?

12. **a.** Do the following diagrams represent isotopes of the same element? Explain.

These Bohr-Rutherford models differ by a key feature.

   b. What are the mass numbers of these atoms? Explain your reasoning.

13. Determine the number of protons, neutrons, and electrons in each of the following atoms. Identify each element as a metal, a non-metal, or a metalloid.

   a. $^{7}_{3}Li$

   b. $^{30}_{15}P$

   c. $^{28}_{13}Al$

   d. $^{13}_{6}C$

   e. $^{28}_{14}Si$

   f. $^{35}_{17}Cl$

14. Describe the process that Mendeleev used to create his periodic table.

15. Describe the properties of non-metals. Where are non-metals located in the periodic table?

16. Describe the number of valence electrons in each atom as you move down Group 2 in the periodic table.

17. What arrangement of valence electrons makes an atom non-reactive?

18. How many valence electrons are in an atom of each of the following elements?

   a. hydrogen

   b. boron

   c. chlorine

   d. helium

   e. phosphorus

   f. beryllium

   g. silicon

   h. sulfur

19. What determines the size of an atom?

20. Based on its position in the periodic table, which atom in each pair of elements is larger?

   a. sodium or lithium

   b. chlorine or bromine

   c. nitrogen or fluorine

Thinking and Investigation (T/I)

21. Which metal is more reactive: potassium or rubidium? Explain.

22. Elements within a group in the periodic table have similar properties. In which two groups in the periodic table would you expect to find elements with the widest range of properties? Explain your reasoning.

23. What would have happened if Rutherford had placed the screen to detect where the particles went after hitting the gold foil only where he had expected them to go? How might Rutherford's conclusions have changed?

24. Argon, potassium, and calcium have naturally occurring isotopes that have the same mass number, 40. Explain how this is possible.

25. How did Thomson's model of the atom differ from Rutherford's model?

Communication (C)

26. Draw each of the following models of the atom. Make sure that you show the key features and indicate any negatively or positively charged regions.

   a. the Rutherford model

   b. the Bohr model

   c. the Thomson model

27. Draw a Bohr-Rutherford model for each of the following atoms.

   a. $_2^4$He

   b. carbon-13

   c. an aluminum atom with a mass number of 28

   d. an atom that has an atomic number of 19 and a mass number of 41

28. BIG IDEAS The use of elements and compounds has both positive and negative effects on society and the environment. As a contributing author to an on-line environmental magazine, you have been asked to write an article about the effects of metals on people's health. Write a short paragraph to discuss the positive and negative effects.

29. BIG IDEAS Elements and compounds have specific physical and chemical properties that determine their practical uses. Discuss how the properties of gold make it useful in the aerospace industry.

Application (A)

30. Elements cannot be broken down into smaller particles by physical or chemical methods. How does this help when isolating elements for industrial uses?

31. Deuterium is a naturally occurring isotope of hydrogen that contains one neutron.

   a. Draw a Bohr-Rutherford model of deuterium and write the standard atomic notation for this element.

   b. Deuterium is an element in a compound called heavy water. Research what heavy water is. Why do you think it is called heavy water?

   c. As part of your research, determine what heavy water is used for in the National Research Universal (NRU) reactor at the Chalk River Laboratories in Chalk River, Ontario.

Chapter 6 Understanding the Properties of Compounds

What You Will Learn

In this chapter, you will learn how to...

- **explain** the difference between ionic compounds and molecular compounds
- **demonstrate** an understanding of the important properties of ionic and molecular compounds
- **assess** the social, environmental, and economic impacts of the use of some common compounds

Why It Matters

Modern scientists study thousands of new and increasingly complex compounds. A central part of this important research is knowing how the elements in a compound are chemically bonded together. This information can be used to predict and determine the properties and applications of a compound.

Skills You Will Use

In this chapter, you will learn how to...

- **investigate** the properties of ionic and molecular compounds
- **explore** the chemistry of rusting
- **construct** three-dimensional models of molecules

As this climber scales the rock face, high above the ground, she depends on the properties of different compounds to keep her safe. She uses chalk–a white, powdery compound–to absorb the sweat on her hands and improve her grip. She also uses a rope made from a strong, lightweight, and flexible type of compound. All compounds are composed of two or more elements that are chemically combined. The way that the elements are combined, however, can differ. This plays a large part in determining their properties and practical uses.

Bouncing Glue

In the 1940s, an engineer was trying to develop a new kind of rubber. One of his early attempts produced a compound that is similar to what you will make in this activity. The compound did not have the properties he wanted, so he considered it a failure. Years later, however, it became a popular toy. What toy do you think it became?

The mixture you make will gradually harden.

Safety Precautions

- Wear safety goggles and a lab apron.
- Clean up any spills immediately, and inform your teacher.

Materials

- 10 mL of Elmer's® glue
- 10 mL of water
- 100 mL beaker
- tablespoon
- wooden stir stick
- food colouring
- 10 mL of 4% borax solution

Procedure

1. Read over the Procedure, and then make a table to record your observations. Give your table a title.

2. Place 10 mL of glue and 10 mL of water in the beaker. Stir vigorously with the stir stick. Add one or two drops of food colouring, and stir to make sure that it is thoroughly mixed in.

3. Add 10 mL of borax solution, and immediately begin stirring with the stir stick. The material should start to become slimy.

4. After a few more minutes of stirring, the material should be hard enough to place in your hand. Continue kneading the material until it does not harden anymore.

5. Try to do different things with the material, such as bouncing it and stretching it. Can you think of any other tests to perform on the material? Record your observations.

Questions

1. Are all the glue balls made by the class the same, or are there differences? If there are differences, what do you think is responsible for them?

2. Based on your observations, what popular toy do you think the inventor's "mistake" became?

Study Toolkit

These strategies will help you use this textbook to develop your understanding of science concepts and skills. To find out more about these and other strategies, refer to the Study Toolkit Overview, which begins on page 561.

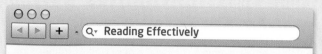
Reading Effectively

Making Inferences

Often, a text does not contain *all* the details related to a particular topic. Some details or connections between ideas may be implied rather than stated explicitly. The writer relies on the reader to make inferences, or to "read between the lines."

Making an inference involves combining information in the text with prior knowledge. For example, the table below shows one inference you could make about the following text: "Your body relies on dissolved ions for many vital processes. For example, sodium ions and potassium ions are important for the transmission of nerve impulses and the control of muscular contractions."

Information in Text	+ Prior Knowledge	= Inference
The human body relies on sodium and potassium for many vital processes.	I don't take sodium and potassium supplements, but I'm healthy.	Some of what we eat or drink regularly must contain sodium and potassium.

Use the Strategy

Read the second paragraph in the section titled "Solubility" on page 225. Create a table like the one above to make an inference about electrolytes.

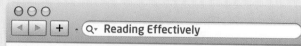
Reading Effectively

Monitoring Comprehension

As you read, stop periodically to *monitor*, or check, whether you understand what you have just read. Place a sticky note beside each chunk of text. When you finish reading, put a ✔ on the sticky note if you understand what you have just read, and an ✗ if you do not. For each chunk of text that you *do* understand, restate the main idea. For each chunk that you *do not* understand, reread the text. Try to pinpoint what aspect is confusing to you:

- If a word or term is confusing, check the margin, the Glossary, or a dictionary for a definition.

- If a concept is confusing, examine the visuals on the page to see if they help to explain the concept.

- If a formula or definition is confusing, look for examples in the text that might help you understand.

Use the Strategy

1. Read the paragraphs on the next page.

2. Put a ✔ or an ✗ on a sticky note beside the paragraph.

3. If you put a ✔ on the sticky note, restate the main idea. If you put an ✗ on the sticky note, follow the steps above. If you still do not understand, ask a classmate or your teacher for help.

Word Study

Creating a Word Map

One strategy you can use to learn a new word is to create a **word map**.

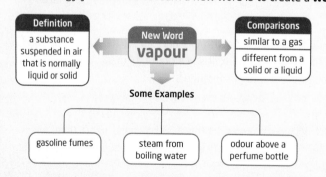

Use the Strategy

1. As you read this chapter, create a word map for the word "bond."

2. Compare your word map with a partner's word map.

3. If your partner has any information that helps you understand the word better, add this information to your word map.

6.1 Ionic Compounds

Key Terms
ion
chemical bond
ionic bond
ionic compound

Each winter, they come out and prowl the icy streets of your community, leaving behind a trail of small, white crystals. Salt trucks, like the one in **Figure 6.1**, spread salt to keep the roads from getting icy. This means, however, that a great deal of road salt is dumped into the environment. Each winter, the Ontario Ministry of Transportation spreads between 500 000 and 600 000 tonnes of salt on the roads. This mass is equivalent to over 300 000 cars!

Why is salt used to reduce ice on roads? How can we avoid or minimize the effects of road salt on the environment? The answers lie in the important properties of road salt—an ionic compound—and the potential alternatives.

Figure 6.1 Road salt is used to keep roads safe for motorists, but it has negative effects on the environment.

Forming Ions

In Chapter 5, you learned that the reactivity of elements is influenced by the arrangement of their valence electrons. Noble gases are the least reactive because their electron arrangements are very stable. This stability is because the outer energy level of electrons is full. Some of the other elements can achieve a full outer energy level, and therefore more stability, by either gaining or losing electrons.

When an atom loses or gains electrons, the balance between positive and negative charges no longer exists and the atom becomes charged. An atom that becomes charged is called an **ion**. As shown in **Figure 6.2**, when an atom loses electrons, it forms an ion that is positively charged because it now has more protons than electrons. Conversely, when an atom gains electrons, it forms an ion that is negatively charged because it now has more electrons than protons.

ion a positively or negatively charged atom or molecule

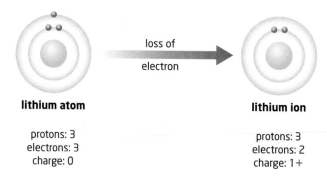

lithium atom

protons: 3
electrons: 3
charge: 0

lithium ion

protons: 3
electrons: 2
charge: 1+

Figure 6.2 When this atom loses an electron, it becomes an ion with more protons than electrons.

The charge on an ion is equal to the sum of the charges on its protons and electrons. For example, consider a sodium ion that has 11 protons (11+) and 10 electrons (10–). The sum of the charges is +1. The ion is represented as Na^+. When ion charges are 1+ or 1–, the number is not included. It is important to remember that an atom cannot lose or gain protons, only electrons.

The periodic table lists the charges that ions of each element can have. For example, as shown in **Figure 6.3**, the only ion charge for magnesium in the periodic table is 2+. This ion is represented as Mg^{2+}.

12	2+
Mg	
Magnesium	
24.3	

Figure 6.3 An element's square in the periodic table shows what charges an ion of the element might have.

Ionic Bonds

Compounds consist of two or more different elements that are chemically linked together. These chemical links are called **chemical bonds**. One type of chemical bond is the **ionic bond**, which is formed by the attraction between oppositely charged ions. When an **ionic compound** forms, one or more electrons from one atom are transferred to another atom. This electronic rearrangement produces oppositely charged ions that are attracted to each other. An ionic bond forms between the two ions, creating a neutral compound. In the formation of ionic compounds, the loss and gain of valence electrons between the reacting elements allows each ion to have a full outer energy level of electrons.

chemical bond a chemical link between two atoms, which holds the atoms together

ionic bond a chemical bond that forms between oppositely charged ions

ionic compound a compound made of oppositely charged ions

Recognizing Ionic Compounds

Knowing the types of elements that form ionic compounds and understanding the reasons for this will allow you to identify most ionic compounds. Ionic compounds are usually composed of a metal and one or more non-metals. This is because atoms of metals tend to lose electrons and form positive ions, while atoms of non-metals tend to gain electrons and form negative ions.

Sodium chloride, shown in **Figure 6.4**, is an ionic compound that you consume every day. Sodium, an alkali metal in Group 1, readily loses an electron to form Na^+. It forms an ionic bond with chlorine, a halogen in Group 17 of the periodic table, which readily gains an electron to form Cl^-. The Bohr-Rutherford diagrams in **Figure 6.4** show the electron transfer that occurs in this reaction. Notice how oppositely charged ions form a compound that is neutral. This reaction is an example of how two hazardous substances can be combined to produce an edible product—table salt.

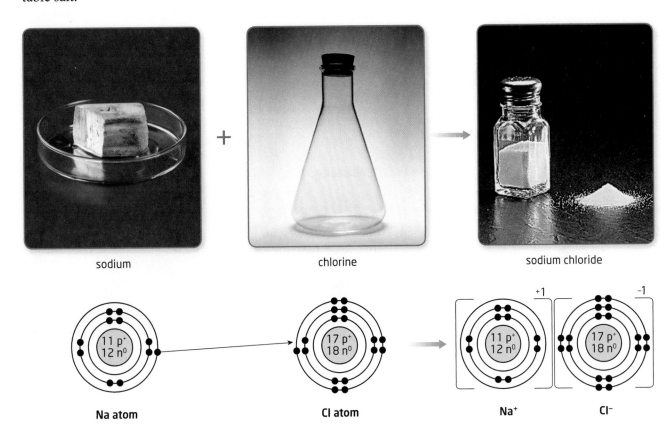

sodium   chlorine   sodium chloride

Na atom   Cl atom Na^+ Cl^-

Figure 6.4 When one electron is transferred from sodium to chlorine, both ions end up with a stable electron arrangement. The sodium ion has a charge of 1+ because it has one more proton than the number of electrons. The chloride ion has a charge of 1− because it has one more electron than the number of protons.

What Does Sodium Fluoride Do?

The next time you brush your teeth, look at the list of ingredients on the tube of toothpaste. As shown in **Figure 6.5**, you will probably see an ionic compound named sodium fluoride in the list. This compound is very similar to sodium chloride, the ionic compound just discussed. Sodium fluoride is made of sodium ions (Na^+) and fluoride ions (F^-) and is represented by the formula NaF. The fluoride in sodium fluoride helps to strengthen tooth enamel (the tough outer layer on teeth) and reduce cavities. Because of these benefits, every province in Canada approved adding fluoride to drinking water. Communities that did this experienced a significant decline in the rate of tooth decay.

There is now a controversy, however, associated with adding fluoride to drinking water. The issue revolves around determining the optimum level of exposure to this chemical. Today, people can be exposed to several different sources of fluoride in drinking water, toothpaste, beverages that are made using fluoridated water, and fluoride that is released into the environment from natural and industrial processes. Some scientists suggest that too much fluoride can have negative effects, such as cancer, fragile bones, and improper brain development in children. While many scientists disagree about how harmful fluoride can be, communities are now paying closer attention to the level of fluoride in their water.

Go to **scienceontario** to find out more

Figure 6.5 **A** Sodium fluoride is an ingredient in most toothpastes. It is included to help strengthen teeth and reduce **B** cavities.

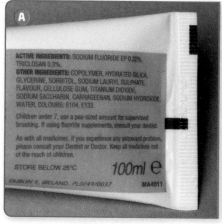
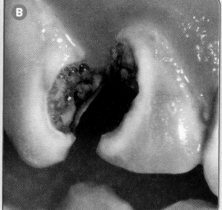

Learning Check

1. Which two types of elements usually form ionic compounds?

2. If an atom loses an electron, what kind of particle does it become?

3. Describe the electron arrangement in each atom and compound in **Figure 6.4**.

4. The ions that make up an ionic compound are attracted to each other because they have opposite charges. Describe an everyday situation that involves charged objects sticking together.

Properties of Ionic Compounds

Ionic bonds tend to be very strong, so they require a large amount of energy to break. The strength of these bonds helps to explain many of the properties of ionic compounds.

Physical States

Most ionic compounds exist in a solid arrangement called a *crystal lattice*, shown in **Figure 6.6**. A crystal lattice is a regular repeating pattern of ions. Since each ion in an ionic compound is strongly attracted to the ions around it, almost all ionic compounds are solid at room temperature. Because a large amount of energy is needed to melt most ionic compounds, they tend to have very high melting points. For example, the melting point of sodium chloride is 801°C, and the melting point of sodium fluoride is 993°C.

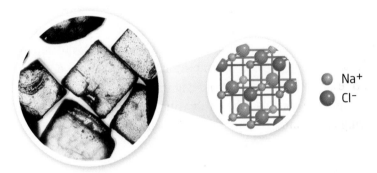

Na⁺
Cl⁻

Figure 6.6 The ionic compound sodium chloride exists as a crystal lattice, which consists of a regular repeating pattern of Na⁺ and Cl⁻ ions. Note that this diagram only shows part of the crystal lattice.

The liquid state of most ionic compounds is too hot for us even to observe. The "liquid" version you are most familiar with is actually the aqueous state—ionic solids that have been dissolved in water and exist as solutions. The gaseous state is almost non-existent for most ionic compounds.

Solubility

Many ionic compounds are soluble in water. An ionic compound dissolves because the water separates the positive and negative ions from each other, causing the ionic bonds to break. When the ions are in solution, as shown in **Figure 6.7**, they are able to move about.

The solubility of ionic compounds in water is essential for most living things on Earth. The human body is an aqueous environment. Your body relies on dissolved ions for many vital processes. For example, sodium ions (Na^+) and potassium ions (K^+) are important for the transmission of nerve impulses and the control of muscular contractions. Carbonate ions (CO_3^{2-}) are essential in blood. Severe dehydration can be caused by extreme exercising, working outside in the sunlight on very hot days, or vomiting and diarrhea. When dehydration occurs, not only water but also essential ions, called electrolytes, are lost. In such cases, it is important to replenish the electrolytes as well as the water. For example, fluid supplements that are recommended for people who become dehydrated due to illness contain potassium ions and sodium ions.

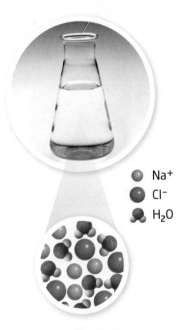

Na⁺
Cl⁻
H₂O

Figure 6.7 When an ionic compound dissolves, the ions exist as separate particles.

Solubility and Plant Fertilizers

Study Toolkit

Making Inferences Read the paragraphs on this page. Draw a table like the one shown on page 220 to make an inference about fertilizers and the environment. This will help you gain a better understanding of fertilizer use and its impact on society.

Ionic compounds also play a vital role in the health of plants and crops. Many crops are treated with fertilizers that provide nitrogen, phosphorus, and potassium in the form of ionic compounds, such as ammonium nitrate (NH_4NO_3), ammonium phosphate ($(NH_4)_3PO_4$), and potassium chloride (KCl). All three nutrients, which are water soluble, are taken in through the roots of the plants and are necessary for plant growth.

Fertilizers provide many benefits, which include faster plant growth and the ability to grow more plants in less space. As a result, farms can produce more crops with less spoilage and lower labour costs. This helps to reduce the cost of the food that is produced from the crops, making the food more affordable for consumers.

Although fertilizers provide benefits in food production, overusing them can create problems. If plants do not take up all the dissolved fertilizers, the ionic compounds in the fertilizers can be carried by water into nearby streams and lakes, shown in **Figure 6.8**. As discussed in Chapter 1, the overuse of fertilizers can introduce excess nutrients and affect ecosystems by disrupting such things as the nitrogen and phosphorus cycles. For example, additional nutrients can increase the growth of algae. After the algae die, microscopic organisms use the oxygen dissolved in the water to decompose their remains. As a result, little or no oxygen is left in the water, and fish and other living organisms may die from lack of oxygen.

Figure 6.8 Fertilizers can improve plant growth, increase crop yields, and restore nutrients to the soil. Excessive run-off, however, can have harmful effects on ecosystems.

1. Farm run-off adds nutrients from crops.
2. Suburban run-off adds nutrients from fertilized lawns.
3. Algae bloom forms due to excessive nutrients.
4. Oxygen in water is used up when algae decompose.
5. Fish die from lack of oxygen.

Conductivity

A substance can conduct an electric current if charged particles, such as electrons or ions, are free to move around. Metals are good electrical conductors because they have electrons that are free to move throughout them. In Chapter 10, the principles of conductivity and uses for conducting materials are discussed in more detail.

Ionic compounds are also good electrical conductors—under the right conditions. In the solid state, an ionic compound is a poor conductor because the ions are locked into position in their crystal structure. In the liquid state, however, the ions of an ionic compound are free to move around. So, an ionic compound is a good conductor when it is melted. Similarly, when an ionic compound has been dissolved in water, the ions are free to move around and will conduct electricity. For example, pure water is a poor conductor. In comparison, tap water tends to have quite a few naturally occurring ionic compounds dissolved in it and, therefore, is a better conductor than pure water. Salt water is a very good conductor, as seen in **Figure 6.9**.

Study Toolkit

Monitoring Comprehension
Read the two paragraphs on this page. Use the Monitoring Comprehension strategy on page 220 to check whether you understand what you have just read.

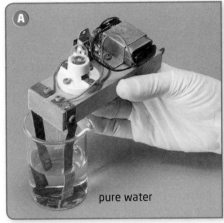
pure water

salt water

Figure 6.9 A Pure water is a poor conductor, so the bulb does not light. The sodium and chloride ions that are present in **B** salt water can conduct an electric current, so the bulb lights up.

Learning Check

5. Sketch the ionic compound sodium fluoride as it exists in the solid state.

6. What solvent do most ionic compounds dissolve in? Draw a sketch that represents the ions when an ionic compound is dissolved in this solvent.

7. Explain why the human body can conduct electricity.

8. Give two examples of ionic compounds that you use every day.

Road Salt

When road salt, shown in **Figure 6.10**, is used in the winter, it dissolves into any water on the road. Normally, water becomes ice at a temperature of 0°C, which is called the freezing point of water. When salt is added to the water, however, it interacts with the water and makes ice formation more difficult. A lower temperature is needed for ice to form. Therefore, road salt lowers the freezing point of water on the road and prevents the formation of ice. In addition, the saltwater mixture forms a layer between the road and the snow and ice. As vehicles drive on the road, their tires break up the snow and ice, which can then be more easily plowed from the road. Ultimately, using road salt makes the road safer for vehicles. It reduces injuries and deaths due to poor road conditions and also reduces the medical and insurance costs associated with accidents.

Activity 6-2 is another example of how we can use the ability of salt to lower the freezing point of water, but in an enjoyable way.

Sense of place

Sifto Canada's salt mine in Goderich, Ontario, reaches a depth of 533 m, is about 2.4 km wide, and extends 3.2 km into Lake Huron. The chambers from which the salt is removed have ceilings that are nearly 14 m high.

Figure 6.10 Cities and towns in Ontario use stockpiles of road salt to reduce the build-up of ice on roads.

Activity 6-2

Making Ice Cream

In this activity, you will take advantage of the ability of salt to lower the freezing point of water as you convert a mixture into ice cream.

Safety Precautions

- Wear safety goggles.
- Alert your teacher if you have an allergy to any ingredients in ice cream.
- Do not eat the ice cream, unless instructed by your teacher.

Materials

- measuring cups and spoons
- plastic spoons
- 5 mL of sugar
- 60 mL of milk
- 2 drops of vanilla extract
- 250 mL resealable plastic bag
- 500 mL of ice
- 150 mL of rock salt (sodium chloride)
- 1 L resealable plastic bag
- thermometer
- sheet of newspaper

Procedure

1. Read over the procedure. Then make a table to record your observations. Give your table a title.

2. Put the sugar, milk, and vanilla extract into the 250 mL plastic bag, and seal the bag.

For ice cream to form, the temperature must be below 0°C.

3. Place the ice and salt in a 1 L plastic bag. Measure the temperature of the ice. Place the smaller bag with the ingredients inside the larger bag. Top up the larger bag with ice, and then seal it closed. Wrap the bag in the newspaper.

4. Rock the large bag covered in newspaper back and forth.

5. Every 5 min, unwrap the bag and measure the temperature of the ice and saltwater mixture. Record the temperature and your observation of what the ice cream ingredients look like. The ice cream should form in about 15 to 20 min.

Questions

1. What was the temperature of the ice and saltwater mixture at the point when the ice cream had formed?

2. Why was sodium chloride added to the ice?

The Harmful Effects of Road Salt

Although road salt is very effective for reducing ice on roads, there are negative effects associated with its use. For example, the presence of salt on a road attracts animals, such as the moose in **Figure 6.11**. This causes hazardous conditions for both drivers and animals.

Conductivity and Rusting

The increased conductivity of water when it contains dissolved salt leads to increased corrosion, or rusting, of iron. Bridges must be regularly painted to keep rust from forming. Cars and trucks must also be protected because steel is an alloy of iron. This is why, in areas such as Ontario, anti-corrosion products are very popular. They are applied as protective coatings to help "rustproof" vehicles.

> **Suggested Investigation**
>
> Inquiry Investigation 6-A, What Causes Rusting of Iron Nails?, on page 249

Figure 6.11 Although salt improves driving conditions, it attracts animals to roads.

Effects of Road Salt on Ecosystems

When salt is used on roads, it can be quite harmful to local ecosystems. When the ice and snow melt, the road salt enters the environment through the soil, ground water, and surface water. The chart in **Figure 6.12** shows the numerous pathways that road salt can take into our environment. High levels of salt in the soil can inhibit or slow plant growth, which can eventually affect the animals that rely on the plants for food. Once in the waterways, high salt concentrations can affect aquatic plant and animal species. Even high levels of salt in drinking water can lead to increased salt consumption by people, which can negatively affect health.

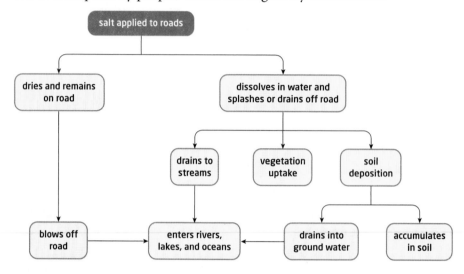

Figure 6.12 Salt that is used on roads may eventually find its way into the environment, along different pathways.

Although the most extensively used road salt is sodium chloride, calcium chloride and magnesium chloride are also used. All three of these compounds can leave high concentrations of chloride ion residue, which is particularly damaging. Although de-icing alternatives that have a lower impact on the environment have been studied, salts such as sodium chloride remain the most popular. Therefore, as shown in **Figure 6.13**, deciding how to use road salt most effectively is important for many towns and cities in Canada.

Figure 6.13 Deciding how to manage road-salt application involves carefully balancing two major factors.

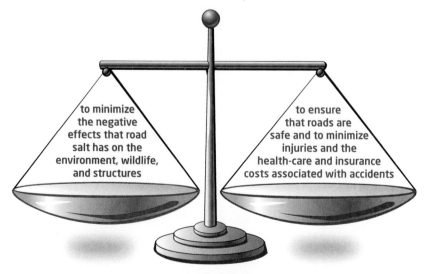

Section Summary

- The formation of ions involves the loss or gain of electrons. The ion(s) formed by an atom will depend on its atomic structure and the number of valence electrons.

- Ionic compounds form when there is a transfer of electrons between atoms. An ionic bond is the attraction that holds positive ions and negative ions together.

- Most ionic compounds are composed of a metal and a non-metal. Ionic compounds have high melting points and tend to be soluble in water. Ionic compounds are good electrical conductors when melted or when dissolved in water.

- Road salt is used in the winter to reduce icy driving conditions. Nevertheless, because of its harmful effects on the environment, the frequency and amount of road salt used should be carefully considered.

Review Questions

K/U **1.** How can a negative ion form from an atom?

K/U **2.** Identify each of the following compounds as ionic or not ionic.

    a. KCl   **b.** CO_2 **c.** CF_4 **d.** NaI

T/I **3.** Is an ionic compound likely to form between fluorine and chlorine? Explain your reasoning.

C **4.** Write an explanation for a classmate about why ionic compounds tend to have high melting points.

K/U **5.** In what form are the nutrients in fertilizers? What are important nutrients that fertilizers provide?

T/I **6.** Ionic compounds tend to be good conductors of electric current, but the light on the conductivity tester in the photograph on the right is not glowing. Why does the ionic compound shown not conduct electric current? What could you do to make the light glow?

K/U **7.** According to **Figure 6.12**, what are two ways that road salt can enter rivers and lakes?

A **8.** Which area do you think has more problems with rust: a town along the Atlantic Ocean or a town in a remote area of the Northwest Territories? Explain.

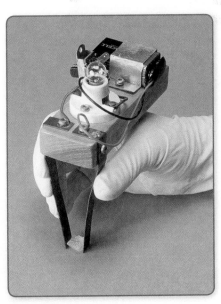

The light is not glowing because this substance does not conduct electricity.

6.2   Molecular Compounds

Instead of throwing out that wrapper, eat it! Imagine if you could eat the protective wrapping on your food instead of throwing it out. Think of the amount of trash this would eliminate. Scientists are working on the development of edible films made from dairy products, like the one shown in **Figure 6.14**. Edible films are made from casein, a protein that is in milk and other dairy products. They are transparent and shiny, and they can extend the shelf life of food by preventing exposure to moisture and oxygen, just like plastic wrap. They are an example of another class of compounds, called molecular compounds. Like ionic compounds, molecular compounds have a specific type of chemical bond, which gives them characteristic properties.

Figure 6.14 This food technologist is preparing an edible plastic film, similar to these green breath-freshening strips.

Covalent Bonds

A **molecular compound** forms when atoms share a pair of electrons to form a **covalent bond**. In a covalent bond, the shared electrons are attracted to the nuclei of both atoms. The attraction of the nuclei for the shared electrons holds the atoms together. Unlike ionic compounds, electrons are not transferred between atoms, and the atoms remain uncharged. A covalent bond is like a tug-of-war game, as shown in **Figure 6.15**. Two teams are joined by their mutual pull on the rope.

Figure 6.15 The mutual pull of the two teams on the shared rope is an analogy for the attraction of two atoms on the electrons that are shared in a covalent bond.

Filling Outer Energy Levels by Sharing

The formation of a molecular compound is based on the same principle as the formation of an ionic compound: the stability that is associated with a full outer energy level of electrons. There is an important difference, however. The atoms that form a molecular compound achieve full outer energy levels, and therefore more stability, by sharing their valence electrons, as shown in **Figure 6.16**.

covalent bond

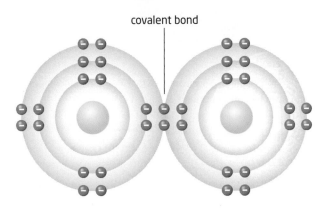

Figure 6.16 Covalent bonds involve the sharing of valence electrons to form full outer energy levels of electrons.

Recognizing Molecular Compounds

Simple covalent compounds are usually composed of two or more non-metals. One familiar molecular compound is water, shown in **Figure 6.17**. The smallest particle of water is a **molecule** of water. Each molecule of water is composed of two hydrogen atoms and one oxygen atom, represented as H_2O. The Bohr-Rutherford models for water in **Figure 6.18** show each hydrogen atom forming a covalent bond with the oxygen atom by sharing a pair of electrons. The covalent bonding of each hydrogen atom to the oxygen atom produces filled outer energy levels for all three atoms. In the Bohr-Rutherford model, the shared electrons are shown between the atoms.

Figure 6.17 A water molecule consists of two hydrogen atoms (shown in white) that are joined by covalent bonds to an oxygen atom (shown in red).

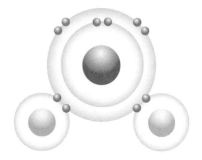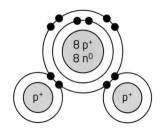

Figure 6.18 These Bohr-Rutherford models for water show how the covalent bonds between hydrogen and oxygen involve sharing a pair of valence electrons.

Molecules

Molecular compounds are so called because they exist as molecules. By definition, a molecule is the smallest unit of a pure substance that has two or more atoms covalently bonded. Not all molecules, however, are compounds. Recall, from Chapter 4, that compounds are defined as being composed of two or more *different* elements. Molecules can include two or more atoms of the *same* element that are covalently bonded. For example, the oxygen in the air you breathe exists as two oxygen atoms that are covalently bonded, shown in **Figure 6.19**. It is represented as O_2 and referred to as a molecule of oxygen, *not* a compound.

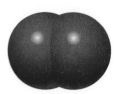

Figure 6.19 Oxygen in the air you breathe exists as a molecule composed of two oxygen atoms that are covalently bonded.

Naming Molecular Compounds

The names of most molecular compounds reflect the elements that are in the compounds, as well as the number of each element. Consider carbon monoxide and carbon dioxide, shown in **Figure 6.20**. Both compounds are composed of the elements carbon and oxygen. Notice, however, that their names include the prefixes *mono-* and *di-*, which are used to indicate the number of oxygen atoms present in a molecule of each compound. So, carbon *mon*oxide has the formula CO because *monoxide* means one oxygen. Carbon *di*oxide has the formula CO_2 because *dioxide* means two oxygens.

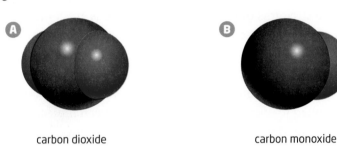

carbon dioxide   carbon monoxide

Figure 6.20 **A** Carbon dioxide and **B** carbon monoxide are molecular compounds that differ in composition by one oxygen atom. Nevertheless, carbon monoxide is a toxic gas. Detectors, like the one shown here, are recommended in homes that are heated using fossil fuels to warn residents about unsafe levels of carbon monoxide.

Although the only difference between their names is a prefix, carbon dioxide and carbon monoxide are compounds with vastly different properties. Carbon dioxide is a gas that is exhaled every time you breathe. It is also used to carbonate drinks. Carbon monoxide, however, is a highly toxic gas that interferes with the body's ability to transport oxygen. Carbon monoxide is generated by burning fuels such as gasoline, wood, and natural gas.

Table 6.1 lists some common prefixes and the number that each prefix represents. You will learn more about naming molecular compounds and determining their chemical formulas in Grade 10.

Table 6.1 Prefixes Used for Molecular Compounds

Prefix	Number	Prefix	Number
mono-	1	hexa-	6
di-	2	hepta-	7
tri-	3	octa-	8
tetra-	4	nona-	9
penta-	5	deca-	10

The Properties of Molecular Compounds

There are many different types of molecular compounds. This makes it difficult to generalize about the properties of all molecular compounds. Nevertheless, there are some properties that are shared by a large number of molecular compounds and that are quite different from the properties of ionic compounds. A key reason for many of the differences in properties is the weaker attraction *between* molecules.

Recall that an ionic compound behaves like one large structure. Each ion is surrounded by ions of opposite charge, and the strong attractions between oppositely charged ions exist throughout the crystal. Although the strengths of ionic and covalent bonds are about the same, the attraction between molecules in a molecular compound are weak, as shown in **Figure 6.21**. These attractions are much weaker than the attraction between ions in an ionic crystal.

When a molecular compound is melted or vaporized, enough energy must be supplied to overcome the attraction between molecules. Because the attraction is weak, most molecular compounds have relatively low melting and boiling points. The weak attraction between molecules also explains the relative softness of molecular compounds. In addition, because molecular compounds do not have free electrons or ions, they are poor conductors of electricity and heat, compared with ionic compounds. **Figure 6.22** shows just one of many ways that the properties of molecular compounds can be taken advantage of, for practical applications.

Figure 6.22 Molecular compounds are poor conductors of electricity. This makes them useful as insulating covers over electrical wires.

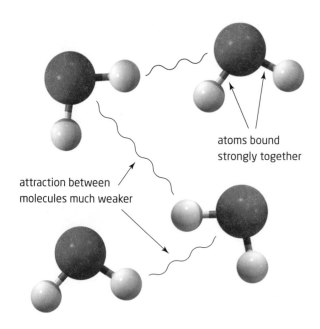

atoms bound
strongly together

attraction between
molecules much weaker

Figure 6.21 In molecular compounds, such as water, the attraction between the molecules is much weaker than the strength of the covalent bonds between the atoms.

Solubility

Another general difference between ionic and molecular compounds is solubility. Many molecular compounds do not dissolve as well as ionic compounds in water. For example, carbon dioxide is a molecular compound that gives soft drinks their fizz, as shown in **Figure 6.23**. Only very small amounts of carbon dioxide gas, however, can dissolve in water. To make the carbon dioxide gas dissolve better, soft drinks are packed under high pressure. When you open a bottle or can, and consequently reduce the pressure inside, the carbon dioxide begins to come out of solution and the soft drink starts to go flat.

Suggested Investigation

Inquiry Investigation 6-B, Properties of Ionic and Molecular Compounds, on page 250

Figure 6.23 The bubbles that you see in a soft drink are carbon dioxide gas that is coming out of solution.

Learning Check

1. Which type of elements are molecular compounds composed of?

2. What happens to electrons in a covalent bond?

3. Identify the elements in each covalent molecular, and state the number of atoms of each element.

   a. silicon tetrachloride

   b. sulfur hexafluoride

4. Why would wearing gloves made from a molecular compound, such as rubber, help to prevent an electrician from being electrocuted?

Plastics

Plastics are made of molecular compounds called *polymers*. If you think about all the different things that are made from plastic, it becomes obvious that there are a large number of different types of plastic.

Ethylene, a molecular compound composed of the elements hydrogen and carbon, is a common starting material for a class of plastics called polyethylenes. Numerous items, such as shopping bags, toys, bottles, and containers, are made with this class of plastics. The different types of polyethylene plastic are grouped based on their density and how many ethylene molecules are joined together. If you look on the bottom of a plastic milk jug, such as the one shown in **Figure 6.24**, you will probably see the letters *HDPE*, which stand for high-density polyethylene.

Figure 6.24 This milk jug is made of high-density polyethylene.

STSE **Case Study**

Taking a Stand on Plastic Bags

Leaf Rapids, Manitoba, a community of about 550 people, had a problem with plastic bags. The discarded bags were scattered all along the lakeshore, trails, and roads, and some bags were even left dangling from trees. The litter was an eyesore in the community, and it cost the community nearly $5000 a year to clean up. The problems with the plastic bags did not end, however, when they were cleaned up.

Plastic bags are not biodegradable. The plastic simply changes into smaller pieces over time. The small, broken-down particles contain toxic materials that can leach into water and soil. The toxic materials are found not only in landfill sites, but also anywhere that plastic ends up as litter.

A Plan of Action

In May 2006, the Leaf Rapids town council began a program to reduce the use of plastic bags. Consumers were charged three cents for each single-use plastic shopping bag they took home from a store. To help consumers stop using plastic bags, the town gave each household five reusable cloth bags.

Then, in April 2007, Leaf Rapids became the first community in Canada to ban most plastic bags in retail stores. According to By-Law 462, "retailers in the Town of Leaf Rapids will not be permitted to give away or sell plastic shopping bags that are intended for single use." Breaking this by-law could mean a fine of $1000.

Leaf Rapids officials estimated that the ban would mean preventing 50 000 to 100 000 bags from ending up in landfills each year. The ban had almost full support from town residents. A year after the ban, the mayor announced that the program was a success. The town was much tidier.

Consumers in Ontario use an estimated 2.5 billion plastic bags each year.

Environmental Concerns

Plastics provide a wide range of products that have many benefits, from convenient food packaging to bottles that keep medicines safe. Each year, millions of tonnes of plastics are produced. The durability of most plastics, however, poses problems for the environment because plastics do not easily degrade. Recycling efforts have reduced the amount of plastics entering landfills, but only some plastics are able to be recycled at this time. For example, many products made from polyethylene plastics are not biodegradable—they are not broken down naturally by living organisms. Chemicals in the plastics slowly leach out over time in landfills. As well, discarded plastics are hazardous to wildlife on land and in the ocean, as shown in **Figure 6.25**.

Suggested Investigation
Data Analysis Investigation 6-C, Classification of Household Substances, on page 252

Figure 6.25 Animals can be harmed if they eat discarded plastic or if they become trapped in pieces of plastic, such as plastic rings.

Alternatives to Plastic

Are paper bags an eco-friendly alternative to plastic bags? Not necessarily. According to the David Suzuki Foundation, one paper bag uses more energy to make and produces more waste than two plastic bags. The Foundation suggests using reusable cloth bags instead of either plastic or paper bags.

The next time you go shopping, you have a choice. You can bring a cloth bag for your purchase, you can carry your purchase without a bag, or you can accept your purchase in a plastic or paper bag. What will you do? Will you take a stand on plastic bags?

Your Turn

1. According to this case study, why might a community consider imposing a charge or a ban on plastic bags?

2. Banning plastic bags is one way to reduce the amount of plastic that is tossed into the garbage. With a partner, brainstorm a list of other solutions.

3. Research what other communities are doing to help reduce the use of plastic bags. Based on your research, write a proposal that describes what could be done in your community.

Not for Everyone

In May 2007, The *Toronto Star* newspaper asked its readers if they thought that plastic shopping bags should be banned. Only about 18 percent of the people who responded agreed with a ban. Other responses included

- concern about not being able to use plastic shopping bags as garbage-bin liners or "stoop and scoop" bags for dog walking

- concern about why plastic bags were being targeted instead of other single-use disposable items

- support for a voluntary reduction instead of a ban

Many people are now using alternatives to plastic shopping bags.

Activity 6-3

Cornstarch Plastic

Starch particles are very long chains of sugar molecules. Starch, therefore, is a natural polymer. Under certain conditions, the long chains become tangled with each other, to form a solid material. How do you think it could be useful?

Safety Precautions

- Wear safety goggles and a lab apron.
- Do not eat anything you use or produce in this activity.
- Make sure that you dispose of any waste materials according to your teacher's instructions.

Materials

- 75 mL of cornstarch
- 250 mL beaker
- 45 mL of water
- sturdy spoon or stir stick
- graduated cylinder

Procedure

1. Read over the procedure, and then make a table to record your observations. Give your table a title.

2. Place the cornstarch in the beaker. Add the water, and stir. When the water and cornstarch are completely mixed, the mixture should be difficult to stir.

3. Shape the mixture into a ball. Observe what happens when you let the ball just sit in your open hand. Record your observations.

4. Apply a small but sudden force to the ball, using your fingers or an object such as a spoon. How does the mixture respond to the sudden application of force? Record your observations.

5. Dispose of the materials as directed by your teacher.

Questions

1. How does the mixture behave if it is allowed to sit undisturbed?

2. What does the mixture do when a sudden force is applied?

3. How do you think a mixture, like the one you made, could be useful?

Making a Difference

As captain of her high school's 2007 Envirothon team, Dayna Corelli helped to develop an award-winning proposal that was reviewed by the city of Sudbury. Dayna's team was concerned that watering lawns and cleaning streets was wasting water. They were also concerned that the city's infrastructure could not handle heavy rainfall, which was causing storm sewers to overflow and dump raw sewage into the Great Lakes. Since reviewing the proposal, as well as recommendations from other groups, Sudbury has restricted lawn watering, made street cleaning more efficient, and improved infrastructure. The Envirothon team's proposal also recommended that the city develop a plan to capture methane, which is produced in landfills, and explore its potential as an energy source.

Dayna has worked on other campaigns to promote recycling, energy efficiency, water conservation, and anti-idling. In 2008, she received a Toyota Earth Day scholarship. Dayna is now studying chemical engineering at Laurentian University.

What changes could your municipality make to improve water quality and energy conservation?

Section Summary

- Most simple molecular compounds are composed of two or more atoms of different elements. These elements are usually two or more non-metals.

- The attraction between molecules is much weaker than the attraction between oppositely charged ions in an ionic crystal. This contributes to the differences in the properties of ionic compounds and some molecular compounds.

- Many molecular compounds tend to have low melting points and low solubility in water, compared with ionic compounds. Many molecular compounds are also poor conductors of heat and electricity.

- Plastics are a large class of human-made molecular compounds. Their numerous uses include shopping bags, containers, and fabrics. There are, however, many environmental concerns associated with the use of plastics.

Review Questions

K/U **1.** Identify each of the following compounds as molecular or ionic.

    a. carbon disulfide

    b. lithium carbonate

    c. OCl_2

    d. P_2O_5

T/I **2.** Is a molecular compound likely to form from two metals? Explain your reasoning.

T/I **3.** Why is the term "covalent" appropriate for describing the bonds in a molecular compound?

K/U **4.** Does the model on the right correctly represent a molecular compound? Why or why not?

A **5.** The prefixes that are used for naming molecular compounds are also used in many common everyday words. List three everyday words that contain one of the prefixes in **Table 6.1**, and explain why the prefix is used.

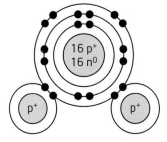

This is a Bohr-Rutherford model.

K/U **6.** What is an important difference between how molecules interact and how ions in a crystal lattice interact? How does this contribute to making the properties of ionic compounds and molecular compounds very different?

K/U **7.** Why are most molecular compounds poor electrical conductors?

C **8.** Suppose that you are given a pamphlet about polymers. The pamphlet claims that polymers are destructive and will ruin the environment. Write a short response, based on your study of molecular compounds.

6.3 Modelling Compounds

The Michael Lee-Chin Crystal at the Royal Ontario Museum in Toronto, shown in **Figure 6.26**, is an impressive accomplishment. Architects and designers, with a wide variety of knowledge and artistic abilities, relied on models throughout the design and construction process. Two-dimensional models, in the form of floor plans, blueprints, and drawings, helped to show how spaces would be arranged within the building and how the building would look from the outside. Three-dimensional models were also used to get a different perspective. These models showed how the building would fit on the available land and what the relative scale of the components would be when the construction was complete. Each type of model has its benefits and its limitations. Like architecture and design, science relies on two-dimensional and three-dimensional models, which can be used to illustrate the important features of compounds.

Figure 6.26 To build the Michael Lee-Chin Crystal at the Royal Ontario Museum, models were used at different stages to convey different types of information.

Two-dimensional Models: Bohr-Rutherford Diagrams

The simplest models of compounds are models that can be drawn on paper. These are two-dimensional models, which indicate height and width. Two-dimensional models are useful for showing what happens during the formation of ionic and molecular compounds.

In the previous chapter, you learned how to draw Bohr-Rutherford models of atoms. You also saw examples of Bohr-Rutherford models for compounds earlier in this chapter, when you learned about the formation of ionic and molecular compounds. These models are helpful for understanding how ions form and how atoms share electrons.

The Bohr-Rutherford model in **Figure 6.27** represents the formation of potassium chloride, KCl. The single electron in the fourth energy level of the potassium atom transfers to the chlorine atom, to fill chlorine's third energy level. After the transfer, the potassium ion has a positive charge, the chloride ion has a negative charge, and both ions have full outer energy levels of electrons.

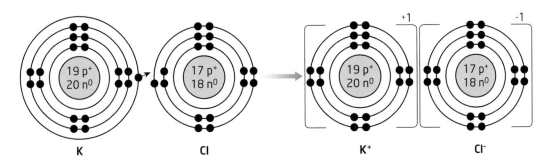

Figure 6.27 The single valence electron of the potassium atom transfers to the chlorine atom. The resulting ions form the ionic compound potassium chloride.

The Bohr-Rutherford model for the molecular compound carbon dioxide (CO_2) is shown in **Figure 6.28**. Notice that each oxygen atom shares two pairs of electrons with the carbon atom. This sharing of electrons results in full outer energy levels for the oxygen atoms and the carbon atom. When two atoms share two pairs of electrons, the covalent bond between them is called a *double bond*. You will learn more about this type of bond in future chemistry courses. You will practise drawing Bohr-Rutherford models for ionic and covalent compounds in Activity 6-4.

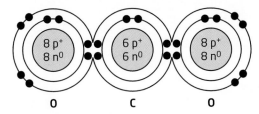

Figure 6.28 Each oxygen atom shares two of its electrons with the carbon atom to form a molecule of carbon dioxide.

Activity 6-4

Representing Compounds Using Bohr-Rutherford Models

Bohr-Rutherford models can be used as two-dimensional representations of how ionic and molecular compounds form. How do Bohr-Rutherford models depict the difference between ionic compounds and molecular compounds?

Materials

- Bohr-Rutherford models of NaCl, H_2O, KCl, and CO_2 (in **Figures 6.4**, **6.18**, **6.27**, and **6.28**).
- periodic table

Procedure

1. Examine the Bohr-Rutherford models for ionic and molecular compounds in **Figures 6.4**, **6.18**, **6.27**, and **6.28**. Use these models to help you draw models of the compounds in this activity. In your models, be sure to show the following details:

   - In your models for ionic compounds, be sure to show the transfer of electrons, the formation of ions, and the joining of oppositely charged ions to form ionic bonds.

   - In your models for molecular compounds, be sure to show the electrons that are shared between atoms, creating a covalent bond.

2. Using a periodic table, draw Bohr-Rutherford models for the compound formed from each of the following pairs of elements.

   a. sodium and fluorine

   b. nitrogen and three hydrogens

   c. sulfur and two hydrogens

   d. lithium and chlorine

Questions

1. If a non-metal has six electrons in its outer energy level, how many single electrons from other atoms does it have room for?

2. A certain non-metal consistently forms three covalent bonds. How many single electrons does it have in its outer energy level?

3. What part of a Bohr-Rutherford model of an atom illustrates the difference between how ionic compounds form and how molecular compounds form?

Three-dimensional Models

A two-dimensional model does not show the three-dimensional characteristics of a compound, such as the spacial arrangement of each atom in the molecule. Three-dimensional models indicate height, width, and depth. There are a variety of three-dimensional models, ranging from ball-and-stick models to computer-generated images, that can show what a compound looks like. These types of models are analogous to three-dimensional models used by architects, such as the one shown in **Figure 6.29**.

Figure 6.29 This three-dimensional model of the Lee-Chin Crystal at the Royal Ontario Museum provided a more realistic view of what the extension would look like.

Ball-and-Stick Models

Although simple craft materials can be used to model molecular compounds, model kits are available. One benefit of using a model kit is that the balls representing the atoms of different elements have holes in the correct positions and at the proper angles for joining them. This helps to show how the atoms in a molecule are arranged in three-dimensional space. The shape of a molecule has a strong influence on the properties of the compound, so being able to see the shape is important. Compare the Bohr-Rutherford model and the ball-and-stick model of each molecular compound in **Figure 6.30** to see how the models convey different information. In Activity 6-5, you will use a model kit to build ball-and-stick models for several molecular compounds.

Study Toolkit

Making Inferences Read the paragraph on this page. Draw a table like the one on page 220 to make an inference about three-dimensional models of compounds. This will help you gain a better understanding of the information that three-dimensional models can provide.

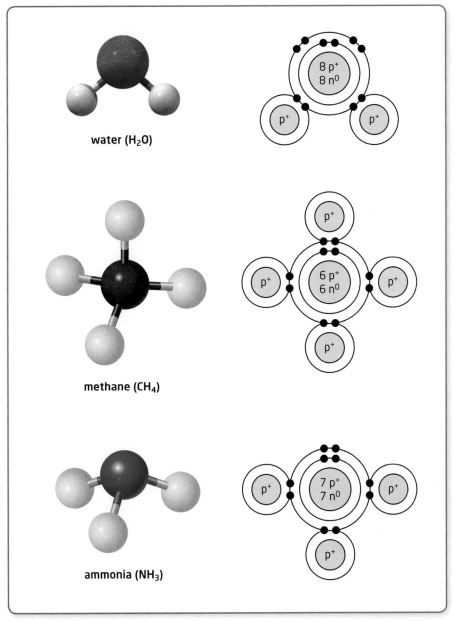

water (H_2O)

methane (CH_4)

ammonia (NH_3)

Figure 6.30 The three-dimensional ball-and-stick models better reflect the true shapes of these molecules.

Activity 6-5

Ball-and-Stick Models

Two-dimensional models, such as Bohr-Rutherford models, provide helpful information about the bonds between atoms. This information can be used to make three-dimensional models. What information do you think three-dimensional models can provide?

Safety Precautions

- Be careful when joining the pieces in the model kit. Excessive force could break them.

- Make sure that you keep track of all the pieces in the model kit, so that none are lost.

Materials

- molecular model kit

Molecular model kits contain pieces that represent atoms (balls) and bonds (sticks).

Procedure

1. Create a table to place the sketches of Bohr-Rutherford models and ball-and-stick models that you will make in this activity.

2. Sketch Bohr-Rutherford models for each of the following compounds: H_2O, O_2, CO_2, NH_3, and CH_4. Have your teacher check your models. You will refer to your models as you build your three-dimensional models.

3. Your teacher will give you a molecular model kit. The ball-shaped pieces in the model kit represent the atoms. The stick-like pieces represent the electron pairs or covalent bonds between the atoms. Place the stick-like pieces between the atoms, using your Bohr-Rutherford model as a guide for how the atoms are connected.

4. Draw a quick sketch of your three-dimensional model, and label it with the chemical formula of the molecule.

5. Build a model of every compound listed in step 2. Remember to sketch each model that you build.

Questions

1. What information does the ball-and-stick model provide that the two-dimensional model does not?

2. Compare and contrast ball-and-stick models with Bohr-Rutherford models.

Space-Filling Models

The relative sizes of atoms can be used to create more accurate three-dimensional models of atoms, ions, and molecules. The space-filling model in **Figure 6.31** is one example of a three-dimensional model that shows the relative sizes of the atoms.

Computer-generated three-dimensional models, like the one in **Figure 6.32**, are extensively used to study large, complex biological molecules, such as proteins and DNA. By building and studying three-dimensional models, scientists can learn more about how these molecules carry out life's essential processes and how chemicals can interact with them and interfere with their activities.

Figure 6.31 This space-filling model of water is a more accurate representation of the relative sizes of the oxygen (red) atom and hydrogen (grey) atoms than a Bohr-Rutherford model or a ball-and-stick model would be.

Go to **scienceontario** to find out more

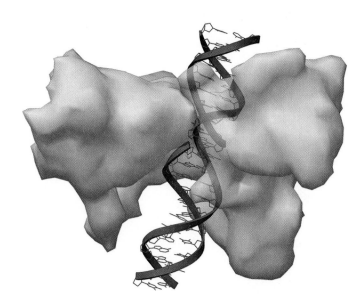

Figure 6.32 Being able to view DNA as a three-dimensional structure allows scientists to speculate on how other molecules can interact with it. This model shows a molecule, called a protein (in grey), interacting in a specific way with DNA.

Section Summary

- Bohr-Rutherford models are two-dimensional models of compounds. A Bohr-Rutherford model shows the electron arrangement within each atom of a compound.

- Three-dimensional models provide valuable information about compounds, including the spatial arrangement of the atoms or ions.

- Two types of three-dimensional models are ball-and-stick models and space-filling models. Ball-and-stick models show the overall shape of a molecule, and space-filling models emphasize the relative sizes of the atoms or ions.

Review Questions

K/U **1.** What type of model shows all the electrons in each atom of a compound?

T/I **2.** Examine the Bohr-Rutherford model of carbon tetrafluoride on the right. How many electrons are used in covalent bonds in the molecule? How many electrons in the outer energy levels of the atoms are not in bonds?

K/U **3.** What are two ways to model compounds in three dimensions?

A **4.** What three-dimensional model can you easily make using materials you can find at home?

T/I **5.** Compare and contrast the usefulness of the two-dimensional models and three-dimensional models in **Figure 6.30**.

C **6.** Write an argument for why there is not one best way to model compounds.

T/I **7.** You could make a ball-and-stick model of a compound from a model kit or from gumdrops and toothpicks. Analyze the benefits and limitations of each of these materials for making a model of a compound.

A **8.** Which type of model would be best to use to determine if a new pain medicine is the correct size and shape to bind to a particular location on a nerve cell? Explain your reasoning.

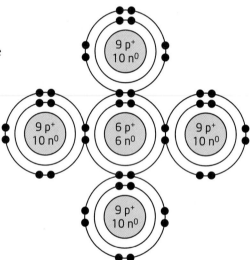

This Bohr-Rutherford model represents carbon tetrafluoride.

Safety Precautions

- Wear safety goggles and a lab apron.
- Clean up all spills immediately.
- Agitate the test tubes safely and effectively.

Materials

- fine sandpaper
- 3 clean, dry nails
- 3 clean, dry test tubes
- 3 clean, dry rubber stoppers
- water
- table salt
- test-tube rack

Set up the test tubes in this way. Leave them undisturbed for one or two days.

Science Skills

Go to **Science Skills Toolkit 7** for information about creating data tables.

What Causes Rusting of Iron Nails?

Garden sheds, tools, lawn furniture, bicycles, and other items that are left outside can be quickly damaged by rust. The cost of the damage can add up to hundreds of dollars each year. In this investigation, you will find out whether certain conditions promote the rusting process.

Question

What conditions cause rust to form?

Procedure

1. Lightly sand each nail to remove any protective coating that the manufacturer may have added.

2. Place one clean, dry iron nail into each of three clean, dry test tubes. You will expose the iron to three different sets of conditions.

3. Stopper one test tube, and label it "dry." Add enough water to the other two test tubes so that the height of the water in each test tube is about 2 cm. Stopper the second test tube, and label it "water." Add a tiny pinch of salt to the third test tube, stopper the test tube, and label it "salt plus water." Lay the stoppered test tubes on their sides, and gently roll the test tubes to distribute the water and the salt. Carefully observe all three nails, and record your observations.

4. Place the test tubes upright in a test-tube rack. Allow them to sit unopened for one or two days.

5. Observe the three iron nails. Are there any similarities in their appearance? Are there any differences? Record your observations.

Analyze and Interpret

1. Identify the control that was used in this investigation.

2. Which set of conditions caused the greatest amount of rusting? Which set of conditions caused the least amount of rusting?

Conclude and Communicate

3. What advice would you give to a home-owner who wanted to minimize the damage caused by rusting?

Extend Your Inquiry and Research Skills

4. **Inquiry** Is oxygen necessary for rusting to occur? Write a hypothesis as a tentative answer to this question. Design an experiment you could perform to test your hypothesis.

Inquiry Investigation 6-B

Skill Check

Initiating and Planning

✓ **Performing and Recording**

✓ **Analyzing and Interpreting**

✓ **Communicating**

Safety Precautions

- Wear safety goggles and a lab apron.
- Cautiously test for odour. Do not smell directly. Take a deep breath and hold it. Waft some air near the mouth of the test tube toward your nose, and then breathe out. This way, you should avoid inhaling any gas.
- Treat the hot plate carefully. Do not leave it turned on for more than 2 min. Allow it to cool for 15 min before moving it.
- To unplug the hot plate, do not pull on the cord. Pull on the plug.

Materials

- 6 test tubes
- 6 samples of compounds
- glass plate or watch glass
- scoop
- plastic water bottle
- hot plate
- aluminum foil
- distilled water
- conductivity tester
- tongs

Properties of Ionic and Molecular Compounds

You encounter hundreds of compounds every day. Although each compound has unique properties, there are some similarities in these properties that can help you to tell what kind of compound it is. In this investigation, you will test six different compounds to determine whether they are ionic or molecular.

Question

How can you use properties to identify compounds as ionic or molecular?

Procedure

1. Label six test tubes with the letters A to F. Place samples of six different compounds in the labelled test tubes. Use just enough of each compound to fill the rounded bottom of the test tube.

2. Prepare a table similar to the one shown. Your table should take up one full sheet of paper so that you have enough space for all your observations. Give your table a title.

Substance	A	B	C	D	E	F
Odour						
Crush						
Hardness						
Melting						
Solubility						
Conductivity						
TOTAL						

3. Perform each of the following tests on each compound. At each test step, analyze all the compounds before moving on to the next test. If a substance responds like an ionic compound, record a score of zero (0) in your table. If a substance responds like a molecular compound, record a score of one (1). Also record short, descriptive observations for each test in your table.

Odour test: Take a deep breath and hold it. Waft some of the air near the mouth of the test tube toward your nose, and then breathe out. Does the compound have a noticeable odour?

Crush test: Place one or two grains of the compound on a glass plate or watch glass. Press on the compound with a scoop or another metal tool. Ionic compounds withstand considerable force and then crush suddenly into a gritty powder (score 0). Molecular compounds that are solids are often more flexible and crush like wax or plastic (score 1).

Hardness test: Rub some of each compound on a clear plastic water bottle. Ionic compounds are often hard enough to scratch the plastic (score 0). Molecular compounds are seldom hard enough to scratch the plastic (score 1).

Melting test: Your teacher will give you a cold hot plate. Spread a small square of aluminum foil over the surface of the hot plate. Carefully place one small piece (no larger than a half a grain of rice) of each substance on the aluminum. Place the samples as far apart as possible. Plug the hot plate in the electric outlet. Be sure to hold the plug away from the metal terminals. Turn on the hot plate. Ionic compounds do not melt, except at very high temperatures (score 0). Molecular compounds tend to melt and even vaporize at relatively low temperatures (score 1). Turn off the hot plate after 2 min. When the hot plate has cooled, pull out the plug. Do not pull on the cord.

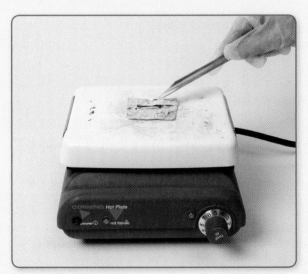

Place each substance on a piece of aluminum foil that is placed on the hot plate.

Solubility test: Each test tube should still contain most of the original substance. Add 10 mL of water to each of the test tubes. Many ionic compounds will dissolve in water, although there are exceptions (score 0). Many molecular solids are insoluble in water (score 1), although again there are exceptions.

Conductivity test: Use a conductivity tester to test the conductivity of the solution in each test tube. When ionic compounds dissolve, the resulting solution will conduct electricity (score 0). When molecular compounds dissolve, the resulting solution will usually not conduct electricity (score 1). Make sure that you clean the probes of the conductivity tester between readings.

4. Clean up your work area. Dispose of all the compounds as indicated by your teacher. Return each piece of equipment to its place.

Analyze and Interpret

1. Add up the scores for each compound. A low score, near 0, indicates that the compound is ionic. A high score, near 6, indicates that the compound is molecular. What patterns do you see?

2. If a compound has a score of 2, 3, or 4, use your descriptive observations to help you decide whether it is ionic or molecular.

Conclude and Communicate

3. Your teacher will tell you the names and formulas of the compounds. Do the names reflect the ionic and molecular classifications that you suggested based on your observations?

Extend Your Inquiry and Research Skills

4. **Inquiry** If you could perform only two tests to identify ionic and molecular compounds, which two tests would you choose? Explain your thinking.

5. **Research** Do sports drinks contain ionic compounds? Which test would you perform to find out?

Skill Check

Initiating and Planning

Performing and Recording

✓ **Analyzing and Interpreting**

✓ **Communicating**

Classification of Household Substances

There are numerous common household substances. As you saw for laboratory chemicals, these substances can also be classified according to whether or not they have ionic or molecular properties. A group of students studied the properties of common household substances. Some of their data are listed in the table below.

Properties of Common Substances

Materials	Melting Point (°C)	Solubility in Water	Conductivity of Solution
Baking soda	Decomposes	Yes	Yes
Cooking oil	−5	No	No
Table salt	801	Yes	Yes
Lip balm	40	No	No
Wax	50	No	No
Sugar	170	Yes	No
Dishwasher soap (powder)	851	Yes	Yes

Question

Which of these household substances have ionic properties, and which have molecular properties?

Analyze and Interpret

1. Examine the substances in the table above. Look for substances that have similar properties.

2. Based on the qualitative and quantitative data, sort the substances into two groups: "ionic properties" and "molecular properties." You may need to have a third group that cannot be identified as either.

Conclude and Communicate

3. Identify the substances that had molecular properties and the substances that had ionic properties. Were there substances that could not be classified? If so, explain why they could not be classified.

Extend Your Inquiry and Research Skills

4. **Research** Determine how the physical properties listed for these common household substances make them useful and/or hazardous in the home.

Chapter 6 Summary

6.1 Ionic Compounds
Key Concepts

- The formation of ions involves the loss or gain of electrons. The ion(s) formed by an atom will depend on its atomic structure and number of valence electrons.
- Ionic compounds form when there is a transfer of electrons between atoms. An ionic bond is the attraction that holds positive ions and negative ions together.

- Most ionic compounds are composed of a metal and a non-metal. Ionic compounds have high melting points and tend to be soluble in water. Ionic compounds are good electrical conductors when melted or when dissolved in water.
- Road salt is commonly used to keep roads safe in the winter by reducing icy driving conditions. Nevertheless, because of its harmful effects on the environment, the frequency and amount of road salt used should be carefully considered.

6.2 Molecular Compounds
Key Concepts

- Most simple molecular compounds are composed of two or more atoms of different elements. These elements are usually two or more non-metals.
- The attraction between molecules is much weaker than the attraction between oppositely charged ions in an ionic crystal. This contributes to the differences in the properties of ionic compounds and some molecular compounds.

- Molecular compounds tend to have low melting points and low solubility in water, compared with ionic compounds. Many molecular compounds are also poor conductors of heat and electricity.
- Plastics are a large class of human-made molecular compounds. Their numerous uses include shopping bags and containers. There are, however, many environmental concerns associated with the use of plastics.

6.3 Modelling Compounds
Key Concepts

- Bohr-Rutherford models are two-dimensional models of compounds. A Bohr-Rutherford model shows the electron arrangement within each atom of a compound.
- Three-dimensional models can provide valuable information about compounds, including the spatial arrangement of the atoms or ions.

- Two types of three-dimensional models are ball-and-stick models and space-filling models. Ball-and-stick models show the overall shape of a molecule, and space-filling models emphasize the relative sizes of the atoms or ions.

Chapter 6 Review

Reviewing Key Terms

Match each key term listed below to its definition.

a. covalent bond   **e.** molecular compound

b. ionic bond   **f.** ion

c. molecule   **g.** chemical bond

d. ionic compound

1. a positively or negatively charged atom (6.1)

2. a chemical link between two atoms, which holds the atoms together (6.1)

3. a chemical bond in which one or more pairs of electrons are shared by two atoms (6.2)

4. the smallest discrete particle of a pure substance, which has one or more shared pairs of electrons (6.2)

5. a chemical bond that forms between oppositely charged ions (6.1)

6. a compound formed when atoms of two or more different elements share electrons (6.2)

7. a compound made of oppositely charged ions (6.1)

Knowledge and Understanding K/U

8. Why are some atoms more stable when they gain or lose an electron?

9. Indicate whether the formation of each ion involved a loss or gain of electrons, and state the number of electrons that were lost or gained.

    a. Mg^{2+} **c.** S^{2-}

    b. Al^{3+} **d.** I^-

10. Identify the types of elements that make up an ionic compound and the types of elements that make up a molecular compound.

11. Give two examples of ionic compounds.

12. Give two examples of molecular compounds.

13. Write formulas for the following compounds, and identify each compound as ionic or molecular.

    a. water

    b. carbon dioxide

    c. sodium chloride

    d. oxygen difluoride

14. Identify each compound as ionic or molecular.

    a. $SrBr_2$

    b. CS_2

15. Use a table to list the similarities and differences between carbon dioxide and sodium chloride.

16. Describe how electrons are involved in forming the bonds in ionic and molecular compounds.

17. State the number that each prefix represents.

    a. di-   **c.** hexa-

    b. penta-   **d.** nona-

18. The following models represent molecules of water.

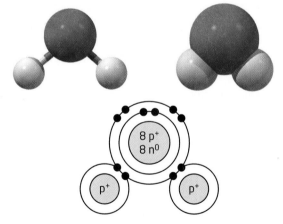

    a. Write the name of each type of model.

    b. Identify the model(s) that represent(s) water in three dimensions.

    c. Which model clearly shows that four valence electrons are not part of the covalent bonds?

19. Salt is used on many Ontario roads to make the roads safe for driving in icy conditions.

   a. What kind of salt is used? What are the properties of this salt that make it valuable for de-icing?

   b. What are some of the negative consequences of using road salt?

Thinking and Investigation T/I

20. How does the total positive charge in an ionic compound compare with the total negative charge in the compound? Explain your reasoning.

21. Why do most ionic compounds have very high melting points?

22. Why is it incorrect to say that the low melting point of a molecular compound is due to its weak covalent bonds?

Communication C

23. Draw a Bohr-Rutherford model for each of the following.

   a. KCl

   b. NaF

   c. O_2

   d. $SiCl_4$

24. **BIG IDEAS** Elements and compounds have specific physical and chemical properties that determine their practical uses. You see an advertisement in a newspaper that claims a new product, which is a molecular compound, can replenish electrolytes when dissolved in water. Write a brief letter to the Better Business Bureau, explaining why this is likely to be false advertising.

25. **BIG IDEAS** The use of elements and compounds has both positive and negative effects on society and the environment. Make a table to summarize the positive and negative effects of the use of plastics on society.

Application A

26. To prevent excess fertilizer from being washed into nearby bodies of water, your friend suggests creating a fertilizer that does not dissolve in water.

   a. Why would this be an ineffective fertilizer?

   b. What could be some social, economic, and environmental effects associated with using an ineffective fertilizer?

27. Which compound would you expect to have a higher melting point: sulfur dichloride or calcium chloride? Explain your reasoning.

28. The table below contains information about three common molecular compounds.

Bond Angles in Molecular Compounds

Compound	Formula	Bond angle
Methane (main component of natural gas)	CH_4	109.5°
Ammonia (used as a fertilizer)	NH_3	107.0°
Water (necessary for living organisms)	H_2O	104.5°

   a. Draw a Bohr-Rutherford model for each compound in this table.

   b. Based on your models, complete a table like the one below.

Electron Arrangements and Bond Angles

Compound	Formula	Number of Valence Electrons in Covalent Bonds	Number of Valence Electrons Not in Covalent Bonds	Bond Angle

   c. Describe the relationship between the bond angle and the number of pairs of valence electrons around the central atom that are not in covalent bonds.

Science at Work

Canadians in Science

Carol Ann Budd traces her interest in science to classroom experiments that she conducted as a student in Sudbury, Ontario. Fascinated by how chemicals and compounds reacted, she decided to study engineering chemistry at Queen's University in Kingston, Ontario. Today, she is a registered professional engineer and a research scientist in private industry. Of Anishinabe heritage, Carol Ann is also a director of CASTS, the Canadian Aboriginal Science and Technology Society. Here's what Carol Ann has to say about scientific research in Canada.

Carol Ann Budd is a professional engineer and research scientist.

In Carol Ann Budd's Words

To continue its growth beyond its natural resources base, our country needs a lot of activity in research and development. I enjoy making a contribution by having a career focused on product research in plastics and polymers. Right now, I lead a team working to develop improved synthetic fibres to make better passenger air bags in automobiles.

Through CASTS programs, I use laboratory demonstrations to encourage students to take an interest in science and technology and to imagine where that interest might lead them. They could end up with jobs in pure science or in a related field, such as health, medicine, or business. In my work in product research, knowledge of chemistry and scientific principles is essential. Communication skills are also important. My co-workers and I need to communicate our findings clearly to persuade business leaders and investors to create new or better products based on our research.

More than ever, we need to think about scientific research in a broad context because of social and environmental issues that challenge us. With their strong ties to the land, Aboriginal cultures remind us to respect Earth's resources and to consider potential future consequences of our actions. We need to ask, 'What effect will we have seven generations from now?' Increasingly, the scientific community needs to be sensitive to important environmental and social issues in order to help solve them.

To encourage student interest in science and technology, Carol Ann Budd organizes and conducts laboratory demonstrations in schools.

Chemistry at Work

The study of chemistry contributes to these careers, as well as many more!

Food Technologist

Food technologists use applied chemistry to develop new food products and ingredients. They prepare recipes and help to design the steps needed to produce new foods. They also help to ensure that packaging protects food and maintains its quality. An especially important part of food technology is testing products to ensure that they are safe for people to eat.

Chemistry Teacher

Research Scientist

Chemical Technologist

Chemistry

Forensic Scientist

Environmental Chemist

Pharmacist

Pharmacists dispense medication that medical doctors prescribe. In some provinces, regulations allow pharmacists to refill prescriptions without having to get a doctor's approval first. As well, pharmacists play an important role in health care by providing information about medication. They answer questions about medication and possible side effects, and they give advice on how to take medication correctly.

Occupational Safety Officer

Occupational safety officers monitor safety practices and train workers in how to handle chemicals properly. They also keep any legally required records about the storage and use of chemicals. If a hazardous spill occurs, occupational safety officers coordinate evacuation and clean-up efforts.

Go to **scienceontario** to find out more

Over To You

1. Provide some examples of research and development activities that you think are important to Canada. Explain why you think they are important.

2. In a small group, discuss whether research chemists have an obligation to ensure chemicals used to manufacture products are safely produced, used, and disposed of. Write a brief paragraph, summarizing your point of view.

3. From the list of careers in chemistry and related fields, choose one that interests you. Use library or Internet resources to research information about the career and what you would need to do to pursue it. **What essential skills would you need for this career?**

Work

Learning

Life

Inquiry Investigation

Rust Prevention

Because of its strength and availability, iron is one of the most widely used metals. But if you have ever left a bicycle outside in the rain, you know that iron rusts. Tendency to rust is a chemical property that causes the iron to become weaker as the reddish-brown rust flakes away. Rusting is a chemical change in which iron reacts with oxygen and water to form the compound iron oxide. Many millions of dollars are spent on technologies to slow or prevent the formation of rust.

Inquiry Question

Although iron rusts, other substances do not. How can you use the chemical properties of other materials to prevent iron from rusting?

Initiate and Plan

1. Suggest two different materials you could use to prevent iron from rusting. You might choose one of the following: plastic wrap, petroleum jelly, nail polish, or another material of your choice. Remember to set up your inquiry so that you test one variable at a time, comparing it to a control.

2. List the materials you will need, the steps in your procedure, and any safety precautions you should take.

3. Decide how you will rate the extent of rusting.

4. For each material you are testing (in other words, for each variable), write a hypothesis that
   • describes the results you expect to see; and
   • explains why you expect those results, based on the physical properties of the materials you are testing.

5. Have your teacher approve your investigation.

Perform and Record

6. Conduct your investigation. Record your results.

Analyze and Interpret

1. Compare the success of each material at preventing rusting.

2. What applications might there be for your discovery?

3. Identify any sources of uncertainty in your inquiry.

Communicate Your Findings

4. Present your results using both a visual and a written component.

Assessment Criteria

Once you complete your project, ask yourself these questions. Did you...

• **T/I** follow the procedure safely and record data accurately?

• **T/I** ensure that your evidence clearly refutes or supports the prediction for each variable tested?

• **T/I** identify sources of uncertainty?

• **A** make a connection between the science and practical application of the results?

• **C** communicate your results using appropriate language?

An Issue to Analyze

The Impact of Metal Mining

Ontario is the largest producer in Canada of nickel, gold, platinum, and cobalt. Ontario is also a significant producer of copper, zinc, and silver. In 2005, over $4 billion worth of metal was produced in Ontario.

> **Issue**
> Do the benefits of metal mining justify the costs?

Initiate and Plan

1. Research on-line to find active metal mining operations in Ontario. Choose one operation (a single mine and metal) to analyze. Have your teacher approve your choice.

2. Before doing any further research, consider how the mining operation might both benefit and harm the local community, Ontario, and Canada.

3. Think of some questions to focus your research. To do this, consider the issue from different perspectives: social, technological, scientific, political, financial, and environmental. Consider researching some or all of the following questions:

   • Who is involved in this issue? (In other words, who are the stakeholders?)

   • How many jobs does the mine provide?

   • How do the metal's properties and its applications benefit society?

   • How does the mining operation affect the environment?

   • How do the products made from the metal affect the environment?

   • What does the mining company do to reduce its impact on the environment?

4. Decide how you will perform your research. What research sources will you use?

Perform and Record

5. Conduct your research to find answers to your questions.

Analyze and Interpret

1. On any issue there are differences of opinion. Based on your research, state your position on the issue and justify your position.

   • Should the mine be closed down? Why, and what proposals will you make to address the negative effects of its closing?

   • Should the mine remain open but with changes to how it operates? Why, and what changes would you suggest?

   • Should the mine continue to operate with no changes? How do you justify any negative effects the mine has?

Communicate Your Findings

2. Decide on a format in which to present your position and findings to your class, such as a newspaper article, a poster, or a podcast. If there is controversy about the project, you might act as moderator in a class debate.

> ### Assessment Criteria
> Once you complete your project, ask yourself these questions. Did you...
> • **K/U** demonstrate knowledge of issues specific to metal mining?
> • **T/I** formulate research questions effectively?
> • **A** identify varying perspectives and stakeholders?
> • **A** take a position, based on supporting evidence from several perspectives and propose an alternative solution if your position differs from what is currently being done?
> • **A** provide a rationale if the position you take suggests no changes?
> • **C** present your report clearly using appropriate language?

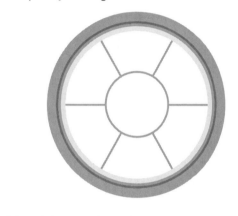
Knowledge and Understanding K/U

For questions 1 through 5, select the best answer.

1. Which of the following is a chemical property?

a. density   c. solubility

b. reactivity with water   d. boiling point

2. Who was the first scientist to discover that atoms are divisible?

a. Mendeleev   c. Thomson

b. Rutherford   d. Dalton

3. A sodium atom is composed of 11 protons, 12 neutrons, and 11 electrons. Which of the following describes the particles that make up an ion of this isotope of sodium?

a. 11 protons, 12 neutrons, and 10 electrons

b. 10 protons, 12 neutrons, and 11 electrons

c. 11 protons, 11 neutrons, and 10 electrons

d. 11 protons, 13 neutrons, and 12 electrons

4. In which family would you expect to find an element that is very reactive with water and whose atoms have one valence electron?

a. halogens   c. alkaline-earth metals

b. noble gases   d. alkali metals

5. Which of the following is a molecular compound?

a. CCl_4 c. KCl

b. $MgCl_2$ d. NaI

6. Describe each of the following physical properties of matter, and provide an example of each one.

a. boiling point

b. electrical conductivity

c. solubility

7. A sample has a mass of 15 g and a volume of 6.0 cm³. Calculate the density of the sample.

8. Iron has a density of 7.87 g/cm³. What is the mass of a 2.50 cm³ piece of iron?

9. A laboratory technician has measured the following data for two liquids that are insoluble in each other.

Liquid A: 5.0 mL has a mass of 6.8 g
Liquid B: 2.5 mL has a mass of 2.3 g

If these liquids are added to the same flask and allowed to separate into two layers, which liquid would be on top? Explain why.

10. Identify two physical properties and one chemical property of water.

11. What is the charge associated with each type of particle?

a. a proton

b. an electron

c. an ion formed by gaining an electron

12. Describe the relative mass of a proton, a neutron, and an electron.

13. How does an atom's valence electrons influence the element's chemical properties?

14. Draw a Bohr-Rutherford model for each atom or ion.
    a. Na
    b. Ar
    c. C
    d. S^{2-}
    e. Mg^{2+}
    f. P^{3-}

15. Determine the number of protons, electrons, and neutrons in each atom.
    a. $^{13}_{6}C$
    b. $^{52}_{24}Cr$
    c. $^{32}_{16}S$
    d. $^{14}_{7}N$

16. Using standard atomic notation, provide an example of an isotope of each atom in question 15.

17. Distinguish among the terms *atomic number*, *atomic mass*, and *mass number*.

18. Explain how the size of the atoms changes as you move down a family in the periodic table.

Thinking and Investigation T/I

19. List the steps you would take to deal with each situation safely.
    a. While you are using a hot plate to heat a liquid, the fire alarm sounds.
    b. You are heating a test tube in the flame of a Bunsen burner when you notice that your test tube has a chip near the top.

20. Describe the laboratory tests that are used to identify each of the following gases.
    a. hydrogen
    b. oxygen
    c. carbon dioxide

21. Explain why sodium metal would not be a good material to use for a water bottle.

22. Use the information in the following table to answer the questions below.

Atomic Properties

Element	Number of Valence Electrons	Atomic Mass	Atomic Number
A	6	16.0	8
B	2	40.1	20
C	8	39.9	18

a. Which element is located farthest to the left in the periodic table? Explain your reasoning.

b. Which element is a noble gas? Explain your reasoning.

c. Which element is most likely to form negative ions? Explain your reasoning.

d. Which element appears latest in the periodic table? Explain your reasoning.

e. Which element has the highest electrical conductivity? Explain your reasoning.

23. Use the following Bohr-Rutherford model to answer the questions below.

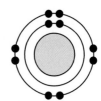

a. If this model represents an atom, what element is it?

b. If this model represents an ion with a charge of 3−, what element is it?

c. If this model represents an ion with a charge of 2+, what element is it?

24. Compare elements and compounds. Clearly describe the relationship between them.

25. Make a table to compare ionic compounds and molecular compounds. Include their properties, as well as how their valence electrons are involved in bonding.

26. Use the following Bohr-Rutherford models to answer the questions below.

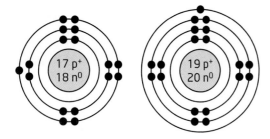

   a. Do these models represent neutral atoms or ions? Explain.

   b. If these two elements combine, is the compound that forms ionic or molecular? Explain.

   c. Draw a Bohr-Rutherford model for the compound that forms if these two elements combine. Label the type of bond that forms.

   d. What is the name of the compound that forms?

Communication C

27. Organize the following models of the atom in the order they were developed. Write the names of the models, from earliest to latest, across the width of a page in your notebook. Under each name, draw a sketch of the model and briefly describe the experimental evidence that supported the model.

| Thomson's model | Dalton's model | Bohr's model | Rutherford's model |

28. Use library and/or Internet resources to research the different types of polyethylene. Create a table to summarize the properties and uses of each type.

29. Sketch an outline of the periodic table, and identify the following on your outline.

   a. metals   **d.** alkali metals

   b. non-metals   **e.** alkaline-earth metals

   c. noble gases   **f.** halogens

Application A

30. The following graph shows the solubility of six compounds. represented by the letters A, B, C, D, E, and F.

Effect of Temperature on Solubility

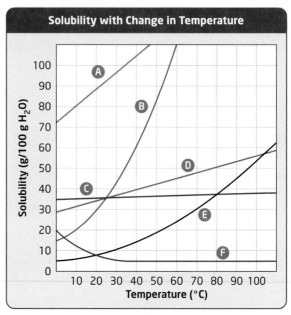

   a. Which compound is the most soluble at 20°C?

   b. Which compound's solubility is least affected by changes in temperature between 0°C and 30°C?

   c. Which compound's solubility increases as the temperature decreases?

31. How has the presence of mercury in waterways affected the environment and the lives of Aboriginal peoples in Canada?

32. Use the chart in **Figure 6.12** on page 230 and your knowledge of the properties of salt to develop a road-salt application strategy. Your strategy should focus on reducing the use of road salt and its effects on the environment.

33. A scientist wants to develop a new drug that interacts with a specific site on DNA. Describe how molecular models can help to accomplish this.

Literacy Test Prep

Read the selection below and answer the questions that follow it.

Aluminum Production

Aluminum is an extremely useful material because of its properties. Aluminum has a low density compared with other metals, so it forms very strong, lightweight alloys with other metals. It is very reactive but does not corrode. Aluminum is easy to work with, so it can be flattened and bent to the desired shape. It also has very good thermal and electrical conductivity.

Aluminum is obtained from a compound called aluminum oxide, which comes from bauxite that is mined. A large amount of electrical energy is needed to process the bauxite and aluminum oxide. Although bauxite is not mined in Canada and must be imported, our abundant hydroelectric power plants allow Canada to be one of the world's primary producers of aluminum.

Each year, approximately 1.5 billion kg of aluminum are used to produce beverage cans in North America. This requires about 5 billion kilowatt-hours of electricity–the same amount of electricity that is used by over half a million homes each year. Recycling the aluminum in cans, however, requires only 5 percent of the energy needed to make new aluminum. Also, unlike most other metals, 100 percent of the aluminum can be recycled.

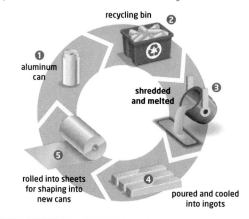

Multiple Choice

In your notebook, record the best or most correct answer.

34. Canada is a large producer of aluminum because Canada has many

a. bauxite mines

b. hydroelectric power stations

c. beverage canning factories

d. deposits of elemental aluminum

35. Aluminum is extremely useful because of all the following properties **except**

a. its ability to form alloys

b. its high thermal conductivity

c. its ability to be easily shaped

d. its high density

36. What is the correct order in the production of aluminum beverage cans?

a. bauxite → aluminum oxide → cans

b. aluminum oxide → bauxite → aluminum → cans

c. bauxite → aluminum → aluminum oxide → cans

d. bauxite → aluminum oxide → aluminum → cans

37. The purpose of the information in the last paragraph is to

a. encourage the reader to recycle aluminum cans

b. organize information about the production of aluminum

c. inform the reader of worldwide aluminum use

d. recommend that the reader use less energy in the home

38. The purpose of the diagram is to show

a. how many aluminum cans are recycled each year

b. how much energy is saved by recycling an aluminum can

c. how an aluminum can is recycled into aluminum foil

d. how an aluminum can is recycled into another can

Written Answer

39. Aluminum is used to manufacture parts for airplanes. Describe two properties of aluminum that you think are important in the production of these parts. Use specific details from the selection to support your answer.

UNIT
3
The Study of the Universe

BIG IDEAS

- Space exploration has generated valuable knowledge but at enormous cost.
- Different types of celestial objects in the solar system and universe have distinct properties that can be investigated and quantified.
- People use observational evidence of the properties of the solar system and the universe to develop theories to explain their formation and evolution.

Canadarm2, shown here supporting an astronaut, plays a major role in constructing the International Space Station (ISS). The ISS is a large complex of laboratories orbiting in space. Aboard the ISS, researchers from many countries investigate the effects of space travel on humans and materials. Scientists also investigate Earth and space itself from the ISS.

Despite their great contributions to scientific knowledge, space research and exploration are tremendously expensive. For example, Canadarm2 cost $600 million to design and build. Other benefits help offset such costs, however. For example, robotic expertise gained by developing Canadarm2 led to neuroArm, shown in the inset photograph. This robotic device allows brain surgeons to operate on their patients with great precision.

In this unit, you will learn about space exploration and our current understanding of the universe, including the solar system.

Why is it important to find out how space travel affects people and materials?

Chapter 7
The Night Sky

Chapter 8
Exploring Our Stellar Neighbourhood

Chapter 9
The Mysterious Universe

Get Ready for Unit 3

Concept Check

1. Match each term with its correct definition below.

   a. planet   **e.** star

   b. meteorite   **f.** Earth

   c. Moon   **g.** comet

   d. asteroid belt

   i. Earth's natural satellite

   ii. emits light

   iii. located between Mars and Jupiter

   iv. much of its surface is covered with water

   v. has a tail consisting of gas and dust

   vi. orbits stars and reflects light

   vii. stony or metallic matter that has fallen to Earth

2. With a partner, brainstorm ways in which stars differ from planets. Organize your comparisons in a table like the one below. Alternatively, make a Venn diagram to compare and contrast stars and planets.

   Comparing Stars and Planets

Characteristics of Stars (like our Sun)	Characteristics of Planets

3. It takes 11.86 Earth-years for Jupiter to revolve around the Sun. Each Jupiter day is 9 h, 50 min, and 30 s long.

   a. Which of the above statements describes Jupiter's period of rotation?

   b. Which statement describes Jupiter's period of revolution?

   c. What are the periods of rotation and revolution for Earth?

4. Match each cause to an effect in the table below. Write each of your answers as a complete sentence in your notebook.

   Cause-and-Effect Relationships

Cause	Effect
a. Earth's rotation on its axis causes …	**i.** the seasons
b. Earth's revolution around the Sun causes …	**ii.** ocean tides
c. The Moon's gravitational pull on Earth causes …	**iii.** Earth's orbit
d. Earth's tilt on its axis causes …	**iv.** day and night
e. The Sun's gravitational pull on Earth causes …	**v.** yearly periods

5. Each of the following space technologies is illustrated below. Match each technology to its corresponding illustration.

   a. *Discovery* space shuttle

   b. Atlas V rocket

   c. the Hubble Space Telescope

   d. the International Space Station

Inquiry Check

Scientific and technological advances have allowed humans to adapt to life in space. However, astronauts face many challenges while living in space. For example, some of the needs that must be met while living on the International Space Station are the following:

a. elimination of human waste

b. regular exercise to maintain muscle and bone density

c. a long-term supply of drinkable water

6. **Think Critically** Using jot notes, add three to five more challenges to the list.

7. **Analyze** How might some of these challenges be overcome? Choose one challenge from the list above and one from your own list, and discuss your recommendations in a small group.

8. **Think Critically** The average stay for an astronaut on the International Space Station is six months. Why do you think astronauts remain on the International Space Station for this period of time?

Numeracy and Literacy Check

Astronomers commonly use scientific notation to express the sizes of objects in space and distances between them. For example, the diameter of the Moon is 3475 km, or 3.475×10^3 km.

9. **Convert** The diameter of Earth is 12 756 km. Express this measurement in scientific notation.

10. **Compare** How much larger is the diameter of Earth compared to the diameter of the Moon?

11. **Writing** While risky and expensive, space exploration technology is beneficial. For example, the technology used for fuel pumps in space shuttles is also used to make better artificial hearts. Write a brief letter to the editor of your local newspaper expressing your opinion on the money spent by the federal government for space exploration (see table). Support your viewpoint with examples.

Federal Spending in Canada in 2004

Area	Money Spent (millions of dollars)
Environmental initiatives	900
Defence	9 800
Health care	99 000
Space exploration	308

Looking Ahead to the Unit 3 Project

At the end of this unit, you will have an opportunity to apply what you have learned in an inquiry or research project. Read the Unit 3 Projects on pages 390–391. Start a project folder now (either paper or electronic). Store ideas, notes, news clippings, websites, and lists of materials that might help you to complete your project.

Inquiry Project
Investigate how to simulate a cosmic event.

An Issue to Analyze
Decide whether Canada should continue to fund costly space missions.

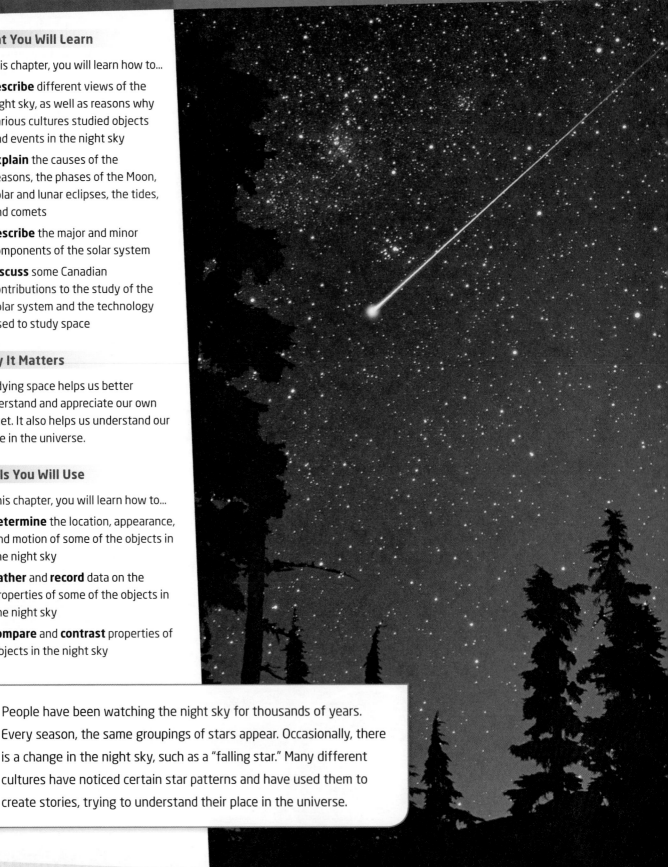

Chapter 7 The Night Sky

What You Will Learn

In this chapter, you will learn how to...

- **describe** different views of the night sky, as well as reasons why various cultures studied objects and events in the night sky
- **explain** the causes of the seasons, the phases of the Moon, solar and lunar eclipses, the tides, and comets
- **describe** the major and minor components of the solar system
- **discuss** some Canadian contributions to the study of the solar system and the technology used to study space

Why It Matters

Studying space helps us better understand and appreciate our own planet. It also helps us understand our place in the universe.

Skills You Will Use

In this chapter, you will learn how to...

- **determine** the location, appearance, and motion of some of the objects in the night sky
- **gather** and **record** data on the properties of some of the objects in the night sky
- **compare** and **contrast** properties of objects in the night sky

People have been watching the night sky for thousands of years. Every season, the same groupings of stars appear. Occasionally, there is a change in the night sky, such as a "falling star." Many different cultures have noticed certain star patterns and have used them to create stories, trying to understand their place in the universe.

Activity 7-1

Create Your Own Constellation

Constellations are star patterns that represent different people and objects in the night sky. Many cultures have their own stories about what the constellations represent. For example, the constellation shown here is Leo, the lion. According to Greek mythology, Hercules slayed a gigantic lion. As a thank you to Hercules, the Greek gods placed the lion in the sky. Does the star pattern look like a lion to you? In this activity, you will create your own constellation and a story to go with it.

Leo, the lion

Materials

- blank paper
- coloured markers

Procedure

1. Use the following questions to plan your constellation:
   - What object, animal, or person will your constellation represent?
   - What shape will your constellation be, and how many stars will it have?
   - Will your constellation be visible all year long or only in a certain season?
2. Name your constellation.
3. Write a story about your constellation, and draw a picture of it.
4. Trade constellation stories and pictures with your classmates.

Questions

1. Do your interpretations of your classmates' constellations match their stories?
2. Why do you think different cultures created stories about the constellations?

Study Toolkit

These strategies will help you use this textbook to develop your understanding of science concepts and skills.
To find out more about these and other strategies, refer to the Study Toolkit Overview, which begins on page 561.

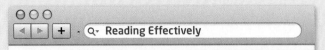

Making Connections to Prior Knowledge

You may already know some facts about the universe, from reading other texts, from the news, or from your own experiences. This prior knowledge can help you understand new information in this chapter. As you read, ask yourself these questions:

- What personal experience does this remind me of? (connect text to self)

- What else have I read about this? (connect text to text)

- What have I heard about meteorites lately? (connect text to world)

You can use a **concept map** like the one below to organize your connections to prior knowledge.

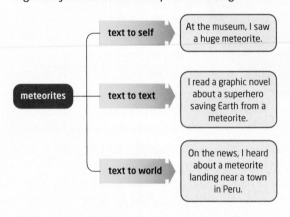

Use the Strategy

Think of what you know about Earth's moon. Make some connections to your prior knowledge about this topic. Then draw a concept map to show the connections.

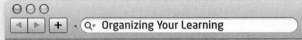

Identifying Cause and Effect

Non-fiction text sometimes explains *why* something happens (the cause), or what happens *as a result of* something (the effect). Some causes can have multiple effects, such as in the following passage: "The impact [cause] produced an explosion [effect] with energy equivalent to approximately 1000 atomic bombs. This amount of energy probably generated hurricane-force winds [effect] up to 40 km from the impact site. Falling rock [effect] resulting from the impact would have destroyed everything within a 10 km radius."

You can use a **graphic organizer** like the one below to identify causes that have multiple effects.

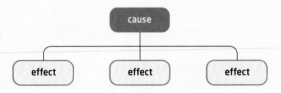

Use the Strategy

Turn to the section titled "Asteroid and Meteorite Impacts" on page 302. Draw a cause-and-effect graphic organizer to show the multiple effects of the object that entered Earth's atmosphere above Siberia.

Word Origins

Some English words originated from words in ancient languages, such as Greek and Latin. One strategy for figuring out the meaning of a new word is to study its origin. For example, if you know that *helios* means Sun in Greek, you might figure out that *heliocentric* means "centred around the Sun."

Use the Strategy

1. Think about the word *geocentric*. *Geo* comes from the Greek word for Earth. Predict what *geocentric* means.

2. Apply this strategy to other unfamiliar words as you read through this chapter.

7.1 Ancient Astronomy

Key Terms
calendar
celestial object
astronomer
revolution
rotation

The first people to notice the sky must have been very impressed with its reliability. The Sun sets every night and rises every morning. The Moon goes through the same phases every month. The stars sweep across the night sky with the changing seasons and return with exact timing to the same position in the sky every year.

People began developing technologies based on observations of the sky. For example, the Maya civilization in Mexico's Yucatan region built the pyramid in **Figure 7.1** around 1000 years ago. As the Sun sets on the first day of spring and fall, the light and shadow create the appearance of a diamond-backed snake gradually moving down the stairs of the pyramid. The shadows end at a statue of a snake's head. This phenomenon does not happen on the first day of winter and summer.

Human survival depends on the reliability of the Sun rising every morning and the seasons returning every year. It must have been very frightening for early sky watchers when unexpected events, such as a solar eclipse, occurred in the sky. During a solar eclipse, the Moon passes in front of the Sun and temporarily blocks the Sun's light. (You will learn more about eclipses in Section 7.3.) If unexpected events can occur in the sky, then maybe the reliability of the Sun and the changing seasons were not as dependable as the early sky watchers had hoped.

Figure 7.1 This pyramid has four stairways, each with 91 stairs. These stairs, plus the platform on top, add to a total of 365, representing the 365 days of the year.

Early Calendars and Sky Observations

calendar a way of showing days, organized into a schedule of larger units of time, such as weeks, months, seasons, or years; usually a table or a chart

Careful long-term observations of the sky by early sky watchers led to the first calendars. A **calendar** is a way of showing days. The days are organized into a schedule of larger units of time, such as weeks, months, seasons, or years. Calendars like the stepped pyramid in **Figure 7.1** allowed people to predict yearly events, such as when the seasons change. This, in turn, allowed people to predict other important events, such as spring rains, the annual flooding of rivers and lakes, and the migration of birds, insects, and herds of animals. Predicting rains and floods allowed some cultures to plan watering for agriculture (farming). Predicting locations of herds of animals allowed other cultures to plan hunting.

Fishers, mariners, and travellers knew the fixed patterns of the stars in the sky and used them to help them find their way, or navigate, on land and water. The ancient Egyptians relied on a star called Sirius to let them know when the Nile river was about to flood. Sirius rises just before dawn at the same time every year before the annual flooding of the Nile.

Early Astronomers

Our earliest ancestors paid a great deal of attention to the sky and took great care not to offend the deities (gods) who they believed ruled the skies. The sky watchers closely watched the sky for signs that the deities might be getting restless. If something unusual happened, such as the eclipse in **Figure 7.2**, people interpreted this to mean that they needed to do something to please the deities and return order to the sky. From these early needs grew the role of celestial priests and priestesses. Celestial priests and priestesses studied **celestial objects**, such as the Sun and other stars, the Moon, and the planets. They learned to predict celestial events, such as seasons and eclipses.

celestial object any object that exists in space, such as a planet, a star, or the Moon

Figure 7.2 Scientists know from historical records that early sky watchers were terrified by the sight of the Moon blocking the Sun's light and sending Earth into darkness. They did not understand what was happening, and they were afraid of the unknown.

Mesopotamian Astronomers

Over 6000 years ago, civilizations developed in the region between the Tigris and Euphrates Rivers. These two rivers flow through what is now the country of Iraq. The civilizations that developed in this region—the Assyrians, the Babylonians, and the Sumerians—were called Mesopotamians. The Mesopotamians were the first **astronomers** for whom we have evidence of detailed astronomical observations. They kept detailed records of the sky as early as 6000 years ago. Their calendars were thorough although not perfectly accurate.

With the invention of the calendar, the first civilizations were born. Having a calendar meant that organized agriculture was possible. Having organized agriculture meant that societies could produce extra food. Producing extra food meant that other people in these societies could be freed up from farming to focus on specializing their skills in diverse areas such as woodworking and metallurgy (the science of working with metals).

astronomer a scientist who studies astronomy, which is the study of the night sky

Today's Year

Today, our year is determined by counting the number of days required for the Sun to return to exactly the same place in the sky with respect to the background stars. In other words, our year is determined by the amount of time it takes for Earth to make one **revolution** around the Sun. This means that the year is 365.24 days long. The year is further divided into 12 months and 52 weeks, with seven days in each week.

The months have different numbers of days. If you add up the total number of days in each month, you actually get only 365 days. Every four years, an extra day is added in February to account for the accumulation of the quarter days. The year in which this happens is called a leap year.

revolution the time it takes for an object to orbit another object; Earth's revolution around the Sun is 365.24 days

Early Clocks

People were also interested in understanding and recording time during a single day. One day is the average time it takes for Earth to make one **rotation** on its axis with respect to the Sun, for example, from noon until noon.

The first clocks were simply pillars and sticks in the ground. People used the shadows they cast to tell the time of day. Early sky watchers had to use shadows because watching the Sun directly is dangerous. The sunlight can damage the eyes and even cause blindness. People monitored the position and length of the shadow cast by a stick or pillar as the Sun moved across the sky. As cultures progressed, they replaced the early stick "clocks" with sundials, such as the one shown in **Figure 7.3**.

rotation the turning of an object around an imaginary axis running through it

Figure 7.3 As Earth rotates, the shadow of the straight edge moves and aligns with the hour markers.

Inferring Earth's Spherical Shape

Today, you can look at photographs of Earth taken from space and see that Earth is a sphere. This is not obvious when standing on Earth's surface. Earth is so large that it looks flat. The ancient Egyptians thought that Earth was flat and supported by mountains at four different places. The ancient Inuit also thought that Earth was flat, stationary, and at the centre of the universe. The ancient Chinese believed that Earth was a square surrounded by one huge ocean.

Originally, the ancient Greeks thought that Earth floated in the ocean like a piece of wood floats in water. Two ancient Greek philosophers, Eratosthenes and Aristarchus (310–230 B.C.E.), hypothesized that Earth is spherical. They also hypothesized that the apparent flatness of Earth is an illusion created by Earth's enormous size. Their hypotheses were based on three pieces of evidence.

Disappearing Ships

The first piece of evidence was well known in the time of the ancient Greeks (and probably much earlier, but not recorded). Look at **Figure 7.4**. As a ship sailed out into the Mediterranean Sea, the hull disappeared below the horizon (the line where the sky and Earth seem to meet). But the masts and the sails of the ship were still visible. Eventually, the masts and the sails also disappeared below the horizon as the ship moved farther away.

Figure 7.4 Ancient Greek philosophers observed that the hull of a ship drops out of sight and appears to descend below the horizon as the ship sails farther away.

The Changing Sky

The second piece of evidence was the changing appearance of the sky as travellers journeyed farther north and south. When travelling farther north, travellers saw stars rising farther above the northern horizon. When travelling farther south, they saw stars they had never seen before rising above the southern horizon. This is shown in **Figure 7.5**.

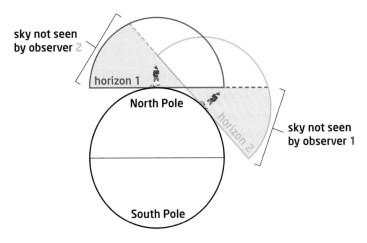

Figure 7.5 As ancient travellers moved in a north-south direction, they noticed changes in their view of the sky. Observer 1 sees a different view of the sky than observer 2.

Earth's Curved Shadow

The third piece of evidence was the shape of Earth's shadow. During an eclipse of the Moon, the Moon passes through Earth's shadow. The ancient Greeks knew about eclipses of the Moon. They noticed that the shape of Earth's shadow is always curved, as shown in **Figure 7.6**. Only a circular or spherical object can cast a curved shadow. In addition, using this knowledge, Aristarchus calculated the relative sizes of the Moon and Earth. Aristarchus also figured out the relative size of the Sun and its relative distance from Earth compared with Earth's distance from the Moon.

Study Toolkit

Identifying Cause and Effect The three pieces of evidence leading to the realization that Earth is a sphere can be seen as effects. You can use a cause-and-effect graphic organizer, such as the one on page 270, as an aid to show this. How does using a graphic organizer help you better understand the material?

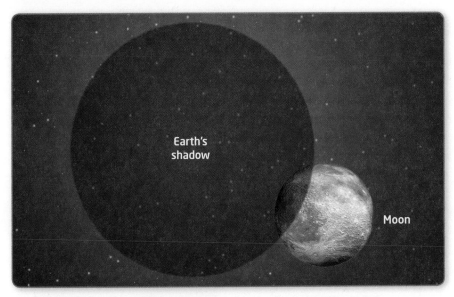

Figure 7.6 During a lunar eclipse, the Moon passes through Earth's shadow.

Section Summary

- Early sky watchers paid a lot of attention to the sky. This enabled them to develop accurate calendars, which they used to predict the seasons and other events that were important to them in their daily lives.

- Different cultures have different reasons for watching the sky. For example, the ancient Egyptians watched for a star called Sirius to rise every year because they knew that the Nile River would flood soon after.

- Earth's revolution around the Sun takes 365.24 days. Earth's rotation on its axis takes 24 hours.

- Careful observations of ships "disappearing" below the horizon, the changing appearance of the sky when travelling, and Earth's shadow viewed during eclipses led the early Greeks to infer that Earth is a sphere.

Review Questions

K/U **1.** What does the term *celestial object* mean? Give two examples.

C **2.** What unit of time does one revolution of Earth around the Sun correspond to? Include a simple diagram in your answer.

K/U **3.** Give two examples of why early cultures depended on their observations of the sky.

C **4.** In an email to a friend, explain how calendars were helpful to ancient civilizations.

C **5.** A friend believes that Earth is flat. Construct an argument to convince your friend that Earth is a sphere.

A **6.** What do you think a ship would look like if it sailed farther and farther away on a flat surface? How do you think this observation helps to prove that Earth is not flat?

T/I **7.** Imagine that you are standing at the North Pole and see a star directly overhead. Where do you think the star would be if you were standing at the equator? Review **Figure 7.5**.

T/I **8.** Large sailing ships have a lookout post, called a crow's-nest, on one of their masts. Why is the crow's-nest as high on a mast as possible?

A crow's-nest

7.2 The Constellations

Key Terms
constellation
light-year
apparent magnitude
latitude

When you look up on a clear, moonless night in a location far away from city lights, you can see thousands of stars, some twinkling very brightly and others shining more faintly. Most cultures imagined that the patterns formed by the stars in the night sky represented different people, animals, and objects. For example, the ancient Greeks gave the first star pattern in **Figure 7.7** the name "Orion." Orion was a mythological hunter. The Inuit interpreted the pattern of the three stars in Orion's belt as a bear and two hunters. The topmost star in the belt is the bear escaping by climbing high in the sky. The other two stars are the hunters chasing the bear. A third hunter came back to Earth because he dropped a mitten. He remained and tells the story.

Patterns in the Night Sky

Many groups of stars seem to form distinctive patterns. These patterns are called **constellations**. The stars in a constellation appear to lie close to each other and at exactly the same distance from Earth. They look close together because they lie on the same line of sight. They may, in fact, be light-years apart. A **light-year** is a unit of distance. It represents the distance that light travels in one year. At the speed of 300 000 km/s, light travels about 9.5×10^{12} km in one year.

constellation a group of stars that seem to form a distinctive pattern in the sky

light-year the distance that light travels in one year, about 9.5×10^{12} km

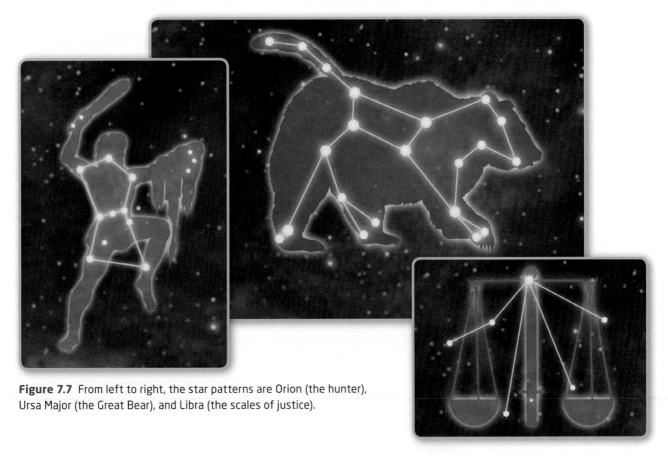

Figure 7.7 From left to right, the star patterns are Orion (the hunter), Ursa Major (the Great Bear), and Libra (the scales of justice).

Random Stars in Space

Figure 7.8 shows the constellation Cassiopeia as it appears from Earth. The figure also shows that the stars appear to be unrelated in space.

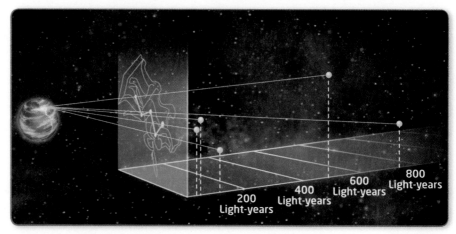

Figure 7.8 The stars in Cassiopeia are many light-years apart.

Apparent Magnitude

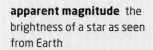
apparent magnitude the brightness of a star as seen from Earth

Star maps, such as the one shown in **Figure 7.9**, show constellations and individual stars. Star maps also represent the stars by dots of varying sizes. The larger the dot, the brighter the star is. Astronomers use the term *apparent magnitude* when they are describing the brightness of a star. A star's **apparent magnitude** is its brightness as seen from Earth.

The magnitude scale for star brightness was first developed by the ancient Greek astronomer Hipparchus, around 130 B.C.E. He assigned the number 1 to the brightest star he could see and the numbers 2 through 6 for sequentially fainter stars. A star of magnitude 6 is about the faintest star that the unaided human eye can see.

Hipparchus devised his stellar (star) magnitude scale based on the assumption that a magnitude 5 star was ⅕ the brightness of a magnitude 1 star. Similarly, a magnitude 3 star was ⅓ the brightness of a magnitude 1 star. A difference of five magnitudes actually represents a brightness difference of about 100. Today, the stellar magnitude scale goes beyond magnitude 6 and into the minus range, as well. The Sun, the brightest object in the sky, has an apparent magnitude of –26.

Figure 7.9 A star map shows the relative locations of stars in the sky at a certain time of night on a certain date.

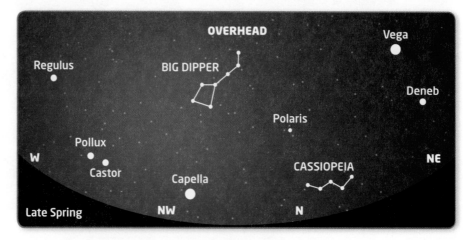

Names of Constellations

The International Astronomical Union (IAU) is responsible for naming and classifying celestial objects. The IAU lists 88 official constellations. The star patterns in **Figure 7.7** are all constellations. Other examples of constellations are Cancer (the crab), Cassiopeia (the queen), and Ursa Minor (the Little Bear). Many of the constellation names, especially in the northern hemisphere, are ancient Greek and Latin names that represent mythological figures. For example, Cassiopeia is Greek for seated queen. The Romans used Latin names, such as Capricornus, which is Latin for sea goat.

Smaller groups of stars that form patterns within a constellation are called *asterisms,* from the Greek word *aster,* meaning star. An example of an asterism is the Big Dipper, seen in **Figure 7.10**. The Big Dipper is one of the most visible star patterns in the northern sky. It is part of the large constellation Ursa Major (the Great Bear).

Go to **scienceontario**
to find out more

Figure 7.10 In the Big Dipper, the four bright stars at the lower right form the bowl of the dipper (a ladle or scoop). The three bright stars at the upper left of the bowl form the handle of the dipper.

The Big Dipper

Many cultures recognize the star pattern in the Big Dipper. The ancient Chinese saw the Big Dipper as a chariot for the emperor of the heavens. The early Egyptians saw the thigh and leg of a bull. For several North American Aboriginal cultures, such as the Algonquin, Iroquois, and Narragansett, the bowl of the Big Dipper is a bear. The stars in the handle are hunters who are following the bear. According to some stories, because the bear is low enough in early autumn evenings to brush the maple trees, blood from its wounds turns the leaves red. Another culture, the Snohomish, have a story that tells how three hunters chasing four elk became the seven brightest stars of the Big Dipper. One of the hunters is accompanied by a dog, which you can see if you look carefully at the middle star in the handle.

Sense of place

The Algonquin live in the Ottawa River Valley, at the current border between Ontario and Québec. The Iroquois live in the northeastern United States and eastern Canada. The Narragansett live in western Rhode Island, in the eastern United States. The Snohomish live along the coast of Washington State.

Polaris and the Pointer Stars

The Big Dipper's two end stars are called the pointer stars because they point toward Polaris, the North Star. You can see the pointer stars in **Figure 7.11**. The next time you go out and look at the night sky, find Polaris using the pointer stars.

For thousands of years, long before the invention of the compass, people in the northern hemisphere used Polaris to tell direction. Earth's rotational axis points to Polaris. So, as Earth rotates eastward on its axis, Polaris does not appear to move, unlike the other stars. During the night, the stars seem to revolve counterclockwise around Polaris, as shown in **Figure 7.12**. If you can see Polaris, then you know which way is north. Once you know which way is north, you can figure out the other directions: east, south, and west.

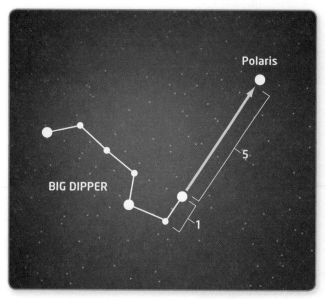

Figure 7.11 The distance from the pointer stars to Polaris is about five times the distance between the two pointer stars.

Figure 7.12 This time-exposure image, taken over several hours, shows how the stars in the northern sky appear to revolve counterclockwise around Polaris, the North Star.

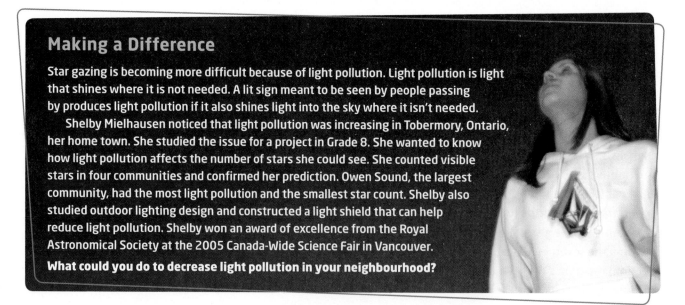

Making a Difference

Star gazing is becoming more difficult because of light pollution. Light pollution is light that shines where it is not needed. A lit sign meant to be seen by people passing by produces light pollution if it also shines light into the sky where it isn't needed.

Shelby Mielhausen noticed that light pollution was increasing in Tobermory, Ontario, her home town. She studied the issue for a project in Grade 8. She wanted to know how light pollution affects the number of stars she could see. She counted visible stars in four communities and confirmed her prediction. Owen Sound, the largest community, had the most light pollution and the smallest star count. Shelby also studied outdoor lighting design and constructed a light shield that can help reduce light pollution. Shelby won an award of excellence from the Royal Astronomical Society at the 2005 Canada-Wide Science Fair in Vancouver.

What could you do to decrease light pollution in your neighbourhood?

Viewing Different Constellations

Due to Earth's revolution around the Sun, you see different constellations in the evening sky at different times of the year. The effect of Earth's orbital motion is illustrated in **Figure 7.13**.

Suggested Investigation

Inquiry Investigation 7-B, The Changing View of the Night Sky, on pages 308–309

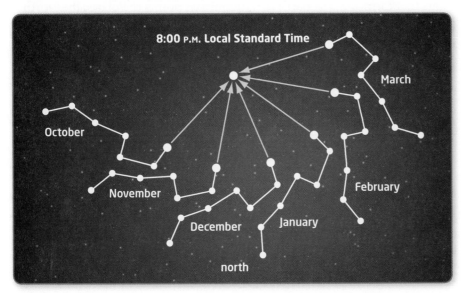

Figure 7.13 The westward creep of the constellations around Polaris is due to Earth's eastward orbit around the Sun.

The constellations that you can see also depend on your **latitude**. As you move northward, constellations along the southern horizon slip below the horizon so that you cannot see them. As you move southward, constellations, formerly unseen, rise above the southern horizon. For thousands of years, travellers have used the constellations to navigate on sea and on land. In **Figure 7.14**, compare the altitudes of contellations at two different latitudes.

As European explorers sailed the oceans and entered the southern hemisphere in the 1600s and 1700s, they saw new star patterns that they had never seen before. The explorers created new constellations and gave them names such as "the Telescope," "the Microscope," and "the Sextant," after technologies that were important to the explorers at the time.

latitude the location above or below the equator

Figure 7.14 A The latitude of Ottawa, Ontario, is about 45°N, and **B** the latitude of Miami, Florida, is about 25°N. Polaris, in the Little Dipper, is very low in Miami compared with Ottawa.

Section Summary

- Constellations are groupings of stars that form distinctive patterns. The stars in these groupings appear to be close to each other, but they are not.

- A star's apparent magnitude is its brightness as seen from Earth.

- The Big Dipper is an asterism, which is a smaller grouping of stars within a constellation.

- Earth's rotational axis points to Polaris, the North Star. For thousands of years, travellers have used Polaris and the constellations to navigate.

- Different cultures have different interpretations of the night sky.

- A light-year is the distance that light travels in one year.

Review Questions

K/U **1.** Compare and contrast the terms *constellation* and *asterism* in a Venn diagram. Give an example of each.

C **2.** Draw the Big Dipper star pattern, and list two cultures that recognize this pattern.

K/U **3.** What is a star's apparent magnitude?

K/U **4.** Why do the stars in the northern hemisphere appear to revolve around Polaris?

K/U **5.** Define the term *light-year*.

T/I **6.** Do you think any of the constellations in **Figure 7.7** look like the person, animal, or object they represent? Explain your answer.

C **7.** Using a diagram, explain how people use Polaris and the constellations to navigate.

T/I **8.** Copy the diagram of the Big Dipper into your notebook. The numbers are distances from Earth, in light-years, of the stars. Show that the stars in the Big Dipper are not close together. Use **Figure 7.8** as a guide.

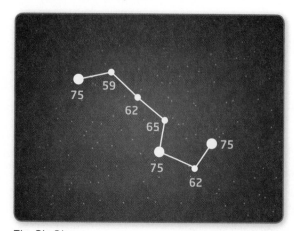

The Big Dipper

7.3 Movements of Earth and the Moon

Key Terms

tides
ellipse
phases of the Moon
eclipse
lunar eclipse
solar eclipse
gravitational force

An understanding of Earth and its movements is important. Understanding Earth's rhythms is critical to understanding the life cycles of all living things on Earth. The seasons are a result of Earth's revolution around the Sun, combined with Earth's tilt. The study of our closest neighbour in space, the Moon, is also important. The Moon is responsible for the tides that occur on Earth. The **tides** are the rising and falling of ocean waters. The orbit of the Moon around Earth results in the phases of the Moon, as well as eclipses.

Earth's Motion

As you learned earlier, Earth undergoes two different types of motion through space: rotation and revolution. As a result of Earth's rotation, everything in the night sky appears to rise in an easterly direction and set in a westerly direction. As a result of Earth's revolution around the Sun, you see different constellations at different times of the year.

The path of Earth's orbit around the Sun is not a perfect circle. It is an ellipse. An **ellipse** is a curve that looks like a stretched circle. A circle has one centre point and a radius, both of which define the size and shape of the circle. An ellipse has two points called focal points, which define the shape of the ellipse. The Sun is at one focal point of Earth's elliptical orbit, as shown in **Figure 7.15**. So, at one point in Earth's elliptical orbit, Earth is closest to the Sun. At another point, Earth is farthest from the Sun.

tides the rising and falling of ocean waters as a result of the Moon's gravity and Earth's gravity

ellipse a curve that is generally referred to as an oval or the shape of an egg

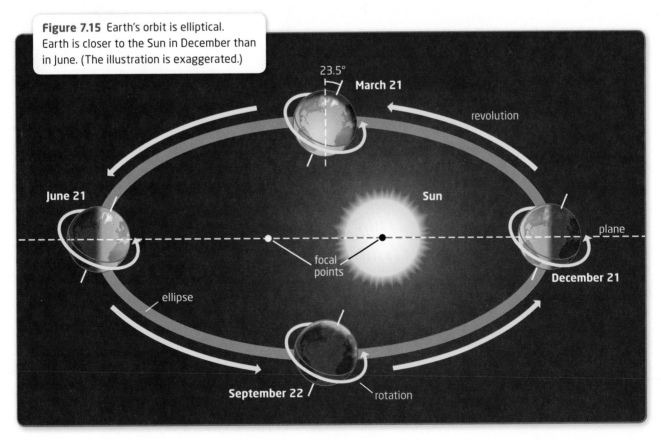

Figure 7.15 Earth's orbit is elliptical. Earth is closer to the Sun in December than in June. (The illustration is exaggerated.)

Why Do We Experience Seasons?

Earth does not rotate in an upright position. Rather, its axis is tilted 23.5° from the flat plane of Earth's orbit. The tilt does not change. In the summer months, the northern hemisphere is tilted toward the Sun. In the winter months, the northern hemisphere is tilted away from the Sun. The opposite happens in the southern hemisphere. Some people believe that the seasons are a result of Earth's distance from the Sun.

As a result of Earth's tilt, sunlight strikes Earth's surface at different angles. Areas that receive sunlight at larger angles receive more sunlight for longer periods of time. Look at **Figure 7.16A**, which shows the northern hemisphere in June. The solar energy reaches Earth's surface at a large angle and for longer periods of time than the solar energy that reaches the southern hemisphere. **Figure 7.16B** models the energy coverage with a flashlight. **Figure 7.16C** shows the approximate height of the Sun in Ontario around the start of each season.

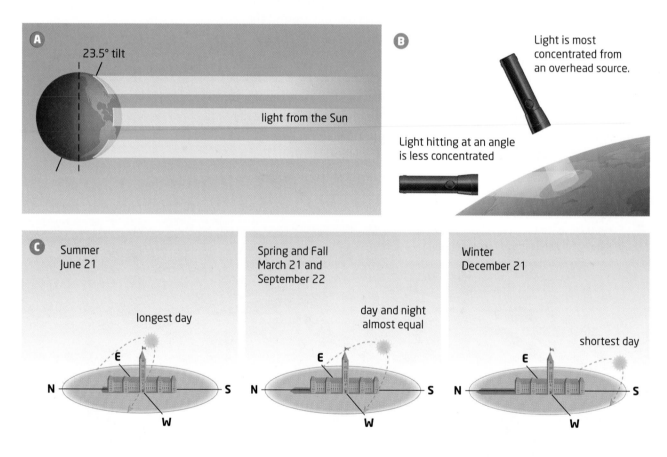

Figure 7.16 **A** During the summer in the northern hemisphere, when Earth is tilted toward the Sun, the northern hemisphere receives solar radiation at a higher angle for longer periods of time. **B** A flashlight models the Sun's energy coverage. **C** The Sun is higher in the sky for a longer period of time in the summer in the northern hemisphere.

Activity 7-2

Angle of Sunlight

In the winter in the northern hemisphere, the Sun delivers less heat to a flat patch of Earth's surface, so the temperatures are lower. How can a flashlight and a piece of paper model the amount of energy reaching Earth's surface? In this activity, you will model the Sun's effect on a patch of Earth.

Materials

- flashlight with a wide beam
- sheet of graph paper
- ruler
- protractor
- notebook

Procedure

1. Make a data table like the one below.

Data Table

Angle of Flashlight from the Vertical	Area (number of squares)
90°	
75°	
60°	
45°	
30°	
15°	

2. Your teacher will turn off the lights in the classroom.

3. While your partner shines the flashlight directly onto a sheet of graph paper, estimate the area that the flashlight beam illuminates by counting the illuminated (lit) squares on the paper.

4. Repeat step 3, but change the angle. Tilt the flashlight 15° from the vertical. Use a ruler as a marker for the vertical. Use a protractor to measure the angle. Alternate roles with your partner, so both of you have turns holding the flashlight and counting the squares.

5. Repeat step 3 until you have tried angles between 90° and 15° in increments of 15°.

6. Use your data to plot a line graph of the illuminated area (*x*-axis) against the angle of the beam (*y*-axis).

Questions

1. What angle caused the light to be spread over the largest area?

2. Why do you need to place the flashlight at a constant distance from the graph paper?

3. Which factor affects Earth's seasons—distance from the Sun or angle of sunlight?

4. How does this model demonstrate the effect of latitude on energy from the Sun?

Learning Check

1. Why do the stars appear to rise in the east and set in the west?

2. What is an ellipse, and what significance does it have regarding Earth's orbit? Review **Figure 7.15**.

3. Why are latitudes just above and below the equator always hot?

4. Why do you think it is important to understand Earth's motion through space?

The Moon's Motion

During the night, the Moon appears to move across the sky with the stars and the planets, due to Earth's rotation. The Moon also appears to move from west to east as it moves in its orbit.

The Moon makes a complete orbit around Earth in about 29.5 days. As the Moon completes one orbit around Earth, the Moon rotates only once on its axis. As a result, you always see the same side of the Moon. You never see the other side. The other side of the Moon is nicknamed "the dark side of the Moon." However, the other side does receive sunlight for about two weeks, so a better term is "far side of the Moon." It was not until 1959 that humans got their first glimpse of the far side of the Moon. At that time, the Union of Soviet Socialist Republics (most of which is present-day Russia) launched a spacecraft that passed behind the Moon and photographed the far side of the Moon.

The Moon is always half-illuminated by the Sun. But how much of the illumination you see depends on where the Moon is relative to Earth. The amount of illumination you see is classified as the **phases of the Moon**. **Figure 7.17** shows the main phases of the Moon: new Moon, waxing crescent, first quarter, waxing gibbous, full Moon, waning gibbous, and third quarter. *Waxing* means increasing, *waning* means decreasing, and *gibbous* means that the amount of light we see illuminating the Moon is between half-lit and fully lit.

phases of the Moon the monthly progression of changes in the appearance of the Moon, which result from different portions of the Moon's sunlit side being visible from Earth

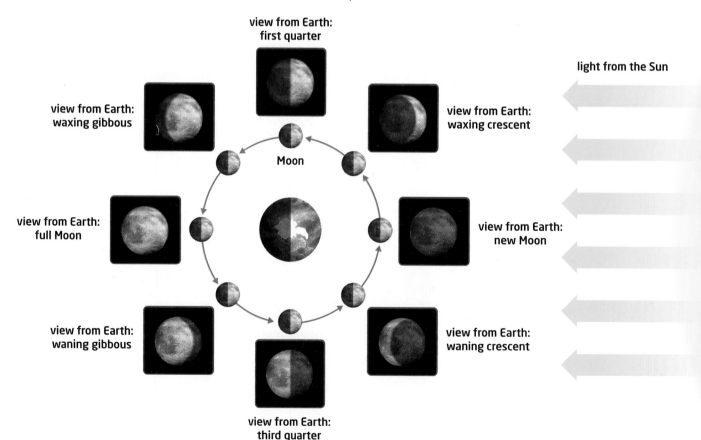

Figure 7.17 The relative positions of Earth and the Moon provide the phases of the Moon. (This diagram is not drawn to scale.)

Eclipses

When one celestial object passes directly in front of another celestial object, as seen from Earth, there is an **eclipse**. There are two main types of eclipses that you can see from Earth: lunar eclipses and solar eclipses.

Lunar Eclipses

Earth's shadow is divided into two parts: the umbra and the penumbra. As shown in **Figure 7.18**, the umbra is the inner shadow, and the penumbra is the outer shadow. During a total **lunar eclipse**, the full Moon passes through the umbra portion of Earth's shadow, so Earth is between the Sun and the Moon. On average, there are two lunar eclipses every year. If a lunar eclipse is occurring, you can watch it from anywhere on Earth where you can see the Moon. A lunar eclipse is perfectly safe to watch.

eclipse the phenomenon in which one celestial object moves directly in front of another celestial object

lunar eclipse the phenomenon in which the full Moon passes into Earth's shadow

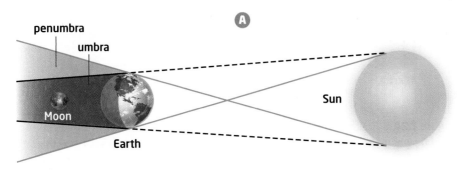

Figure 7.18 **A** If the Moon passes through Earth's umbra, a total lunar eclipse occurs. If the Moon passes through only the penumbra or part of the umbra, a partial lunar eclipse occurs. **B** During a total lunar eclipse, the Moon sometimes looks reddish.

As you have learned, the Moon orbits Earth once a month. So, why is there not a lunar eclipse every full Moon? The answer is that the orbit of the Moon is tilted, or inclined, approximately 5° to Earth's orbit about the Sun, as shown in **Figure 7.19**. The full Moon usually passes above or below Earth's shadow.

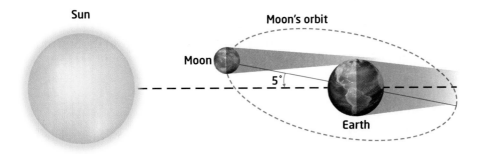

Figure 7.19 The Moon's orbit is tilted approximately 5° to Earth's orbit. Note that the angle is exaggerated in this diagram to help you see the tilt of the Moon's orbit relative to Earth and the Sun. Also, the sizes of the Sun, the Moon, and Earth are not drawn to scale.

Solar Eclipses

solar eclipse the phenomenon in which the shadow of the Moon falls on Earth's surface

A **solar eclipse** occurs whenever the shadow of the Moon falls on Earth's surface. During a solar eclipse, the Moon is between the Sun and Earth. This can only happen during a new Moon. **Figure 7.20** shows the positions of the Sun, the Moon, and Earth during a solar eclipse. Like lunar eclipses, solar eclipses occur, on average, twice a year. But unlike lunar eclipses, the shadow of the Moon on Earth is quite small. To see a solar eclipse, you have to be in a very specific, and often very remote, place on Earth's surface. For this reason, solar eclipses seem to be quite rare.

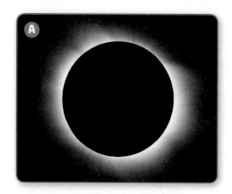

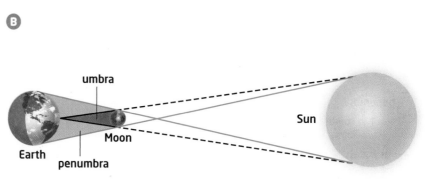

Figure 7.20 A This total solar eclipse happened on March 29, 2006. **B** If you are in a location where the umbra touches Earth's surface, you will see a total solar eclipse. If you are in a location where the penumbra touches Earth's surface, you will see a partial solar eclipse. (This diagram is not drawn to scale.)

The diameter of the Sun is about 400 times larger than the diameter of the Moon. But during a total solar eclipse, the Moon can cover the Sun completely. The reason this is possible is that the Sun is about 400 times farther from Earth than the Moon is. As a result, the Sun and the Moon appear to be about the same size in the sky.

It is never safe to look at the Sun with the unaided eye. The radiation from the Sun can burn your retina and blind you. (You will learn more about the Sun in Chapter 8.) During a solar eclipse, as the Moon starts to cover the Sun, the Sun is still visible and still dangerous. It is not safe to watch a solar eclipse when any portion of the Sun is still visible. Experienced astronomers project the image of the Sun onto a light-coloured surface. Some use binoculars to focus the image of the Sun onto a sidewalk or a sheet of paper.

Suggested Investigation

Inquiry Investigation 7-A, Modelling the Moon's Movement, on page 307

Learning Check

5. Define the terms *umbra* and *penumbra*. Explain how they relate to solar eclipses or lunar eclipses.

6. Why does a lunar eclipse only happen when the Moon is full?

7. In your notebook, make a simple diagram that shows how a total solar eclipse happens. Review **Figure 7.20** if necessary.

8. Why do you always see the same side of the Moon?

Tides

The Moon's motion is also responsible for tides. Tides in the open ocean are about half a metre to a metre high. Tides along coastal areas, however, can vary greatly. The Bay of Fundy, which lies between New Brunswick and Nova Scotia, is a good example of this. Tides in the Bay of Fundy can reach 16 m. **Figure 7.21** shows high and low tide at a location in the Bay of Fundy. The Bay of Fundy is one of only a few places in the world with a range in tide heights that is great enough to harness tidal energy.

What Causes Tides?

Tides are caused by the force of gravity. The amount of the force of gravity, or **gravitational force**, between two objects depends on the masses of the objects and the distance between them. The larger the masses, the greater the gravitational force is. But the farther the objects are from each other, the less the gravitational force is. The Moon is held in orbit around Earth by gravity. The Moon's gravity pulls on Earth, and Earth's gravity pulls on the Moon, resulting in tides.

Note that it is not the direct pull of the Moon's gravity that causes the tides. Rather, it is the *difference* between the force of gravity on the side of Earth nearest the Moon and the force of gravity on the side of Earth *farthest* from the Moon. The result is a stretching effect on Earth. This stretching effect is called a *tidal force*. See **Figure 7.22**.

To understand how this effect results, imagine three people holding hands and running as fast as they can to catch a bus. If the person in the middle is between the slowest person and the fastest person, he or she will experience a very large stretching force. How does this analogy relate to the tides? The side of Earth that is closest to the Moon experiences the largest gravitational pull. The centre of Earth feels less gravitational pull because it is farther from the Moon. The side of Earth farthest from the Moon experiences the least gravitational pull.

gravitational force the force of attraction between all masses in the universe

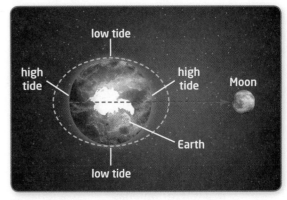

Figure 7.22 The Moon's gravitational pull on the side of Earth nearest the Moon is stronger than on the side of Earth farthest from the Moon.

Figure 7.21 High tide is shown in **A**, and low tide is shown in **B**.

Section Summary

- The tilt of Earth's axis, combined with Earth's motion around the Sun, gives rise to the seasons.
- We see different phases of the Moon, depending on where the Moon is in relation to Earth.
- During a lunar eclipse, the Moon passes through Earth's shadow.
- During a solar eclipse, the Moon passes in front of the Sun.
- The tides are a result of the difference between the force of gravity on the side of Earth nearest the Moon and the force of gravity on the side of Earth farthest from the Moon.

Review Questions

K/U **1.** Create a Venn diagram to compare the terms *rotation* and *revolution*.

C **2.** Draw the illustration at the right. Add the following labels: Sun, rotation, revolution, December, June.

K/U **3.** Earth is farthest from the Sun in its orbit in June, but the northern hemisphere is warmer in the summer than in the winter. Explain why.

C **4.** In a diagram, indicate at which Moon location Earth would experience the following.

   a. a new Moon phase   **c.** a solar eclipse

   b. a full Moon phase   **d.** a lunar eclipse

C **5.** Describe why tides occur. Include tidal force in your description, as well as a diagram.

A **6.** Why is it safe to watch an eclipse of the Moon but not an eclipse of the Sun?

K/U **7.** Why is there not a lunar eclipse every month?

T/I **8.** The graph shows the hours of daylight for five different latitudes in the northern hemisphere:

   a. For all latitudes, which date has the greatest number of hours of daylight?

   b. On which two dates are day and night always equal in length for all latitudes?

   c. For latitude 70°N, does the Sun set between June 1 and July 15? Explain your answer.

   d. Based on the graph, infer the date on which there is the least amount of daylight for all latitudes in the southern hemisphere.

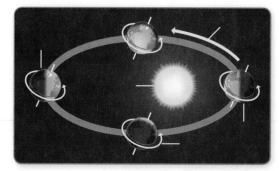

Earth's orbit around the Sun

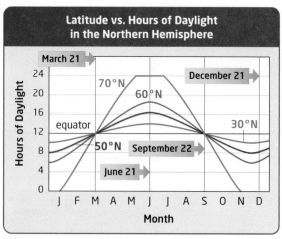

The latitudes 0° (equator), 30°N, 50°N, 60°N, and 70°N are shown.

7.4 Meet Your Solar System

Key Terms
planet
solar system
retrograde motion
astronomical unit
orbital radius

The ancient Greeks noticed that five objects appeared to wander through the constellations. They were observing the five planets that you can see without binoculars or a telescope: Mercury, Venus, Mars, Jupiter, and Saturn. The ancient Greeks thought that these objects were special because they were not fixed against the background sky, like the stars appear to be. The word *planet* is from the Greek word for wanderer.

The Planets

You have probably learned about the planets (shown in **Figure 7.23**) in earlier studies. There is now a more formal definition for the term *planet*. The International Astronomical Union defines a **planet** as an object that orbits one or more stars (and is not a star itself), is spherical, and does not share its orbit with another object. The planets, the Sun, and other smaller objects (see Section 7.5) make up the **solar system**. The Sun's gravitational pull keeps the objects in the solar system in orbit around the Sun.

planet an object that orbits one or more stars (and is not a star itself), is spherical, and does not share its orbit with another object

solar system a group of planets that circle one or more stars

Models of the Solar System

The first model of the solar system stated that Earth was the centre of all planetary motion, with the planets and the Sun travelling in perfect circles around Earth. This model is called the *geocentric model* (*geo* means Earth). The geocentric model was based largely on the work of Ptolemy, a Greek astronomer in the second century c.e. The geocentric model remained the main model for almost 1500 years.

In the 1500s, Polish astronomer Nicolaus Copernicus (1473–1543) presented new observations and a new model for the solar system, called the heliocentric model. The *heliocentric model* (*helio* means Sun) places the Sun in the centre of the solar system and has the planets orbit the Sun in perfect circles. German astronomer Johannes Kepler (1571–1630) revised the heliocentric model by demonstrating that the orbits of the planets are ellipses.

Figure 7.23 The eight planets are shown to scale of size but not to scale of distance.

Sun · asteroid belt · Jupiter · Saturn · Uranus · Neptune · Venus · Mars · Earth · Mercury

Classifications of the Planets

The planets Mercury, Venus, Earth, and Mars are called the *inner planets*. Sometimes they are called the *terrestrial* (Earth-like) planets. They are relatively small and have solid cores and rocky crusts. Farther away, large clumps of gas, ice, and dust formed what are called the *outer planets*: Jupiter, Saturn, Uranus, and Neptune. These planets are known for their large gaseous bands and cold temperatures. They are also called the *gas giants*.

> ### Learning Check
>
> 1. Define the term *planet*.
>
> 2. List and describe two models of the solar system.
>
> 3. Compare and contrast the inner planets and the outer planets in a Venn diagram.
>
> 4. In a group, brainstorm what you think might happen if the Sun were not at the centre of the solar system.

Planetary Motion

Venus and Mercury stay near the Sun. They can be seen only in the early evening or early morning. In comparison, on any given night, Mars, Jupiter, and Saturn move westward along with the fixed stars due to Earth's rotation. At certain times, however, these three planets "wander" against their starry background in a slow, looping motion that lasts several weeks.

This apparent change in direction is called **retrograde motion**. Retrograde motion is produced when Earth catches up with and passes an outer planet in its orbit. Earth is on an inside track and moves faster than the outer planets. Every time it catches up to an outer planet and moves between the outer planet and the Sun, the planet appears to make a looping motion, which is shown for Mars in **Figure 7.24**.

retrograde motion the movement of an object in the sky, usually a planet, from east to west, rather than in its normal motion from west to east

Figure 7.24 This diagram shows the position of Mars compared with the background stars during a period of retrograde motion. Each point represents the planet's new position every 10 days over the retrograde period.

Distances between the Planets

Large distances keep the planets well separated from each other. In fact, the planets lie so far apart that kilometres are not a meaningful way to measure the distances between them. Using kilometres would result in huge numbers that are difficult to work with. It would be like using millimetres to measure the longest hallway in your school or describing the cost of groceries in pennies. For this reason, astronomers created a unit for measuring distances in the solar system: the **astronomical unit (AU)**. The AU is equal to the average distance between Earth and the Sun—about 150 million kilometres. Therefore, by definition, Earth is 1 AU from the Sun. The average distance between the Sun and an object orbiting the Sun is called the **orbital radius**. The orbital radius is expressed in astronomical units.

The planets share many similar characteristics, but they also have many differences. The planet profiles that follow, in **Figure 7.25**, will give you a better idea of Earth's planetary neighbours. Note that Pluto is no longer considered a planet. You will learn why in Section 7.5.

astronomical unit the average distance between Earth and the Sun, about 150×10^6 km

orbital radius the average distance between the Sun and an object that is orbiting the Sun

Suggested Investigation

Data Analysis Investigation 7-C, Gravity on Other Planets, on page 310

Activity 7-3

Modelling the Solar System

The solar system is so vast and empty that it is impossible to draw the sizes of the Sun and planets and the distances between them to the same scale on a regular piece of paper. How can you model distances in the solar system? In this activity, you and your classmates will create a scale model of the solar system using the data in the table.

Materials

- calculator
- construction paper
- coloured markers or pencils
- scissors
- long white paper tape
- glue or tape
- metre stick

Diameters and Distances in the Solar System

Celestial Object	Diameter (km)	Distance from Sun (km)
Sun	1 392 530	
Mercury	4 879	57 909 711
Venus	12 104	108 209 570
Earth	12 756	149 600 000
Mars	6 792	227 039 534
Jupiter	142 980	778 294 598
Saturn	120 540	1 423 872 155
Uranus	51 120	2 876 160 232
Neptune	49 530	4 515 865 992

Procedure

1. Work in groups of three or four. Calculate the scale diameter of the Sun and each planet using the scale 1 cm = 10 000 km. Calculate the scale distance of each planet from the Sun using the scale 20 cm = 149 600 000 km. Organize your data in a table, and give your table a title.

2. Cut out the Sun and each planet from construction paper according to the scaled sizes you calculated in step 1.

3. Lay the long white paper tape on the floor. Attach the Sun and each planet to the paper tape. Space them according to your distance scale. The Sun should start the tape.

Questions

1. According to the scale you used for your model, how far (in metres) from the Sun is Neptune?

2. Using the data table on this page, calculate the distance of each planet from Earth. Then calculate how long it would take for an airplane to reach each planet from Earth. Use the speed 800 km/h. Add your data to the table you made in step 1.

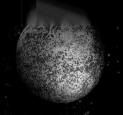

Mercury, a rocky ball covered in craters, is only slightly larger than our Moon. At only 0.39 AU from the Sun, Mercury is the planet closest to the Sun (see Table 7.1). Because Mercury does not have an atmosphere, there are huge differences between day and night surface temperatures. The extreme heating and freezing that result from these temperature differences cause the rock to expand and contract, forming immense cracks in Mercury's surface.

Venus

Venus is often called Earth's sister planet because its size and composition are similar to Earth's. The surface features of Venus are not visible from Earth because the planet is continuously shrouded in thick clouds. Sulfur mixes with moisture in Venus's atmosphere to rain down as sulfuric acid (acid rain). Venus's atmosphere also contains carbon dioxide and nitrogen. In 1990, the *Magellan* spacecraft began scanning the surface of Venus using radar. Data from *Magellan* revealed that large areas of Venus are very flat, while other areas have volcanoes, lava flows, and cracks called rifts. Venus is significantly hotter than Mercury because Venus's atmosphere traps the heat from the planet.

Earth

Our little blue planet, third from the Sun, is home to the only life that scientists have discovered so far in the universe. Besides having a suitable atmosphere and temperatures for life to survive, Earth is the only place known to have water in three phases: liquid, solid, and gas. Water covers nearly three quarters of Earth's surface. Running water, atmospheric effects (such as wind), and plate tectonics (movements of Earth's crust) constantly shape the surface of Earth. Earth's atmosphere contains mainly nitrogen, oxygen, and water vapour.

Mars

Mars is often called the red planet because the iron in its surface rocks gives it a rusty colour. Mars has a volcano that is three times higher than Mount Everest. Mount Everest is 8850 m high! There is also a canyon that is 8 km deep, which would stretch from Vancouver to Toronto, over 3300 km. The winds on Mars move at speeds of up to 900 km/h. On Earth, the strongest hurricanes have wind speeds of up to 250 km/h. Dust storms can cover the whole planet and last for weeks. Mars has two polar ice caps. Mars's very thin atmosphere is made mostly of carbon dioxide.

Table 7.1 Properties of the Inner Planets

Planet	Orbital Radius (AU)	Radius (km)	Mass (relative to Earth)	Average Surface Temperature (°C)	Period of Rotation (relative to 1 Earth day)	Period of Revolution (relative to 1 Earth year)	Number of Moons
Mercury	0.39	2440	0.05	179	58.90	0.24	0
Venus	0.72	6052	0.82	467	244.00	0.62	0
Earth	1.00	6378	1.00	17	1.00	1.00	1
Mars	1.52	3396	0.11	−63	1.03	1.88	2

Jupiter

The largest planet in the solar system is Jupiter. Its mass is 2.5 times greater than the total mass of all the other planets combined. See Table 7.2. Jupiter's Great Red Spot has been visible from Earth for more than 300 years. This spot, which is as large as three Earths, is a storm in the clouds of hydrogen and helium that form the planet's outer layers and atmosphere. Despite Jupiter's immense size, it has the shortest day of any of the planets, turning once on its axis every 10 hours. If Jupiter were 100 times more massive, it might have formed into a small, faint star. Jupiter has rings made of ice particles, but the rings are very thin.

Saturn

Saturn is easily identified by its elaborate system of rings. Saturn's rings are ice particles, which range in size from tiny specks to the size of a house. These rings are 250 000 km wide, but they can be as thin as 10 m. A sheet of paper the size of Toronto would have the same thickness-to-width ratio as Saturn's rings. The planet itself, including its atmosphere, is composed mainly of hydrogen and some helium.

Uranus

Uranus is one of the gas giants. It is the fourth most massive planet in the solar system. Its composition is similar to the composition of Jupiter and Saturn, including a ring system composed of ice and dust. Uranus gets its distinctive blue-green colour from the methane gas in its atmosphere. (Methane absorbs red light and reflects blue-green light.) Its atmosphere also contains hydrogen and helium. Uranus has an unusual rotation–it is flipped on its side. As a result, it appears to be rolling through its orbit around the Sun.

Neptune

Neptune is the outermost planet and the third most massive. Its composition and atmosphere are similar to those of Uranus, but Neptune is a darker blue colour. Neptune also has a very thin ring system made of ice particles.

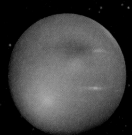

Figure 7.25

Table 7.2 Properties of the Outer Planets

Planet	Orbital Radius (AU)	Radius (km)	Mass (relative to Earth)	Average Surface Temperature (°C)	Period of Rotation (relative to 1 Earth day)	Period of Revolution (relative to 1 Earth year)	Number of Moons
Jupiter	5.20	71 490	317.8	−150	0.41	11.86	61
Saturn	9.54	60 270	95.2	−170	0.45	29.46	60
Uranus	19.18	25 560	14.5	−215	0.72	84.01	27
Neptune	30.06	24 765	17.1	−235	0.67	164.8	13

Section Summary

- Two models of the solar system are the geocentric model and the heliocentric model.
- The planets share many similar characteristics, but they also have many differences.
- The inner, or terrestrial, planets are rocky and small. The outer planets, or gas giants, are made of gases and are huge.
- The astronomical unit is defined as the average distance between Earth and the Sun.

Review Questions

K/U **1.** Create a mnemonic device (memory aid) to help you remember the order of the planets from the Sun.

K/U **2.** According to the heliocentric model of the solar system, which celestial object is holding all the other celestial objects in orbit?

T/I **3.** If the Sun revolved around Earth, as in the geocentric model, what do you think the path of the Sun across the sky would look like?

K/U **4.** Explain why astronomers devised the astronomical unit.

T/I **5.** Compare the atmospheres of the planets by copying and completing the table for all the planets. What similarities and differences can you see among the planets?

Planetary Atmospheres

Planet	Composition of Atmosphere
Mercury	
Venus	
Earth	
Mars	

K/U **6.** Why does it seem that Uranus rolls on its side?

K/U **7.** Would a year on the planet Saturn be longer or shorter than a year on Earth? Explain your answer.

T/I **8.** Use **Tables 7.1** and **7.2** to compare the properties of the planets.

    a. Create a bar graph to compare the radii (plural of radius) of the planets. Put the planets on the *x*-axis and the radius (in kilometres) on the *y*-axis. Why are the outer planets called the gas giants?

    b. Create a bar graph to illustrate the distances of the planets from the Sun. Put the planets on the *x*-axis and the distances (in astronomical units) on the *y*-axis.

7.5 Other Objects in the Solar System

Key Terms
comet
asteroid
meteoroid
meteor
meteorite

The Moon and the planets are the most noticeable objects in the night sky. Comets, dwarf planets, meteoroids, and asteroids are other important objects in the solar system. **Comets** are composed of dust, ice, and rock. In 1994, the world watched as chunks of comet Shoemaker-Levy 9 hit Jupiter, as illustrated in **Figure 7.26**. Each impact left a mark the size of Earth in Jupiter's atmosphere. Canadian astronomer David Levy co-discovered this comet with Carolyn and Eugene Shoemaker, an American husband-and-wife astronomer team.

comet an object composed of rocky material, ice, and gas; comes from the Kuiper Belt and Oort Cloud

Trans-Neptunian Objects

Objects that circle the Sun beyond the orbit of Neptune are called *trans-Neptunian objects*. They are located in the Kuiper [pronounced KI-per] Belt, shown in **Figure 7.27**. The Kuiper Belt is a disc-shaped group of millions of small objects orbiting the Sun. Astronomers theorize that the Kuiper Belt is composed of fragments of material left over from the formation of the solar system (similar to the dust around the edges of a patio after it has been swept). Dutch astronomer Gerard Kuiper (1905–1973), after whom the Kuiper Belt is named, predicted that such an area might have existed when the solar system formed.

Figure 7.26 Comet Shoemaker-Levy 9 hit Jupiter in 1994 (artist's depiction).

Figure 7.27

Recent findings of objects beyond Pluto, in a vast disk called the Kuiper Belt, have forced scientists to rethink what features define a planet.

(Note: Buffy (XR190) is a nickname used by its discoverer. EL61 is an official number assigned to an unnamed body.)

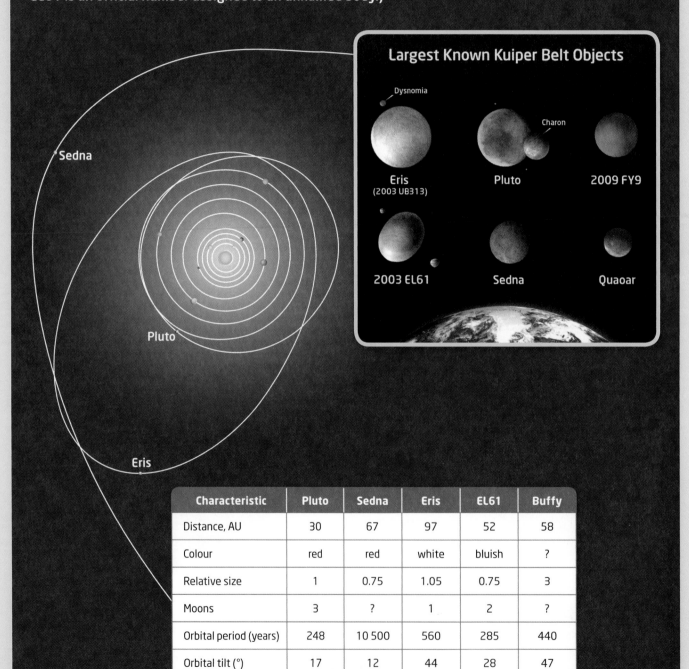

Largest Known Kuiper Belt Objects

Dysnomia

Charon

Eris
(2003 UB313)

Pluto

2009 FY9

2003 EL61

Sedna

Quaoar

Sedna

Pluto

Eris

Characteristic	Pluto	Sedna	Eris	EL61	Buffy
Distance, AU	30	67	97	52	58
Colour	red	red	white	bluish	?
Relative size	1	0.75	1.05	0.75	3
Moons	3	?	1	2	?
Orbital period (years)	248	10 500	560	285	440
Orbital tilt (°)	17	12	44	28	47
Orbital eccentricity	0.25	0.85	0.43	0.19	0

The Plight of Pluto

The Kuiper Belt contains the former planet Pluto and other small objects that are similar in composition and size. Astronomers think that Pluto is composed of rock and ice, and estimate its diameter to be 2300 km. Pluto has three known moons. Astronomers refer to Pluto and similar objects in the Kuiper Belt as *dwarf planets*. The largest Kuiper Belt object is Eris. It is almost 2700 km in diameter and has its own moon.

In 2006, the IAU promoted Eris to dwarf planet status. At the same time, Pluto was demoted to dwarf planet because its orbit sometimes crosses Neptune's orbit. That ended Pluto's 76-year history as the solar system's ninth planet.

The Oort Cloud

At the farthest reaches of the Sun's gravitational influence lies a spherical cloud of small icy fragments of debris called the Oort [pronounced ORT] Cloud. The Oort Cloud is between 50 000 AU and 100 000 AU from the Sun. It is roughly one quarter of the distance between the Sun and Proxima Centauri, the nearest star. In 1952, Dutch astronomer Jan Hendrik Oort (1900–1992) revived the theory of the Oort Cloud's existence, proposed in 1932 by Estonian astronomer Ernst Öpik (1893–1985).

Comets

Most comets originate in the Kuiper Belt and the Oort cloud. Every so often, a comet gets too close to Jupiter. Jupiter's gravitational force will either capture the comet, as you saw in **Figure 7.26**, or nudge the comet to change its orbit and enter the inner solar system. When a comet comes close to the Sun, the radiation from the Sun releases the gases and particles in the comet. The wind from the Sun pushes the gases and particles away, forming a tail, as seen in **Figure 7.28**.

○○○

Study Toolkit

Making Connections to Prior Knowledge Think about what you already know about comets. Make some connections to your prior knowledge about this topic. Then draw a concept map, like the one on page 270, to show the connections.

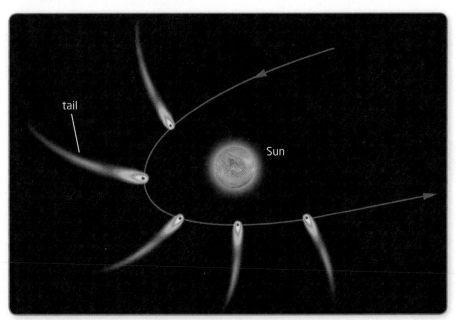

Figure 7.28 A comet's tail always points away from the Sun.

Comet Tails

See the image of comet Hale-Bopp in **Figure 7.29**. The whitish tail is sunlight reflecting off the particles that have been released. These particles, generally called debris, stay in the comet's orbit. The blue tail is made of gases and is called the gas tail. The blue tail is also called the ion tail because the gases have been ionized by the Sun's radiation. It is perfectly safe to view a comet.

Table 7.3 Examples of Periodic Comets

Comet	Period (years)	Closest Approach to the Sun (AU)
Encke	3.30	0.34
Wild 2	6.41	1.59
Halley	76.1	0.59
Swift-Tuttle	133.28	0.96
Hale-Bopp	2533	0.91

Figure 7.29 Comets are named after their discoverers. Comet Hale-Bopp was discovered by two people at the same time: Thomas Bopp from Stanfield, Arizona, and Alan Hale from Cloudcroft, New Mexico.

Go to **scienceontario** to find out more

Some comets visit the Sun just once. Others orbit the Sun, and they are called periodic comets. See **Table 7.3**. In 1999, NASA (the National Aeronautics and Space Administration, in the United States) launched a spacecraft called *Stardust* to meet Comet Wild 2 [pronounced VILT 2]. *Stardust* collected samples from this comet using the aerogel mentioned at the beginning of Chapter 4, and returned the samples to Earth.

Asteroids

asteroid a small object that ranges in size from a tiny speck, like a grain of sand, to 500 km wide; most asteroids originate in the asteroid belt between Mars and Jupiter

Asteroids are small, non-spherical objects that are believed to be debris left over from the formation of the solar system. Most asteroids orbit the Sun in a band, called the asteroid belt, between Mars and Jupiter. See **Figure 7.30A**. Asteroids range in size from a tiny speck, like a grain of sand, to about 500 km wide. An object called Ceres, which is 1000 km wide, is in the asteroid belt. The IAU has promoted Ceres to the status of dwarf planet. Some asteroids even have their own moon, as seen in **Figure 7.30B**.

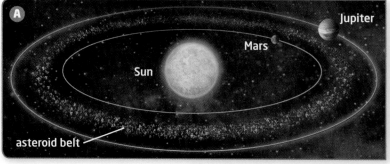

Figure 7.30 A Thousands of asteroids orbit in the asteroid belt. **B** The asteroid Ida has its own moon, named Dactyl. Dactyl is to the right of the potato-shaped Ida.

Meteoroids, Meteors, and Meteorites

Meteoroids are pieces of rock moving through space. Astronomers think that meteoroids are rocky chunks that have broken off asteroids and planets. When meteoroids collide with Earth's atmosphere, they burn up due to atmospheric friction, forming **meteors**. When Earth passes through an area where there is a lot of excess material, such as debris left over from a comet, a meteor shower results, such as the one shown in **Figure 7.31**.

meteoroid a piece of rock moving through space

meteor a meteoroid that hits Earth's atmosphere and burns up

⊖○○

Study Toolkit

Word Origins The word *meteor* is from the Greek word *meteoron*, meaning "high in the air." Research the suffixes *oid* and *ite*. How does knowing the meaning of these suffixes help you remember the meaning of the words *meteoroid* and *meteorite*?

Figure 7.31 Meteors in meteor showers seem to come from certain constellations, which is how meteor showers are named. This is an image of the Leonid meteor shower.

The most famous meteor shower is the Perseid meteor shower, which occurs around August 12 every year. In 1862, two American astronomers, Lewis Swift and Horace Tuttle, discovered a comet, which today bears their names: Comet Swift-Tuttle. In 1865, the Italian astronomer Giovanni Schiaparelli realized that the debris left along the orbital path of Comet Swift-Tuttle is responsible for the Perseid meteor shower.

Some people call meteors "shooting stars," but they are not stars. They are meteoroids that are colliding with Earth's atmosphere. Meteoroids that survive the impact with the atmosphere and reach the ground are called **meteorites**. Scientists estimate that about 100 000 metric tonnes of material from meteorites reaches Earth's surface annually.

meteorite a meteoroid that is large enough to pass through Earth's atmosphere and reach the ground, without being totally burned up

Learning Check

1. What are trans-Neptunian objects?

2. Why is the gas tail of a comet also called an ion tail?

3. What is an asteroid?

4. In 2004, NASA's *Stardust* spacecraft returned samples of Comet Wild 2 to Earth. Why do you think astronomers are so interested in learning about comets?

Asteroid and Meteorite Impacts

An asteroid about the size of a mountain struck Earth 65 million years ago. As a result, there were catastrophic changes to Earth's atmosphere. Some scientists think that these changes are responsible for global mass extinctions of thousands of species, including the dinosaurs. See **Figure 7.32**.

Figure 7.32 A About 65 million years ago, a large asteroid struck Earth. **B** So much debris must have been thrown into the atmosphere that Earth must have been dark for years. **C** Global mass extinctions likely resulted from the darkness.

There are several impact craters on Earth, and many are in North America. About 39 million years ago, an object about 2 km in diameter hit Devon Island, Nunavut. It left the crater, known as Haughton Crater, shown in **Figure 7.33A**. More recently, about 40 000 to 50 000 years ago, a huge impact produced the Barringer Meteorite Crater in Arizona, shown in **Figure 7.33B**. The impact produced an explosion with energy that was equivalent to about 1000 atomic bombs. This amount of energy probably generated hurricane-force winds up to 40 km from the impact site. Falling rock resulting from the impact would have destroyed everything within a 10 km radius.

Haughton Crater

Figure 7.33 A The object that hit Devon Island, Nunavut, about 39 million years ago left this crater, 23 km in diameter. **B** About 40 000 to 50 000 years ago, a large meteorite struck the marshy swamps in the southwest region of North America. Today, visitors can see the crater in what is now the desert of Arizona in the United States.

Tunguska Devastation

Much more recently, on June 30, 1908, in Tunguska, Siberia, an object entered Earth's atmosphere and destroyed an area more than 2000 km². To put this in perspective, the city of Kingston, in Ontario, covers 1900 km². **Figure 7.34** shows an example of the devastation. The object flattened nearly 100 million trees and killed tens of thousands of forest mammals, including several large herds of reindeer. The explosion was probably caused by an object that was about 50 m in diameter. No remnants of the object have been recovered. Scientists speculate that some pieces may be at the bottom of Lake Cheko, in Siberia.

Figure 7.34 This photograph was taken after the Tunguska event. Such events happen about once every 200 to 1000 years.

Activity 7-4

Making Craters

How can you model a crater left by an object hitting Earth with flour and marbles? In this activity, you will demonstrate how an object can create a crater after hitting another object.

CAUTION: Clean up any flour spills immediately. Do not throw the marbles.

Materials

- newspaper
- shallow, rectangular pan
- sand
- flour
- cocoa powder
- 3 marbles, each a different size
- metric ruler

Procedure

1. Place the newspaper on the floor, and place the pan on the newspaper.

2. Half-fill the pan with sand, and then cover the sand with a layer of flour. Sprinkle a thin layer of cocoa powder over the layer of flour.

3. Hold out a large marble at shoulder level. Drop the marble into the mixture. Do not throw the marble. If any flour splashes onto the floor, clean it up immediately because it will make the floor slippery.

4. Observe and record what happens to the flour. Carefully remove the marble. Measure the width of the crater that was formed. Do not add more cocoa powder yet.

5. Repeat steps 3 and 4 with the other two marbles, but drop the marbles in a different area of the flour mixture.

6. Sprinkle another layer of cocoa powder on top of the flour. Repeat steps 3 to 5 but from knee height.

7. Sprinkle another layer of cocoa powder on top of the flour. Repeat steps 3 to 5. This time, drop the marbles from knee height, but angle them to give them some horizontal motion.

Questions

1. Why was it important to drop the three different marbles from the same height each time you completed steps 3 to 5?

2. What affected the size of a crater?

3. What did you notice when the marble hit with some horizontal motion?

Making craters

Looking Back

In this chapter, you learned that people have been observing the night sky and learning its patterns for thousands of years. In time, different cultures began building technologies, such as stepped pyramids and sundials, to predict motions of celestial objects. Understanding the motions of celestial objects allowed people to navigate and to predict the seasons and important events, such as flooding and the return of animal herds.

You also learned about the planets and other celestial objects. For example, each gas giant has dozens of moons. How do astronomers know this, when most of the moons are too small to be seen from Earth? How did scientists get an image of a small asteroid and its even smaller moon?

STSE Case Study

Can We Prevent the Next Big Impact?

In 1942, astronomers discovered a new group of asteroids. These near-Earth objects (NEOs) travel inside Earth's orbit. Many appear in the sky close to the Sun. Earth-based telescopes cannot see them because the NEOs set a few minutes after the Sun does, but before the sky gets dark. Scientists estimate that there are between 200 000 and 500 000 undiscovered NEOs larger than 100 m. These NEOs are large enough to cause a very bad day if one were to collide with Earth.

Finding NEOs

A Canadian project is underway to send a small satellite with a telescope into Earth orbit in 2010 to find NEOs. NEOSSat (Near-Earth Object Surveillance Satellite) will be the world's first space telescope to look for NEOs.

Many people and organizations are involved in the design, construction, launching, and use of NEOSSat. The Canadian Space Agency, university teams, and industry teams are all working together. Defence Research

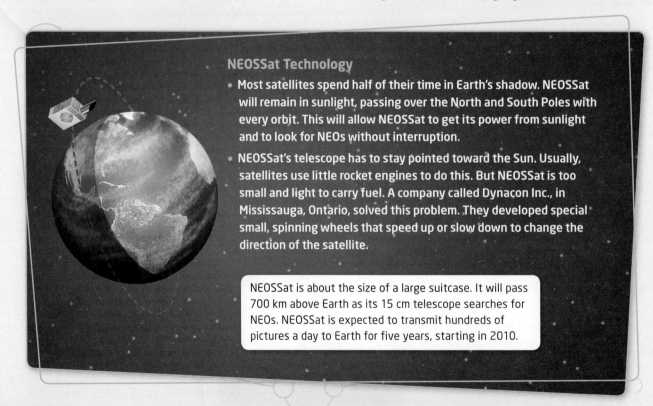

NEOSSat Technology

- Most satellites spend half of their time in Earth's shadow. NEOSSat will remain in sunlight, passing over the North and South Poles with every orbit. This will allow NEOSSat to get its power from sunlight and to look for NEOs without interruption.

- NEOSSat's telescope has to stay pointed toward the Sun. Usually, satellites use little rocket engines to do this. But NEOSSat is too small and light to carry fuel. A company called Dynacon Inc., in Mississauga, Ontario, solved this problem. They developed special small, spinning wheels that speed up or slow down to change the direction of the satellite.

NEOSSat is about the size of a large suitcase. It will pass 700 km above Earth as its 15 cm telescope searches for NEOs. NEOSSat is expected to transmit hundreds of pictures a day to Earth for five years, starting in 2010.

Looking Forward

By the 1600s, theories and technologies had progressed extensively. Astronomers had a better understanding of the motions of some celestial bodies, and they had access to telescopes, thus opening the window to the universe even more. In just a few hundred years, technologies advanced from telescopes on the ground to sending astronauts to the Moon, putting telescopes and other technologies in space, and even planning a crewed mission to Mars. In Chapter 8, you will learn about some of these technologies and how they contribute to our understanding of space and the Sun and other stars, as well as some of the risks and hazards associated with space exploration. You will also learn how stars live and die.

Development Canada and the Canadian Space Agency are paying the $12 million bill. This sounds very expensive, but it is a lot cheaper than some modern ground-based telescopes. And NEOSSat will be able to do what those telescopes cannot–find hard-to-detect NEOs.

NEOSSat's Limitations

NEOSSat will only be able to detect objects that are 100 m in diameter or larger. This is larger than the objects thought to have caused the Tunguska and Barringer Meteorite Craters. Scientists think that these objects were about 50 m in diameter. As you can see in the photograph at the right, even much smaller asteroids can create large craters. So, even when NEOSSat has completed its mission, Earth will still be vulnerable to the impact of objects from space.

What happens if NEOSSat does detect a 1 km asteroid on a collision course for Earth? Unfortunately, the answer today is nothing. It may be decades before scientists develop the technology to deflect an oncoming asteroid. But the chances of a collision happening any time soon are slim. And if NEOSSat discovers an asteroid that passes harmlessly by Earth, scientists may be able to send a spacecraft to collect a sample and bring it back to Earth. Such a sample could be material left over from the birth of the solar system.

Your Turn

1. The design of NEOSSat is an example of technological problem solving.

   a. Why will NEOSSat be able to look for NEOs, while Earth-based telescopes cannot?

   b. Describe one technological challenge that designers of NEOSSat have faced and how they solved it.

2. Suppose that NEOSSat discovers an object, 1 km in diameter, that is likely to hit Earth off Canada's east coast in a few months. What steps could be taken to minimize loss of life?

3. "Funding for NEOSSat is a waste of money." Do you agree or disagree? List reasons to support your opinion. Then write a letter to your local MP to express your concern or support for NEOSSat funding.

In September 2007, an asteroid only 1 to 2 m in diameter created this 20 m crater near Carancas, Peru.

20 m

Section Summary

- In addition to planets, the solar system contains many different objects, such as dwarf planets, asteroids, comets, and meteors.

- There is a very real danger that an asteroid or a large meteor will hit Earth again.

- The Canadian Space Agency and Canadian businesses are building a satellite that will help to detect near-Earth objects that could be harmful if they hit Earth.

Review Questions

K/U **1.** What happens to a comet as it approaches the Sun?

K/U **2.** Why is Pluto no longer considered to be a planet?

C **3.** Write a convincing argument to support this statement: "Shooting stars are not really stars."

K/U **4.** Complete the following table.

Definition Table

Object	Definition
asteroid	
meteoroid	
	a streak in the night sky
	the leftover matter when a meteoroid hits Earth's surface

K/U **5.** In terms of origin, what is the difference between a comet and most asteroids?

A **6.** Study **Figure 7.32** and its caption. Create a sequence of events graphic organizer like the one shown here. Complete your graphic organizer to describe the causes and effects that may have resulted in the destruction of several species, including the dinosaurs.

T/I **7.** How are comets related to meteor showers?

T/I **8.** Asteroids orbit the Sun like planets do. Why are asteroids not considered to be planets?

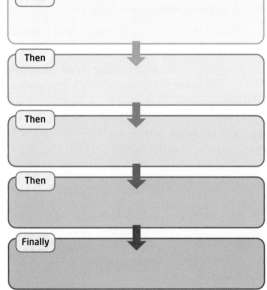

Sequence of Events

First

Then

Then

Then

Finally

Sequence of events graphic organizer

Inquiry Investigation 7-A

Skill Check

Initiating and Planning

✓ Performing and Recording

✓ Analyzing and Interpreting

✓ Communicating

Safety Precautions

- Do not look at or let your eyes get in the path of the projector light.
- Do not touch the projector or the light. They can get very hot.
- To unplug the projector, pull on the plug, not the cord.

Materials

- flashlight or overhead projector
- volleyball
- baseball
- string, about 0.5 m
- wide-point, water-soluble black marker
- large sheet of white paper

Set-up for the investigation if using an overhead projector

Modelling the Moon's Movement

In this investigation, you will model the motion of the Moon relative to Earth and the Sun.

Question

How does the Moon's position affect its phases?

Procedure

1. Lay the white paper on a large flat surface, such as four flat-topped student desks, pushed together.

2. Using a piece of string as a compass, draw a large circle on the paper to represent the orbit of the Moon.

3. Place the volleyball in the centre of the circle to represent Earth.

4. Place the light source at a height that is the *same level as the table* and about 3 m away. The light source is your simulated Sun.

5. Place the baseball on the circle so that it lies exactly between the volleyball and the light source. The baseball represents the new Moon phase in this position.

6. Assuming that the North Pole is at the top of the volleyball, move the baseball around the circle at 45° intervals in a counterclockwise direction. On the sheet of paper, write the lunar phase that the position of the baseball represents at each interval.

Analyze and Interpret

1. Can you see a full Moon during the day? Explain your answer.

2. Can you see a new Moon? Explain your answer.

Conclude and Communicate

3. At which phase of the Moon is a lunar eclipse possible?

4. At which phase of the Moon is a solar eclipse possible?

5. This model suggests that there should be an eclipse every month. In reality, there are usually only two lunar eclipses and two solar eclipses every year. Explain why.

Extend Your Inquiry and Research Skills

6. **Inquiry** Using direct observations, track the movement of the Moon over a period of one month in a notebook. How do your observations compare with the observations you made in this investigation?

Inquiry Investigation 7-B

Skill Check

Initiating and Planning

✓ **Performing and Recording**

✓ **Analyzing and Interpreting**

✓ **Communicating**

Safety Precautions

- Always observe the night sky with a trusted and responsible adult present.
- Check the forecasted weather conditions for your area, and dress appropriately.

Materials

- star maps for each season from your teacher
- a list of the visible planets from your teacher
- coloured pencils
- flashlight with a red filter, such as red cellophane (Red light does not interfere with night vision.)
- a clipboard or hard surface to use under the star maps

The Changing View of the Night Sky

Some constellations and stars are visible throughout the year but change position in the night sky. Other constellations and stars are only visible in certain seasons. As the planets orbit the Sun, they become visible from Earth in different parts of the night sky. The path that they follow through the sky is called the *ecliptic*. The ecliptic passes through 12 constellations, called the constellations of the zodiac, as shown in the diagram on page 309.

In this investigation, you will observe the motions of Polaris and one of three bright seasonal stars (Sirius in Canis Major, Vega in Lyra, or Regulus in Leo). Depending on the time of year, you may be able to observe Venus, Jupiter, or Saturn. You will use direct observation and star maps. Go to Appendix B to learn more about using star maps.

Questions

- Why are some constellations and stars visible throughout the year, while others are visible only in certain seasons?
- Why can you only observe Venus just before sunrise or just after sunset?

Hypotheses

- Some constellations and stars are visible throughout the year because they are close to Polaris. Other constellations and stars are only visible during a certain season because of Earth's revolution around the Sun.
- You can only observe Venus just before sunrise or just after sunset because it is so close to the Sun.

Procedure

1. Make a table like the one below. When observing a star or planet, estimate its direction (north, south, east, or west) and its height above the horizon in degrees. For example, halfway up from the horizon to overhead is 45°, one third of the way up is 33°, two thirds of the way up is about 67°, and overhead is 90°. Record the date and time of your observation, as well as a description of the object's appearance (for example, bright, whitish, reddish, twinkling).

Observation Table

Object	Direction and Height	Constellation	Date and Time of Observation	Appearance
Betelgeuse	south, about 50°	Orion	January 15, 9:00 P.M.	orangish, twinkling

2. Observe Polaris and the star for the season. You will have to check the star maps to determine which of the seasonal stars you can see. Record your observations in your table. Make the same observations again a few hours later, and record those observations as well.

3. Observe Venus and either Jupiter or Saturn (whichever is visible). Record your observations, and mark the positions of the planets on the appropriate star map.

Analyze and Interpret

1. a. Compare the positions of Polaris and your seasonal star using your observations. Which star does not appear to change position? Explain your answer.

   b. Which stars can you only see at certain times of the year?

2. In which seasons are the following constellations visible in the early evening: Orion, Leo, Scorpius, and Pegasus?

3. a. When did you observe Venus?

   b. In which constellation is Jupiter or Saturn? Determine the approximate length of time that Jupiter or Saturn will be in this constellation by dividing the planet's period (in years) by 12 (the number of zodiacal constellations).

4. How are the planets similar to the brighter nearby stars? How are they different?

Conclude and Communicate

5. Why will you never see a planet near the Big Dipper?

6. Why can you only observe Venus just before sunrise or just after sunset, while Jupiter or Saturn can be observed throughout the night? Compare your answer to the hypothesis.

7. Why are some constellations and stars visible throughout the year, while other constellations and stars are only visible during a certain season? Compare your answer to the hypothesis.

Extend Your Inquiry and Research Skills

8. **Inquiry** In this investigation, you observed and noted the motion of celestial objects. What new scientific questions has this experience made you think of?

9. **Research** Research star maps. What is the history of star maps?

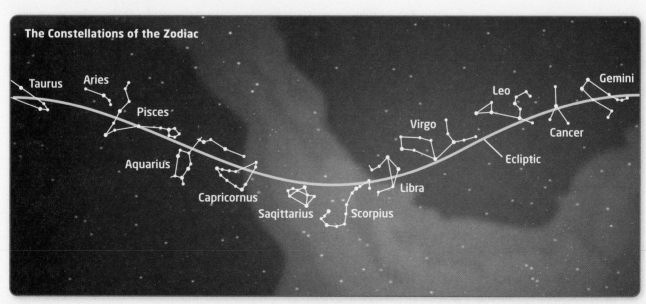

The Constellations of the Zodiac

Skill Check

✓ Initiating and Planning

✓ Performing and Recording

✓ Analyzing and Interpreting

✓ Communicating

Science Skills
Go to **Science Skills Toolkit 7** for information about creating data tables.

Gravity on Other Planets

You have probably seen pictures of astronauts bouncing along the surface of the Moon. Even with their bulky spacesuits and oxygen tanks, they can jump much higher and drop back down more slowly than they could on Earth. The reason why astronauts can bounce this way on the Moon but not on Earth is because the Moon's gravity is different from Earth's gravity. In this investigation, you will compare the gravity on different planets.

Astronaut bouncing on the Moon

Question

Which characteristics of a planet cause the planet to have more or less gravity: atmosphere, mass, and/or orbital radius?

Hypothesis

Write your own hypothesis.

Organize the Data

1. Make a table to record values of the planetary characteristics. Include a column headed "Gravity (Earth = 1.00)." Give your table a title.

Analyze and Interpret

1. Complete your table by conducting research on the Internet or using other sources. Enter the value for the gravity of each planet in terms of Earth's gravity. So, the value under "Gravity" for Earth is 1.00.

2. Does a planet's gravity depend on its atmosphere, mass, or orbital radius? Explain your answer.

Conclude and Communicate

3. Which characteristics affect a planet's gravity?

Extend Your Inquiry and Research Skills

4. **Research** What is your weight on Earth? Research what your weight would be on other planets in the solar system.

Chapter 7 Summary

7.1 Ancient Astronomy

Key Concepts

- Early sky watchers paid a lot of attention to the sky. This enabled them to develop accurate calendars, which they used to predict the seasons and other events that were important to them in their daily lives.
- Earth's revolution around the Sun takes 365.24 days. Earth's rotation on its axis takes 24 hours.

- Different cultures have different reasons for watching the sky. For example, the ancient Egyptians watched for a star called Sirius to rise every year because they knew that the Nile River would flood soon after.
- Careful observations of ships "disappearing" below the horizon, the changing appearance of the sky when travelling, and Earth's shadow viewed during eclipses led the early Greeks to infer that Earth is a sphere.

7.2 The Constellations

Key Concepts

- Constellations are groupings of stars that form distinctive patterns. The stars in these groupings appear to be close to each other, but they are not.
- A star's apparent magnitude is its brightness as seen from Earth.
- The Big Dipper is an asterism, which is a smaller grouping of stars within a constellation.

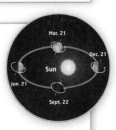

- Earth's rotational axis points to Polaris, the North Star. For thousands of years, travellers have used Polaris and the constellations to navigate.
- Different cultures have different interpretations of the night sky.
- A light-year is the distance that light travels in one year.

7.3 Movements of Earth and the Moon

Key Concepts

- The tilt of Earth's axis, combined with Earth's motion around the Sun, gives rise to the seasons.
- We see different phases of the Moon, depending on where the Moon is in relation to Earth.
- During a lunar eclipse, the Moon passes through Earth's shadow.

- During a solar eclipse, the Moon passes in front of the Sun.
- The tides are a result of the difference between the force of gravity on the side of Earth nearest the Moon and the force of gravity on the side of Earth farthest from the Moon.

7.4 Meet Your Solar System

Key Concepts

- Two models of the solar system are the geocentric model and the heliocentric model.
- The planets share many similar characteristics, but they also have many differences.

- The inner, or terrestrial, planets are rocky and small. The outer planets, or gas giants, are made of gases and are huge.
- The astronomical unit is defined as the average distance between Earth and the Sun.

7.5 Other Objects in the Solar System

Key Concepts

- In addition to planets, the solar system contains many different objects, such as dwarf planets, asteroids, comets, and meteors.

- There is a very real danger that an asteroid or a large meteor will hit Earth again.
- The Canadian Space Agency and Canadian businesses are building a satellite that will help to detect near-Earth objects that could be harmful if they hit Earth.

Make Your Own Summary

Summarize the key concepts of this chapter using a graphic organizer. The Chapter Summary on the previous page will help you identify the key concepts. Refer to Study Toolkit 4 on pages 566–567 to help you decide which graphic organizer to use.

Reviewing Key Terms

1. The Mesopotamians were the first _____ for whom we have evidence of detailed astronomical observations. (7.1)

2. Earth _____ on its axis and _____ around the Sun. (7.1)

3. Groups of stars that seem to form distinctive patterns are called _____ . (7.2)

4. During a _____ , the new Moon completely blocks the Sun. (7.3)

5. A _____ is a celestial object that orbits one or more stars, is spherical, and does not share its orbit with another object. (7.4)

6. _____ is the apparent motion of a planet opposite to the usual east-to-west motion. (7.4)

7. A _____ that survives impact with the atmosphere and reaches the ground is called a _____ . (7.5)

Knowledge and Understanding K/U

8. Why was recording the movement of stars in the night sky important to early sky watchers?

9. Why does the Moon have phases?

10. Identify the phases of the Moon that are shown in the diagram below.

A   B   C

11. Why can you not see the new Moon?

12. Describe how a total eclipse of the Sun would look from the Moon. Include a diagram with your description.

13. Draw a diagram of the solar system, like the one shown below. Complete your diagram by labelling each object.

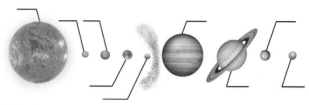

The solar system

14. Why are the distances between objects in the solar system not measured in light-years?

15. What name do astronomers give to the average distance between Earth and the Sun?

16. The planets are classified as the inner planets and the outer planets. What do you think this classification is based on?

17. Describe characteristics that all the outer planets share.

18. Describe the difference between Pluto and the eight planets.

19. What causes "shooting stars," the streaks of light that cross the night sky?

20. Compare and contrast asteroids and meteoroids.

21. Describe a comet. Include a diagram and a definition in your description. Explain where comets originate and why comets have two tails.

Thinking and Investigation T/I

22. The same side of the Moon is always visible from Earth because the Moon rotates at about the same rate as it revolves around Earth. Would a person living in a lunar colony experience day and night? Explain your answer.

23. A solar eclipse always occurs about two weeks before or after a lunar eclipse. Explain why.

Communication C

24. **BIG IDEAS** Different types of celestial objects in the solar system and universe have distinct properties that can be investigated and quantified. Create a table with planetary facts. Include mass, diameter, period of rotation, moons, average surface temperature, atmosphere (yes/no), special features (such as rings), orbital radius, and any other characteristics that interest you. Prepare a brochure using the information in your table. Include drawings of the planets. A hypothetical space agency will use the brochure to select a planet to research, by sending a spacecraft to it.

25. **BIG IDEAS** People use observational evidence of the properties of the solar system and the universe to develop theories to explain their formation and evolution. Explain how studying objects in the Oort Cloud and Kuiper Belt can help astronomers understand the solar system.

26. **BIG IDEAS** Space exploration has generated valuable knowledge but at enormous cost. Assess the NEOSSat program. Write an editorial for the school newspaper in which you express your opinion on Canada's financial and technological contributions.

27. Draw a diagram to show the difference between rotation and revolution.

28. Explain why constellations appear to move through the night sky.

29. Describe why Earth experiences seasons. Include a drawing that shows why the surface of Earth warms in the summer and cools in the winter.

Application A

30. Sometimes a halo appears around the Moon. Some people say that the halo means bad weather is approaching. Research the causes of the halo on the Internet or in other sources.

31. Suppose that astronomers spotted a large rock at approximately the same distance as the Moon is from Earth, on a collision course with Earth. How much time would there be to prepare? Would there be minutes, days, months? Follow these steps to estimate an answer:

a. Earth takes about 30 000 000 s to orbit the Sun. Consider Earth's orbit to be circular, with a radius of 150 000 000 km. Estimate Earth's orbital speed.

b. Suppose that Earth runs into an asteroid orbiting at the same speed as Earth, in the opposite direction. How fast would the object appear to be approaching Earth?

c. How long would the object take to cover the 400 000 km distance between Earth and the Moon?

Chapter 8 Exploring Our Stellar Neighbourhood

What You Will Learn

In this chapter, you will learn how to...

- **discuss** a range of technologies used to study objects in the sky
- **assess** some of the costs, hazards, and benefits of space exploration
- **describe** the Sun's composition and energy source, and **explain** how the Sun's energy warms Earth and supports life on the planet
- **compare** star temperatures and colours, and **understand** how stars evolve

Why It Matters

Improvements in technology increase our ability to observe and to travel farther into space.

Skills You Will Use

In this chapter, you will learn how to...

- **interpret** the composition of the Sun and other stars by examining their spectra
- **plan** and **conduct** a simulation that illustrates the relationship between a star's distance from Earth and its brightness
- **compare** and **contrast** properties of stars by using a graph to determine star properties based on their spectral type

Space technology is progressing at an amazing rate, enabling astronomers to explore further and further. In 1969, the first humans walked on the Moon. By 1972, 12 humans had walked on the Moon. Some have even driven on the Moon! Now, more than 400 men and women have travelled into space. Sophisticated technology has provided close-up images of every planet in the solar system, the first images of planets around other stars, and dramatic images of the Sun.

Activity 8-1

Preparing for a Trip to the Moon

Many scientists believe that the next major step in human exploration of space will be a base on the Moon. If you travelled to the Moon, what would you need? In this activity, you will plan a trip to the Moon and plan your needs for a base on the Moon.

There are many factors to consider when planning a trip to the Moon.

Materials
- large sheets of paper
- markers

Procedure

1. Working in a small group, analyze what you would need for the three-day trip to the Moon, as well as what you would need once you reach the Moon. The following questions will guide you in deciding your needs.

    a. How many crew members and passengers will there be?

    b. Will there be any specialists (such as doctors or engineers)?

    c. What will your spaceship need (for example, spacesuits, fuel, oxygen supply, food, medical supplies, entertainment)?

    d. What will your needs be when you reach the Moon (think about shelter, oxygen, food supplies, water)?

    e. How will you get home?

2. Sketch the results of your discussion on the paper provided.

Questions

1. As a class, discuss the technological problems that would have to be solved before establishing a base on the Moon.

2. Do you think there should be a limit on the total number of passengers on your trip? Explain your answer.

3. Do you think families should be allowed to take your trip? Explain your answer.

Study Toolkit

These strategies will help you use this textbook to develop your understanding of science concepts and skills. To find out more about these and other strategies, refer to the Study Toolkit Overview, which begins on page 561.

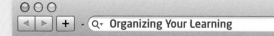

Making Study Notes

Study notes are brief statements that explain the most important ideas and details of a text in your own words. Use whatever format helps you remember the information: point form, sentences, or graphic organizers. The T-chart below shows the most important idea and supporting details of the first paragraph on page 330.

Main Idea	Supporting Details
Space travel is both expensive and risky.	• It takes years to design and test the equipment and software. • A fire in the *Apollo 1* spacecraft led to the death of all three astronauts inside.

Use the Strategy

Read the first paragraph under the heading "Satellites" on page 325. After reading, draw a T-chart like the one shown above. In your chart, write the main idea of the paragraph. Then list the supporting details. Finally, write a sentence in your own words to summarize the paragraph.

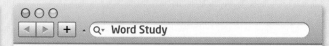

Compound Words

A compound word is made of two smaller words joined together. Recognizing the smaller words and knowing their meanings can help you figure out the meaning of the compound word. For example, *blackout* is made up of *black*, meaning without any light, and *out*, meaning outside. So, *blackout* literally means "without any light outside." Note that some compound words have meanings that are different from the combination of their smaller parts. Consider the context of the compound word, too.

Use the Strategy

Think about the compound word *wavelength*. Identify the two smaller words that make up this compound. Use their meanings to figure out the meaning of the compound word. Be sure that your meaning makes sense in a scientific context.

Interpreting Diagrams

A diagram is a simplified drawing that uses symbols to represent objects, directions, and relationships. Reading the labels of a diagram can help you understand these symbols.

To interpret a diagram, first read the title or caption to understand the main idea of the diagram. Then consider how each part illustrates the main idea. For example, the caption of the figure on the right tells you about the function and structure of a refracting telescope. The labels and the picture show how each part of the telescope collects light and focusses it for the observer.

Use the Strategy

Examine **Figure 8.20** on page 336. Read the caption to identify the main idea of the diagram. Explain how each labelled part on the diagram contributes to your understanding of the main idea.

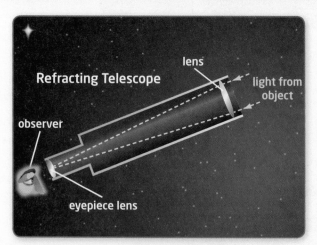

Telescopes let you see light from distant objects, such as stars, more clearly. A refracting telescope uses a lens to collect light. A smaller lens in the eyepiece magnifies the image.

8.1 Exploring Space

Key Terms
electromagnetic radiation
refracting telescope
reflecting telescope
satellite
ethics

Throughout human history, curiosity and the need to understand the world around us have driven people to explore. People also explore to find new resources, such as minerals, and places to live. People started exploring on land. Then various civilizations built boats and ships to explore the world further. Next came exploration of the North and South Poles and the oceans. In the mid-20th century, humans ventured into space. On July 20, 1969, American astronaut Neil Armstrong was the first human to step onto the Moon, followed by Edwin (Buzz) Aldrin, who is shown in Figure 8.1. The third member of the *Apollo 11* crew, Michael Collins, stayed in orbit around the Moon in another vehicle while Armstrong and Aldrin explored the surface for two hours.

Challenges of Space Travel

It is very difficult and costly to send humans into space because everything is so far away. Humans need enough food and air for long trips. Other challenges include protecting them from the extreme cold of space, and trying to ensure that the spacecraft do not break down and leave humans stranded in space. One alternative to sending humans into space is exploring space from Earth using telescopes and other instruments. Another alternative is sending instruments, such as planetary orbiters, landers, and satellites, instead of people. Instruments are expensive, but sending them is less expensive and less risky than sending humans because, for example, instruments do not need food and companionship.

Figure 8.1 In this image, American astronaut Buzz Aldrin is about to step onto the Moon's surface.

Exploring Space with Telescopes

As you learned in Chapter 7, people began exploring space simply by watching the sky. As new technologies, such as telescopes, were invented, people began using the technologies to explore space further. Galileo Galilei (1564–1642) was one of the first to turn the telescope to the sky. Today, there are many types of telescopes and other instruments used to explore space.

The telescopes that astronomers use to study space all detect electromagnetic radiation. **Electromagnetic radiation** is varying types of energy waves. The electromagnetic spectrum, shown in **Figure 8.2**, is the range of all forms of electromagnetic radiation. Visible light is a form of electromagnetic radiation, as are X rays, microwaves, and radio waves. Cellphone signals are radio waves. All forms of electromagnetic radiation travel at the speed of light (3.00×10^8 m/s).

electromagnetic radiation
radiation consisting of electromagnetic waves that travel at the speed of light (such as visible light, radio waves, and X rays)

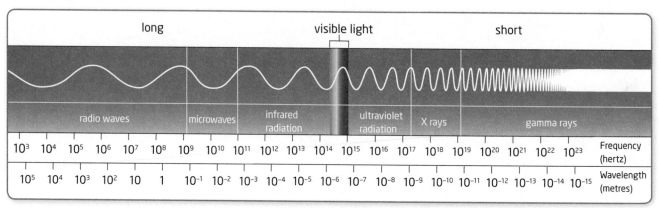

Figure 8.2 Radiation with shorter wavelengths is associated with higher energy. In optics (the science of light), the term *wavelength* is associated with the word colour.

Activity 8-2

An Astronomer's View

You might think that exploring space with a telescope is easy because the stars seem so bright and space is dark. However, Earth's atmosphere changes incoming starlight and prevents the formation of perfect images. How can you model looking through Earth's atmosphere? In this activity, you will model looking through Earth's atmosphere by using plastic wrap.

Materials
• piece of plastic wrap, about 15 cm long

Procedure
1. Place an opened book in front of you and observe how clear the text is from a distance of 1.0 m.

2. Hold the piece of plastic wrap in both hands, close to your eyes. Keep it taut.

3. Look at the same text from step 1 through the plastic wrap at the same distance.

4. Fold the plastic wrap in half, and look at the text again through both layers at the same distance.

Questions
1. In a sentence or two, compare reading text through plastic wrap to an astronomer viewing stars through Earth's atmosphere.

2. How many times do you think you would have to fold the plastic wrap before the wrap becomes opaque? (Remember that each fold doubles the number of layers of plastic wrap.)

3. Find the relationship between layers of plastic and distance from the text needed to read the text.

Optical Telescopes

An optical telescope is a telescope that detects visible light. There are two main types of optical telescopes. **Refracting telescopes**, shown in **Figure 8.3**, use a lens to collect light. **Reflecting telescopes**, also shown in **Figure 8.3**, use a curved mirror to collect light.

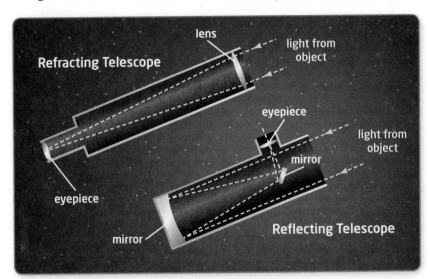

Figure 8.3 When using an optical telescope, the observer views the image of the object through the eyepiece, which is a lens that magnifies the image.

Non-optical Telescopes

There are other types of telescopes that detect non-visible radiation. One example is a radio telescope, shown in **Figure 8.4**. A radio telescope detects radio waves. Radio waves can penetrate clouds, so an advantage of using radio telescopes over using optical telescopes is that radio telescopes can be used on cloudy days. Another advantage is that they can also be used at night.

Radio telescopes are large receivers, similar to the satellite dishes attached to some homes. Radio waves coming from a distant object are collected and focussed on the receiver. An organization called the SETI (Search for Extraterrestrial Intelligence) Institute uses a group of radio telescopes to search for signs of intelligent life on other planets.

Figure 8.4 This 26 m radio telescope is part of the Dominion Radio Astrophysical Observatory near Penticton, British Columbia. The observatory is owned and operated by Canada's National Research Council.

Telescopes in Space

Much of the radiation that reaches Earth from space is absorbed by Earth's atmosphere and does not reach Earth's surface. As illustrated in **Figure 8.5**, for example, infrared radiation with a wavelength of 1 mm is absorbed about 50 km above Earth's surface. Therefore, in order to explore space in more detail, some telescopes need to be placed above Earth's atmosphere. There are several telescopes in space. Some examples are the Chandra X-ray Observatory, the Spitzer Space Telescope (which detects infrared radiation), and the Hubble Space Telescope (HST). The HST has provided many of the beautiful images in this unit.

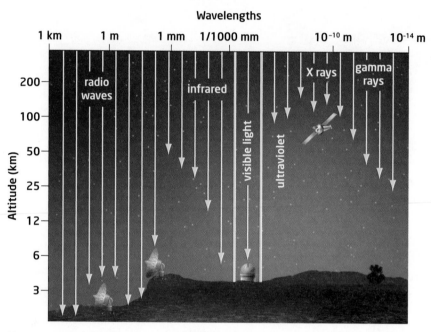

Figure 8.5 Only small portions of the electromagnetic spectrum from space reach Earth's surface. Therefore, telescopes need to be above Earth's atmosphere to detect the portions that do not reach Earth's surface.

The advantages and disadvantages of placing telescopes in space compared with Earth-based telescopes are summarized in **Table 8.1**.

Table 8.1 Advantages and Disadvantages of Placing Telescopes in Space

Advantages	Disadvantages
• They are above Earth's atmosphere, so they can detect parts of the electromagnetic spectrum that do not reach Earth's surface. • They can take long exposures of certain parts of the sky without being affected by daylight and bad weather. This allows the telescopes to detect faint astronomical objects not otherwise detectable on the ground.	• Launching telescopes into space is very expensive. • Telescopes in space are subjected to extremes of hot and cold. Such extremes cause the metals used in the instruments to expand and contract. Over time, the materials weaken. Once in space, telescopes are difficult or impossible to repair and upgrade. • Without a solid base, telescopes in space are difficult to point accurately and to keep pointing in any direction. Earth-based telescopes are anchored to the ground. • Compared with Earth-based telescopes, the working lives of space telescopes are very short, sometimes lasting only a few years.

MOST: Canada's "Humble" Space Telescope

MOST (Microvariability and Oscillations of STars) is Canada's first space telescope. It is pictured in **Figure 8.6** beside its older cousin, the HST. **Table 8.2** compares the HST and MOST. MOST was designed and built by the University of British Columbia, Dynacon Inc., and the University of Toronto Institute for Aerospace Studies, Space Flight Lab. The $10 million in funding was provided by the Canadian Space Agency (CSA). MOST's purpose is to study stars that are similar to the Sun, one star at a time for about eight weeks per star. To keep it pointing in one direction for that length of time, MOST uses Dynacon's reaction wheels, which were mentioned with the NEOSSat satellite in Chapter 7. MOST was expected to study 10 stars and last one year. It has provided data on over 1500 stars and is now expected to last until 2015.

Another telescope in space, called SOHO (SOlar Heliospheric Observatory), gathers data on the Sun. Astronomers have learned much about the Sun and other stars from SOHO and other technologies, such as spectroscopy. You will learn more about spectroscopy, the Sun, and other stars in Sections 8.2 and 8.3.

Table 8.2 A Comparison of the HST and MOST

	Hubble Space Telescope	MOST
Cost and year of launch	$10 billion; 1990	$10 million; 2003
Dimensions and mass	13.2 m × 4.2 m (about the size of a large school bus); 11 110 kg	65 × 65 × 30 cm (about the size of a suitcase); 60 kg
Instruments	7 science instruments; diameter of the primary optical mirror: 2.4 m	telescope mirror diameter: 15 cm
Altitude above Earth	600 km	820 km
Power	solar energy	solar energy

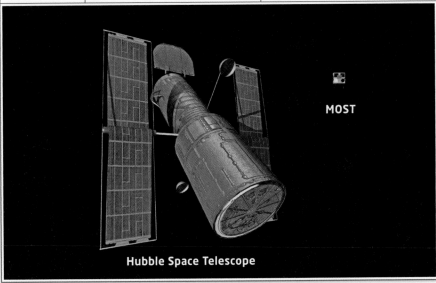

MOST

Hubble Space Telescope

Figure 8.6 The tiny MOST satellite is so successful that it received the Alouette Award in 2008 for its outstanding contributions to space technology and research. (Alouette was Canada's first satellite, launched in 1962.)

Studying Objects in Different Wavelengths

A range of telescopes can reveal different types of information about an object. For example, **Figure 8.7** shows the planet Saturn in four different wavelengths. A comparison of Saturn in visible light, shown in **Figure 8.7A**, with Saturn in ultraviolet radiation, **Figure 8.7B**, reveals that Saturn has auroras (the glowing areas at the poles), like Earth. The view in infrared, **Figure 8.7C**, shows detailed features in Saturn's atmosphere. The different colours represent different heights and compositions of Saturn's clouds. The radio wave image in **Figure 8.7D** indicates that the planet emits (gives off) radio waves (the red) and that the rings (the blue) absorb this radiation.

Study Toolkit

Making Study Notes A T-chart such as the one on page 316 could be used to organize the information in the first paragraph on this page. A T-chart is helpful because it shows the main idea and supporting details.

Figure 8.7 **A** is Saturn in visible light, **B** is Saturn in ultraviolet, **C** is Saturn in infrared, and **D** is Saturn in radio wavelengths. The colours in **B**, **C**, and **D** are false. Astronomers add the colours to show different features.

Learning Check

1. Why is it risky to send humans into space?

2. Compare and contrast space telescopes and Earth-based telescopes.

3. How do telescopes that detect non-optical radiation contribute to our understanding of space? Review **Figure 8.7**.

4. Neil Armstrong's first words on the Moon were, "That's one small step for [a] man, one giant leap for mankind." What do you think his words mean?

Planetary Orbiters and Landers

Orbiters are observatories that orbit other planets. They are equipped with digital cameras that provide high-resolution images not obtainable from Earth. Orbiters have fairly short operational life expectancies, such as 2 or 3 years, but some have lasted as long as 10 years. One example of an orbiter is *MESSENGER* (MErcury Surface, Space ENvironment, GEochemistry, and Ranging), shown in **Figure 8.8**. NASA launched *MESSENGER* in 2004 to explore Mercury.

The *Mars Climate Orbiter*

Sending instruments into space has some risks. In December 1998, NASA launched an orbiter to Mars called the *Mars Climate Orbiter* (MCO). The MCO was supposed to go into orbit around Mars. Once in orbit, the MCO was to act as a Martian weather satellite and communicate with the *Mars Polar Lander*. A *lander* is a spacecraft designed to land on a planet. The *Mars Polar Lander* was launched in January 1999 and was scheduled to land on Mars in December 1999. In September 1999, as the MCO approached Mars to go into orbit, NASA engineers lost communication with it, and never heard from it again.

Look at **Figure 8.9**. The blue line is the MCO's intended orbit, and the red line is the actual path that the MCO followed. A team of engineers at NASA's Jet Propulsion Laboratory (JPL) was responsible for monitoring the MCO's orbit. The JPL team used metric units, such as kilometres, for their data. The contractor for the MCO, Lockheed Martin, sent data to JPL in imperial units, such as miles. As a result, the MCO went into an orbit that was too low, and it burned up in the atmosphere of Mars. The *Mars Polar Lander* also failed: it crash-landed on Mars. The total cost of the MCO mission was U.S. $327.6 million, and the total cost of the Mars Polar Lander mission was U.S. $120 million.

Figure 8.8 In January 2008, the spacecraft *MESSENGER* was close enough to Mercury to start sending back images of Mercury's heavily cratered surface.

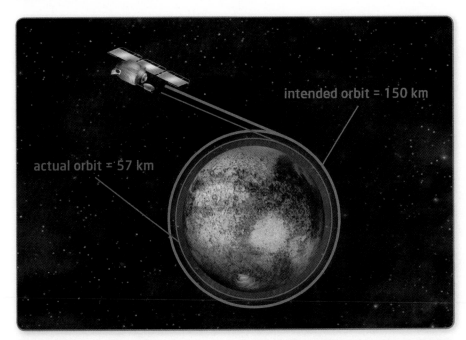

intended orbit = 150 km

actual orbit = 57 km

Figure 8.9 As a result of an error in communication, NASA lost the *Mars Climate Orbiter*. (This image is not to scale.)

Landers

Landers cannot move around. Therefore, they can sample only a fraction of the environment on the planet being explored. NASA's *Phoenix Lander* is shown in **Figure 8.10**. Most landers are designed to last for a few months, although in exceptional cases they have been known to last many months longer than what they were designed for. Landers, like orbiters, are expensive. They must be able to land safely on a surface. This added complexity contributes significantly to the cost of the project. As you read on the previous page, sometimes landers do not land safely.

One of the sets of instruments that *Phoenix* took is a weather station that was designed and built by a team from York University (Toronto), Dalhousie University (Halifax), Optech Inc. (Vaughan), the University of Alberta (Edmonton), and the CSA. The weather station collected data on clouds, fog, and dust in the Martian atmosphere—giving a weather report from Mars! In November 2008, winter began on Mars. The amount of sunlight reaching the northern polar cap began to decline, so the weather station stopped working. *Phoenix* required sunlight to power its computers and run its instruments.

The Lidar Instrument

One of the instruments in the weather station is called lidar, which stands for Light Detection and Ranging. The lidar instrument, which is about the size of a shoebox, uses laser technology. The thin, green vertical line in **Figure 8.10** is the lidar's laser beam. The laser shot quick pulses of light into the Martian atmosphere, and the light bounced off clouds and dust particles. The laser light then returned to an optical telescope in the instrument. The Canadian science team ran the laser for 15 min, four times a day. The data that the team collected gave information on the movement, size, and composition of Martian clouds and dust particles above the weather station.

Go to **scienceontario** to find out more

Figure 8.10 The *Phoenix Lander* was the first spacecraft to land in the northern polar region of Mars. The CSA invested $37 million in the weather station. This picture is an artist's conception of *Phoenix* on Mars.

Satellites

A **satellite** is a human-made object or vehicle that orbits Earth, the Moon, or other celestial bodies. Satellites are an important part of your daily life. The weather reports on television, the Internet, and the radio use data from weather satellites. When you watch television, telephone a friend, and use the Internet, communications satellites are likely playing a role (see **Figure 8.11**). Communications satellites transmit television, telephone, and radio signals around the world. Canada has been part of the communications satellite industry since 1972, when it launched its first communications satellite, *Anik 1*. Canada is an extremely large country, with its towns and cities spread far apart. Communications satellites are important to unite the country.

Figure 8.11 Without satellite technology, both **A** computers and **B** cellphones could not access the Internet to the extent possible today.

Global Positioning System (GPS) Satellites

Satellites also provide services for search and rescue. Using a small, hand-held GPS unit, as shown in **Figure 8.12**, you can use satellite technology to find out where you are on Earth. More than two dozen GPS satellites (called NAVSTAR, for navigation satellite tracking and ranging) are now spread out in orbit around Earth, about 20 200 km above Earth's surface. As a result, there are always at least three above the horizon, wherever you are in the world, whatever the time of day.

Figure 8.12 You need never get lost again. Hand-held GPS units are becoming more and more popular with hikers.

GPS technology is now commonly used in all kinds of vehicles, even in farmers' combines (large tractors). The GPS unit in a farmer's combine monitors the farmer's field at evenly spaced time intervals, for example, every 10 min. The unit gives information on factors such as soil needs, differences in types of soil, and soil moisture. Such data allow the farmer to fine-tune the fertilizing and watering needs for the whole farm.

Remote-sensing Satellites

Satellites that are generally less than 700 km above Earth's surface are called low-Earth-orbit satellites. They take about 90 min to complete a single orbit. They can survey Earth quickly and cover a lot of surface. This is very useful for the sciences of meteorology (study of weather), climatology (study of climates), oceanography (study of oceans), and hydrology (study of water). The process of gathering data about Earth using instruments mounted on satellites is called *remote sensing*.

ENVISAT

ENVISAT (ENVIronmental SATellite) is a remote-sensing satellite launched in 2002 by the European Space Agency (ESA). The CSA and several Canadian companies contributed to the funding, design, and construction of ENVISAT.

For example, EMS Technologies, in Sainte-Anne de Bellevue, Québec, designed and manufactured one of ENVISAT's remote-sensing instruments. The instruments can capture data even through cloud cover and during the long, dark winters at the poles. Scientists now have a better understanding of shrinking Arctic sea ice and Antarctic ice shelves. **Figure 8.13** shows changes in the Arctic ice in 2008. Scientists also use ENVISAT data to monitor the heights of oceans, land surfaces, and major lakes and rivers.

Additional Uses of ENVISAT Data

Scientists use ENVISAT data to help manage resources and prevent disasters. For example, the ESA maintains a World Fire Atlas, which makes fire maps available on-line in near-real time. The atlas uses ENVISAT data. The maps are used for assessing damage and the risk of fires, and deciding how to fight fires efficiently.

ENVISAT data have even helped in a race to the North Magnetic Pole. When 16 teams skied 500 km from Resolute Bay to the North Magnetic Pole in the 2005 Scott Dunn Polar Challenge, they used ENVISAT maps that showed the extent and types of ice.

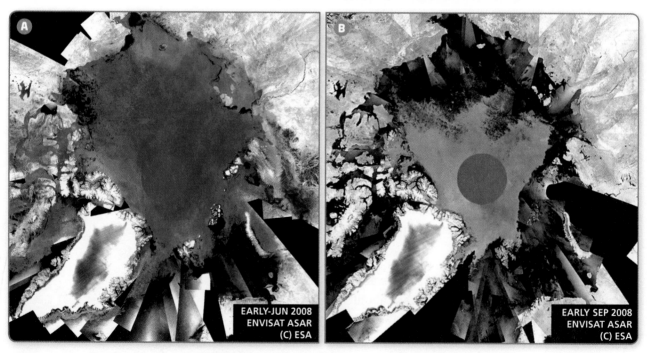

EARLY-JUN 2008
ENVISAT ASAR
(C) ESA

EARLY SEP 2008
ENVISAT ASAR
(C) ESA

Figure 8.13 These ENVISAT images show the changes in ice cover between June, in part **A**, and September, in part **B**, in 2008. The blue represents areas covered with ice, and the grey represents areas with no ice.

Geosynchronous Satellites

Geosynchronous satellites orbit Earth in an eastward direction at an altitude of 35 800 km above the equator. At this altitude, it takes 24 hours for a geosynchronous satellite to complete one orbit. Since Earth also turns in an eastward direction and makes one rotation in 24 hours, the satellite appears to stay over a single location above the equator. As a result, these satellites are also called "geostationary" satellites (*geo* means Earth). The rotation of Earth combined with the orbital motion of the satellite creates the illusion that the satellite is stationary in the sky. The advantage is that the receivers on the ground do not have to move to track the satellite. The best-known geosynchronous satellites are the ones that broadcast television programs and satellite radio.

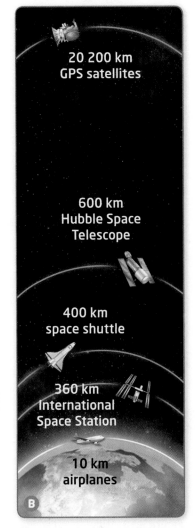

20 200 km
GPS satellites

600 km
Hubble Space
Telescope

400 km
space shuttle

360 km
International
Space Station

10 km
airplanes

B

Figure 8.14 A Travelling at more than 27 000 km/h, the ISS circles Earth in about 90 min. Part **B** shows the altitudes of the ISS and other spacecraft.

> ### Learning Check
>
> 5. Compare the altitudes and purposes of remote-sensing, GPS, and geosynchronous satellites.
>
> 6. List three alternatives to sending humans into space.
>
> 7. Compare the advantages and disadvantages of using a lander over using an orbiter.
>
> 8. The CSA invested $37 million in the weather station on Mars. Do you think it was worth the investment? Explain your answer.

The International Space Station

Since the late 20th century, more countries have begun to partner in space exploration to share the costs. Numerous partnerships between private businesses and governments, including Canada, have been formed to complete the International Space Station (ISS).

Construction of the ISS began in 1993. It is being built piece by piece from components delivered by NASA's space shuttle and rockets from Russia. Its orbit is about 360 km above Earth. **Figure 8.14A** shows the ISS, and **Figure 8.14B** shows the altitude of the ISS compared with the altitudes of other spacecraft.

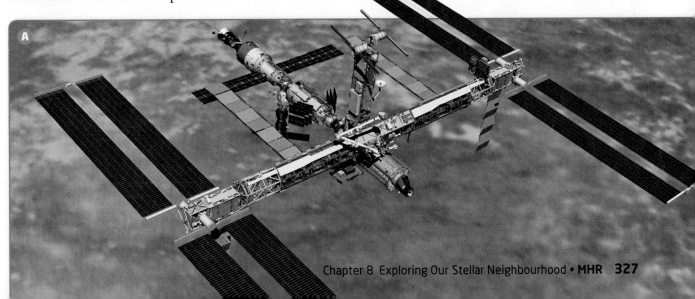

A

A Laboratory in Space

The ISS is a space-based laboratory. It provides many opportunities for research in the microgravity environment. Microgravity is the condition of weightlessness experienced by all objects in space, including people and spacecraft. Scientists at the CSA are known around the world for their work in microgravity research.

The crew members who stay on the ISS conduct experiments, such as growing protein crystals. Research on growing protein crystals will help scientists determine protein structure and function. Pharmaceutical companies may be able to use this research to develop treatments for diseases.

Canadian Contributions to the ISS

One of the largest successes in the U.S. space program has been the robotic fixtures that were designed and built in Canada: Canadarm, Canadarm2, and Dextre, shown in **Figure 8.15**. The Canadarms are used on NASA's space shuttles to help with the construction of the ISS.

Canada's robotic technology has resulted in benefits on Earth, too. For example, MD Robotics, the company that built the Canadarms, has used this technology in another arm—the Light Duty Utility Arm. This robotic arm handles radioactive waste in underground storage tanks.

Canada's Astronauts

Figure 8.16 As of 2009, Canada has three active astronauts: Chris Hadfield (top), Julie Payette (middle), and Robert Thirsk (bottom).

As of this book's printing, Canada has three active astronauts: Chris Hadfield, Julie Payette, and Robert Thirsk, shown in **Figure 8.16**. Hadfield has been an astronaut since 1992, and he was the first Canadian to operate the Canadarm in orbit. Payette has also been an astronaut since 1992 and was the first Canadian to travel to the ISS. Thirsk has been an astronaut since 1983. He studies the effects of space conditions on animal and plant life. Canada's retired astronauts are Roberta Bondar, Marc Garneau, Steve MacLean (now president of the CSA), Bjarni Tryggvason, and Dave Williams.

Making a Difference

Roberta Bondar fulfilled a childhood dream after she boarded the space shuttle *Discovery* in 1992. She also became Canada's first female astronaut and the first neurologist in space.

Roberta spent eight days conducting experiments and researching connections between how the human body recovers after being in space and neurological conditions, such as Parkinson's disease and stroke.

Roberta has studied agriculture and zoology at the University of Guelph and neurobiology at the University of Western Ontario and the University of Toronto. She earned a medical degree from McMaster University with a specialty in neurology.

Roberta is an inspiring role model for students all across Canada. Which Canadian role model has made the biggest impact on you and your dreams for the future?

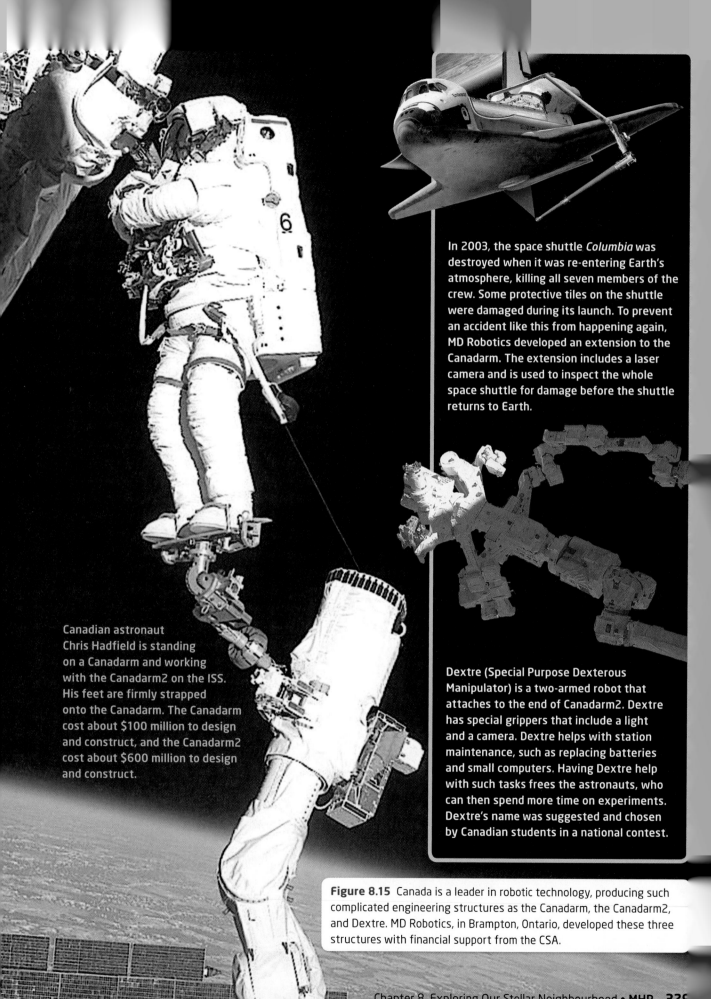

In 2003, the space shuttle *Columbia* was destroyed when it was re-entering Earth's atmosphere, killing all seven members of the crew. Some protective tiles on the shuttle were damaged during its launch. To prevent an accident like this from happening again, MD Robotics developed an extension to the Canadarm. The extension includes a laser camera and is used to inspect the whole space shuttle for damage before the shuttle returns to Earth.

Canadian astronaut Chris Hadfield is standing on a Canadarm and working with the Canadarm2 on the ISS. His feet are firmly strapped onto the Canadarm. The Canadarm cost about $100 million to design and construct, and the Canadarm2 cost about $600 million to design and construct.

Dextre (Special Purpose Dexterous Manipulator) is a two-armed robot that attaches to the end of Canadarm2. Dextre has special grippers that include a light and a camera. Dextre helps with station maintenance, such as replacing batteries and small computers. Having Dextre help with such tasks frees the astronauts, who can then spend more time on experiments. Dextre's name was suggested and chosen by Canadian students in a national contest.

Figure 8.15 Canada is a leader in robotic technology, producing such complicated engineering structures as the Canadarm, the Canadarm2, and Dextre. MD Robotics, in Brampton, Ontario, developed these three structures with financial support from the CSA.

The Costs of Space Exploration

It takes years of designing and testing the equipment, spacesuits, and computer software needed to send people and vehicles into space. As a result, space exploration is very expensive. Sending humans into space is also extremely risky. Tragic accidents have occurred. For example, the first Apollo mission—*Apollo 1*—did not even get off the ground. In 1967, there was a fire in the spacecraft on the ground during a test three weeks before launch, leading to the deaths of all three astronauts inside. In another accident, the Russian cosmonaut (the Russian equivalent of an astronaut) Vladimir Komarov died when his spacecraft crashed when returning to Earth, also in 1967.

The Ethics of Space Exploration

The term **ethics** means the set of moral principles and values that guide a person's activities and help him or her decide what is right and what is wrong. When discussing space exploration and the use of space resources, such as rock samples from the Moon and other celestial bodies, it is important to consider the ethical issues related to space exploration. Closely tied to ethical issues are environmental and political issues.

Sense of Value

NASA's budget in 2008 was just over U.S. $17 billion, most of which went to salaries. How does this compare with the budget of the city or town you live in?

ethics the set of moral principles and values that guide a person's activities and help him or her decide what is right and what is wrong

STSE Case Study

Space Junk

Earth is not the only place where humans have dumped their garbage–we have also created a garbage problem in space. There are now millions of pieces of garbage, called space junk, orbiting our planet.

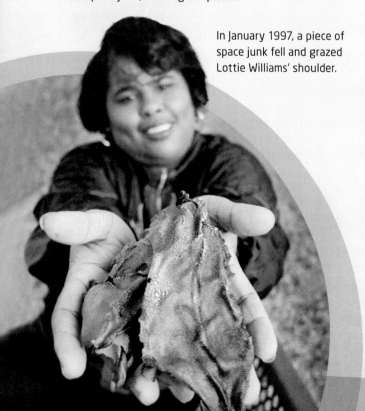

In January 1997, a piece of space junk fell and grazed Lottie Williams' shoulder.

Most pieces of space junk are very small, but they move at speeds of up to 8 km/s. At these extremely high speeds, a collision with even a very small piece of junk can cause a lot of damage. Mission controllers have sometimes had to change the flight paths of space shuttles to avoid dangerous collisions. But scientists cannot track the millions of pieces of junk all the time, and the risk of a collision with a piece of this debris is now the biggest threat to space shuttle missions. Space junk can also cause costly damage to functioning satellites.

According to NASA, about one piece of space junk returns to Earth every day, and there is a one-in-a-trillion chance a person will be hit by falling junk. There have been no reported cases of people being killed by space junk, but there have been reports of large pieces of junk falling to Earth.

Reducing Space Junk

Space agency scientists are researching ways to clean up and reduce the amount of space junk. One solution for reducing the amount of space junk is to send spacecraft into orbit to try to collect it. Another solution is to slow the orbit of a piece of space junk using lasers, so that it will fall back to Earth. Unfortunately, these strategies are too expensive or technically difficult to put into practice. Until we find a way to get rid of the orbiting junk, sending astronauts and equipment into space will become riskier.

Issues to Consider

Table 8.3 outlines some of the questions that we must consider if we are to prevent the unethical use of space and its resources in the future.

Table 8.3 Issues Related to Space Exploration

Ethical	• How do we ensure that space resources will be used to help all humankind, rather than just to provide an advantage for one country or another? • Do humans have the right to explore other environments around the solar system? • Do humans have the right to take materials from other bodies in the solar system?
Environmental	• How will space exploration affect Earth's natural systems? • Who is responsible for policing environmental impacts? • Who is responsible for cleaning up any damage or debris caused by space exploration and development?
Political	• Who owns space resources? • Should countries share technology and resources? • Who should decide how space resources will be used?

Sources of Space Junk

Earth is surrounded by a halo of space junk.

- Millions of small bits and pieces, such as paint chips, nuts and bolts, and other tiny fragments, have broken off telescopes, satellites, and spacecraft.

- An American astronaut's extra glove floated off during the first U.S. spacewalk in 1965, and in 2008 an astronaut lost a tool kit.

- Some countries have intentionally exploded their own satellites. For example, in 2007, China tested its anti-satellite capabilities by destroying one of its own satellites, creating hundreds of new pieces of garbage.

- New pieces of space junk form when objects already in orbit collide with each other.

- Old satellites and other equipment, such as rocket stages, have remained in orbit but are no longer functioning.

Your Turn

1. What is space junk, and why is it such a problem?

2. Some people think that space junk is similar to pollution and other environmental problems on Earth. Create a Venn diagram to illustrate the similarities and differences between space junk and pollution on Earth.

3. You are a reporter for a local newspaper who has been assigned to write about a large piece of space junk that has landed in a field outside of town. Write a newspaper article that describes what happened and why space junk is dangerous.

Section Summary

- There are two basic types of optical telescopes. Refracting telescopes collect light using a lens, and reflecting telescopes collect light using mirrors.
- There are also telescopes that detect non-visible radiation.
- Alternatives to human exploration of space are telescopes, planetary orbiters, landers, and satellites.

- There are hazards, risks, benefits, and ethical issues related to exploring space and developing space technology.
- The Canadian government, Canadian companies, and individual Canadians have contributed to the exploration of space in many different ways.

Review Questions

K/U **1.** List two reasons why astronomers collect electromagnetic radiation from objects in space using telescopes instead of visiting the objects.

C **2.** In a graphic organizer, show the advantages and disadvantages of using robots and satellites instead of humans to explore space.

K/U **3.** List two risks of space exploration.

K/U **4.** Canadian individuals, Canadian companies, and the Canadian government are active in space research.

  a. List three Canadian contributions to space exploration.

  b. List three Canadian individuals who have contributed to space exploration.

K/U **5.** How have Canadians contributed to the development and use of satellite technology? Include an example in your answer.

A **6.** The image on the right was taken by ENVISAT in late 2007. The coastline is southern California. What is the image showing, and how is this helpful?

C **7.** The term *geostationary satellite* is not really accurate. Argue why this is so.

T/I **8.** Study **Figure 8.5** on page 320. Predict what this drawing would look like if Earth's atmosphere were replaced with the atmosphere of Mars. Include a sketch. How would this affect the design of a space suit?

T/I **9.** In **Table 8.3** on page 331, nine questions are posed. In your opinion, which three questions are the most difficult to answer? Explain your choices.

The ENVISAT satellite took this image of southern California in October 2007.

8.2 Exploring the Sun

Key Terms

solar nebula theory
star
nebula
protostar
nuclear fusion
photosphere
sunspot
solar wind

The Sun is the most important celestial object for life on Earth. It is not surprising that astronomers use some of the technological tools described in Section 8.1, such as the SOHO satellite, to learn as much as they can about the Sun. In spite of the Sun's importance, people generally take for granted that it will continue to shine steadily and reliably every day, year after year, allowing us to enjoy each day from sunrise to sunset (**Figure 8.17**).

The Formation of the Sun and the Solar System

One major question about the Sun is, Where did it come from? The current theory regarding how the Sun, other stars, and planets form is called the **solar nebula theory**. This theory says that stars and planets form together. A **star** is a celestial body made of hot gases, mainly hydrogen and some helium. When a star forms, such as the Sun, its hot core remains surrounded by gas and dust—called a **nebula**—that have not been pulled into the centre. Sometimes this leftover material just drifts off into space. In other cases, it remains in the nebula, bound to the star by gravity.

solar nebula theory the theory that describes how stars and planets form from contracting, spinning disks of gas and dust

star a celestial body made of hot gases, mainly hydrogen and some helium

nebula a vast cloud of gas and dust, which may be the birthplace of stars and planets

Figure 8.17 Kayaking on a lake allows for unobstructed views of sunrises, sunsets, and the night sky.

How the Solar System Formed

As you read this paragraph, refer to **Figure 8.18**. Gravity can set the gas and dust particles in the nebula into motion around the core of the young star, which is called a protostar (**Figure 8.18A**). The **protostar** is a hot and condensed object. The particles begin to gather in the centre of the spinning cloud. You can see a similar effect if you stir a glass of water that has a small amount of sand at the bottom—the more you stir, the more the sand gathers in the middle of the bottom of the glass. The spinning nebula begins to contract, and tiny grains start to collect, building up into bigger, rocky lumps called planetesimals (**Figure 8.18B**). If the planetesimals can survive collisions with each other, they may build up and eventually develop into full-fledged planets like those in our solar system (**Figure 8.18C**).

Evidence for the Formation of the Solar System

The early solar system was a very cluttered and disorganized place. Dust and rocky materials ranging from particles the size of grains of sand to balls of rock the size of planets orbited the new Sun. Collisions were common in this crowded, jumbled environment. Stray rocks and dust that had not fallen into the Sun pounded the planets and their moons. The cratered surfaces of the Moon and Mercury are evidence of this pounding.

protostar hot, condensed object at the centre of a nebula

Study Toolkit

Making Study Notes After you read the paragraph on evidence for the formation of the solar system, you could arrange your notes in a T-chart, like the one on page 316. A T-chart illustrates the text's main idea and supporting details.

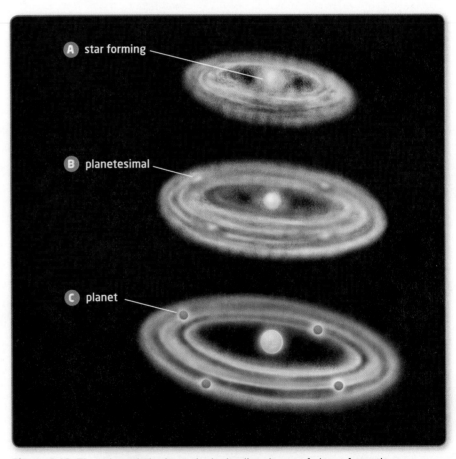

A star forming

B planetesimal

C planet

Figure 8.18 The solar nebula theory is the leading theory of planet formation.

A Flat, Rotating Disk

Over time, as the nebula spins, it flattens into a disk-like shape while spinning in one direction. Astronomers theorize that any planets and other bodies that form at this stage would form in the flat plane of the disk. As a result, they would rotate and revolve around the star in the same direction. All the planets in the solar system are more or less in the plane of the disk, most rotate in the same direction, and they all revolve around the Sun in the same direction.

Using various technologies and tools such as telescopes, astronomers have also discovered flattening dust clouds around young stars that are beyond our solar system. This evidence strongly supports the solar nebula theory.

Extrasolar Planets

The solar nebula theory indicates that planets are by-products of star formation, so planets should be fairly common. In fact, astronomers have discovered over 300 planets orbiting stars other than the Sun. These are called *extrasolar planets*. There are several techniques that astronomers use to detect extrasolar planets. For example, astronomers have discovered some extrasolar planets by detecting changes in a star's light levels as the planet orbits the star. When the planet is between the star and the observer on Earth, the amount of light coming from the star decreases slightly.

In 2008, astronomers took the first images of extrasolar planets, which you can see in **Figure 8.19**. The star is HR 8799 (labelled **a**) in the constellation Pegasus. Canadian astronomer Christian Marois, of the Herzberg Institute of Astrophysics in Victoria, British Columbia, and colleagues developed a way to separate a star's bright light from the light emitted by the still-forming planets. Otherwise, the light from a star is so bright that it prevents astronomers from seeing the planets. The image in **Figure 8.19** was taken at the Keck Observatory in Hawaii.

How the Sun Formed

As a star-forming nebula collapses and contracts, the gas compresses. As a result of the compression, the temperature of the protostar increases. When the temperature reaches around 10 000 000°C, nuclear fusion begins. During **nuclear fusion**, hydrogen nuclei combine to form helium nuclei. It takes enormous pressure and temperatures to do this. Such conditions only exist in the cores of stars. Note that nuclear fusion is not a chemical or physical reaction—it is a nuclear reaction.

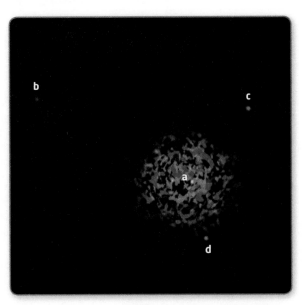

Figure 8.19 The extrasolar planets are labelled in order of discovery, so **a** is the star, which was discovered first. Then planets **b**, **c**, and **d** were discovered, all of which are larger than Jupiter.

nuclear fusion the process of energy production in which hydrogen nuclei combine to form helium nuclei

A Growing Sun

Go to **scienceontario** to find out more

Once the fusion process begins, the protostar starts to consume the hydrogen fuel. Helium from nuclear fusion begins to build up in the protostar's core. The core continues to heat up, which increases the pressure and temperature. At the same time, there is always a balancing act going on with gravity. The pressure is always trying to balance with gravity pulling matter toward the core. When gravity and pressure are balanced, the result is a stable star such as the Sun, as shown in **Figure 8.20**.

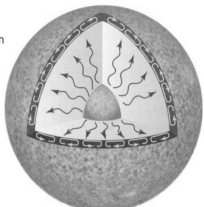

Figure 8.20 Energy in the Sun is transferred mostly by radiation from the core outward to about 86 percent of its radius. The outer layers transfer energy in convection currents.

When the Sun has converted about 10 percent of its hydrogen to helium, the helium in the core will accumulate and also begin to undergo fusion. At this point, the Sun will physically change, as will be described in Section 8.3. Solar astronomers (astronomers who study the Sun) know that the Sun can produce energy by nuclear hydrogen fusion for about 10 billion years. This estimate is based on the energy output of the Sun and the mass of hydrogen it contains. The Sun is now about five billion years old, so you might say the Sun is in mid-life.

Helium is denser than hydrogen, so helium settles in the Sun's core. As the Sun continues to fuse hydrogen into helium, the helium core grows larger. The region of hydrogen fusion, which lies around the helium core like the shell on an egg, also grows larger. So the Sun is getting larger. Solar astronomers estimate that the Sun is 30 percent larger today than when it was a protostar about five billion years ago.

Learning Check

1. Why is the theory shown in **Figure 8.18** called the solar nebula theory?

2. List three pieces of evidence that support the solar nebula theory.

3. Define *protostar*.

4. Name and describe the process that fuels the Sun.

Features of the Sun

Since the Sun is really a large sphere of gas, it has no surface as such. The area recognized as the surface is called the **photosphere**. The photosphere is several thousand kilometres deep.

Sunspots

For centuries, observers of the Sun have noticed dark spots on the photosphere, called sunspots. **Sunspots** are areas of strong magnetic fields. A magnetic field is a region of force around a magnetically charged area, such as a magnet. When you observe a compass needle pointing toward north, you are seeing evidence of Earth's magnetic field. Like Earth, the Sun has a magnetic field, although the Sun's magnetic field is much more complicated than Earth's.

Sometimes, when charged particles disturb the Sun's photosphere, sunspots appear. Sunspots are not actually dark—they are bright. They look dark because they are a different temperature from the photosphere, and one temperature contrasts with the other. The photosphere is about 6000°C, and sunspots are about 4500°C.

Evidence of a Rotating Sun

Astronomers have observed that sunspots that form near the Sun's north and south poles take about 35 days to complete one rotation, and sunspots that form near the Sun's equator take about 27 days to complete one rotation. Based on these observations, astronomers infer that not only does the Sun rotate, but it rotates faster at its equator than at its poles. This means that the Sun does not rotate as a solid body the way Earth does. **Figure 8.21** shows the movement of a group of sunspots across the photosphere.

Sunspots usually start off small, gradually grow larger and sometimes form in clusters, eventually fade, and then disappear altogether. Sunspots occur in 22-year cycles, peaking in number at intervals of about every 11 years. The precise time at which the maximum sunspot activity occurs is difficult to predict.

> **photosphere** the surface layer of the Sun
>
> **sunspot** an area of strong magnetic fields on the photosphere

⊖ ○ ○

Study Toolkit

Compound Words Think about the compound word *sunspot*. If you identify the two smaller words that make up this compound word, you can use their meanings to figure out the meaning of *sunspot*.

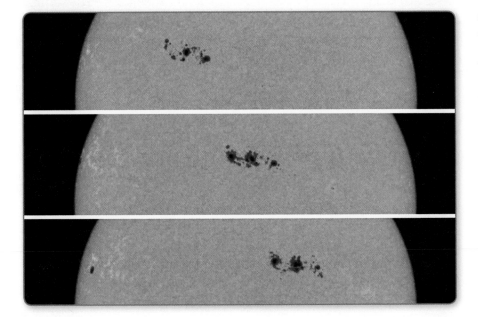

Figure 8.21 Notice how sunspots move as the Sun rotates. The SOHO satellite took the top image on July 15, the middle image on July 16, and the bottom image on July 17, 2007.

Solar Flares

Occasionally, solar flares can occur where there are complex groups of sunspots. A solar flare, seen in **Figure 8.22A**, is an event in which magnetic fields explosively eject intense streams of charged particles into space. If one of these streams, called the **solar wind**, hits Earth, the results can be quite spectacular. On the one hand, these events, called solar storms, can disrupt telecommunications and damage electronic equipment aboard spacecraft. They can also overload the electrical power network, causing large-scale power blackouts. The radiation from a solar storm can also be harmful to astronauts.

On the other hand, solar flares usually result in beautiful auroras, as shown in **Figure 8.22B**. Auroras are shimmering curtains of green and/or red light in Earth's polar regions. They result when the high-energy charged particles are carried past Earth's magnetic field, generating electric currents that flow toward Earth's poles. These electric currents charge gases in Earth's upper atmosphere, producing the light in auroras. Auroras at Earth's North Pole are called aurora borealis. Auroras at Earth's South Pole are called aurora australis.

Figure 8.22 A Solar flares eject intense blasts of charged subatomic particles toward Earth. The SOHO satellite took this X-ray image of the Sun. **B** When the charged particles from the Sun collide with Earth's upper atmosphere, spectacular auroras can result.

Learning Check

5. Name the two most abundant elements that the Sun is composed of, and identify which element is in the higher proportion.

6. What is the difference between a solar flare and the solar wind?

7. Explain why sunspots look dark.

8. If you were an astronaut on the International Space Station, would you be concerned about solar flares? Why or why not?

The Importance of the Sun

The Sun is needed for all life on Earth. The Sun's energy drives most processes on Earth that support our daily activities, like finding sufficient food and providing ourselves with adequate shelter.

Solar energy powers the winds and ocean currents. It also drives all weather, from soft summer winds to gigantic hurricanes. Sunlight provides the energy required for photosynthesis. Photosynthesis is the process in which green plants provide all the vital oxygen in the atmosphere and all the food at the base of the food chain.

Heating Earth

The Sun's energy, or solar energy, is not just visible light. The Sun emits radiation from across the entire electromagnetic spectrum, such as microwaves, radio waves, light waves, X rays, and gamma rays. Recall from **Figure 8.5** on page 320 that most of the radiation that reaches Earth's surface is visible light and shorter-wavelength infrared radiation. This radiation goes through a cycle, shown in **Figure 8.23**. Earth's surface absorbs most of the visible light. While absorbing the visible light, Earth also emits longer-wavelength infrared radiation to the atmosphere. In turn, the atmosphere absorbs and emits infrared radiation. The process of reflecting and absorbing energy warms Earth's surface.

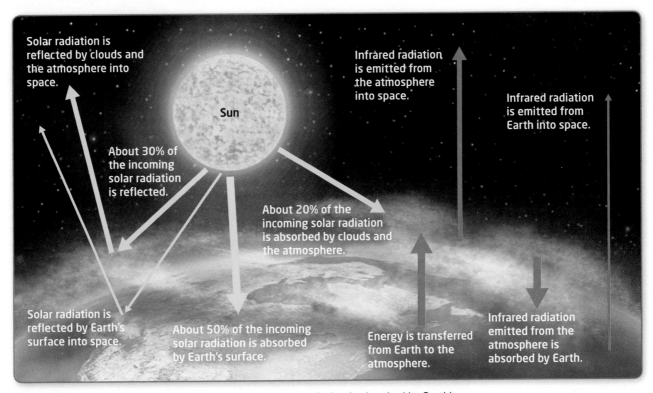

Figure 8.23 About 20 percent of the total incoming solar radiation is absorbed by Earth's atmosphere. About 30 percent is reflected by Earth's atmosphere, clouds, and surface and ocean features. About 50 percent is absorbed by Earth's surface and ocean features.

Section Summary

- The solar nebula theory says that the Sun and the solar system formed from a spinning, contracting disk of gas and dust particles.

- Evidence supporting the solar nebula theory consists of heavily cratered objects, most planets rotating in about the same direction, most planets revolving in the same direction and in about the same plane, and the existence of other planets around other stars.

- The Sun's energy source is hydrogen. It converts matter into energy through nuclear fusion.

- Sunspots can produce solar flares, which send gigantic beams of charged particles into space.

- Charged particles from the Sun that enter Earth's atmosphere produce auroras, but the charged particles can also damage electronic equipment, cause large-scale power blackouts, and pose a danger to astronauts.

- Energy absorbed and emitted by Earth's surface heats Earth and keeps it warm.

Review Questions

C **1.** In your notebook, draw the stages of the formation of the Sun and the solar system. Review **Figure 8.18**.

K/U **2.** List the types of radiation emitted by the Sun.

T/I **3.** The pie chart on the right shows the current composition of the Sun. Predict how the sizes of the pie portions for hydrogen and helium will change as the Sun gets older. Explain your reasoning.

K/U **4.** List three reasons why the Sun's energy is important to us.

K/U **5.** Give an example of the result of the Sun's energy interacting with Earth's atmosphere.

C **6.** In a pie chart, indicate the portions of solar radiation that are absorbed and reflected by Earth's surface features, oceans, and atmosphere. Refer to **Figure 8.23**.

K/U **7.** How does the Sun keep Earth's surface warm?

A **8.** What are the impacts of solar flares on technology, society, and the environment?

T/I **9.** Using the graph below, estimate the year of the next peak in sunspot activity.

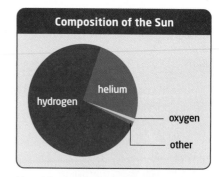

Use this pie chart to answer question 3.

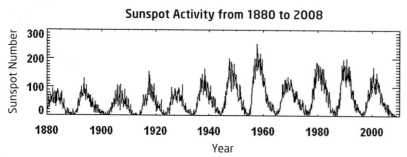

8.3 Exploring Other Stars

When you look at the night sky, you see that some stars are brighter than others, as shown in **Figure 8.24**. But are the stars brighter because they are emitting more light, or are they brighter because they are closer to Earth? A star can seem brighter than another because it is larger or because it is closer to Earth. The closest stars to Earth are not necessarily the brightest.

How Bright Is That Star?

Astronomers refer to luminosity when talking about the brightness of stars. A star's **luminosity** is a measure of the total amount of energy it radiates per second. The star that astronomers know the best is the Sun, so it is helpful to compare other stars with the Sun. Astronomers have found that some stars are about 10 000 times less luminous than the Sun, while others are more than 30 000 times more luminous than the Sun.

Another term referring to a star's brightness is absolute magnitude. A star's **absolute magnitude** is defined as how bright the star would be at a distance of 32.6 light-years from Earth. The absolute magnitude of the Sun is about 4.7. (Recall from Chapter 7 that a 4.7 magnitude star is not that bright.) This means that, compared with other stars, the Sun is rather faint.

Key Terms
luminosity
absolute magnitude
spectroscope
spectral lines
Hertzsprung–Russell (H-R) diagram
main sequence
white dwarf
supernova
neutron star

luminosity a star's total energy output per second; its power in joules per second (J/s)

absolute magnitude the magnitude of a star that we would observe if the star were placed 32.6 light-years from Earth

Figure 8.24 The night sky is filled with stars at all levels of brightness.

The Colour and Temperature of Stars

Stars in the night sky generally look like small points of white light. If you were able to view them through a powerful telescope, however, you would see that some are bluish, some are bluish-white, and some are yellow, orangish, or reddish.

Astronomers use the colour of a star to determine the star's surface temperature. (Think of a stove element that has become so hot that it turns red.) Recall from Section 8.2 that the temperature of the Sun's photosphere is about 6000°C. The Sun is yellow, so astronomers infer that yellow stars have a similar surface temperature. Bluish stars are much hotter. The surface temperature of a bluish star typically varies between 21 000°C and 35 000°C. On the other end of the scale, the temperatures of reddish stars are typically much cooler, about 3300°C.

The Composition of Stars

How do astronomers know that the Sun and other stars are made of hydrogen and helium? They use a spectroscope to analyze the light from stars. A **spectroscope** is an instrument that produces a pattern of colours and lines, called a spectrum, from a narrow beam of light. In the 1820s, Joseph von Fraunhofer, a German optician, used a spectroscope to observe the Sun's spectrum and noticed hundreds of lines. These lines are called **spectral lines**. He mapped the Sun's spectrum completely, although he did not know what the spectral lines meant. Today, astronomers know that a star's spectrum identifies the elements within the star's photosphere, as shown in **Figure 8.25**.

Suggested Investigation

Plan Your Own Investigation 8-A, The Brightness of Stars, on page 350

spectroscope an optical instrument that produces a spectrum from a narrow beam of light, and usually projects the spectrum onto a photographic plate or a digital detector

spectral lines certain specific wavelengths within a spectrum characterized by lines; spectral lines identify specific chemical elements

Figure 8.25 Every element is uniquely identified by its spectrum. A nanometre (nm) is 10^{-9} m.

Suggested Investigation

Inquiry Investigation 8-B, Using Spectral Analysis to Identify Star Composition, page 352

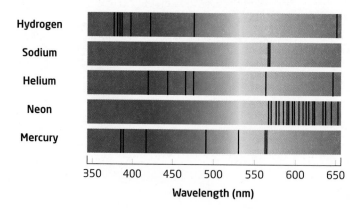

Wavelength (nm)

Learning Check

1. Write a definition for luminosity.

2. Does a star's apparent brightness depend on just its distance from Earth? Explain your answer.

3. List four properties of stars.

4. What can you learn about a star by looking at its spectrum? Review **Figure 8.25**.

The Mass of Stars

Determining the mass of stars was not possible until astronomers discovered that most of the stars seen from Earth are binary stars. *Binary stars* are two stars that orbit each other. The Sun is unusual in that it is not part of a binary star system. By knowing the size of the orbit of a binary pair and the time the two stars take to complete one orbit, astronomers were then able to calculate the mass of each star. Star mass is expressed in terms of *solar mass*. The Sun is 1 solar mass. Other stars range from 0.08 solar masses to over 100 solar masses.

The Hertzsprung-Russell Diagram

As astronomers learned more about the properties of stars, they began to look for patterns in the data. In the 1920s, two astronomers were studying data from large numbers of stars visible from Earth. Ejnar Hertzsprung in the Netherlands and Henry Norris Russell in the United States were working independently of each other. But both observed that each star type has certain properties. These relationships can be shown on a graph called the **Hertzsprung–Russell (H-R) diagram**. Their graph had star colour (ranging from blue to red) on the *x*-axis. Absolute magnitude (ranging from dimmer to brighter) was on the *y*-axis of their graph. **Figure 8.26** shows an H-R diagram in which the absolute magnitude has been replaced by the luminosity. Astronomers discovered from the H-R diagram that there are several different categories of stars.

> **Hertzsprung-Russell (H-R) diagram** a graph that compares the properties of stars

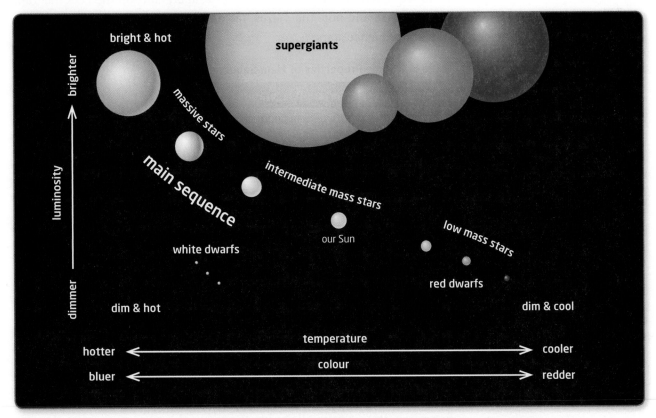

Figure 8.26 Hertzsprung-Russell diagrams like this one show trends in the evolution of stars. For example, most cool stars are much dimmer than hot stars, and most hot stars tend to be more massive than cool stars.

The Main Sequence

main sequence a narrow band of stars on the H-R diagram that runs diagonally from the upper left (bright, hot stars) to the lower right (dim, cool stars); about 90 percent of stars, including the Sun, are in the main sequence

The central band of stars stretching from the upper left to the lower right of the H-R diagram in **Figure 8.26** is called the **main sequence**. The main sequence accounts for about 90 percent of the stars that you can see from Earth. What about the 10 percent of known stars not in the main sequence? Hertzsprung and Russell found that some stars were cooler but very bright. The star Antares, for example, shown in **Figure 8.27**, has a surface temperature of only 3500°C, but it is the 15th brightest star in the night sky.

Figure 8.27 Antares is a bright supergiant located approximately 600 light-years from Earth. Its surface temperature is relatively cool, yet it is extremely bright.

When placed on the H-R diagram, the cool, bright stars are far above the main sequence. Find these red giants and supergiants on the H-R diagram in **Figure 8.26** and note their sizes. **Table 8.4** summarizes some properties of main-sequence stars.

Table 8.4 Some Properties of Main-Sequence Stars

Colour	Surface Temperature (°C)	Mass*	Luminosity*
Blue	35 000	40	405 000
Blue-white	21 000	15	13 000
White	10 000	3.5	80
Yellow-white	7 500	1.7	6.4
Yellow	6 000	1.1	1.4
Orange	4 700	0.8	0.46
Red	3 300	0.5	0.08

* These properties are relative to the Sun.

Questions about why some stars are not in the main sequence led astronomers to wonder how these stars came to be. Were they special, rare types of stars that formed in a different way? Or were they examples of main-sequence stars that had gone through dramatic changes at some stage in their life? Astronomers have worked out the basic features of star formation. But, as you will read in the rest of this section, there are lots of details missing, and many puzzles still remain.

Suggested Investigation

Data Analysis Investigation 8-C, Building an H-R Diagram, on page 354

How Stars Evolve

Stars, in general, do not change very rapidly. Stars like the Sun shine for billions of years with little or no change. Nevertheless, stars radiate huge amounts of energy into space, and they cannot do that forever. Eventually, they run out of fuel. In the final stages of a star's life, it becomes a white dwarf, a neutron star, or a black hole. What the star evolves into depends on its initial mass on the main sequence. **Figure 8.28** illustrates the evolution of different types of stars. Refer to this figure as you read the following text.

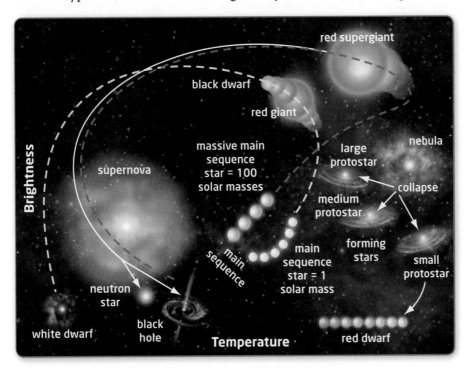

Figure 8.28 A star's life cycle depends on its initial mass.

Low-Mass Stars

Low-mass stars (red dwarfs) have less mass than the Sun. They consume their hydrogen slowly over a period that may be as long as 100 billion years. During that time, they lose significant mass, essentially evaporating. In the end, all that remains of them is a very faint **white dwarf**. While white dwarfs no longer produce energy of their own, they are incredibly hot. It takes tens of billions of years for them to cool down. Astronomers theorize that when they do cool down, they will become nothing more than dark embers called black dwarfs. The universe is not old enough to contain any black dwarfs.

white dwarf a small, dim, hot star

Intermediate-Mass Stars

Intermediate-mass stars, such as the Sun, consume their hydrogen faster than low-mass stars, over a period of about 10 billion years. When their hydrogen is used up, the core collapses. As the core contracts, the temperature increases and the outer layers begin to expand. The expanded layers are cooler and appear red. At this phase the star is called a red giant. In about five billion years the Sun will become a red giant. It will become so large that its diameter will extend out to the current orbit of Mars. Eventually, the layers will disappear into space, and the Sun will become a white dwarf.

High-Mass Stars

Stars that are 12 or more solar masses are high-mass stars. These stars consume their fuel even faster than the intermediate-mass stars. As a result, high-mass stars die more quickly and more violently. In massive stars, the core heats up to much higher temperatures. Heavier elements form by fusion, and the star expands into a supergiant. Eventually, iron forms in the core. Since iron cannot release energy through fusion, the core collapses violently, and a shock wave travels through the star. The outer portion of the star explodes, producing a **supernova**. A supernova can be millions of times brighter than the original star was. **Figure 8.29** shows the remains of a supernova.

During a supernova explosion, the heavier elements formed are ejected into the universe. Some of these elements become parts of new stars, and some form planets and other bodies. Your body, in fact, contains many atoms that were fused in the cores of old stars.

Supernova Discovery

In 1987, Canadian astronomer Ian Shelton discovered a supernova while working at a University of Toronto observatory in Chile. Shelton was examining images of stars, and he noticed something unusual in one of them. He decided to step outside and look up. Among thousands of stars he spotted a bright one that was not previously visible. See **Figure 8.30**. Shelton had discovered a supernova. Called SN 1987A, the supernova was the closest one to Earth since 1604. SN 1987A is 163 000 light-years from Earth.

Depending on the initial mass of the star before it became a supernova, the remaining star will become either a neutron star or a black hole.

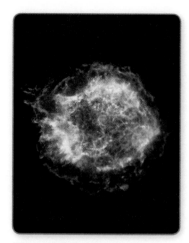

Figure 8.29 This image shows what is left of a star in the constellation Cassiopeia. The star exploded at the end of its life.

supernova a massive explosion in which the entire outer portion of a star is blown off

Figure 8.30 The image on the left shows the supernova discovered by Ian Shelton. The image on the right shows the same area before the supernova.

Neutron Stars

If the star began with a mass of about 12 to 15 solar masses, the core will shrink to approximately 20 km in diameter. In such stars, the pressure is so great that electrons are squeezed into protons, and the star eventually becomes a **neutron star**. The first neutron star to be discovered is in the centre of the Crab Nebula. The Crab Nebula is shown in **Figure 8.31A**.

The Crab Nebula is the remnant of a supernova explosion that occurred in 1054. Chinese historical records from that year reveal that Chinese astronomers observed it. They called it a "guest star." Astronomers have since discovered that the neutron star in the Crab Nebula is spinning about 30 times per second. **Figures 8.31B** and **C** show that as the neutron star spins, it sends pulses of radiation into space. The Crab Nebula neutron star was among the first discoveries of a type of neutron stars called pulsars. *Pulsars* send *pulses* of radiation toward Earth, much like an extremely fast-sweeping searchlight.

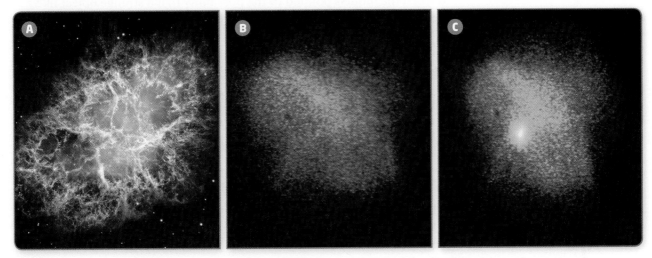

Figure 8.31 **A** The Crab Nebula in visible light. In **B**, the beam is pointing away from Earth. In **C**, you can see a pulse of radiation. This pulsar flashes about 30 times per second. The images in **B** and **C** are from the Einstein X-ray Observatory (in space).

Learning Check

5. What is the fate of the Sun? Review **Figure 8.28**.

6. Can a star less massive than the Sun become a supernova? Explain your answer.

7. What is a neutron star?

8. The Canadian songwriter Joni Mitchell wrote, "We are stardust" in her song called "Woodstock". She was being factual as well as poetic. Explain why.

Black Holes

The most spectacular deaths happen to stars whose initial masses are more than 25 solar masses. The remnant of the supernova explosion is so massive that nothing can compete with the crushing force of gravity. The remnant is crushed into a black hole. A *black hole* is a tiny patch of space that has no volume, but it does have mass. Therefore, there is still gravity. In fact, the gravitational force of a black hole is so strong that nothing can escape it. Even light cannot escape a black hole's gravity.

Black holes are among the strangest objects in the universe. Astronomers predicted the existence of black holes before the first one was discovered. Recall how Mendeleev's periodic table modelled the elements that were known at the time. Mendeleev's model led to predictions of missing elements, which then led to discoveries. In a similar way, scientists build mathematical models of how stars evolve and eventually die. The models seemed to fit what scientists were seeing, so when the models pointed to the possibility that a strange object like a black hole could exist, scientists started looking for them.

Finding a Black Hole

Go to **scienceontario** to find out more

When astronomers say they have detected a black hole, they do not mean that they have seen one. What they mean is that they have detected the *gravitational effects* of an object whose mass and size match those predicted by physics. For example, black holes that exist in congested regions of space sometimes swallow up matter and compress it until enormous temperatures are reached before it disappears. When this happens, the black hole emits intense radiation that uncloaks the normally invisible black hole. Astronomers look for the telltale signature of black holes devouring gas, dust, and stars using radio, X-ray, and gamma ray telescopes.

Dr. Tom Bolton, of the University of Toronto, identified the first black hole in 1972. The name of the black hole is Cygnus X-1. Astronomers now know that black holes are everywhere. They may exist in the core of every galaxy. You will learn more about galaxies in Chapter 9.

Section Summary

- A star's apparent brightness depends on its luminosity and distance from Earth.

- Hertzsprung and Russell independently discovered that each type of star has specific properties. They organized their findings into what is now called a Hertzsprung–Russell (H-R) diagram.

- The main sequence is a narrow band of stars on the H-R diagram that runs diagonally from the upper left (bright, hot stars) to the lower right (dim, cool stars). About 90 percent of stars are on the main sequence, including the Sun.

- A star's position on the main sequence is determined by its initial mass.

- A star will become a white dwarf, a neutron star, or a black hole, depending on its initial mass.

- Canadian researchers contribute to our understanding of space.

Review Questions

K/U   **1.** If a star's surface temperature is around 7200°C, what colour is the star?

C   **2.** Create a poster to describe the Hertzsprung–Russell diagram.

K/U   **3.** Place the following in order from youngest to oldest: A. star; B. nebula; C. red giant; D. white dwarf.

K/U   **4.** Why are the more massive stars the only important contributors in enriching the universe with heavy elements?

C   **5.** Pick one type of star, and write a short story on its life cycle.

A   **6.** Copy the table on the right into your notebook. Complete the table after studying **Figure 8.26**. Refer to **Table 8.4** as well.

A   **7.** Describe one contribution from a Canadian researcher to the study of space. Say how the contribution is important to the study of space.

T/I   **8.** Why do you think Chinese astronomers called the 1054 supernova explosion a "guest star"?

Star Properties

Star	Colour	Approximate Surface Temperature (°C)	Bright or Dim
Aldebaran		3 300	
Arcturus		4 700	
Betelgeuse		3 300	
Polaris		7 500	
Proxima Centauri		3 300	
Rigel		21 000	
Sirius		10 000	

Plan Your Own Investigation 8-A

Skill Check

✓ Initiating and Planning

✓ Performing and Recording

✓ Analyzing and Interpreting

✓ Communicating

Safety Precautions

- Do not short circuit the batteries. The batteries will become very hot, and their usable lifetime will be shortened.

- Use only incandescent bulbs.

- Do not exceed 4.5 V when hooking up the bulbs.

- Work carefully if you perform this investigation in a darkened room.

Materials

- six 1.5 V C or D battery cells, set up with one, then two, and then three in series (that is, 1.5 V, 3.0 V, and 4.5 V); see the illustration

- 6 hook-up wires with clips

- three 5 V (4.8 V) incandescent flashlight bulbs

- 3 base sockets for bulbs

- 3 battery holders

- sufficient connecting wires with connecting clips for 3 lamps

- metric tape measure

The Brightness of Stars

Is a star bright because it is close? Or is a star bright because it is luminous? Are both distance and luminosity important? In this investigation, you will plan and conduct a simulation to determine the relationship between star brightness and star distance from Earth. You will set up your simulation as though you are a designer at a science centre and are preparing a display for the general public. Your display cannot be longer than 4 m.

Question

What is the relationship between star brightness and star distance from Earth?

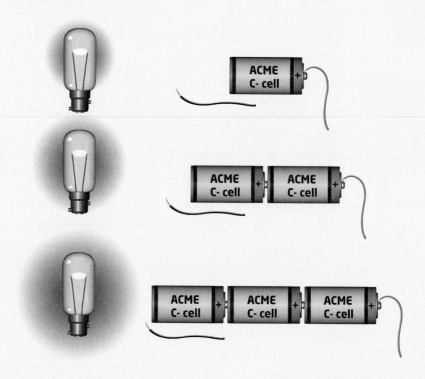

Prediction

Predict the relationship between distance and brightness, and predict how the flashlight bulbs must be arranged in order to have the same apparent brightness.

Plan and Conduct

1. Brainstorm about how you might perform this investigation. Write an outline of how the display will be built.

2. Make a prediction. Give a reason why you believe your prediction is correct.

3. Create a data table for collecting your data. Give your table a title.

4. Have your teacher approve your investigation method, outline, data table, and safety precautions.

5. Carry out your investigation. Remember to record your observations in your data table.

6. Repeat your investigation several times to collect more data.

Analyze and Interpret

1. Describe the relative positions of the lamps when they all have the same apparent brightness as seen by an observer.

Conclude and Communicate

2. Explain how the properties that you discovered can be used to help astronomers find the distances from Earth to the stars.

3. Evaluate the tools, techniques, and processes that you used to gather evidence. What improvements could you make?

4. From your observations, write a general statement about the relationship between distance and brightness.

5. Write the display plaque that explains to visitors the purpose of the display.

Extend Your Inquiry and Research Skills

6. **Inquiry** What are the benefits and limitations of the model in this experiment? If you were to design a new model, what modification would you make?

7. **Research** Simulations are important in the study of space. Research the advantages and disadvantages of using simulations.

Inquiry Investigation 8-B

Skill Check

Initiating and Planning

✓ Performing and Recording

✓ Analyzing and Interpreting

✓ Communicating

Materials

• ruler

Using Spectral Analysis to Identify Star Composition

Recall from your previous chemistry studies that a spectroscope separates white light into its rainbow colours, like a prism. A star's spectrum shows dark lines across the colours, as shown in the diagram below. These lines reveal that some wavelengths of light have "disappeared." The wavelengths have been absorbed by gases in the star's atmosphere. Each element absorbs certain wavelengths, producing a unique pattern of dark lines—like a bar code—on a spectrum. For example, the diagram below shows the spectrum for the element carbon.

In this investigation, you will examine the simplified spectra of five known chemical elements and use that information to interpret the composition of the Sun and three "mystery" stars.

The spectral lines for carbon are illustrated here.

Question

What are the Sun and the three mystery stars made of?

Prediction

The composition of the stars can be predicted by analyzing their spectra.

Procedure

1. The diagram illustrates the spectral patterns for five elements. Study these spectra to familiarize yourself with their patterns.

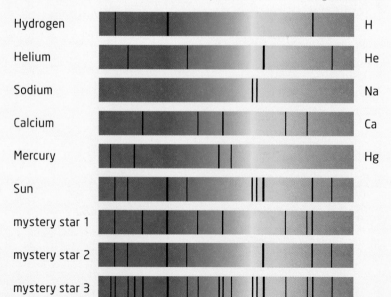

2. Examine the spectra for the Sun and the three mystery stars in the diagram. Using a ruler to help you line up the spectral lines, compare the spectral patterns of the known elements to those of the Sun and the three unknown stars. Then answer the following questions.

Analyze and Interpret

1. Which elements are present in the Sun's spectrum?

2. In which two mystery stars is calcium (Ca) present?

3. Which mystery star contains sodium (Na)?

4. Only one mystery star contains mercury (Hg). Which one is it?

5. Which mystery star's composition is least like that of the Sun?

Conclude and Communicate

6. In a paragraph, briefly describe how a star's composition can be inferred by analyzing its spectral pattern.

Extend Your Inquiry and Research Skills

7. Inquiry Suppose you were to analyze the light from the full Moon with a spectroscope. Predict the spectra that you would see. Explain your answer.

8. Research Research how astronomers use spectroscopy in their work.

Data Analysis Investigation 8-C

Data for H-R Diagram

Spectral Type	Absolute Magnitude
O5	−5.7
O9	−4.5
B0	−4.0
B2	−2.45
B5	−1.2
A0	+0.65
A2	+1.3
F0	+2.7
F2	+3.6
F8	+0.44
G2	+4.7
G8	+5.5
K0	+5.9
K2	+6.4
K5	+7.35
M0	+8.8
M2	+9.9
M5	+12.3

Building an H-R Diagram

Some H-R diagrams plot absolute magnitude on the *y*-axis instead of luminosity. In this investigation, you will build an H-R diagram from the data in the table. You will use your H-R diagram to predict the absolute magnitudes of main-sequence stars.

Question

How can you predict the absolute magnitudes of stars in the main sequence if you know whether the star is hot or dim?

Hypothesis

Hotter stars have higher absolute magnitudes.

Organize the Data

Your teacher will give you a blank H-R diagram. To make it easier to refer to the different types of main-sequence stars, astronomers developed a series of star types based on their spectra. These are called spectral types and are named O, B, A, F, G, K, and M. They are further broken into subcategories, using numbers, such as O5 and B2. Using the table of data at the left, graph each spectral type against its absolute magnitude on the blank H-R diagram.

Analyze and Interpret

1. What pattern do you see on your graph?

2. The Sun's spectral type is about G2. Use your chart to predict the Sun's absolute magnitude.

3. The star Vega's spectral type is A0. Use your chart to predict Vega's absolute magnitude.

4. A star's spectral type is B5. Use your chart to predict its absolute magnitude.

Conclude and Communicate

5. Summarize how you can use this pattern to predict a main-sequence star's absolute magnitude if you know the star's spectral type.

6. Was the hypothesis supported by the data? Why or why not?

Extend Your Inquiry and Research Skills

7. **Research** Research why astronomers use absolute magnitude instead of apparent magnitude on H-R diagrams.

Chapter 8 Summary

8.1 Exploring Space

Key Concepts

- There are two basic types of optical telescopes. Refracting telescopes collect light using a lens, and reflecting telescopes collect light using mirrors.
- There are also telescopes that detect non-visible radiation.
- Alternatives to human exploration of space are telescopes, planetary orbiters, landers, and satellites.
- There are hazards, risks, benefits, and ethical issues related to exploring space and developing space technology.
- The Canadian government, Canadian companies, and individual Canadians have contributed to the exploration of space in many different ways.

8.2 Exploring the Sun

Key Concepts

- The solar nebula theory says that the Sun and the solar system formed from a spinning, contracting disk of gas and dust particles.
- Evidence supporting the solar nebula theory consists of heavily cratered objects, most planets rotating in about the same direction, most planets revolving in the same direction and in about the same plane, and the existence of other planets around other stars.
- The Sun's energy source is hydrogen. It converts matter into energy through nuclear fusion.
- Sunspots can produce solar flares, which send gigantic beams of charged particles into space.
- Charged particles from the Sun that enter Earth's atmosphere produce auroras, but the charged particles can also damage electronic equipment, cause large-scale power blackouts, and pose a danger to astronauts.
- Energy absorbed and emitted by Earth's surface heats Earth and keeps it warm.

8.3 Exploring Other Stars

Key Concepts

- A star's apparent brightness depends on its luminosity and distance from Earth.
- Hertzsprung and Russell independently discovered that each type of star has specific properties. They organized their findings into what is now called a Hertzsprung-Russell (H-R) diagram.
- The main sequence is a narrow band of stars on the H-R diagram that runs diagonally from the upper left (bright, hot stars) to the lower right (dim, cool stars). About 90 percent of stars are on the main sequence, including the Sun.
- A star's position on the main sequence is determined by its initial mass.
- A star will become a white dwarf, a neutron star, or a black hole, depending on its initial mass.
- Canadian researchers contribute to our understanding of space.

Chapter 8 Review

Reviewing Key Terms

1. Light from a star is a form of _____ _____. (8.1)

2. _____ telescopes use mirrors to collect light, and _____ telescopes use lenses to collect light. (8.1)

3. Once a _____ reaches a temperature of 10 000 000°C, the process of _____ _____ begins. (8.2)

4. _____ are dark areas on the Sun's surface. (8.2)

5. The Sun is located in the band of stars called the _____ _____ in a _____ _____ diagram. (8.3)

6. After the Sun becomes a red giant, it will contract and eventually become a _____ _____. (8.4)

7. A massive star will end up as either a _____ _____ or a _____ _____, depending on the star's initial mass. (8.4)

Knowledge and Understanding K/U

8. How have partnerships between the Canadian government and Canadian businesses contributed to the development of technology used in space research and exploration?

9. Describe how an event on the Sun can affect Earth. Use an example in your answer.

10. To answer these questions, refer to **Figure 8.15**, which shows some Canadian contributions to the International Space Station.

    a. Give an example of a hazard that humans face when they are in space.

    b. What technology was developed in response to the hazard in part (a)?

11. Describe how the Sun is necessary for life as we know it.

12. Copy the figure below into your notebook, and fill in the three missing percentages.

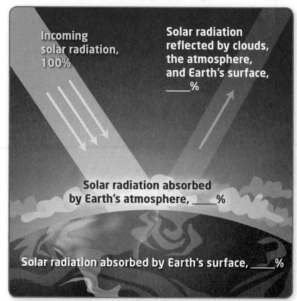

This diagram shows what happens to solar radiation when it reaches Earth.

13. Explain why the Sun is about 30 percent larger today than about five billion years ago.

14. Solar flares are associated with what features on the Sun's photosphere?

15. What evidence is there that the Sun rotates?

16. Describe how a star's spectrum is useful.

17. In a graphic organizer of your choice, list the evidence that supports the solar nebula theory.

18. Using the information in **Table 8.2**, compare and contrast MOST and the Hubble Space Telescope. Use a comparison strategy of your choice.

19. Create a Hertzsprung–Russell diagram like the one below in your notebook. Label the diagram with the following terms: main sequence, red giants, supergiants, and white dwarfs. Also, label the axes with the missing words.

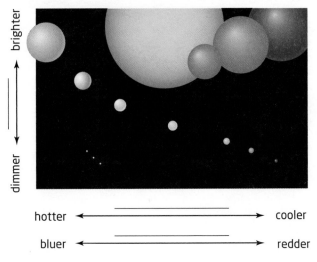

A Hertzsprung–Russell diagram

Thinking and Investigation T/I

20. To launch humans into space requires very specialized systems. List the essential systems that aerospace engineers must include in a spacecraft to support humans in space, but that would not normally be needed for unpiloted spacecraft.

21. Why are white dwarfs hot as well as dim?

22. It is a common misconception that if a star turns into a black hole, the newly formed black hole will begin to gobble up everything around it. Explain why this assumption is false.

23. Why do you think the MOST satellite is called "Canada's Humble Space Telescope"?

Communication C

24. **BIG IDEAS** People use observational evidence of the properties of the solar system and the universe to develop theories to explain their formation and evolution. Describe, using an example from this chapter, how astronomers use observational evidence to develop a theory to explain the formation of the solar system.

25. **BIG IDEAS** Space exploration has generated valuable knowledge but at enormous cost. In this chapter, you learned about some of the risks associated with space exploration as well as some of the knowledge gained. Express your opinion on the pros and cons of space exploration in an e-mail to a friend.

26. Review the issues in **Table 8.3**. Take a position on whether you think it is ethical to send people to Mars. State your position in writing, and support it with your reasons.

27. Describe the important stages of a star's life. Use any method of presentation you wish.

Application A

28. In what ways do satellites benefit your life and the lives of your family and friends?

29. The Canadarm is an essential component of both the space shuttle system and the International Space Station. Research the Canadarm by visiting the Canadian Space Agency's website. Identify one medical benefit that has resulted from the development of Canadarm technology.

30. Robots on other planets can be controlled from Earth, but it takes several minutes for the instruction to reach the robot because of the vast distances between planets.

   a. A camera on a Mars rover detects a hole directly in its path 100 m ahead (the length of a football field). Mars is located relative to Earth such that the signal takes 20 min to get to Earth. The technician on Earth sends a "stop" command. If the rover travels at 10 cm/s, will it stop before the hole? What is the maximum safe speed for the rover to operate to avoid missing the hole? (**Hint:** $v = d/t$, where v is speed, d is distance, and t is time.)

   b. Suggest a way in which the risk to rovers on distant planets might be minimized.

Chapter 9   The Mysterious Universe

What You Will Learn

In this chapter, you will learn how to...

- **identify** the three main types of galaxies
- **describe** the shape and size of the Milky Way galaxy
- **describe** the evidence that supports the big bang theory and an evolution model of the universe
- **identify** spinoff technologies that have resulted from studying space

Why It Matters

Gaining a better understanding of the universe gives us more insight into the possible origin of everything around us.

Skills You Will Use

In this chapter, you will learn how to...

- **model** the size of the Milky Way galaxy
- **model** the expanding universe
- **estimate** the age of the universe
- **evaluate** the costs and benefits of space exploration

There has been an explosive growth in technology for space exploration. This technology has revealed that the universe is a mysterious place, with black holes, exploding stars, and colliding galaxies, such as those pictured here. The planets, stars, and galaxies that we see, however, make up only about 4 percent of the universe. What could make up the rest of the universe?

Matter in Motion

A galaxy is a huge collection of stars, planets, gas, and dust held together by gravity. Like stars and planets, galaxies also rotate. Can you model galaxy rotation? In this activity, you will model the rotational motion of a galaxy using different materials to simulate stars.

Safety Precautions

Materials

- 600 mL beaker or plastic cup
- warm water
- medicine dropper
- small samples of food colouring, cocoa powder, and powdered milk

Add a few drops of food colouring to the swirling water.

Procedure

1. Create a table to record your sketches. Include a row for each sample and three columns: "First Rotation," "Slower Rotation," and "Faster Rotation." Give your table a title.

2. Put on the safety goggles and apron.

3. Pour warm water into the beaker until the beaker is approximately half full. Carefully holding the beaker in one hand, lift it up and make the water swirl by slowly moving the beaker in small circles.

4. With the water still swirling, put the beaker back on the table. Carefully place a few drops of food colouring on the centre of the water surface.

5. Observe what happens. Sketch your observations in your table immediately, while the water is still swirling.

6. Discard the water. Then repeat steps 3 to 5 twice, first swirling the water more slowly than before and then swirling it faster than before.

7. Repeat steps 3 to 5 for each of the dry materials, adding a pinch of each material to the water.

Questions

1. How did the different materials react when they were dropped in the swirling water?

2. How did changing the speed of rotation affect the pattern you observed?

3. Infer how this activity is similar to galaxy motion.

Study Toolkit

These strategies will help you use this textbook to develop your understanding of science concepts and skills.
To find out more about these and other strategies, refer to the Study Toolkit Overview, which begins on page 561.

Reading Effectively

Skim, Scan, or Study

Not all parts of a textbook should be read at the same speed. In general, the speed at which you read a chunk of text is determined by your purpose for reading. The table below shows three reading speeds, each suiting a different purpose for reading.

Purposes of Reading Speeds

Purpose	Reading Approach (Skim, Scan, or Study)
Preview text to get a general sense of what it contains.	Read quickly (skim).
Locate specific information.	Read somewhat quickly (scan).
Learn a new concept.	Read slowly (study).

Sometimes, you can determine your reading approach by the placement, treatment, or features of the text. For example, text placed at the beginning of a chapter or unit is often meant to stimulate interest and may not include important definitions or concepts. Marginal text with a heading such as "Sense of Time" can probably be skimmed. But text with several **boldfaced** words should be read slowly and carefully.

Use the Strategy

Turn to Section 9.3, "Unsolved Mysteries." With a partner, identify two sections of text that should be read slowly and carefully. Then identify two sections of text that could be skimmed. Make sure you can justify your choices based on the placement, treatment, or features of the text.

Organizing Your Learning

Using Graphic Organizers

Sometimes changing text into a visual format can help you understand and remember it. Graphic organizers come in many forms (see page 566 in this textbook). You can even design your own to organize important information and relationships. Circles and squares can be used to indicate different levels of importance. Lines and arrows can show sequence or cause-and-effect relationships. For example, the text below can be "translated" into the following graphic organizer.

"There has been an explosive growth in technology for space exploration. This technology has revealed that the universe is a mysterious place, with black holes, exploding stars, and colliding galaxies...."

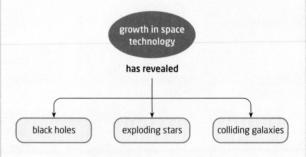

Use the Strategy

Turn to the section called "Star Clusters" on page 363. Draw a graphic organizer to show the information in the first two paragraphs. Be sure to reflect the relative importance of the facts and the relationships among them.

Word Study

Base Words

Understanding a word's *base* can help you understand the word's meaning. For example, if you do not know what *radiation* means, you might think about the word's base, which is *radiate*. If you know that *radiate* means "emit energy," you might be able to figure out that *radiation* is "the process of emitting energy" or the energy itself.

Use the Strategy

Think about the word *globular*. What is the base? Use that word to predict the meaning of *globular*. Use a dictionary to check your prediction.

9.1 Galaxies

Key Terms
Milky Way
galaxy
star cluster
open cluster
globular cluster
Local Group
supercluster

If you have viewed the night sky far from city lights, you have probably seen the Milky Way. On very clear nights, you can see the bright and dark areas shown in **Figure 9.1**. The **Milky Way** is a galaxy, and it includes the solar system. A **galaxy** is a collection of stars, gas, dust, and planets held together by gravity. Brightest in the summertime, the Milky Way appears as a hazy white band extending from the southern horizon and across the sky overhead. The ancient Greeks gave the Milky Way its name. They imagined that the white band was milk, spilled by the goddess Hera while she was feeding her son Heracles.

The Discovery of Galaxies

William Herschel (1738–1822) was a multi-talented British astronomer. He discovered the planet Uranus, and he coined the word *asteroid*. He and his sister, Caroline, were famous for building and selling fine telescopes. When William Herschel pointed one of his best telescopes at the Milky Way around 1780, he expected to see fuzzy white clouds. He was astonished to see a huge number of stars. Larger telescopes showed even more stars. Herschel had discovered that the Milky Way is a gigantic system of stars that we know today as a galaxy. Every star that you see in the sky on a clear night is part of the Milky Way.

Milky Way the galaxy that includes the solar system; appears as a hazy white band in the night sky

galaxy a huge collection of stars, planets, gas, and dust that is held together by gravity

Figure 9.1 In a dark sky on a clear night, the Milky Way looks like a band of white in the night sky.

The Shapes of Galaxies

A galaxy forms when gravity causes a large, slowly spinning cloud of gas, dust, and stars to contract (become smaller). The Sun is one of an estimated 100 billion stars in the Milky Way. All the stars in the universe belong to a galaxy.

Galaxies come in different shapes and sizes. Generally, they are classified as either spiral or elliptical, according to their appearance. Galaxies that do not fit into these general classifications are called irregular galaxies.

- A *spiral galaxy*, when viewed from above, looks like a pinwheel. It has many long "arms" spiralling out from a centre core. When viewed from the side, a spiral galaxy looks like a plate with a bulge in the middle, as if it had an orange inserted in its centre. **Figure 9.2A** shows a spiral galaxy viewed from above, and **Figure 9.2B** shows a spiral galaxy viewed from the side.

- *Elliptical galaxies* range in shape from a perfect sphere to a stretched-out ellipse. Some elliptical galaxies, for example, are similar in shape to a football, and others are similar in shape to a cigar. **Figure 9.2C** shows an elliptical galaxy. Elliptical galaxies contain some of the oldest stars in the universe. Astronomers believe that well over half of all galaxies are elliptical. The largest galaxies in the universe are elliptical.

- *Irregular galaxies* are galaxies that do not have a regular shape, such as spiral arms or an obvious central bulge. They are made up of newly forming stars and old stars. The galaxy in **Figure 9.2D** is an irregular galaxy.

Figure 9.2 A This is an image of a spiral galaxy as it looks from above. **B** This is an image of a spiral galaxy as it looks from the side. **C** This is an image of an elliptical galaxy taken by the Hubble Space Telescope. **D** This image of an irregular galaxy was also taken by the Hubble Space Telescope.

Understanding the Milky Way Galaxy

It has taken astronomers many years to learn about the Milky Way galaxy. William Herschel started putting together the pieces of the puzzle. By counting stars, Herschel figured out the approximate shape of the Milky Way galaxy. Herschel proposed that the Milky Way is a huge disk of billions of stars, flattened like a dinner plate, in which the Sun is embedded. He also proposed that the Sun might be at the centre of the Milky Way.

Star Clusters

In the early 20th century, American astronomer Harlow Shapley (1885–1972) helped to put together more pieces of the puzzle. While studying the Milky Way, he was also studying star clusters. A **star cluster** is a collection of stars held together by gravity. There are two types of star clusters: open clusters and globular clusters. Both types are shown in **Figure 9.3**. **Open clusters** contain 50 to 1000 stars and appear along the main band of the Milky Way. **Globular clusters** contain 100 000 to 1 000 000 stars. The stars in a globular cluster are arranged in a spherical shape. Globular clusters appear around the centre of the Milky Way.

Shapley became interested in globular clusters in particular. He reasoned that globular clusters should be evenly distributed around the galaxy. He noticed, however, that they appear only in the direction of the constellations Hercules, Scorpius, Ophiuchus, and Sagittarius—not all around us. Shapley reasoned that his observations could only be explained if he were observing the globular clusters from a position well away from them. He concluded that the Sun must be nowhere near the globular clusters.

star cluster a collection of stars held together by gravity

open cluster a collection of 50 to 1000 stars; open clusters appear along the main band of the Milky Way

globular cluster a collection of 100 000 to a million stars, arranged in a distinctive spherical shape; globular clusters appear around the centre of the Milky Way

Study Toolkit

Skim, Scan, or Study
The text on this page contains three boldfaced terms. What does that tell you about the speed at which you should read the text?

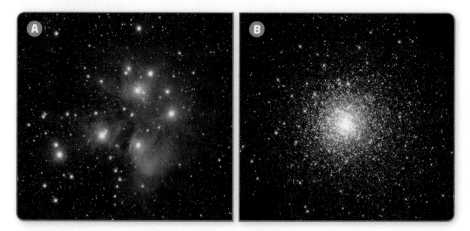

Figure 9.3 A The Pleiades open star cluster is in the constellation Taurus.
B Globular clusters contain many more stars than open clusters.

The Diameter of the Milky Way Galaxy

Recall from Chapter 8 that radio waves can travel through clouds. Radio waves can also travel through the dust and gas between the stars. By mapping the galaxy with radio waves, astronomers have been able to determine its diameter and shape. Astronomers have determined that the diameter of the Milky Way galaxy is about 100 000 light-years and the shape of the Milky Way is disk-like. Recall from Chapter 7 that a light-year is the distance that light travels in one year: 9.5×10^{12} km.

The Centre of the Milky Way Galaxy

Using radio waves as well as infrared radiation, astronomers next confirmed that the centre of the Milky Way galaxy is surrounded by a bulge of stars. Around the bulge, there is a sphere of globular clusters, as shown in **Figure 9.4**. When Shapley was observing globular clusters, he was looking toward the centre of the Milky Way galaxy from a position well away from the centre of the halo of globular clusters that surround the galaxy.

Figure 9.4 Globular clusters form a sphere around the centre of the Milky Way galaxy.

The Shape of the Milky Way Galaxy

Knowing that the Milky Way galaxy has a disk-like shape, with a central bulge of stars, astronomers have concluded that it is a spiral galaxy. Recent observations suggest that the Milky Way has two major spiral arms and numerous minor arms. The Sun is approximately 28 000 light-years from the centre region of the Milky Way. Astronomers estimate that the visible mass of the Milky Way galaxy is about 200 billion solar masses.

Today, astronomers know much more about the structure of our galaxy. Thanks to telescopes that can detect radiation from different parts of the electromagnetic spectrum, astronomers have been able to take images of various regions of the Milky Way, as shown in **Figure 9.5**.

Figure 9.5 The dark, reddish-brown areas across the centre of this image of the Milky Way galaxy are called lanes. Lanes are enormous clouds of gas and dust. The gas and dust block the light from the background stars in the galaxy.

The Local Group

The Milky Way belongs to a group of about 40 galaxies called the **Local Group**. Some of these galaxies are shown in **Figure 9.6**. The diameter of the Local Group is about 10 million light-years. The Milky Way and Andromeda galaxies are the largest galaxies in the Local Group. Most of the galaxies in this group are small ellipticals and companions to the larger galaxies.

Local Group the small group of galaxies that includes the Milky Way

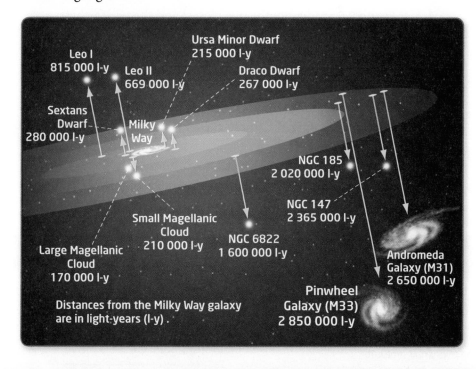

Figure 9.6 This image shows some of the galaxies in the Local Group. The yellow arrows are scaled to help you visualize the distances of each galaxy from the Milky Way.

Activity 9-2

How Big Is the Milky Way Galaxy?

The Milky Way galaxy, in which the solar system is located, is many times larger than the solar system. How large is the Milky Way galaxy, relative to the size of the solar system? In this activity, you will compare the size of the Milky Way galaxy with the size of the solar system.

Materials
- calculator

Procedure

1. The diameter of the Milky Way galaxy is approximately 6.33×10^9 AU. Calculate the diameter of the Milky Way in light-years. (1 AU = 1.58×10^{-5} light-years)

2. The Kuiper Belt has a diameter of 50 AU. Calculate the diameter of the Kuiper Belt in light-years.

3. Using the scale 1 mm = 1 light-year, how large is the Milky Way?

4. The Sun is approximately 28 000 light-years from the centre of the Milky Way. Based on the scale that you used in step 3, what is the distance, in millimetres, from the centre of the Milky Way to the Sun?

5. Based on the scale that you used in step 3, what is the diameter of the Kuiper Belt?

Questions

1. Suppose that you built a model of the Milky Way, using your results in this activity. Describe the approximate size of your model.

2. Would it be a problem to show the solar system in your model of the Milky Way? Why or why not?

3. How would you change your model to include Earth?

Galaxy Superclusters

supercluster a gigantic cluster of 4 to 25 clusters of galaxies, which is hundreds of millions of light-years in size

Just as stars occur in clusters within galaxies, galaxies also occur in clusters throughout the universe. These clusters form **superclusters**, which may contain 4 to 25 clusters of galaxies and may span hundreds of millions of light-years across the universe. Astronomers hypothesize that there may be more than 125 billion galaxies, and nearly all of them seem to be organized in clusters.

Activity 9-3

Counting Galaxies by Sampling

Have you ever wondered how scientists know how many hairs are on the average cat? Counting every hair on a cat would take a very long time. A mature house cat has about 3 million hairs (a reasonable number). It would take more than a month, counting one per second, 24 h a day, non-stop, to count every hair. A better and more accurate strategy is to estimate the number using a technique called sampling. In this activity, you will use sampling to estimate the number of galaxies that the Hubble Space Telescope (HST) can observe in a small area of the sky.

This image of galaxies is from the HST.

Materials
- image of galaxies taken by HST

Procedure

1. Your teacher will give you a copy of the image shown above. Each group will study one section of the image.

2. Tally the number of galaxies in your section. Every small smudge on the image is a galaxy, except the smudges that have "spikes" radiating from them. The spiked smudges are stars. (The spike effect is produced by the brightness of the stars in the lens of the camera.)

3. Collect the tallies for the other sections, add all the tallies together, and calculate the average number of galaxies per section.

4. Astronomers use degrees to represent measurements in the sky. For example, when measuring in degrees, the diameter of the full Moon is one half a degree, where the distance between the east horizon and the west horizon is 180°. One section in the image represents approximately 2.2×10^{-4} square degrees in the sky. The total area of the sky is 4.13×10^4 square degrees. Estimate the total number of galaxies in the universe as follows:

Total number of galaxies

$$= \frac{\text{total area of the sky in square degrees}}{\text{area of one section}} \times \text{average number per section}$$

$$= \frac{4.13 \times 10^4 \text{ square degrees}}{2.2 \times 10^{-4} \text{ square degrees}} \times \text{average number per section}$$

Questions

1. Approximately how many galaxies can HST see in this image?

2. Why is it better to average the tallies for all the sections to get the average number per section rather than use the results for a single section?

3. Why is sampling more practical than trying to do a more detailed count?

Section Summary

- Galaxies are generally classified as spiral, elliptical, or irregular. They occur in clusters throughout the universe. These clusters form superclusters, which may contain 4 to 25 clusters.

- The Milky Way galaxy is a spiral galaxy, about 100 000 light-years in diameter. It is part of the Local Group of about 40 galaxies.

- Astronomers used improved technology, such as telescopes that were able to detect different parts of the electromagnetic spectrum, to learn more about the Milky Way galaxy and other galaxies.

Review Questions

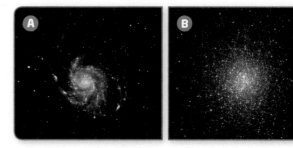

T/I **1.** Identify image A and image B on the right.

K/U **2.** What is the Local Group?

K/U **3.** Explain the difference between a galaxy cluster and a galaxy supercluster.

K/U **4.** William Herschel thought that the Sun was in the centre of the Milky Way galaxy. Was he correct? Why or why not?

C **5.** In a Venn diagram, compare open star clusters with globular star clusters.

C **6.** Draw a cartoon of what you would expect to see while riding in a spaceship looking down on the Milky Way galaxy.

C **7.** Review **Figure 9.2** and **Figure 9.3**. Describe the similarities and differences between globular clusters and galaxies.

K/U **8.** Copy the illustration below into your notebook. Add the following labels: Sun's location, bulge, 100 000 light-years, 28 000 light-years, globular clusters, disk.

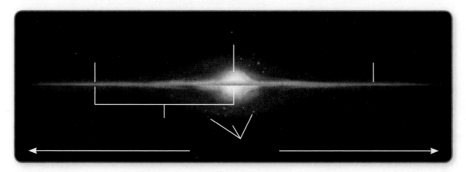

This illustration is a side view of the Milky Way galaxy.

Key Terms

cosmology
Doppler effect
redshift
blueshift
big bang
cosmic microwave
   background (CMB)
   radiation

cosmology the study of the universe

9.2 The Universe

People have long wondered about the origin of the universe. How did the universe begin? Is it changing? Will it come to an end one day? **Cosmology** is the study of the universe. Cosmologists try to answer such questions about the universe. Using technology such as the Hubble Space Telescope and two satellites called COBE and WMAP, cosmologists have been able to see backward in time, to almost the very beginning of the universe. For example, the Hubble Space Telescope image in **Figure 9.7** shows many galaxies that are so old they must have formed shortly after the universe formed. In this section, you will learn how cosmologists and other astronomers, such as Edwin Hubble, have unravelled some of the universe's secrets and developed a theory about the formation of the universe.

Edwin Hubble

American astronomer Edwin Hubble (1889–1953) began his career as a high school teacher. Then he became a lawyer. He finally turned his attention to astronomy. Using the 2.5 m Mount Wilson Observatory telescope and later the 5 m Mount Palomar telescope (both in California), he photographed and recorded distant galaxies and studied their spectra.

Figure 9.7 This image is called the Hubble Deep Field. Most of the galaxies in this image are several billions of years old.

The Doppler Effect

Hubble noticed something unusual about the spectra of galaxies. The spectral lines were slightly displaced from their normal positions. This is known as the **Doppler effect**. An example of the Doppler effect is the change in pitch of an ambulance siren as the ambulance approaches you, passes you, and then moves away. When the ambulance is moving toward you, the siren's sound waves are compressed, resulting in a higher frequency, or pitch. When the ambulance is moving away from you, the siren's sound waves are lengthened, resulting in a lower pitch. Light waves behave in a similar way.

Doppler effect the change in frequency of a light source due to its motion relative to an observer; also, the change in pitch of a sound due to the motion of the source relative to an observer

Redshift and Blueshift

Look at **Figure 9.8**. In spectrum A, the star is not moving. In spectrum B, the spectral lines have shifted toward the blue end of the spectrum. In spectrum C, the spectral lines have shifted toward the red end of the spectrum. (Spectra were introduced in Chapter 8.)

Longer wavelengths are associated with the red end of the spectrum. Since the wavelength of light from an object moving away from an observer is lengthened, toward the red end of the visible spectrum, astronomers say that the spectrum of the object is **redshifted**. Shorter wavelengths are associated with the blue end of the spectrum. Since the wavelength of light from an object moving toward an observer is shortened, toward the blue end of the visible spectrum, astronomers say that the spectrum of the object is **blueshifted**.

Hubble's study of the spectra of the observable distant galaxies revealed that the spectral lines of most of these galaxies are redshifted. Redshifted galaxies are moving away from the Milky Way galaxy. In honour of Hubble's observations, the first large space telescope was named the Hubble Space Telescope.

redshift the effect in which objects moving away from an observer have their wavelengths lengthened, toward the red end of the visible spectrum

blueshift the effect in which objects moving toward an observer have their wavelengths shortened, toward the blue end of the visible spectrum

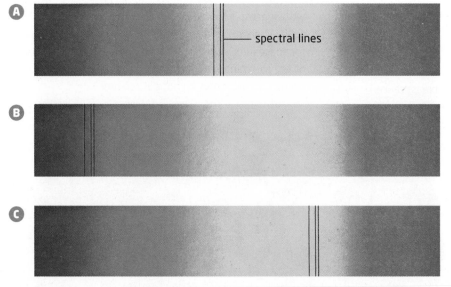
spectral lines

Figure 9.8 The spectral lines indicate the direction of motion of a star. In **A**, the star is not moving. In **B**, the lines have shifted toward the blue end of the spectrum, indicating that the star is moving toward the observer. In **C**, the spectral lines have shifted toward the red end of the spectrum, indicating that the star is moving away from the observer.

The Expanding Universe

In 1929, Edwin Hubble and American astronomer Milton L. Humason (1891–1972) discovered a relationship between a galaxy's redshift and its distance from Earth. They discovered that the speed of a galaxy, which is determined from its redshift, is proportional to the distance of the galaxy from Earth. One explanation for this observation is that all the galaxies (or the space they take up) began their outward motion at the same time. The galaxies that are moving twice as fast are now twice as far away.

Examine the graph shown in **Figure 9.9**. The straight line in the graph means that the speed of a galaxy is proportional to the galaxy's distance from Earth. This relationship is called the *Hubble law*. The slope of the line in the graph is called the *Hubble constant*. The Hubble constant is the rate at which the universe is expanding. (Like the Hubble Space Telescope, the Hubble law and the Hubble constant were named in honour of Edwin Hubble.) Russian-American physicist George Gamow (1904–1968) realized the significance of the speed–distance relationship: the universe is expanding.

> **Suggested Investigation**
>
> Inquiry Investigation 9-B, Modelling the Expanding Universe, on page 384

STSE Case Study

Space Exploration Spinoffs

Exploring space is a costly enterprise. Some space agencies spend billions of dollars a year, most of which goes to salaries. However, space exploration has generated some unexpected and useful spinoffs. A spinoff is a product that was originally invented and designed for one use but has been adapted for other everyday uses.

- The star-mapping technology used by the Hubble Space Telescope is now being used to detect breast cancer tumours in the early stages. This technology is an alternative to detection by surgery. It saves time and money and is not painful.

- Spacesuits have generated spinoffs such as breathing equipment for firefighters and specialized diving suits. U.S. Navy divers, for example, can now use suits designed with spacesuit technology to dive into ocean chemical spills. Thanks to the European Space Agency technology for spacesuits, some race-car crews now have suits made of fire-resistant materials. These suits also have a cooling system, so the crews do not get too hot.

> The materials used to make the suits worn by racing crews are similar to the materials used to make spacesuits.

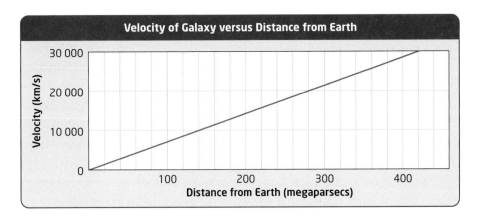

Velocity of Galaxy versus Distance from Earth

(Graph: y-axis labelled "Velocity (km/s)" with values 0, 10 000, 20 000, 30 000; x-axis labelled "Distance from Earth (megaparsecs)" with values 100, 200, 300, 400. A straight line rises from the origin to approximately 30 000 at 420 megaparsecs.)

Figure 9.9 The value of the Hubble constant is the slope of the line. (**Note:** The unit that is used for distance is the megaparsec, which is 3.26×10^6 light-years. Astronomers prefer to use the megaparsec in graphs such as this.)

Learning Check

1. Review **Figure 9.8**. Define the term *redshift*.

2. If a galaxy is moving away from you, is its spectrum blueshifted? Explain your answer.

3. What evidence supports the expansion of the universe?

4. Explain the Doppler effect using the siren of a passing firetruck as an example.

NASA technology has resulted in eye-controlled computer technology, allowing someone with cerebral palsy, for example, to have more independence.

- During the Apollo rocket launches, the astronauts experienced extreme vibrations and high gravitational forces. As a result, they had limited arm and leg movement and found it difficult to control the switches. So, NASA developed eye-controlled switches. People who are confined to wheelchairs can now use this technology to write, speak, send e-mails, and even control their environment, for example, by turning up the heat.

- Astronauts on space walks need protection from the intense solar radiation. The Canadian Space Agency developed a radiation monitor, called the EVARM, to track astronauts' exposure to radiation from the Sun. This technology is now used in cancer treatment. The EVARM is placed on the part of the body receiving the radiation treatment to help doctors track how much of the radiation is reaching the tumour.

- To protect satellites from the extreme cold in space, NASA uses a very thin, lightweight, and shiny insulating material. This material reflects some of the infrared radiation to protect the instruments but absorbs some of the radiation to keep the instruments warm. Different businesses now manufacture this material as various products available to the public. One example is a protective blanket for marathon runners, which keeps the runners warm after the run.

Your Turn

1. What is a spinoff?

2. Name one hazard that astronauts face while in space. What technology was developed to protect astronauts from this hazard, and how has this technology been adapted for use on Earth?

3. Choose a spinoff from the case study. Research both the technology that generated the spinoff and the spinoff itself. Evaluate the costs and benefits of the technology and the spinoff. Organize your research in a graphic organizer of your choice.

The Big Bang Theory

Cosmologists observe that, at some time in the distant past, the universe was extremely compact, small, and unimaginably dense. Modern satellites can look back in time, almost to the very beginning of the universe. The observations from these satellites show that the universe began its expansion about 14 billion years ago. Therefore, the universe is about 14 billion years old. Cosmologists theorize that *there was no before*—that time and space both began 14 billion years ago.

No one knows what caused the "beginning." But whatever the cause, many cosmologists believe that the universe began in an event called the *big bang*. According to the **big bang** theory, the universe began expanding with unimaginable violence from a hot and incredibly dense state to its present state. British astronomer Sir Fred Hoyle (1915–2001) originally coined the term *big bang* as an insulting term. Hoyle did not believe that evidence for the big bang was very strong. Therefore, he thought that the big bang probably did not happen. There is now convincing evidence that the big bang may have actually occurred.

Evidence of the Big Bang

One piece of evidence to support the big bang theory is Hubble and Humason's distance–redshift relationship. Scientists have confirmed the expansion of the universe with their observations of very large distances and, therefore, a very early time in the history of the universe.

A second piece of evidence to support the big bang theory is the **cosmic microwave background (CMB) radiation**, which is radiation left over from the big bang.

To understand CMB radiation, imagine what happened to the radiation in the universe as the universe expanded. Initially, the universe was very hot. It was filled with gamma rays—electromagnetic radiation with very short wavelengths. As the universe expanded, the wavelengths of the gamma rays stretched. As the wavelengths stretched, the radiation changed from gamma rays to visible light. As the universe continued to expand, the wavelengths of the radiation stretched further until they slipped into other parts of the electromagnetic spectrum.

Today, the CMB radiation that astronomers observe has a very short wavelength, only about 1.07 mm. As you can see in **Figure 9.10**, this is in the microwave part of the electromagnetic spectrum.

big bang the event that may have triggered the expansion of the universe 14 billion years ago

cosmic microwave background (CMB) radiation the radiation left over from the big bang, which fills the universe

Figure 9.10 Today, the universe is filled with microwaves, the radiation left over from the big bang.

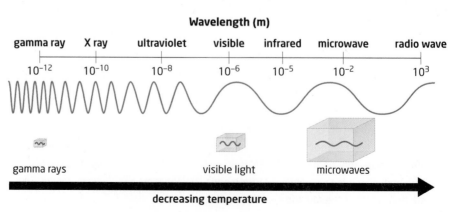

Uncovering the CMB Radiation Evidence

In 1948, Gamow predicted that the CMB radiation in the universe had cooled to about –269°C. In 1965, two American scientists, Robert Wilson and Arno Penzias, accidentally discovered this background radiation. Wilson and Penzias were working for the Bell Telephone Labs in New Jersey, in the United States. They were looking for sources of "noise" (such as static from a radio) that could interfere with satellite communications. In the process, they accidentally discovered the microwave noise that was produced by radiation left over from the big bang. The temperature of the CMB radiation was about –270°C, surprisingly close to Gamow's prediction. Wilson and Penzias's discovery was so important that they won the Noble Prize for physics in 1978.

COBE and WMAP

The two images in **Figure 9.11** are all-sky, false-colour maps of the cold microwave background radiation. They are called *false-colour maps* because the colours are added to indicate slight differences in temperature, like the colours that show different elevations in a contour map of Earth. The colours are not observable colours. Microwaves are not in the visible part of the spectrum.

The images in **Figure 9.11** were taken by two different NASA satellites: COBE (COsmic Background Explorer, launched in 1989) and WMAP (Wilkinson Microwave Anisotropy Probe, launched in 2001). Both satellites were designed to measure the CMB radiation left over from the big bang. The satellites had to be above the atmosphere to detect this radiation. The WMAP image has more detail. In fact, the detailed data gathered by WMAP confirmed the data gathered by COBE. The tiny temperature variations in the WMAP map, indicated by the different colours, are exactly what scientists expected.

Figure 9.11 Both images show the CMB radiation, represented mostly in green. The colours represent slight variations in temperature. Blue is colder, and yellow-red is warmer. The temperature variations are only a few millionths of a degree Celsius (10^{-6} °C).

Looking Back in Time

Go to **scienceontario** to find out more

Modern telescopes can see enormous distances into the universe, which means that they can see very far back into the past. The reason for this is the finite speed of light. For example, light from the Sun takes about 8 min to reach Earth. So, we always see the Sun *as it was* 8 min ago. The nearest stars are about 4 light-years away. Thus, their light takes 4 years to reach us. We see these stars *as they were* 4 years ago. Looking at galaxies that are 10 billion light-years away gives us a view of the universe as it was 10 billion years ago.

A Young Universe

The COBE and WMAP images are pictures of the CMB radiation (now cooled to about –270°C) when the universe was a mere 380 000 years old (about 0.002 percent of its present age). At that time, the universe was remarkably small. Yet, from our point of view in space and time, the tiny universe (in the past) appears to be a huge distant shell that surrounds us. We see it in all directions, at a very great (redshifted) distance when it was, in fact, very small.

Suggested Investigation

Inquiry Investigation 9-A, Estimating the Age of the Universe, on page 382

Evolution of the Universe

Astronomers have collected enough observations from different types of telescopes to piece together a fairly detailed picture of how the universe has evolved since the big bang. Of course, the details are always being refined because new discoveries are made with surprising regularity. **Figure 9.12** presents a time line of the evolution of the universe from the big bang until the present.

Figure 9.12 This time line is an artist's representation of the universe from the big bang to the present.

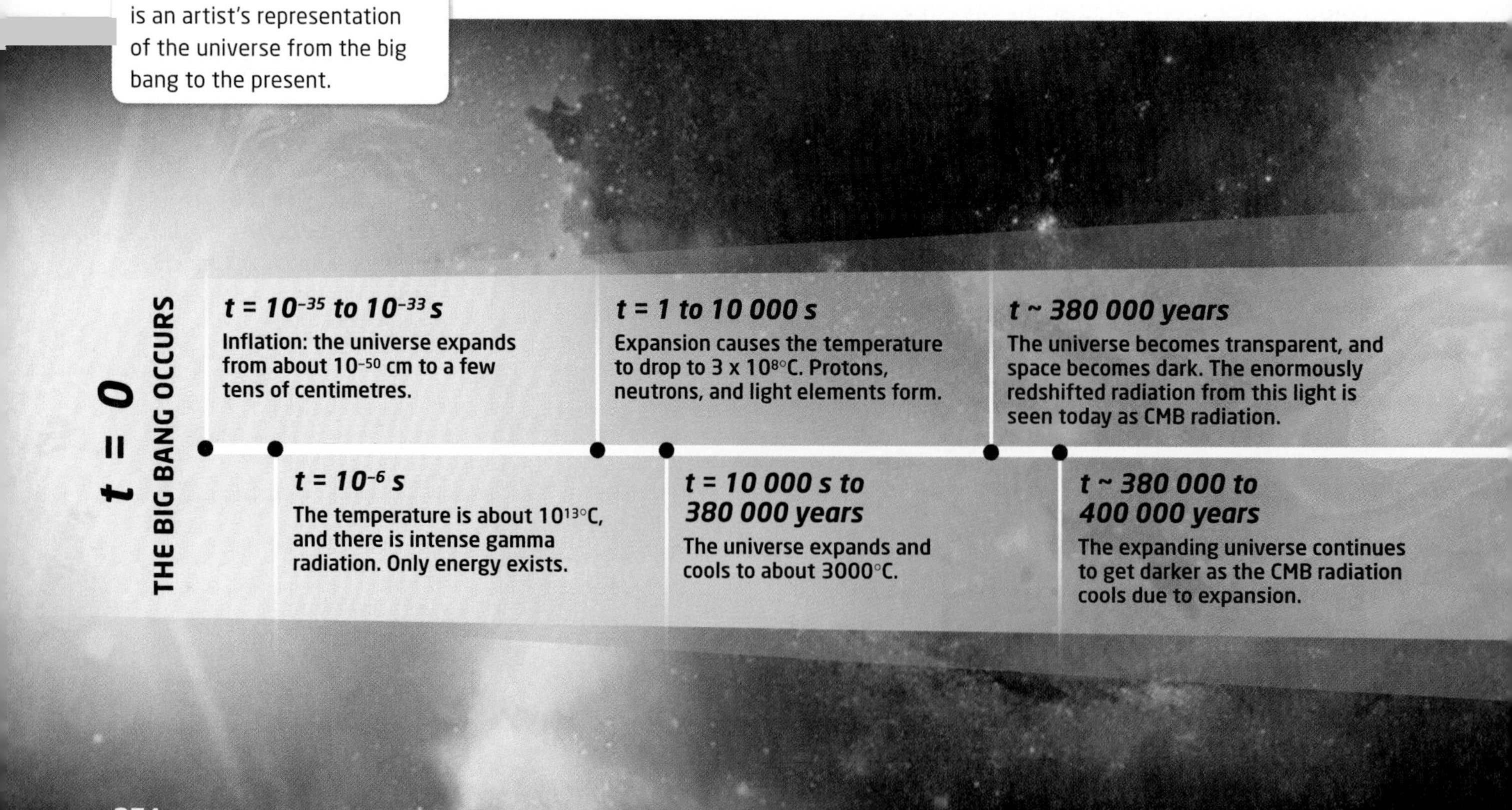

$t = 0$
THE BIG BANG OCCURS

$t = 10^{-35}$ to 10^{-33} s
Inflation: the universe expands from about 10^{-50} cm to a few tens of centimetres.

$t = 1$ to $10\,000$ s
Expansion causes the temperature to drop to 3×10^{8}°C. Protons, neutrons, and light elements form.

$t \sim 380\,000$ years
The universe becomes transparent, and space becomes dark. The enormously redshifted radiation from this light is seen today as CMB radiation.

$t = 10^{-6}$ s
The temperature is about 10^{13}°C, and there is intense gamma radiation. Only energy exists.

$t = 10\,000$ s to $380\,000$ years
The universe expands and cools to about 3000°C.

$t \sim 380\,000$ to $400\,000$ years
The expanding universe continues to get darker as the CMB radiation cools due to expansion.

The James Webb Space Telescope

Around 2014, NASA will be retiring the Hubble Space Telescope (HST). However, in 2013, NASA plans to launch its replacement: the James Webb Space Telescope (JWST). You can see a comparison of the HST's main mirror and the JWST's mirror in **Figure 9.13**. The JWST will see even farther than the HST can. Its mission will be to find the first galaxies that formed after the big bang. The Canadian Space Agency is a partner in the development of the JSWT, along with NASA and the European Space Agency

primary mirror in
James Webb Space
Telescope

primary mirror in
Hubble Space
Telescope

Figure 9.13 The mass of the JWST's mirror is half the mass of the HST's primary mirror, even though the HST's primary mirror is a lot smaller.

CERN

In September 2008, an organization called CERN (Conseil Européen pour la Recherche Nucléaire), in Switzerland, began the full-scale operation of the world's most powerful machine for studying particles at high energies. This machine, called the Large Hadron Collider (LHC), can conduct experiments at energies that approach the energies found in the universe 10^{-12} s after the big bang. Scientists hope to unravel some of the secrets of the very early universe by studying what happens at these incredibly high energies.

Designing and building machines such as the LHC takes a great deal of creativity. Sometimes, other technologies have to be invented to make the machines and to enable scientists to share the information they learn. The technologies can then be modified and used by the public. For example, scientist Tim Berners-Lee invented the World Wide Web at CERN so that all the scientists could share their information on their computers.

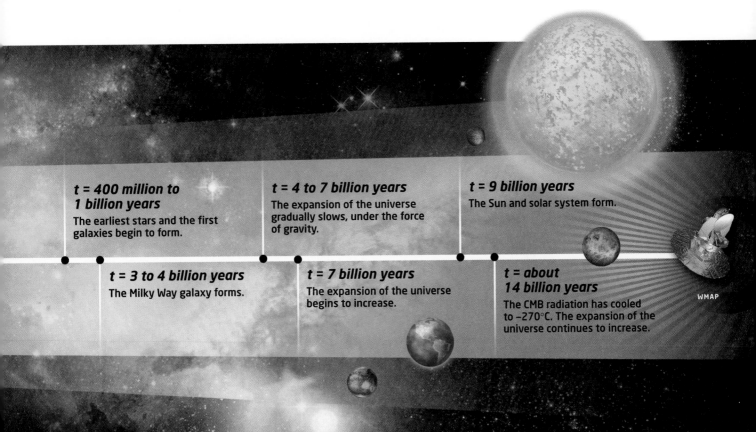

t = 400 million to 1 billion years
The earliest stars and the first galaxies begin to form.

t = 3 to 4 billion years
The Milky Way galaxy forms.

t = 4 to 7 billion years
The expansion of the universe gradually slows, under the force of gravity.

t = 7 billion years
The expansion of the universe begins to increase.

t = 9 billion years
The Sun and solar system form.

t = about 14 billion years
The CMB radiation has cooled to −270°C. The expansion of the universe continues to increase.

WMAP

Section Summary

- Edwin Hubble's observations of galaxies led to the discovery that the universe is expanding.

- Exploring space has generated valuable spinoff technologies.

- The most widely accepted theory of the beginning of the universe is called the big bang theory. According to this theory, an unimaginably tiny volume of space suddenly and rapidly expanded to an immense size about 14 billion years ago.

Review Questions

C **1.** What did Edwin Hubble discover about the spectra of the galaxies he observed? Support your answer with a diagram.

K/U **2.** What does the redshift suggest about the motion of galaxies?

K/U **3.** State the main idea of the big bang theory.

K/U **4.** How does cosmic microwave background radiation support the big bang theory?

T/I **5.** How does the pattern shown in the WMAP image in **Figure 9.11** indicate that microwave radiation is not the same everywhere in the universe?

T/I **6.** Analyze the graph below, and describe what happened to the universe from 10^{-45} s to 10^{-5} s.

K/U **7.** What other evidence, in addition to cosmic microwave background radiation, supports the big bang theory?

A **8.** If the World Wide Web had not been invented, how do you think your life would be different?

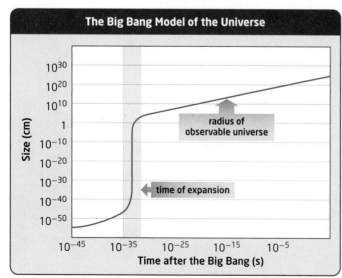

This graph shows the size of the universe versus time after the big bang.

9.3 Unsolved Mysteries

The universe imagined by the ancient Greeks was, by their standards, huge. It contained the entire world—Earth, the Sun, the Moon, the planets, and all the stars. Their estimate of its size, however, was nowhere near the immense size estimated by astronomers today.

Over time, astronomers have revised their view of the universe. First, astronomers included the Milky Way galaxy of an unimaginable size. Then, they expanded their view to include an unknown number of galaxies. Today, astronomers are piecing together the story of the universe—its evolution, age, and size. As you will discover in this section, however, in spite of everything that astronomers have discovered, the universe still holds many mysteries and secrets. One of these mysteries is dark matter, illustrated in **Figure 9.14**.

Dark Matter

The structure of the Andromeda galaxy is similar to the structure of the Milky Way. Thus, astronomers have studied the Andromeda galaxy extensively, hoping to learn more about the Milky Way. By examining the total amount of light that the stars in the Andromeda galaxy emit, astronomers have been able to estimate the total mass of this galaxy with a high degree of confidence. The mass of the Andromeda Galaxy is about the same mass as the Milky Way galaxy.

Figure 9.14 A This image, taken by the Hubble Space Telescope, shows a galaxy cluster called Cl 0024+17. **B** This image shows the same galaxy cluster, except there is a blue ring around the cluster. The lighter blue overlay is a computer-generated model that shows where the mysterious dark matter must be.

Dark Matter and the Andromeda Galaxy

Just as the stars in the Milky Way orbit the centre of our galaxy, the stars in the Andromeda galaxy, shown in **Figure 9.15A**, orbit its centre. Using the estimated mass of the Andromeda galaxy, astronomers predicted the speeds of the stars at various distances from its centre. To verify their predictions, astronomers studied the spectra of the stars within the galaxy. Their results were astonishing. The stars are moving much faster than predicted.

One way that astronomers could explain the speed of the stars was by assuming that the galaxy contains about 90 percent more mass than can be accounted for by visible matter. Visible matter is everything that can be seen—all the planets, stars, and galaxies. Astronomers could not see the missing mass. Wherever this mass was located, it did not emit any light. So, the missing mass was at first called *dark matter*. The name was meant to be temporary, but it stuck. Astronomers still refer to the missing mass as dark matter. **Dark matter** is the most abundant form of matter in the universe. Except for the effects that astronomers have observed, dark matter has not been detected. Its true identity is unknown.

dark matter the most abundant form of matter in the universe; invisible to telescopes

The Search for Dark Matter

The search for dark matter has been going on since the 1990s. Its elusiveness is partly due to the fact that it only seems to interact with visible matter through its weak gravitational effects. Because dark matter interacts so weakly, it does not conform to the shape of a spiral galaxy. It seems to form a huge spherical halo around the Andromeda galaxy, as shown in **Figure 9.15B**.

Figure 9.15 A The Andromeda galaxy is about 2.5 million light-years from Earth.
B Astronomers hypothesize that there must be at least eight or nine times more dark matter than visible matter in the Andromeda galaxy.

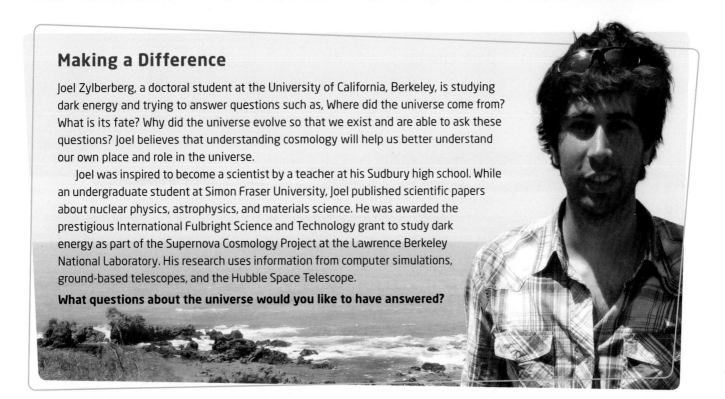

Making a Difference

Joel Zylberberg, a doctoral student at the University of California, Berkeley, is studying dark energy and trying to answer questions such as, Where did the universe come from? What is its fate? Why did the universe evolve so that we exist and are able to ask these questions? Joel believes that understanding cosmology will help us better understand our own place and role in the universe.

Joel was inspired to become a scientist by a teacher at his Sudbury high school. While an undergraduate student at Simon Fraser University, Joel published scientific papers about nuclear physics, astrophysics, and materials science. He was awarded the prestigious International Fulbright Science and Technology grant to study dark energy as part of the Supernova Cosmology Project at the Lawrence Berkeley National Laboratory. His research uses information from computer simulations, ground-based telescopes, and the Hubble Space Telescope.

What questions about the universe would you like to have answered?

Dark Matter and the Milky Way Galaxy

The hypothesis about the halo of dark matter around the Andromeda galaxy led astronomers to wonder if the Milky Way galaxy is also sitting in the centre of a huge halo of dark matter. They think that it is. One clue comes from the motion of the galaxies within the Local Group. Astronomers have estimated the mass of the Milky Way to be about 200 billion solar masses. Yet the motion of small, nearby galaxies that are orbiting the Milky Way indicates that the mass of the Milky Way is at least 10 times larger than the estimated mass. This means that only 10 percent of the Milky Way is made of visible matter.

Go to **scienceontario** to find out more

When astronomers study other galaxies that are in groups or clusters, they find that the motion of the galaxies can only be accounted for by assuming that the galaxies are surrounded by huge halos of dark matter. Visible matter makes up only 4 percent of the universe. Astronomers theorize that dark matter makes up about 23 percent of the universe, nearly six times more than visible matter. As described on the next page, dark energy makes up the rest of the universe.

Learning Check

1. What is dark matter?

2. Why do astronomers study the Andromeda galaxy?

3. Review **Figure 9.14**. What does the lighter blue overlay represent?

4. Why do you think understanding dark matter is important to astronomers when they make models of the structure of the universe?

Dark Energy

At the end of the 20th century, astronomers were observing light from extremely bright Type Ia supernovae, like the one shown in **Figure 9.16**. Type Ia supernovae are explosions of white dwarf stars. The absolute magnitudes of Type Ia supernovae are well known and quite reliable. Astronomers plotted their absolute magnitudes against their redshifts and got quite a shock. The Type Ia supernovae were too faint. That is, the supernovae were farther away than astronomers had inferred.

Astronomers had predicted that, after the big bang, the expansion of the universe should be gradually slowing down under the influence of gravity. But the Type Ia supernovae data show that the expansion of the universe began accelerating about 7 billion years ago and continues to accelerate. For some reason, something began to overcome the effects of gravity that was originally slowing the expansion and is now causing the rate of expansion to increase. Without understanding the cause of this "anti-gravity" effect, scientists have simply called it **dark energy** to reflect its elusive and mysterious nature. Dark energy makes up 73 percent of the entire universe. Although it now has a name, astronomers do not understand its real nature.

dark energy a form of energy that makes up nearly three quarters of the universe; has the effect of increasing the expansion of the universe

Sense of place

Earth, the sky, and the stars constituted the entire universe of the early sky watchers. Today, we know that we inhabit a rock that orbits an average star, in one of hundreds of billions galaxies in an expanding universe. What do you think our place in the universe is?

Figure 9.16 The Type Ia supernova is the bright object at the lower left of the galaxy. Details of this supernova led scientists to hypothesize the existence of dark energy.

Section Summary

- The motions of stars and galaxies within clusters indicate that there are huge amounts of unseen matter, called dark matter, around each galaxy.
- Dark matter makes up about 23 percent of the universe—nearly six times more than visible matter.

- Dark energy makes up about 73 percent of the universe. Astronomers theorize that dark energy is responsible for the increased expansion of the universe.

Review Questions

T/I **1.** Draw a pie graph showing the breakdown of dark matter, visible matter, and dark energy in the universe. Give your graph a title.

K/U **2.** Why do astronomers think there is dark matter in the universe?

K/U **3.** What evidence do astronomers have for the existence of dark matter?

K/U **4.** Compared with visible matter, how much dark matter do scientists predict to be in the universe?

T/I **5.** In images such as the one shown below, the dark matter is added by an artist or it is generated by computer.

    a. With the variety of telescopes that can detect different parts of the electromagnetic spectrum, why can astronomers not take an image of the dark matter around a galaxy? Explain your answer.

    b. Why is dark matter shown as a halo around a galaxy? Explain your answer.

K/U **6.** Why do astronomers theorize that there is dark energy in the universe?

T/I **7.** How would the brightness of Type Ia supernovae observed at large redshifts have appeared to astronomers if there were no dark energy?

T/I **8.** Dark energy makes up most of the universe, yet its effects were not detected until the late 1990s. Suggest a reason why its effects were undetected for so long.

This is a computer-generated image of dark matter around the Andromeda galaxy.

Inquiry Investigation 9-A

Skill Check

Initiating and Planning

✓ Performing and Recording

✓ Analyzing and Interpreting

✓ Communicating

Materials

• ruler

• calculator

Math Skills

Go to **Math Skills Toolkit 3** for information on graphing.

Estimating the Age of the Universe

There is a relationship between a galaxy's redshift and its distance from Earth. When this relationship is plotted, the slope of the line gives the Hubble constant, H. Once you have a value for H, you can estimate the age of the universe, in years, using the equation $\frac{10^{12}}{H}$. The units of the Hubble constant are kilometres per second per megaparsec (km/s/Mpc). See below for information about parsecs.

The spectra of six galaxies are shown below. Each spectrum contains a pair of spectral lines. The spectral lines are normally seen in the far ultraviolet part of the spectrum. Due to the motion of each galaxy, however, these lines have been redshifted. The amount they are redshifted depends on the velocity of the galaxy. The velocity of each galaxy can therefore be determined from the redshifted position of the absorption lines.

Note that the terms *velocity* and *speed* are not exactly the same. *Velocity* is speed associated with a direction. Astronomers use *velocity* because galaxy motion is associated with a direction: either toward Earth (blueshift) or away from Earth (redshift). Also note that the distances given for the spectra are in megaparsecs. A parsec is 3.26 light-years, so a megaparsec is 3.26×10^6 light-years. Astronomers use megaparsecs for graphs of this type.

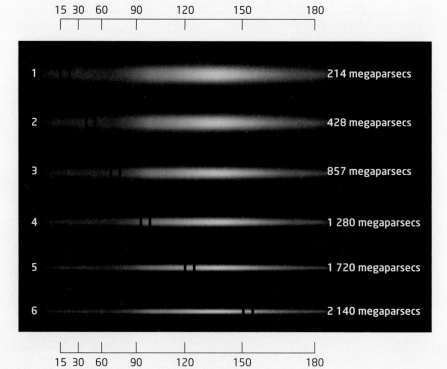

The spectra from six galaxies are shown here.

Question

How can you estimate the age of the universe?

Hypothesis

If galaxy velocity and galaxy distance data are known, then the age of the universe can be estimated by plotting these data and using data from the graph in an equation.

Procedure

1. Make a table like the one shown. Give your table a title.

Galaxy	Distance from Earth (megaparsecs)	Velocity (thousands of km/s)
1	214	15
2		
3		
4		
5		
6		

2. Refer to the spectra in the figure. Use the redshifted position of the spectral lines to determine the velocity of each galaxy. To do this, use a ruler to line up the centre of the left spectral line with the velocity scales at the top and bottom of the chart. The velocity scales give the galaxy's velocity in thousands of kilometres per second. Record the velocity and distance of each galaxy in your table. The first entry has been done for you.

3. Use the data in your table to plot a line graph of galaxy velocity (in thousands of km/s) against galaxy distance (in megaparsecs). Put galaxy distance on the *x*-axis and galaxy velocity on the *y*-axis. See the Math Skills Toolkit on page 557 for more information about graphing.

4. Draw a line of best fit through the points.

5. The slope is the Hubble constant, *H*. Calculate the slope of the line, which is the rise over the run. For help calculating slopes, see the graph below.

Analyze and Interpret

1. The age of the universe is given by the equation $\frac{10^{12}}{H}$. Use your value of the Hubble constant from step 5 to estimate the age of the universe in years.

Conclude and Communicate

2. How does the age of the universe that you calculated compare with the currently accepted age of slightly less than 14 billion years?

Extend Your Inquiry and Research Skills

3. **Inquiry** Predict the age you would calculate if you used the spectral line on the right. Repeat this investigation to check your prediction.

4. **Research** Research the Hubble constant, including the controversy surrounding it and how its value has changed over time.

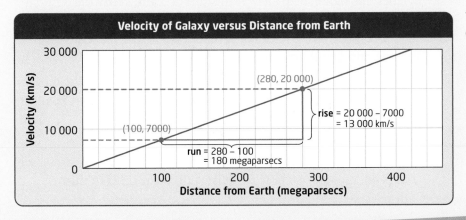

Velocity of Galaxy versus Distance from Earth

(280, 20 000)

rise = 20 000 − 7000
= 13 000 km/s

(100, 7000)

run = 280 − 100
= 180 megaparsecs

Velocity (km/s)

Distance from Earth (megaparsecs)

This graph can help you calculate the slope of a line.

Inquiry Investigation 9-B

Skill Check

✓ Initiating and Planning

✓ Performing and Recording

✓ Analyzing and Interpreting

✓ Communicating

Materials

- marker, black or blue
- balloon (light colours only and with no marks on it)
- clothespin
- string
- ruler

Distance	M1	M2	M3
From A to B			
From A to C			
From A to D			
From A to E			
From A to F			

Modelling the Expanding Universe

In this investigation, you will model the concept of universe expansion.

Question

If all the galaxies around Earth are moving away from Earth, does this mean that the Milky Way galaxy is at the centre of the universe?

Prediction

Write your own prediction based on what you learned in this chapter.

Procedure

1. Make a table like the one shown. Give your table a title.

2. Use a marker to draw six dots on an uninflated balloon. Draw three dots on each side of the balloon, and make each dot about the size of the eraser at the end of a pencil. Label the dots A to F. The dots represent individual clusters of galaxies.

3. Partially inflate the balloon, and twist and clip the opening shut with a clothespin. (Do not tie the balloon.) Using a piece of string and a ruler, measure the distance between dot A and each of the other five dots. Record these distances in your table under "M1."

4. Unclip the balloon, inflate it some more, and then tightly reclip it. Measure the new distances between dot A and the other dots. Record your results in the table under "M2."

5. Inflate the balloon one last time, until it is almost completely full. Measure the distances, and record them in the table under "M3."

Analyze and Interpret

1. What pattern do you see in the three sets of measurements you took as you inflated the balloon?

2. Does this model help answer the question and verify the prediction? Why or why not?

Conclude and Communicate

3. From your observations, what can you conclude about the motion of galaxy clusters relative to one another, as the universe expands?

Extend Your Inquiry and Research Skills

4. **Research** Dark energy is causing the universe to expand. Research dark energy to learn how scientists initially reacted to this discovery.

Chapter 9 Summary

9.1 Galaxies

Key Concepts

- Galaxies are generally classified as spiral, elliptical, or irregular. They occur in clusters throughout the universe. These clusters form superclusters, which may contain 4 to 25 clusters.
- The Milky Way galaxy is a spiral galaxy, about 100 000 light-years in diameter. It is part of the Local Group of about 40 galaxies.
- Astronomers used improved technology, such as telescopes that were able to detect different parts of the electromagnetic spectrum, to learn more about the Milky Way galaxy and other galaxies.

9.2 The Universe

Key Concepts

- Edwin Hubble's observations of galaxies led to the discovery that the universe is expanding.
- Exploring space has generated valuable spinoff technologies.
- The most widely accepted theory of the beginning of the universe is called the big bang theory. According to this theory, an unimaginably tiny volume of space suddenly and rapidly expanded to an immense size about 14 billion years ago.

9.3 Unsolved Mysteries

Key Concepts

- The motions of stars and galaxies within clusters indicate that there are huge amounts of unseen matter, called dark matter, around each galaxy.
- Dark matter makes up about 23 percent of the universe—nearly six times more than visible matter.
- Dark energy makes up about 73 percent of the universe. Astronomers theorize that dark energy is responsible for the increased expansion of the universe.

Make Your Own Summary

Summarize the key concepts of this chapter using a graphic organizer. The Chapter Summary on the previous page will help you identify the key concepts. Refer to Study Toolkit 4 on pages 566–567 to help you decide which graphic organizer to use.

Reviewing Key Terms

Match each key term listed below to its definition.

a. big bang

b. cosmic microwave background

c. cosmology

d. dark energy

e. dark matter

f. galaxy

g. Milky Way galaxy

1. A(n) _____ is a huge collection of stars, planets, gas, and dust held together by gravity. (9.1)

2. The galaxy that includes our solar system is called the _____. (9.1)

3. The study of how the universe began and evolved is called _____. (9.2)

4. According to the _____ theory, the universe began from an incredibly dense state. (9.2)

5. The universe has cooled to a chilly –270°C during its billions of years of expansion. The leftover radiation from the big bang is called the _____ radiation. (9.2)

6. Stars in the outer regions of galaxies are revolving around the centre faster than expected. This evidence suggests that much of the matter within each galaxy must be in the form of _____. (9.3)

7. Recent observations have revealed the presence of a mysterious energy that is causing increased expansion of the universe. This energy is called _____. (9.3)

Knowledge and Understanding K/U

8. Arrange the following objects in order of size, from smallest to largest: galaxy cluster, universe, star, galaxy, globular cluster.

9. What led William Herschel to conclude that the Sun is part of a huge galaxy of stars?

10. Identify each celestial object below.

11. Which type of galaxy do astronomers consider to be the oldest?

12. What surprising discovery was made by Edwin Hubble?

13. What conclusion can be drawn from the fact that the universe is observed to be expanding?

14. List two spinoff technologies from the exploration of space.

15. What prediction was made by George Gamow and subsequently verified by Robert Wilson and Arno Penzias?

16. Arrange the following statements in order of time, from earliest to most recent.

    a. The Sun and solar system formed.

    b. The cosmic microwave background radiation cooled to –270°C.

    c. The Milky Way galaxy formed.

    d. The earliest stars formed.

    e. The big bang happened.

17. If dark matter cannot interact with ordinary matter, how do scientists know that it exists?

18. How is dark matter distributed in galaxies?

19. Why do astronomers think that the universe must have started from something compact and dense?

Thinking and Investigation `T/I`

20. The sphere of stars around a galaxy is made exclusively of old stars. What does that tell you about galaxy formation?

21. Use **Figure 9.9** on page 371 to calculate the rate of the expansion of the universe.

22. Consider three identical galaxies. Galaxy A is coming toward us, galaxy B is going away from us, and galaxy C is not moving, relative to the Milky Way galaxy. How will their line spectra be different?

23. Make a concept map showing the life history of a massive star.

Communication `C`

24. **BIG IDEAS** Different types of celestial objects in the solar system and universe have distinct properties that can be investigated and quantified. Explain how the properties of globular clusters were investigated and how the resulting discoveries led to further understanding of the Milky Way galaxy.

25. **BIG IDEAS** Astronomers use observational evidence of the properties of the solar system and universe to develop theories that explain their formation and evolution. Explain how astronomers used observational evidence to support the big bang theory.

26. **BIG IDEAS** Space exploration has generated valuable knowledge, but at an enormous cost. Research rechargeable tools. Describe how and when rechargeable tools became a spinoff technology from NASA's space program.

27. NASA usually allows shuttle missions to take place if the chance of a catastrophic collision with space junk is not greater than one in 200. Do you think space missions with a greater chance of a catastrophic collision are worth the risk to human life or the huge expense? Work with a partner to complete a chart outlining the costs and benefits of space exploration that carries a risk of collision with space junk.

28. Organize the evidence that supports the big bang theory in a graphic organizer.

Application `A`

29. Identify three careers related to astronomy and space exploration in this chapter.

30. Why do celestial objects that are farther away sometimes look younger than if they were closer to us?

31. In the science fiction television series *Star Trek*, the writers felt that the crew of the starship *Enterprise* would grow bored if they had to wait decades between adventures. So, the writers invented "warp drive" to get the crew around the galaxy much faster. Warp 9.9 is about 3000 times faster than the speed of light. In reality, this is impossible. In science fiction, however, it is fun. Calculate how long it would take the crew of the *Enterprise*, at warp 9.9, to

a. reach the nearest star, about 4 light-years away

b. reach the centre of the Milky Way galaxy

c. go to the far side of the galaxy

d. go around the galaxy at the Sun's distance from the centre of the galaxy

Science at Work

Canadians in Science

Roberto Abraham first began to explore astronomy at the age of 12 with a small backyard telescope. Today, Roberto is an astrophysicist and professor based at the University of Toronto. He has access to modern telescopes in places such as Hawaii and Chile, and he is a world leader in astronomy. Roberto is making important contributions to science through his research. For example, he worked on an international study of distant regions of the universe. This study helped advance theories about how galaxies formed and evolved. Here are some of Roberto's thoughts about Canada's participation in space research.

As a leading Canadian astrophysicist, Roberto Abraham is helping to unlock mysteries about how the universe was formed.

> ### In Roberto Abraham's Words
>
> Canada has emerged as a leader in astronomy and space research and will continue to stay at the forefront. The Canadian Space Agency is one of the main partners developing the James Webb Space Telescope. It is a next-generation successor to the Hubble telescope and will be launched in 2013. From its position about 1.5 million kilometres from Earth, the Webb telescope will significantly expand what we can see in the universe.
>
> Telescopes are as close as we can get to a time machine. It is endlessly fascinating to me to explore our past through images that have taken billions of years to reach Earth. Everything in our vast and complex universe developed from the simplest of elements: hydrogen and helium. There is so much to learn about the processes that brought us from there to here, and that will carry us into the future.
>
> This is the golden age of astronomy and cosmology. Improved technology is helping us to peer deeper into space, to go back in time farther than ever in the quest to solve mysteries about how the universe developed. The more we explore, the more we must revise our notions about the universe and how it formed. And with every discovery we are reminded that there is much more to discover. For students interested in careers in astronomy and cosmology, this is an exciting time to get involved.

Roberto Abraham and a colleague are shown here at the Mont-Mégantic Observatory in Québec. This observatory is the largest of its kind in eastern North America.

Space Science at Work

The study of space science contributes to these careers, as well as many more!

Display Designer

Display designers at planetariums, science centres, and museums create exhibits that explain the universe in non-technical terms. These exhibits often include a variety of techniques to engage viewers, such as three-dimensional models, graphics, scale models, photographs, games, and videos. Designers usually have technical skills and a degree or diploma in art and graphic design.

Circles:
- Astronomer
- Cosmologist
- Electronics Technician
- Space Science
- Satellite Communications Operator
- Astronaut

Project Manager

Project managers in the Canadian Space Program coordinate the work of individuals and teams on projects related to space technology and innovation, including space missions. Project managers organize schedules, monitor work performance, and manage costs. They also oversee processes to analyze and solve any problems that arise. They usually have technical expertise in a related field such as civil, computer, or mechanical engineering.

Aerospace Engineer

Aerospace engineers contribute to the design, construction, testing, and operation of spacecraft. They specialize in areas such as aerodynamics and propulsion. Aerospace engineers often work in teams to develop highly complex spacecraft for space exploration.

Go to **scienceontario** to find out more

Over To You

1. Why does Roberto Abraham say that telescopes are as close as we can get to a time machine?

2. Roberto Abraham says that Canada has emerged as a leader in the study of space. Conduct research to find one example of a recent discovery in space science by Canadian scientists, and explain why you think this discovery is important.

3. Imagine that you are a reporter for a popular television science show for children. What questions would you ask Roberto Abraham if you were interviewing him for the show?

4. Choose a space-science career that interests you. If you wish, you may choose a career from the list above. Research the career, including how you would prepare for it. **What essential skills would you need for this career?**

Work · Learning · Life

Unit 3 Projects

Inquiry Investigation

Simulating a Cosmic Event

In July 1994, astronomers from all over the world watched in awe as Comet Shoemaker-Levy 9 (SL9) slammed into the southern hemisphere of Jupiter. Comet SL9 had originally orbited the Sun. It came close enough to Jupiter, however, to be captured by Jupiter's gravitational pull and it had begun to orbit Jupiter instead. The collision allowed scientists to make observations about Jupiter, especially about the chemical composition of its atmosphere. Many of these observations had never been possible before.

Inquiry Question

How could you simulate a cosmic event?

Initiate and Plan

1. Make a list of cosmic events that could take place in the outer solar system or in other galaxies.

2. Select and research one cosmic event in your list. Have your teacher approve your choice.

3. Make a hypothesis about what the "Before," "During," "Soon After," and "Long After" observations of this cosmic event might be from Earth and/or space.

4. With your teacher's approval, select the materials you will use to create a simulation of this cosmic event.

Perform and Record

5. Create your simulation in the form of an electronic slideshow, storyboard, poster, dramatic skit, video performance, physical model, or graphic novel.

6. Label or identify the components of your simulation clearly.

Analyze and Interpret

1. Analyze your predicted observations. Use the following guiding question to support your analysis: How might the cosmic event you simulated affect the outer solar system, the night sky, or the solar system near Earth?

2. Evaluate the design of your simulation. Use the following questions to guide your evaluation: Does your design represent the event as it would likely occur? How would you improve your design if you could?

Communicate Your Findings

3. Present your simulation to the class. Include all your observations and analyses.

Assessment Criteria

Once you complete your project, ask yourself these questions. Did you...

- **K/U** develop an accurate list of cosmic events?
- **T/I** state a hypothesis related to possible observations of a cosmic event clearly and accurately?
- **T/I** select an appropriate design and appropriate materials to simulate the cosmic event?
- **T/I** present a reasonable analysis of the possible observations related to the cosmic event based on reliable research sources?
- **T/I** include in your analysis a description of how accurately the simulation reflects real cosmic events and possible improvement to the design?
- **C** organize the information presented in a clear and logical manner?
- **C** select a format appropriate for your purpose and audience?

An Issue to Analyze

Canadian Space Missions: To Go or Not to Go?

The mandate of the Canadian Space Agency is

To promote the peaceful use and development of space, to advance the knowledge of space through science, and to ensure that space science and technology provide social and economic benefits for Canadians.

Suppose that you work for the Canadian federal government. Your job is to ensure that taxpayers' funds are used as effectively and responsibly as possible for space research.

Issue
Should taxpayers' funds be used for space research and exploration?

Initiate and Plan

1. Research and select three space missions in which Canadians have been involved. For example, Canadian astronaut Dave Williams made a record three space walks during the *Endeavour* space mission in August 2007.

Perform and Record

2. List some hazards, benefits, and costs of each mission, using a risk-benefit-cost analysis chart. Include the following perspectives in your chart: economic, political, scientific, technological, and environmental.

Analyze and Interpret

1. Evaluate each mission based on the following criteria:
   - Did the benefits of the mission outweigh the risks and costs (economic perspective)?
   - Have the mission and the spinoffs from the mission been peaceful (political perspective)?
   - Did the mission help advance knowledge of space and space science (scientific perspective)?
   - Have Canadians benefited from the results of the mission? (technological perspective)
   - Did the mission harm Earth's atmosphere or environment in any way? (environmental perspective)

2. Based on your findings and analysis, decide whether Canada should continue to contribute to space research and technology. Provide supporting evidence from the varying perspectives to support your position on this issue.

Communicate Your Findings

3. Write and deliver a speech to explain your position and recommend a future course of action. Consider your intended audience, for example, members of Parliament.

Assessment Criteria

Once you complete your project, ask yourself these questions. Did you...

- **A** describe the risks, costs, and benefits of each of the three space missions thoroughly from varying perspectives?

- **A** support your position on the issue of space exploration and space technology with evidence from varying perspectives?

- **C** use an appropriate graphic organizer to summarize and clarify connections from a variety of perspectives in support of your position?

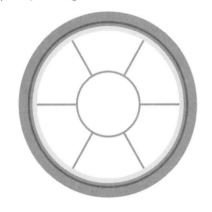
Knowledge and Understanding K/U

For questions 1 through 5, select the best answer.

1. The model of the solar system that places the Sun at the centre is called the
   - **a.** geocentric model
   - **b.** solar nebula theory
   - **c.** heliocentric model
   - **d.** big bang model

2. Which instrument does an astronomer use to analyze the spectrum of a star?
   - **a.** a refracting telescope
   - **b.** a reflecting telescope
   - **c.** a radio telescope
   - **d.** a spectroscope

3. If a star is the same mass as the Sun, for how many years can it fuse hydrogen into helium?
   - **a.** 5 billion years
   - **b.** 10 billion years
   - **c.** 15 billion years
   - **d.** 20 billion years

4. Which type of galaxy is the largest?
   - **a.** elliptical
   - **c.** irregular
   - **b.** spiral
   - **d.** the Milky Way

5. Dark matter and dark energy, respectively, make up which percentages of the universe?
   - **a.** 73 percent and 23 percent
   - **b.** 23 percent and 73 percent
   - **c.** 10 percent and 86 percent
   - **d.** 86 percent and 10 percent

6. Use the diagram below to answer the questions that follow.

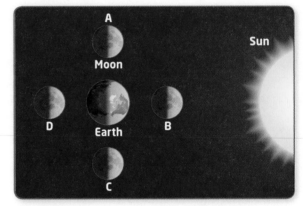

The Moon is shown in four different positions in its orbit.

   - **a.** In which position is the Moon at third quarter?
   - **b.** In which position is the Moon at first quarter?
   - **c.** For a lunar eclipse to occur, in which position in its orbit must the Moon be?
   - **d.** For a solar eclipse to occur, in which position in its orbit must the Moon be?

7. Astronomers have a model for how stars are born.
   - **a.** How do stars form? Include a diagram to support your answer.
   - **b.** What condition is required within a star to cause the fusion of hydrogen into helium?

8. Draw a concept map to summarize the model that represents how astronomers theorize stars and planetary systems form. Include the name of the model.

9. What are two advantages of using a radio telescope compared with using an optical telescope?

10. Using Internet or print resources, research the information you need to complete the final column in the table below.

Magnitude and Distance of Stars

Star	Apparent Magnitude	Absolute Magnitude	Distance from Earth (light-years)
Star A	–26	4.7	0.000 02
Sirius	–1.5	1.4	
Alpha Centauri	0.01	4.4	
Rigel	0.1	–7.0	
Betelgeuse	0.4	–5.0	
Capella	0.8	–0.8	

a. What is star A in the table?

b. Which star appears brightest in the nighttime sky to an observer on Earth?

c. Which star appears brightest from a distance of 32.6 light-years from Earth?

d. According to the table, are the stars that are closest to Earth always the brightest? Explain your answer.

11. Will the Sun become a black hole in 5 billion years? Explain your answer.

12. What property of a star has the greatest effect on the star's life cycle?

13. Summarize the life cycles of stars in a graphic organizer of your choice.

14. Describe observational and theoretical evidence related to the origin and evolution of the universe.

15. Dark matter and dark energy make up a significant portion of the universe.

a. Why are dark matter and dark energy so mysterious?

b. What are the effects of dark matter and dark energy?

Thinking and Investigation T/I

16. The astronomical unit is the average distance between Earth and the Sun. Why is this measurement not exact?

17. Mercury is heavily cratered, Mars has fewer craters on its surface, and Earth has very few craters. Account for these differences.

18. Why do you think an energy source other than solar energy is necessary to fuel spacecraft that explore the outer reaches of the solar system?

19. What observational clues do astronomers use to determine the spectral type of a star?

20. The Canadarm and the Canadarm2 cannot support their own weight on Earth, yet they move massive objects in space. Explain why.

21. The cosmic microwave background radiation is very cold, but it has arisen from an unimaginably hot event. Explain why.

22. The GPS system consists of a large fleet of satellites in Earth orbit, as shown in the diagram below.

a. Why are so many satellites needed?

b. There are 32 GPS satellites in orbit, but only 24 are in operation at any one time. Suggest a reason for this.

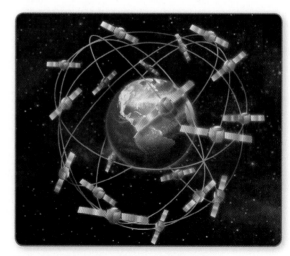

There are 32 GPS satellites orbiting Earth.

Unit 3 Review

Communication C

23. Building and maintaining the International Space Station is incredibly expensive. Sending a crewed mission to Mars will be even more expensive. Suggest some arguments for and against these projects.

24. Using a diagram, illustrate and explain the Doppler effect.

25. Choose three planets that you would like a spacecraft to explore. Explain what you would have the spacecraft explore on these planets. Give reasons to support your answer.

26. Use the following terms to complete the cause-and-effect graphic organizer below: aurora borealis, electric currents, electronic equipment, electrical power network, gases in Earth's magnetic field, intense stream of charged particles.

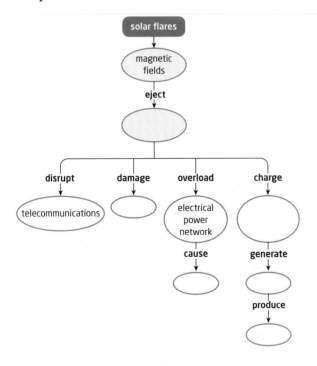

27. Refer to the diagram of the Milky Way galaxy below. Explain the reasoning used by Harlow Shapley to determine that the Sun is located at a significant distance from the centre of the Milky Way galaxy.

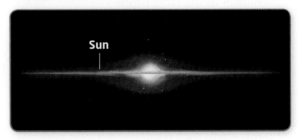

28. Explain how the rate of expansion between two points is proportional to their distance. Use a diagram or an example of an expandable surface, such as a balloon or a rubber sheet, to illustrate your explanation. Then relate the rate of expansion between two points to Hubble's law.

Application A

29. Can other planets have seasons? Explain your answer.

30. Explain how the positions of the stars and the Sun can be used for navigation.

31. "Calendars are a prerequisite for civilization." Explain why this statement is true.

32. In your opinion, should the Government of Canada continue to spend money on developing and launching satellite technology? Explain your answer.

33. Assess some of the costs, hazards, and benefits of space exploration. Formulate an opinion, and present your opinion in a graphic organizer of your choice.

Literacy Test Prep

Read the selection below and answer the questions that follow it.

Helioseismology

If you tapped a bell and watched the surface of the bell closely, you might be able to see the surface vibrating very quickly. These vibrations cause the sound of the bell. Helioseismology is the study of the vibrations in the Sun. (*Seismo* means vibration, and *helio* means Sun.) Helioseismologists have learned that stars, including the Sun, "ring" like a bell. They study the interior of the Sun because this is where the sounds are produced.

In the interior of the Sun, the process of convection starts the sounds. Convection is a method of transferring energy through the movement of particles. Boiling water in a pot is an example of convection. The water molecules move up from the bottom of the pot to the surface of the water. In the Sun, the flow of energy starts in nuclear reactions in the core. The energy moves out from the core until it reaches the photosphere and escapes. The particles that transfer the energy in the Sun are gas particles. Solar convection produces huge bubbles on the photosphere. The noise from the convection is then trapped and filtered inside the Sun to produce the "ringing."

You cannot hear the ringing of the Sun for two reasons. First, the sound is too low for our ears to detect. Second, sound needs a medium in which to travel. Sound cannot travel through the vacuum of space. So how can helioseismologists detect the sound of the Sun? Vibrations inside the Sun cause parts of the outside of the Sun to move up and down. Astronomers use special cameras to watch this movement.

This image of the Sun shows the parts of the Sun that are vibrating. The blue parts are moving toward the observer, and the red parts are moving away from the observer. **Note:** These colours were added.

Multiple Choice

In your notebook, record the best or most correct answer.

34. Paragraph 1 does *not*

   a. introduce the term *helioseismology*

   b. state that the Sun makes a sound

   c. discuss earthquakes

   d. state what helioseismologists study

35. Helioseismology is the study of

   a. earthquakes on Earth

   b. vibrations in the Sun

   c. vibrations in a bell

   d. vibrations in Earth

36. Paragraph 2 relates to paragraph 1 because paragraph 2

   a. explains why you cannot hear the ringing of the Sun

   b. relates the ringing of the Sun to the ringing of a bell

   c. describes how helioseismologists know that the Sun produces sound

   d. provides a sequence of explanations that clarify the information in paragraph 1

37. The image of the Sun on the left depicts the Doppler effect of the up-and-down motions of the photosphere because

   a. blueshifted motion is shown in blue, and redshifted motion is shown in red

   b. redshifted motion is shown in blue, and blueshifted motion is shown in red

   c. blueshifted motion is shown in blue, and redshifted motion is shown in blue

   d. blueshifted motion is shown in red, and redshifted motion is shown in red

Written Answer

38. Summarize this selection. Include the main idea and one relevant point that supports it.

BIG IDEAS

- The production and consumption of electrical energy has social, economic, and environmental implications.

- Static and current electricity have distinct properties that determine how they are used.

- Electricity is a form of energy produced from a variety of non-renewable and renewable sources.

Televisions, microwaves, computers, lights, toasters—these are just a few everyday items that rely on electricity. If you have ever experienced a blackout, you realize just how much you depend on a reliable source of electricity. But generating electricity comes at a cost to the environment. For example, coal burning power plants produce greenhouse gases. Alternative sources of electricity, such as windmills, have far less impact, but they cannot yet supply enough energy to meet Ontario's needs.

Conservation is one way to reduce the environmental costs of generating electricity. Turning off lights and computers when they are not in use, switching to energy-efficient devices, and air-drying laundry are all simple ways to reduce the electricity we consume every day.

In this unit, you will learn what electricity is, how it is produced, and the effects of its consumption.

What are some sustainable ways to produce and use electricity?

Chapter 10
Static Charges and Energy

Chapter 11
Electrical Circuits

Chapter 12
Generating and Using Electricity

Get Ready for Unit 4

Concept Check

1. Using the words below, complete each sentence in your notebook.

current	parallel	static
energy	series	transformed

a. Electricity is a form of ▢▢▢▢▢ .

b. Electricity can be ▢▢▢▢▢ into other forms of energy.

c. ▢▢▢▢▢ electricity is the build-up of an electric charge on the surface of an object.

d. ▢▢▢▢▢ electricity can be described as electric charge in motion.

e. In a ▢▢▢▢▢ circuit, there are multiple paths along which the charge can flow.

f. In a ▢▢▢▢▢ circuit, there is a single path along which the charge can flow.

2. Examine the illustration below. Identify materials that are either insulators or conductors of electricity. Record your answers in a two-column chart with the headings "Insulating Materials" and "Conducting Materials."

3. Electrical energy can be converted into other forms of energy. Match each device in column A below with the type of energy conversion in column B that occurs when the device is turned on.

Column A	Column B
a. MP3 player	**i.** mechanical energy and sound energy
b. toaster oven	**ii.** light energy and sound energy
c. television set	**iii.** heat and light energy
d. blender	**iv.** sound energy

4. In the illustration below, three students are using electrical devices.

Identify the following components of the circuit that powers each device. Write your answers in your notebook.

a. a load: ▢▢▢▢▢▢▢

b. a power source: ▢▢▢▢▢▢▢

c. a switch: ▢▢▢▢▢▢

Inquiry Check

5. Plan You predict that a rubber balloon will allow a static charge to build up on it, if the balloon is rubbed with another object. Design a test you could perform to show the balloon's ability to hold a static charge.

6. Analyze Use the circuit diagrams below to complete each sentence in your notebook.

   a. Circuit ▨ is a series circuit.

   b. Circuit ▨ has two loads.

   c. Circuit ▨ shows how electricity flows in our homes.

   d. In circuit ▨, all loads will stop working if one of the loads burns out.

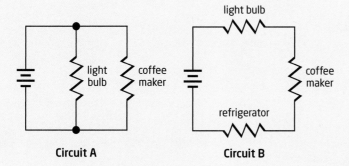

Circuit A   Circuit B

Numeracy and Literacy Check

7. Analyze The Ontario Energy Board sets the price of electricity in Ontario based on the time of day.

Electricity Use Pricing in Ontario (2008)

Day	Time	Use	Price Rate (cents per kW•h)
Weekends and holidays	All day	Non-peak	4.0
Summer weekdays (May 1st–Oct 31st)	7 A.M.–11 A.M.	Non-peak	7.0
	11 A.M.–5 P.M.	Peak	8.0
	5 P.M.–7 A.M.	Non-peak	5.0
Winter weekdays (Nov 1st–Apr 30th)	7 A.M.–11 A.M.	Peak	8.0
	11 A.M.–5 P.M.	Non-peak	7.0
	5 P.M.–8 P.M.	Peak	8.0
	8 P.M.–7 A.M.	Non-peak	5.0

   a. When are the most expensive times for electricity use?

   b. When are the least expensive times for electricity use?

8. Writing Write a school PA announcement encouraging students and staff to reduce their daily electricity use.

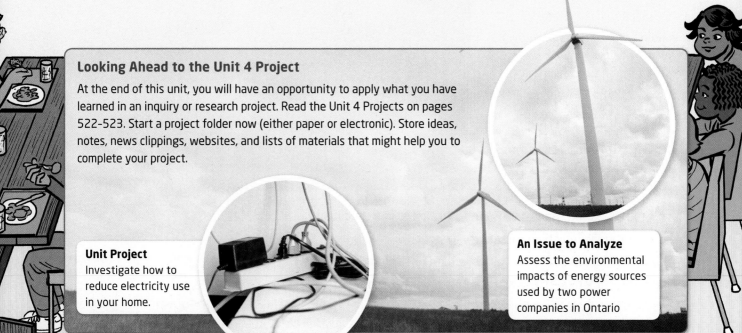

Looking Ahead to the Unit 4 Project

At the end of this unit, you will have an opportunity to apply what you have learned in an inquiry or research project. Read the Unit 4 Projects on pages 522–523. Start a project folder now (either paper or electronic). Store ideas, notes, news clippings, websites, and lists of materials that might help you to complete your project.

Unit Project
Investigate how to reduce electricity use in your home.

An Issue to Analyze
Assess the environmental impacts of energy sources used by two power companies in Ontario

Chapter 10 Static Charges and Energy

What You Will Learn

In this chapter, you will learn how to...

- **relate** your understanding of the atom to the study of electricity and static charges
- **explain** the characteristics of conductors and insulators, and **learn** how different materials allow static charges to be collected or discharged
- **apply** your understanding of electrostatics to describe technologies that control or use static electricity

Why It Matters

Photocopiers, static cling, and lightning are all examples of static electric charges. To someone who lived just 100 years ago, computer scanners and photocopiers might seem to be magical. Each of these inventions, however, is based on our understanding of static charges.

Skills You Will Use

In this chapter, you will learn how to...

- **conduct** experiments to investigate the formation of static charges by friction, contact, and induction, and explain your results with diagrams
- **predict** and **verify** the nature and behaviour of static charges
- **plan** and **carry out** experiments to compare conductivities

A lightning storm can instantly cut all the lights in a community, except those running on emergency batteries or generators. Lightning strikes trigger more than a third of all electrical power outages. Modern electrical science began with attempts to understand lightning and electric charges.

Activity 10-1

Lightning in a Glow Tube

You have seen a lightning bolt light up the sky. In this activity, you will see an electric charge light up a glow tube. How can you use common materials to generate an electric charge that will light up a glow tube?

Materials

- masking tape
- foam cup
- aluminum pie pan
- foam plate
- wool cloth
- neon glow tube

Procedure

1. Work with a partner. Use masking tape to fasten the open end of a foam cup to the inside of an aluminum pie pan, as shown in the set-up.

2. Vigorously rub an upside-down foam plate with a piece of wool cloth for at least 20 s.

3. While holding the cup, place the aluminum pie pan on top of the foam plate.

4. Use a finger of your other hand to touch the aluminum pie pan. Then lift the pie pan away from the plate, using only the foam cup. Do not put down the pie pan.

5. Your partner will hold one of the two metal leads of a neon glow tube in her or his fingers and then touch the other lead to the aluminum pie pan that you are holding.

Questions

1. When you touched the aluminum pie pan with your finger in step 4, did you experience a small electric shock? What could have caused this?

2. Was the glow tube glowing before it touched the pie pan? Did the glow tube glow briefly in step 5? If so, did the glow tube continue to glow after it touched the aluminum pie pan? Explain your observations.

Study Toolkit

These strategies will help you use this textbook to develop your understanding of science concepts and skills. To find out more about these and other strategies, refer to the Study Toolkit Overview, which begins on page 561.

○ ○ ○   ◀ ▶ + · Q▾ Reading Graphic Text

Interpreting Diagrams

A diagram can help readers understand complex ideas or explanations. A diagram is a simplified drawing that shows a concept or a process. Symbols are a common feature of diagrams. In the diagrams in this chapter, a plus sign (+) is used to indicate a positive electric charge. A minus sign (-) is used to indicate a negative electric charge. In the diagram below, the number of plus signs is equal to the number of minus signs. These symbols indicate, therefore, that the charges balance. The doorknob is not charged.

Use the Strategy

Browse through this chapter and locate two other diagrams with plus and minus signs. What do the diagrams represent? Discuss your thoughts with a classmate.

○ ○ ○   ◀ ▶ + · Q▾ Organizing Your Learning

Identifying the Main Idea and Details

The main ideas of a text are supported and explained by *details*, such as facts or examples. It is important to be able to differentiate between the main idea and its supporting details. Phrases such as *for example* and *for instance* are clues that a detail will follow. If you cannot decide whether a sentence is the main idea or a detail, ask yourself, "Is this information the most important thing I need to know, or does this information help me understand the most important thing?"

Use the Strategy

Read the first paragraph in Section 10.1. Determine the main idea and find two supporting details. Compare your findings with those of a partner. Discuss how you decided what the main idea of this paragraph is and what the supporting details are.

○ ○ ○   ◀ ▶ + · Q▾ Word Study

Word Families

Recognizing that a word belongs to a certain word family can help you grasp the meaning of the word. Words can be related by a common base word. For example, the words in the table below all have a common base: *electro*, meaning electricity. When you see this base in a word, you know that the word has something to do with electricity. If you know or can figure out the meaning of the combining part of the word, you will understand the whole word.

Use the Strategy

Some other words in this chapter also have *electro* as their base. Copy the chart below into your notebook, and add words to it as you read. Try to predict the definition of new words *before* you read their definitions in the text. Check your predictions in the text or in the Glossary at the back of this book.

Analyzing Parts of Words

Word	Base	Combining Part	Definition of Whole Word
electron	electro	on	particle in an atom with a negative electric charge
electroscope	electro	scope	instrument for detecting an electric charge
electrostatic	electro	static	having to do with electric charges that tend to be stationary

10.1 Exploring Static Charges

You have probably experienced static cling. It results from small charges and can be a minor nuisance, such as when clothes come out of a dryer stuck together, as shown in **Figure 10.1**. At other times, static cling can be useful. For example, it causes plastic wrap to stick to your lunch. However, charges can be dangerous. Lightning bolts are giant sparks caused by the build-up of large static charges. Static charges on the surfaces of objects must be reduced in many situations to protect people and equipment. For example, people who work with computers must reduce the net static charges on objects to avoid damaging sensitive circuits. In this section, you will learn how static charges are caused, how they can be used, and how they can be removed.

Charging by Friction

Electricity is a form of energy that results from the interaction of charged particles, such as electrons or protons. The word *static* means stationary, or not moving. Thus **static charge (static electricity)** refers to an electric charge that tends to stay on the surface of an object, rather than flowing away quickly. Static charges build up as different materials rub together, as in a clothes dryer. This process is called **charging by friction**. Rubbing a piece of wool cloth on a foam plate, rubbing a rubber balloon against a sweater, and combing your hair with a plastic comb are all examples of charging by friction.

When objects become charged by friction, one material has a stronger attraction to electrons (which are negatively charged) than another material, and therefore pulls electrons off the material that has the weaker attraction for them. As a result, both materials become charged due to an excess or a deficit (shortage) of electrons.

Key Terms

electricity

static charge
  (static electricity)

charging by friction

electrostatic series

insulator

conductor

semiconductor

ground

electricity a form of energy that results from the interaction of charged particles, such as electrons or protons

static charge (static electricity) an electric charge that tends to stay on the surface of an object, rather than flowing away quickly

charging by friction a process in which objects made from different materials rub against each other, producing a net static charge on each

Figure 10.1 In an electric clothes dryer, friction causes charges to build up on the clothes.

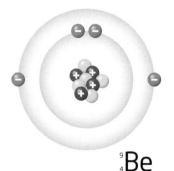

$^9_4$Be

Figure 10.2 This is the Bohr-Rutherford model of a beryllium atom. In the Bohr-Rutherford model of an atom, electrons revolve around the nucleus in definite orbits.

Go to **scienceontario** to find out more

The Bohr-Rutherford Model of the Atom

In 1897, British physicist J. J. Thomson discovered some of the properties of a basic unit of matter that caused charge. Thomson named this particle the *electron*.

In the early 20th century, Danish physicist Niels Bohr and New Zealand physicist Ernest Rutherford developed the Bohr-Rutherford model of the atom. In this model, shown in **Figure 10.2**, atoms consist of three types of particles: protons, neutrons, and electrons. A central, relatively massive nucleus contains the protons and neutrons. Protons are positively charged. Neutrons, as their name suggests, are electrically neutral and so are not a source of static charge. Electrons move in the outer parts of the atom, relatively far from the nucleus. They are negatively charged. (For more on the structure of the atom, see Chapter 5.)

Causes of Electric Charges

Most objects are electrically neutral because they contain equal numbers of positively charged protons and negatively charged electrons. When two neutral objects made from different materials rub against each other, as shown in **Figure 10.3**, electrons from the atoms in one material can transfer to atoms in the other material. It is only electrons that transfer, because they have a small mass and are relatively far from the nucleus.

The Bohr-Rutherford model of the atom explains the following conclusions:

- Particles that carry electric charges can be neither created nor destroyed.
- Any net charge on a solid object, whether it is positive or negative, results from the transfer of electrons between this object and another object.
- Compared with a neutral object, an object with an excess of electrons (more electrons than protons) has a negative charge.
- Compared with a neutral object, an object with a deficit of electrons (fewer electrons than protons) has a positive charge.
- Different materials hold on to their electrons with different strengths.

Sense of scale

In **Figure 10.2**, + or – symbols indicate single charges. However, in most diagrams, such as **Figure 10.3**, + or – symbols indicate a very large number of charges that have either a net positive or net negative charge.

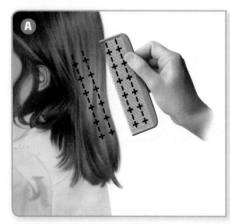
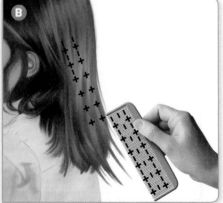

Figure 10.3 Look carefully at the + and - symbols. **A** Before combing, both the girl's hair and the plastic comb are neutral. **B** After combing, the girl's hair is positively charged, and the comb is negatively charged.

An Electrostatic Series

An **electrostatic series**, like **Table 10.1**, is a list of materials that have been arranged according to their ability to hold on to electrons. An electrostatic series is based on data from experiments. Scientists determine whether the charges on two materials, after they are rubbed together, are positive or negative. The material with atoms that have a stronger hold on electrons ends up with a negative charge. The other material, whose atoms have a weaker hold on electrons, loses its electrons to the first material and becomes positively charged. In **Table 10.1**, materials that are closer to the bottom of the list become negatively charged after being rubbed with materials that are closer to the top of the list, which become positively charged.

electrostatic series a list of materials that have been arranged according to their ability to hold on to electrons

Table 10.1 Electrostatic Series of Some Common Materials

Material	Strength of Hold on Electrons
Glass	Weak
Human hair	
Nylon	
Wool	
Fur	
Silk	
Cotton	
Lucite (a clear plastic)	
Rubber balloon	
Polyester	
Foam	
Grocery bags (low density polyethylene)	
Ebonite (a hard form of rubber)	Strong

Sense of Value

Conductors can also be ordered by their conductivity. The following metals are listed in order, from greater to lesser conductivity: silver, copper, gold, aluminum, chromium, molybdenum, tungsten, zinc.

- Different sources often list the materials in a different order, because the surface layer on a material can slightly change its properties. If you rub together two materials that are far apart in an electrostatic series, however, you can accurately predict the charge on each that will result.

- Different animals have fur with slightly different characteristics. For example, rabbit fur holds on to electrons more strongly than cat fur.

Note that cotton holds on to its electrons more strongly than nylon. Thus, when nylon socks and cotton shirts are dried together in a clothes dryer, the nylon socks become positively charged and the cotton shirts become negatively charged. This difference in charge is what causes "static cling."

> When an object is said to have a positive charge, it means that the object has a net positive charge. An object with a net positive charge has many more protons than electrons. Likewise, an object with a net negative charge has many more electrons than protons.

Suggested Investigation

Plan Your Own Investigation 10-A, Comparing Conductivity, on page 429

○○○

Study Toolkit

Word Families Why do you think several words in this chapter have *conduct* as their base?

insulator a material in which electrons cannot move easily from one atom to another

conductor a material in which electrons can move easily between atoms

semiconductor a material in which electrons can move fairly well between atoms

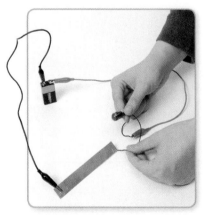

Figure 10.4 The light on a conductivity tester glows brightly if the material being tested is a good conductor.

Learning Check

1. When you comb your hair with a plastic comb, which object, the hair or the comb, holds on to its electrons more tightly? What is the charge on this object?

2. If you comb your hair vigorously, how is the amount of charge on your hair and the comb affected? Why?

3. If leather is rubbed with polyester, the polyester becomes negatively charged. Would you place leather above or below polyester in an electrostatic series? Refer to **Table 10.1**.

4. In the winter, removing a wool hat can give your hair a static charge. Use **Table 10.1** to predict the type of charge on your hair.

Anti-static Sheets

Clothes are made from many different materials, such as cotton, wool, and nylon. These materials hold on to their electrons with different strengths. A clothes dryer generates static charges on the different materials when they tumble and rub against each other as the dryer drum rotates. In other words, charging by friction occurs. An anti-static sheet is a small piece of cloth that contains a waxy compound. Hot air from the dryer vaporizes the waxy compound, which then coats the clothes. This causes the clothes to behave as if they were made from the same material, so no static charges build up.

Insulators and Conductors

Each material listed in the electrostatic series shown in **Table 10.1** is a non-metal and an **insulator**. An electrical insulator is a material in which electrons cannot move easily from one atom to another. Metals and other materials in which electrons can move easily between atoms are classified as electrical **conductors**. There are some non-metals, such as silicon, in which electrons can move fairly well. These non-metals are called **semiconductors**. The degree to which electrons move between atoms is different in all materials, so different materials have different conductivities.

Because different materials have different conductivities, they can be used for different applications. For example, copper and aluminum are conductors that are used in wire. Another conductor, mercury, is used in switches. Insulators, which include wood, rubber, and plastic, are used to make the coverings and connectors for wires, wall socket protectors, and screwdriver handles.

Using a Conductivity Tester

You can use a conductivity tester to distinguish between an insulator and a conductor. A conductivity tester consists of a battery that is connected to a light and two contact points. When the contact points touch a material that conducts electricity, as shown in **Figure 10.4**, electrons flow through the light and the light goes on.

Water: Insulator and Conductor

You may have noticed that static charges are more common during the winter when the air is dry. Dry air is a good insulator, but moist air is a fair conductor. In the summer, static charges tend to be reduced by the transfer of electrons to or from water molecules in the moist air.

Pure water is a good insulator, but water is such a good solvent that it is rarely pure, even when it falls as rain. Water from a faucet contains dissolved substances that make it a fairly good conductor. This is why you should never use an electrical device, such as a radio plugged into an outlet, in a bathroom. If the radio fell into the bathtub while you were bathing, an electric current would flow through the water and you could be electrocuted. Similarly, a stream of water can be a conductor. If a stream of water from a garden hose hit an electrical device plugged into an outlet outside, the water would become a conductor. The person holding the hose could be electrocuted. With these facts in mind, look at **Figure 10.5**.

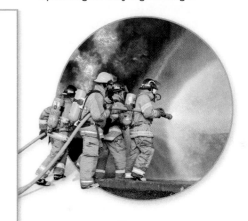

Figure 10.5 Firefighters spray mist on a fire that might involve live electrical equipment operating on very high voltage.

Learning Check

5. Refer to **Table 10.1**. Which types of materials are good insulators and good conductors? Give two examples of each type.

6. Explain how a conductivity tester works.

7. Your friend says that every material must be either a good insulator or a good conductor. Is your friend correct? Write a sentence to explain why you agree or disagree.

8. Refer to **Figure 10.5**. Why could a steady stream of water electrocute a firefighter? Why do you think the mist is safer?

Grounding: Removing Static Charges

The simplest way to remove the net static charge on an object is to put it in contact with what is called a **ground**. A ground has a very large number of charges. It can supply electrons to a positively charged object and can remove electrons from a negatively charged object. The object becomes neutral. The ground, which had been neutral, remains neutral. A conductor is grounded if electrons are free to flow between the conductor and Earth.

Earth is only a fair conductor. However, Earth's capacity to absorb or supply electrons is so great that Earth remains neutral when electrons are transferred between it and a charged object.

You can ground many kinds of charged objects by touching them. This is because your fingers conduct electrons. Your body can receive or supply enough electrons to neutralize the charge on those objects. You feel only a small shock or no shock at all. **Figure 10.6** shows the symbol for a ground.

ground an object that can supply a very large number of electrons to, or can remove a very large number of electrons from, a charged object, thus neutralizing the object

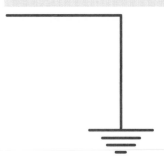

Figure 10.6 This symbol for a ground indicates a material that can discharge a conductor.

Shocking Results

When a relatively large number of electrons flow rapidly through your hand, you feel a shock. What happens if you walk on a carpet while wearing socks in the winter, when the air is dry? If you touch a metal doorknob, you may experience a shock, as shown in **Figure 10.7**. This happens because your body has an electric charge. One way to eliminate the shock is to rub your hand over the doorframe, if it is wood, before touching the doorknob. Wood is an insulator. Therefore, few electrons can transfer at any one point of contact between your hand and the doorframe. Rubbing your hand over the wood doorframe transfers relatively few electrons at each point you touch. The charge is slowly reduced, and you do not feel a shock. The flow of electrons is shown in **Figure 10.7C**. How would these diagrams change if you had a positive charge when you approached the door?

Figure 10.7 **A** The hand has a negative charge (a surplus of electrons). **B** If the hand touches the metal doorknob, there is a rapid transfer of electrons, and a shock is felt. **C** If the hand touches the wooden doorframe, there is a slower transfer of electrons, and no shock is felt.

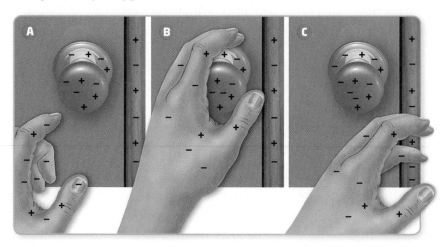

In many situations, static charges are a serious hazard, and people or equipment must be grounded. For example, electrical equipment can be easily damaged by static charges. Many computer hard drives have lost data or been damaged when they were touched by someone with a static charge. People who assemble electronic equipment and work on computer circuit boards must be grounded, as shown in **Figure 10.8**.

Figure 10.8 Both the people and the electrical equipment are grounded to eliminate the risk of a rapid transfer of electrons to the sensitive equipment.

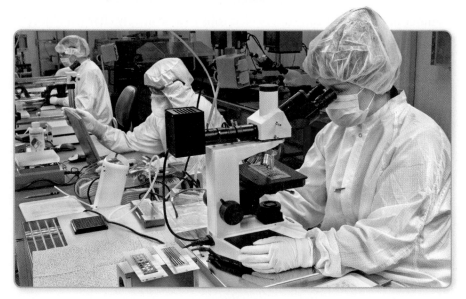

Grounded for Good

Static electricity can be generated by friction in many ways. When the discharge could result in a spark that would be dangerous, precautions must be taken to reduce the build-up of charges. For example, sparks from an electrostatic discharge have caused explosions at grain elevators, flour mills, and coal mines. Surgeons use electrical equipment and sometimes insert devices, such as pacemakers, that could be damaged by sparks. Some of the gases that are used for anesthesia are explosive, and thus sparks must be avoided. In an operating room, insulating materials, such as rubber footwear and wool blankets or clothing, are not allowed. Clothing worn by surgeons and nurses is made using fibres that conduct well, and the operating room is kept at relatively high humidity.

A moving vehicle produces friction between the rubber tires and the highway surface, as well as dust and the air. Each of these sources of friction can generate static charges on the vehicle, which is not grounded because of the insulating properties of the rubber tires. To guard against a spark that could cause an explosion, a fuel tanker truck is always grounded before the fuel is transferred, as in **Figure 10.9**. Also, some trucks have chains that touch the road and keep the truck grounded.

Figure 10.9 This fuel truck must be grounded before it can be fuelled.

Section 10.1 Review

Section Summary

- Static charge (static electricity) is an electric charge that tends to stay on an object's surface.
- Friction can cause a static charge when objects made from different materials rub together.
- Protons are positively charged, and electrons are negatively charged.
- Any net charge on a solid object results from the transfer of electrons between it and another object.
- An object with more electrons than protons has a negative charge. An object with fewer electrons than protons has a positive charge. An object with equal numbers of electrons and protons is neutral.

- An electrostatic series describes how strongly different materials hold on to their electrons.
- In electrical insulators, such as most non-metals, electrons cannot move easily between atoms.
- In electrical conductors, such as metals, electrons can move easily from one atom to another.
- A ground is connected to Earth and can supply a very large number of electrons to, or can remove a very large number of electrons from, a charged object.

Review Questions

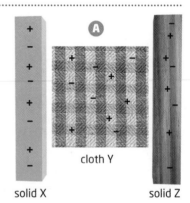

solid X   cloth Y   solid Z

K/U **1.** Use the Bohr-Rutherford model of the atom to explain how an insulator differs from a conductor.

C **2.** Draw two sketches of the same balloon with charges indicating that the balloon is (a) negative and (b) positive.

K/U **3.** If you want to avoid charge build-up on your hair, should you use a plastic comb or an aluminum comb? See **Figure 10.3**.

K/U **4.** Nylon socks and a silk blouse are tumbled in a clothes dryer. Use the electrostatic series to predict the type of charge on each.

K/U **5.** List two materials that are electrical conductors and two materials that are insulators. For each material, give an example of how its electrical properties are useful.

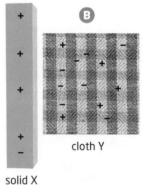

cloth Y   solid X

T/I **6. a.** Diagram **A** on the right shows the initial charges on two solid objects (X and Z) and a cloth (Y) made from different materials. What type of net charge is on each?

     b. In diagram **B**, solid X has been rubbed with the cloth. Which material has the greater hold on electrons?

     c. In diagram **C**, solid Z has been rubbed with the cloth. Rank the three materials, from greatest to least, according to their ability to hold on to electrons.

T/I **7.** Rainwater contains dissolved substances that allow it to conduct electricity. Why would you not be electrocuted if you walked under an electric transmission line during a rainstorm?

A **8.** Why is the flooring in an operating room made of a conducting material? Should the floor be waxed?

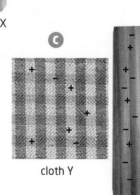

cloth Y   solid Z

10.2 Charging by Contact and by Induction

Key Terms
electroscope
charging by contact
laws of electric charges
electric field
induced charge separation

A charged comb can be used to attract small pieces of paper that are electrically neutral. As the comb approaches the pieces of paper, some of the pieces jump off the table and onto the comb. Although the charged comb and the neutral pieces of paper are not initially in contact, there must be an attraction between them. Why does a charged comb attract small pieces of neutral paper? Why may some of the pieces fly off the comb later?

Detecting Charges

An **electroscope** is a simple device that is used to detect the presence of electric charges. In schools, the pith ball electroscope and the metal leaf electroscope are commonly used. Both types are shown in **Figure 10.10**.

A pith ball electroscope consists of a small, light ball suspended by a piece of cotton thread. Pith is an insulator, so in an electroscope it must be covered by a conducting substance. If a charged object comes close to the pith ball, there is an electric force between them. Because the pith ball has a small mass, this electric force is strong enough to cause the pith ball to move. You can make a similar electroscope using a piece of cereal. Tie a cotton thread to the cereal and hang the thread from a rod or stand, like the one in a pith ball electroscope.

Metal leaf electroscopes are available with different designs, but all have the same key parts. They consist of a sphere (sometimes a flat plate) that is connected to a rod, which has metal leaves attached to it. The sphere, rod, and leaves are all made of metal, which allows electrons to move freely. The rod and the leaves are usually enclosed in a glass container to shield the leaves from air currents. An insulator, such as a rubber stopper, isolates the rod from the glass container. The leaves of a metal leaf electroscope spread apart when a charge is near the sphere or when the electroscope has a charge.

electroscope a device for detecting the presence of an electric charge

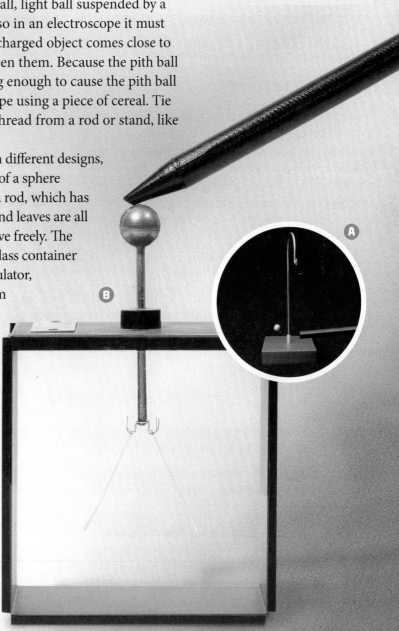

Figure 10.10 Electroscopes show the presence of a net electric charge. **A** In a pith ball electroscope, the ball is covered with a conducting substance. **B** The key parts of a metal leaf electroscope—the sphere, the rod, and the leaves—are all made of metal.

Charging by Contact

charging by contact
generating a charge on a neutral object by touching it with a charged object

Charging by contact takes place when contact is made between a neutral object and an object that is charged. **Figure 10.11** illustrates charging by contact in two ways. **Figure 10.11A** shows a negatively charged object and a neutral pith ball. On contact, electrons flow from the negatively charged object into the pith ball. After the object and the pith ball have touched, the negatively charged object has a reduced charge, but it is still negative. The pith ball is now negatively charged.

Examine **Figure 10.11B** to see how touching a neutral pith ball with a positively charged object gives the pith ball a positive charge.

○○○

Study Toolkit

Identifying the Main Idea and Details Finding the main idea and details in the paragraph on the right can help you understand the concept of charging by contact.

> An object that becomes charged by contact always gets the same type of charge that is on the object that charges it.

Activity 10-2

Detecting Static Charge Using an Electroscope

How do electroscopes detect static charges? In this activity, you will use an electrostatic series to predict how the net charge on objects made from different materials will change when you rub them together. Then you will observe how a pith ball electroscope and a metal leaf electroscope detect the presence of a known static charge.

Safety Precautions

If you are allergic to animal fur, do not handle it.

Materials

- different materials listed in the electrostatic series in **Table 10.1** on page 405
- metal leaf electroscope
- pith ball electroscope

Procedure

1. Skim through the steps of this activity, and then create an appropriate data table to record your observations.

2. Use the electrostatic series to predict the type of charge on all the materials that you plan to rub together. Record your predictions.

3. Choose two of the materials. Rub them together to create two oppositely charged materials. Bring one of the materials toward the sphere of a metal leaf electroscope, without making contact. Record your observations of the electroscope leaves. Now remove the charged material and see what happens to the leaves.

4. Touch the sphere of the metal leaf electroscope with the charged material, and record the position of the leaves.

5. Remove the charged material, and again record the position of the leaves.

6. Touch the sphere of the metal leaf electroscope with one of your fingers, and record what happens to the leaves.

7. Repeat steps 3 through 6, using a material with a different charge.

8. In steps 3 through 7, you used a metal leaf electroscope. Repeat step 3, using a pith ball electroscope. Record what happens to the pith ball as you bring a charged material close to it. Then allow the pith ball and the charged material to make contact, and record your observations.

Questions

1. Compare the metal leaf electroscope with the pith ball electroscope. How does each electroscope indicate the presence of an electric charge?

2. What happened to the leaves of the metal leaf electroscope when a charged object made contact with the sphere? Did it make a difference whether the charged object had a positive charge or a negative charge?

3. What happened in step 6, when you touched the sphere of the metal leaf electroscope with your finger? Explain your observation.

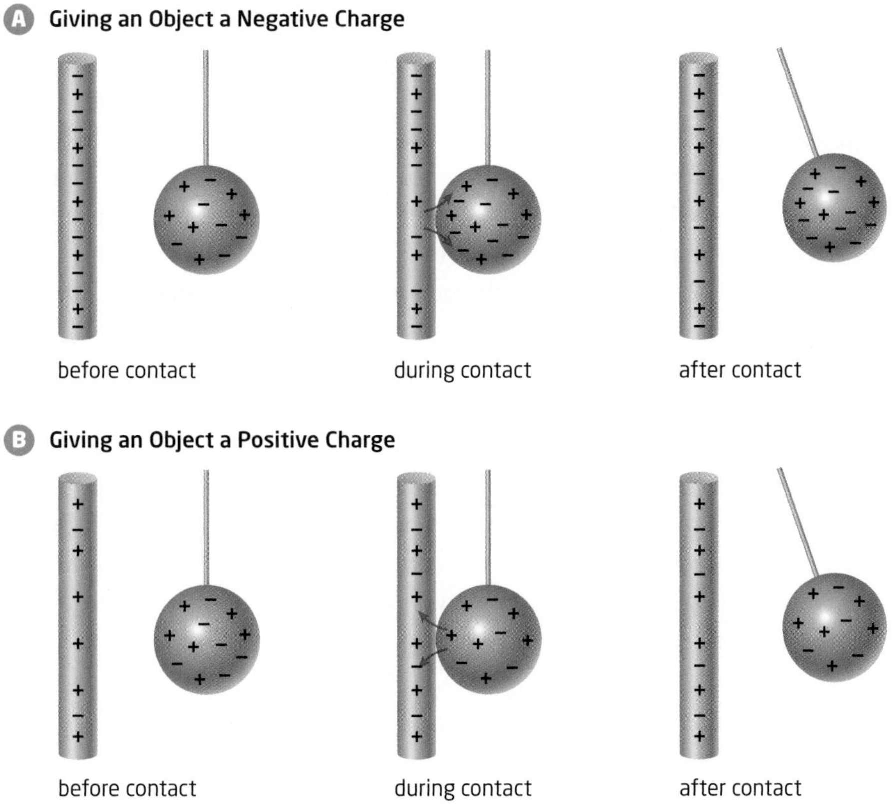

A Giving an Object a Negative Charge

before contact   during contact   after contact

Figure 10.11 A change in the net charge of an object is the result of the movement of electrons either onto or off the object. In **A**, contact with a negatively charged object gives a neutral pith ball a negative charge. In **B**, contact with a positively charged object gives a neutral pith ball a positive charge.

B Giving an Object a Positive Charge

before contact   during contact   after contact

The Laws of Electric Charges

As you know, an object may be positively or negatively charged, or it may be electrically neutral. The net charge on a solid object is best described in terms of the electrons in its atoms, because the electrons are the charged particles that can move from atom to atom and from one material to another. Protons are bound in the nucleus, and thus cannot move from one atom to another. Scientists have established the **laws of electric charges** through experiments using objects with known charges and an electroscope. These three laws are summarized in **Figure 10.12**.

> **laws of electric charges**
> laws that describe how two objects interact electrically when one or both are charged

Laws of Electric Charges

1. Like charges repel.

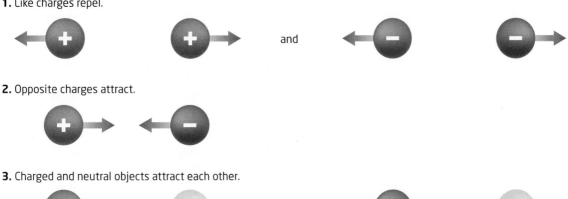

and

2. Opposite charges attract.

3. Charged and neutral objects attract each other.

and

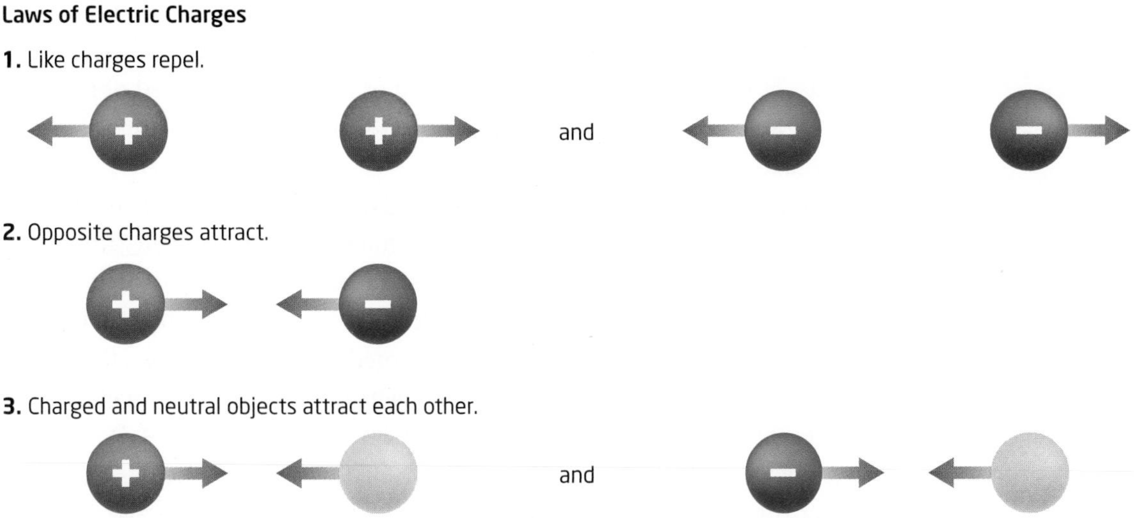

Figure 10.12 The three laws of electric charges describe how two objects interact electrically when one or both are charged.

The Amount and Type of Charge

The amount of net charge on an object depends on the difference between the number of protons and the number of electrons that it contains. The size of the electric force between two charged objects is directly proportional to the amount of charge on each object. This is true whether the electric force is an attraction that pulls the objects toward each other or a repulsion that pushes them apart.

If the distance between two charged objects is increased, the electric force between them will decrease. The force of gravity is similar in this way. Increasing your distance from Earth in a spaceship would result in a decreased force of gravity between you and Earth.

To determine whether an object is charged and, if so, what type of charge it has, you must observe repulsion between it and another object. Once you observe repulsion occurring, you can be certain that the object is charged. Then you can use the laws of electric charges to determine the type of charge (positive or negative). If the object with an unknown charge is attracted to both positive and negative charges, you know that the object is neutral.

Figure 10.13 A charged object produces an electric field, which gives rise to electrical forces near the object. The arrows in these diagrams represent the direction of the force on a second, positively charged object that is in the field of the central object. The length of each arrow represents the relative magnitude of the force on an object in the field. In **A**, a positively charged object repels positive objects in its field. In **B**, a negatively charged object attracts positive objects in its field.

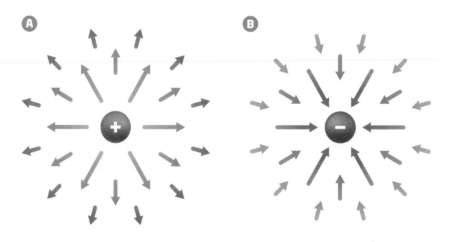

Electric Fields

The laws of electric charges describe the electrical interactions between objects. How is it possible for a positively or negatively charged object to exert an electric force on another object if the two objects are not in contact?

You are familiar with the force of gravity, which exists between any two objects that have mass, even though they may not be in contact. Similarly, electric forces exist between two objects that are not in contact if at least one of them is charged. These forces are transmitted by an **electric field**. It is a property of the space around a charged object, where the effect of its charge can be felt by other objects. An electric field produces an electric force on any other objects that are in the field. See **Figure 10.13**.

Objects with greater net charges have stronger electric fields. The greater the distance from a charged object, the weaker the electric field of the object is. Also, all electric forces between two objects are transmitted through the electric field at the speed of light.

electric field a property of the space around a charged object, where the effect of its charge can be felt by other objects

Suggested Investigation

Plan Your Own Investigation 10-B, Be a Charge Detective, on page 430

Go to **scienceontario** to find out more

Charging by Induction

A third method of charging is charging by induction. When a charged object is close to a neutral object, the electric field of the charged object produces a force on the neutral object. According to the laws of electric charges, the force is attractive. Although the charged object exerts a force on the protons and electrons in a solid neutral object, only electrons can move in the solid. Thus, the charged object causes (induces) electrons in the neutral object to move. An **induced charge separation** is the movement of electrons in a substance, caused by the electric field of a nearby charged object, without direct contact between the substance and the object.

Figure 10.14 shows what happens when a negatively charged rod is brought near a neutral pith ball. The electric field of the rod is strong enough to have an effect on the pith ball. The result is an induced charge separation on the pith ball. The force from the rod causes some of the electrons on the pith ball to move away from the side that is closer to the rod. This side of the pith ball thus has a positive charge. The attractive force between the rod and this positive side of the ball is stronger than the repulsive force between the rod and the other, negative side of the ball, because the negative side of the ball is farther away from the rod. Therefore, even though the ball has equal numbers of positive and negative charges overall, it is attracted to the negatively charged rod.

induced charge separation the movement of electrons in a substance, caused by the electric field of a nearby charged object, without direct contact between the substance and the object

Study Toolkit

Word Families What base do the words *induced* and *induction* share? How does knowing the meaning of the base help you remember the meanings of the words?

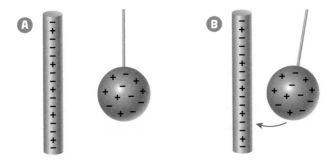

Figure 10.14 A The rod is negatively charged, and the pith ball is neutral.
B The induced charge separation on the pith ball causes it to swing toward the rod.

Activity 10-3

Drawing Charges You Cannot See

How can you draw diagrams to explain induced charges? In Part 1 of this activity, you will draw diagrams to show the movement of electrons when a positively charged object is brought close to a neutral pith ball electroscope. In Part 2 of this activity, you will draw diagrams to show the induced charge separation caused by the electric field of a charged object when it is moved close to a metal leaf electroscope.

Materials

- paper
- coloured pencils

Procedure

Part 1 The Effect of a Positively Charged Object

1. Copy diagram **A** into your notebook to show a positively charged rod and a neutral pith ball before they interact.

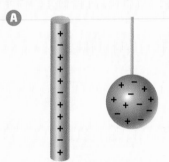

2. Make a second drawing to show the charged rod after it has been moved closer to the pith ball. Include charges on the rod and the pith ball.

3. Below your second drawing, answer the following questions. As you answer these questions, check your drawing and make corrections if necessary.

   a. How does the position of the positive charges in your second drawing compare with their position in the first drawing?

   b. What type of charge is on the side of the pith ball that is closer to the charged rod? How does this charge compare with the charge on the rod?

   c. Considering all the charges on the pith ball, is it neutral or charged? Does your second drawing show this?

Part 2 The Effect of a Negatively Charged Object

4. Diagram **B** shows a neutral metal leaf electroscope and a charged rod before they interact. Sketch a diagram like this in your notebook. What kind of charge is on the rod?

5. Diagram **C** shows the same charged rod close to the sphere of the metal leaf electroscope. No charges are shown, however. The leaves of the electroscope are spread apart, as you observed in Activity 10-2 when you brought a charged material close to a metal leaf electroscope. Copy and complete this diagram to show the positions of the charges on the metal leaf electroscope and the rod.

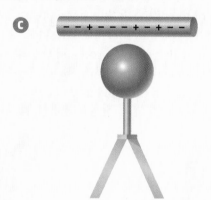

Questions

1. Explain why an induced charge separation causes the leaves on a metal leaf electroscope to spread apart.

2. What do you think will happen to the charges on the electroscope when the charged rod is withdrawn?

3. Summarize what you need to know about charges when you draw diagrams to explain static and induced charges.

Section Summary

- An electroscope is a device that is used to detect the presence of an electric charge.
- There are three laws of electric charges:
  1. Like charges repel.
  2. Opposite (unlike) charges attract.
  3. Neutral objects and charged objects are attracted to each other.

- An object that is charged by contact has the same type of charge as the charging object.
- An electric force between two objects is transmitted by an electric field.
- An induced charge separation is the movement of electrons in a substance, caused by the electric field of a nearby charged object.

Review Questions

K/U **1.** Compare and contrast charging by contact, charging by friction, and charging by induction.

C **2.** The leaves of a metal leaf electroscope are slightly separated, indicating that it is charged. When you bring a positively charged rod near the sphere, the leaves spread farther apart. What charge is on the electroscope? Draw diagrams to explain your answer.

K/U **3.** See **Figure 10.13**. How does the strength of an object's electric field change with distance?

K/U **4.** A metal leaf electroscope has a sphere, rod, and leaves. Why would the electroscope not work if any of these parts were made using an insulator?

A **5.** You can charge a balloon by rubbing it against your clothing. Then you can stick the charged balloon to a wall.

    a. Is the wall charged by contact or by induction? Explain.

    b. Why does the balloon eventually fall from the wall?

C **6.** When you bring a negatively charged ebonite rod near a pith ball electroscope, the pith ball moves toward the rod. Is the pith ball positively charged? Explain.

T/I **7.** You are given two objects made from different materials. How could you use a pith ball electroscope to learn which material holds on to its electrons more strongly?

T/I **8.** The diagram on the right shows representative charges on a rod and two identical metal spheres.

    a. What is the charge on the rod?

    b. Draw a diagram to show the rod close to the spheres. Indicate the resulting charges.

    c. Keep the rod near one sphere, and move the other sphere away. Draw a diagram to show the charges on the rod and the spheres.

    d. Remove the rod. Draw the charges on the spheres and the rod.

Key Terms

ion

lightning rod

electrostatic precipitator

Van de Graaff generator

radiation dosimeter

Figure 10.15 Laser printers, scanners, and photocopiers use electric charges to print images.

ion a charged atom or group of atoms

10.3 Charges at Work

Do you have an electric dust and pollen filter in your home, or do you know someone who does? This appliance uses electric charges to clean the air. Several office machines, such as the photocopier shown in **Figure 10.15**, also use static charges. Electric charges are used in many applications to control pollution, reduce waste, and monitor workers' safety. On a much larger scale, the first atom smashers (**Figure 10.16**) used large charges to accelerate and separate subatomic particles. In this section, you will learn about some important applications of static charges, many of which involve induced charges. One of the first applications of static charges was a lightning conductor. You will begin this section by studying lightning bolts, which carry large charges that must be discharged safely.

Lightning

Over 250 years ago, Benjamin Franklin showed that a lightning bolt is a gigantic electrical discharge. A moderate thunderstorm briefly generates electrical energy that is equivalent to the output of a small nuclear generating plant. Every electrical discharge is caused by a transfer of charge.

A storm cloud is a complicated mix of raindrops and ice particles, as shown in **Figure 10.17A**. Strong updrafts in the centre of a storm cloud carry smaller raindrops and ice particles upward. At the same time, gravity causes larger, heavier raindrops and hailstones to fall. The raindrops, ice particles, and hailstones collide. Charge is transferred, and **ions**, which are charged atoms or groups of atoms that have gained or lost one or more electrons, are formed.

The negative charge at the bottom of a cloud induces a positive charge in the ground and buildings below it, as shown in **Figure 10.17B**. A charged stream, called a stepped leader, forms, as in **Figure 10.17.C**. When a large enough flow of negative charge is within about 100 m of the ground, a large flow of positive ions, called a return stroke, jumps from the ground, as shown in **Figure 10.17D**. Momentarily, the humid air becomes a superheated conductor. This creates a glow, which you see as lightning, and causes a shock wave of expanding gases, which you hear as thunder. A stepped leader and return stroke may occur many times in what appears to be a single lightning strike. There may also be lightning between or within clouds. See **Figure 10.17E**.

Figure 10.16 This pear-shaped atom smasher was built at the Westinghouse Electric and Manufacturing Company in East Pittsburgh, Pennsylvania, in 1937. It generated enormous static charges, which were used to study subatomic particles.

Figure 10.17

Storm clouds can form when humid, warm air rises to meet a colder air mass. As these air masses churn together, the stage is set for the explosive electrical display we call lightning. Lightning strikes when negative charges at the bottom of a storm cloud are attracted to positive charges on the ground.

A Air currents in the storm cloud cause charge separation. The top of the cloud becomes positively charged, and the bottom becomes negatively charged.

B Negative charges on the bottom of the cloud induce a positive charge on the ground below the cloud by repelling negative charges in the ground.

C When the bottom of the cloud has accumulated enough negative charges, the attraction of the positive charges below causes electrons in the bottom of the cloud to move toward the ground.

D When the electrons get close to the ground, they attract positive ions that surge upward, completing the connection between the cloud and the ground. This is the spark you see as a lightning flash.

E

LIGHTNING BETWEEN OR WITHIN CLOUDS never strikes Earth and can occur much more often in a storm than cloud-to-ground lightning.

How Does a Lightning Rod Work?

Lightning takes the path of least resistance between a cloud and the ground, usually striking the highest object in an area. This explains why a tall building, a tree, or a person who is standing in an open field or sitting in a boat on a lake is the most likely to be hit by lightning.

A lightning strike carries a very large electric current, which will damage any unprotected building, tree, or person it hits. In Canada, lightning strikes cause about one third of all forest fires and about 10 deaths each year. They occur most frequently in June, July, and August, when warm, humid air masses collide with cooler air masses. Buildings can catch fire if they are hit by a lightning bolt.

Since lightning cannot be prevented, many buildings have a lightning rod on top. A **lightning rod** is a metal sphere or point that is attached to the highest part of a building and connected to the ground. A thick, insulated copper wire connects the lightning rod to a metal plate or bare metal cable in the ground. A lightning rod is especially important in rural areas, where a house or barn may be the tallest building, as shown in **Figure 10.18**.

lightning rod a metal sphere or point, attached to the highest part of a building and connected to the ground

Go to **scienceontario** to find out more

○○○

Study Toolkit

Interpreting Diagrams
How do the + and – symbols help you understand the function of a lightning rod?

cable buried beneath the surface of the ground

conducting cable insulated from the building

Figure 10.18 A lightning rod becomes positively charged by induction. To protect the building, the cable that is attached to the lightning rod is insulated. Below the surface of the ground, the cable is bare, allowing the charge to be conducted into the ground.

Lightning Rods and Safety

A lightning rod has two functions: to reduce the likelihood of a lightning strike and, if a strike occurs, to conduct the charge safely to the ground. Ideally, a lightning rod reduces the likelihood of a lightning strike. The charges streaming between the cloud and the lightning rod tend to neutralize each other, and this may be enough to prevent lightning from striking. If lightning does strike, however, it will likely hit the lightning rod rather than the building to which the lightning rod is attached. Charge from the lightning bolt will then be safely conducted to the ground.

Lightning produces visible light and an expanding shock wave of air that you hear as thunder. The light and sound wave are formed at the same instant, but they travel at very different speeds. This explains why you hear the thunder after you see the flash of light. Environment Canada suggests that you take shelter in a building or a metal vehicle when you can count 30 s or less between the flash of light and the thunder.

Sense of *time*

The speed of light is about 300 000 km per second, so the flash of light reaches you almost immediately. The speed of sound is much less–about one third of a kilometre per second. So, when you can count 30 seconds between seeing a lightning bolt and hearing thunder, the storm is about 10 km away.

Learning Check

1. Refer to **Figure 10.18**. Why does lightning tend to strike the tallest building nearby?

2. Briefly describe the two functions of a lightning rod.

3. What is an ion? How can positive ions move through the air?

4. What are some of the hazards of a lightning strike?

Using an Electric Charge to Reduce Pollution and Waste

In 1907, Frederick Cottrell patented the first industrial application that made use of the principles of electrostatics (the study of static electricity). Cottrell was a chemistry professor who wanted to remove sulfuric acid droplets from smokestacks. Sulfuric acid, smoke, and ash are by-products of ore smelters, coal-burning plants, and cement kilns. Cottrell invented an **electrostatic precipitator**, a type of cleaner that removes unwanted particles and liquid droplets from a flow of gas. An electrostatic precipitator can be very effective for reducing pollution from smokestacks, such as those shown in **Figure 10.19**.

electrostatic precipitator a type of cleaner that removes unwanted particles and liquid droplets from a flow of gas

Figure 10.19 Most of the "smoke" you see coming from the smokestacks on this steel plant in Hamilton, Ontario, is condensing steam. However, the emissions also contain harmful substances that an electrostatic precipitator can remove.

How an Electric Precipitator Works

Figure 10.20 A An electrostatic precipitator consists of a series of plates and highly charged wires. It can reduce air pollution from dust particles and liquid droplets. B In this view, the positively charged wires cannot be seen because they run between the plates.

An electrostatic precipitator, like the one illustrated in **Figure 10.20**, makes use of the laws of electric charges. Dust particles and liquid droplets in a polluted gas become positively charged when they come in contact with a wire that has a strong positive charge. The positively charged particles and droplets induce a negative charge on the collection plates. When they collide with the collection plates, they are neutralized and collected in large containers called hoppers.

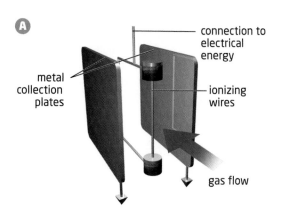

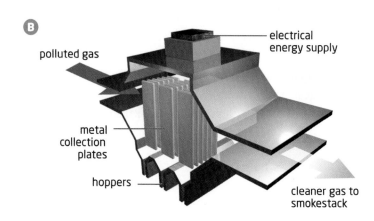

STSE Case Study

E-waste

Electronics companies are constantly marketing new models of computers, cellphones, and MP3 players. The new models are sleeker and run faster, and they have more memory, better interfaces, and more creative features. They tempt customers with leading-edge technology, inspiring customers to discard their old devices for new ones. What happens to the discarded electronic products?

Electronics that are no longer used can become a hazardous waste called e-waste. E-waste is becoming a serious threat to human and environmental health. Many electronic products, including televisions and computers, have parts that are made from heavy metals, such as mercury, lead, and cadmium. These toxic elements can build up in landfills and can end up in ground water.

Although most e-waste can be recycled, little of it is. Much of the e-waste that is recycled is shipped to developing countries for recycling. Often the recycling methods are dangerous. For example, to collect the glass in computer monitors, workers smash the monitors, releasing toxic lead dust. As well, workers use dangerous acids and open fires to recover valuable metals from the e-waste.

International agreements exist to prevent dangerous recycling. E-waste from developed countries, however, is still being sent to countries that allow the use of high-risk recycling methods. It is cheaper for companies to export the e-waste than to pay for safer recycling methods.

To combat e-waste, many countries, including Canada, are adopting a policy called Extended Producer Responsibility. This policy makes companies responsible for their products when consumers are finished with them.

Electrostatic Spray Painting

Look at the objects around you. You can probably see objects made from metal, plastic, wood, and fabric. Most of the manufactured products you see have some kind of coating. For example, think about the painted surface on a car, the enamel finish on a refrigerator, and the flame retardant on some fabrics. For economic and environmental reasons, manufacturers want to apply only as much coating as necessary, with no waste. The solution is to use an electrostatic spray. The paint or powder is given a charge as it leaves the nozzle of the sprayer. The object to be coated is either grounded or given a charge that is opposite to the charge of the particles in the spray. Thus, the particles are attracted to the object being coated, minimizing the amount of over-spray. In **Figure 10.21**, paint leaving the spray gun is given a negative charge. The car fender being painted has a positive charge.

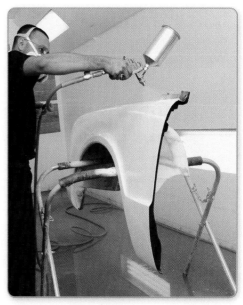

Figure 10.21 Electrostatic spray painting is a good environmental and economic choice because it reduces over-spraying.

How can you help to reduce e-waste?

- Wait longer before replacing electronic devices.
- Upgrade computers and other electronic devices instead of discarding them.
- Donate used electronic devices to charity.
- Buy from electronics manufacturers that take back old devices and safely recycle the materials in them.
- Choose electronic devices that last longer and are made from safer materials.

According to Environment Canada, discarded electronic products create 140 000 tonnes of waste in Canada each year. This is 4.5 kg of electronic waste per Canadian.

Your Turn

1. Create a PMI chart of the advantages and disadvantages of living in a world where billions of people use cellphones. Your chart should have three columns: P for the plus (advantages), M for the minus (disadvantages), and I for interesting points that you consider neither entirely positive nor entirely negative.

2. Research the company that makes your favourite electronic product. What are the company's policies regarding recycling? Is the company responsible for its products at the post-consumer stage? How do the company's policies affect your opinion of its products?

3. Find out more about the Extended Producer Responsibility policy. How do companies pay for the extra costs involved? Create a pamphlet for an electronics company to promote its Extended Producer Responsibility policy. Your pamphlet should highlight the benefits to consumers, as well as explain any costs.

The Van de Graaff Generator

A **Van de Graaff generator** is a device that can accumulate and transfer very large charges, as shown in **Figure 10.22**. The basic operation of the generator is shown in **Figure 10.23**. The sphere rests on an insulated column. Inside the column is a rubber belt that runs over two rollers. A motor drives the lower roller, and, as the belt moves over it, charging by friction takes place. Charges stick to the belt and are carried up as the belt rotates. Near the top roller is a metal collecting comb, which is attached to the inside of the metal sphere. The charged belt induces a redistribution of charges in the comb, and charges accumulate on the metal sphere.

Van de Graaff generators have been used in atom smashers since the 1930s. A Van de Graaff generator can accelerate particles to very high speeds. Beams of high-speed particles can be focussed so they crash into each other, breaking the particles into fragments and sometimes forming new subatomic particles. Van de Graaff generators have also been used to test the electronic circuits used in space technology.

Figure 10.22 The girl in the photograph has received a large charge from the Van de Graff generator.

Study Toolkit

Interpreting Diagrams If the metal sphere becomes positively charged, why does this illustration show some – symbols on the sphere?

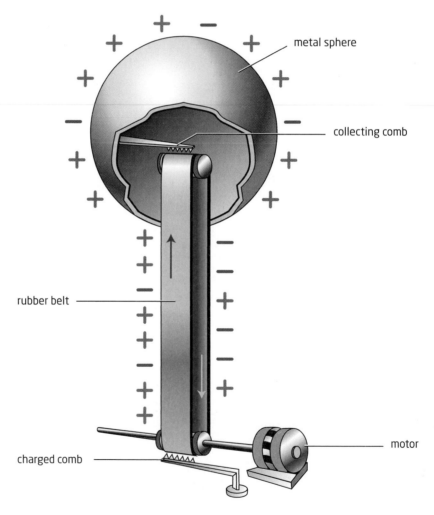

Figure 10.23 In a Van de Graaff generator, positive charges are collected on the metal sphere.

Photocopiers, Laser Printers, and Scanners

Selenium is an element that is essential for good health. It also has a peculiar and useful electrical property. In 1873, Willoughby Smith was the chief engineer at the Telegraph Construction and Maintenance Company in Britain. Smith began testing selenium as a possible material for use in telegraph cables. He was puzzled to find that bars made of selenium did not give consistent results when their conductivity was measured. Eventually, Smith discovered that different light conditions affected the ability of selenium to conduct. Selenium is only a fair conductor in the dark, but it becomes a very good conductor when exposed to light.

Chester Carlson, an American inventor, used this unique property of selenium in the first photocopier machine, which he patented in 1942. In a photocopier, laser printer, or scanner, an electrostatic image is made on an aluminum drum coated with selenium. As you read through the description in **Figure 10.24** of how a photocopier works, try to identify the parts of the photocopier and the principles involved.

Figure 10.24 The parts of a photocopier use the principles of electrostatics.

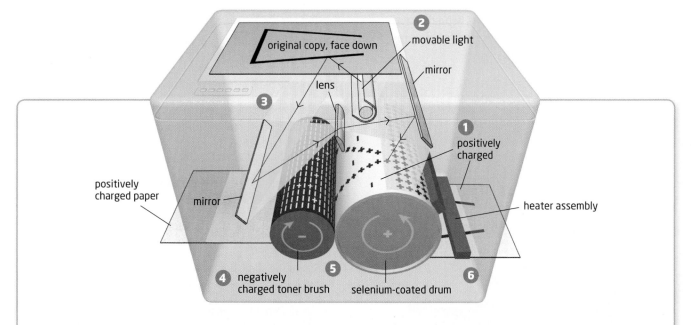

1. The sheet of paper to be copied is placed face down on the glass surface of the copier. When the copy button is pressed, the selenium-coated drum is given a positive charge in the darkness.

2. A bright light moves across the paper. An optical system, which consists of mirrors and a lens, projects an image of the paper on the selenium-coated drum.

3. Light reflects from white portions of the paper being copied. Where the reflected light strikes the drum, selenium conducts charge. Electrons from the aluminum base of the drum move to these light areas, neutralizing the charge that was there. Dark areas on the drum, representing the information being copied, retain a positive charge. The surface of the drum contains an electrostatic image of the information being copied.

4. The machine spreads toner over the surface of the drum. Toner is a fine black powder, consisting of pigments that coat tiny plastic beads. (The pigments give the powder its black colour.) The toner is attracted to the positive parts of the drum, which represent an image of the paper being copied.

5. As the drum rotates, it pulls a sheet of paper from the input tray. The sheet of paper is given a larger positive charge than the drum. The toner is transferred to the paper as the paper presses against the drum.

6. The paper next passes through heated Teflon® rollers. The heat melts the plastic beads in the toner, and the rollers press the black powder into the paper. As the copy emerges from the machine, it is still warm.

Learning Check

5. Explain how electrostatic spray painting works.

6. What electrical property of selenium is used in photocopiers and laser printers?

7. What function does a Van de Graaff generator play in an atom smasher?

8. How does an electrostatic precipitator reduce pollution?

Activity 10-4

A Static Spice Separator

As you know, a static charge attracts a neutral material. How can an electrostatic charge be used to separate particles that have different masses?

Materials

- salt
- pepper
- plastic spoon or ruler
- paper
- wool cloth

Procedure

1. Spread a mixture of salt and pepper in a thin layer on a sheet of paper.

2. Rub the plastic spoon or ruler with the wool cloth.

3. Slowly bring the charged plastic down toward the salt and pepper mixture. Record your observations.

Questions

1. Which substance in the mixture collected on the charged plastic?

2. Explain why the salt and pepper can be separated using a charged object.

3. Could the same principle be used to separate nuts from their shells (after first cracking the shells)? Explain.

4. An electrostatic separator is any device that can use an electrostatic charge to separate different particles that have different masses. Propose another application for an electrostatic separator.

This activity depends on the relationship between electric charge and mass.

Radiation Dosimeters

A **radiation dosimeter** is a small device that detects and measures exposure to radiation. People who work with radioactive materials or equipment that produces radiation often need to wear a radiation dosimeter. Astronauts wear a radiation dosimeter when they are above Earth's atmosphere, which protects Earth from radiation emitted by the Sun. Nuclear and solar radiation and X rays can be very hazardous, and the damage tends to be cumulative. A single high exposure, or a large dose accumulated over time, places a worker at risk.

There are different types of radiation dosimeters. Some dosimeters are like a photographic film. Radiation darkens the film, just as higher levels of light produce a darker image on a photograph. Other dosimeters resemble a metal leaf electroscope surrounded by a gas. Imagine a charged metal leaf electroscope, with its leaves fully spread apart. Normally a gas is a non-conductor, but radiation knocks electrons from the gas atoms. When this happens, the gas surrounding the electroscope becomes a conductor and there is a charge transfer between the gas and the electroscope. As the charge is conducted away from the electroscope, the leaves come closer together and return to the non-charged position. The pen-style dosimeter shown in **Figure 10.25** uses these principles. It consists of a fibre surrounded by a gas.

radiation dosimeter a small device that detects and measures exposure to radiation

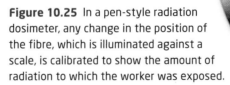

Figure 10.25 In a pen-style radiation dosimeter, any change in the position of the fibre, which is illuminated against a scale, is calibrated to show the amount of radiation to which the worker was exposed.

Making a Difference

Katie Pietrzakowski was brushing her hair when she came up with the idea for her award-winning science fair project. She observed how different particles were attracted to her brush and wondered if these forces of attraction could be used to clean recycled grey water.

Grey water is household waste water from sinks, showers, washing machines, and dishwashers. It can be collected and re-used for lawn irrigation. Re-using grey water helps to conserve water safely and appropriately. Using a system she designed, Katie found that introducing an electric field to grey water could reduce the particulates suspended in the water.

Katie took her project, "Shock the Grey," to the 2006 Canada Wide Science Fair in Saguenay, Québec. There, she won a bronze medal in the Junior Earth and Environmental Sciences division and a scholarship to the University of Western Ontario. Katie is now a high school student in Sault Ste. Marie and hopes to become a teacher.

What other uses for grey water can you think of, to help conserve water?

Section Summary

- A lightning rod is a metal sphere or point that is attached to the highest part of a building and connected to the ground.

- A lightning rod reduces the likelihood of a lightning strike. If there is a lightning strike, the lightning is more likely to strike the lightning rod than the building it protects, and then to be conducted to the ground.

- An electrostatic precipitator removes unwanted dust particles and liquid droplets from a flow of gas.

- An electrostatic separator uses induced charges to separate particles that have different masses.

- A Van de Graaff generator is capable of generating very large charges.

- In the dark, selenium is only a fair conductor. When exposed to light, it becomes a very good conductor. Selenium-coated drums are used in photocopiers, laser printers, and scanners.

- A radiation dosimeter is a small device that detects and measures exposure to radiation.

Review Questions

T/I **1.** Why does lightning follow a jagged path?

K/U **2.** Make a table about a lightning rod's parts and their functions.

C **3.** Write a short brochure for an electrostatic air purifier, describing how it removes dust and pollen from air.

A **4.** Sandpaper is usually made from an abrasive material, such as aluminum oxide or silicon carbide, which is attached to a backing of cotton, polyester, or rayon. How could electrostatics be used to attach abrasive grains to the sticky coating on a backing of polyester "paper"?

K/U **5.** Briefly describe a Van de Graaff generator and two of its uses.

K/U **6.** See **Figure 10.24**. In a photocopier, why does the toner spread from the drum to the paper?

K/U **7.** Air and other gases are normally good insulators. Explain how a gas can become a good conductor.

T/I **8.** The diagram at the right shows parts of a pen-style dosimeter. A particle of radiation has just entered the dosimeter and is about to strike one of the gas molecules shown.

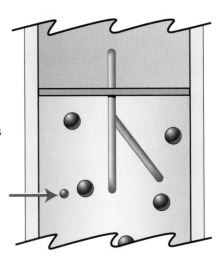

   a. Suppose that the movable fibre has a positive charge. The gas molecule is neutral, because the radiation has not yet hit it. Draw a diagram to show the charges on the dosimeter and the gas molecule.

   b. Draw one or more diagrams to show what the radiation does to the gas molecule. Also show why the movable fibre indicates a decrease in the charge on the dosimeter.

Skill Check

✓ Initiating and Planning

✓ Performing and Recording

✓ Analyzing and Interpreting

✓ Communicating

Suggested Materials

- conductivity tester
- aluminum (strip or wire)
- coated wire
- copper wire
- small block of wood
- graphite
- metal comb
- nylon comb
- beaker
- distilled water
- tap water
- salt
- stir stick

Comparing Conductivity

The transmission and use of electrical energy involves insulators, conductors, and semiconductors. For example, the wire that connects a computer to a wall plug consists of a conducting metal covered with an insulating plastic. Inside the computer, there are semiconductors. In this investigation, you will compare the conductivity of different materials and group together those with similar electrical properties.

Question

With a partner, brainstorm two or three scientific questions you can answer by testing the conductivity of the suggested materials.

Plan and Conduct

1. With your partner, decide how to use the conductivity tester to classify each material as a good conductor, a poor conductor (insulator), or a semiconductor.

2. Make a table to record your observations. List the materials you will be testing in your table. For the coated wire, include both the exposed wire and the coating on the wire.

3. Get your teacher's approval before continuing with your investigation.

Analyze and Interpret

1. List the materials you tested under the following categories: conductors, insulators, and semiconductors.

Conclude and Communicate

2. Write one or two sentences explaining what your results showed.

Extend Your Inquiry and Research Skills

3. **Research** Gases, such as air, are normally insulators. Under certain conditions, a gas can become a very good conductor, called a plasma. Learn more about plasmas, and write a paragraph to summarize where they are found and how they form.

Science Skills

Go to **Science Skills Toolkit 2** to learn more about scientific inquiry.

Plan Your Own Investigation 10-B

Skill Check

✓ Initiating and Planning

✓ Performing and Recording

✓ Analyzing and Interpreting

✓ Communicating

Safety Precautions

- If you use a glass rod, handle it carefully and make sure that it cannot roll off your table. Do not use a glass rod that is chipped or cracked.

- If you are allergic to animal fur, do not use this material.

Suggested Materials

- pith ball electroscope
- some materials from **Table 10.1** in Section 10.1
- some materials that are not in **Table 10.1** (for example, wood, paper, plastic wrap, a plastic compact disc case)

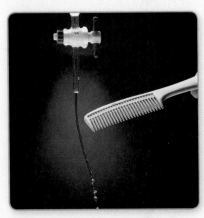

You can bend a small stream of water by using a charged object. The closer a charged object is to the stream of water, the more the stream of water is deflected.

Be a Charge Detective

When two different materials are rubbed together, both materials become charged by friction. The material with the stronger hold on its electrons becomes negatively charged. The material with the weaker hold on its electrons becomes positively charged. The electrostatic series in **Table 10.1** lists several materials according to their ability to hold on to electrons.

Question

How can new materials be added in the correct places in the electrostatic series?

Plan and Conduct

1. Plan how to use materials from **Table 10.1** to give a pith ball electroscope a known charge.

2. Decide how to use the charged pith ball electroscope and the laws of electric charges to infer the type of charge on a material that has an unknown charge.

3. Brainstorm how to add a new material in the correct place in the electrostatic series.

4. Create a data table to record your observations.

5. Have your teacher approve your investigation method and data table.

6. Conduct your investigation.

Analyze and Interpret

1. Compare your electrostatic series with the electrostatic series developed by your classmates. How can you resolve differences in the order of the materials?

2. Why are some materials difficult to place in an electrostatic series?

Conclude and Communicate

3. Write a sentence or two summarizing the electrical characteristics of two different materials that result in the formation of static charge when they are rubbed together.

Extend Your Inquiry and Research Skills

4. **Inquiry** A charged object can bend a small stream of water, as shown in the photograph. Particles dissolved in water allow induced charges to form. How would you predict the temperature of the water might affect the amount of bending? How would you test this?

Chapter 10 Summary

10.1 Exploring Static Charges

Key Concepts

- A static charge (static electricity) is an electric charge that tends to stay on the surface of an object.
- A static charge can be generated by friction when objects rub together.
- Protons are positively charged, and electrons are negatively charged.
- Particles that carry electric charges can be neither created nor destroyed.
- Any net charge on a solid object results from the exchange of electrons with another object.
- A neutral object has the same number of protons and electrons. An object with an excess of electrons has a negative charge. An object with a deficit of electrons has a positive charge.

- Different materials hold on to their electrons with different strengths.
- In electrical insulators, such as non-metals, electrons cannot move easily from one atom to another.
- In electrical conductors, such as metals, electrons can move easily from one atom to another.
- A ground is a conductor that allows the transfer of electrons to Earth, thus eliminating the charge on an object.

10.2 Charging by Contact and by Induction

Key Concepts

- An electroscope detects the presence of an electric charge.
- An object that is charged by contact has the same type of charge as the charging object.
- There are three laws of electric charges: like charges repel; opposite (unlike) charges attract; neutral objects and charged objects are attracted to each other.

- An electric force between two objects is transmitted by an electric field.
- An induced charge separation is the movement of electrons in a substance, caused by the electric field of a nearby charged object, without direct contact between the substance and the object.

10.3 Charges at Work

Key Concepts

- A lightning rod is attached to the highest part of a building and connected to the ground. It reduces the likelihood of a lightning strike and protects buildings.
- An electrostatic precipitator removes unwanted dust particles and liquid droplets from a flow of gas.

- A Van de Graaff generator is used to generate very large charges.
- Selenium, a light-sensitive element, is used in copiers, printers, and scanners.
- A radiation dosimeter detects and measures radiation.

Make Your Own Summary

Summarize the key concepts of this chapter using a graphic organizer. The Chapter Summary on the previous page will help you identify the key concepts. Refer to Study Toolkit 4 on pages 566–567 to help you decide which graphic organizer to use.

Reviewing Key Terms

1. A list of materials that have been arranged according to their ability to hold on to electrons is a(n) _____ . (10.1)

2. Metals and other materials in which electrons can move easily between atoms are classified as electrical _____ . Non-metals are classified as _____ . (10.1)

3. Electric charges can be detected in a laboratory using a device called a(n) _____ . (10.2)

4. The force exerted between two charged objects is transmitted through space by a(n) _____ . (10.2)

5. A(n) _____ can reduce the chances of a lightning strike. (10.2)

6. An _____ uses a static charge to remove unwanted particles and liquid droplets from a flow of gas. (10.3)

Knowledge and Understanding K/U

7. Explain why two electric charges may interact, even though there is no contact between them.

8. Explain why a strip of polyethylene had a negative charge after it was rubbed with a piece of silk cloth.

9. Touching a ground to a charged object causes the object to become neutral. Explain why.

10. Explain, on an atomic level, how an insulator differs from a conductor.

11. Why is the electric charge on a solid object always explained in terms of an excess or deficit of electrons?

12. If a neutral object has no net charge, why is it attracted to a charged object that is placed nearby?

13. Suggest a reason why most homes in a city do not need to be protected by a lightning rod.

14. Which law of electric charges is applied in electrostatic spray painting?

15. Why are Van de Graaff generators used in atom smashers?

Thinking and Investigation T/I

16. A strip of acetate has a positive charge after it is rubbed with wool. A piece of lead has a negative charge after it is rubbed with wool, but a positive charge after it is rubbed with silk. A piece of copper has a negative charge after it is rubbed with silk. Arrange acetate, copper, and lead in order, according to their ability to hold on to electrons. Give reasons for your order.

17. Experiments were performed with three balloons, labelled X, Y, and Z. The results of bringing two different pairs of balloons close together are shown below.

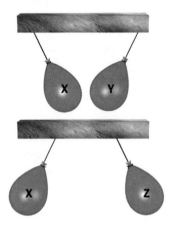

What can you infer about the type of charge (definitely charged, possibly charged, definitely neutral, or possibly neutral) on each balloon?

18. A student saw a metal leaf electroscope with its leaves spread apart and concluded that the electroscope must have a permanent charge. She decided to try an experiment. She rubbed an ebonite rod with fur to give the rod a permanent charge. Then she brought the rod close to the sphere on the electroscope. She observed that the leaves collapsed. When she brought the rod even closer, without making contact, the leaves began to spread apart again. What was the charge on the metal leaf electroscope before the experiment began?

Communication Ⓒ

19. **BIG IDEAS** Explain the statement "electric charge is neither created nor destroyed." Describe how the movement of *one* type of particle can result in the formation of *two* different types of electric forces.

20. **BIG IDEAS** Modern materials used in homes, offices, and businesses have contributed to increased problems with electrostatic discharge. Write a pamphlet for architects and home renovation companies, explaining how to anticipate these problems. Include specific suggestions for how to reduce the build-up of static charges.

21. **BIG IDEAS** A petroleum refinery has developed an electrostatic separator to remove small solid particles from oil. Make a diagram to show how this separator uses the properties of static electricity.

22. The wood, paper, and pulp industry is one of many industries that require knowledge of materials and coatings. Find out what courses are offered at colleges and universities in Canada to prepare for a career in this industry.

Application Ⓐ

23. Why does wiping a television or computer screen with a wool cloth cause dust to build up again within a few days?

24. Electrostatic precipitators are used by industries and power plants to remove particles from gases. Use the Internet to identify a factory or power plant that has an electrostatic precipitator. Research the cost of the electrostatic precipitator and the amount of particulate emissions it removes from the atmosphere. Also find out what happens to the removed solids and how the environment is improved by removing them from the waste gases.

25. a. What evidence shows that the child in drawing **A** has a static charge? What do you think generated the charge?

   b. What is different about the materials that were used to build the slides in the two drawings?

   c. Cochlear implants are electronic devices that are surgically implanted into the ears to give people who are profoundly deaf partial hearing. Why can some playground equipment damage these implants?

Chapter 11 Electric Circuits

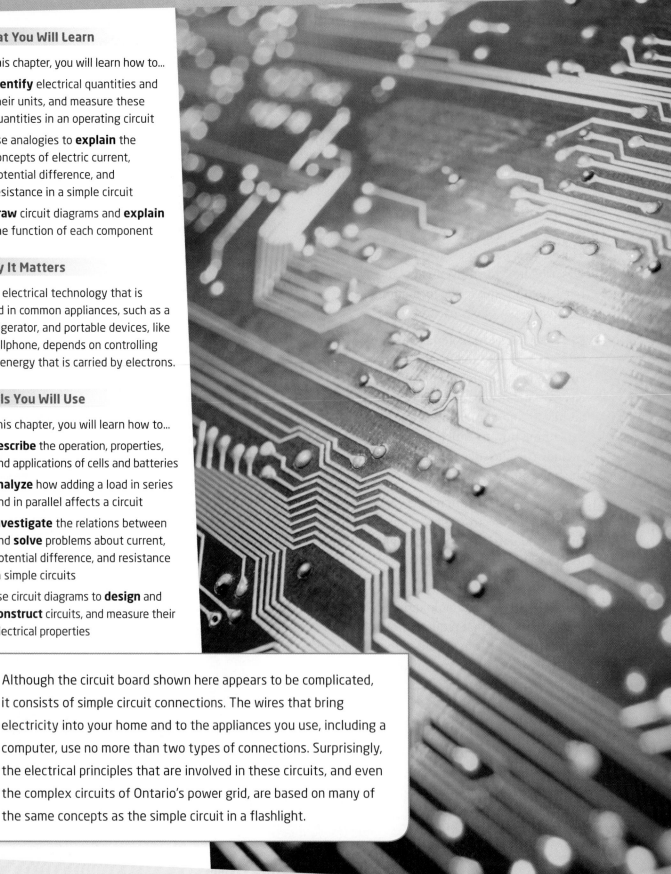

What You Will Learn

In this chapter, you will learn how to...

- **identify** electrical quantities and their units, and measure these quantities in an operating circuit
- use analogies to **explain** the concepts of electric current, potential difference, and resistance in a simple circuit
- **draw** circuit diagrams and **explain** the function of each component

Why It Matters

The electrical technology that is used in common appliances, such as a refrigerator, and portable devices, like a cellphone, depends on controlling the energy that is carried by electrons.

Skills You Will Use

In this chapter, you will learn how to...

- **describe** the operation, properties, and applications of cells and batteries
- **analyze** how adding a load in series and in parallel affects a circuit
- **investigate** the relations between and **solve** problems about current, potential difference, and resistance in simple circuits
- use circuit diagrams to **design** and **construct** circuits, and measure their electrical properties

Although the circuit board shown here appears to be complicated, it consists of simple circuit connections. The wires that bring electricity into your home and to the appliances you use, including a computer, use no more than two types of connections. Surprisingly, the electrical principles that are involved in these circuits, and even the complex circuits of Ontario's power grid, are based on many of the same concepts as the simple circuit in a flashlight.

Activity 11-1

Shed Light On It

A simple flashlight contains a dry cell to provide electrical energy, an on-off switch, and a light bulb. How are these components connected to operate the flashlight?

Safety Precautions

- If you notice that any wire in the circuit is hot, disconnect the wire from the cell. Inform your teacher.

Materials

- D cell in cell holder
- flashlight bulb in a holder
- switch
- 3 connecting wires
- strip of aluminum foil

Procedure

1. Make sure that the switch is in the open position. Use connecting wires to join the cell, flashlight bulb, and switch.

2. Close the switch. Record the intensity (low, medium, or high) of the bulb.

3. With the switch still closed, unscrew the flashlight bulb from its holder and record what happens to the bulb.

4. Tighten the flashlight bulb into its holder. With the switch closed, remove one of the connecting wires. Record the intensity of the bulb.

5. Use the strip of aluminum foil to replace the connecting wire you removed. Observe the intensity of the bulb, and compare it with its intensity when the wire was used.

Questions

1. Draw a diagram to show the bulb, switch, cell, and connecting wires when the flashlight bulb was glowing.

2. Describe three different ways that you can make a flashlight bulb stop glowing. What do these different ways have in common?

3. How is a strip of aluminum foil similar to a connecting wire?

Study Toolkit

These strategies will help you use this textbook to develop your understanding of science concepts and skills. To find out more about these and other strategies, refer to the Study Toolkit Overview, which begins on page 561.

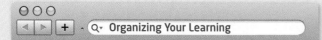

Identifying Cause and Effect

Identifying causes and effects can help you understand why things happen. Sometimes, many simultaneous causes lead to an effect, which itself becomes a cause of a second effect. A cause-and-effect map can help you organize such relationships. For example, read the section "Electric and Hybrid Vehicles" on the next page and study the cause-and-effect map below:

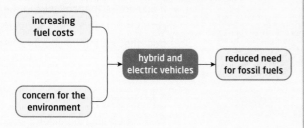

Use the Strategy

1. Read the first paragraph of the section titled "Factors That Affect the Resistance of Wires" on page 465.

2. Make a cause-and-effect map showing the relationship between the resistance of two wires made from the same metal, with the same diameter, but with different lengths.

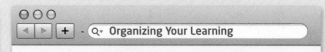

Comparing and Contrasting

Comparing and contrasting new concepts can help you understand them. Venn diagrams and charts are two ways to organize this information graphically. For example, the chart below shows the differences and similarities between a series circuit and a parallel circuit.

	Differences	Similarities
series circuit	There is *only one* path along which electrons can flow.	Both are closed paths along which electrons that are powered by an energy source can flow.
parallel circuit	There is *more than one* path along which electrons can flow.	

Use the Strategy

1. Create a chart with *resistance* and *load* in the first column.

2. Write the everyday definition for each word in the second column.

3. As you read this chapter, fill in the third column with the scientific definition of each word.

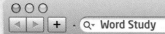
Word Study

Multiple Meanings

Words can have more than one meaning, depending on their context. The chart below shows some words that you may have seen in a non-scientific context. It includes their everyday meanings *and* their scientific meanings, specifically in the context of a unit about electricity.

Use the Strategy

1. Read the text on page 458 titled "Measuring Current and Potential Difference."

2. Make a chart to show the similarities and differences between ammeters and voltmeters.

Word	Everyday Meaning	Scientific Meaning (Physics)
cell	Small room in a prison	A device that converts chemical energy into electrical energy
current	(1) Going on now (2) Water moving in one direction	A flow of electricity
terminal	Building at an airport	Site on a cell that must be connected to other components to form an electric circuit

11.1 Cells and Batteries

As you know, electrons are involved in all static charges. Electrons are also involved in the circuits of electrical devices. An **electric circuit** is a closed path along which electrons that are powered by an energy source can flow. To function, a circuit requires a source of electrical energy, which is often a cell or a battery.

Electric and Hybrid Vehicles

The first electric cars, such as the one shown in **Figure 11.1**, were built a century ago. Yet today, most of the vehicles on the road are powered by gasoline or diesel derived from fossil fuels. However, increasing fuel costs and concern for the environment have led to the development of hybrid and electric vehicles. In the future, electricity will play a key role in transportation. Electric vehicles are powered only by batteries, while hybrid vehicles use a combination of batteries and a fossil-fuel engine. In a hybrid vehicle, a small combustion engine burns fossil fuel, and an electric motor assists the combustion engine when the car is accelerating. This helps to reduce the need for fossil fuels.

Key Terms

electric circuit
voltaic cell
battery
electrode
electrolyte
dry cell
wet cell
primary cell
secondary cell
fuel cell

electric circuit a closed path along which electrons that are powered by an energy source can flow

Figure 11.1 American inventor Thomas Edison, shown here with his son, experimented with electric cars about 100 years ago. Scientists and engineers are trying to improve the batteries that are used in electric and hybrid vehicles today.

Figure 11.2 When Volta invented this "pile," it had no practical uses.

voltaic cell a source of energy that generates an electric current by chemical reactions involving two different metals or metal compounds separated by a solution that is a conductor

battery a connection of two or more cells

electrode one of two metal terminals in a cell or battery

electrolyte a solution or paste that conducts charge

Voltaic Cells

Most of the batteries that are used today are similar in principle to the battery constructed by Alessandro Volta, an Italian physicist, around 1800. He stacked alternating discs made of silver and zinc, separated by a piece of cloth soaked in salt water. Volta invented the first battery, which became known as a Voltaic "pile," shown in **Figure 11.2**.

From Cells to Batteries

The AA or D "battery" that you insert into a flashlight or portable radio is actually a **voltaic cell** (also called a cell). It generates an electric current by chemical reactions that involve two different metals or metal compounds separated by a conducting solution. A **battery** is a connection of two or more cells. You make a battery when you place two or more cells in a flashlight.

In a voltaic cell or battery, the two metal terminals are called **electrodes**. The electrodes must be made of different metals, with different abilities to hold on to electrons. The electrodes are immersed in a conducting solution or paste, called an **electrolyte**. You may have seen a "lemon clock," shown in **Figure 11.3A**, which has these features.

In a voltaic cell, chemical reactions take place at the surface of each electrode that is in contact with the electrolyte. The chemical reactions depend on the metals that are used, but the operation of every cell involves the movement of electrons and ions. **Figure 11.3B** shows what happens in a lemon cell that has aluminum and copper electrodes. The aluminum atoms give up three electrons, forming Al^{3+} ions. The Al^{3+} ions leave the aluminum electrode, enter the electrolyte solution, and move toward the copper electrode. As this happens, the strip of aluminum slowly disintegrates. The disintegration of an electrode is one factor that can limit the life of a cell. The electrons that are released by the aluminum atoms move through the connecting wires to the copper electrode.

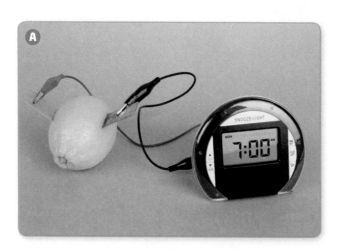

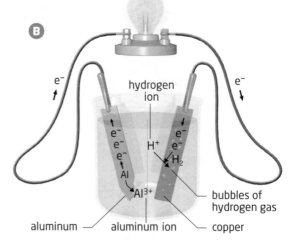

Figure 11.3 A The strips inserted in the lemon are made of different metals and function as electrodes. The lemon juice is the electrolyte. **B** In a cell, electrons flow from one electrode, through connecting wires, to the other electrode. The electrode that loses electrons forms positive ions, and these ions enter the electrolyte. At the other electrode, electrons combine with ions in the electrolyte.

Types of Cells

Because a battery is made up of cells that are connected together, batteries and cells are classified in the same way. One way they are classified is based on the electrolyte they contain: either dry or wet.

Dry Cells

Most of the cells you use are classified as dry cells. A **dry cell** contains an electrolyte that is a paste. A German scientist named Carl Gassner invented the first practical dry cell in 1887. Gassner's cell used zinc and carbon as electrodes. The electrolyte was made from a paste of plaster of Paris and a chemical called ammonium chloride. The inexpensive zinc-carbon cell in common use today, shown in **Figure 11.4A**, has changed little since Gassner's invention. The first major advance in dry cells came in 1959, with the alkaline cell, shown in **Figure 11.4B**. Alkaline cells are more expensive than zinc-carbon cells, but they have the advantage of lasting much longer. "Button" cells are either silver-oxide cells or zinc-air cells, shown in **Figures 11.4C** and **11.4D**.

Suggested Investigation

Inquiry Investigation 11-A, Constructing and Comparing Voltaic Cells, on page 472

dry cell a cell that contains an electrolyte that is a paste

Sense of Value

Today's alkaline batteries last 40 times longer than the first 1959 model.

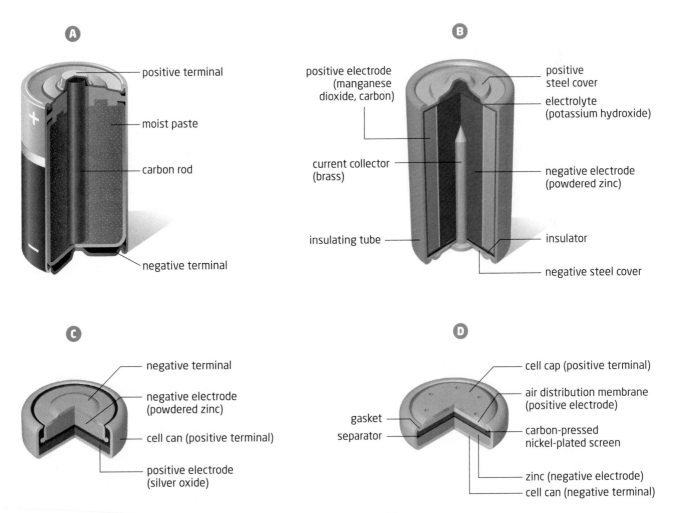

Figure 11.4 Different types of primary cells are used in calculators, hearing aids, computers, and toothbrushes. Four types of dry cells are shown: **A** a zinc-carbon cell, also called a D cell, **B** an alkaline cell, **C** a silver-oxide cell, and **D** a zinc-air cell.

Wet Cells

A **wet cell** contains a liquid electrolyte. Volta's pile was a wet cell because the electrolyte was a salt solution. Most wet cells use a solution of sulfuric acid as an electrolyte, because sulfuric acid is an inexpensive, strong acid. However, sulfuric acid is a corrosive liquid, and contact with the skin may cause injury.

Primary and Secondary Cells

A second way that cells are classified depends on whether they can be recharged. A **primary cell** can be used only once, and then it is discarded. All the cells that are shown in **Figure 11.4** are primary cells. A **secondary cell** can be recharged many times. In a secondary cell, an electric current is passed in the opposite direction through the cell from another source. The charging current reverses the chemical reactions that take place in the cell, essentially restoring the cell to full capacity. The lead-acid battery that is used in trucks, automobiles, motorcycles, and wheelchairs is a secondary wet cell. **Figure 11.5** shows this and other common secondary cells.

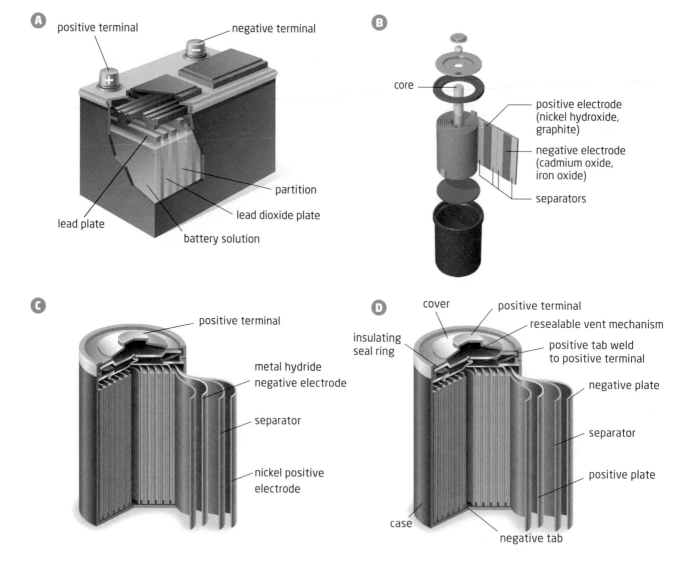

Figure 11.5 These are four examples of secondary cells: **A** a lead-acid battery, **B** a nickel-cadmium cell, **C** a nickel-metal hydride cell, and **D** a lithium-ion cell.

Table 11.1 Cells and Batteries in Common Use

Name	Primary/ Secondary	Dry/Wet	Typical Uses	Pros	Cons
Zinc-carbon	Primary	Dry	Flashlights, small radios, music players	Is inexpensive	Gives poor performance at low temperature
Alkaline	Primary	Dry	Flashlights, small radios, music players	Lasts longer than zinc-carbon cells	Is more expensive than zinc-carbon cells
Silver-oxide	Primary	Dry	Calculators, watches, hearing aids, pagers	Is small and long-lasting	Is relatively expensive
Zinc-air	Primary	Dry	Hearing aids, pagers	Has a long shelf life if sealed	Requires oxygen from the air
Lead acid	Secondary	Wet	Cars, trucks, motorcycles, snowmobiles	Delivers high current; is inexpensive	Is heavy; contains a corrosive electrolyte; has a short storage life
Nickel-cadmium	Secondary	Dry	Portable power tools, laptop computers, shavers, toothbrushes	Can be recharged 500 to 700 times	Is an environmental hazard because of the cadmium
Nickel-metal hydride	Secondary	Dry	Portable power tools, laptop computers, shavers, toothbrushes	Can be recharged 300 to 400 times; is good for high-demand applications, such as cameras and power tools	Is relatively expensive
Lithium-ion	Secondary	Dry	Cellphones, laptop computers	Can be recharged 300 to 400 times; has an excellent shelf life; is good at high and low temperatures	Is relatively expensive

Activity 11-2

Make a CELLection

There are many cells and batteries that can be used to provide electrical energy. For some applications, more than one type of cell can be used. What properties would you consider important if you were selecting a cell for each of the following applications?

Applications

- key holder with a light
- golf cart
- travel alarm clock
- camcorder
- portable drill
- child's singing teddy bear
- flashlight
- pacemaker
- snowblower
- engine starter
- scuba diver's light
- road-hazard warning light

Procedure

1. Design a table with four headings: Application, Properties of Cells That Could Be Used, Recommended Cell, and Reasons for Recommendation.

2. Research the meanings of these properties: storage, capacity, recharge life.

3. Using the information in **Table 11.1** and other sources, recommend a cell for each application. Consider the properties you listed in Procedure step 2, as well as cost and environmental impact.

Questions

1. Which cells have the least impact on the environment? Explain your reasoning.

2. Did you recommend primary cells or secondary cells more often? Explain your choices.

3. Think about the portable devices you use and the cells that provide them with electrical energy. Would you change the type of cell you use for any of these devices? Explain your reasoning.

Fuel Cells

fuel cell a cell that generates electricity through the chemical reactions of fuel that is stored outside the cell

A **fuel cell** generates electricity through the chemical reactions of fuel that is stored outside the cell. A hydrogen fuel cell combines hydrogen that is stored in a tank or cartridge with oxygen from the air. The only by-products of the reaction are heat and water. Fuel cells were originally developed for the U.S. space program, to help keep astronauts warm and provide them with drinking water. Fuel cells are capable of providing the energy for automobiles, buses, and small devices such as cellphones.

Figure 11.6 Fuel cell cars and buses are quiet and non-polluting. The fuel cells are expensive, however, and require hydrogen gas, which must be produced from other sources.

STSE Case Study

Electric Avenue

As gasoline gets more costly, in terms of both price and environmental effects, consumers are looking for alternatives to gasoline-burning vehicles. Electric cars, which make more efficient use of energy, are one answer. Because electric engines run only on batteries, they emit no greenhouse gases while running. The generation of the electricity they use, however, does produce some carbon dioxide emissions.

Toronto-based ZENN Motor Company, whose name stands for "zero emission, no noise," produces fully electric cars. The ZENN car is manufactured in St. Jérôme, Québec. It is a hatchback low-speed vehicle (LSV), powered by six heavy-duty lead-acid batteries. Its top speed is 40 km/h, it can hold two people, and it costs $16 900. Its range (the distance it can travel on fully charged batteries) is 50 to 80 km.

Advantages of Electric Cars

As well as the advantage of emitting no greenhouse gases, electric cars have several other advantages over gasoline-burning vehicles. To charge an electric car, it is plugged into a normal wall socket. A ZENN car is 80 percent charged in four hours and completely charged in eight hours. Depending on how much an electric car is used, its battery pack will last three to five years. When an electric car is not moving, such as in a traffic jam, it does not use its stored power or produce any exhaust.

The ZENN electric car is a low-speed vehicle that is powered only by batteries. It is manufactured in Canada. Québec and British Columbia were the first provinces to allow it on city streets.

Fuel Cell Vehicles

Ballard Power Systems, based in Burnaby, British Columbia, develops and manufactures hydrogen fuel cells. Ballard is cooperating with other companies to work on a new fuel cell for use in cars. Fuel cells are also being developed for use in public transportation, as shown in **Figure 11.6**.

Go to **scienceontario** to find out more

Learning Check

1. Sketch and label the main parts of a voltaic cell.

2. Refer to **Table 11.1** on page 441. Give an example of
   a. a dry primary cell   **b.** a wet secondary cell

3. Is a fuel cell a primary cell or a secondary cell? Explain.

4. A soil tester for plants uses a meter to display moisture content when the end of a probe is placed in the soil. No batteries are needed. How does the soil tester work?

Relative Energy Consumption and Costs

A gasoline-burning car wastes fuel and releases carbon dioxide when it is stuck in traffic because its engine is still running. On average, only 12 percent of the energy that is produced by burning gasoline goes toward making a car move. An electric engine that is charged by the power generated at an oil-burning generating plant converts twice as much energy to making a car move. As well, because an electric car has fewer moving parts, it needs less maintenance. Considering all the costs, a ZENN car costs less than two cents per kilometre to operate. A conventional car can cost 10 times as much per kilometre.

Disadvantages of Electric Cars

One concern with electric cars is that charging them increases our electricity needs and may have a significant effect on the environment if the energy source is fossil fuels. If the power that is used to charge the batteries, however, comes from renewable sources, such as wind or solar energy, an electric car is a very "green" method of transportation.

Another concern with electric cars is their limited range. Once the batteries are out of power, completely recharging them takes several hours. More high-tech batteries exist, but their cost is much greater. The range of electric cars is not a major concern for short distances, however, and electric cars are not intended for use on highways.

Getting Greener

Electric cars are an important step toward reducing the use of the internal combustion engine and achieving more efficient and environmentally friendly methods of transportation.

Your Turn

1. Suppose your family is discussing what kind of car to purchase. What would you tell your parents about the pros and cons of an electric vehicle?

2. Why does the source of power that is used to charge an electric vehicle make a difference to its energy efficiency and the amount of carbon compounds it releases? What could government and power utilities do to make electric cars an even greener method of transportation in your area?

3. Write a persuasive letter to your MPP explaining why you think low-speed electric cars should or should not be allowed on Ontario roads.

How can we meet our transportation needs in an environmentally friendly way?

- Drive an electric car, especially for short distances.
- Carpool to school or work.
- Combine errands and other trips to reduce the amount driven.
- Use public transportation.
- Get some exercise—walk or ride a bicycle.

Solar Cells

The Sun will continue to supply energy for billions of years. Earth receives more energy from the Sun in one hour than all the energy consumed by humans in a year. How can the Sun's energy be harnessed and stored for use at night and on cloudy days, at a reasonable cost?

A **solar cell** converts sunlight into electrical energy. For example, when sunlight strikes a semiconductor, such as silicon, electrons are knocked loose from the atoms. A few small solar cells can provide enough energy for a calculator or an ornamental garden light, and large solar panels can operate a communications satellite. For several years, the Ontario government has been encouraging renewable energy projects through a program called the Renewable Energy Standard Offer Program (RESOP). This program has been modelled after a program in Germany. An example of a solar farm is shown in **Figure 11.7**.

Figure 11.7 These solar panels and tower are part of the Solar 2 farm in California.

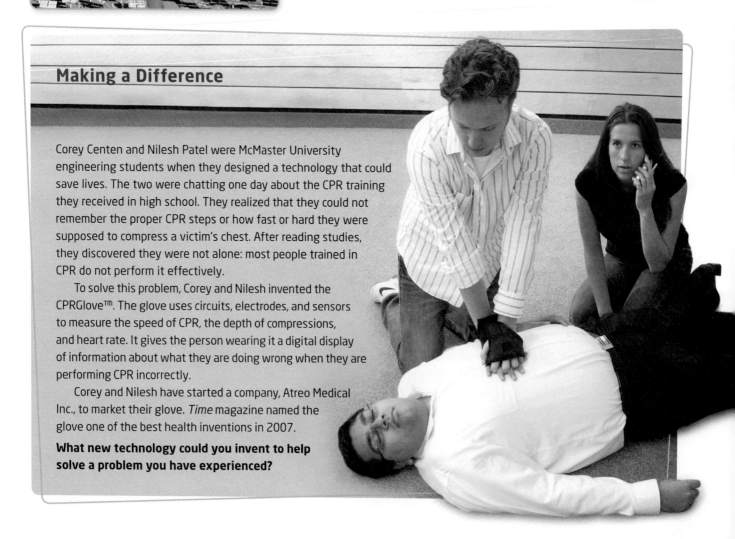

Making a Difference

Corey Centen and Nilesh Patel were McMaster University engineering students when they designed a technology that could save lives. The two were chatting one day about the CPR training they received in high school. They realized that they could not remember the proper CPR steps or how fast or hard they were supposed to compress a victim's chest. After reading studies, they discovered they were not alone: most people trained in CPR do not perform it effectively.

To solve this problem, Corey and Nilesh invented the CPRGlove™. The glove uses circuits, electrodes, and sensors to measure the speed of CPR, the depth of compressions, and heart rate. It gives the person wearing it a digital display of information about what they are doing wrong when they are performing CPR incorrectly.

Corey and Nilesh have started a company, Atreo Medical Inc., to market their glove. *Time* magazine named the glove one of the best health inventions in 2007.

What new technology could you invent to help solve a problem you have experienced?

Section Summary

- In a voltaic cell, chemical reactions involve two different metals or metal compounds (called electrodes), and a conducting solution or paste (called an electrolyte).

- A battery is a connection of two or more cells.

- A dry cell contains an electrolyte that is a paste, whereas a wet cell contains an electrolyte that is a liquid solution.

- A primary cell can be used only once, and then it is discarded, whereas a secondary cell can be recharged many times.

- A fuel cell generates electricity using chemical reactions of fuel stored outside the cell.

- A solar cell converts sunlight, a renewable energy source, into electrical energy.

Review Questions

A **1.** Compare the consequences to the environment of using an electric car and a hybrid car.

K/U **2.** Explain why the electrodes in a cell must be made from different materials (usually metals). See **Figure 11.3**.

K/U **3.** List two ways in which batteries are classified.

K/U **4.** What is an electrolyte? Explain the function of an electrolyte in a cell.

T/I **5.** Part of a voltaic cell is shown in the diagram on the right.

   a. Describe the role of electrons in a voltaic cell.

   b. Which electrode will lose mass as the cell operates? Explain your answer.

T/I **6.** A flashlight can be powered by zinc-carbon cells, alkaline cells, or rechargeable cells. Design an experiment to find out which type of cell lasts longest.

C **7.** Write a pamphlet advising consumers what cell is best to use in a flashlight, based on use and cost.

T/I **8.** What would need to be done before hydrogen fuel cells can be practical for general use in automobiles?

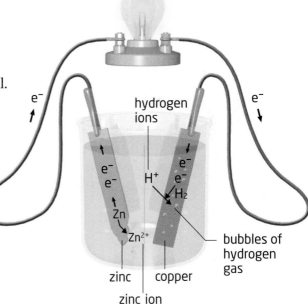

Key Terms

terminal

switch

open circuit

electric current

coulomb (C)

ampere (A)

electrical resistance

resistor

load

potential difference
(voltage)

volt

11.2 Electric Circuits: Analogies and Characteristics

Beginning with a set of ideas based on observations, scientists often make a model or develop an analogy to represent what they think is happening. Some models are physical representations, such as a model of a water molecule or of the solar system, like the one shown in **Figure 11.8**. Many models are mathematical, such as a model of climate change.

Models and Analogies

Models and analogies represent parts of reality. An analogy makes a comparison between two existing things that are similar in some ways but different in others. For example, the flow of water is an analogy for an electric current. A model is something that is constructed to give a simplified representation of an object or a process. You have seen models of an atom or a molecule. These models give a basic sense of what they are representing, but do not include many of the details.

Models and analogies allow scientists to make predictions that can be tested and thus can guide future experiments. In this section, you will examine different analogies and models for what happens when a battery or its components are connected in a circuit.

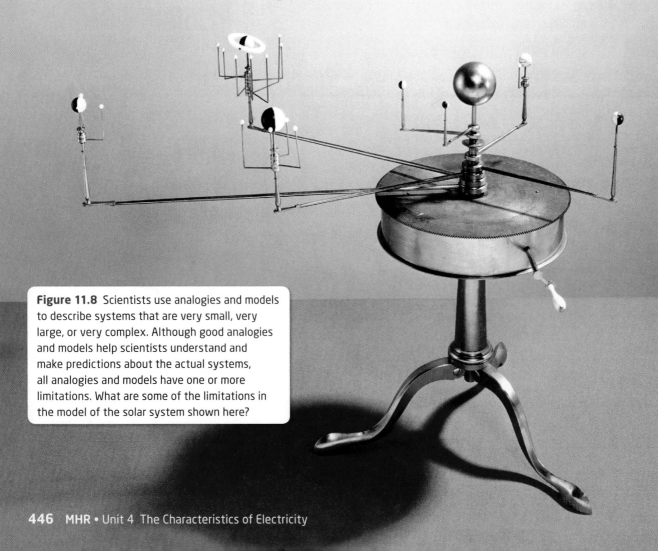

Figure 11.8 Scientists use analogies and models to describe systems that are very small, very large, or very complex. Although good analogies and models help scientists understand and make predictions about the actual systems, all analogies and models have one or more limitations. What are some of the limitations in the model of the solar system shown here?

Electric Circuits

As you learned in Section 11.1, an electric circuit is a closed path along which electrons can flow from and return to an energy source. The two locations in a cell that must be connected to other components are the positive **terminal** and the negative terminal, which are shown in **Figure 11.9**. Another way to state this is that the cell has two types of poles: a positive pole and a negative pole. In a flashlight, you may have discovered that the way the cell is connected in the circuit affects the operation of the flashlight bulb. As you investigate circuits, you will need to distinguish between the two terminals.

Switches and Wires

A **switch** is a control device. It is a conductor that can complete or break the circuit it is connected to. A switch is not essential for a circuit to operate, but it is usually included for convenience. A connecting wire is a conductor that joins different circuit components, such as a bulb and a switch. The connecting wires you will use in the investigations are metal wires, usually made from copper or aluminum, covered with an insulator made of plastic or rubber. On a circuit board, the connecting wires are strips of metal that are printed on the board.

Open Circuits

Electrons do not flow through any part of a circuit where there is a gap or break. Opening a switch creates a gap, and any devices that are connected to the switch, such as a light bulb, will stop working. There are many ways that a gap or break can occur in a circuit, but all have the same effect as opening a switch. An **open circuit**, shown in **Figure 11.10**, is one in which there is a gap or break in the circuit.

For example, if a bulb is loose and does not make contact with the base of its socket, the circuit is open and the bulb will not glow. A break in the filament of an incandescent bulb, which emits light because of the high temperature of the filament, also creates an open circuit. This is the most common reason why a bulb does not glow. In an incandescent bulb, electrical energy heats the tungsten filament to roughly 2500°C.

terminal location on a cell that must be connected to other components to form a circuit

switch a control device that can complete or break the circuit to which it is connected

open circuit a circuit that contains a gap or break

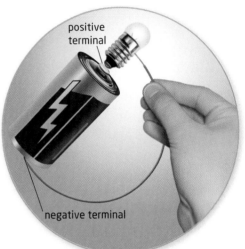

Figure 11.9 This is the simplest circuit that can make a flashlight bulb glow. The casing, filament, and base of the bulb are connected to form part of a circuit.

circuit (closed)

open circuit

Figure 11.10 A circuit, which is the same as a closed circuit, allows electrons to flow from and return to an energy source. When there is a break in the circuit, the result is an open circuit through which current does not flow.

The Movement of Electrons

If a conductor, such as a metal wire, is not part of an electric circuit, its electrons move in random directions, frequently colliding with other electrons or with ions. Thus, as shown in **Figure 11.11**, although the conductor's electrons move very fast, the electrons do not flow in one direction along the wire.

The chemical reactions that occur inside a cell cause charges to separate. An excess of electrons builds up at one electrode, thus making it negatively charged. The other electrode has a deficit of electrons and hence is positively charged. This charge separation produces an electric field along the wires and components in the circuit to which the cell is connected. The electric field moves through the circuit at almost the speed of light, exerting a force on the electrons and protons in the circuit.

Electrons Flow in One Direction in a Circuit

In a solid, only the free electrons are able to move. The electric field produced by the cell forces the free electrons to move, overall, in one direction, although there are still collisions among the electrons, as shown in **Figure 11.12**. The instant a circuit is completed, the electrons begin to flow, just as when you turn on a fan, it forces molecules in air to move in one direction.

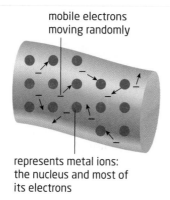

Figure 11.11 If a conductor is not connected to a source of electrical energy, the electrons move in random directions.

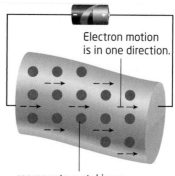

Figure 11.12 The cell produces an excess of electrons at the negative terminal, producing an electric field in the conductor. The electric field causes the electrons to move in one direction through the wire.

Electric Current

electric current the rate of movement of electric charge

Electric current refers to the rate of movement of electric charge. In an electric circuit, the current is due to the flow of electrons. The flow of water in a river is an analogy for the flow of electrons through a conductor. If you were standing on a river bank, you might think about how much water is passing by. It is unlikely that you would think about the flow of water in terms of the number of individual molecules passing by per second. Instead, you might think about a very large amount of water, such as cubic metres of water, passing by per second.

Unit of Charge

The electric charge passing by a point in a circuit is measured in terms of a very large number of electrons. The unit of electric charge is the coulomb. One **coulomb (C)** is the quantity of charge that is equal to the charge of 6.25×10^{18} electrons.

coulomb (C) the quantity of charge that is equal to the charge of 6.25×10^{18} electrons

Activity 11-3

Charged Cereal and Moving Marbles

As soon as you switch on a lamp, the light bulb begins to glow. Thus, the energy that is carried by the electrons in the circuit must be transmitted almost immediately. Does this mean that the electrons in the circuit are moving very quickly?

Safety Precautions

- If you are allergic to animal fur, do not handle this material.

Materials

- ebonite rod
- fur
- cereal
- insulating thread
- scissors
- retort stand with a clamp and rod
- marbles or ball bearings
- tubing (open at both ends)

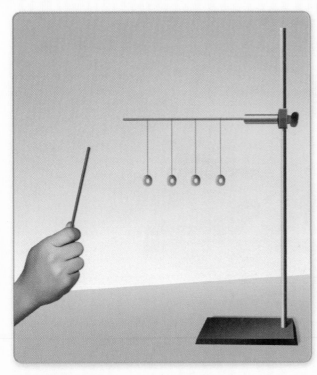

This simple cereal electroscope can be used to represent the very rapid transmission of electric force.

Procedure

1. Put together a retort stand, clamp, and rod so that the rod extends over the base of the stand.

2. Cut four identical lengths of thread. Tie one piece of cereal to each piece of thread, and then tie the other end of the thread to the rod. You should have four pieces of cereal suspended at the same height, as shown.

3. Rub the ebonite rod with fur. Then charge each piece of cereal by contact with the ebonite rod.

4. Rub the ebonite rod with fur again to make sure that it has a good charge. Bring the rod close to the end of the suspended pieces of cereal and observe what happens to the other pieces.

5. Fill a horizontal piece of tubing with marbles (or ball bearings).

6. Add one more marble (or ball bearing) to one end of the tube. Record what happens at the other end of the tube.

Questions

1. Summarize how each analogy represents the flow of electrons through a conductor in a circuit. Explain where the electrons that move through the circuit come from, and where the energy that powers the movement of the electrons comes from.

2. How did each analogy represent the flow of energy through the conductor?

3. What does each analogy predict about the movement of electrons in a circuit, compared with how fast the interactions between electrons carry energy through the circuit?

4. What represented the cell in each analogy?

5. Describe some of the limitations of each analogy.

6. In what ways is each analogy similar to your own ideas about electricity?

Amperes and Ammeters

The unit of electric current is the **ampere (A)** [pronounced AM-pir]. A current of 1.0 A in a circuit means that 1.0 C of charge passes a given point in the circuit every second. The current through a small flashlight bulb that is connected to one AA cell is about 0.3 A. Thus, 1.88×18^{18} electrons pass a given point each second. The units for charge and electric current honour the work of two French scientists, Charles Augustin de Coulomb (1736–1806) and André Marie Ampère (1775–1806). Electric current is measured using an ammeter, such as the one shown in **Figure 11.13**.

Electric Fields and Circuits

The separation of charges between the two electrodes in a cell gives rise to an electric field. This field transmits an electric force through a circuit at almost the speed of light, causing electrons at every point in the circuit to flow almost immediately. Thus, a light bulb in the circuit goes on at once.

Conventional Current

Electrical engineers often describe the direction of electric current as the direction in which a positive charge would move. The positive charge description is called conventional current. Both *conventional current* and *electron flow* can be used to describe electric circuits, as long as each is used consistently. In this text, electrical current is described as electron flow.

Sense of time

In one way, water flowing in a river is a poor analogy for electric current. Imagine water flowing in a river at a slow walking pace, about 1 m/s. This is about 10 000 times faster than the drift of electrons in a circuit that is connected to a cell. Snails move faster than electrons! If electron drift is only about 0.01 cm/s, why does a light bulb glow as soon as you close the switch that is controlling it?

Figure 11.13 An ammeter measures the current at one location in a circuit.

Electrical Resistance

The free electrons in a solid move when an electric field is produced by a cell. The electrons do not get very far, however, before colliding with ions or other electrons in the solid. These collisions interfere with the flow of electrons. **Electrical resistance** is a property of a substance that hinders electric current and converts electrical energy to other forms of energy. In many circuits, a **resistor** is used to decrease the electric current through a component by a specific amount. **Figure 11.14** shows a model for electrical resistance. How could this analogy be modified to represent a material with a lower resistance?

The molecular make-up of a material determines the number of collisions that occur between electrons and atoms or ions. Thus, the resistance to electric current varies for different materials. In general, metals have lower resistance than non-metals, and this is why metal wires are used to make circuit connections. Among metals, only silver has a lower electrical resistance than copper. Copper is used for connections in many circuits, however, because it is less expensive than silver.

electrical resistance the property of a substance that hinders electric current and converts electrical energy to other forms of energy

resistor a device used in an electric circuit to decrease the current through a component by a specific amount

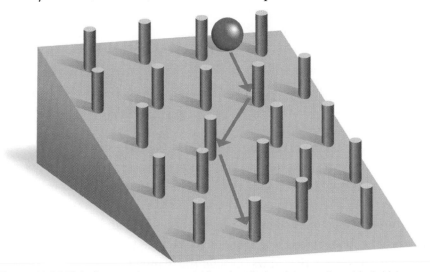

Figure 11.14 This diagram shows a model for electrical resistance. A marble (which represents an electron) collides with pegs (which represent the metal ions in a conductor). Earth's gravity makes the marble move in one general direction, just as the electric field of a cell makes the electrons in a conductor move in one general direction through a circuit.

Loads

load a resistor or any other device that transforms electrical energy into heat, motion, sound, or light

When electrons collide with metal ions, some energy is converted into heat. We make use of the electrical energy that is transformed into light in the filaments of incandescent light bulbs. We make use of the electrical energy that is transformed into heat in the heating elements of toasters, hair dryers, and room heaters. A **load** is a resistor or any other device that transforms electrical energy into heat, motion, sound, or light.

Potential Difference (Voltage)

Go to **scienceontario** to find out more

Cells that provide electrical energy for portable devices come in a wide variety of sizes. You may have noticed that AAA, AA, C, and D cells are all marked "1.5 V." This value is related to the amount of work that is done on each coulomb of charge that moves between the terminals of the cell. Thus, each cell shown in **Figure 11.15** does the same amount of work on a coulomb of charge in a circuit.

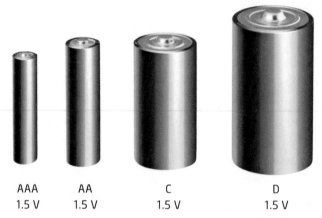

AAA	AA	C	D
1.5 V	1.5 V	1.5 V	1.5 V

Figure 11.15 These cells give electrons in a circuit the same amount of energy. They have different sizes because they contain different quantities of materials. The D cell on the right will last longer than the other cells because it contains the most electrolyte material.

Electric Potential Energy

Potential energy is the energy due to the position of an object in a field that the object interacts with. It is called *potential* energy because it has the potential, to do work. Electric potential energy is the potential energy of charge that interacts with an electric field. The amount of electric charge is analogous to the weight of the box in **Figure 11.16**.

Cells cause chemical reactions that do work on the electric charge, analogous to lifting the box. When a charge flows through a flashlight bulb, it enters the filament with a certain amount of energy and exits with less energy. This is analogous to what happens when a box on a higher shelf tumbles to a lower shelf. The energy of the heat and light that are produced at the filament of a light bulb is equal to the change in the energy of the charge that flows through the filament.

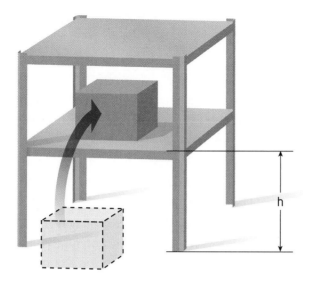

Figure 11.16 The box has gravitational potential energy. If you want to lift the box to put it on a shelf, you have to do some work. The changes in energy when the box moves up or down are analogous to the changes in the energy of a charge moving through a power source and then through a load in a circuit.

Potential Difference and the Volt

The difference between the electric potential energy per unit of charge at two points in a circuit is called **potential difference**.

Potential difference is often referred to as *voltage*. However, what is being described is the *difference* in electric potential energy per unit of charge between two points. There is no such thing as voltage at a single point in a circuit. In the SI system of measurement, all forms of energy are measured in joules (J). As you know, the coulomb (C) is the unit of electric charge. Potential difference is the difference in potential energy per coulomb of charge between two points in a circuit.

$$\text{potential difference} = \frac{\text{difference in potential energy (J)}}{\text{charge (C)}}$$

Thus, the units for potential difference are J/C. This combination of units is called the **volt** (V), named to honour the work of Alessandro Volta (1745–1827). For example, a cell marked "1.5 V" will do 1.5 J of work moving a coulomb of electrons from the negative terminal, through the circuit, to the positive terminal. A voltmeter is used to measure potential difference. **Figure 11.17** shows a *multimeter,* which can be set to act as a voltmeter

An electric charge does not lose energy when it moves along a perfect conductor with no resistance. Connecting wires used in circuits have such low resistance that, for most purposes, they can be considered perfect conductors. The potential difference along the length of the connecting wires you will use in your investigations is so small that it can be neglected. You can check this when you measure the properties of a circuit.

> **potential difference**
> (voltage) the difference between the electric potential energy per unit of charge at two points in a circuit
>
> **volt** the unit for potential difference, equivalent to one joule (J) per coulomb (C)

Figure 11.17 When set as a voltmeter, this multimeter measures the potential difference between two points in a circuit.

Section Summary

- An electric circuit is a closed path along which electrons powered by an energy source can flow.
- In a circuit that is connected to a cell, electrons move very slowly from the negative terminal to the positive terminal in the external circuit.
- The electric field in an operating circuit transmits energy at almost the speed of light.

- Electric current is the rate of flow of electric charge in a circuit, and it is measured in amperes (A) using an ammeter.
- Electrical resistance is a property of a substance that hinders electric current and converts electrical energy to other forms of energy.
- Potential difference (voltage) is the difference between the electric potential energy per unit of charge at two points in a circuit, and it is measured in volts (V) using a voltmeter.

Review Questions

A **1.** Compare and contrast a water tap in your home and an electrical switch.

K/U **2.** Refer back to **Figure 11.15**. Why does a D cell last longer than an AA cell?

K/U **3.** Is the potential difference between the terminals of a cell in a circuit fixed, or does it depend on the components that are connected in the circuit?

K/U **4. a.** What combination of units is equivalent to the ampere?

    b. What combination of units is equivalent to the volt?

C **5.** Using a diagram, explain how the current through two different conductors can be different, even though the electrons in each conductor are moving at the same speed.

T/I **6.** In the circuit shown on the right, the bulbs are identical.

    a. When the switch is closed, how will the energy converted into light and heat by bulb **A** compare with the energy converted into light and heat by bulb **B**?

    b. What will happen to the intensity of each bulb if a wire is connected between points **P** and **Q**?

K/U **7.** What is an electrical load? Give several examples of electrical loads.

K/U **8.** Why is the potential difference between two points in a good conductor so small that it can be neglected?

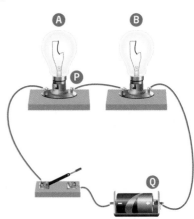

11.3 Measuring the Properties of Simple Circuits

Key Terms
circuit diagram
series circuit
parallel circuit

On a hot afternoon in August 2003, the lights went out across Ontario, as shown in **Figures 11.18A** and **B**. Much of Ontario and parts of the northeastern and midwestern United States went without electricity for up to two days. In the end, 50 million people were affected. Eleven people died as a result of the blackout, and the event cost an estimated $6 billion.

A key cause of the event was a faulty alarm system at a utility company in Ohio that meant operators could not respond quickly to the failure of a power line. Reliable systems for measuring electric circuits both complex and simple are crucial to the safe operation of electrical systems at home and across the continent. **Figure 11.18C** below shows measurements of Ontario's electrical grid.

In this section, you will learn how to read and draw circuit diagrams and how to use a voltmeter and an ammeter.

B during the blackout

A before the blackout

Figure 11.18 The satellite images in **A** and **B** show the light visible from space before and during the vast blackout of August 2003. In **C**, the electrical energy distribution grid for Ontario is monitored in this control room in Mississauga. The operators rely on accurate measurements to keep Ontario supplied with electricity.

C

Circuit Diagrams

circuit diagram a diagram that uses standard symbols to represent the components in an electric circuit and their connections

A practical way to describe a circuit is to draw a circuit diagram. A **circuit diagram** uses standard symbols to represent the components of an electric circuit and their connections. **Figure 11.19** shows the components in a flashlight and the corresponding circuit diagram.

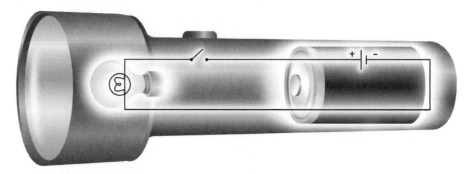

Figure 11.19 The symbol for a cell is two parallel lines of different lengths. The shorter line represents the negative terminal of the cell. The switch is usually shown in the open position so that it is not mistaken for a connecting wire. Note that straight lines are always used to represent the connecting wires.

One Pathway or Multiple Pathways

series circuit a circuit in which there is only one path along which electrons can flow

parallel circuit a circuit in which there is more than one path along which electrons can flow

Circuit diagrams show how the various components of a circuit are connected. In a **series circuit**, there is only one path along which electrons can flow. The specific places in a series circuit where components are connected to the conducting wires are called series connections. **Figure 11.20A** shows a series circuit with two light bulbs. Place your finger on the negative terminal of the cell in the circuit diagram. Trace your finger along the components in the circuit, back to the positive terminal of the cell. As you can see, there is only one way to trace the circuit from the negative terminal to the positive terminal. This is characteristic of all series circuits.

By comparison, in a **parallel circuit**, there is more than one path along which electrons can flow. **Figure 11.20B** shows a parallel circuit with two light bulbs. The specific parts of a parallel circuit where there are more than one pathway are called parallel connections. Most circuits are a combination of series and parallel connections.

Figure 11.20 In **A**, there is only one path along which electrons can flow. This is a series circuit. In **B**, there is more than one path along which electrons can flow. This is a parallel circuit.

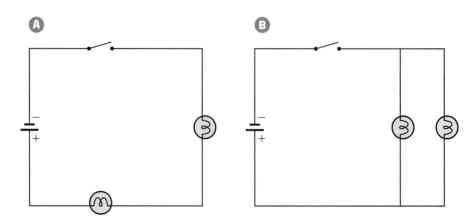

Symbols for Specific Components

Figure 11.21 shows images of the circuit components you will see in this chapter, as well as their symbols.

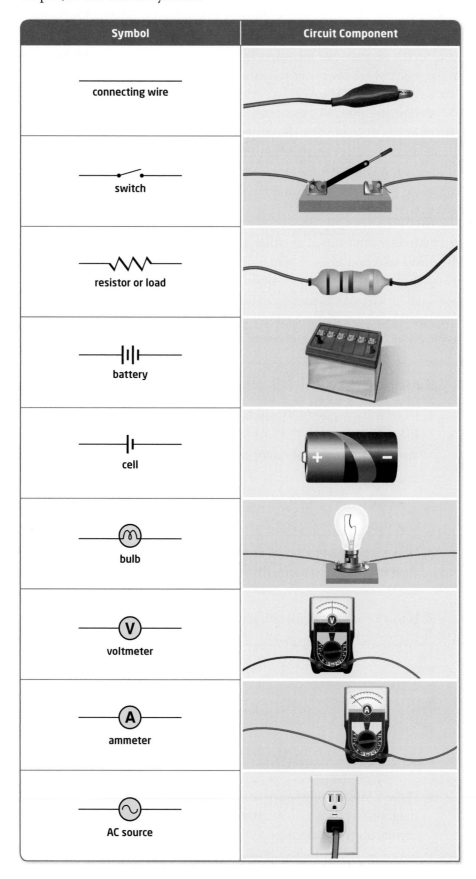

Symbol	Circuit Component
connecting wire	
switch	
resistor or load	
battery	
cell	
bulb	
voltmeter	
ammeter	
AC source	

Figure 11.21 Circuit symbols are used to represent the various components of a circuit. When joined together, the symbols make a circuit diagram. No special symbols for a multimeter or probeware (which can be used to measure voltage, current, and resistance) are shown because, when you use these meters, you must first select the property you need to measure. For example, when a circuit diagram shows the symbol for an ammeter, you need to select the current function on a multimeter.

Measuring Current and Potential Difference

An ammeter measures the current (in amperes, A) at *a particular location* in a circuit. Recall the analogy between electric current and the current of water in a river. If you were standing on a river bank, you could estimate the current, or total flow of water passing by in a certain amount of time. In a circuit, an ammeter measures the flow of electric charge (the current) at the point where the meter is connected in the circuit. Thus, *an ammeter is always connected in series.*

A voltmeter measures the potential difference (in volts, V) between two points in a circuit. The electric potential on one side of a load, such as a bulb or a resistor, is greater than the electric potential on the other side of the load. A voltmeter measures this difference. A voltmeter is *always connected in parallel* to measure the potential difference across the load.

Multimeters

A multimeter can be used as either an ammeter or a voltmeter. When the meter selection is set to read current, the meter must be connected in series. As you might expect, when the meter selection is set to read potential difference, the meter connection must be in parallel with the load. Many different meters are used in schools. In this textbook, instructions are given for ammeters and voltmeters.

Learning Check

1. Draw a symbol to represent each of the following components of a circuit. See **Figure 11.21** on page 457.

    a. a cell (including labels for the positive and negative terminals)

    b. a flashlight bulb

    c. a load

    d. a switch

2. Why must an ammeter be connected in series with a load, rather than in parallel, to correctly measure the current through the load?

3. Is this a parallel circuit or a series circuit? Explain your answer.

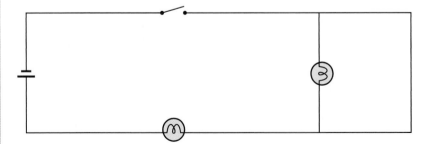

4. Write a brief analogy (two or three sentences) or draw a diagram to compare a road system with series and parallel connections in a circuit.

Activity 11-4

Measuring Current and Potential Difference in a Series Circuit

In this activity, you will build a basic circuit. Then you will measure current using an ammeter. You will also measure the potential difference between various points in the circuit using a voltmeter.

Safety Precautions

- Ask your teacher to check the connections to the ammeter and voltmeter before you close the switch.

Materials

- switch
- 6 connecting wires
- cell
- flashlight bulb
- voltmeter
- ammeter

Procedure

1. Make sure that the switch is in the open position. Use three wires to build the basic circuit on the right. Be sure to connect the switch to the negative pole of the cell. Check with your teacher, and then close the switch briefly to make sure that the flashlight bulb glows. Then open the switch.

2. Use two additional wires to connect a voltmeter across the cell. Make sure that the pole terminals on the meter connect to the same pole terminals on the cell.

3. Insert an ammeter in the circuit to measure the current leaving the cell. To do this, go to the switch and disconnect the wire between the cell and the switch.

4. Connect the loose wire to the negative pole of the ammeter. Use another wire to connect the positive pole of the ammeter to the switch.

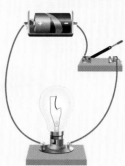

5. After your teacher has checked your circuit connections, close the switch and record the current and potential difference. When you have done this, open the switch.

6. Connect the voltmeter across the switch and measure the potential difference when the switch is closed.

7. Measure and record the current entering the flashlight bulb and the potential difference across the bulb.

Questions

1. How does the voltage of the cell compare with the voltmeter reading across the flashlight bulb? Explain your observation.

2. Explain your reading of the potential difference across the switch when the switch was closed.

3. Explain the relationship between your two ammeter readings.

Electrical Energy and Gravitational Energy

A battery consists of cells that are connected. If you connect the cells in series, the positive terminal of one cell is connected to the negative terminal of another cell. This is what you do when you put two or more cells in a flashlight.

> The potential difference across a battery of cells in series is the sum of the potential differences across each cell.

An Analogy for Potential Difference

As an analogy, think about a box on a table. The weight of the box represents an electric charge. The height of the box above the floor represents the potential difference between the terminals of a cell. Adding a second cell, which increases the potential difference in a circuit, is like stacking a second shelf on the first shelf and moving the box so that it is on top of the second shelf. This analogy is illustrated in **Figure 11.22**.

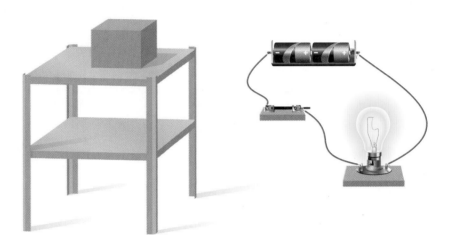

Figure 11.22 When a box is raised to a greater height, its gravitational potential energy is increased. When cells are connected in series, each cell increases the total potential difference across the battery.

Cells, Batteries, and Potential Difference

The potential difference that is generated by a cell is limited to a few volts because of the metals that are used for the electrodes. When a larger potential difference is required to operate a motorized toy or the starter motor on a car, several cells are connected in series to make a battery. As **Figure 11.23A** illustrates, a 9 V battery is made up of six smaller cells, each generating 1.5 V. The battery that is used to start a car is usually a 12 V battery, made up of six 2 V lead-acid cells, as shown in **Figure 11.23B**.

Figure 11.23 A The familiar 9 V battery contains six 1.5 V cells connected together. **B** An automobile battery contains six 2 V cells.

Section Summary

- Circuit diagrams use standard symbols to represent the components of an electric circuit and their connections in the circuit.

- At a series connection, there is only one path along which electrons can flow.

- At a parallel connection, there is more than one path along which electrons can flow.

- An ammeter measures current and is connected in series.

- A voltmeter measures potential difference and is connected in parallel between the terminals of a load.

- Each pole connection on a meter must trace back to the same type of terminal at the electrical source.

- The potential difference across a battery of cells in series is the sum of the potential differences across each cell.

Review Questions

K/U **1.** State the type of connection at each labelled point in the circuit on the right.

K/U **2.** Why is it important to be able to trace the pole connection on a meter back to the same type of pole at the electrical source?

C **3.** Draw the circuit symbol that would represent the 9 V battery shown in **Figure 11.23A**.

A **4.** Predict the potential difference that is generated by a battery with a 1.5 V cell in series with a 2.0 V cell.

C **5.** Draw a circuit diagram for the circuit shown on the lower right.

K/U **6.** Does gravity have an effect on the potential difference of a battery? Explain your answer.

T/I **7. a.** Consider a 6 V battery. How many cells would you expect to find inside the battery?

b. Why should you not connect a 6 V battery into a circuit that requires a D cell?

T/I **8.** In electric circuits, both electrons and energy are conserved.

a. What does it mean to say that something is conserved?

b. A certain battery can supply 6 J of energy to every coulomb of charge moving through a circuit. If the circuit consists of two identical flashlight bulbs in series, what can you predict about the total energy that is consumed by the bulbs?

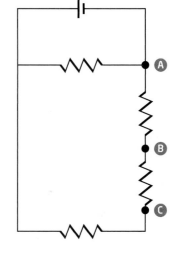

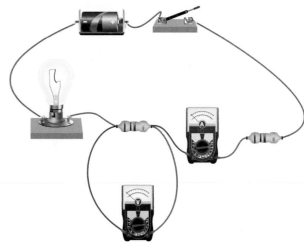

11.4 Measuring Electrical Resistance

The most common component inside most of the devices you use—including a computer, a television, and a radio—is a simple resistor. The filament of an incandescent bulb is also a type of resistor. We use the filament of a bulb for the light it produces, although more energy is transformed into heat than into light. Some energy is transformed into heat by the resistors inside a computer, and this is why a computer is warm when it is being used. The resistors in **Figure 11.24** control current and potential difference in circuits. People who design and check circuits need to know how a resistor affects the potential difference and current in a circuit.

Ohm's Law

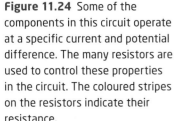

Ohm's law the ratio of potential difference to current is a constant called *resistance*

Georg Ohm, a German physicist, measured the current and potential difference in circuits that contained metal wires. When he changed the potential difference across a wire, he measured a different current through it. Ohm discovered that for most wires, the ratio of potential difference (*V*) to current (*I*) is a constant. The constant is called the resistance (*R*).

$$R = \frac{V}{I}$$

Known as **Ohm's law**, this relationship is often written as $V = IR$.

One consequence of Ohm's law is that the larger the resistance in a particular circuit is, the smaller the current is. Thus, a resistor *resists*, or reduces, the current in a circuit. A resistor is an electrical component with a specific resistance.

Figure 11.24 Some of the components in this circuit operate at a specific current and potential difference. The many resistors are used to control these properties in the circuit. The coloured stripes on the resistors indicate their resistance.

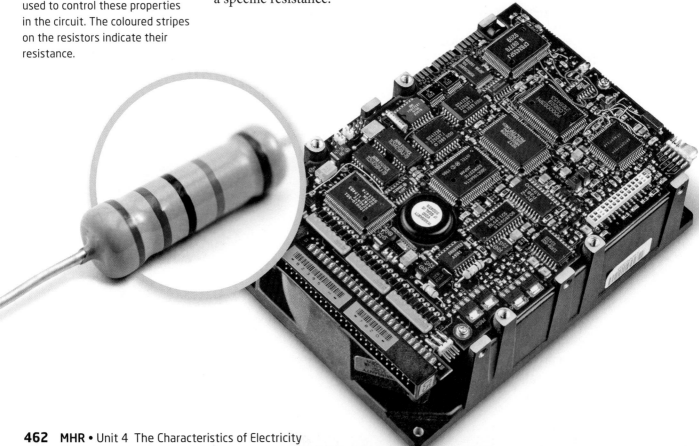

Methods of Changing Potential Difference

When Ohm did his experiments, he added cells in series to change the potential difference between the ends of a wire. You could use the same method as Ohm, or substitute different batteries in the circuit, or connect a variable power supply. Your teacher will give you instructions.

The Units of Resistance

Substituting units into the Ohm's law equation gives the units for resistance:

$$V = IR$$

$$R = \frac{V}{I}$$

$$\text{units:} \quad \frac{\text{volt}}{\text{ampere}} = \frac{\text{V}}{\text{A}} = \Omega$$

Thus, the unit for resistance is volt per ampere (V/A). This combination of units is called the **ohm**, in honour of Ohm's discovery. The symbol for the ohm is the Greek letter omega, Ω. If a potential difference of 1 V across the ends of a load results in a current of 1 A through the load, then the load has a resistance of 1 Ω.

Solving Problems using Ohm's Law

The colour bands on a resistor are a code for the value of the resistance. A technician can determine whether a resistor has failed by using a multimeter or Ohm's law to find its resistance and compare it to the resistance indicated by the colour code.

ohm (Ω) the unit for resistance, equivalent to one volt per ampere (V/A)

Suggested Investigation

Inquiry Investigation 11-D, Testing Ohm's Law, on page 478

Sample Problem: Determining Resistance

Problem

A technician is checking the circuits on a vehicle. The technician measures the current entering a component as 0.47 A. The potential difference across the component is 12 V. What is its resistance?

Solution

Current, $I = 0.47$ A

Potential difference, $V = 12$ V

$$V = IR$$

$$R = \frac{V}{I} = \frac{12\ \text{V}}{0.47\ \text{A}} = 25.53\ \text{V/A} = 26\ \Omega$$

The resistance of the component is 26 Ω.

Check Your Solution

The numerical value of the answer is reasonable. The current is roughly half an ampere. Estimating, 12 V ÷ 0.5 A is 24 Ω, in the range of the answer given. The answer has two significant digits, the same as in each given measurement. The units, V/A, are equivalent to the unit given in the answer, ohm (Ω).

GRASP
Go to **Science Skills Toolkit 9** to learn about an alternative problem solving method.

GRASP

Go to **Science Skills Toolkit 9** to learn about an alternative problem solving method.

Sample Problem: How Many Cells?

Problem

An electric toy has a resistance of 120 Ω and requires a current of 0.050 A to work properly. How many 1.5 V cells does the toy require?

Solution

The toy is an electric load. First, find the potential difference across the toy. Then determine how many cells it requires.

Finding potential difference:

$$R = 120 \ \Omega$$
$$= 120 \ \text{V/A}$$

$$I = 0.050 \ \text{A}$$
$$V = IR$$
$$= 0.050 \ \text{A} \times 120 \ \text{V/A}$$
$$= 6.0 \ \text{V}$$

Finding number of cells:

$$\text{Number of cells} = \frac{6.0 \ \text{V}}{1.5 \ \text{V/cell}}$$
$$= 4 \ \text{cells}$$

The toy requires four 1.5 V cells.

Check Your Solution

The number of cells is reasonable for an electric toy.

Practice Problems

1. In the graph on the left, the potential difference between the ends of a resistor in a circuit is plotted against the current through the resistor. What is the value of the resistance?

2. A television that is plugged into a wall socket has a potential difference of 120 V across its terminals. If the television uses a current of 1.45 A, what is its resistance?

3. A toaster uses a current of 10.4 A when it is plugged into a 110 V outlet. What is the resistance of the heating coils?

4. How will the current passing through a resistor change when the potential difference across the resistor is doubled?

5. The filament of a flashlight bulb has a resistance of 40 Ω. If a 6.0 V battery is used in the circuit, what is the current?

6. A circuit board has a resistance of 12 Ω and requires a current of 0.25 A. What potential difference is required to operate the circuit board?

Potential Difference vs. Current for a Resistor

Factors That Affect the Resistance of Wires

Ohm found that the resistance of different wires of the same length are different, as shown in **Figure 11.25A**. The resistance of wires made from the same metal, with the same diameter, increases in direct proportion to their length. If the only variable is the length of the wire, doubling its length will double its resistance, as shown in **Figure 11.25B**. For wires made from the same metal, with the same length, Ohm found that the resistance decreases as the diameter of the wire increases, as shown in **Figure 11.25C**.

Temperature also affects resistance. Resistance is caused when a current of free electrons collides with the ions and other electrons in a substance. If the temperature increases, these atoms and ions move much more rapidly about their fixed positions. The number of collisions between the free electrons in a current and the atoms and ions in the substance is greater at a higher temperature. Thus, the resistance is greater. This is shown in **Figure 11.25D**.

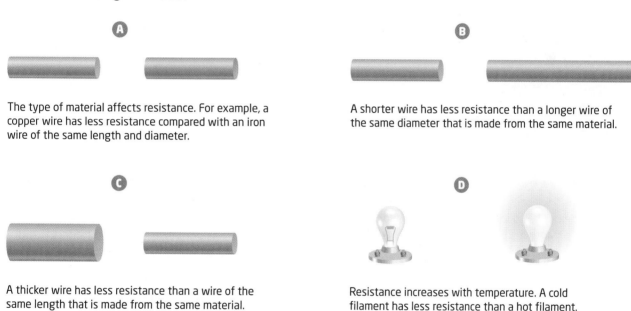

A

The type of material affects resistance. For example, a copper wire has less resistance compared with an iron wire of the same length and diameter.

B

A shorter wire has less resistance than a longer wire of the same diameter that is made from the same material.

C

A thicker wire has less resistance than a wire of the same length that is made from the same material.

D

Resistance increases with temperature. A cold filament has less resistance than a hot filament.

Figure 11.25 Several factors affect the resistance of wires.

Learning Check

1. What is the unit of electrical resistance?

2. State three characteristics of a copper wire that affect its electrical resistance. See **Figure 11.25**.

3. How will the intensity of a flashlight bulb change if you add a resistor in series with the bulb? Explain your answer.

4. The resistance of the incandescent light bulb in a lamp is about 100 times greater than the resistance of the cord on the lamp. Which properties of the bulb account for this difference?

Superconductors

superconductor a material through which electric charge can flow with no resistance

non-ohmic not following Ohm's law

The resistance of a wire increases as its temperature increases. How does its resistance change if the temperature becomes very low? Heike Kamerlingh Onnes, a Dutch physicist, was the first person to liquefy helium. By chance, he discovered that mercury loses all of its electrical resistance at the temperature of liquid helium. Many other metals have the same property. When electric charge can flow through a material with no resistance, the material is called a **superconductor**. A superconducting wire does not transform electrical energy into heat. If wires that were superconducting at room temperature could be made, they would vastly increase the efficiency of supplying electrical energy.

A magnet can be made with a coil of wire that is carrying an electric current. Very powerful magnets are made using superconducting wires, which are cooled to a few degrees above absolute zero by liquid helium. These magnets are used to accelerate particles. When beams of particles smash together at almost the speed of light, scientists can investigate the fundamental nature of matter and the forces within atoms. The collider shown in **Figure 11.26** was built beneath the border between Switzerland and France. It uses nearly 7000 superconducting magnets and 96 tonnes of liquid helium.

Non-ohmic Conductors

Electrical resistance is the ratio of the potential difference between the ends of a load to the current through the load. If this ratio changes as the potential difference varies, the load does not have constant resistance. Thus, it does not obey Ohm's law, so it is called a **non-ohmic** conductor.

The filament of an incandescent bulb is non-ohmic because its resistance increases with temperature. The greater the resistance of the filament is, the more electrical energy is converted into light energy and the brighter the bulb glows. The graph of the potential difference between the connections to an incandescent bulb and the current through the bulb is not a straight line. **Figure 11.27** compares a graph for an ohmic load with a graph for a non-ohmic load, such as an incandescent light bulb.

Go to **scienceontario** to find out more

Figure 11.26 The enormous magnet in the Large Hadron Collider at the European Centre for Nuclear Research (CERN) is the largest superconducting magnet ever built. It uses a current of 21 000 A, but it has a potential difference of only about 9 V.

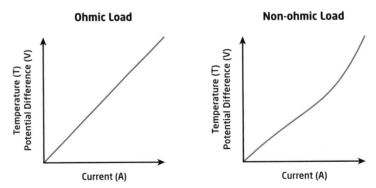

Figure 11.27 A resistor that obeys Ohm's law has constant resistance, as shown in the graph on the left. The current through the filament of a light bulb does not increase as much as would be expected according to Ohm's law, because its resistance increases as temperature increases, as shown in the graph on the right.

Section Summary

- Ohm's law states that, for most conductors, the ratio of potential difference (V) to current (I) is a constant called the resistance (R).

- A resistor is an electrical component with a specific resistance.

- The unit of electrical resistance is the ohm (Ω). One ohm is equivalent to one volt per ampere (V/A).

- Four factors affect the resistance of a wire:

  1. the type of material

  2. the length (A longer wire has greater resistance.)

  3. the diameter (A wire with a larger diameter has lower resistance.)

  4. the temperature (A hotter wire has greater resistance.)

- A superconductor is a material through which electric charge can flow with no resistance.

- A non-ohmic conductor does not obey Ohm's law.

Review Questions

A **1.** The current in an automobile headlight, which is connected to a 12 V battery, is 0.80 A. What is the resistance of the headlight?

K/U **2.** The resistance of a particular circuit board is 5.0 Ω. What potential difference must be supplied to the circuit board if it requires a current of 0.030 A to operate?

K/U **3.** An electric motor has a resistance of 7.41 Ω. What current is there through the motor when it is connected to a 100 V source?

A **4.** If you happen to be looking at the filament of an incandescent light bulb just before it burns out, you might notice that the filament glows brighter just before it burns out. Explain these observations.

C **5.** You have been asked to write part of the user's manual for an electric lawn mower. Explain why the user of an electric lawn mower must not connect several extension cords together when using a lawn mower, and why the extension cord must have wires that are relatively thick.

T/I **6.** When connected in the same circuit, two incandescent light bulbs glow with different intensities. Compare the filaments in the two light bulbs.

A **7.** Why is it very important that the wires used in incandescent light bulbs have a specific constant diameter?

T/I **8.** Refer to **Figure 11.27**. Does a superconducting wire obey Ohm's law? Explain your answer.

11.5 Series and Parallel Circuits

There is electric current through all the bulbs around the mirror shown in **Figure 11.28**, except for the bulb that is not glowing. The bulb that is not glowing has probably "burned out," but it could be loose. In either case, the result is an open circuit. Since the other bulbs are on, the bulb that is not glowing must be in parallel with them. Otherwise, the circuit through those bulbs would be broken and charges would not be able to flow through them. The bulbs are turned on or off by a single switch. Thus, the switch must be in series with the circuit for the bulbs. The source of electricity, the switch, and the bulbs are an example of a circuit that combines series and parallel connections.

Loads in Series

The potential difference (in volts) between the terminals of a cell is the energy required (in joules) to move one coulomb of charge around the circuit. Loads, such as bulbs, transform electrical energy into other forms of energy. The total energy that is transformed by the current through the entire circuit must equal the work that is done by the cell. The current is the same at all points in a series circuit, and the potential difference between the terminals of a cell must equal the sum of the potential differences between the connections to all the loads in series with the cell (**Figure 11.29**).

$$I_T = I_1 = I_2 = I_3 \qquad V_T = V_1 + V_2 + V_3 \qquad R_T = R_1 + R_2 + R_3$$

Adding loads in series is similar to increasing the length of a wire. If length is the only difference between two wires, the longer wire has greater resistance. Thus, you can use Ohm's law to predict that the resistance will increase as more loads are added to a series circuit.

Figure 11.28 Circuits that contain both series and parallel connections are found in almost every application that uses electric current.

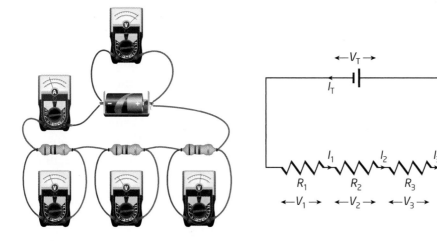

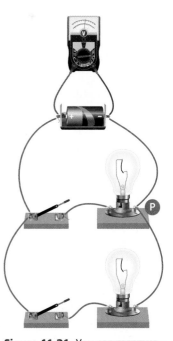

Figure 11.29 When loads are connected in series, the sum of the individual resistances is equal to the total resistance. Note that ammeters connected at I_1, I_2, and I_3 would all show the same reading as the ammeter at I_T.

Decreased Current, Decreased Glow

Adding more bulbs in series to a circuit increases the total resistance of the circuit. This has an effect on the intensity of light bulbs in the circuit, as is shown in **Figure 11.30**.

Suggested Investigation

Inquiry Investigation 11-B, Loads in Series, on page 474

Figure 11.30 As more bulbs in series are added to this circuit, each bulb will glow with less intensity. All the bulbs in each arrangement will glow with the same intensity as each other *if they are identical.*

Loads in Parallel

At a parallel connection, there is more than one path along which electrons can flow. If you drink a liquid through two straws, more liquid will reach your mouth in the same amount of time than if you drank through one straw. The analogy between two straws in a drink and a parallel connection in a circuit suggests that the total resistance of two loads connected in parallel is less than the resistance of either load.

Figure 11.31 shows a series-parallel circuit that can be used to operate two bulbs independently. If only one switch is closed, the circuit operates as a simple series circuit. The bulb in series with the closed switch will glow, while the bulb in series with the open switch will not glow. Now imagine that both switches are closed, and place a finger on the negative terminal of the cell. Move your finger along the connecting wire. At the point marked P, you can choose which path you trace with your finger. This is characteristic of a parallel connection. The current entering a parallel connection divides. Thus, the sum of the currents through each path of a parallel connection equals the current entering the connection.

Figure 11.31 You can measure the potential difference and current in this circuit to find out the characteristics of a parallel connection.

Measuring Potential Difference

Now think about how you would measure the current and potential difference in the circuit in **Figure 11.31**. Recall that a voltmeter must be connected in parallel between the ends of a load. When you connect a voltmeter, the basic circuit does not change. You might connect the voltmeter between the terminals of the cell or between the connections to a bulb. Each bulb is connected to the cell with a switch and connecting wires. There is negligible potential difference across these components when the switch is closed, because their resistance is negligible. Thus, allowing for experimental error, the voltmeter will measure the same potential difference across each bulb and between the terminals of the cell.

Measuring Current

Recall that an ammeter must be connected in series at a point in a circuit. Connecting an ammeter always involves disconnecting the basic circuit at the point where you want to measure the current. Imagine that you have a pair of scissors and you could cut the basic circuit to insert the ammeter. To measure the current through a bulb, imagine making a cut in the circuit at different points, as shown in **Figure 11.32**. The points where you decide to cut the circuit do not matter, because the current in a series connection is the same at any point. To "cut" the circuit in **Figure 11.32**, trace along a wire to a connection, disconnect the circuit at the connection, and insert the ammeter.

The resistance of the ammeter is very small, so adding it to the circuit does not affect the current. The easiest connection for an ammeter is between the switch and the bulb. You could make the ammeter connection, however, at point P. At this point, two connecting wires would be attached to the negative terminal of the ammeter. As in **Figure 11.33**, a wire from the positive terminal on the ammeter to the bulb would complete the series connection. **Figure 11.33** shows the relationships among the current, potential difference, and resistance of loads that are connected in parallel.

$$I_T = I_1 + I_2 + I_3 \qquad\qquad V_T = V_1 = V_2 = V_3$$

Suggested Investigation

Inquiry Investigation 11-C, Loads in Parallel, on page 476

Study Toolkit

Identifying Cause and Effect Drawing a cause-and-effect map can help you understand how inserting an additional parallel connection into a circuit affects the current and resistance in each parallel path.

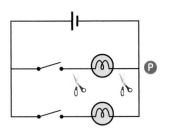

Figure 11.32 An ammeter can be inserted at different points in this circuit.

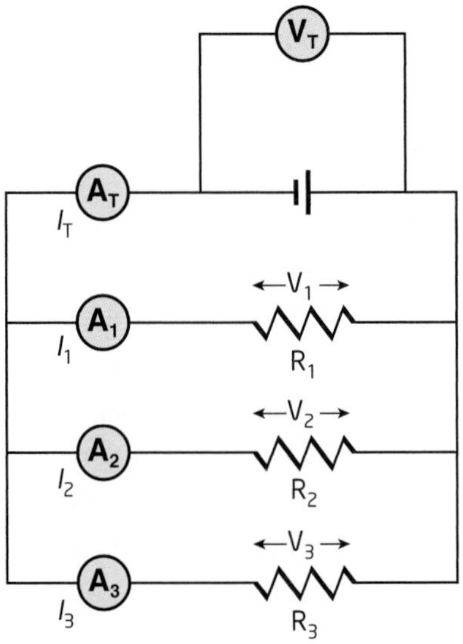

Figure 11.33 This diagram shows the relationships among the current, potential difference, and resistance in a circuit that contains loads in parallel.

Section Summary

- The current is the same at any point in a series connection: $I_T = I_1 = I_2 = I_3$.
- The potential difference across loads in series is the sum of the potential differences across all the loads: $V_T = V_1 + V_2 + V_3$.
- The resistance of loads that are connected in series is equal to the sum of the resistances of all the loads: $R_T = R_1 + R_2 + R_3$.

- The potential difference is the same between the terminals of any load in a parallel connection: $V_T = V_1 = V_2 = V_3$.
- The current entering loads that are connected in parallel is equal to the sum of the currents entering all the loads: $I_T = I_1 + I_2 + I_3$.
- The resistance of loads that are connected in parallel is less than the resistance of the smallest load: $R_T < R_1$; $R_T < R_2$; $R_T < R_3$.

Review Questions

K/U **1.** Two loads are connected in series. Must the potential differences between the connections on the loads be the same? Must the current through each load be the same? Explain.

K/U **2.** Two loads are connected in parallel. Must the potential differences between the connections on the loads be the same? Must the current through each load be the same? Why?

C **3.** Draw the diagram for the circuit shown in **Figure 11.30**.

C **4.** Draw a circuit diagram that contains three cells connected in series to a flashlight bulb. If each cell is 1.5 V, what is the potential difference across the bulb?

K/U **5.** How does the current leaving the cell in a parallel circuit compare with the current in a series circuit, if both circuits have the same type of cell and the same number of identical flashlight bulbs?

T/I **6.** Will each of two bulbs connected in parallel be as bright as a single bulb connected to a cell? Why? In this question, assume that all bulbs are identical and both cells are identical.

A **7.** A set of lights has a bulb that can be inserted near the plug to make all the lights flash on and off. If one of the regular bulbs burns out, the other bulbs still operate. Explain why.

T/I **8.** In the circuit diagram on the right, the flashlight bulbs are identical. Describe what you would expect to observe in each of the following situations.

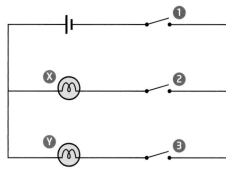

a. switch 1 closed, switches 2 and 3 open

b. switches 1 and 2 closed, switch 3 open

c. switches 1 and 3 closed, switch 2 open

d. all switches closed

Inquiry Investigation 11-A

Safety Precautions

- The electrolyte is a caustic liquid. You must wear safety goggles during this activity to protect your eyes. Wash any spills of electrolyte on your skin or clothing by using plenty of cold water.

- Wear gloves when using steel wool to clean the metal strips.

Materials

- variety of metal strips (for example, aluminum, copper, iron, zinc)
- steel wool
- small beaker (100 mL)
- electrolyte: vinegar or dilute sulfuric acid (about 40 mL)
- 2 large paper clips
- voltmeter or multimeter (if available, probeware may be used to measure voltages)
- connecting leads
- light-emitting diode (optional)
- paper towel

Science Skills

Go to **Science Skills Toolkit 10** to learn about using an ammeter and voltmeter.

Constructing and Comparing Voltaic Cells

In this investigation, you and your classmates will use a variety of metal strips to make different voltaic cells. You will make one or more cells (as directed by your teacher), and then combine the results to compare the potential difference produced by different cells.

Question

Which combination of metal electrodes forms a cell with the greatest voltage?

Prediction

The following metals are listed in order of decreasing ability of their atoms to hold on to electrons: aluminum, zinc, iron, nickel, copper. Predict which pair of metals will make a voltaic cell that generates the greatest voltage.

Procedure

1. In your notebook, prepare a table like the one shown below to record your results. The table will depend on the metals available for your class to use for electrodes, so you may need to change the entries shown.

Cell Voltage (V)

Metals	Aluminum	Zinc	Iron	Copper
Zinc				
Iron				
Copper				

2. Your teacher will assign one or more pairs of metal strips for you to use as electrodes. Wear gloves and clean each metal strip with a piece of steel wool to make the surface shiny.

3. Pour about 40 mL of the electrolyte solution into the beaker. Place a pair of metal strips into the beaker that contains the electrolyte. Use large paper clips to attach the metal strips to the beaker as shown. Record any observation that indicates a chemical reaction between the electrolyte and either of the electrodes.

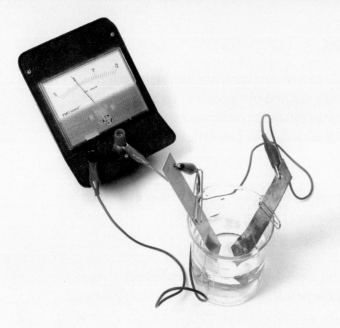

4. Connect leads from the meter (or probeware) to the electrodes. Examine the meter carefully. If it appears that the needle is not moving, or is tending to move to a value less than zero, reverse the connections. The voltage produced by a cell may be less than 1.0 volt. Record the cell voltage in your table.

5. Remove the electrodes from the electrolyte solution. Rinse the electrodes in running water, and then dry them using a paper towel.

6. Repeat steps 2–5 for each pair of metal electrodes assigned for you to test.

7. Dispose of the electrolyte solution as directed by your teacher, and return the other materials.

8. Share your data with other groups to fill in the table with voltage data for every possible combination of electrodes.

Analyze and Interpret

1. Identify the pair of electrodes that generated the greatest voltage. Did this pair match your prediction?

2. In step 4, what did you observe to indicate that a chemical reaction took place?

Conclude and Communicate

3. If you were planning to manufacture a voltaic cell, which factors would you consider when choosing the electrodes?

Extend Your Inquiry and Research Skills

4. **Inquiry** The figure below shows a battery consisting of two cells, each made using copper and zinc electrodes. Note that the zinc electrode in one cell is connected to the copper electrode in the next cell. If necessary, more cells can be connected in the same way. Conduct an experiment to find out how many cells are required to make a light-emitting diode (LED) glow. The light will only glow with the positive lead on the LED connected to the copper electrode as shown.

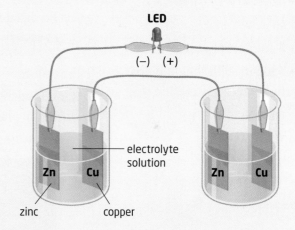

5. **Research** A thermocouple is another device that relies on two different metals to produce a potential difference. Research how thermocouples work, and list applications where these devices are used.

Inquiry Investigation 11-B

Skill Check

Initiating and Planning

✓ **Performing and Recording**

✓ **Analyzing and Interpreting**

✓ **Communicating**

Safety Precautions

- If a bulb is glowing very brightly, open the switch to prevent the bulb from burning out, and inform your teacher.

Materials

- battery (6 V)
- battery (9 V) (optional)
- switch
- 8 connecting leads
- 3 identical flashlight bulbs in holders
- ammeter
- voltmeter

Math Skills

Go to **Math Skills Toolkit 2** to learn about significant digits and rounding.

Loads in Series

In this activity, you will observe and compare the brightness of identical bulbs as they are connected together in series. You will take measurements of potential difference and current, and use your data to make general statements about the properties of a series circuit.

Question

How are the current, potential difference, and resistance of a circuit affected as more loads (bulbs) are connected in series?

Predictions

a. Predict a relationship between the potential difference across a cell or battery and the potential difference across each load in a series circuit.

b. Predict a relationship between the current leaving the cell or battery and the current through each load in a series circuit.

c. Predict a relationship between total resistance and the resistance of each load in a series circuit.

Procedure

If it is available, use probeware to measure the potential difference and current in place of a voltmeter and ammeter.

1. Copy the table below into your notebook and give it a title.

Number of Bulbs	Comparative Brightness	Current (A)	Potential Difference (V)			
			Across the Cell	Across Each Bulb		
				1	2	3
2						
3						

2. Connect the circuit diagram shown below, using a 6 V battery. Make sure the switch is in the open position.

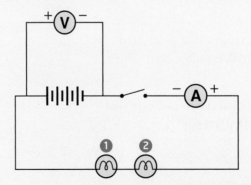

3. Close the switch long enough to compare the brightness of the bulbs and take readings on the ammeter and voltmeter. Record your observations of the current in the circuit and the potential difference across the battery.

4. With the switch open, disconnect the voltmeter and connect it across bulb 1. Close the switch and record the potential difference across the bulb. Repeat this procedure to measure and record the potential difference across bulb 2.

5. Open the switch. Add a third bulb in series with the others, between bulb 2 and the ammeter.

6. Reconnect the voltmeter across the battery, then repeat step 3.

7. Measure and record the potential difference across each bulb.

8. Use the ammeter to measure and record the current between bulbs 2 and 3.

Analyze and Interpret

1. As more bulbs are connected in series in a circuit, what happens to
- **a.** the brightness with which each glows?
- **b.** the current leaving the source?
- **c.** the potential difference across the source?
- **d.** the potential difference across each load?

2. In a series circuit, how does the current between two loads compare with the current from the source?

3. Calculate the total resistance in the circuit, using the ammeter and voltmeter readings from step 6.

4. Calculate the resistance of each bulb, using the potential difference measurements from step 7 and the current through each bulb that you measured in step 8.

5. Evaluate your predictions. Do your data support or refute your predictions? Explain.

Conclude and Communicate

6. Summarize the relationship between the current leaving the source and the current through each load in a series circuit.

7. Write a word equation for the relationship between the potential difference across the source and the potential difference across each load in a series circuit that has three loads.

8. Write a word equation for the relationship between the total resistance and the resistance of each load in a series circuit that has three loads.

Extend Your Inquiry and Research Skills

9. Inquiry Predict the effect of replacing the 6 V battery with a 9 V battery on the
- **a.** brightness of the bulbs
- **b.** potential difference across each bulb
- **c.** current through each bulb

If time permits, perform the experiment using three bulbs in series.

10. Research A dimmer switch, like an ordinary on-off switch, is in series with the light it controls. Older dimmer switches use a variable resistance to control the light level. Use the Internet or library resources to find out how they work, and why this type of switch wastes energy. Write a summary of your findings.

Skill Check

Initiating and Planning

✓ Performing and Recording

✓ Analyzing and Interpreting

✓ Communicating

Safety Precautions

• If a bulb is glowing very brightly, open the switch to prevent the bulb from burning out.

Materials

• 1.5 V cell
• switch
• 10 connecting leads
• 3 identical flashlight bulbs in holders
• voltmeter
• ammeter

Science Skills

Go to **Science Skills Toolkit 4** to learn about estimating and measuring.

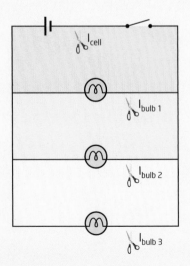

Loads in Parallel

In this activity, you will take measurements of potential difference and current, and use your data to make general statements about the properties of a parallel circuit.

Question

How are the current, potential difference, and resistance of a circuit affected as more loads (bulbs) are connected in parallel?

Predictions

a. Predict a relationship between the potential difference across a source and the potential difference across each load in a parallel circuit.

b. Predict a relationship between the current leaving a source and the current through each load in a parallel circuit.

c. Complete the following sentence: The total resistance of a circuit containing loads connected in parallel should be (greater/smaller) _____ than the resistance of any load in the circuit.

Procedure

Note: If available, use probeware to measure the potential difference and current in place of a voltmeter and ammeter.

1. Copy the table below into your notebook and give it a title.

Measurements of Potential Difference and Current			
Potential Difference (V)		**Current (A)**	
Across Cell	Across Each Bulb	Leaving Cell	Through Each Bulb
	#1		#1
	#2		#2
	#3		#3

2. Connect the circuit shown on the left in stages, as indicated by the colour scheme. Make sure the switch is in the open position.

3. Close the switch and compare the brightness of the bulbs. Record your observation.

4. Open the switch. Connect a voltmeter between the terminals of the cell. Imagine cutting the circuit at the location marked I_{cell}, and insert an ammeter there.

5. Check the terminal connections for both meters. Close the switch. Record the potential difference across the cell, and the current leaving the cell.

6. Open the switch and disconnect both meters. Reconnect the basic circuit.

7. Measure the potential difference between the connections for each bulb, and the current entering each bulb. If you are unsure of how to do this, refer to the circuit diagram and look over steps 4 to 6 and follow similar procedures for each bulb.

Analyze and Interpret

1. When loads (in this case, flashlight bulbs) are connected in parallel to a cell, how does the potential difference across each load compare with the potential difference across the cell?

2. In a parallel circuit, how does the current through each path compare with the current entering the parallel connection?

3. Calculate the resistance of each bulb. Show your calculations.

4. Evaluate your predictions. Do your data support or refute your predictions? Explain.

Conclude and Communicate

5. Summarize the relationship between the current leaving the source and the current through each load in a parallel circuit that has three loads.

6. Write a word equation for the relationship between the potential difference across the source, and the potential difference across each load, in a parallel circuit that has three loads.

Extend Your Inquiry and Research Skills

7. **Inquiry** Determine a way to use your data to find the resistance of the circuit as a whole.

8. **Research** Conduct research to find a relationship between the resistance of the circuit and the resistance of each load connected in parallel. Check your data to see if they show the same relationship, and show your work.

Inquiry Investigation 11-D

Skill Check

✓ Initiating and Planning

✓ Performing and Recording

✓ Analyzing and Interpreting

✓ Communicating

Testing Ohm's Law

In this investigation, you will measure the potential difference across a resistor in a circuit and the current through the resistor. By changing the potential difference, you will learn about the relationships among current, potential difference, and resistance.

Safety Precautions

- Before taking the first measurement, ask your teacher to check your circuit.
- As you do this activity, bring a finger close to the resistor, without touching it. If the resistor is hot, open the switch and tell your teacher.

Materials

- resistor
- ammeter
- voltmeter
- cells, batteries, or a variable power supply
- 6 connecting leads

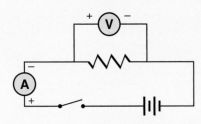

Question

If you change the potential difference in a circuit, how does it affect the current and resistance?

Procedure

1. Design a table to record the potential difference between the ends of the resistor and the current through it. Include the units.

2. Record the colour bands on the resistor in order. The last colour you record will probably be gold or silver.

3. Connect a basic circuit as shown in the diagram.

4. Make sure the range selector switch on both the ammeter and voltmeter are set to the highest values.

5. Close the switch and dial the range selector on the ammeter to smaller values to take a reading. Record the current through the resistor. Repeat this procedure for the voltmeter, and record the potential difference between the ends of the resistor.

6. Open the switch and select the highest range on both meters. Change the potential difference of the source of electricity.

7. Repeat steps 5 and 6 until you have at least four sets of data.

Analyze and Interpret

1. Explain the relationship between the slope of your graph and the resistance of the resistor.

Conclude and Communicate

2. How does changing the potential difference in a circuit affect the current and resistance?

Extend Your Inquiry and Research Skills

3. **Inquiry** Compare and contrast this experiment with the experiments that Ohm performed.

4. **Research** Conduct research to learn about non-ohmic resistors. Write a brief paragraph explaining their applications.

11.1 Cells and Batteries

Key Concepts

- A cell generates an electric current through chemical reactions that involve two electrodes and an electrolyte.

- Cells are classified as dry or wet, and as primary or secondary.

- A battery is a connection of two or more cells.

11.2 Electric Circuits: Analogies and Characteristics

Key Concepts

- An electric circuit is a closed path along which electrons that are powered by an energy source can flow.

- Electrical resistance is a property of a substance that hinders electric current and converts electrical energy to other forms of energy.

- An electric current is the flow of electric charge in a circuit.

- Potential difference is the difference between the electric potential energy per unit of charge at two points in a circuit.

11.3 Measuring the Properties of Simple Circuits

Key Concepts

- Circuit diagrams represent the components and connections in an electric circuit.

- Each pole connection on a meter must trace back to a terminal at the electrical source that has the same polarity.

- At a parallel connection, there is more than one path along which electrons can flow.

- At a series connection, electrons can flow along only one path. At a parallel connection, electrons can flow along more than one path.

11.4 Measuring Electrical Resistance

Key Concepts

- Four factors affect the resistance of a wire: the type of material; the length (a longer wire has greater resistance); the diameter (a wire with a larger diameter has lower resistance); and the temperature (a hotter wire has greater resistance.)

- A resistor is an electrical component with a specific resistance.

- Ohm's law states that, for most conductors, the ratio of potential difference (V) to current (I) is a constant called the resistance (R).

- A non-ohmic conductor does not obey Ohm's law.

11.5 Series and Parallel Circuits

Key Concepts

- In a series connection, the current is the same at any point. The total resistance is the sum of the resistances of all the loads.

- The potential difference across loads in series is the sum of the potential differences across all the loads.

- The current entering a parallel connection of loads is the sum of the currents through all the loads. The total resistance is less than the smallest resistance of any load.

- The potential difference is the same between the terminals of any load in a parallel connection.

Make Your Own Summary

Summarize the key concepts of this chapter using a graphic organizer. The Chapter Summary on the previous page will help you identify the key concepts. Refer to Study Toolkit 4 on pages 566-567 to help you decide which graphic organizer to use.

Reviewing Key Terms

1. A(n) ░░░░░░░ cell consists of two ░░░░░░░ and a(n) ░░░░░░░ . (11.1)

2. The lithium ion cell in a camera is classified as a dry cell and a(n) ░░░░░░░ . (11.1)

3. If there is no current in a circuit that is attached to a source of electricity, it is a(n) ░░░░░░░ . (11.2)

4. The ░░░░░░░ is a unit that is equivalent to a coulomb per second. (11.2)

5. Any device that transforms electrical energy into heat or other forms of energy is called a(n) ░░░░░░░ . (11.2)

6. In a(n) ░░░░░░░ , the current divides among different pathways. (11.3)

7. When electric charge flows through a material with no resistance, the material is a(n) ░░░░░░░ . (11.4)

8. The ratio of potential difference to current is called ░░░░░░░ . (11.4)

Knowledge and Understanding K/U

9. Compare and contrast a wet cell and a dry cell.

10. Compare and contrast a cell and a battery.

11. Explain how a fuel cell differs from other types of cells.

12. Which one of these two wires has the greater resistance: a wire that is long and thin, and made of silver; or a wire that is short and thick, and made of copper? Give reasons for your choice.

13. Explain how a circuit with only series connections differs from a circuit with a parallel connection.

14. Describe two changes you could make to a circuit that would increase the current.

15. State four properties of a wire that affect the resistance of the wire. Describe how a change in each property will change the resistance of the wire.

16. If you connect additional resistors in parallel in the same circuit, will the resistance of the circuit be larger or smaller? Explain your answer.

Thinking and Investigation

17. Examine the graphs below.

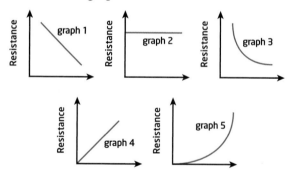

a. When the horizontal axis represents the length of wire, which graph best shows the relationship between resistance and length? State your reasoning.

b. When the horizontal axis represents the current, which graph represents a conductor that obeys Ohm's law? Explain your answer.

18. Write Ohm's law in a form that can be used to calculate

a potential difference

b resistance

c current

19. Ayisha was investigating the electric circuit in a flashlight. She wanted to find out the relationships among the number of cells, the potential difference across the bulb, and the current in the circuit. Her data are recorded in the table below.

Measurements in a Flashlight Circuit

Number of Cells	Potential Difference (V)	Current (A)
1	1.52	0.10
2	3.01	0.15
3	4.47	0.18
4	5.99	0.20

a. Plot the data, with potential difference on the vertical axis and current on the horizontal axis. Give your graph a title.

b. Draw the line of best fit for the data.

c. At first, Ayisha was not sure that the bulb was working because she could not see it glowing with one cell in the circuit. With four cells, however, the bulb glowed brightly. Explain these observations.

d. Explain the shape of your graph.

20. In the circuit diagram below, which bulb(s) will be off if the switch is in the open position? State your reasoning.

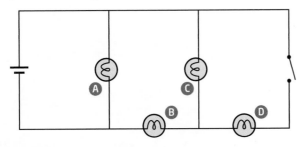

21. Two different flashlight bulbs, labeled A and B, with filaments of the same material, are connected in series to a 6 V battery. The filament in bulb A is longer than the filament in bulb B.

a. Which bulb glows brighter?

b. Which bulb has the greater current through it?

c. Which bulb has the greater potential difference between its terminals?

d. Which bulb has the greater resistance?

Communication C

22. 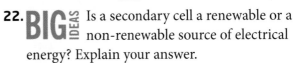 Is a secondary cell a renewable or a non-renewable source of electrical energy? Explain your answer.

23. **BIG IDEAS** Write an essay in which you predict the social, economic, and environmental implications of using electrical energy to power vehicles rather than gasoline or diesel.

24. **BIG IDEAS** Relatively few applications make use of static electricity, while many applications use current electricity. Describe the properties of static and current electricity that account for this difference.

25. A working knowledge of electronics and computers is required in a number of trades, such as automotive service technician. Talk to a technician with these skills and summarize what work they do, the training they received, and their apprenticeship program.

Application A

26. Bulbs that flash on and off are often used in advertising.

a. Draw a diagram of a circuit used for this purpose.

b. What is the effect on the brightness of the other bulbs in a circuit when a flashing bulb is connected in series?

c. What is the effect on the brightness of the other bulbs when a flashing bulb is connected in parallel?

27. A fluorescent light tube contains a gas at low pressure, usually mercury vapour. Research the purpose of a device called a ballast, which is in series with the fluorescent tube and increases the resistance of the circuit.

28. A multimeter can be used to measure the resistance of a load in one step. Outline how this is possible.

Chapter 12 Generating and Using Electricity

What You Will Learn

In this chapter, you will learn how to...

- **compare** direct current and alternating current, and **describe** how alternating current can be used safely
- **explain** why Ontario has different types of generating plants, and **assess** methods of energy production
- **produce** an action plan to reduce your consumption of electricity and its environmental impact

Why It Matters

Changing the ways you use electricity can help to reduce the amount of electricity that generating plants must produce, their impact on the environment, and your energy costs.

Skills You Will Use

In this chapter, you will learn how to...

- **demonstrate** an understanding of electrical safety
- **gather** data on electrical energy consumption, and use spreadsheet software to record the data
- **analyze** data and **interpret** graphs related to the generation and use of electrical energy

The giant "solar wall" shown here was created for the 2008 Olympic village in Beijing, China. The solar energy stored during the day produces enough electricity to power the wall's image display all night long. Today, most of the electricity we use comes from non-renewable, unsustainable sources. But scientists and engineers are finding ways to ensure that energy sources like solar energy can help us produce renewable and sustainable electricity in the future.

Activity 12-1

Generating an Electric Current

In almost all cases, the electricity that you use at home probably began with a spinning generator. In this activity, you will demonstrate the principle that enables generating plants to supply electricity to your home. Do you think a magnet can generate an electric current? How?

Materials

- wire coil
- 2 connecting wires
- ammeter (centre zero)
- bar magnet

Procedure

1. Connect the coil of wire to the ammeter, as shown here.

2. Rapidly move one pole of the bar magnet into the coil of wire. Record the direction in which the ammeter needle moves.

3. Rapidly pull the bar magnet out of the coil of wire. Record the direction in which the ammeter needle moves.

4. Repeatedly move the magnet into and out of the coil of wire. Observe and record the movement of the ammeter needle.

5. With the magnet stationary and inside the coil, move the coil of wire back and forth. Observe and record the movement of the ammeter needle.

Questions

1. Compare the movement of the ammeter needle when the magnet was moved into the coil with the movement of the needle when the magnet was pulled out of the coil.

2. Is there a current in the circuit when the magnet and the coil are stationary, relative to each other? Explain your reasoning.

3. Based on the movement of the ammeter needle, what do you think was happening to electrons in the circuit when the magnet was moved into and out of the coil of wire?

4. Compare the effect on the ammeter needle when you moved the magnet in step 4 with the effect when you moved the coil of wire in step 5.

Study Toolkit

These strategies will help you use this textbook to develop your understanding of science concepts and skills. To find out more about these and other strategies, refer to the Study Toolkit Overview, which begins on page 561.

◀ ▶ + · Q▾ Organizing Your Learning

Using Graphic Organizers

When studying for a test, organize information in a way that makes sense to *you*. Different graphic organizers can be used for different purposes, as shown below.

Purpose	Possible Graphic Organizers	Pages Where Sample Is Shown
To organize a main idea and supporting details	Web	Page 566
To show cause and effect, the steps in a process, or a sequence	Cause-and-effect map Flowchart	Page 567
To organize information about a word or an idea	Web Word map	Page 566 At right
To compare and contrast	Venn diagram	Page 567
To analyze a series of numbers or results	Graph Table	Page 48 Page 440
To summarize	Chart	Page 136

Use the Strategy

1. Identify the main idea and two supporting details in the first paragraph on page 485.

2. Organize this information using a **web**.

3. Organize the same information using a **chart**.

4. Which graphic organizer better helps you understand and remember the information better? Why?

◀ ▶ + · Q▾ Word Study

Creating a Word Map

A **word map** like this one can help you understand a new word or concept.

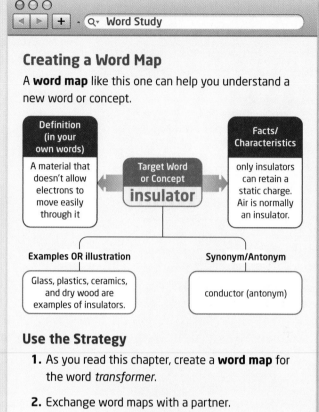

Use the Strategy

1. As you read this chapter, create a **word map** for the word *transformer*.

2. Exchange word maps with a partner.

3. Add any new information to your map that helps you understand the word or concept better.

◀ ▶ + · Q▾ Reading Effectively

Making Inferences

Making inferences about what is written means figuring out some things that a writer did not state directly. It involves connecting your prior knowledge with information from the text and visuals. As you read, ask yourself questions to help you identify any information that may be missing. For example, read page 485. Why did engineers build the generating station under the city? To answer that question, you could make these inferences:

- It was probably easier to access a water source under the city.

- The water would not have to be pumped above ground before being converted to electrical power.

Use the Strategy

Read page 485. Write three questions about information that may be missing and then make three inferences.

12.1 Electricity at Home

Key Terms
direct current (DC)
alternating current (AC)
transformer
circuit breaker
fuse

If you get up in the middle of the night, you expect to see the glow of an alarm clock. You also expect to see street lights or lights from other buildings outside. To supply electricity day and night, the generators at the Adam Beck hydroelectric plant in Niagara Falls run all the time. When construction of the Adam Beck plant began in 1917, it was the largest construction project ever undertaken in North America. Over the next four years, water was diverted from the Niagara River, a canal was constructed, and two very large generators were built. As the demand for electricity grew, more generators were added. Then, in 1954, a second generating station, built under the city of Niagara Falls, was opened.

In 2006, the world's largest hard-rock-boring machine began boring a huge tunnel under the city, as shown in **Figure 12.1**. Grade 6 science students from Port Weller Public School in St. Catharines named the rock-boring machine that is being used "Big Becky." This name is a clever play on the name of the generating station. When completed, the tunnel will supply water to increase hydroelectric generating capacity.

Figure 12.1 These photographs show the new tunnel project and the hydroelectric plants at Niagara Falls. A huge tunnel, which is being bored through rock under the city of Niagara Falls, will increase the capacity of the Sir Adam Beck generating station to generate hydroelectric energy.

Generating and Distributing Electricity

To understand how electrical energy is generated and how it reaches your home, you need to understand the properties of two different kinds of electric current.

Direct Current and Alternating Current

The current from a cell is called **direct current (DC)**. As you learned in Chapter 11, in DC, charged particles in a circuit travel in only one direction. In a circuit containing a cell, electrons move from the negative terminal to the positive terminal.

Moving a magnet into and out of a coil of wire generates a current in the coil. The current moves in one direction when a pole of the magnet is inserted into the coil, and in the opposite direction when the magnet is removed from the coil. This kind of current is called **alternating current (AC)**. In AC, electrons move back and forth, but there is no net movement of electrons in either direction.

The Advantages of Alternating Current

Across the country, hundreds of kilometres of wire cables carry huge quantities of electrical energy. To transmit this energy, with a relatively low loss of energy as heat, requires a low current and a high potential difference. There is a potential difference of several hundred thousand volts between the ground and the wires on a transmission tower.

Appliances and other devices in your home run on much lower voltage. An electric stove uses 220 to 240 V. Most other appliances in your home use 110 to 120 V. Thus, there is a need to change the potential difference. A simple electrical device called a **transformer** can change the potential difference of an alternating current. Transformers, however, do not work with direct current. This is one reason we use alternating current in our homes, businesses, and factories.

Many electronic devices, such as MP3 players and cellphones, use rechargeable batteries to supply DC. When you plug one of these devices into a wall outlet, a transformer reduces the potential difference from 110 V to the potential difference needed. Special circuits change the reduced AC output into DC to recharge the battery.

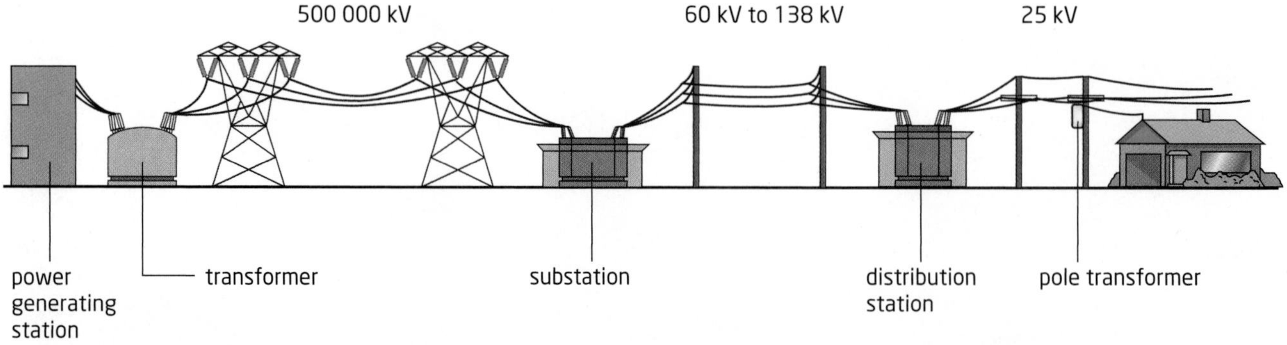

direct current (DC) current in which charged particles travel through a circuit in only one direction

alternating current (AC) current in which electrons move back and forth in a circuit

transformer an electrical device that changes the size of the potential difference of an alternating current

○○○

Study Toolkit

Making Inferences Why do you think electrical energy is transmitted over long distances, despite the costs of doing so?

500 000 kV   60 kV to 138 kV   25 kV

power generating station — transformer   substation   distribution station   pole transformer

Figure 12.2 The electrical wires in your home are part of a circuit that includes power generation, transmission across the country, and distribution from substations.

From the Generating Plant to Your Meter

As shown in **Figure 12.2**, the electrical energy produced at a power plant begins with a source of energy, which is then used to spin the shaft of a generator. The source of energy may be moving water, wind, or steam produced by the burning of fossil fuels or the heat of nuclear reactions. Energy from the generator's shaft moves a magnet and a coil of wire relative to each other. This generates an electric field that causes electrons to move.

Electric current is generated at 20 000 V or less. Transformers increase the voltage to 115 000 V, 230 000 V, or 500 000 V before the current is sent to transmission lines, as shown in **Figure 12.3**. Transformers that increase potential difference are called step-up transformers. Various substations then use step-down transformers to distribute electricity to groups of users.

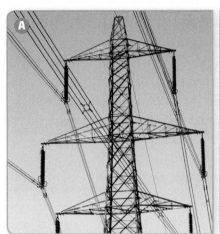

Figure 12.3 **A** The thin wires at the top of the tower are grounded to help protect the system from lightning strikes. The high voltage is between *adjacent* wires, not between the ends of a single wire. Insulators stop adjacent wires from touching. **B** Transformers step down the voltage before a line is connected to the meter at your home. In towns and cities, wiring is underground and step-down transformers are often inside green boxes. **C** In rural areas, cylindrical pole transformers are the norm.

Go to **scienceontario** to find out more

Learning Check

1. What is the difference between direct current and alternating current?

2. A doorbell is connected to a 110 V supply, but it operates on only about 12 to 14 V. What kind of transformer does it have?

3. Refer to **Figure 12.3**. What are the two main advantages of supplying alternating current to homes and businesses?

4. Outline the sequence of events as electricity is sent from a generator to a device you used at home this morning. Explain how the electricity was generated, transmitted, and used.

The Meter and Distribution Panel

A box or pole transformer reduces the potential difference from 7200 V to 120 V. From the transformer, three wires go to your home. Two of the wires are "live" or "hot," and therefore insulated. They carry alternating current. The third wire is the ground. It is neutral and not insulated.

The wires from the street transformer are in series with a meter and a distribution panel. The meter registers the amount of electrical energy that is used in your home. By reading the meter, shown in **Figure 12.4A**, the utility company can determine how much to charge for your energy use and for a proportion of other costs, such as distribution, maintenance, and repair. Many apartment and condominium buildings have only one meter, so the cost of electricity is averaged among all the units.

After passing through the meter, the electrical supply is connected to a distribution panel. The distribution panel consists of circuit breakers, shown in **Figure 12.4B**, or fuses in older homes. **Circuit breakers** and **fuses** are safety devices that are placed in series with other circuits, which lead to the appliances and wall outlets in your home. A circuit may lead to a single appliance, such as an electric oven that operates at 240 V, or to several lights and wall outlets, which supply 120 V. As **Figure 12.5** shows, circuits with several lights and wall outlets are connected in parallel. The circuit breaker at the distribution panel is in series with the parallel connections.

circuit breaker a safety device that is placed in series with other circuits, which lead to appliances and outlets

fuse a safety device that is found in older buildings and some appliances; like a circuit breaker, it is placed in series with other circuits, which lead to appliances and outlets

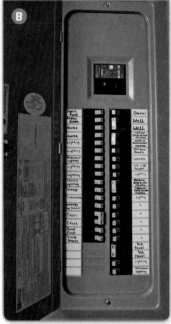

Figure 12.4 A All electrical energy use is metered. **B** In a typical home, the meter is in series with the wires from the street transformer and a distribution panel like the one shown here.

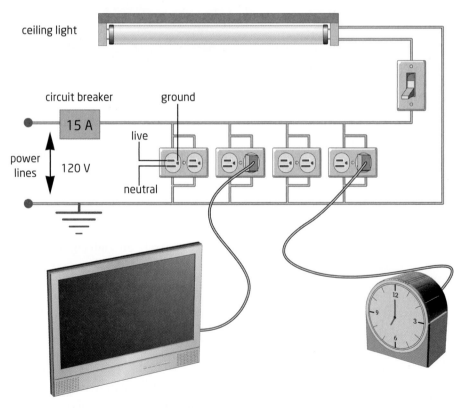

Figure 12.5 Most of the circuits in your home are series-parallel combinations. A circuit breaker or fuse at the distribution panel is always connected in series. Lights and wall outlets in each room, such as the kitchen, are connected in parallel.

Characteristics of Alternating Current

The electricity that is supplied to your home from the street transformer consists of two "live" or "hot" wires and a neutral ground wire. When an electrician wires an appliance that needs 240 V, the two live wires and the ground wire are used. Each live wire provides a potential difference of 120 V. When the potential difference in one wire is +120 V, however, the potential difference in the second wire is –120 V. Thus, the potential difference between the two wires is 240 V. Lights and wall outlets, which operate at 120 V, use only one of the two live wires, as well as the ground.

The current through a toaster (**Figure 12.6**) switches direction as the potential difference alternates. Electrons in direct current move very slowly, at about 0.01 cm/s. Electrons in alternating current do not flow in one direction along the wires at all. They only move back and forth. Many electrical devices that you use at home, such as a kettle, hair dryer, and toaster, convert electrical energy into heat.

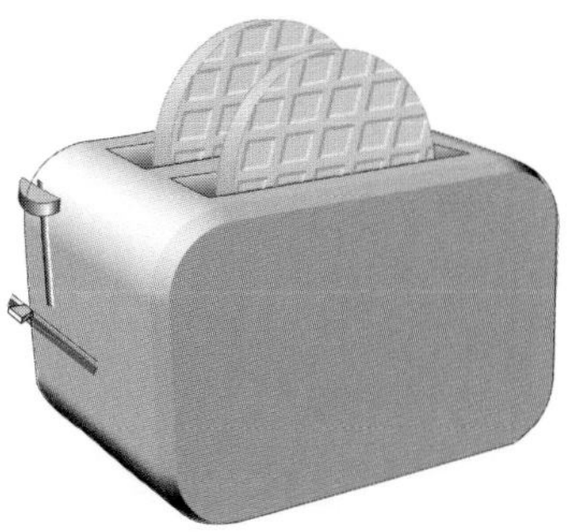

Figure 12.6 Many appliances make use of the heat that is generated by an alternating current.

An Analogy for Alternating Current

The analogy shown in **Figure 12.7** may help you understand how electrons in alternating current convert electrical energy into heat. Imagine an exercise bicycle. In this analogy, the pedals represent a source of electrical energy, and the tire represents electrons in a circuit. If you cranked the pedals in one direction, representing a direct current source, the tire would move in one direction. If the tire rubbed against an object, friction would make the tire very hot.

Now imagine that you turn the pedals first in one direction and then in the opposite direction, analogous to an alternating current. The tire moves back and forth. Again, if the tire rubbed against an object, the tire would become very hot.

Similarly, the electric field that is generated by alternating current generators changes direction. The electric field travels through a circuit at almost the speed of light, exerting a force on electrons in the circuit. The electrons have no net movement through an alternating current circuit because the direction of the field is always changing.

Although the electrons in AC do not always flow in one direction, the energy they carry is equivalent to the energy of a DC source that has the same current and potential difference.

Suggested Investigation

Technology Investigation 12-A, Designing a Staircase Circuit, on page 513.

Figure 12.7 The tire can rotate in one direction, analogous to direct current. It can also turn back and forth, analogous to alternating current. In both cases, the tire has energy.

Electrical Safety in the Home

Elecricity can be dangerous if used incorrectly. The combination of potential difference and current is the significant hazard. You can easily generate a potential difference of thousands of volts between you and the ground by scuffing your feet across a carpet while wearing socks. Because the current is very small, you experience only a small shock if you touch a doorknob. A wall outlet at 120 V can be lethal, however, because it can supply a large current. Your home has several features that help to protect you from a large current. **Table 12.1** summarizes some important safety devices.

Table 12.1 Electrical Safety Equipment in the Home

Device	Safety Purpose	How It Works	Example
Circuit breaker	Limits the amount of current to a set value; prevents overheating in wires and possible resulting fires	Main circuit breaker is in series with meter and with parallel connections to other breakers; when a current is too large, a part of the circuit breaker is heated, and then bends and breaks contact with another part, opening the circuit; the circuit breaker must then be reset	
Fuse	Limits the amount of current to a set value; prevents overheating in wires and possible resulting fires	Contains a metal conductor that melts at a temperature corresponding to a set amount of current, which creates an open circuit and stops the current; must be replaced	
Ground fault circuit interrupter	Replaces wall outlet when it is within 2 m of water source	Contains a circuit breaker that trips if there is any difference in current between the right (hot) slot and the left (neutral) slot	
Wall outlet and plug	Prevents shock resulting from faulty appliances	Outlet contains three slots, including a round one that is grounded; plug's round prong is electrically connected to appliance's metal frame; if a loose wire is connected to the frame, it sets up a large current that trips a circuit breaker connected to the outlet	
Surge protector	Prevents damage to circuits in electronic devices during power surges caused by lightning	Current above a pre-set maximum causes resistance of part of the surge protector to drop rapidly, diverting the current to ground	
Power bar with switch	Allows all appliances connected to the power bar to be turned off with one switch	Each outlet on the power bar is connected in parallel; the switch is in series with the wall outlet	

Section Summary

- Electrical energy is always generated from another source of energy.

- In direct current, charged particles travel through a circuit in only one direction. In alternating current, electrons move back and forth in a circuit.

- Alternating current is generated when a magnet and a coil of wire are moved relative to each other.

- Alternating current can be transmitted at high potential difference over long distances, with only a small loss of electrical energy.

- Transformers can increase (step up) or decrease (step down) potential difference, but they only work with alternating current.

- Circuit breakers and fuses are safety devices that limit the current to appliances and wall outlets in your home.

Review Questions

K/U **1.** Explain why it is not accurate to speak of electrons flowing in an alternating current.

K/U **2.** A microwave oven requires 3000 V to operate. How could this potential difference be obtained if the microwave oven is plugged into a 120 V wall outlet?

A **3.** Older transmission lines are made from copper cable. What advantages does copper have compared with aluminum? Why is aluminum used to make transmission lines today?

T/I **4.** What advantage does a circuit breaker have, compared with a fuse? Refer to **Table 12.1**.

T/I **5.** Describe at least two different situations that could result in a large current in a household circuit.

T/I **6.** Why is it not safe to plug an appliance with a three-prong plug into an extension cord with a two-slot socket?

C **7.** Research electrical hazards in a home. Prepare a safety sheet that could be given to parents of school-age children.

T/I **8.** Why can birds stand safely on a 230 000 V transmission line, as shown on the right, whereas someone who is trimming a tree and touches the same line will be electrocuted?

This bird is unharmed as it perches on the live transmission line.

Key Terms

electrical power

watt (W)

kilowatt (kW)

electrical energy

kilowatt-hour (kW·h)

EnerGuide label

smart meter

time of use pricing

phantom load

efficiency

Figure 12.8 This is a typical electrical energy bill for a home in Ontario. It includes many charges that are based on how much energy was used. The difference between the meter readings at the beginning and end of a time period indicates the energy that was used by the customer.

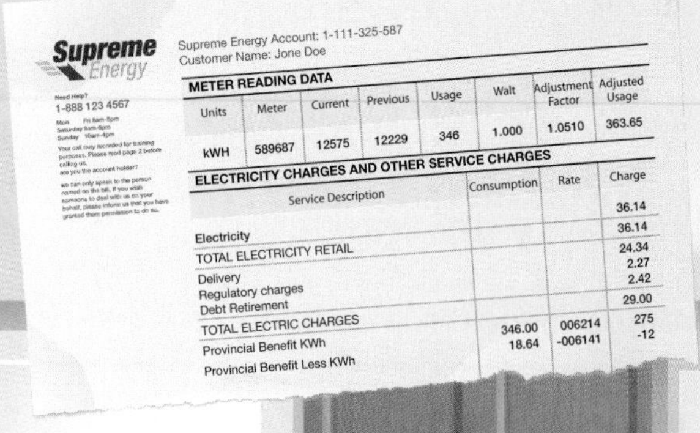

12.2 Using Electrical Energy Wisely

Choosing appliances carefully and choosing when to use them can make a big difference in the financial and environmental cost of electrical energy.

What You Pay For

A typical electrical energy bill is shown in **Figure 12.8**. It includes charges for the energy used, charges related to the cost of distributing the energy, and administration charges. **Figure 12.9** illustrates some of the savings that can be made by the choices of appliances and lighting in your home.

The energy bill in **Figure 12.8** shows the energy that was used as the difference between two readings—346 kW·h. It also shows an adjustment factor of 1.0510. This adjustment factor represents an allowance for the energy "lost" (converted to heat in wires and transformers) during transmission. The adjusted usage is 346 kW·h × 1.0510 = 363.65 kW·h, which is the amount of energy that the customer must pay for.

The amount of electrical energy that is used in your home depends on three factors: the power ratings of the appliances and devices used, the settings on the appliances and devices (such as high, medium, or low), and the amount of time that each appliance or device is used. The *cost* of electricity depends on the amount of energy that is used and the price that is charged for it.

Refrigerator:
More than 50%

Dishwasher:
More than 50%

Electric stove:
About 20%

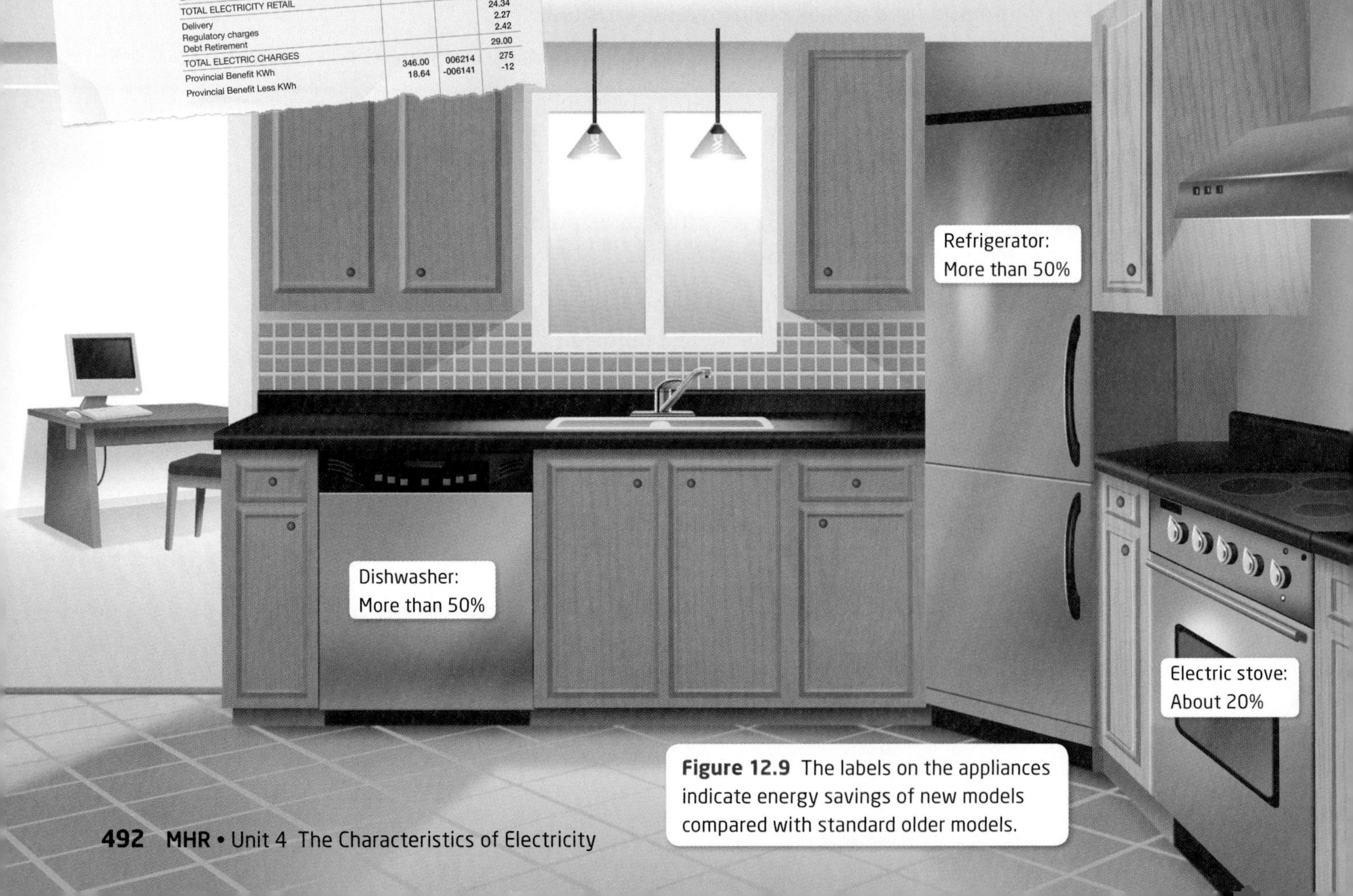

Figure 12.9 The labels on the appliances indicate energy savings of new models compared with standard older models.

Power Ratings

One factor that affects the amount of electrical energy used in your home is the power ratings of your appliances and devices. **Figure 12.10** shows the ratings of some compact fluorescent bulbs. A brighter bulb has a higher rating. **Table 12.2** lists several appliances and their typical power ratings. The actual power rating of any particular appliance appears on a label on the outer casing of the appliance. The value given there is usually the maximum power used. The **electrical power** of an appliance is its rate of use of electrical energy. Electrical power is measured in **watts (W)**, although the practical unit for most appliances is the **kilowatt (kW)**, which is 1000 watts.

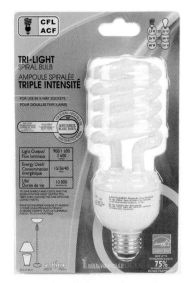

electrical power the rate at which an appliance uses electrical energy

watt (W) a unit of electrical power

kilowatt (kW) a practical unit of electrical power; 1 kW = 1000 W

Appliance Settings

A second factor that affects the amount of electrical energy used by appliances and devices is their settings. The actual power used may be different from the power rating, depending on the setting or what the appliance is doing. For example, the wash cycle of a clothes washer requires more power than the spin cycle.

Figure 12.10 Bulbs with lower power ratings are used for areas that need less light, such as storage rooms.

Go to **scienceontario** to find out more

Table 12.2 Typical Power Ratings of Appliances

Appliance	Typical Power Rating (kW)
Clock	0.0050
Clothes dryer	5.0
Clothes washer	0.50
Coffee maker	1.0
Computer with monitor and printer	0.20
Dishwasher	1.8
DVD player	0.040
Freezer	0.34
Light: Incandescent (60 W) Compact Fluorescent (60 W equivalent)	0.060 0.018
Microwave oven	1.5
Electric stove: Self-cleaning Not self-cleaning	3.2 3.5
Refrigerator: Older model Energy Star®	0.40 0.35
Stereo	0.030

Television: Cathode Ray Tube (CRT)
        Liquid Crystal Display (LCD)
        Plasma
	0.20
	 0.12
	 0.28

Toaster	1.1
Toaster oven	1.2
Vacuum cleaner: Portable Central vacuum	0.80 1.6
Video game console	0.10

Amount of Use

A third factor that affects the amount of electrical energy used in your home is how long each appliance or device is used. Obviously, leaving a bulb on for 10 h consumes 10 times as much energy as leaving the same bulb on for 1 h. The **electrical energy** that is used is calculated by multiplying the power rating of an appliance or device (in kW) by the amount of time that the appliance or device is used (in hours, h). Thus, the practical unit of electrical energy is the **kilowatt-hour (kW·h)**. Note that the kW·h combines the units for power × time. The joule, which is the unit for any form of energy, also combines the units for power × time: J = W·s.

EnerGuide Labels

In Canada, any household appliance that is sold must have an **EnerGuide label**. As in **Figure 12.11**, the label shows how much energy an appliance uses in one year of normal use. The Canadian Standards Association tests major appliances to make sure they meet minimum energy efficiency standards.

Consumers should use the EnerGuide label to help them make an informed choice when they purchase a refrigerator, freezer, stove, dishwasher, clothes washer, dryer, or room air conditioner. Products earn an Energy Star® rating when they use 10 to 50 percent less energy (and water, for appliances such as clothes washers and dishwashers), compared with a standard product in the same category. **Table 12.3** shows the typical energy that is used in one year by various appliances.

electrical energy the energy that is used by an appliance at a given setting; determined by multiplying the power rating of an appliance by the length of time it is used

kilowatt-hour (kW·h) the practical unit of electrical energy

EnerGuide label a label that gives details about how much energy an appliance uses in one year of normal use

Table 12.3 Annual Energy Used for Common Household Appliances in Canadian Homes

Appliance	Typical Annual Energy Used (kW·h/year)
Electric clothes dryer	912
Clothes washer:	
Older model	573
Energy Star®	267
Dishwasher:	
Older model	457
Energy Star®	422
Freezer	344
Electric stove:	
Self-cleaning	622
Not self-cleaning	694
Refrigerator:	
Older model	465
Energy Star®	411

Figure 12.11 This front-loading clothes washer uses far less electrical energy in one year of normal use than a top-loading model does. The indicator arrow shows how this appliance compares with other appliances in the same category. The farther left the indicator arrow is, the lower the cost to use the appliance is. This appliance has earned an Energy Star® rating.

Cost of Electrical Energy

The cost of electrical energy depends on the amount of energy that is used and the price that is charged for it. This cost is calculated by multiplying the amount of energy used (in kW·h) by the price (in ¢/kW·h).

Sample Problem: Cost of Using a Hair Dryer

Problem

A hair dryer is rated at 1200 W. On average, it is used for 10 min each school day in the morning, when the cost of electrical energy is 8.8¢/kW·h. What is the cost of using the hair dryer on all five school days during one week?

Solution

Part 1: Power = $1200 \text{ W} = \dfrac{1.20 \text{ W}}{1000 \text{ W/kW}} = 1.20 \text{ kW}$

Time = $10 \dfrac{\text{min}}{\text{day}} \times 5 \text{ days} = \dfrac{50 \text{ min}}{60 \text{ min/h}} = 0.833 \text{ h}$

Energy used = power × time = $1.20 \text{ kW} \times 0.833 \text{ h} = 1.0 \text{ kW·h}$

Part 2: Rate = 8.8 ¢/kW·h

Cost = energy use × rate

= $1.0 \text{ kW·h} \times 8.8 \dfrac{¢}{\text{kw·h}} = 8.8 ¢$

The hairdryer costs 9¢ to use on all five school days.

Check Your Solution

The final answer has the correct units, and the cost is reasonable.

Sense of Value

In the first stage of generating electrical energy from fossil fuel, the fuel is burned to turn water into steam at a power station. The steam is then used to drive turbines in a generator; transformers step up the voltage as the energy is fed to transmission lines; and the energy is then distributed. By the time the energy reaches consumers, about 70 percent of it has been lost to heat.

GRASP

Go to **Science Skills Toolkit 9** to learn about an alternative problem solving method.

Practice Problems

1. Convert the following power ratings to kW.

   a. hot plate 1300 W   **b.** ceiling fan 60 W   **c.** coffee maker 900 W

2. Convert the following times to hours.

   a. 5 min   **b.** 20 min   **c.** 70 min

3. How much energy is used when a 1.25 kW toaster oven is used for a total of 3 h in a month?

4. The estimated average energy that is used to operate a clothes dryer for a year is 912 kW·h. If the average rate to operate the dryer is 7.15 ¢/kW·h, what is the average cost per year?

5. Calculate the cost of watching television for 3 h at night at a rate of 8.8¢/kW·h. The television has a power rating of 150 W.

Smart Meters

A **smart meter**, shown in **Figure 12.12**, records the total electrical energy used each hour. The data are sent to the utility company automatically. Ontario plans to replace all older meters with smart meters by 2010. Then, all electricity bills for residences will be based on time of use pricing.

Time of Use Pricing

Time of use pricing is a system of pricing in which the price that is charged for each kW·h of energy used is different at different times of the day or week. **Figure 12.13** shows typical time of use intervals and the price charged for energy that is used during each interval. There are three different time of use prices, which correspond to off-peak, mid-peak, or on-peak use. These intervals are adjusted twice each year because the demand for electricity changes with the seasons. In the summer, the demand is greater during the middle of weekdays, when many people are using air conditioners. In the winter, the demand is greater in the morning and evening, when people need light and heat.

The price of electrical energy is lowest on weekends and holidays. Thus, even if the amount of energy used is the same, its total cost varies.

Figure 12.12 Smart meters encourage conservation by making us think about how and when we use electrical energy.

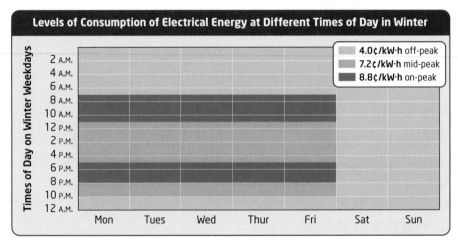

Figure 12.13 Different time of use prices reflect the changing cost of generating electricity throughout the day.

Learning Check

1. What factors determine the amount of electrical energy that is consumed by an appliance?

2. Use the data in **Table 12.2** to determine which appliance uses the most electrical energy: a clothes dryer that operates for 30 min or a freezer that operates for 24 h.

3. Explain how you would use an EnerGuide label to help you choose a new refrigerator.

4. How can you use information about time of use prices to reduce your family's energy bill?

Phantom Loads

Many appliances are in stand-by mode when they are not switched on. For example, if you have a remote control to turn on a television, the television must be able to sense the signal, which requires energy. The electricity that is consumed by an appliance when it is turned off is called the **phantom load**. Clock displays, such as those on microwaves and coffee makers, and external power adapters also require phantom loads. External power adapters plug into wall outlets and change the electricity to low voltage alternating or direct current. If you touch an external power supply, as shown in **Figure 12.14**, you will notice that it is quite warm. It is estimated that an average home has a phantom load of about 50 W.

A meter, such as the one shown in **Figure 12.15**, can be used to measure the power ratings of appliances. The meter plugs into a wall outlet, and an appliance can be plugged into an outlet in the meter. The meter will display the power that is drawn by the appliance when it is on or off. The easiest way to prevent a phantom load is to unplug an appliance.

Electrical Devices, Energy, and Efficiency

An efficient electrical device does what you want it to do, with a minimum conversion of energy to unwanted forms. For example, you do not want heat from a computer or a TV set. The **efficiency** of an electrical device is the ratio of useful energy output to total energy input, expressed as a percentage:

$$\text{Percent efficiency} = \frac{\text{useful energy output}}{\text{total energy input}} \times 100\%$$

The total energy input for an electrical appliance is its power multiplied by the time it is on. The energy that is absorbed when a known amount of water is heated is relatively easy to determine. This method is used to find the energy output of water-heating appliances.

Sense of scale

When your body is at rest (in a classroom, for example), it is generating heat that is roughly equivalent to the energy output of one 60 W incandescent bulb (or four 15 W compact fluorescents). Thus, you and 16 of your classmates generate about 1 kW of heat.

Suggested Investigation

Data Analysis Investigation 12-C, A "Dry" Investigation, on page 515

Figure 12.14 External power adapters are sometimes called wall warts. These adapters are inefficient and give off a substantial amount of heat.

Figure 12.15 You can measure the power that an appliance uses by connecting it to a watt-meter. You can also use the meter to measure the phantom load (if there is one) when an appliance is turned off.

The Unit of Electrical Energy

The SI unit of energy is the joule (J). One joule is equivalent to a power of one watt operating for one second (W·s). Thus, 1 J = 1 W·s. This is a small amount of energy, so a unit of one thousand joules, the kilojoule, is more convenient to use. Thus, 1 kJ = 1 kW·s. The energy input to an electrical device is usually stated as its power (in kW) multiplied by the time (in s) that it operates.

Study Toolkit

Using Graphic Organizers
How can using a Venn diagram help you compare and contrast an incandescent bulb and a compact fluorescent bulb?

GRASP
Go to **Science Skills Toolkit 9** to learn about an alternative problem solving method.

Sample Problem: Electric Kettle or Microwave?

Problem

To compare the efficiency of a microwave with the efficiency of an electric kettle, Sara placed 500 mL of water into each. Sara's teacher helped her calculate the energy required to boil the water, which was 168 kJ. The kettle, which had a power rating of 1.5 kW, took 132 s to boil the water. The microwave had a power rating of 1.2 kW and took 280 s to boil the water. Which is more efficient?

Solution

You need to calculate the efficiency of the microwave and the electric kettle.

The useful energy is 168 kJ.

Kettle: Energy input = 1.5 kW × 132 s = 198 kW·s = 198 kJ

$$\text{Percent efficiency} = \frac{168 \text{ kJ}}{198 \text{ kJ}} \times 100\% = 85\%$$

Microwave: Energy input = 1.2 kW × 280 s = 336 kJ

$$\text{Percent efficiency} = \frac{168 \text{ kJ}}{336 \text{ kJ}} \times 100\% = 50\%$$

The kettle is more efficient than the microwave for heating water.

Check Your Solution

The solution is reasonable. The microwave took about twice as long to boil the water, while its power rating is not much less.

Practice Problems

1. The spin cycle of a clothes washer operates for 3 min at a power of 300 W. The useful output from the washer is 40 kJ. What is the efficiency of the washer?

2. An AC power adapter operates at 28.6 W·s. The output from the adapter is 1.04 W·s. What is its efficiency?

3. Two nuclear reactors provide 3200 MW of power. If the transmission system loses 5.1% of the energy produced, how much power from these two reactors would customers receive?

4. A motor is 80 percent efficient. How much useful work can the motor do if it is supplied with 200 kW·h of energy?

The Efficiency of Light Sources

In Ontario alone, the electricity wasted by the use of incandescent bulbs is enough to power 600 000 homes. As you can see in **Figure 12.16**, incandescent light bulbs are hugely inefficient. Fortunately, there are other ways to convert electricity into light.

Figure 12.16 Different light sources have a variety of advantages and disadvantages.

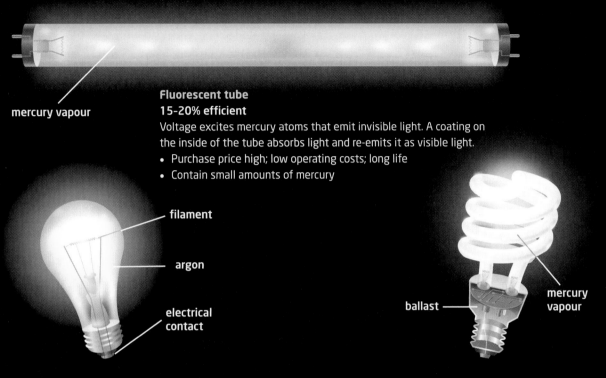

mercury vapour

Fluorescent tube
15-20% efficient
Voltage excites mercury atoms that emit invisible light. A coating on the inside of the tube absorbs light and re-emits it as visible light.
- Purchase price high; low operating costs; long life
- Contain small amounts of mercury

filament

argon

electrical contact

ballast

mercury vapour

Incandescent light bulb
5-8% efficient
A long, thin tungsten filament is heated to about 2200°C. The filament gradually evaporates, but the process is slowed by argon or other inert gas.
- Low purchase price; high operating costs; short lifetime

Compact fluorescent light bulb (CFL)
15-20% efficient
Fluorescent bulbs are coiled to fit into the space of an incandescent bulb.
- Purchase price high; low operating costs; long life
- Contains small amounts of mercury

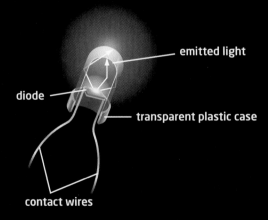

emitted light

diode

transparent plastic case

contact wires

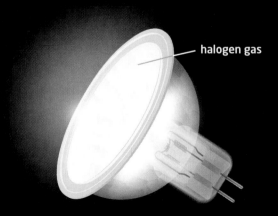

halogen gas

Light-emitting diode (LED)
25-50% efficient
A semiconductor chip (diode) emits light that is focused by a plastic case.
- Purchase price high; very low operating costs; very long life

Halogen lamp
20% efficient
A tungsten filament, whose evaporation is slowed by a gas, often iodine, is heated to more than 2500°C.
- Lasts longer than incandescent bulb

Section Summary

- The electrical power of an appliance is the rate at which it uses electrical energy. The practical unit for electrical power is the kilowatt (kW).

- The electrical energy that is used by an appliance at a given setting is calculated by multiplying its power rating (in kW) by the amount of time that it is used (in hours, h). The practical unit of electrical energy is the kilowatt-hour (kW·h).

- The cost of electrical energy is calculated by multiplying the amount of energy that is used (in kW·h) by the price (in ¢/kW·h).

- Smart meters allow a utility company to charge a different amount for each kW·h of energy that is used at different times of the day.

- The electricity that is consumed by any appliance or device when it is turned off is called the phantom load.

- The efficiency of an electrical device is the ratio of useful energy output to total energy input:

$$\text{Efficiency} = \frac{\text{useful energy output}}{\text{total energy input}}$$

Review Questions

K/U **1.** What is the difference between electrical power and electrical energy?

K/U **2.** What are the three factors that determine the total amount of electrical energy consumed in a home?

T/I **3.** Look at **Figure 12.13** on page 496. Why is there a high demand for electricity between 5:00 P.M. and 8:00 P.M. in the winter?

T/I **4.** If you go away on a vacation, why might your family still be billed for electrical energy used in your home?

K/U **5.** A water pump operates for 1 h, and its output is 1700 kJ of useful energy. Calculate the efficiency of the water pump, if it has a power rating of 1200 W.

T/I **6.** Refer to the table on the right. How much energy is consumed in 12 h by an electric toothbrush that is plugged in but is not in use?

K/U **7.** Some sources claim that lighting accounts for up to 15 percent of home electricity costs. Explain how you would collect and analyze data to test this claim.

T/I **8.** A 60 W incandescent bulb costs $1.25 and has an average lifetime of 1500 h. A 15 W compact fluorescent bulb, which gives the same amount of light, costs $4.00 and has an average lifetime of 10 000 h. Compare the lifetime cost of buying and operating the incandescent bulb with the lifetime cost of buying and operating the compact fluorescent bulb. Assume that the average cost of electrical energy is 8.0 ¢/kW·h.

C **9.** Based on your answer to question 8, make an argument for which bulb is the more economical choice.

Typical Phantom Loads of Some Common Appliances

Appliance	Typical Phantom Load (W)
Cable television	12.5
Computer and printer	7.0
Electric toothbrush	1.6
Microwave	3.0
Cordless telephone	2.5

12.3 Meeting the Demand for Electricity

Key Terms
base load
hydroelectric power
  generation
intermediate load
peak load
renewable energy source
non-renewable energy
  source

A great deal of planning is required to make sure that Ontario has the ability to provide electricity now, and will continue to be able to in the future. About 10 to 20 years are needed to plan and build a generating station. During this time, existing plants need to be upgraded or replaced.

Meeting the Minimum Demand

Ontario must plan carefully to ensure that the daily demand for electricity is matched by the supply. During the early hours of the morning, when most people are asleep and many businesses are not operating, a minimum amount of electrical power is generated **(Figure 12.17)**. In Ontario, this minimum amount is about 12 000 MW. 1 MW = 1 megawatt = 10^6 W. The continuous minimum demand for electrical power is called the **base load**. In this context, the term load refers to the demand for electrical power. To meet the base load demand, large reliable generators are used because their turbines can be run using the least expensive fuel. Off-peak prices are charged when base load generators can meet the demand for electricity. In Ontario, the base load is generated mainly by hydroelectric and nuclear generating stations, but also by some coal-fired generating stations.

base load the continuous minimum demand for electrical power

Demand, Supply, and Price for Electricity

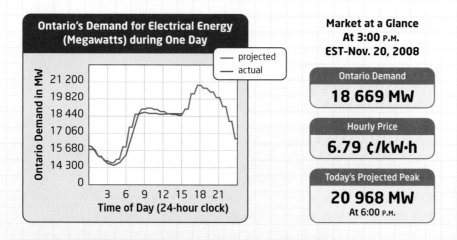

Ontario's Demand for Electrical Energy (Megawatts) during One Day

— projected
— actual

Ontario Demand in MW: 21 200, 19 820, 18 440, 17 060, 15 680, 14 300, 0

Time of Day (24-hour clock): 3 6 9 12 15 18 21

Market at a Glance
At 3:00 P.M.
EST-Nov. 20, 2008

Ontario Demand
18 669 MW

Hourly Price
6.79 ¢/kW·h

Today's Projected Peak
20 968 MW
At 6:00 P.M.

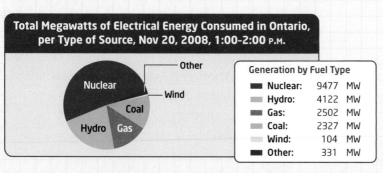

Total Megawatts of Electrical Energy Consumed in Ontario, per Type of Source, Nov 20, 2008, 1:00–2:00 P.M.

Other
Nuclear
Wind
Coal
Hydro
Gas

Generation by Fuel Type
Nuclear:	9477	MW
Hydro:	4122	MW
Gas:	2502	MW
Coal:	2327	MW
Wind:	104	MW
Other:	331	MW

Figure 12.17 In Ontario, the Independent Electricity System Operator (IESO) manages the generation, transmission, and distribution of electricity. The graph shows the demand for electricity at different times on a particular day. The chart shows how much electrical power was supplied by various sources.

Hydroelectric Power Generation

Hydroelectric power generation relies on a large source of water to provide the energy needed to turn turbines. There are two types of hydroelectric plants: dam stations and run-of-river stations. At a dam station, water that falls between different levels is used to turn turbines. At a run-of-river station, water that is flowing in a river is used. The generating stations at Niagara Falls are run-of-river stations. **Figure 12.18** shows a dam station.

Advantages and Disadvantages of Hydroelectric Power

Hydroelectric generating stations have a number of advantages. There are no combustion emissions and no fuel costs. Once constructed, a hydroelectric station has very low operating costs. The process is about 90 percent efficient because there are almost no heat transformations, which waste useful energy. In comparison, a generating station that burns fossil fuels (coal, oil, or natural gas) is about 30 percent efficient. In addition, hydroelectric generators can be brought on line quickly, which makes them useful for peak-load generation. Hydroelectric energy is a **renewable energy source**. This is a source of energy that can be renewed in a relatively short period of time. A **non-renewable energy source**, such as fossil fuels, cannot be renewed as quickly as it is used up.

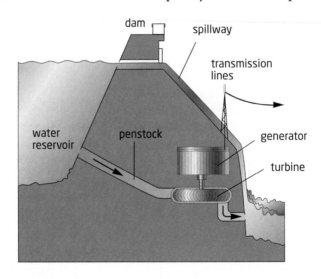

Disadvantages of Hydroelectric Power

Hydroelectric stations also have disadvantages. When reservoirs are built to store water in dams, large areas of land must be flooded. For example, the La Grande Phase 1 portion of the James Bay hydroelectric project in Québec covers 11 400 km², which includes 9700 km² of flooded land that had been home to the Cree people. Another disadvantage is that when land is flooded, the submerged vegetation decays. This can lead to the production of methane, a potent greenhouse gas. Mercury, a toxic metal, is released from the soil and vegetation and is taken up by whatever fish manage to survive.

hydroelectric power generation the generation of electrical power using a source of moving water

renewable energy source a source of energy that can be replaced in a relatively short period of time

non-renewable energy source a source of energy that cannot be replaced as quickly as it is used

Figure 12.18 The turbine and generator transform the energy of moving water into electrical energy.

Go to **scienceontario** to find out more

Sense of Value

Ontario currently has over 60 hydroelectric generating stations, which have the capacity to supply 21 percent of the province's demand for electricity. There are very few remaining sites, where new hydroelectric stations could be built.

Generation from Nuclear Fuel

About 51 percent of Ontario's capacity to generate electricity comes from three nuclear stations. The heat from nuclear reactions generates steam, which turns turbines that are connected to generators. **Figure 12.19** shows the components of a nuclear generating station. Because nuclear energy is relatively inexpensive, it is suitable for meeting base load demand.

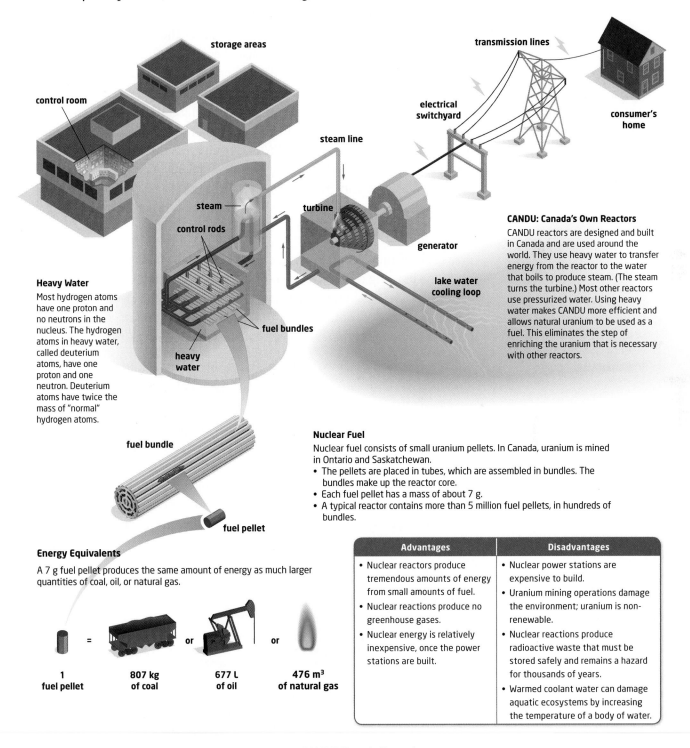

Heavy Water

Most hydrogen atoms have one proton and no neutrons in the nucleus. The hydrogen atoms in heavy water, called deuterium atoms, have one proton and one neutron. Deuterium atoms have twice the mass of "normal" hydrogen atoms.

CANDU: Canada's Own Reactors

CANDU reactors are designed and built in Canada and are used around the world. They use heavy water to transfer energy from the reactor to the water that boils to produce steam. (The steam turns the turbine.) Most other reactors use pressurized water. Using heavy water makes CANDU more efficient and allows natural uranium to be used as a fuel. This eliminates the step of enriching the uranium that is necessary with other reactors.

Nuclear Fuel

Nuclear fuel consists of small uranium pellets. In Canada, uranium is mined in Ontario and Saskatchewan.
- The pellets are placed in tubes, which are assembled in bundles. The bundles make up the reactor core.
- Each fuel pellet has a mass of about 7 g.
- A typical reactor contains more than 5 million fuel pellets, in hundreds of bundles.

Energy Equivalents

A 7 g fuel pellet produces the same amount of energy as much larger quantities of coal, oil, or natural gas.

1 fuel pellet	=	807 kg of coal	or	677 L of oil	or	476 m³ of natural gas

Advantages	Disadvantages
• Nuclear reactors produce tremendous amounts of energy from small amounts of fuel. • Nuclear reactions produce no greenhouse gases. • Nuclear energy is relatively inexpensive, once the power stations are built.	• Nuclear power stations are expensive to build. • Uranium mining operations damage the environment; uranium is non-renewable. • Nuclear reactions produce radioactive waste that must be stored safely and remains a hazard for thousands of years. • Warmed coolant water can damage aquatic ecosystems by increasing the temperature of a body of water.

Figure 12.19 In Canada, all active nuclear reactors are CANDU (Canada Deuterium Uranium) reactors. They are located in Ontario, Québec, and New Brunswick. The ones in Ontario are in Tiverton, Newcastle Township, and Pickering.

Meeting Intermediate and Peak Demand

Although nuclear energy is very useful for supplying base load, nuclear reactors cannot be turned on and off quickly. How is power generated as thousands of people wake up, turn on lights, and prepare breakfast?

Generators are designed to provide an alternating current that goes through 60 cycles every second. As electrical demand increases, the generators slow down. To keep the alternating current close to 60 cycles per second, more generators are brought on line. The reverse process happens when the demand for electricity begins to fall. Thus, to meet intermediate and peak loads, smaller generators that are capable of coming on line quickly are used. **Intermediate load**, between roughly 15 000 MW and 20 000 MW, is met by generating stations that burn fossil fuels. The increased fuel costs are passed along to consumers as mid-peak rates. **Peak load**, above 20 000 MW, is met by using hydroelectric and gas turbines, which can be turned on and off quickly. Again, the cost of providing electricity increases, especially if the electricity must be purchased from outside Ontario. Thus, the higher on-peak rates apply.

Power Generation from Coal

In a coal-burning generating station, as shown in **Figure 12.20**, the heat from the burning coal is used to boil water, which circulates in tubing in a boiler. The steam turns the blades of turbines, which are connected to generators. Most of the energy of the fossil fuel is converted to heat rather than to the turbine motion as the fuel burns and the water boils.

Advantages and Disadvantages of Power Generation from Coal

On the plus side, there are large known reserves of coal. In addition, the economic costs of generating electrical energy from coal are very low. However, the conversion of energy from coal to electricity is very inefficient. Burning coal produces gases that contribute to acid rain, particulates, and other emissions, including carbon dioxide, a greenhouse gas. And coal is non-renewable, meaning that eventually, supplies will run out. Reliance on coal can be decreased if people shift more of their use of electricity to off-peak hours, when most power generation does not require fossil fuels.

intermediate load
a demand for electricity that is greater than the base load and is met by burning coal and natural gas

peak load the greatest demand for electricity, which is met by using hydroelectric power and natural gas

Sense of place

Nanticoke generating station, located on the north shore of Lake Erie in Haldimand County, is the largest coal-burning generating station in North America. This station has a generating capacity of 4000 MW and burns crushed coal. It is the single largest source of carbon dioxide in North America.

Figure 12.20 Ontario has five generating stations that burn fossil fuels. These stations use coal or natural gas to heat water into steam.

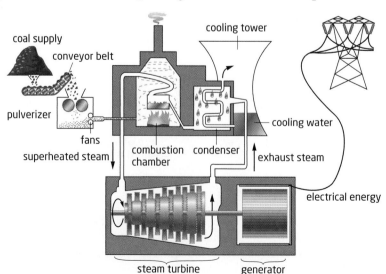

Section Summary

- Base load is the continuous minimum demand for electrical power. It is met by using large generators that run on the least expensive fuels.

- Intermediate load and peak load are met by using smaller generators that can be turned on and off quickly.

- Ontario obtains most of its electrical energy from nuclear, hydroelectric, and fossil fuel-burning stations.

- The rate that is charged for electricity changes when the cost of the fuel that is used to generate the electricity changes.

Review Questions

K/U **1.** The demand for electricity varies at different times.

    a. What is base load?

    b. Why does only base load need to be supplied on holidays and weekends?

K/U **2.** Explain why hydroelectric generating stations can be used to supply both base load and peak load.

T/I **3.** Uranium is mined at the Elliot Lake mine in Ontario, which is shown on the right. It is also mined in Saskatchewan, but there are no nuclear power stations there. Suggest a possible reason for this.

K/U **4.** Examine the data in **Figure 12.17**. Calculate the contribution of each fuel type as a percentage of the total.

A **5.** In general, electricity must be used as it is generated. Hydroelectric stations can pump water into a dam reservoir when the demand is off-peak. Suggest a reason for doing this.

T/I **6.** The sources of electricity that are used have an effect on the overall environmental impact.

    a. Once constructed, which type of generating station has the least effect on the environment? Explain.

    b. Which type has the greatest effect on the environment, after it is constructed? Explain.

A **7.** If hybrid and electric cars become more popular, which type of load demand is likely to increase the most? Explain your answer.

T/I **8.** Use the data given in **Figures 12.13** and **12.17** to estimate the mid-peak demand for electricity.

About one quarter of the world's supply of uranium comes from Ontario mines. The operation shown here is in Elliot Lake.

Key Terms

wind farm

solar energy

photovoltaic effect

biomass energy

12.4 Sustainable Sources of Electricity

A pie chart, like the one in **Figure 12.17** on page 501, shows how electricity is generated in Ontario. The chart is updated as the demand for power changes during the day. At the present time, our generating stations use mostly nuclear power, hydroelectric power, gas, and coal. What will this pie chart look like in the future, as some generating stations need to be replaced and Ontario's population grows?

There are very few remaining sites that are suitable for developing new hydroelectric stations, and the other types of generating stations make significant impacts on the environment. Future plans include conservation and the increased use of renewable forms of energy.

Wind energy, for example, presently contributes only about 1 percent of electrical energy, but there is the potential for a much greater contribution. As **Figure 12.21** shows, wind turbines can make both large and small contributions to our energy needs.

In this section, you will learn how electricity can be generated using renewable forms of energy and how electrical energy can be conserved.

Figure 12.21 Some wind generators are part of large wind farms that are linked to the power grid. Other wind generators, like the one shown in the inset photograph, are used to provide electricity to a single home or farm.

Renewable Sources of Energy

Electrical energy is always generated from another source of energy. Fossil fuels like coal, oil, and natural gas took millions of years to form, and their supplies are limited. Uranium, the fuel that is used to generate nuclear energy, was present when Earth formed, and no more will be produced by natural processes. As you learned in section 12.3, these are examples of non-renewable energy sources. However, there are many energy sources that are renewable. Hydroelectric power is one example. Others include wind, solar, ocean (tides and waves), biomass, and geothermal.

Wind Turbines

Figure 12.21 shows many large wind turbines at one location, called a **wind farm**. A single turbine, which may supply electricity to a farm, home, or small business, operates in much the same way. The most common type of wind turbine in Canada is mounted on a tower, usually 30 m or more above the ground, to take advantage of greater wind speeds. The height above the ground also reduces turbulence, or irregular air motion, which results from wind blowing around buildings.

wind farm many large wind turbines at one location

How Wind Turbines Work

Figure 12.22 shows the main parts of a large wind turbine. A wind turbine begins producing electricity when the wind speed is about 13 km/h (kilometres per hour). The power that is generated increases with wind speed until it reaches a maximum at about 55 km/h. For safety reasons, the controller activates a brake to shut down the turbine when the wind speed reaches 90 km/h or more. The controller contains circuits that maintain output from the generator at a frequency of 60 cycles a second alternating current.

The Promise of Wind Energy

The potential for generating electricity from wind turbines is good in Ontario and other parts of Canada. In particular, Ontario's Great Lakes provide very good sites for wind farms. At the end of 2008, Ontario led all the provinces in the capacity to generate electricity from wind, with more than 950 MW—providing enough energy to supply nearly 250 000 homes.

When wind turbines are installed and connected to the grid, the cost of running them is very low. The major technical disadvantage of generating electricity from wind is that the wind speed at any location may vary during the day. There are also concerns that wind turbines spoil the view, are noisy, and can be a danger to birds and humans nearby.

Figure 12.22 The gears in the gear box increase the speed of rotation of the shaft. The motor and the gears that are next to it control the direction of the blades. A large turbine can generate a few megawatts of electrical power. Most smaller turbines do not have a system of gears.

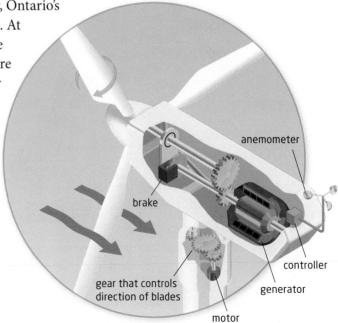

anemometer

brake

controller

gear that controls direction of blades

generator

motor

Solar Energy

The Sun is the ultimate source of all the different forms of energy we use, except nuclear and geothermal energy. Fossil fuels are the result of energy from the Sun being captured by vegetation millions of years ago. Today, the Sun is the energy source of biomass, wind, and hydroelectric generators. Usually, however, the term **solar energy** means energy that is directly converted from the Sun's energy into electricity.

The Photovoltaic Effect

In 1839, the French physicist Edmund Becquerel discovered that certain materials produce an electric current when they are exposed to light. This is called the **photovoltaic effect**. Photovoltaic materials in a solar cell generate direct current when light strikes their surface. You may have a calculator or wristwatch, or an external light on your home, that uses solar cells. **Figure 12.23** shows a parking meter that uses solar cells.

The Sun emits enormous amounts of energy. The challenge is to collect and convert this solar energy to electrical energy efficiently and cost-effectively. Above the atmosphere, the energy that is received from the Sun averages 1367 W/m². Thus, a 1 m² solar cell, operating at 100 percent efficiency, could easily supply the power necessary to operate most electrical appliances. At Earth's surface, this efficiency is about half. We receive only about 700 W/m².

---

solar energy energy that is directly converted from the Sun into electricity

photovoltaic effect the generation of a direct current when certain materials are exposed to light

Sense of Value

According to the Canadian Energy Research Institute, in 2003, solar photovoltaic was the most expensive form of electricity generation in Canada, at a cost of as high as 80 ¢/kW·h. Coal was among the cheapest, at no more than 7 ¢/kW·h. However, it was estimated that by 2030, the cost of solar photovoltaic energy would decrease by up to 65 percent.

STSE Case Study

Off the Grid and Living Green

Alternative energy sources such as solar and wind power make it possible to generate your own electricity supply.

Comparison of Energy-Efficient and Standard Appliances

Appliance	Average Energy Consumption (kW·h/year)	Consumption of Most Energy-efficient Model (kW·h/year)
Refrigerator	465	347
Dishwasher	457	344
Clothes washer	573	264

Cam and Brenda Snell live year-round in Silver Islet, Ontario, about 80 km from Thunder Bay and 8 km from the nearest power lines. Silver Islet is not connected to the power grid, which means that the community does not draw electricity from Ontario's network of generating stations and transmission lines.

Many local residents use gas generators when they need electricity. The Snells, however, decided to power their house with renewable energy sources. They installed a solar/wind hybrid system consisting of four 75 W photovoltaic cells (solar panels) on the roof of their house and a 1300 W two-blade wind turbine on a cliff behind their house. In addition, the Snells purchased energy-efficient appliances.

Solar Energy at Earth's Surface

To find out the useful amount of solar energy that a solar cell would receive, its position on Earth needs to be considered, as well as weather and seasonal changes, including the number of daylight hours. For Ontario, the average energy at Earth's surface is between 3.3 and 5.0 kW·h/m^2.

Costs of Solar Energy

The commercial solar cells that are now available are, at best, about 25 percent efficient. A single family home might have a roof area of about 30 m^2 facing the Sun. Thus, assuming that 4.0 kW·h/m^2 of energy is available on an average day, the electrical energy that could be generated is 4.0 kW·h/m^2 × 30 m^2 × 0.25 = 30 kW·h. In a 24 h period, only 1.7 kW of power is available, much less than what is usually needed in a home.

This example illustrates two of the problems with solar energy: it is not very concentrated, compared with other sources, and solar cells are not very efficient. A third disadvantage is the high cost of solar energy systems. Solar cells generate DC, and batteries are needed to store energy for use at night and on cloudy days. To supply energy to the grid, or to appliances that use AC, special electronics are required to convert DC to AC. The advantage, of course, is that the fuel is free, and there is very little negative impact on the environment.

Figure 12.23 Solar cells are becoming more common on our streets. They are used in parking meters, shown here, as well as traffic signals.

Combining Solar and Wind Energy

The solar and wind parts of the hybrid system complement each other well. In the summer, when the days are longer and there are more hours of sunlight, the solar panels provide most of the Snells' electricity. In the winter, the area is quite windy, so the wind generator takes over.
If excess energy is produced by the solar panels or wind generator, it can be stored in a bank of four lead-acid batteries. If there are long stretches without enough sunshine or wind, the Snells have a propane generator they can use. This is seldom necessary, however.

The Snells' total investment was about $40 000, which included the solar cells, the wind generator, the batteries, and all the other necessary electrical equipment. Bringing hydro wires into the community would have cost the Snells more. Since the Snells are not paying an electricity bill every month, they figure that their system will pay for itself in 20 to 25 years. Their choice was not just about saving money, however. It was about reducing their impact on the environment. Regardless of whether we live on or off the power grid, that is a choice all Canadians need to make.

Your Turn

1. Where do you see opportunities (big or small) in your community to generate electricity from renewable energy sources?

2. By purchasing electricity from a company called Bullfrog Power, residents of Ontario continue to draw power from the Ontario energy grid but also support locally generated renewable energy. Purchasing electricity from Bullfrog Power currently adds about $1 per day to an average electricity bill. Despite the extra cost, would you switch to an energy provider like Bullfrog Power? Why or why not?

3. Ontario has started a system called net metering. Research this system, and write a newspaper article that explains how net metering works in Ontario.

Ocean Wave Energy

Ocean waves can be used to generate electricity. The oceans on Canada's east and west coasts could meet our need for electrical energy many times over. The vertical rise and fall of the waves can be used to compress an air column, which drives a turbine that is connected to a generator. Canada is one of several countries that are investigating ways to generate electricity using ocean waves.

Tidal Energy

At Annapolis Royal, in Nova Scotia, a large natural basin and tides that change the height of the water by several metres are being used to generate electricity, as shown in **Figure 12.24**. A dam was built, with gates that allow water to enter the basin. At high tide, the gates are closed, trapping water in the basin. When the tide retreats, lowering the water level, the gates are opened. As the water leaves the basin, it turns turbines. One problem is that tides vary on a 15-day cycle. Another is the presence of boat traffic. Also, tidal stations only generate electricity for about 10 hours each day, as the tide is moving in or out. However, tides are predictable, unlike winds.

Biomass Energy

Biomass energy refers to energy that is generated from plant and animal matter. The burning of plant matter at biomass stations adds carbon dioxide to the atmosphere, but the process is said to be "carbon neutral." This is because plant combustion returns to the atmosphere only as much carbon as the plants absorbed during their growth. Compared with burning fossil fuels, especially coal, the use of biomass energy results in much less acid rain, and no heavy metals are emitted. A large and convenient supply of biomass is not available, however, unless agricultural land and forests are used for this purpose.

Geothermal Energy

Geothermal energy is produced from naturally occurring steam and hot water that is heated by hot rocks and trapped under Earth's surface. When pumped to the surface, the steam drives turbines to generate electricity. There are few, if any, emissions from geothermal plants and they can provide base-load electricity with low running cost. However, suitable reservoirs of very hot water are deep underground, and the cost of drilling to extract the water is high. In Canada, the best prospects for geothermal energy are in British Columbia.

biomass energy energy that is generated from plant and animal matter

Figure 12.24 The Annapolis Royal generating station is the only modern tidal generating station in North America.

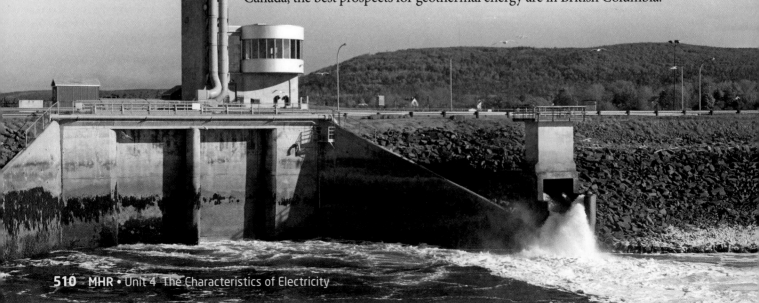

Conserving Electrical Energy

As you know, electrical energy is generated using other forms of energy. Each form of energy has an economic cost and an environmental cost. Switching energy use to off-peak times lowers the costs and reduces the effects on the environment. Using less electricity saves even more, both in costs and in effects on the environment. Governments and utility companies have a key role to play in energy conservation. For example, to meet projected demand, the Ontario government might decide to spend $1 billion to build a new generating station. An alternative is to offer incentives that encourage conservation and to pass legislation that requires change.

Ontario introduced the Great Refrigerator Roundup program in 2007 to remove older, inefficient refrigerators, freezers, and window air conditioners. The EnerGuide program, which gives consumers information about new appliances, was initiated by Natural Resources Canada. In some regions of Ontario, residents can sign up for the "peaksaver® program. This program allows the local utility company to install a device, operated wirelessly, that reduces the electricity used by a central air-conditioning unit.

The common incandescent bulb, used in homes for about 100 years, will be banned for sale in Ontario beginning in 2012. Smart meters will provide homeowners with the information they can use to reduce their energy bills. None of these initiatives can be successful, however, without individual action.

Suggested Investigation

Plan Your Own Investigation 12-D, Every Kilowatt Counts, on page 516

Go to **scienceontario** to find out more

Making a Difference

For their 2008 science project, Pinky Langat and Chris Palmer investigated dye-sensitized solar cells (DSSCs) because these cells mimic photosynthesis. They had both been amazed by the efficiency of photosynthesis when they studied it in biology class. DSSCs can be cheaper and less hazardous to produce than other types of solar cells. Pinky and Chris investigated how DSSCs could be made as efficient as possible. They produced and tested DSSCs using different components to increase electrical efficiency. Their work produced a unique design that improved efficiency by 10 percent.

Pinky and Chris won several awards at the Canada Wide Science Fair for their project, "A Bright Future for Energy: Optimizing Dye-Sensitized Solar Cells." Pinky is now studying biochemistry and international relations at McGill University. Chris is studying engineering at Queen's University and is a member of the Queen's Fuel Cell Team.

What organizations could you join to help promote government and corporate funding of research into sustainable energy technologies?

Section Summary

- Renewable sources of energy can be renewed within a reasonably short period of time.

- In Ontario, the renewable energy sources that contribute to electrical energy are wind, hydroelectric, and solar energy.

- Other renewable energy sources include waves, tides, biomass, and geothermal.

- Solar photovoltaic cells are semiconductor materials that generate a direct current when light shines on them.

Review Questions

K/U **1.** Explain the difference between renewable and non-renewable energy sources. Give an example of each.

A **2.** Refer to **Figure 12.22**. What is the function of the controller in a wind turbine?

K/U **3.** What are the advantages and disadvantages of photovoltaic cells?

K/U **4.** Why are photovoltaic cells sometimes used to provide electrical energy for a home or business in a remote location?

T/I **5.** Solar cells are commonly used to provide electricity for satellites. What advantages do solar cells have in space, compared with similar solar cells on Earth's surface?

K/U **6.** Why is biomass combustion considered to be carbon neutral?

A **7.** Contact your local utility company to find out how it helps its customers conserve energy. Make a summary, and identify any energy-saving incentives that would benefit your family.

T/I **8.** Examine the map below. What conditions in the Bay of Fundy make it a possible source of tidal energy?

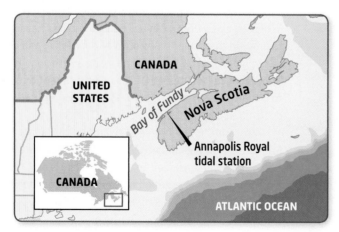

The Annapolis Royal tidal station is located on the Bay of Fundy.

Skill Check

✓ Initiating and Planning

✓ Performing and Recording

✓ Analyzing and Interpreting

✓ Communicating

Safety Precautions

Materials

• battery (6 V)

• connecting wires

• flashlight bulb in holder

• 2 three-connection switches

A staircase circuit allows you to turn a light on or off at two different locations.

Designing a Staircase Circuit

Many AC circuits are similar to DC circuits. In this investigation, you will design and build a circuit with two switches that control a single light. Your circuit will be similar to a circuit for a staircase light that can be turned on or off by operating either of two switches placed at the top and bottom of the staircase.

Challenge

Design a circuit that can be used to switch a light bulb on or off using two switches. Construct and test your circuit.

Design Criteria

a. Use a minimum number of connecting wires to construct your circuit.

b. You must be able to turn the light on or off using either of the two switches.

Plan and Construct

1. Draw diagrams of possible circuits. Decide which circuit will work best.

2. Have your teacher approve your design. Then connect and test your circuit.

3. If your circuit does not operate properly, check the connections and your circuit diagram. If necessary, modify your circuit and try again.

4. Demonstrate your circuit to your teacher and then to your classmates.

Evaluate

1. Did your first circuit work properly? If not, explain why not.

2. What precaution would you expect an electrician to take before wiring switches in your home?

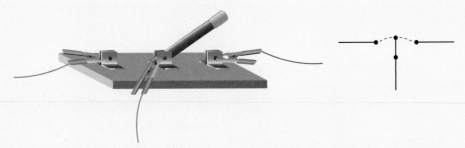

In this investigation, you will use switches with three connections, as shown.

Real World Investigation 12-B

Skill Check

Initiating and Planning

✓ Performing and Recording

✓ Analyzing and Interpreting

✓ Communicating

Science Skills

Go to **Science Skills Toolkit 7** to learn more about Creating Data Tables.

An Electrical Energy Audit

You can calculate the energy that your family uses in one week by adding up the energy consumed by all the appliances and devices used. If you cannot find the power rating of an appliance or device in your home, use typical data from **Table 12.2**.

Question

Which appliances in your home consume the most energy?

Organize the Data

Make a table to record your family's use of electrical appliances and lighting. Give your table a title. Some appliances are never turned off. For these appliances, enter 24 h multiplied by the number of days you monitor your energy use.

Appliance or Device	Power		Time on	Time off	Time Used	Energy Used
	(W)	(kW)			(h)	(kW·h)

Analyze and Interpret

1. Record the date and the meter reading for your home.

2. One week later, record the date and the final meter reading. Calculate the energy used. Then calculate your family's daily consumption of electricity.

3. Calculate and record the total energy used in the chart. Treat all the lighting as one device. **Note:** This gives only an approximate estimate. A power rating refers to usage at full power.

4. Compare the value you calculated for energy use in step 2, based on the meter readings, with the value you calculated in step 3 by adding the energy used by all the appliances and devices. Explain the likely causes of any difference between the two values.

Conclude and Communicate

5. List the six appliances or devices in your home that consume the most electrical energy.

6. List the appliances or devices in your home that could be replaced with energy-saving models.

Extend Your Inquiry and Research Skills

7. **Research** Use the Internet to find out the time of use prices in effect during your audit. Then use your time and energy data to calculate the cost of using each appliance.

Data Analysis Investigation 12-C

Skill Check

✓ Initiating and Planning

  Performing and Recording

✓ Analyzing and Interpreting

✓ Communicating

Anywhere High School (AHS)

- AHS has 1500 students and staff who wash their hands four times each school day, using two paper towels each time.

- The washrooms at AHS have a total of 16 paper-towel dispensers, which cost $25 each.

- A case of brown paper towels costs $30 and contains 4000 towels.

- Brown paper towels are made from recycled paper products but are sent to a landfill after being used. A case has a mass of 10 kg.

Erehwon High School (EHS)

- EHS is identical to AHS but has electric hot-air hand dryers.

- Each of the 16 dryers cost $80.

- The dryers are rated at 1.5 kW and provide hot air for 30 s.

- Each dryer uses 2 W in stand-by mode throughout the school year.

- The school pays an average of $0.08/kW·h for electrical energy.

A "Dry" Investigation

When you are in a public restroom and need to dry your hands, should you use paper towels or an electric hot-air hand dryer? In this investigation, you will compare the use of paper towels with the use of hot-air hand dryers at two high schools.

Question

Which is the least expensive and most environmentally friendly way to dry your hands during a school year (about 200 days)?

Organize the Data

Make a table to summarize the data on the left.

Analyze and Interpret

1. a. How many paper towels are used during the school year at AHS?

  b. How many cases of paper towels are used?

  c. What is the annual mass of paper towels that go to a landfill?

  d. What is the annual cost of paper towels?

  e. What was the cost of the paper towel dispensers?

2. a. At EHS, how many hours do the dryers operate per year?

  b. How much energy (in kW·h) is used to operate the dryers?

  c. What is the cost of the electricity used to operate the dryers?

  d. What was the cost of installing the hand dryers?

3. a. The hot-air hand dryers remain connected all year, which is 8760 h. What is the total number of hours that all the dryers at EHS are connected?

  b. For how many hours are the dryers in stand-by mode?

  c. How much energy is consumed in stand-by mode?

  d. What is the cost of the electricity used in stand-by mode?

Conclude and Communicate

4. Compare the total annual cost of using power towels and electric hot-air hand dryers.

Extend Your Inquiry and Research Skills

5. Inquiry Although the amount of CO_2 emitted by generating electricity varies with the type of station, an overall estimate is 0.5 kg CO_2 per kW·h. Calculate the mass of CO_2 emitted by generating the electricity for the hand dryers. Compare this with the mass of the paper towels sent to a landfill.

Plan Your Own Investigation 12-D

Skill Check

✓ Initiating and Planning

✓ Performing and Recording

✓ Analyzing and Interpreting

✓ Communicating

Suggested Materials

- copy of a recent electricity bill
- computer and spreadsheet program

Every Kilowatt Counts

The electricity bill is a very important part of many families' budget. Electricity costs can be reduced by using appliances during off-peak times and by using less electricity.

Question

What steps can you take to reduce your family electricity costs?

Plan and Conduct

1. Refer to your work on Real World Investigation 12-B, An Electrical Energy Audit.

2. Identify which major appliances in your home, if any, could be replaced. Predict the annual savings if you replaced one.

3. Examine your electrical energy audit for your family. Outline ways your family could save by changing your use of major appliances to off-peak times. Estimate the annual savings if you did this.

4. Gather information about ways to conserve electrical energy from your local utility company and the Internet.

5. Divide your family use of electricity into various categories, such as lighting, heating, entertainment, and food preparation. For each category, identify ways to reduce energy use or switch to off-peak use. Include phantom loads in your investigation.

Analyze and Interpret

1. Make three recommendations for reducing the family's electricity bill. Estimate total annual savings (in kW·h and dollars) if your family follows each recommendation. Show your calculations.

2. There are about 4.6 million households in Ontario. Estimate the annual energy savings if each household reduced its electrical energy use by the same amount you estimated for your family.

Conclude and Communicate

3. Evaluate the processes you used to gather information and make decisions. Explain any improvements you could make.

Extend Your Inquiry and Research Skills

4. **Inquiry** Compare the output from a medium-sized generating station (500 MW) with the reduction in electrical generation that would be possible if all the households in Ontario followed your conservation recommendations.

12.1 Electricity at Home

Key Concepts

- Electrical energy is always generated from another source of energy.

- In direct current, charged particles travel through a circuit in only one direction. In alternating current, electrons move back and forth in a circuit.

- Alternating current is generated when a magnet and a coil of wire are moved relative to each other.

- Alternating current can be transmitted at high potential difference over long distances, with only a small loss of electrical energy.

- Transformers can increase (step up), or decrease (step down) voltage, but they only work with alternating current.

- Circuit breakers and fuses are safety devices that limit the current to appliances and wall outlets in your home.

12.2 Using Electrical Energy Wisely

Key Concepts

- The electrical power of an appliance is the rate at which it uses electrical energy. The practical unit for electrical power is the kilowatt (kW).

- The electrical energy that is used by an appliance is calculated by multiplying its power rating (in kW) by the amount of time that it is used (in hours, h). The practical unit of electrical energy is the kilowatt-hour (kW·h).

- The cost of electrical energy is calculated by multiplying the amount of energy that is used (in kW·h) by the price (in ¢/kW·h).

- Smart meters allow a utility company to charge a different amount for each kW·h of energy that is used at different times of the day.

- The electricity that is consumed by any appliance or device when it is turned off is called the phantom load.

- The efficiency of an electrical device is the ratio of useful energy output to total energy input, or useful output to total input, expressed as a percentage.

12.3 Meeting the Demand for Electricity

Key Concepts

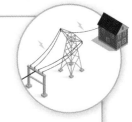

- Base load is the continuous minimum demand for electrical power. It is met using large generators that run on the least expensive fuels.

- Intermediate load and peak load are met by using smaller generators that can be turned on and off quickly.

- Ontario obtains most of its electrical energy from nuclear, hydroelectric, and fossil fuel-burning stations.

- The rate that is charged for electricity changes when the cost of the fuel that is used to generate the electricity changes.

12.4 Sustainable Sources of Electricity

Key Concepts

- Renewable sources of energy can be renewed within a reasonably short time period.

- In Ontario, the renewable energy sources that contribute to electrical energy are wind, hydroelectric, and solar energy.

- Solar photovoltaic cells are semiconductor materials that generate a direct current when light shines on them.

- Biomass energy refers to the generation of electricity from plant and animal matter.

Make Your Own Summary

Summarize the key concepts in this chapter using a graphic organizer. The Chapter Summary on the previous page will help you identify the key concepts. Refer to Study Toolkit 4 on pages 566–567 to help you decide which graphic organizer to use.

Reviewing Key Terms

Match each key term listed below to its definition. The terms may be used once, more than once, or not at all.

Definition

1. technology that is used to change the voltage of an alternating current

2. device that is used to protect a circuit by opening a switch when the current exceeds a safe maximum value

3. the practical unit of electrical energy

4. something that helps you choose a new electric washing machine

5. the clock on an electric coffee maker

6. a demand that is met using fossil-fuel-burning generators, which can be turned on and off quickly

7. a renewable source of energy that involves the indirect conversion of energy from the Sun

8. its practical unit is the kW

Terms

a. biomass energy

b. phantom load

c. electrical energy

d. electrical power

e. EnerGuide label

f. fuse

g. intermediate load

h. kW

i. kW·h

j. circuit breaker

k. solar energy

l. transformer

Knowledge and Understanding K/U

9. When there is alternating current in a circuit, electrons move back and forth. Explain how AC can transfer energy.

10. Why is AC, rather than DC, used to supply electrical energy in Canada?

11. What are the functions of the two vertical slots and the round hole in a wall outlet?

12. A freezer consumes 340 kW·h of electrical energy in a year, and the average rate charged is 6.0 ¢/kW·h. What is the cost to operate this freezer for a year?

13. Energy conversions take place at a fossil-fuel generating station. Which of these energy conversions lower the efficiency of the station the most?

14. How is a surge protector the same as a power bar? How is it different?

15. Is the connection to a circuit breaker in series or in parallel? Explain.

16. What is the source of the energy that is available from oceans (tides and wave energy)?

17. What factors affect the energy that can be obtained from a solar panel?

18. Which source of energy that is used to generate electricity results in the greatest emission of gases to the atmosphere?

Thinking and Investigation T/I

19. Calculate the efficiency of a 23 W compact fluorescent bulb that generates 5.0 W of useful light energy.

20. An electric water heater is 90 percent efficient. If the output from the heater to the water is 6.5 kW, what is the power input to the heater?

21. Compare and contrast the methods used to generate electricity from different energy sources.

22. The following table compares the environmental costs of generating electricity from various sources. The cheapest source is wind energy (given a value of 1), and the other sources are compared with it.

Environmental Costs of Generating Electrical Energy from Various Sources

Source	Comparative Environmental Cost
Fossil fuels	114-609
Nuclear	120-1200
Solar	44
Wind	1

a. Wind and solar energy are renewable resources. Why do you think the environmental cost of a solar plant is so much greater than the environmental cost of a wind farm?

b. A considerable range is given for the environmental cost of nuclear energy. This cost includes the costs of construction, operation, waste disposal, and closing down the plant at the end of its life. Research these costs, and briefly summarize your findings. Explain why a wide range is quoted for the environmental cost of nuclear energy.

23. More electrical energy may be required in the future to charge electric vehicles. Which type of generating plant would you expect Ontario to build to meet this need? Why?

Communication C

24. A letter to the editor of your local newspaper states that in a northern climate such as Ontario's, incandescent bulbs provide necessary heat as well as light. How would you explain, in a follow-up letter, why although that is true, people should still replace incandescent with fluorescent lighting?

25. **BIG IDEAS** Electricity is a form of energy produced from a variety of non-renewable and renewable sources. To reduce environmental impact, we should generate electrical energy using clean, renewable sources, rather than non-renewable ones. Describe the promise and challenge of using wind turbines, solar panels, ocean energy, and geothermal energy to generate electricity.

26. **BIG IDEAS** The production and consumption of electrical energy has social, economic, and environmental implications. How is the slogan "every kilowatt counts" relevant to you as a consumer of electrical energy? How is the slogan relevant to the environment?

27. **BIG IDEAS** Static and current electricity have distinct properties that determine how they are used. Describe some of the uses of each type of electricity. Which of these types of electricity do you think has more practical applications (or more important practical applications)? Explain.

28. Men and women work in a variety of fields with the general heading of "electrician." Find out what these fields are, and what education and training are required. Using what you find out, create a brochure that could be placed on a careers bulletin board at your school.

Application A

29. Suppose that the capacity of an existing power plant is going to be doubled. Currently, electricity is carried from the plant by 350 kV transmission lines. Outline two ways that the increased energy could be distributed when the capacity of the plant is doubled.

30. Explain why a fire can result if a 15 A fuse is replaced with a fuse that has a higher rating.

31. What sources of electrical energy can best be developed in Ontario in the future? Explain.

Science at Work

Ben used metal from one of his grandfather's engineering projects to create the Uno.

Canadians in Science

Thanks to a high school science project, Ben Gulak from Milton, Ontario, is going places. Ben combined his interests in motorcycles and science to invent a battery-powered riding machine that he named the Uno. With its two wheels positioned side by side, the Uno looks like a radically redesigned unicycle. It is controlled by simply leaning forward or backward to speed up or slow down.

Ben's invention earned him a top award at an international science fair and put him on the cover of *Popular Science* magazine. Ben is studying mechanical engineering at the Massachusetts Institute of Technology (MIT). In addition, he is working on plans to bring his eco-friendly invention to the market.

In Ben Gulak's Words

I started thinking about battery power during a visit to China. Seeing so many gasoline-fueled motorcycles and scooters gave me the idea to design a vehicle that has less effect on the environment. I am now on my third model, or prototype, as I work through some design and engineering challenges. I would like to have a product with appeal especially in Asia, Europe, and South America. In those regions, motorcycles and scooters really are part of the culture and are needed by many people to get around.

Engineering has interested me for a long time. I learned a lot from my grandfather, who was an engineer and inventor. Participating in a science fair also helped. It allowed me to meet many knowledgeable, skilled professionals. If you show a real interest in science and discovery, people in the scientific community are more than eager to offer guidance. My advice to students thinking about a science career is to check out every opportunity. Ontario has excellent mentoring programs linked to terrific resources at post-secondary institutions and science organizations.

An interest in transportation technology leads to many career opportunities. This is a great time to look at green technology, with governments and the private sector funding a lot of research. In today's environment, we can't afford not to look at energy efficiency and sustainability. I think there are possibilities that we haven't even considered yet. Today, you can buy electric sports cars that, 20 years ago, no one thought were possible. Who knows where technology will take us in the next 20 years?

The Uno, developed by Ben Gulak, uses wheelchair motors.

Electricity at Work

The study of electricity contributes to these careers, as well as many more!

Electronic Service Technician

Construction Inspector

Powerline Technician

Electricity

Robotics Engineer

Mechanical Engineer

Electrician

Electricians install, maintain, repair, and test electrical circuits in residential, commercial, and industrial settings. Electricians make sure that wiring, outlets, switches, and other devices work safely to provide the energy that lights homes, runs office equipment, and powers factories. In Ontario, many electricians have trade certification. People who meet trade standards in terms of training, education, and experience can become certified.

Power Station Operator

Power station operators run systems and equipment that generate electricity for distribution in power grids. They monitor energy systems and adjust electricity output to meet changes in energy demand. They also monitor production equipment in hydroelectric dams, nuclear reactors, and oil-fired or gas-fired turbines, to ensure that the equipment runs safely and efficiently. Entry-level operators usually have a high school diploma. Senior-level operators may have a diploma from a technical college or a university degree in either engineering or physical science.

Electrical Engineer

Electrical engineers design, build, and test electrical and electronic equipment. They also participate in leading-edge research to build better power generators, improve telecommunications technology, and enhance computer systems. Electrical engineers usually have undergraduate or post-graduate degrees in science or engineering.

Go to **scienceontario** to find out more

Over To You

1. Imagine that you have a background in electrical systems and are working with Ben Gulak. Write a short paragraph that describes some of the challenges you would face in designing a machine that, like the Uno, operates on battery power.

2. Ben refers to mentoring programs that help Ontario high school students interested in careers in science and technology. Research one of these programs, and share your findings with the class.

3. From the list of careers related to electricity, choose one that interests you. Use Internet and print resources to research this career. **What essential skills would you need for this career?**

Inquiry Investigation

Designing an Electrical Makeover

Devise a "green" design to improve the electrical plan of a room in your home.

> **Inquiry Question**
> How might you reduce electricity use in your home?

Initiate and Plan

1. Select two rooms in your home. List the devices that require electricity in each room.

2. Explain how these devices are connected in a circuit. Include a description of the role of each of the following components: switch, fuse, electrical source, load, resistor. Summarize the information in a table.

Perform and Record

3. Draw a schematic diagram that supports your explanation.

4. Design and build a circuit board that models the wiring in each room. Test your circuit board to ensure that it works.

5. Determine the maximum current draw for each room. To do this, check the size and number of fuses or circuit breakers that service the room from the distribution panel.

Analyze and Interpret

1. Which room uses more electricity? Provide evidence to support your answer.

2. Alter the design of the room that uses more electricity so that it uses less electricity. Consider these criteria:
   - Flexibility
   - Cost-effectiveness
   - Safety

3. Draw a new schematic diagram for your "greener" room. Include at least one power bar or surge protector for all non-essential loads, and create a special label for this in your schematic diagram. Consider the types of lighting you choose, the size and type of television and/or computer monitor (if applicable), and the power requirements for the other devices.

Communicate Your Findings

4. Prepare a summary of your "greener" room design. Include your schematic diagram and an explanation of your new electrical plan. Present your summary using a visual format of your choice.

Assessment Criteria

Once you complete your project, ask yourself these questions. Did you...

- **K/U** describe accurately the components of the electrical circuit in the selected rooms of the home?

- **C** draw accurate schematic diagrams?

- **C** organize effectively the details about the components of the circuit?

- **C** present the summary of the "greener" room using an appropriate visual format?

- **C** use proper scientific conventions and vocabulary?

- **T/I** design a functional circuit board for each room using safe practices?

- **T/I** accurately determine the current values for each room using appropriate information from the distribution panel?

- **T/I** accurately identify with supporting evidence the room that uses more electricity?

- **A** accurately evaluate the circuit design for the "greener" room according to criteria of flexibility, safety, and cost-effectiveness?

An Issue to Analyze

A "Greener" Power Generation Mix

Since the turn of the 21st century, more and more non-traditional sources of electrical energy have been appearing in Ontario. Wind generators dot rural landscapes, and solar panels are becoming more common. Many large power-generation companies, however, still produce electricity from traditional sources of energy. In 2007, Ontario Power Generation produced electrical energy from 64 hydroelectric, five fossil-fuel (coal), and three nuclear generating stations. Despite these statistics, power generation companies in Ontario are making an effort to become "greener."

Issue

In what ways can one power generation company be "greener" than another?

Initiate and Plan

1. Imagine that you are a representative of a consumer organization. Research information about power generation companies that provide electricity to home-owners in Ontario. Choose two companies that produce electricity from distinctly different sources of energy.

Perform and Record

2. Create a table for each company. List the types of energy sources each uses to generate power. Include these headings to describe each energy source:

   - Traditional or non-traditional source of energy
   - Number of power generation plants
   - Total power output
   - Reliability

3. Create a separate table that focuses on the environmental impacts of the energy sources used by each company. Include these headings:

   - Renewable or non-renewable resource
   - Disruption of ecosystems involved (for example, scarring the landscape, rerouting waterways, laying pipelines)

- Dependence on other resources (for example, scarce or non-renewable resources required, fuel needed for transportation)
- Type of pollution produced (for example, air, water, thermal)
- Waste production (for example, amount, type, treatment and/or containment required, danger level)
- "Greener" sources for the future

Analyze and Interpret

1. Reorganize your findings in a risk-benefit-cost analysis chart for each company.

2. Based on your findings, decide which power generation company is currently "greener." Write your decision as a concluding statement.

Communicate Your Findings

Write a report for your organization that compares the two companies in terms of their environmental impact.

Assessment Criteria

Once you complete your project, ask yourself these questions. Did you...

- **A** clearly define your issue and position with supporting evidence?
- **A** describe multiple perspectives on the issue?
- **A** identify using an accurate and concise concluding statement which company is "greener" based on a summary of the risk-benefit-cost analysis?
- **C** gather and cite information from a variety of sources, including electronic, print, and/or human resources using an accepted form of academic documentation?
- **C** communicate findings using appropriate scientific vocabulary?
- **C** communicate information effectively for both your audience and purpose?

Unit 4 Review

Use this bicycle wheel graphic organizer to connect what you have learned in this unit to the Big Ideas, found on page 399. Draw one bicycle wheel for each Big Idea and write the Big Idea in the centre. Between the spokes of the wheel, briefly describe six examples of that Big Idea.

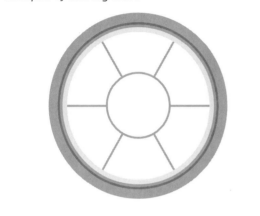

Knowledge and Understanding K/U

For questions 1 through 4, select the best answer.

1. When glass and silk are rubbed together
   a. protons are transferred from the silk to the glass
   b. electrons are transferred from the silk to the glass
   c. protons are transferred from the glass to the silk
   d. electrons are transferred from the glass to the silk

2. Three different pith balls (labelled P, Q, and R) are charged by contact. Then the pith balls are brought close to each other. Pith balls P and Q repel each other. Pith balls P and R attract each other. Which of these could be the charges on the three pith balls?

	P	Q	R
a.	−	+	+
b.	−	+	−
c.	−	−	+
d.	−	−	−

3. Electrical energy is measured in
   a. amperes
   b. volts
   c. watts or kilowatts
   d. watt-hours or kilowatt-hours

4. Which circuit could be used to measure the resistance of a lamp?

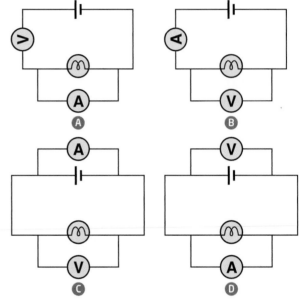

5. People sometimes rub sunglasses with a cloth to clean them. Why is this not a good way to clean sunglasses on a hot, dry day?

6. **a.** Explain why a neutral pith ball, suspended by a cotton thread, moves toward a negatively charged rod that is held nearby.

   b. Explain why this pith ball is strongly repelled after it makes contact with the charged rod.

7. Classify each cell as wet or dry, and as primary or secondary.
   a. zinc-carbon cell
   b. nickel-cadmium cell
   c. lead-acid battery

8. A series circuit consists of a battery that is connected to two loads with different resistances. What are the properties of current and potential difference in this circuit?

9. A parallel circuit consists of a battery that is connected to two loads with different resistances. What are the properties of current and potential difference in this circuit?

10. What environmental problems are associated with using nuclear energy to generate electricity?

11. Distinguish between two different types of energy that are available from the oceans. What is the source of each type of energy?

Thinking and Investigation T/I

12. A friend complains that she sometimes experiences a small shock after using a telephone. She wonders whether the telephone has an electrical fault. You know that your friend often places the telephone handset on one of her shoulders while she talks. What is the likely reason for the shock? Outline a simple investigation to prove your hypothesis.

13. Suppose that you have a part-time job assembling electronic components at a factory. The electronic components arrive at your metal table after sliding through a plastic delivery tube. Some of the components you assemble do not work properly, and the manager thinks that you are responsible for this. Could the parts be faulty before you assemble them? Explain your reasoning. What suggestions would you make to solve the problem?

14. In the circuit below, new 1.5 V AA cells were connected and a series of potential differences were measured as indicated. What value would you predict for each measurement?

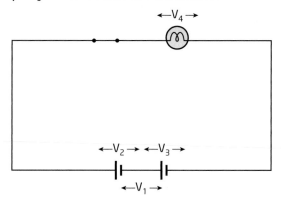

15. The potential difference in an operating electric circuit is doubled, and the resistance is halved. What change takes place in the current?

16. A solar array has an area of 4.0 m by 2.0 m, and the panels are 25 percent efficient at converting sunlight to electricity. On a day when the Sun is providing 5.0 kW·h per square metre, what is the electrical output from the solar array?

17. What is the monthly cost of operating a 60 W security light for 12 h each night? Assume that there are 30 days in a month and the electricity costs 7.0¢/kW·h.

18. An environmental website claims that a large coal-burning plant emits more radioactive materials into the atmosphere than a nuclear plant with the same generating capacity. Use Internet or print resources to investigate this claim. How can radioactive materials be emitted from each type of generating plant? State whether you agree or disagree with this claim.

Communication C

19. Draw a diagram of an electroscope. Identify each labelled part of the electroscope and state which type of material (insulator or conductor) it is.

20. Draw and label two wet cells that are connected in series to make a battery.

21. Draw a Venn diagram. Label one circle "direct current" and the other circle "alternating current." Write as many statements as you can in the three sections of the Venn diagram.

22. The first Earth Hour in Ontario took place between 8:00 P.M. and 9:00 P.M. on Saturday, March 29, 2008. During Earth Hour, people were encouraged to use less electricity. A graph of the demand for electricity on March 29, 2008 is shown below.

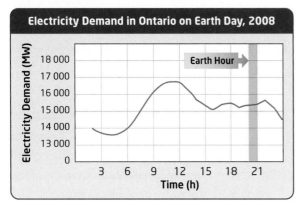

Electricity Demand in Ontario on Earth Day, 2008

During Earth Hour, the demand for electricity actually increased slightly compared with the previous hour's demand. Explain why the organizers of Earth Hour still claimed that Earth Hour was a success.

23. Describe the factors that contribute to the environmental costs of burning fossil fuels to generate electricity.

24. Using the data in the table below, identify the major differences in the energy mix in Ontario and Alberta. Then suggest reasons why these differences exist.

Sources of Electricity

Energy Source	Ontario (%)	Alberta (%)
Nuclear	52	—
Hydroelectric	21	7
Coal	18	49
Gas	8	38
Wind and other	1	6

Application A

25. Suppose that you want to connect speakers in your bedroom to the stereo system in the living room. How will you ensure that the speakers receive the strongest possible signal?

26. The heating element in a toaster is a metal wire. What electrical properties do you expect that the wire has? What other properties are important in this type of application?

27. Some people, especially those living in remote locations, use a small electric generator if there is a power failure. When a refrigerator motor turns on and off, it may cause a fluctuation in the output supplied by the generator to other devices. Explain why this happens and how sensitive equipment, such as a computer, can be protected.

28. Two examples of secondary cells are the lead-acid cell and the lithium-ion cell.

   a. What is a secondary cell?

   b. What properties distinguish a lead-acid cell from a lithium-ion cell?

   c. State one application for each cell.

29. This circuit is used to illuminate four bulbs at the corners of a mirror.

   a. Suggest a reason for having a resistor in series with each bulb.

   b. If one bulb burned out, what change would occur in the brightness of the other three bulbs?

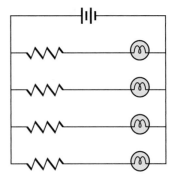

30. A worker received a severe electrical shock when she inserted the end of a plug into the broken socket of a portable machine and then touched the metal casing of the machine. The broken socket allowed the plug to be inserted 90° clockwise from the appropriate connection. Explain why the worker received a shock.

Literacy Test Prep

Read the selection below, and answer the questions that follow it.

Life Cycle Assessment

Life cycle assessment or analysis (LCA) is an assessment of the environmental impact of a product or technology over its full life cycle. It is often referred to as a cradle-to-grave analysis. The LCA for an electricity generating station starts with the environmental impact of mining raw materials for construction and operation. The LCA ends with the demolition and disposal of the station, called its decommissioning.

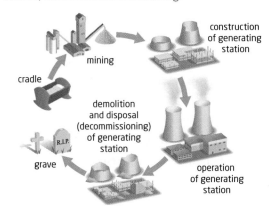

Different types of electricity generating stations can be compared over the lifetime of their operation.

Different kinds of generating stations affect the environment in different ways, but an LCA can be used to make a direct comparison between them. Because CO_2 is an important greenhouse gas, one type of LCA compares how much CO_2 different kinds of stations emit into the atmosphere during their life cycle. All generating stations result in CO_2 emissions over their lifetime, because energy and materials are required for their construction (at "cradle") and decommissioning (at "grave"). Solar-cell production results in relatively large emissions of CO_2 because the silicon that is used to produce the cells is obtained by heating quartz sand to a high temperature.

Comparisons that are based on CO_2 emissions discriminate against fossil-fuel stations, which emit large quantities of CO_2 during their operation. A large coal-burning station may require 3 000 000 tonnes of coal a year. The coal must be mined and transported to the station. About 200 000 m^3 of ash are generated, and about 6 000 000 tonnes of CO_2 are sent into the atmosphere. The capture and storage of CO_2 (for example, in the oceans or underground) would drastically change the LCA for coal-burning stations. This technology, however, has not yet been shown to be practical.

Multiple Choice

In your notebook choose and record the best or most correct answer.

31. In paragraph 2, you learned that
   a. life cycle assessments are only used to compare electricity generating stations
   b. life cycle assessments compare the costs of building different generating stations
   c. cradle-to-grave means the full life cycle of a product or technology
   d. carbon dioxide emissions are one measure for comparing generating stations

32. A life cycle assessment for an electricity generating station
   a. evaluates only the cost of constructing the station
   b. evaluates the cost of decommissioning the station
   c. compares the price of the fuel that is used to operate the station
   d. assesses the environmental impact of the station

33. Carbon dioxide emissions are often used to make a life cycle assessment because
   a. CO_2 is a gas
   b. CO_2 is a greenhouse gas
   c. CO_2 levels are easily measured
   d. fossil fuels emit large quantities of CO_2

34. The diagram reminds us that an LCA
   a. must include cradle-to-grave environmental impacts
   b. emphasizes the emissions during the operation of a generating station
   c. discriminates against fossil-fuel generating stations
   d. shows how mining has the greatest impact on the environment

Written Answer

35. Summarize this selection. Include the main idea and one relevant point that supports it.

Guide to the Toolkits and Appendices

TOOLKITS

Science Skills Toolkit 1 Analyzing Issues—Science, Technology, Society, and the Environment 529

Science Skills Toolkit 2 Scientific Inquiry 532

Science Skills Toolkit 3 Technological Problem Solving 536

Science Skills Toolkit 4 Estimating and Measuring 538

Science Skills Toolkit 5 Precision and Accuracy 542

Science Skills Toolkit 6 Scientific Drawing 543

Science Skills Toolkit 7 Creating Data Tables 545

Science Skills Toolkit 8 Using a Microscope 546

Science Skills Toolkit 9 The GRASP Problem Solving Method 547

Science Skills Toolkit 10 Using Electric Circuit Symbols and Meters . . . 548

Science Skills Toolkit 11 Using Models and Analogies in Science 551

Science Skills Toolkit 12 How to Do a Research-Based Project 552

Math Skills Toolkit 1 The Metric System and Scientific Notation 554

Math Skills Toolkit 2 Significant Digits and Rounding 556

Math Skills Toolkit 3 Organizing and Communicating Scientific Results with Graphs 557

Study Toolkit Overview 561

Study Toolkit 1 Preparing for Reading: Previewing Text Features 563

Study Toolkit 2 Reading Effectively: Monitoring Comprehension 564

Study Toolkit 3 Word Study: Common Base Words, Prefixes, and Suffixes in Science 565

Study Toolkit 4 Organizing Your Learning: Using Graphic Organizers 566

APPENDICES

Appendix A Properties of Common Substances 568

Appendix B Using Star Maps 570

Appendix C Chemistry References 572

Appendix D Numerical Answers and Answers to Practice Problems 573

Science Skills Toolkit 1

Analyzing Issues—Science, Technology, Society, and the Environment

Can you think of an issue that involves science, technology, society, and the environment? How about the use of salt to de-ice roads in the winter? Roads are safer in winter when they are clear of ice and snow.

However, what if you found out that the salt may eventually reach your drinking water and could have negative effects on aquatic ecosystems? How might you use science and technology to solve this problem?

Suppose your town council is in the process of deciding whether to expand its road salting program. How will you analyze this issue and determine what action to take? The concept map on this page shows a process to help you focus your thinking and stay on track.

A Process for Analyzing Issues

Identify the issue.

↓

Gather relevant information.

↓

Identify all the alternatives.

↓

Consider each alternative by clarifying its consequences.

↓

Make a decision.

↓

Evaluate the decision.

Errors of judgement may have been made at any of these steps in the decision-making process.

The decision is the best alternative based on risks/benefits and, thus, probable consequences.

One or more of the steps in the decision-making process were faulty. No action should be taken and the process should be repeated to ensure that the faulty steps are eliminated and replaced by improved thinking.

Take action and communicate the decision.

Identifying the Issue

Soon after hearing the news about the road salting, you go to your friend's house. You find your friend sitting in front of the computer, composing a letter to the town council. In it, your friend is asking that the salting program not be expanded to your area. "I heard that the salt can damage the environment, but how bad can it be?" you ask. "And, isn't it important to make our roads safer?"

Gathering Information

"It is," answers your friend, "but is there some way we can make the roads safer without doing so much harm to the plants at roadsides and to the drinking water in springs and wells? I was going to research to find information about these questions I have written down."

"Whew," you say. "There is an awful lot to think about here. Let's see what we can find out from the Internet."

The Internet and other sources, such as books or experts, are great places to find information about an issue. One thing that is important to do when gathering information is to look for bias. **Bias** is a personal and possibly unreasonable judgement of an issue. For example, a person who makes his or her living putting salt on the roads may have a bias that salt does not harm the environment. It is important to check the source of information to determine whether it is unbiased. Refer to **Science Skills Toolkit 12** for more information about how to research information.

Another important part of gathering information is taking notes so that you can analyze what you have learned. You may read about different viewpoints or solutions and advantages and disadvantages for each one. It is helpful to be able to organize your notes in the form of a graphic organizer such as a concept map, a flowchart, or a Venn diagram. You will find information on using graphic organizers in **Study Toolkit 4** on pages 566–567.

Identifying Alternatives

Your research may lead you to ask new questions about alternative solutions and how successful they might be. For example, you might think about how a combination of salt and sand would work to keep roads clear of ice. Would this be a safer environmental alternative? Answering these questions often leads to more research or possibly doing your own scientific inquiry.

Making a Decision

When you have all of the information that your research can provide, your decision will still involve some very human and personal elements. People have strong feelings about the social and environmental issues that affect them. Something that seems obvious to you might not be so obvious to another person. Even the unbiased scientific evidence you found during your research might not change that person's mind. If you are going to encourage a group to make what you consider a good decision, you have to find ways to persuade the group to think as you do.

Evaluating the Decision

After you have made a decision, it is important to evaluate your decision. Is the decision the best alternative considering the risks and benefits? Have you thought about the possible consequences of the decision and how you might respond to them? If you determine that your decision-making process was faulty—if, for example, you based your decision on information that you later learned was false—you should begin again. If you find that you are comfortable with your decision, the next step is to take action.

Taking Action

Issues rarely have easy answers. People who are affected have differing, valid points of view. It is easier for you to act as an individual, but if you can persuade a group to act, you will have greater influence. In the issue discussed here, you might write a letter to your town council. As a compromise, you might suggest a combination of salt and sand on the roads. Your research can provide you with appropriate statistics. As a group, you could attend a town council meeting or sign a petition to make your views known.

Over time, you can assess the effects of your actions: Are there fewer accidents on the salted/sanded roads? Does less salt end up in the water than when more salt alone is used?

Sometimes taking action involves changing the way you do things. After you have presented your findings to the town council, one of your friends makes you stop and think. "I have noticed you putting a lot of salt out on your sidewalk," your friend says. "You could use a bit of time and muscle power to chip away the ice, but that is not the choice you make." You realize your friend is right—it is not only up to the town council or any other group to act responsibly; it is also up to you and your friends. How easy is it for you to give up an easy way of doing a task in order to make an environmentally responsible decision?

Instant Practice—Analyzing Issues

We live in an energy-intensive society. One of the most common sources of the energy we use is fossil fuels. Complete the following exercise in a group of four.

1. Start by dividing your group into two pairs.

2. One pair will research and record the advantages of using fossil fuels and how this use has affected members of our society in a positive way.

3. The second pair will research and record the disadvantages of using fossil fuels and their negative impacts on society.

4. The pairs will then regroup, and both sides can present their findings. Record key points on a chart for comparison.

5. Determine which pair has the more convincing evidence for its point of view concerning the use of fossil fuels.

6. As a group, research alternative energy sources, including advantages and disadvantages of each. Determine the best alternative, based on the information you found in steps 2 and 3 above.

Science Skills Toolkit 2

Scientific Inquiry

Scientific inquiry is a process that involves many steps, including making observations, asking questions, performing investigations, and drawing conclusions. These steps may not happen in the same order in each inquiry. There is no universal scientific method. However, one model of the scientific inquiry process is shown here:

The Scientific Inquiry Process

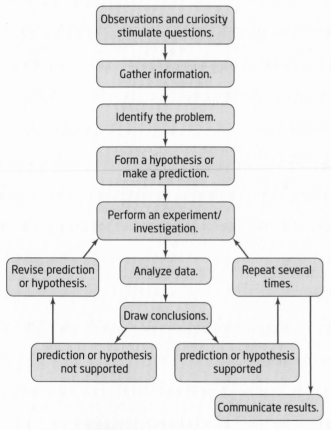

- Observations and curiosity stimulate questions.
- Gather information.
- Identify the problem.
- Form a hypothesis or make a prediction.
- Perform an experiment/investigation.
- Revise prediction or hypothesis.
- Analyze data.
- Repeat several times.
- Draw conclusions.
- prediction or hypothesis not supported
- prediction or hypothesis supported
- Communicate results.

Making Observations and Asking Questions

The rain has stopped, and the Sun is out. You notice that a puddle of water has disappeared from the sidewalk. What happened to that puddle? You could probably quickly answer that question, but how would you prove your answer? You would need to carry out a scientific inquiry.

Gathering Information and Identifying the Problem

First, you might observe what happens to some other puddles. You would watch them closely until they disappeared and record what you observed.

One observation you might make is "The puddle is almost all gone." That would be a **qualitative observation**, an observation in which numbers are not used. A little later, you might also say, "It took five hours for the puddle to disappear completely." You have made a **quantitative observation**, an observation that uses numbers.

Although the two puddles were the same size, one disappeared (evaporated) much more quickly than the other one did. Your quantitative observations tell you that one evaporated in 4 h, whereas the other one took 5 h. Your qualitative observations tell you that the one that evaporated more quickly was in the sun. The one that evaporated more slowly was in the shade. You now have identified one problem to solve: Does water always evaporate more quickly in the sun than in the shade?

Beginning your observations of puddles

Concluding your observations of puddles

Stating a Hypothesis

Now you are ready to make a **hypothesis**, a statement about an idea that you can test, based on your observations. Your test will involve comparing two things to find the relationship between them. You know that the Sun is a source of thermal energy, so you might use that knowledge to make this hypothesis: If a puddle of water is in the sunlight, then the water will evaporate faster than if the puddle is in the shade.

Making a Prediction

As you prepare to make your observations, you can make a **prediction**, a forecast about what you expect to observe. In this case, you might predict that puddles A, B, and C will dry up more quickly than puddles X, Y, and Z.

Performing an Investigation

As you know, there are several steps involved in performing a scientific investigation, including identifying variables, designing a fair test, and organizing and analyzing data.

Identifying Variables "But wait a minute," you think, as you look again at your recorded observations. "There was a strong breeze blowing today. What effect might that have had?" The breeze is one factor that could affect evaporation. The Sun is another factor that could affect evaporation. Scientists think about every possible factor that could affect tests they conduct. These factors are called **variables**. It is important to test only one variable at a time.

You need to control your variables. This means that you change only one variable at a time. The variable that you change is called the **independent variable** (also called the manipulated variable). In this case, the independent variable is the condition under which you observe the puddle (one variable would be adding thermal energy; another would be moving air across it).

According to your hypothesis, adding thermal energy will change the time it takes for the puddle to evaporate. The time in this case is called the **dependent variable** (also called the responding variable).

Often, experiments have a **control**. This is a test that you carry out with no variables, so that you can observe whether your independent variable does indeed cause a change. Look at the illustration below to see some examples of variables.

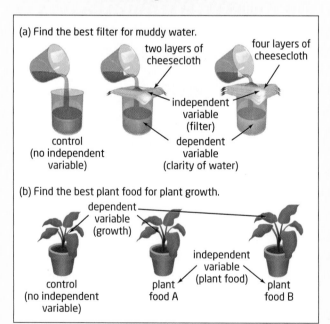

(a) Find the best filter for muddy water.

two layers of cheesecloth

four layers of cheesecloth

independent variable (filter)

dependent variable (clarity of water)

control (no independent variable)

(b) Find the best plant food for plant growth.

dependent variable (growth)

independent variable (plant food)

control (no independent variable)

plant food A

plant food B

Instant Practice—Identifying Variables

For each of the following questions, state your control, your independent variable, and your dependent variable.

1. Does light travel the same way through different substances?

2. Does adding compost to soil promote vegetable growth?

3. How effective are various kinds of mosquito repellent?

Controlling Variables for a Fair Test If you consider more than one variable in a test, you are not conducting a **fair test** (one that is valid and unbiased), and your results will not be useful. You will not know whether the breeze or the Sun made the water evaporate.

THAT'S NOT FAIR!

As you have been reading, a question may have occurred to you: How is it possible to do a fair test on puddles? How can you be sure that they are the same size? In situations such as this one, scientists often use **models**. A model can be a mental picture, a diagram, a working model, or even a mathematical expression. To make sure your test is fair, you can prepare model puddles that you know are all exactly the same. **Science Skills Toolkit 11** gives you more information on using models.

Before you begin your investigation, review safety procedures and identify what safety equipment you may need. Refer to page xiv in this textbook for more information on safety.

Recording and Organizing Data Another step in performing an investigation is recording and organizing your data. Often, you can record your data in a table like the one shown below. Refer to **Science Skills Toolkit 7** for more information on making tables.

Puddle Evaporation Times

Puddle	Evaporation Time (min)
A	37
B	34
C	42
X	100
Y	122
Z	118

Analyzing and Presenting Data After recording your data, the next step is to present your data in a format so that you can analyze it. Often, scientists make a graph, such as the bar graph below. For more information on constructing graphs, refer to **Math Skills Toolkit 3**.

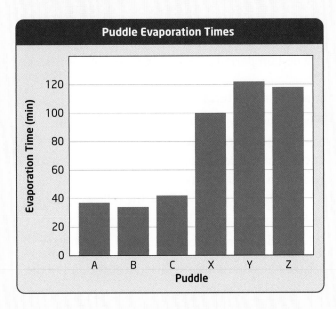

Forming a Conclusion

Many investigations are much more complex than the one described here, and there are many more possibilities for error. That is why it is so important to record careful qualitative and quantitative observations.

After you have completed all your observations, you are ready to analyze your data and draw a **conclusion**. A conclusion is a statement that indicates whether your results support or do not support your hypothesis. If you had hypothesized that the addition of thermal energy would have no effect on the evaporation of water, your results would not support your hypothesis. A hypothesis gives you a place to start and helps you design your experiment. If your results do not support your hypothesis, you use what you have learned in the experiment to come up with a new hypothesis to test.

Scientists often set up experiments without knowing what will happen. Sometimes they deliberately set out to prove that something will *not* happen.

Eventually, when a hypothesis has been thoroughly tested and nearly all scientists agree that the results support the hypothesis, it becomes a **theory**. For example, you will learn about the big bang theory of the origin of the universe in Unit 3 of this textbook.

Science Skills Toolkit 3

Technological Problem Solving

Technology is the use of scientific knowledge, as well as everyday experience, to solve practical problems. Have you ever used a pencil to flip something out of a tight spot where your fingers could not reach? Have you ever used a stone to hammer bases or goal posts into the ground? Then you have used technology. You may not know why your pencil works as a lever or the physics behind levers, but your everyday experiences tell you how to use a lever successfully.

A Process for Technological Problem Solving

People turn to technology to solve problems. One problem-solving model is shown below.

Solving a Technological Problem

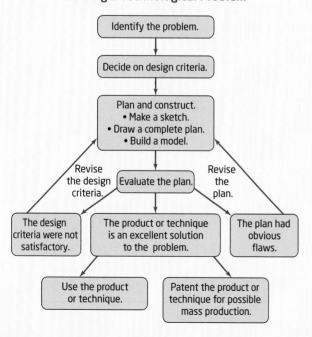

Identifying the Problem

When you used that pencil to move the small item you could not reach, you did so because you needed to move that item. In other words, you had identified a problem that needed to be solved. Clearly identifying a problem is a good first step in finding a solution. In the case of the lever, the solution was right before your eyes, but finding a solution is not always quite so simple.

Suppose school is soon to close for a 16-day winter holiday. Your science class has a hamster whose life stages the class observes. Student volunteers will take the hamster home and care for it over the holiday. However, there is a three-day period when no one will be available to feed the hamster. Leaving extra food in the cage is not an option because the hamster will eat it all at once. What devices could you invent to solve this problem?

First, you need to identify the exact nature of the problem you have to solve. You could state it as follows.

The hamster must receive food and water on a regular basis so that it remains healthy over a certain period and does not overeat.

Identifying Criteria

Now, how will you be able to assess how well your device works? You cannot invent a device successfully unless you know what criteria (standards) it must meet.

In this case, you could use the following as your criteria.

1. The device must feed and water the hamster.

2. The hamster must be thriving at the end of the three-day period.

3. The hamster must not appear to be "overstuffed."

How could you come up with such a device? On your own, you might not. If you work with a team, however, each of you will have useful ideas to contribute.

Planning and Constructing

You will probably come up with some good ideas on your own. Like all other scientists, though, you will want to use information and devices that others have developed. Do some research and share your findings with your group. Can you modify someone else's idea? With your group, brainstorm some possible designs. How would the designs work? What materials would they require? How difficult would they be to build? How many parts are there that could stop working during the three-day period? Make a clear, labelled drawing of each design, with an explanation of how it would work.

Examine all of your suggested designs carefully. Which do you think would work best? Why? Be prepared to share your choice and your reasons with your group. Listen carefully to what others have to say. Do you still feel yours is the best choice, or do you want to change your mind? When the group votes on the design that will be built, be prepared to co-operate fully, even if the group's choice is not your choice.

Get your teacher's approval of the drawing of the design your group wants to build. Then gather your materials and build a **prototype** (a model) of your design. Experiment with your design to answer some questions you might have about it. For example, should the food and water be provided at the same time? Until you try it out, you may be unsure if it is possible (or even a good idea) for your invention to deliver both food and water at the same time. Keep careful, objective records of each of your tests and of any changes you make to your design.

You might find, too, that your invention fails in a particular way. Perhaps it always leaks at a certain point where two parts are joined. Perhaps the food and water are not kept separate. Perhaps you notice a more efficient way to design your device as you watch it operate. Make any adjustments and test them so that your device works in the best and most efficient way possible.

Evaluating

When you are satisfied with your device, you can demonstrate it and observe devices constructed by other groups. Evaluate each design in terms of how well it meets the design criteria. Think about the ideas other groups tried out and why they work better than (or not as well as) yours. What would you do differently if you were to redesign your device?

Science Skills Toolkit 4

Estimating and Measuring

Estimating

How long will it take you to read this page? How heavy is this textbook? You could probably answer these questions by **estimating**—making an informed judgement about a measurement. An estimate gives you an idea of a particular quantity but is not an exact measurement.

For example, suppose you wanted to know how many ants live in a local park. Counting every ant would be very time-consuming. What you can do is count the number of ants in a typical square-metre area. Then, multiply the number of ants by the number of square metres in the total area you are investigating. This will give you an estimate of the total population of ants in that area.

Measuring Length and Area

You can use a metre stick or a ruler to measure short distances. These tools are usually marked in centimetres and/or millimetres. Use a ruler to measure the length in millimetres between points A and C, C and E, E and B, and A and D below. Convert your measurements to centimetres and then to metres.

A •   • B

        • C   • E   • D

To calculate an area, you can use length measurements. For example, for a square or a rectangle, you can find the area by multiplying the length by the width.

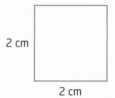

Area of square is 2 cm × 2 cm = 4 cm²

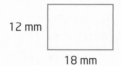

Area of rectangle is 18 mm × 12 mm = 216 mm²

Make sure you always use the same units—if you mix up centimetres and millimetres, your calculations will be wrong. Remember to ask yourself if your answer is reasonable (you could make an estimate to consider this).

> ### Instant Practice—Estimating and Measuring
>
> Imagine that all rulers in the school have vanished. The only measurement tool that you now have is a toothpick.
>
> 1. Estimate the length and width of your textbook in toothpick units. Compare your estimates with a classmate's estimates.
>
> 2. Measure the length and width of your textbook with your toothpick. How close was your estimate to the actual measurement?
>
> 3. If you had a much larger area to measure, such as the floor of your classroom, what could you use instead of toothpicks to measure the area? (Be creative!)
>
> 4. What is your estimate of the number of units you chose (in question 3) for the width of your classroom?

Measuring Volume

The **volume** of an object is the amount of space that the object occupies. There are several ways of measuring volume, depending on the kind of object you want to measure.

As you can see in Diagram A below, the volume of a regularly shaped solid object can be measured directly. You can calculate the volume of a cube by multiplying its sides, as shown on the left in Diagram A. You can calculate the volume of a rectangular solid by multiplying its length × width × height, as shown on the right in Diagram A.

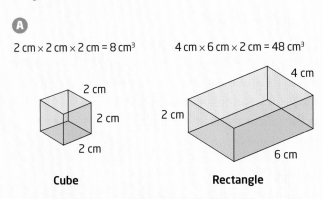

A

$2 \text{ cm} \times 2 \text{ cm} \times 2 \text{ cm} = 8 \text{ cm}^3$

$4 \text{ cm} \times 6 \text{ cm} \times 2 \text{ cm} = 48 \text{ cm}^3$

2 cm
2 cm
2 cm

4 cm
2 cm
6 cm

Cube

Rectangle

Measuring the volume of a regularly shaped solid

If all the sides of a solid object are measured in millimetres (mm), the volume will be in cubic millimetres (mm^3). If all the sides are measured in centimetres (cm), the volume will be in cubic centimetres (cm^3). The units for measuring the volume of a solid are called cubic units.

The units used to measure the volume of liquids are called capacity units. The basic unit of volume for liquids is the litre (L). Recall that 1 L = 1000 mL.

Cubic units and capacity units are interchangeable. For example,

$1 \text{ cm}^3 = 1 \text{ mL}$
$1 \text{ dm}^3 = 1 \text{ L}$
$1 \text{ m}^3 = 1 \text{ kL}$

The volume of a liquid can be measured directly, as shown in Diagram B below. Make sure you measure to the bottom of the **meniscus**, the slight curve where the liquid touches the sides of the container. To measure accurately, make sure your eye is at the same level as the bottom of the meniscus.

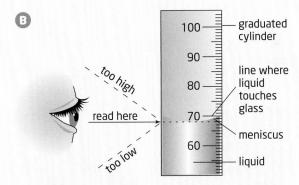

B

100 — graduated cylinder
90
too high
80 — line where liquid touches glass
read here
70
too low
meniscus
60
liquid

Measuring the volume of a liquid

The volume of an irregularly shaped solid object, however, must be measured indirectly, as shown in Diagram C below. This is done by determining the volume of a liquid it will displace.

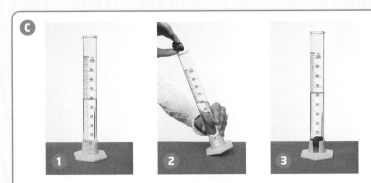

C

1
2
3

1. Record the volume of the liquid.

2. Carefully lower the object into the cylinder containing the liquid. Record the volume again.

3. The volume of the object is equal to the difference between the two volumes of the liquid. The equation below the photographs shows you how to calculate this volume.

Measuring the volume of an irregularly shaped solid
volume of object = volume of water with object – original volume of water
= 85 mL – 60 mL
= 25 mL

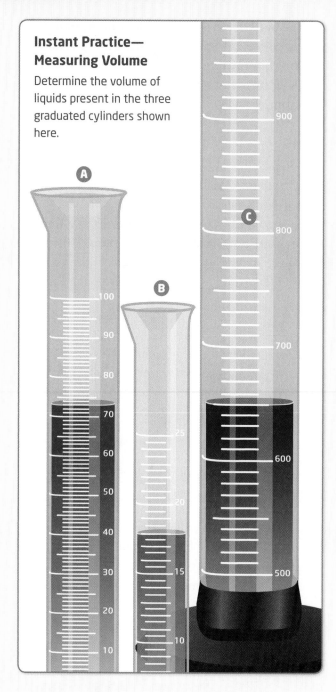

How can you find the mass of a certain quantity of a substance, such as table salt, that you have added to a beaker? First, find the mass of the beaker. Next, pour the salt into the beaker and find the mass of the beaker and salt together. To find the mass of the salt, simply subtract the beaker's mass from the combined mass of the beaker and salt.

Measuring Angles

You can use a protractor to measure angles. Protractors usually have an inner scale and an outer scale. The scale you use depends on how you place the protractor on an angle (symbol = ∠). Look at the following examples to learn how to use a protractor.

Example 1

What is the measure of ∠XYZ?

Solution

Place the centre of the protractor on point Y. YX crosses 0° on the inner scale. YZ crosses 70° on the inner scale. So ∠XYZ is equal to 70°.

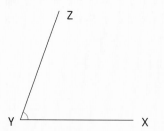

Measuring Mass

Is your backpack heavier than your friend's backpack? You can check by holding a backpack in each hand. The **mass** of an object is the amount of matter in a substance or object. Mass is measured in milligrams, grams, kilograms, and tonnes. You need a balance for measuring mass.

Example 2

Draw ∠ABC = 155°.

Solution

First, draw a straight line, AB. Place the centre of the protractor on B and line up AB with 0° on the outer scale. Mark C at 155° on the outer scale. Join BC. The angle you have drawn, ∠ABC, is equal to 155°.

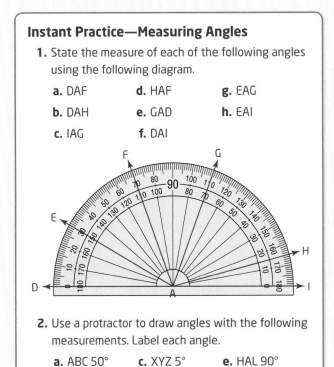

Instant Practice—Measuring Angles

1. State the measure of each of the following angles using the following diagram.

   a. DAF   d. HAF   g. EAG

   b. DAH   e. GAD   h. EAI

   c. IAG   f. DAI

2. Use a protractor to draw angles with the following measurements. Label each angle.

   a. ABC 50°   c. XYZ 5°   e. HAL 90°

   b. QRS 85°   d. JKL 45°

Measuring Temperature

Temperature is a measure of the thermal energy of the particles of a substance. In the very simplest terms, you can think of temperature as a measure of how hot or how cold something is. The temperature of a material is measured with a thermometer.

For most scientific work, temperature is measured on the Celsius scale. On this scale, the freezing point of water is zero degrees (0°C) and the boiling point of water is 100 degrees (100°C). Between these points, the scale is divided into 100 equal divisions. Each division represents one degree Celsius. On the Celsius scale, average human body temperature is 37°C, and a typical room temperature may be between 20°C and 25°C.

The SI unit of temperature is the kelvin (K). Zero on the Kelvin scale (0 K) is the coldest possible temperature. This temperature is also known as absolute zero. It is equivalent to –273°C, which is about 273 degrees below the freezing point of water. Notice that degree symbols are not used with the Kelvin scale.

Most laboratory thermometers are marked only with the Celsius scale. Because the divisions on the two scales are the same size, the Kelvin temperature can be found by adding 273 to the Celsius reading. This means that on the Kelvin scale, water freezes at 273 K and boils at 373 K.

Tips for Using a Thermometer

When using a thermometer to measure the temperature of a substance, here are three important tips to remember.

• Handle the thermometer extremely carefully. It is made of glass and can break easily.

• Do not use the thermometer as a stirring rod.

• Do not let the bulb of the thermometer touch the walls of the container.

Science Skills Toolkit 5

Precision and Accuracy

No measuring device can give an absolutely exact measure. So how do scientists describe how close an instrument comes to measuring the true result?

Precision Quantitative data from any measuring device are uncertain. You can describe this uncertainty in terms of precision and accuracy. The term **precision** describes both the exactness of a measuring device and the range of values in a set of measurements.

The precision of a measuring instrument is usually half the smallest division on its scale. For example, the bottom ruler below is graduated in centimetres, so it is precise to ± 0.5 cm. The length of the object above the ruler would be reported as 9.0 ± 0.5 cm, because it is closer to 9 cm than to 8 cm, and the uncertainty must be included in the measurement. The top ruler below is graduated in millimetres, so it is precise to ± 0.05 cm. The length of the object below the ruler would be reported as 8.7 ± 0.05 cm.

A precise measuring device will give nearly the same result every time it is used to measure the same object. Consider the following measurements of a 50 g weight on a balance. Both give the same average mass, but Scale B is more precise because it has a smaller range of measured values (± 0.3 versus ± 0.5).

Measurements of Mass on Two Scales

	Scale A Mass (g)	Scale B Mass (g)
Trial 1	49.9	49.9
Trial 2	49.8	50.2
Trial 3	50.3	49.9
Average	50.0	50.0
Range	± 0.5	± 0.3

Accuracy How close a measurement or calculation comes to the true value is described as **accuracy**. To improve accuracy, scientific measurements are often repeated and combined mathematically. The average measurements in the table on this page are more accurate than any of the individual measurements.

The darts in diagram A below are very precise, but they are not accurate because they did not hit the bull's-eye. The darts in diagram B are neither precise nor accurate. However, the darts in diagram C are both precise and accurate.

A precise but not accurate   **B** neither precise nor accurate   **C** precise and accurate

Instant Practice—Precision and Accuracy

1. A student measures the temperature of ice water four times, and each time gets a result of 10.0°C. Is the thermometer precise and accurate? Explain your answer.

2. Two students collected data on the mass of a substance for an experiment. Each student used a different scale to measure the mass of the substance over three trials. Student A had a range of measurements that was ±0.06 g. Student B had a range of measurements that was ±0.11 g. Which student had the more precise scale?

Science Skills Toolkit 6

Scientific Drawing

Have you ever used a drawing to explain something that was too difficult to explain in words? A clear drawing can often assist or replace words in a scientific explanation. In science, drawings are especially important when you are trying to explain difficult concepts or describe something that contains a lot of detail. It is important to make scientific drawings clear, neat, and accurate.

Examine the drawing shown below. It is taken from a student's lab report on an experiment to test the expansion of air in a balloon. The student's written description of results included an explanation of how the particle model can explain what happens to the balloon when the bottle is placed in hot water and in ice water. As you can see, the clear diagrams of the results can support or even replace many words of explanation. While your drawing itself is important, it is also important to label it clearly. If you are comparing and contrasting two objects, label each object and use labels to indicate the points of comparison between them.

Making a Scientific Drawing

Follow these steps to make an effective scientific drawing.

1. Use unlined paper and a sharp pencil with an eraser.

2. Give yourself plenty of space on the paper. You need to make sure that your drawing will be large enough to show all necessary details. You also need to allow space for labels. Labels identify parts of the object you are drawing. Place all of your labels to the right of your drawing, unless there are so many labels that your drawing looks cluttered.

3. Carefully study the object that you will be drawing. Make sure you know what you need to include.

4. Draw only what you see, and keep your drawing simple. Do not try to indicate parts of the object that are not visible from the angle of observation. If you think it is important to show another part of the object, do a second drawing, and indicate the angle from which each drawing is viewed.

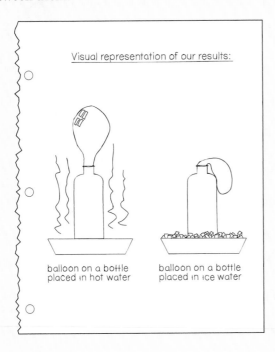

Visual representation of our results:

balloon on a bottle placed in hot water

balloon on a bottle placed in ice water

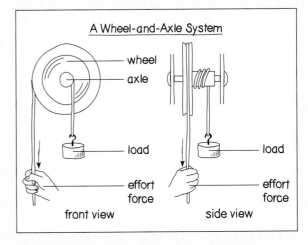

A Wheel-and-Axle System

wheel
axle
load
effort force
front view

load
effort force
side view

5. Shading or colouring is not usually used in scientific drawings. If you want to indicate a darker area, you can use stippling (a series of dots). You can use double lines to indicate thick parts of the object.

6. If you do use colour, try to be as accurate as you can and choose colours that are as close as possible to the colours in the object you are observing.

7. Label your drawing carefully and completely, using lower-case (small) letters. Think about what you would need to know if you were looking at the object for the first time. Remember to place all your labels to the right of the drawing, if possible. Use a ruler to draw a horizontal line from the label to the part you are identifying. Make sure that none of your label lines cross.

8. Give your drawing a title. The drawing of a human skin cell shown below is from a student's notebook. This student used stippling to show darker areas, horizontal label lines for the cell parts viewed, and a title—all elements of an excellent final drawing.

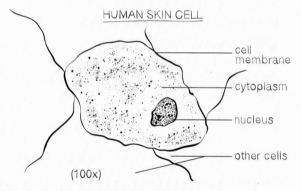

HUMAN SKIN CELL

cell membrane
cytoplasm
nucleus
other cells

(100x)

The stippling on this drawing of a human skin cell shows that some areas are darker than others.

Drawing to Scale

When you draw objects seen through a microscope, the size of your drawing is important. Your drawing should be in proportion to the size of the object as the object appears when viewed through the microscope. This type of drawing is called a **scale drawing**. A scale drawing allows you to compare the sizes of different objects and to estimate the actual size of the object being viewed. Here are some steps to follow when making scale drawings of magnified objects.

1. Use a mathematical compass to draw an accurate circle in your notebook. The size of the circle does not matter. The circle represents the microscope's field of view.

2. Imagine the circle is divided into four equal sections (see the diagram below). Use a pencil and a ruler to draw these sections in your circle, as shown below.

3. Using low or medium power, locate an object under the microscope. Imagine that the field of view is also divided into four equal sections.

4. Observe how much of the field of view is taken up by the object. Note the location of the object in the field of view.

5. Draw the object in the circle. Position the object in about the same part of the circle as it appears in the field of view. Draw the object so that it takes up about the same amount of space within the circle as it takes up in the field of view, as shown in the diagram.

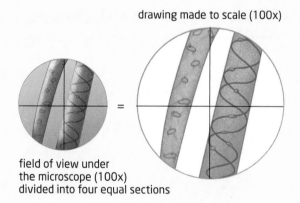

drawing made to scale (100x)

=

field of view under the microscope (100x) divided into four equal sections

> ### Instant Practice—Scale Drawings
>
> Design a scale drawing of your bedroom, using the shape of the floor rather than a circle as in the example given above. Include scale drawings of the furniture in your room. When you are finished, label the fire escape routes.

Science Skills Toolkit 7

Creating Data Tables

Scientific investigation is about collecting information to help you answer a question. In many cases, you will develop an hypothesis and collect data to see if your hypothesis is supported. An important part of any successful investigation includes recording and organizing your data. Often, scientists create tables in which to record data.

Planning to Record Your Data Suppose you are doing an investigation on the water quality of a stream that runs near your school. You will take samples of the numbers and types of organisms at three different locations along the stream. You need to decide how to record and organize your data. Begin by making a list of what you need to record. For this experiment, you will need to record the sample site, the pH of the water at each sample site, the types of organisms found at each sample site, and how many of each type of organism you collected.

Creating Your Data Table Your data table must allow you to record your data neatly. To do this you need to create

- headings to show what you are recording
- columns and rows that you will fill with data
- enough cells to record all the data
- a title for the table

In this investigation, you will find multiple organisms at each site, so you must make space for multiple recordings at each site. This means every row representing a sample site will have at least three rows associated with it for the different organisms.

If you think you might need extra space, create a special section. In this investigation, leave space at the bottom of your table, in case you find more than three organisms at a sample site. Remember, if you use the extra rows, make sure you identify which sample site the extra data are from. Your data table might look like the one at the top of this page.

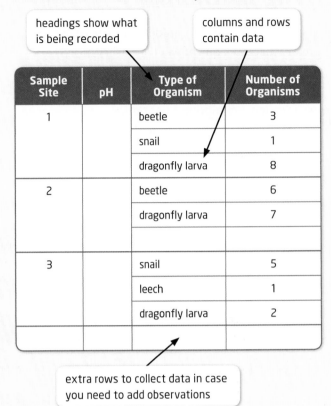

Observations Made at Three Sample Stream Sites

headings show what is being recorded

columns and rows contain data

Sample Site	pH	Type of Organism	Number of Organisms
1		beetle	3
		snail	1
		dragonfly larva	8
2		beetle	6
		dragonfly larva	7
3		snail	5
		leech	1
		dragonfly larva	2

extra rows to collect data in case you need to add observations

Instant Practice—Creating Data Tables

1. You are interested in how weeds grow in a garden. You decide to collect data from your garden every week for a month. You will identify the weeds and count how many there are of each type of weed. Design and draw a data table that you could use to record your data.

2. Many investigations have several different experimental treatments. Copy the following data table into your notebook and fill in the missing title and headings. The investigation tests the effect of increased fertilizer on plant height. There are four plants, and measurements are being taken every two days.

Day 1	Plant 1	5 mL	
	Plant 2	10 mL	10 cm
		15 mL	
		20 mL	

Science Skills Toolkit 8

Using a Microscope

The light microscope is an optical instrument that greatly increases our powers of observation by magnifying objects that are usually too small to be seen with the unaided eye. The microscope you will use is called a compound light microscope because it uses a series of lenses (rather than only one, as in a magnifying glass) and it uses light to view the object.

A microscope is a delicate instrument, so you must use proper procedure and care. This *Science Skills Toolkit* reviews the skills that you will need to use a microscope effectively. Before you use your microscope, you need to know the parts of a microscope and their functions.

A Eyepiece (or ocular lens)

You look through the eyepiece. It has a lens that magnifies the object, usually by 10 times (10×). The magnifying power is engraved on the side of the eyepiece.

B Tube

The tube holds the eyepiece and the objective lenses at the proper working distance from each other.

C Revolving nosepiece

This rotating disk holds two or more objective lenses. Turn it to change lenses. Each lens clicks into place.

D Objective lenses

The objective lenses magnify the object. Each lens has a different power of magnification, such as 4×, 10×, and 40×. (Your microscope may instead have 10×, 40×, and 100× objective lenses.) The objective lenses are referred to as low, medium, and high power. The magnifying power is engraved on the side of each objective lens. Be sure you can identify each lens.

E Arm

The arm connects the base and the tube. Use the arm for carrying the microscope.

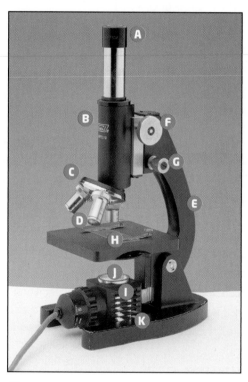

K Light source

Shining a light through the object being viewed makes it easier to see the details. If your microscope has a mirror instead of a light, adjust the mirror to direct light through the lenses. CAUTION: Use an electric light, not sunlight, as the light source for focussing your mirror.

F Coarse-adjustment knob

The coarse-adjustment knob moves the tube up and down to bring the object into focus. Use it only with the low-power objective lens.

G Fine-adjustment knob

Use the fine-adjustment knob with medium- and high-power magnification to bring the object into sharper focus.

H Stage

The stage supports the microscope slide. Stage clips hold the slide in position. An opening in the centre of the stage allows light from the light source to pass through the slide.

I Condenser lens

The condenser lens directs light to the object being viewed.

J Diaphragm

The diaphragm controls the amount of light reaching the object being viewed.

Science Skills Toolkit 9

The GRASP Problem Solving Method

Solving any problem is easier when you establish a logical, step-by-step procedure. One useful method for solving numerical problems includes five basic steps: **Given**, **Required**, **Analysis**, **Solution**, and **Paraphrase**. You can easily remember these steps because the first letter of each word spells the word GRASP.

Example of the GRASP Problem Solving Method

Ruby can afford to spend $45.00 this month on electricity. The company that supplies her home with electrical energy charges 10.9¢ per kWh. Based on her budget, how many kWh of electrical energy can she use in a month?

Given—Organize the given data.

budget = $45.00
cost of electrical energy = 10.9¢/kWh

Required—Identify what information the problem requires you to find.

amount of electrical energy that can be used (kWh)

Analysis—Decide how to solve the problem.

1. Convert cents into dollars. (The units given for Ruby's budget—dollars—do not match the units given for the cost of 1 kWh of electrical energy—cents. Both units need to be the same.)

2. Calculate the number of kWh Ruby can afford to use.

   total cost = amount of energy used × cost per unit of energy

Solution—Solve the problem.

1. Convert units

   $1.00 = 100¢

   10.9¢ =

   $(10.9¢) \times \left(\frac{\$1.00}{100¢}\right) = \$0.109$

2. Use the total cost equation.

   total cost = (amount of energy used)(cost per unit of energy)

   $\frac{\text{total cost}}{\text{cost per unit of energy}} = \frac{(\text{amount of energy used})(\text{cost per unit of energy})}{\text{cost per unit of energy}}$

   $\text{amount of energy used} = \frac{\text{total cost}}{\text{cost per unit of energy}}$

   $\text{amount of energy used} = \frac{\$45.00}{\$0.109}$

   = 413 kWh

Paraphrase—Restate the solution and check your answer.

Restate Ruby has a budget of $45.00 and electrical energy costs 10.9¢, so she can afford to use 413 kWh of electrical energy this month.

Check Multiply the cost of electrical energy by the answer, and you should get $45.00. Round off the numbers to do a quick estimate. If you multiply $0.11 by 400 kWh, you get $44.00, so you know that your answer is reasonable.

Instant Practice—Using GRASP

The company that supplies Ruby's electrical energy raises the price to 11.1 ¢/kWh. Use the GRASP method to calculate how much Ruby's monthly energy bill will be if she uses 375 kWh.

Using Electric Circuit Symbols and Meters

Circuit Diagram Symbols

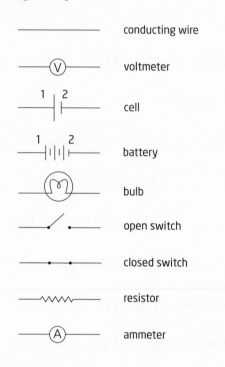

———————	conducting wire
—(V)—	voltmeter
1 2	cell
1 2	battery
—(M)—	bulb
—/ · —	open switch
—· · —	closed switch
—vvvv—	resistor
—(A)—	ammeter

Using Meters to Measure Voltage and Current

Types of Meters

The meters you use in your classroom are either analogue meters or digital meters. **Analogue meters** have a needle pointing to a dial. **Digital meters** display measured values directly as numbers, similar to how a digital watch displays the time directly.

The Terminals of a Meter

All meters have two terminals (connecting points) that you connect to the circuit. The negative terminal (–) is black. The positive terminal (+) is red. In order not to damage the meter, you must take care to connect the meter so that its positive (red) terminal is connected to the positive side of the power source. That is, you should be able to trace from the positive (+) terminal on the meter back to the positive terminal at the source. The negative (–) terminal of the meter is always connected to the negative side of the source. The rule is "positive to positive, and negative to negative."

Connecting an Ammeter

An ammeter is used to measure the electric current in a circuit. Electric current is the amount of charge passing a given point per second. To measure the current at a given location in an electric circuit, the ammeter must be connected so that all the current is allowed to pass through the ammeter. To do this, disconnect one end of a wire to give the same effect as cutting the circuit where you wish to measure the current. Imagine the ammeter and its connecting wires completing the circuit you just disconnected. Make sure the positive terminal on the ammeter traces back to the positive terminal at the source.

A Analogue meters have a needle pointing to different scales.

B Digital meters display the numerical values directly.

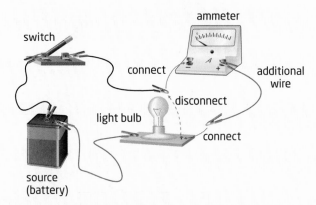

To measure the current through the light bulb, first disconnect the wire connected to the light bulb. Then insert the ammeter into the circuit.

Connecting a Voltmeter

A **voltmeter** is a device used to measure electric potential difference, or voltage, as it is often called. A potential difference exists between two points in a circuit such as across a battery, light bulb, or resistor. When connecting a voltmeter to a circuit, you do not need to disconnect or open the circuit. Potential difference is measured between two points in a circuit. Therefore, connect the terminals of the voltmeter to the two connections on the component where you wish to measure the potential difference. Remember the rule "positive to positive and negative to negative," and make sure you can trace the connections on the voltmeter back to the same type of terminal at the source.

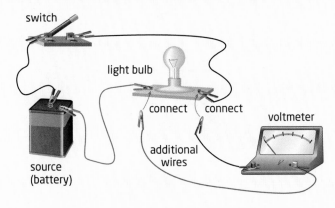

Voltmeters are connected across a component in the circuit.

Connecting a Multimeter

Modern digital meters can also be multimeters. Multimeters can be used to measure voltage, current, and other electrical properties. When using a multimeter, it is important that you position the dial on the correct setting for your application. As well, the connecting wires must be inserted into the correct meter terminals.

Reading a Meter

A digital meter is easy to read since the measured value is displayed directly as numbers. In order to get the most accurate reading on a digital meter, the meter needs to be set to the appropriate scale. The dial on a digital meter has several settings. For example, if the dial is set on the 2 V range, the meter will measure voltages between zero and 2 V. Moving the dial to the 200 V setting will allow the meter to measure between zero and 200 V, but with less accuracy. Therefore, when using meters, you must choose the best setting for your measurement. The best approach is to set the meter on the largest scale to obtain an approximate value. Then lower the scale until you have the highest possible reading without going off scale.

This approach is the same for analogue meters. Some analogue meters have a dial, similar to a digital meter, that is used to change the scale. In other analogue meters, the scale is changed by how the wires are connected to the terminals. Once the scale is selected, you obtain your reading from the most appropriate display on the meter.

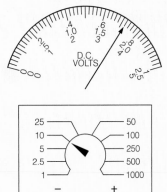

This voltmeter has its dial set at 10 V. To determine the measured potential difference, look for a number at the top of the scale with the same first digit as 10. The top scale has a maximum value of 1, so now the 1 represents 10 V. To read the scale, multiply the number the needle is pointing to by 10. The dial is reporting 7.2 V.

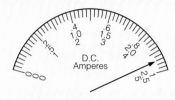

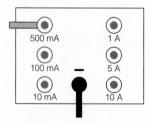

This ammeter has the positive wire connected to the 500 mA scale. The 5 on the bottom scale is the first digit in 500 mA, so the 5 now represents 500 mA. The needle is pointing to 4.7, so the meter is reporting 470 mA of current.

Instant Practice—Using Electric Circuit Symbols and Meters

1. Sketch the following circuit diagram symbols:

   a. battery

   b. light bulb

   c. resistor

   d. open switch

   e. ammeter

   f. voltmeter

2. State the colour that is associated with

   a. the positive terminal of a meter

   b. the negative terminal of a meter

3. When you connect a meter to a circuit, to which side of the power source should you always connect the positive terminal of the meter?

4. For which type of meter do you need to disconnect the circuit before connecting the meter to the circuit?

5. A student wishes to use a meter to determine the most accurate measurement possible without damaging the meter. Describe the correct approach for choosing the appropriate scale.

6. Determine the value of current or voltage indicated by meters A to D shown in the next column on this page.

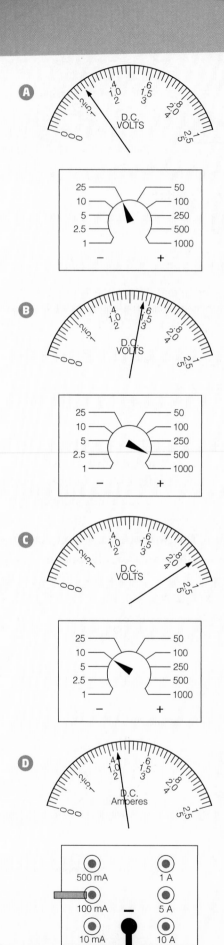

Using Models and Analogies in Science

Scientists often use models and analogies to help communicate their ideas to other scientists or to students.

Using Models

When you think of a model, you might think of a toy such as a model airplane. Is a model airplane similar to a scientific model? If building a model airplane helps you learn about flight, then you could say it is a scientific model.

In science, a model is anything that helps you better understand a scientific concept. A model can be a picture, a mental image, a structure, or even a mathematical formula. Sometimes, you need a model because the objects you are studying are too small to see with the unaided eye. You may have learned about the particle model of matter, for example, which is a model that states that all matter is made of tiny, invisible particles. Sometimes a model is useful because the objects you are studying are extremely large—the planets in our solar system, for example. In other cases, the object may be hidden from view, like the interior of Earth or the inside of a living organism. A mathematical model can show you how to perform a calculation.

Scientists often use models to test an idea, to find out if an hypothesis is supported, and to plan new experiments in order to learn more about the subject they are studying. Sometimes, scientists discover so much new information that they have to modify their models. Examine the model shown in the photograph below. How can this model help you learn about science?

You can learn about day and night by using a globe and a flashlight to model Earth and the Sun.

Instant Practice—Using Models

How does using models help each of the following professionals in their work?
  a. architects
  b. aviation engineers
  c. theatre directors
  d. geographers
  e. landscape designers

Using Analogies

An analogy is a comparison between two things that have some characteristic in common. Scientists use analogies to help explain difficult concepts. For example, scientists sometimes refer to plants as the lungs of Earth. Recall that plants take in carbon dioxide (CO_2) from the atmosphere to use during photosynthesis. Plants then release the oxygen (O_2) produced by photosynthesis back into the atmosphere.

In a sense, the plants are "breathing" for Earth. When animals breathe, they take oxygen into their lungs and give off carbon dioxide.

Instant Practice—Using Analogies

Use an analogy to help explain how organisms in a food web are connected.

How to Do a Research-Based Project

Imagine if your teacher simply stated that he or she wanted you to complete a research-based project on endangered species. This is a really big topic, and it is now your job to decide which smaller aspect of the topic you will research. One way to approach a research project is to break it up into four stages—exploring, investigating, processing, and creating.

Explore—Pick a Topic and Ask Questions

You need to start by finding out some general things about endangered species. Make a list of questions as you conduct your initial research, such as, What factors cause species to become endangered? Why does it matter? What types of species are endangered? Suppose, in the course of your research, you decided to learn more about polar bears. A good research question about polar bears would be, Why are polar bears endangered? An even better question could be, What can I do to help prevent polar bear extinction? Both of these questions are deep and can be subdivided into many subtopics.

Investigate—Research Your Topic

When putting together a research project, it is important to find reliable sources to help you answer your question. Before you decide to use a source that you find, you should consider whether it is reliable or whether it shows any bias.

Sources of Information There are many sources of information. For example, you can use a print resource, such as an encyclopedia from the reference section of the library.

Another approach is to go on-line and check the Internet. When you use the Internet, be careful about which sites you choose to search for information. You need to be able to determine the validity of a website before you trust the information you find on it. To do this, check that the author is identified, a recent publication date is given, and the source of facts or quotations is identified. It is also important that the website is published by a well-known company or organization.

You may also want to contact an expert on your topic. A credible expert has credentials showing his or her expertise in an area. For example, an expert may be a doctor or have a master's degree. Alternatively, an expert could have many years of experience in a specific career or field of study.

No matter which sources you use, it is your responsibility to be a critical consumer of information and to find trustworthy sources for your research.

You should also ask yourself if the sources you are using are primary or secondary.

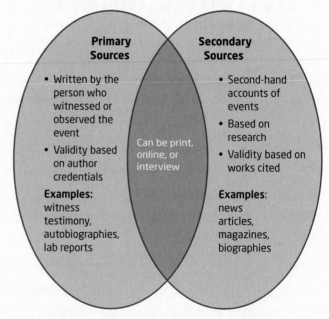

Two other things to check for in a source are reliability and bias. To check for reliability, try to find the same "fact" in two other sources. But keep in mind that even if you cannot find the same idea somewhere else, the source may still be reliable if it is a research paper or if it was written by an author with strong credentials. To check for bias, look for judgemental statements. Does the author tend to favour one side of an issue more than another? Are all sides of an issue treated equally? A good source shows little bias.

Source	Information	Reliability	Bias	Questions I Have
The Canadian Encyclopedia website	Polar bears inhabit ice and coastlines of arctic seas.	• author: Brian Knudsen • secondary source • has links to external sites that are reliable	only lists facts	• Why do they live on ice? • Why don't they move south?
Polar Bears International website	shrinking sea ice habitat	• date at bottom of page 2009 • non-profit organization	designed to save the polar bear	• Why is the ice shrinking?

Recording Information As you find information, jot it down on sticky notes or use a chart similar to the one shown above. Sticky notes are useful because you can move them around, group similar ideas together, and reorganize your ideas easily. Using a different colour for each sub-question is even better! Remember to write the source of your information on each sticky note. In addition to writing down information that you find as you research, you should also write down any questions you think of as you go along.

Process—Ask More Questions and Revise Your Work

Now that you have done some research, what sub-questions have you asked? These are the subtopics of your research. Use the subtopics to find more specific information. If you find that you have two or three sub-questions that have a lot of research supporting them and a few that do not have much research, do not be afraid to "toss out" some of the less important questions or ideas.

Avoiding Plagiarism Copying information word-for-word and then presenting it as though it is your own work is called *plagiarism*. When you refer to your notes to write your project, put the information in your own words. It is also important to give credit to the original source of an idea.

Recording Source Information Research papers always include a bibliography—a list of relevant information sources the authors consulted while preparing them. Bibliographic entries give the author, title, and facts of publication for each information source. Sometimes, you may want to give the exact source of information within

the paper. This is done using footnotes. *Footnotes* identify the exact source (including page number) of quotations and ideas. Ask your teacher how you should prepare your list of works cited and your footnotes.

Create—Present Your Work

Before you choose a format for your final project, consider whether your researched information has answered the question you originally asked. If you have not answered this question, you need to either refine your original question or do some more research! You also need to consider who the audience is for your project. How you format your final project will be very different if it is meant for a Grade 2 class compared to the president of a company or a government official. You could present your project as a computer slide presentation, a graphic novel, a video, or a research paper.

Instant Practice

1. Describe the steps you should follow in preparing a project on the topic of renewable forms of energy.

2. The following example is not an effective question on which to base a research project: *How many moons does Jupiter have?* Modify the question to make it an effective research question.

3. Assume that the target audience for your project is a group of Grade 6 students from a local elementary school. What aspects of your project would you need to modify so that you are reaching the intended audience? What would be the best format to use to present your project to your audience?

Math Skills Toolkit 1

The Metric System and Scientific Notation

Throughout history, people have developed systems of numbering and measurement. When different groups of people began to communicate with each other, they discovered that their systems and units of measurement were different. Some groups within societies created their own unique systems of measurement.

Today, scientists around the world use the metric system of numbers and units. The metric system is the official system of measurement in Canada.

The Metric System

The metric system is based on multiples of 10. For example, the basic unit of length is the metre. All larger units of length are expressed in units based on metres multiplied by 10, 100, 1000, or more. Smaller units of length are expressed in units based on metres divided by 10, 100, 1000, or more.

Each multiple of 10 has its own prefix (a syllable joined to the beginning of a word). For example, *kilo-* means multiplied by 1000. Thus, one kilometre is 1000 metres.

$$1 \text{ km} = 1000 \text{ m}$$

The prefix *milli-* means divided by 1000. Thus, one millimetre is one thousandth of a metre.

$$1 \text{ mm} = \frac{1}{1000} \text{ m}$$

In the metric system, the same prefixes are used for nearly all types of measurements, such as mass, weight, area, and energy. A table of the most common metric prefixes is given at the top of the next column.

Commonly Used Metric Prefixes

Prefix	Symbol	Relationship to the Base Unit
giga-	G	$10^9 = 1\ 000\ 000\ 000$
mega-	M	$10^6 = 1\ 000\ 000$
kilo-	k	$10^3 = 1000$
hecto-	h	$10^2 = 100$
deca-	da	$10^1 = 10$
—	—	$10^0 = 1$
deci-	d	$10^{-1} = 0.1$
centi-	c	$10^{-2} = 0.01$
milli-	m	$10^{-3} = 0.001$
micro-	μ	$10^{-6} = 0.000\ 001$
nano-	n	$10^{-9} = 0.000\ 000\ 001$

Example

There are 250 g of cereal in a package. Express this mass in kilograms.

Solution

$$1 \text{ kg} = 1000 \text{ g}$$
$$250 \text{ g} \times 4 = 1000 \text{ g}$$
$$\frac{1000}{4} \text{ g} = 250 \text{ g}$$
$$\frac{1}{4} \text{ kg} = 0.25 \text{ kg}$$

Instant Practice—Using Metric Measurements

1. A hummingbird has a mass of 3.5 g. Express its mass in mg.

2. For an experiment, you need to measure 350 mL of dilute acetic acid. Express the volume in L.

3. A bald eagle has a wingspan up to 2.3 m. Express the length in cm.

4. A student added 0.0025 L of food colouring to water. Express the volume in mL.

Exponents of Scientific Notation

An exponent is the symbol or number denoting the power to which another number or symbol is to be raised. The exponent shows the number of repeated multiplications of the base. In 10^2, the exponent is 2 and the base is 10. So 10^2 means 10×10.

Powers of 10

	Standard Form	Exponential Form
Ten thousands	10 000	10^4
Thousands	1000	10^3
Hundreds	100	10^2
Tens	10	10^1
Ones	1	10^0
Tenths	0.1	10^{-1}
Hundredths	0.01	10^{-2}
Thousandths	0.001	10^{-3}
Ten thousandths	0.0001	10^{-4}

Why use exponents? Consider this. Mercury is about 58 000 000 km from the Sun. If a zero were accidentally added to this number, the distance would appear to be 10 times larger than it actually is. To avoid mistakes when writing many zeros, scientists express very large and very small numbers in scientific notation.

Example 1

Mercury is about 58 000 000 km from the Sun. Write 58 000 000 in scientific notation.

Solution

In scientific notation, a number has the form $x \times 10^n$, where x is greater than or equal to 1 but less than 10, and 10^n is a power of 10.

58 000 000. ← The decimal point starts here. Move the decimal point 7 places to the left.
$= 5.8 \times 10\ 000\ 000$
$= 5.8 \times 10^7$

When you move the decimal point to the left, the exponent of 10 is positive. The number of places you move the decimal point is the number in the exponent.

Example 2

The electron in a hydrogen atom is, on average, 0.000 000 000 053 m from the nucleus. Write 0.000 000 000 053 in scientific notation.

Solution

To write the number in the form $x \times 10^n$, move the decimal point to the right until there is one non-zero number to the left of the decimal point.

The decimal point starts here. 0.000 000 000 053
Move the decimal point 11 places to the right.
$= 5.3 \times 0.000\ 000\ 000\ 01$
$= 5.3 \times 10^{-11}$

When you move the decimal point to the right, the exponent of 10 is negative. The number of places you move the decimal point is the number in the exponent.

Instant Practice—Scientific Notation

1. Express each of the following in scientific notation.

   a. The approximate number of stars in our galaxy, the Milky Way:
   400 000 000 000 stars

   b. The approximate distance of the Andromeda Galaxy from Earth:
   23 000 000 000 000 000 000 km

   c. The estimated distance across the universe:
   800 000 000 000 000 000 000 000 km

   d. The approximate mass of a proton:
   0.000 000 000 000 000 000 000 0017 g

2. Change the following to standard form.

   a. 9.8×10^5 m

   b. 2.3×10^9 kg

   c. 5.5×10^{-5} L

   d. 6.5×10^{-10} s

Math Skills Toolkit 2

Significant Digits and Rounding

Significant Digits

Significant digits represent the amount of uncertainty in a measurement. The significant digits in a measured quantity include all the certain digits plus the first uncertain digit. In the example below, the length of the rod is between 5.2 cm and 5.3 cm. Suppose we estimate the length to be 5.23 cm. The first two digits (5 and 2) are certain (we can see those marks), but the last digit (0.03) was estimated. The measurement 5.23 cm has three significant digits.

Use these rules to determine the number of significant digits (s.d.) in a measurement.

1. All non-zero digits (1–9) are considered significant.

   Examples:
   - 123 m (3 s.d.); 23.56 km (4 s.d.)

2. Zeros between non-zero digits are also significant.

   Examples:
   - 1207 m (4 s.d.); 120.5 km/h (4 s.d.)

3. Any zero that follows a non-zero digit *and* is to the right of the decimal point is significant.

   Examples:
   - 12.50 m/s^2 (4 s.d.); 60.00 km (4 s.d.)

4. Zeros used to indicate the position of the decimal are *not* significant. These zeros are sometimes called spacers.

   Examples:
   - 500 km (1 s.d.); 0.325 m (3 s.d.); 0.000 34 km (2 s.d.)

5. All counting numbers have an infinite number of significant digits.

   Examples:
   - 6 apples (infinite s.d.); 125 people (infinite s.d.)

Using Significant Digits in Mathematical Operations

When you use measured values in calculations, the calculated answer cannot be more certain than the measurements on which it is based. The answer on your calculator may have to be rounded to the correct number of significant digits.

Rules for Rounding

1. When the first digit to be dropped is less than 5, the preceding digit is not changed.

   Example: 6.723 m rounded to two significant digits is 6.7 m.

2. When the first digit to be dropped is 5 or greater, increase the preceding digit by one.

   Example: 7.237 m rounded to three significant digits is 7.24 m. The digit after the 3 is greater than 5, so the 3 is increased by one.

Adding or Subtracting Measurements

Perform the mathematical operation, and then round off the answer to the value having the fewest *decimal places*.

$$\begin{aligned} \textbf{Example: } x &= 2.3 \text{ cm} + 6.47 \text{ cm} + 13.689 \text{ cm} \\ &= 22.459 \text{ cm} \\ &= 22.5 \text{ cm} \end{aligned}$$

Since 2.3 cm has only one decimal place, the answer can have only one decimal place.

Multiplying or Dividing Measurements

Perform the mathematical operation, and then round off the answer to the least number of *significant digits* of the data values.

$$\begin{aligned} \textbf{Example: } x &= (2.342 \text{ m})(0.063 \text{ m})(306 \text{ m}) \\ &= 45.149\,076 \text{ m}^3 \\ &= 45 \text{ m}^3 \end{aligned}$$

Since 0.063 m has only two significant digits, the answer must have two significant digits.

Math Skills Toolkit 3

Organizing and Communicating Scientific Results with Graphs

In your investigations, you will collect information, often in numerical form. To analyze and report the information, you will need a clear, concise way to organize and communicate the data.

A graph is a visual way to present data. A graph can help you to see patterns and relationships among the data. The type of graph you choose depends on the type of data you have and how you want to present them. You can use line graphs, bar graphs, and pie graphs (pie charts).

The instructions given here describe how to make graphs using paper and pencil. Computer software provides another way to generate graphs. Whether you make them on paper or on the computer, however, the graphs you make should have the features described in the following pages.

Drawing a Line Graph

A line graph is used to show the relationship between two variables. The following example will demonstrate how to draw a line graph from a data table.

Example

Suppose you have conducted a survey to find out how many students in your school are recycling drink containers. Out of 65 students that you surveyed, 28 are recycling cans and bottles. To find out if more recycling bins would encourage students to recycle cans and bottles, you add one recycling bin per week at different locations around the school. In follow-up surveys, you obtain the data shown in **Table 1**. Compare the steps in the procedure with the graph on the next page to learn how to make a line graph to display your findings.

Table 1 Students Using Recycling Bins

Number of Recycling Bins	Number of Students Using Recycling Bins
1	28
2	36
3	48
4	60

Procedure

1. With a ruler, draw an x-axis and a y-axis on a piece of graph paper. (The horizontal line is the x-axis, and the vertical line is the y-axis.)

2. To label the axes, write "Number of Recycling Bins" along the x-axis and "Number of Students Using Recycling Bins" along the y-axis.

3. Now you have to decide what scale to use. You are working with two numbers (number of students and number of bins). You need to show how many students use the existing bin and how many would recycle if there were a second, a third, and a fourth bin. The scale on the x-axis will go from 0 to 4. There are 65 students, so you might want to use intervals of 5 for the y-axis. That means that every space on your y-axis represents 5 students. Use a tick mark at major intervals on your scale, as shown in the graph on the next page.

4. You want to make sure you will be able to read your graph when it is complete, so make sure your intervals on the x-axis are large enough.

5. To plot your graph, gently move a pencil up the y-axis until you reach a point just below 30 (you are representing 28 students). Now move along the line on the graph paper until you reach the vertical line that represents the first recycling bin. Place a dot at this point (1 bin, 28 students). Repeat this process for all of the data.

6. If it is possible, draw a line that connects all of the points on your graph. This might not be possible. Scientific investigations often involve quantities that do not change smoothly. On a graph, this means that you should draw a smooth curve (or straight line) that most closely fits the general shape outlined by the points. This is called a **line of best fit**. A best-fit line often passes through many of the points, but sometimes it goes between points. Think of the dots on your graph as clues about where the perfect smooth curve (or straight line) should go. A line of best fit shows the trend of the data. It can be extended beyond the first and last points to indicate what might happen.

7. Give your graph a title. Based on these data, what is the relationship between the number of students using recycling bins and the number of recycling bins?

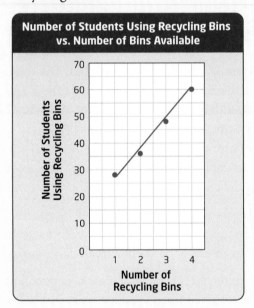

Instant Practice—Line Graph

The level of ozone in Earth's upper atmosphere is measured in Dobson units (all the ozone present in a column of air above a particular point). Using the information in the table below, create a line graph showing what happened to the amount of ozone over Antarctica during a period of 40 years.

Table 2 Ozone Levels in Earth's Upper Atmosphere

Year	Total Ozone (DU)
1960	300
1965	280
1970	280
1975	275
1980	225
1985	200
1990	160
1995	110
2000	105

Constructing a Bar Graph

Bar graphs help you to compare a numerical quantity with some other category at a glance. The second category may or may not be a numerical quantity. It could be places, items, organisms, or groups, for example.

Example

To learn how to make a bar graph to display the data in **Table 3** on the next page, examine the graph in the column next to the table as you read the steps that follow. The data show the area in square kilometres of principal Ontario lakes, not including the Great Lakes.

Table 3 Area Covered by Principal Ontario Lakes

Lake	Area (km²)
Big Trout Lake	661
Lac Seul	1657
Lake Abitibi	931
Lake Nipigon	4848
Lake Nipissing	832
Lake of the Woods	3150
Lake Simcoe	744
Lake St. Clair	490
Rainy Lake	741

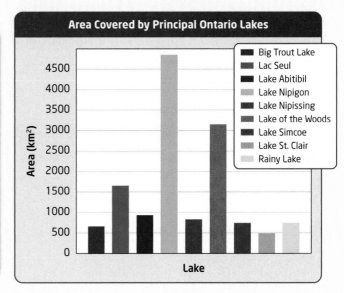

Procedure

1. Draw your x-axis and y-axis on a sheet of graph paper. Label the x-axis "Ontario Lakes" and the y-axis "Area (km²)."

2. Look at the data carefully in order to select an appropriate scale. Write the scale of your y-axis.

3. Decide on a width for the bars that will be large enough to make the graph easy to read. Leave the same amount of space between each bar.

4. Using Big Trout Lake and 661 as the first pair of data, move along the x-axis the width of your first bar, then go up the y-axis to 661. Use a pencil and ruler to draw in the first bar lightly. Repeat this process for the other pairs of data.

5. When you have drawn all of the bars, add labels on the x-axis to identify the bars. Alternatively, use colour to distinguish among them.

6. If you are using colour to distinguish among the bars, you will need to make a legend or key to explain the meaning of the colours. Write a title for your graph.

Instant Practice—Bar Graph

Make a vertical bar graph using the following table of each planet's gravitational force in relation to Earth's gravity.

Table 4 Gravitational Pull of Planets

Planet	Gravitational Pull (g)
Mercury	0.40
Venus	0.90
Earth	1.00
Mars	0.40
Jupiter	2.50
Saturn	1.10
Uranus	0.90
Neptune	1.10

Constructing a Pie Graph

A pie graph (sometimes called a pie chart) uses a circle divided into sections (like pieces of pie) to show the data. Each section represents a percentage of the whole. All sections together represent all (100 percent) of the data.

Example

To learn how to make a pie graph from the data in **Table 5**, study the corresponding pie graph on the right as you read the following steps.

Table 5 Birds Breeding in Canada

Type of Bird	Number of Species	Percent of Total	Degrees in Section
Ducks	36	9.0	32
Birds of prey	19	4.8	17
Shorebirds	71	17.7	64
Owls	14	3.5	13
Perching birds	180	45.0	162
Other	80	20.0	72

Procedure

1. Use a mathematical compass to make a large circle on a piece of paper. Make a dot in the centre of the circle.

2. Determine the percent of the total number of species that each type of bird represents by using the following formula.

$$\text{Percent of total} = \frac{\text{Number of species within the type}}{\text{Total number of species}} \times 100\%$$

For example, the percent of all species of birds that are ducks is

$$\text{Percent that are ducks} = \frac{36 \text{ species of ducks}}{400 \text{ species}} \times 100\% = 9.0\%$$

3. To determine the number of degrees in the section that represents each type of bird, use the following formula.

$$\text{Degrees in "piece of pie"} = \frac{\text{Percent for a type of bird}}{100\%} \times 360°$$

Round your answer to the nearest whole number. For example, the section for ducks is

$$\text{Degrees for ducks} = \frac{9.0\%}{100\%} \times 360° = 32.4° \text{ or } 32°$$

4. Draw a straight line from the centre to the edge of the circle. Use your protractor to measure 32° from this line. Make a mark, then use your mark to draw a second line 32° from the first line.

5. Repeat steps 2 to 4 for the remaining types of birds.

Species of Birds Breeding in Canada

owls · birds of prey · shorebirds · ducks · other · perching birds

Instant Practice—Pie Graph

Use the following data on total energy (oil, gas, electricity, etc.) consumption for 2004 to develop a pie graph to visualize energy consumption in the world.

Table 6 World Energy Consumption in 2004

Area in the World	Consumption (quadrillion btu)
North America	120.62
Central and South America	22.54
Europe	85.65
Eurasia	45.18
Middle East	21.14
Africa	13.71
Eastern Asia and Oceania	137.61

Study Toolkit Overview

At the beginning of every chapter, you will find a Study Toolkit page. Each Study Toolkit page features three of the many helpful study strategies that are described below. Using these strategies can help you understand and remember what you read.

Preparing for Reading

Before you begin to read a chapter, browse through the chapter to get a general sense of what you will be learning.

- *Previewing text features* involves flipping through the chapter to see how it is organized and how the features of the textbook support the main ideas in the chapter.
- *Making connections to visuals* means relating visuals, such as photographs, illustrations, and graphic text, to your own experiences and to the text that accompanies each visual.

Reading Effectively

While you are reading, you can apply these strategies to help you understand what you are reading:

- *Asking questions* helps you engage actively in reading the text and gives you a purpose for continuing to read.
- *Identifying the main idea and details* helps you figure out what is the most important information in the text you are reading. You can also use this strategy after reading, to help you organize what you have learned.
- *Making connections to prior knowledge* helps you relate what you already know to what you are learning.

- *Making inferences* helps you figure out the meaning of the text by combining information in the text with what you already know and by "reading between the lines."
- *Monitoring comprehension* ensures that you stop from time to time as you are reading to ask yourself whether you have understood what you have read.
- *Skim, scan, or study* helps you alter your reading speed based on your purpose for reading.
- *Visualizing* helps you transform a chunk of text into an image in your mind to help you understand and remember details and comparisons in the text.

Reading Graphic Text

Reading tables, graphs, and diagrams is different from reading text. The three strategies below can help you identify elements that are specific to each type of graphic text so you can interpret what the graphic text represents:

- *Interpreting diagrams* requires you to read and understand the parts of the diagram and then relate the parts to each other and to the concepts explained in the text.
- *Interpreting graphs* requires you to understand the organization and functions of the parts of a graph, such as axes, points, and lines. It also requires you to pay attention to the graph's title and caption.
- *Interpreting tables* requires you to examine data that have been organized in rows and columns with explanatory headings. Keep in mind that the title of a table gives information about the table's purpose and meaning.

Word Study

Science textbooks include many words that may be unfamiliar to you. Use the following strategies to help you determine the meanings of new words:

- Identify the *base word*. The base word is the main part of the word, which is distinct from a prefix, suffix, or combining part.
- Examine the smaller words that make up *compound words*.
- *Create a word map* to analyze a word beyond its definition—for example, by identifying its opposites and by listing synonyms for the word.
- Consider the *multiple meanings* of a word when it appears in different contexts.
- Identify the *suffixes* that change the meaning of a word. A suffix is a small word part at the end of a word.
- Analyze *word families* to understand relationships among words that have common parts, such as the same base.
- Look up *word origins* in a dictionary to deepen your understanding of a word.

Organizing Your Learning

Taking notes in class is only the first step in understanding a new concept. You may want to organize what you have learned in a way that helps you remember key concepts and helps you study for tests.

- *Comparing and contrasting* involves identifying the similarities and differences between two concepts or things.
- *Identifying cause and effect* helps you understand why and how events occur, as well as their consequences.
- *Making study notes* means identifying the most important information and recording it in a way that makes sense to you.
- *Summarizing* involves stating the main ideas of a paragraph or a section of text in your own words. You can summarize text using a list, a drawing, point-form notes, a table, or a graphic organizer.
- *Using graphic organizers* helps you to organize information in a visual format.

On the following pages, you will find more information about some of the strategies listed above.

Study Toolkit 1

Preparing for Reading: Previewing Text Features

Before you begin reading a textbook, become familiar with the book's overall structure and features. If you look at the Table of Contents on page v, you will see that this textbook is divided into four *units*. Each unit is divided into three *chapters*. Each chapter is subdivided into numbered *sections*.

As well as the Table of Contents, this textbook has many other features designed to help you find your way while reading. Examine the sample pages below. They include several text features that will help you understand the content.

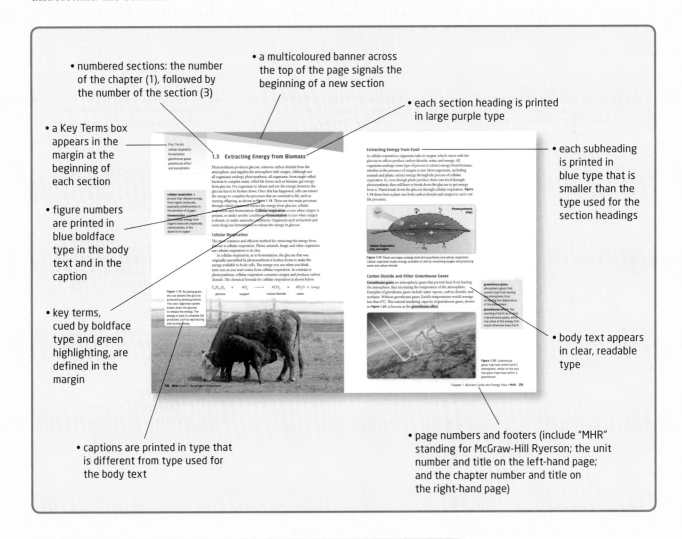

- numbered sections: the number of the chapter (1), followed by the number of the section (3)

- a multicoloured banner across the top of the page signals the beginning of a new section

- each section heading is printed in large purple type

- a Key Terms box appears in the margin at the beginning of each section

- figure numbers are printed in blue boldface type in the body text and in the caption

- key terms, cued by boldface type and green highlighting, are defined in the margin

- each subheading is printed in blue type that is smaller than the type used for the section headings

- body text appears in clear, readable type

- captions are printed in type that is different from type used for the body text

- page numbers and footers (include "MHR" standing for McGraw-Hill Ryerson; the unit number and title on the left-hand page; and the chapter number and title on the right-hand page)

Instant Practice

1. Describe two ways to identify the key terms in a section.

2. Describe two ways to learn more about a visual in this textbook.

Study Toolkit 2

Reading Effectively: Monitoring Comprehension

When you are reading text that contains new ideas and new key terms, stop after each chunk of text to make sure that you understand what you have just read. An effective way to do this is to use the steps in the following flowchart.

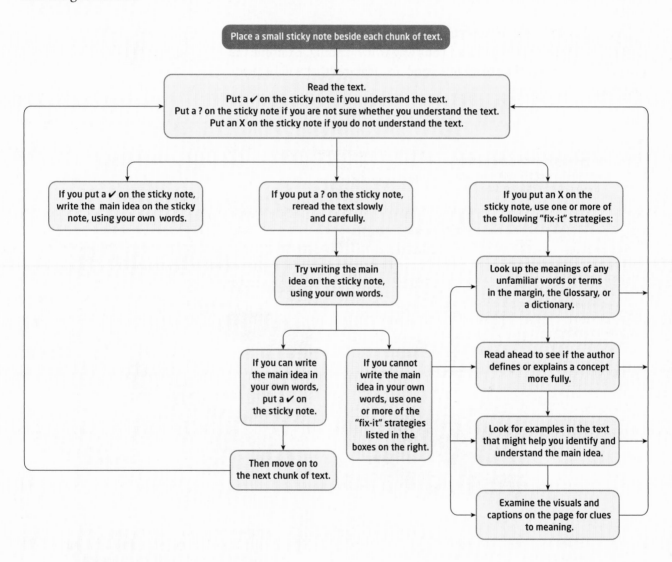

Instant Practice

1. Make a list of steps you could follow if you were not sure that you had understood a section of text. Number your steps.

2. Make a bulleted list of the four "fix-it" strategies, using your own words. Post your list for easy reference.

Study Toolkit 3

Word Study: Common Base Words, Prefixes, and Suffixes in Science

Understanding how words are put together can help you figure out their meanings. The list below includes some common *base words* that are used in science. Also listed are some common *prefixes* and *suffixes*, which change the meaning of a base word when they are combined with the base word.

Base Word	Definition	Example
conduct	To direct or lead	A **semiconductor** allows electrons to move fairly well between atoms.
electr(o)	Having to do with electricity	An **electroscope** is a device for detecting an electric charge.
phot(o)	Having to do with light	A **photometer** measures the amount of light that is emitted from a source.
resist	To hold off; to prevent or oppose	A **resistor** decreases the electric current that is flowing through a component.
sustain	To keep going; to maintain	**Unsustainable** means not able to keep going.
Prefix	**Definition**	**Example**
bio-	Having to do with life	**Biomass** is the total mass of living organisms in a group or an area.
dis-	Not; the opposite of; having an absence of	A **disinfectant** helps to remove and prevent infection.
infra-	Below; beneath	**Infrared** light has a longer wavelength (and thus a lower frequency) than red light.
iso-	Same; equal	An **isotope** has the same number of protons as other atoms of the same element, but a different number of neutrons.
non-	Not; having an absence of	A **non-metal** is an element that does *not* have the properties of a metal.
Suffix	**Definition**	**Example**
-al	Relating to	**Environmental** means relating to the environment.
-ic	Relating to; characterized by	**Atomic** means relating to an atom.
-ity	Having to do with a state or quality	**Reactivity** is the quality of being reactive.
-ion	Having to do with an action or a process	**Evolution** means the process of evolving.
-oid	Resembling; having the form or appearance of	A **metalloid** shares some properties with metals and some properties with non-metals.

Instant Practice

1. Use the table to predict the meaning of *conductivity*.

2. Think of a word that ends in one of the suffixes listed above. (You can browse through this textbook or a dictionary to find a word, if you wish.) Explain the meaning of your word. Compare your word and definition with words and definitions that your classmates suggest.

Study Toolkit 4

Organizing Your Learning: Using Graphic Organizers

When deciding which type of graphic organizer to use, consider your purpose: to brainstorm, to show relationships among ideas, to summarize a section of text, to record research notes, or to review what you have learned before writing a test. Several different graphic organizers are shown on these two pages.

Main Idea Web

A *main idea web* shows a main idea and several supporting details. The main idea is written in the centre of the web, and each detail is written at the end of a line going from the centre.

Spider Map

A *spider map* shows a main idea and several ideas associated with the main idea. It does not show the relationships among the ideas. A spider map is useful when you are brainstorming or taking notes.

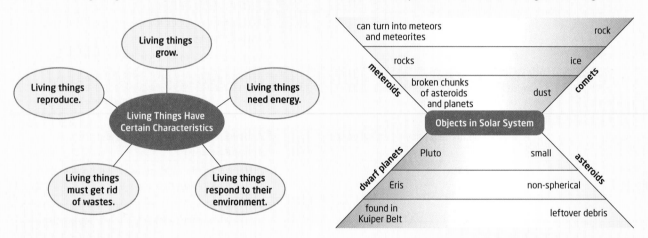

Concept Map

A *concept map* uses shapes and lines to show how ideas are related. Each idea, or concept, is written inside a circle, a square, a rectangle, or another shape. Words that explain how the concepts are related are written on the lines that connect the shapes.

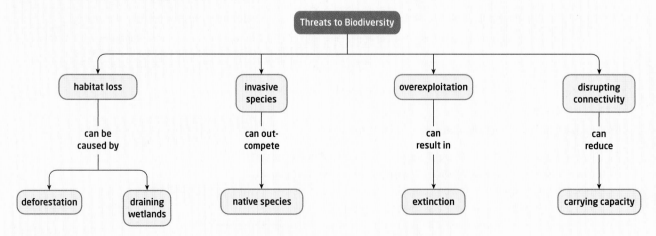

Flowchart

A *flowchart* shows a sequence of events or the steps in a process. A flowchart starts with the first event or step. An arrow leads to the next event or step, and so on, until the final outcome. All the events or steps are shown in the order in which they occur.

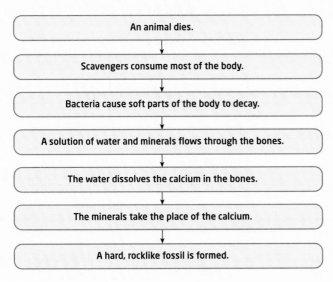

An animal dies.

Scavengers consume most of the body.

Bacteria cause soft parts of the body to decay.

A solution of water and minerals flows through the bones.

The water dissolves the calcium in the bones.

The minerals take the place of the calcium.

A hard, rocklike fossil is formed.

Cycle Chart

A *cycle chart* is a flowchart that has no distinct beginning or end. All the events are shown in the order in which they occur, as indicated by arrows, but there is no first or last event. Instead, the events occur again and again in a continuous cycle.

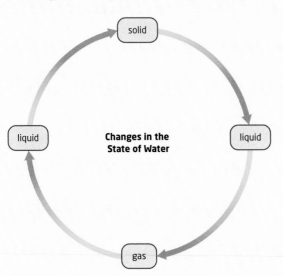

solid

liquid

liquid

Changes in the State of Water

gas

Cause-and-Effect Map

The first *cause-and-effect map* below shows one cause that results in several effects. The second map shows one effect that has several causes.

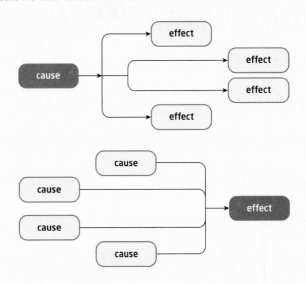

Venn Diagram

A *Venn diagram* uses overlapping shapes to show similarities and differences among concepts.

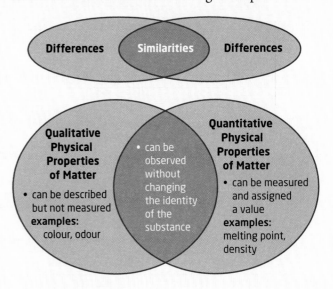

Differences   **Similarities**   **Differences**

Qualitative Physical Properties of Matter
• can be described but not measured
examples: colour, odour

• can be observed without changing the identity of the substance

Quantitative Physical Properties of Matter
• can be measured and assigned a value
examples: melting point, density

Instant Practice

1. Create a Venn diagram that shows the similarities and differences between two of your favourite science topics.

2. Draw a spider map that reflects your prior knowledge about your body's cells.

Appendix A

Properties of Common Substances

KEY TO SYMBOLS:
Common names of substances are enclosed in parentheses.
(*) **water solution of a pure substance**   (e) **element**   (c) **compound**

Name	Formula	Melting Point (°C)	Boiling Point (°C)	Density (g/cm³ or g/mL)	
acetic acid (vinegar) (c)	CH_3COOH	16.6	118.1	–	
aluminum (e)	Al	659.7	2519	2.7	
ammonia (c)	NH_3	–77.8	–33.4	less dense than air	
ammonium nitrate (c)	NH_4NO_3	169.6	210	1.73	
argon (e)	Ar	–189	–185	denser than air	
arsenic (e)	As	–	–	5.727 (grey), 4.25 (black), 2.0 (yellow)	
barium (e)	Ba	727	1897	3.62	
beryllium (e)	Be	1280	2471	1.85	
boron (e)	B	2075	4000	2.37(brown), 2.34 (yellow)	
bromine (e)	Br_2	–7.2	58.8	3.12	
calcium (e)	Ca	845	1484	1.55	
calcium carbonate (limestone) (c)	$CaCO_3$	decomposes at 900°C	–	2.93	
calcium hydroxide (slaked lime) (c)	$Ca(OH)_2$	decomposes at 522°C	–	2.24	
calcium oxide (lime) (c)	CaO	2580	2850	3.3	
carbon (diamond) (e)	C	3500	3930	3.51	
carbon (graphite) (e)	C	4492	4492	2.25	
carbon dioxide (c)	CO_2	–	–	–	
chlorine (e)	Cl_2	–101.6	–34.6	denser than air	
copper (e)	Cu	1084	2562	8.95	
copper(II) nitrate (c)	$Cu(NO_3)_2$	–	–	–	
copper(II) sulfate (bluestone) (c)	$CuSO_4 \bullet 5H_2O$	decomposes at 150°C	–	2.28	
ethanol (ethyl alcohol) (c)	C_2H_5OH	–114.5	78.4	0.789	
fluorine (e)	F_2	–270	–188	–	
gold (e)	Au	1063	2856	19.3	
glucose (c)	$C_6H_{12}O_6$	146	decomposes before it boils	1.54	
helium (e)	He	–272.2	–268.93	–	
hematite (c)	Fe_2O_3	1565	–	5.24	
hydrochloric acid (*)	HCl	varies	varies	varies	
hydrogen (e)	H_2	–259	–253	much less dense than air	
hydrogen peroxide (c)	H_2O_2	–0.4	150.2	1.45	
iodine (e)	I_2	114	184	4.95	
iron (e)	Fe	1535	2861	7.86	
lead (e)	Pb	327.4	1750	11.34	
lithium (e)	Li	179	1340	0.534	
magnesium (e)	Mg	651	1107	1.74	
magnesium chloride (c)	$MgCl_2$	708	1412	2.3	
magnetite (c)	Fe_3O_4	–	–	5.18	
mercury (e)	Hg	–38.9	356.6	13.6	
methane (c)	CH_4	–182.5	–161.5	–	
neon (e)	Ne	–248	–246	–	
nickel (e)	Ni	1455	2913	8.90	
nitrogen (e)	N_2	–209.9	–195.8	slightly less dense than air	
nitrogen dioxide (c)	NO_2	–	–	–	
oxygen (e)	O_2	–218	–183	slightly denser than air	
ozone (e)	O_3	–192.5	–112	denser than air	
platinum (e)	Pt	1769	3824	21.41	
polyethylene (polythene) (c)	$(C_2H_4)n$	–	–	–	
potassium (e)	K	63.5	759	0.86	
propane (c)	C_3H_8	–	–42.17	–	
selenium (e)	Se	217	684.9	4.81	
silicon (e)	Si	1410	3265	2.33	
silicon dioxide (silica) (c)	SiO_2	1600	–	–	
silver (e)	Ag	961	2162	10.5	
sodium (e)	Na	97.5	892	0.971	
sodium chloride (table salt) (c)	NaCl	801	1465	2.16	
sodium fluoride (c)	NaF	988	1695	2.56	
sucrose (sugar) (c)	$C_{12}H_{22}O_{11}$	170	decomposes at 186°C	1.59	
sulfur (brimstone) (e)	S_8	112.8	444.6	2.07	
tin (e)	Sn	231.9	2602	7.31	
titanium (e)	Ti	1666	3287	4.5	
uranium (e)	U	1130	4131	19.05	
water (c)	H_2O	0	100	1.00	
xenon (e)	Xe	–111.9	–107.1	–	
zinc (e)	Zn	419	907	7.14	

DEFINITIONS:

deliquescent: able to absorb water from the air to form a concentrated solution

sublime: to form a vapour directly from a solid

Appearance (at room temperature: 20°C)	Comments
colourless liquid with pungent smell	used in the manufacture of cellulose ethanoate; vinegar is a 5 to 7 percent solution in water
silver-white metal	used in aircraft, cooking utensils, and electrical apparatus
very soluble gas with pungent smell	used as refrigerant and in manufacture of resins, explosives, and fertilizers
white, soluble, crystalline salt	used in explosives and as a fertilizer
inert gas	used in electric lights
grey, black, or yellow solid	used in semiconductors and alloys; compounds are very poisonous and are used in medicine and as pesticides
silver-white solid	used in X-ray diagnosis
hard, white metal	used for corrosion-resistant alloys
brown, amphorous powder or yellow crystals	used for hardening steel and for producing enamels and glasses
red-brown liquid	used to make certain pain-relieving drugs; liquid causes severe chemical burns; vapour is harmful to lungs
soft, white metal that tarnishes easily	very abundant; essential to life
white solid	main ingredient in chalk and marble
white solid	aqueous solution used to test for CO_2
white solid	used in cement and for marking lines on playing fields
colourless, solid crystals	very hard; used for drilling through rock
grey-black solid	very soft; used in lubricants, pencil leads, and electrical apparatus
colourless gas with a faint tingling smell and taste	does not support combustion and is denser than air; used in fire extinguishers and as a refrigerant at −78.5°C
green gas	poisonous; used to kill harmful organisms in water
shiny, reddish solid	soft metal; good conductor of heat
blue, solid crystals	used in pesticides
colourless liquid	derived from fermentation of sugar; used as solvent or fuel; found in wine
greenish yellow gas	similar to chlorine
shiny, yellow solid	very soft metal; highly resistant to tarnishing
white solid	simple sugar; human body converts most sugars and starches to glucose
nonflammable inert gas	used as refrigerant; provides inert atmosphere for welding; used to fill air ships and balloons
rusty red colour	found in iron ore and rusted iron
colourless liquid	corrosive acid; properties vary according to concentration
colourless gas	highly flammable; liquid form used as rocket fuel
colourless liquid	thick and syrupy when pure; an antiseptic
violet-black, solid crystals	crystals sublime readily to form poisonous violet vapour
shiny, silver solid	rusts readily; soft when pure
shiny, blue-white solid	soft metal; forms poisonous compounds
silver-white metal (least dense solid known)	used in alloys; its salts have various medical uses
light, silvery-white metal that tarnishes easily in air	used in alloys and photography; compounds used in medicine; essential to life
white, deliquescent substance	
shiny, black, crystalline solid	strongly magnetic
shiny, silvery liquid	only liquid metal; forms poisonous compounds
odourless, flammable gas formed from decaying organic matter	main constituent in natural gas
colourless, odourless gas	discharge of electricity at low pressures through neon produces an intense orange-red glow
silvery-white, magnetic metal that resists corrosion	used for nickel plating and coinage, in alloys, and as a catalyst
colourless gas	will not burn or support burning; makes up 80 percent of air
brown gas	causes reddish-brown colour in smog
colourless gas	must be present for burning to take place; makes up 20 percent of air
bluish gas	used for purifying air and water and in bleaching; atmospheric layer blocks most of the Sun's ultraviolet light
silver-white solid	used in jewellery; alloyed with cobalt, used in pacemakers
tough, waxy, thermoplastic material	polymer of ethylene; used as insulating material; flexible and chemically resistant
silvery-white, soft, highly reactive, alkali metal	essential to all life; found in all living matter; salts used in fertilizers
colourless gas	flammable; used as fuel
non-metal resembling sulfur; silvery-grey, crystalline solid	used in manufacture of rubber and ruby glass; used in photoelectric cells and semiconductors
steel-grey metalloid similar to carbon in its chemical properties	used in pure form in semiconductors and alloys and in the form of silicates in glass
hard, granular powder; insoluble in water	main constituent of sand; used in clocks and watches as quartz
shiny, white solid	soft metal; best-known conductor of electricity
soft, silvery-white metal; very reactive	used in preparation of organic compounds, as coolant, and in some types of nuclear reactors
white, crystalline solid	used to season or preserve foods
colourless, crystalline substance	used in water fluoridation and as an insecticide
white solid	made from sugar cane or sugar beets
yellow solid	used to make dyes, pesticides, and other chemicals
shiny, slightly yellow solid	soft metal; rust resistant
lustrous white solid	alloys are widely used in the aerospace industry
metallic grey solid	used as a nuclear fuel (usually converted into plutonium)
colourless liquid	good solvent for non-greasy matter
inert gas	used in fluorescent tubes and light bulbs
hard, bluish-white metal	used in alloys such as brass and galvanized iron

Using Star Maps

Star maps help you find your way around the night sky, just like road maps help you find your way around a city. The three star maps on these pages show the night sky in fall, winter, and spring. Notice that each star map is a circle. The circumference of the circle represents the horizon. The centre of the circle is the point directly overhead, called the zenith.

Choosing and Orienting a Star Map

To use a star map, first choose the star map that is appropriate for the season. Then, match its direction to the sky. For example, if you are facing east, rotate the map so that E is at the bottom. The time of night is important, too. The maps tell you what time to look at the sky so the map matches what you see.

Locating Stars and Constellations

Suppose that you are facing north in the fall. Rotate the fall map so that N is at the bottom. The area of the sky just above the N is the northern sky. Start by identifying bright constellations. Here, you can see the constellations Ursa Major (the Big Dipper), Ursa Minor (the Little Dipper), and Cassiopeia. Once you can identify the bright constellations, try to identify their fainter neighbours.

How would you find the bright star Betelgeuse in the fall? The fall star map shows Betelgeuse close to the horizon in the east. Therefore, make sure that you are facing east. Hold the fall star map so that E is at the bottom. You will see Betelgeuse just above the horizon.

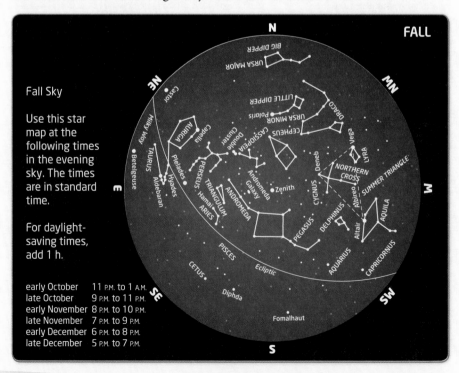

Fall Sky

Use this star map at the following times in the evening sky. The times are in standard time.

For daylight-saving times, add 1 h.

early October	11 P.M. to 1 A.M.
late October	9 P.M. to 11 P.M.
early November	8 P.M. to 10 P.M.
late November	7 P.M. to 9 P.M.
early December	6 P.M. to 8 P.M.
late December	5 P.M. to 7 P.M.

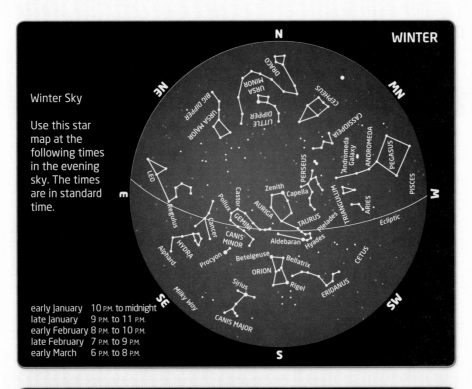

Winter Sky

Use this star map at the following times in the evening sky. The times are in standard time.

early January 10 P.M. to midnight
late January 9 P.M. to 11 P.M.
early February 8 P.M. to 10 P.M.
late February 7 P.M. to 9 P.M.
early March 6 P.M. to 8 P.M.

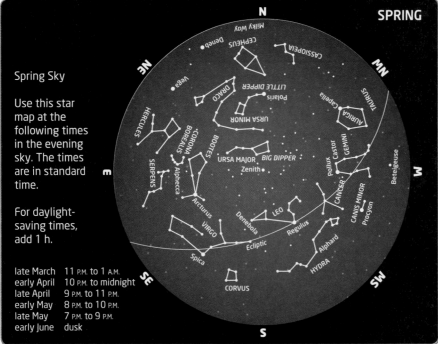

Spring Sky

Use this star map at the following times in the evening sky. The times are in standard time.

For daylight-saving times, add 1 h.

late March 11 P.M. to 1 A.M.
early April 10 P.M. to midnight
late April 9 P.M. to 11 P.M.
early May 8 P.M. to 10 P.M.
late May 7 P.M. to 9 P.M.
early June dusk

Instant Practice—Star Maps

1. Which direction would you face if you wanted to see Leo in January?

2. Name two constellations that you can see in the winter but not in the spring.

3. Write an e-mail to a friend, describing how to use a star map to locate the star Deneb in the spring.

Appendix C

Chemistry References

Names, Formulas, and Charges of Some Polyatomic Ions

Name	Formula
Acetate	CH_3COO^-
Ammonium	NH_4^+
Carbonate	CO_3^{2-}
Chlorate	ClO_3^-
Chlorite	ClO_2^-
Chromate	CrO_4^{2-}
Cyanide	CN^-
Dichromate	$Cr_2O_7^{2-}$
Hydrogen carbonate, bicarbonate	HCO_3^-
Hydrogen sulfate, bisulfate	HSO_4^-
Hydrogen sulfide, bisulfide	HS^-
Hydrogen sulfite, bisulfite	HSO_3^-
Hydroxide	OH^-
Hypochlorite	ClO^-
Nitrate	NO_3^-
Nitrite	NO_2^-
Perchlorate	ClO_4^-
Permanganate	MnO_4^-
Phosphate	PO_4^{3-}
Phosphite	PO_3^{3-}
Sulfate	SO_4^{2-}
Sulfite	SO_3^{2-}

Electron Arrangements of the First 20 Elements

Atom			Ion		
H	1 p	1	H^+	1 p	0
			H^-	1 p	2
He	2 p	2	He	Does not form an ion	
Li	3 p	2, 1	Li^+	3 p	2
Be	4 p	2, 2	Be^{2+}	4 p	2
B	5 p	2, 3	B^{3+}	5 p	2
C	6 p	2, 4	C^{4-}	6 p	2, 8
N	7 p	2, 5	N^{3-}	7 p	2, 8
O	8 p	2, 6	O^{2-}	8 p	2, 8
F	9 p	2, 7	F^-	9 p	2, 8
Ne	10 p	2, 8	Ne	Does not form an ion	
Na	11 p	2, 8, 1	Na^+	11 p	2, 8
Mg	12 p	2, 8, 2	Mg^{2+}	12 p	2, 8
Al	13 p	2, 8, 3	Al^{3+}	13 p	2, 8
Si	14 p	2, 8, 4	Si^{4-}	14 p	2, 8, 8
P	15 p	2, 8, 5	P^{3-}	15 p	2, 8, 8
S	16 p	2, 8, 6	S^{2-}	16 p	2, 8, 8
Cl	17 p	2, 8, 7	Cl^-	17 p	2, 8, 8
Ar	18 p	2, 8, 8	Ar	Does not form an ion	
K	19 p	2, 8, 8, 1	K^+	19 p	2, 8, 8
Ca	20 p	2, 8, 8, 2	Ca^{2+}	20 p	2, 8, 8

Acid-Base Indicators

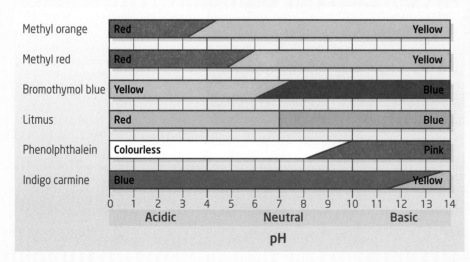

Appendix D

Numerical Answers and Answers to Practice Problems

Unit 1

Section 1.2 Review page 27
5. bunchgrass, 2543 units; grasshopper, 254.3 units; spotted frog, 25.43 units; red-tailed hawk, 2.543 units

Section 2.1 Review page 55
3. 121

Chapter 2 Review pages 84-85
12. 60 years
13. 111.1 days

Chapter 3 Review pages 122-123
12. 65 million years ago

Unit 1 Review pages 128-131
1. d **2.** d **3.** a **4.** c **5.** a
32. b **33.** b. **34.** d **35.** b

Unit 2

Section 4.2 Review page 159
6. 5.02 g/cm^3

Chapter 4 Review pages 174-175
10. 105 g
17. a. 7.13 g/cm^3
b. 0.001 43 g/cm^3
c. 2.70 g/cm^3
22. d = 1.36 g/cm^3

Section 5.2 Review page 193
5. 3 levels

Section 5.4 Review page 211
2. 5 valence electrons

Chapter 5 Review pages 216-217
13. a. 3 p, 4 n, 3 e; metal
b. 15 p, 15 n, 15 e; non-metal
c. 13 p, 15 n, 13 e; metal
d. 6 p, 7 n, 6 e; non-metal
e. 14 p, 14 n, 14 e; metalloid
f. 17 p, 18 n, 17 e; non-metal
18. a. 1 **b.** 3 **c.** 7 **d.** 2
e. 5 **f.** 2 **g.** 4 **h.** 6

Chapter 6 Review pages 254-255
9. a. 2 electrons lost
b. 3 electrons lost
c. 2 electrons gained
d. 1 electron gained
17. a. 2 **b.** 5 **c.** 6 **d.** 9
28. b.

Electron Arrangements and Bond Angles

Compound	Formula	No. of Valence Electrons in Covalent Bonds	No. of Valence Electrons Not in Covalent Bonds	Bond Angle
Methane	CH$_4$	8	0	109.5°
Ammonia	NH$_3$	6	2	107.0°
Water	H$_2$O	4	4	104.5°

Unit 2 Review pages 260-263
1. b **2.** c **3.** a **4.** d **5.** c
7. 2.5 g/cm^3
8. 19.7 g
15. a. 6 p, 7 n, 6 e
b. 24 p, 28 n, 24 e
c. 16 p, 16 n, 16 e
d. 7 p, 7 n, 7 e
34. b **35.** d **36.** d **37.** a **38.** d

Unit 3

Section 7.3 Review page 290
8. a. June 21
b. March 21, September 22
d. June 21

Chapter 7 Review pages 312-313
31. a. 31.4 km/s
b. 62.8 km/s
c. 1 h 46 min

Chapter 8 Review pages 356-357
12. 20% absorbed by atmosphere, 30% reflected, 50% absorbed by Earth's surface
30. a. d = 120 m, v_{max} = 8.3 cm/s

Chapter 9 Review pages 386-387
21. 71.4 km/s/Mpc
31. a. 11.7 h
b. 9.37 years
c. 26.1 years
d. 58.9 years

Unit 3 Review pages 392-395
1. c **2.** d **3.** b **4.** a **5.** b
6. a. C **b.** A **c.** D **d.** B
10.

Magnitude and Distance of Stars

Star	Apparent Magnitude	Absolute Magnitude	Distance (light-years)
Star A	−26	4.7	0.000 02
Sirius	−1.5	1.4	9.0
Alpha Centauri	−0.01	4.4	4.3
Rigel	0.1	−7.0	800
Betelgeuse	0.4	−5.0	520
Capella	0.8	−0.8	42

34. c **35.** b **36.** d **37.** a

Unit 4

Section 11.3 Review page 465
4. 3.5 V
7. a. 3 • 2.0 V, or 4 • 1.5 V
8. b. 6 J/C

Section 11.4 Review page 471
1. 15 Ω
2. 0.15 V
3. 13.5 A

Section 12.2 Review page 500
5. 39%
6. 0.0192 kW•h
8. a. incandescent, $8.45; compact fluorescent, $16.00

Section 12.3 Review page 505
4. nuclear: 50%; other: 2.5%; wind: 1%; gas: 14.5%; coal: 15%; hydro: 17%
8. 20 968 MW

Chapter 12 Review pages 518-519
12. $20.40
19. 22%
20. 7.2 kW

Unit 4 Review pages 524-527
1. d **2.** c **3.** d **4.** b
14. V_1 = 3.0 V, V_2 = V_3 = 1.5 V, V_4 = 3.0 V
16. 10 kW•h
17. $1.51
31. c **32.** d **33.** b **34.** a

Answers to Practice Problems

Chapter 4 page 157
1. 2.70 g/cm^3
2. 1.06 g/cm^3
3. 1.43 × 10^{-3} g/cm^3
4. 6.2 g/cm^3
5. D = 0.67 g/cm^3; it will float on water

Chapter 11 page 468
1. 10 Ω
2. 82.8 Ω
3. 10.6 Ω
4. When potential difference doubles, current doubles.
5. 0.15 A
6. 3.0 V

Chapter 12 page 495
1. a. 1.300 kW
b. 0.060 kW
c. 0.900 kW
2. a. 0.08 h
b. 0.33 h
c. 1.2 h
3. 3.75 kW•h
4. $65.21
5. 4¢

Chapter 12 page 498
1. 74%
2. 3.64%
3. 3036.8 MW
4. 160 kW•h

Glossary

How to Use This Glossary

This Glossary provides the definitions of the key terms that are shown in boldface type in the text. Definitions for other important terms are included as well. The Glossary entries also show the sections where you can find the boldface words. A pronunciation guide, using the key below, appears in square brackets after selected words.

a = mask, back
ae = same, day
ah = car, farther
aw = dawn, hot
e = met, less

ee = leaf, clean
i = simple, this
ih = idea, life
oh = home, loan
oo = food, boot

u = wonder, Sun
uh = taken, travel
uhr = insert, turn

A

abiotic [ae-bih-AW-tik] the non-living parts of an ecosystem (1.1)

absolute magnitude the magnitude of a star that we would observe if the star were 32.6 light-years from Earth (8.3)

acid precipitation rain, snow, or fog that is unnaturally acidic (pH less than 5.6) due to gases in the atmosphere that react with water to form acids (1.3)

aerial insectivore an organism that consumes flying insects (2.4)

alien species a species that is accidentally or deliberately introduced to a new location, usually as a result of human activity (3.3)

alpha particle a positively charged particle emitted from the nuclei of some radioactive elements (5.1)

alternating current (AC) a current in which electrons move back and forth in a circuit (12.1)

ammeter a device that measures the current in one location in a circuit (11.2)

ampere (A) [AM-pir] the unit of electric current, equivalent to one coulomb per second (11.2)

apparent magnitude the brightness of a star as seen from Earth (7.2)

aquatic ecosystem an ecosystem that is water-based, either fresh water or salt water (1.1)

asterism a smaller group of stars that form patterns within a constellation (7.2)

asteroid an object in space that ranges in size from a tiny speck, like a grain of sand, to 500 km wide; most asteroids originate in the asteroid belt between Mars and Jupiter (7.5)

astronomer [uh-STRON-uh-mer] a scientist who studies astronomy (7.1)

astronomical unit [as-truh-NOM-i-kuhl YOO-nit] the average distance between Earth and the Sun, about 150×10^6 km (7.4)

astronomy the study of the night sky (7.1)

atmosphere the layer of gases above Earth's surface (1.1)

atom the smallest particle of an element that retains the identity of the element (5.1)

atomic mass [uh-TOM-ik mas] the average mass of the naturally occurring isotopes of an element (5.3)

atomic number [uh-TOM-ik NUM-ber] the number of protons in the nucleus of an atom (5.2)

atomos [A-toh-mohs] a word used by Greek philosophers, over 2500 years ago, to describe the smallest piece of matter (5.1)

B

base load the continuous minimum demand for electrical power (12.3)

battery a connection of two or more cells (11.1)

big bang the event that may have triggered the expansion of the universe 14 billion years ago (9.2)

binary stars two stars that orbit each other (8.3)

bioaccumulation [bih-oh-uh-KYU-myuh-lae-shuhn] a process in which an organism ingests materials, especially toxins, faster than it eliminates them (1.2, 4.2)

bioaugmentation [bih-oh-awg-mun-TAE-shuhn] the use of organisms to add essential nutrients to depleted soils (3.4)

biocontrol the use of a species to control the population growth or spread of an undesirable species (3.4)

biodiversity the number and variety of organisms found in a specific region (3.1)

biodiversity crisis the current accelerated rate of extinctions on Earth (3.3)

biodiversity hotspot a place where there is an exceptionally large number of species in a relatively small area (3.1)

biomagnification [bih-oh-mag-nuh-fi-KAE-shuhn] a process in which the concentration of ingested toxins increases as it moves from one trophic level to the next (1.2, 4.2)

biomass the total mass of living organisms in a defined group or area (1.2)

bioremediation the use of living organisms to clean up contaminated areas naturally (3.4)

biosphere the regions of Earth where living organisms exist (1.1)

biotic [bih-AW-tik] the living parts of an ecosystem (1.1)

black hole the remnant of a supernova explosion with a gravitational field so strong that nothing can escape its pull (8.3)

blueshift the effect in which objects moving toward an observer have their wavelengths shortened, toward the blue end of the visible spectrum (9.2)

bog a type of wetland in which the water is acidic and low in nutrients (2.2)

Bohr-Rutherford model a model of the atom in which a central positive nucleus is surrounded by electrons in energy levels (5.1, 10.1)

boiling point the temperature at which a liquid turns into a gas (4.2)

bottom-up regulation a process in which the abundance of organisms in lower trophic levels affects the abundance of organisms in higher trophic levels (2.2)

C

calendar a way of showing days, organized into a schedule of larger units of time such as weeks, months, seasons, or years; usually a table or a chart (7.1)

captive breeding the breeding of rare or endangered wildlife in controlled settings to increase the population size (3.2)

carrying capacity the size of a population that can be supported indefinitely by the available resources and services of an ecosystem (2.1)

celestial object [suh-LES-chuhl AWB-jekt] any object that exists in space, such as a planet, a star, or the Moon (7.1)

cell *See voltaic cell*

cellular respiration a process that releases energy from organic molecules, especially carbohydrates, in the presence of oxygen (1.3)

charging by contact generating a net charge on a neutral object by touching it with a charged object (10.2)

charging by friction a process in which objects made from different materials rub against each other, producing a net static charge on each object (10.1)

charisma [ku-RIZ-mah] the ability to attract or keep interest (3.2)

charismatic species [kaer-iz-MA-tik SPEE-sees] an appealing organism used to help draw attention to an environmental problem (3.2)

chemical bond a chemical link between two atoms, which holds the atoms together (6.1)

chemical property the ability of a substance to change or react, and to form new substances (4.3)

chemiluminescence [kem-uh-loo-muh-NES-uhns] the emission of light resulting from a chemical reaction (4.3)

circuit breaker a safety device that is placed in series with other circuits that lead to appliances and outlets (12.1)

circuit diagram a diagram that uses standard symbols to represent the components in an electric circuit and their connections (11.3)

colony collapse disorder the disappearance of mature worker bees that is leaving hives empty, or with only a few young worker bees that cannot maintain the hives alone (2.4)

combustibility the ability of a substance to burn in air (4.3)

comet an object composed of rocky material, ice, and gas; comes from the Kuiper Belt or Oort Cloud (7.5)

community all the populations of the different species that interact in a specific area or ecosystem (3.2)

competition when two or more organisms compete for the same resource in the same location at the same time (1.1)

compound a pure substance made of two or more different elements that are chemically combined (4.1)

conduction the movement or transmission of thermal or electrical energy through a substance (10.1)

conductor a material in which electrons can move easily between atoms (10.1)

connectivity the collection of links and relationships between ecosystems that are separated geographically (2.4)

constellation a group of stars that seem to form a distinctive pattern in the sky (7.2)

consumer an organism that cannot make its own food, so it eats other organisms to survive (1.2)

cosmic microwave background (CMB) radiation the radiation left over from the big bang, which fills the universe (9.2)

cosmology [koz-MAWL-uh-jee] the study of the universe (9.2)

coulomb (C) [KOO-lohm] the quantity of charge that is equal to the charge of 6.25×10^{18} electrons (11.2)

covalent bond [koh-VAE-lent bond] a chemical bond in which two atoms share one or more pairs of electrons (6.2)

covalent compound *See molecular compound*

crystal lattice [KRIS-tul LAT-is] a solid arrangement of a regular repeating pattern of ions (6.1)

D

dark energy a form of energy that makes up nearly three quarters of the universe; has the effect of increasing the expansion of the universe (9.3)

dark matter the most abundant form of matter in the universe; invisible to telescopes (9.3)

daylighting the process of redirecting an underground body of water, such as a creek, to an above-ground channel (3.4)

decomposer an organism that breaks down nutrients in decaying bodies and wastes of organisms, and returns nutrients to abiotic parts of an ecosystem (1.2)

deforestation the practice of clearing forests for logging or other human uses, and never replanting them (3.3)

density the ratio of the mass of a substance to the volume it occupies (4.2)

deposition [dep-uh-ZISH-uhn] the direct change of state from a gas to a solid (4.2)

desertification the change of non-desert land into a desert, which may result from climate change or from unsustainable farming or water use (2.4)

dioxide [dih-OK-sihd] two oxygen atoms (6.2)

direct current (DC) current in which charged particles travel through a circuit in only one direction (12.1)

dominant species a species that is so abundant that it has the biggest biomass of any community member (3.2)

Doppler effect the change in pitch of a sound due to the motion of the source relative to an observer; also, the change in frequency of a light source due to its motion relative to an observer (9.2)

doubling time the period of time that is required for a population to double in size (2.3)

dry cell a cell that contains an electrolyte made of a paste (11.1)

dwarf planet a round, celestial body that orbits the Sun; it may share its orbit with another celestial body, but it is not a satellite (7.5)

E

eclipse the phenomenon in which one celestial object moves directly in front of another celestial object, as viewed from Earth (7.3)

ecological footprint a measure of the impact of an individual or a population on the environment in terms of energy consumption, land use, and waste production (2.3)

ecological niche the way in which an organism occupies a position in an ecosystem, including all the necessary biotic and abiotic factors (2.2)

ecosystem all the interacting parts of a biological community and its environment (1.1)

ecosystem engineer a species that causes such dramatic changes to landscapes that it creates a new ecosystem (3.2)

ecosystem services the benefits experienced by organisms, including humans, that are provided by sustainable ecosystems (2.4)

ecotourism a form of tourism that is sensitive to the health of an ecosystem and involves recreational activities provided by sustainable ecosystems (2.4)

efficiency the ratio of useful energy output to total energy input, expressed as a percentage (12.2)

electric circuit a closed path along which electrons that are powered by an energy source can flow (11.1)

electric current a measure of the number of charged particles that pass by a point in an electric circuit each second (11.2)

electric field a property of the space around a charged object, where the effect of its charge can be felt by other objects (10.2)

electrical energy the energy that is used by an appliance at a given setting; is determined by multiplying its power rating by the length of time it is used (12.2)

electrical power the rate at which an appliance uses electrical energy (12.2)

electrical resistance the property of a substance that hinders electric current and converts electrical energy to other forms of energy (11.2)

electrical source a source of electrical energy that creates potential difference in a circuit (11.2)

electricity a form of energy that results from the interaction of charged particles, such as electrons or protons (10.1)

electrode one of two metal terminals in a cell or battery (11.1)

electrolyte a solution or paste that conducts charge (11.1)

electromagnetic radiation radiation consisting of electromagnetic waves that travel at the speed of light (such as visible light, radio waves, and X rays) (8.1)

electron a negatively charged particle within the atom (5.1)

electroscope a device for detecting the presence of an electric charge (10.2)

electrostatic precipitator a type of cleaner that removes unwanted particles and liquid droplets from a flow of gas (10.3)

electrostatic series a list of materials that have been arranged according to their ability to hold on to electrons (10.1)

element a pure substance that cannot be broken down into simpler parts by chemical methods (4.1)

ellipse a curve that is generally referred to as being oval or the shape of an egg (7.3)

elliptical galaxy a type of galaxy that ranges in shape from a perfect sphere to a stretched-out ellipse (9.1)

EnerGuide label a label that gives details about how much energy an appliance uses in one year of normal use (12.2)

energy level a possible level of energy an electron can have in an atom (5.1)

environmental farm plan a volunteer-membership program in which farmers examine and make plans to reduce environmental impacts of farms (1.1)

equilibrium the balance between opposing forces (2.1)

ethics the set of moral principles and values that guide a person's activities and help him or her decide what is right and what is wrong (8.1)

eutrophication [yoo-troh-fi-KAE-shun] a process in which nutrient levels in aquatic ecosystems increase, leading to an increase in the populations of primary producers (1.1)

evaporation the change of state from a liquid to a gas (4.2)

exponential growth accelerating growth that produces a J-shaped curve when the population is graphed against time (2.1)

extinction the death of all of the individuals of a species (3.3)

extrasolar planet a planet that is orbiting a star other than the Sun (8.2)

F

fermentation a process that releases energy from organic molecules, especially carbohydrates, in the absence of oxygen (1.3)

fuel cell a cell that generates electricity through the chemical reactions of fuel that is stored outside the cell (11.1)

fuse a safety device that is found in older buildings and some appliances; like a circuit breaker, it is placed in series with other circuits that lead to appliances and outlets (12.1)

G

galaxy a huge collection of stars, planets, gas, and dust that is held together by gravity (9.1)

geocentric model [jee-oh-SEN-trik MAW-duhl] a model of the solar system stating that Earth is the centre of all planetary motion, with the planets and the Sun travelling in perfect circles around Earth (7.4)

geothermal energy energy produced from naturally occurring steam and hot water trapped under Earth's surface (12.4)

globular cluster [GLOB-yuh-ler KLUHS-ter] a collection of 100 000 to a million stars that is arranged in a distinctive spherical shape; globular clusters are around the centre of the Milky Way (9.1)

gravitational force the force of attraction between all masses in the universe; the strength of the gravitational force between two objects depends on the masses of the objects and the distance between them (7.3)

greenhouse effect the warming of Earth as a result of greenhouse gases, which trap some of the energy that would otherwise leave Earth (1.3)

greenhouse gas an atmospheric gas that prevents heat from leaving the atmosphere, thus increasing the temperature of the atmosphere (1.3)

ground an object that can supply a very large number of electrons to, or can remove a very large number of electrons from, a charged object, thus neutralizing that object (10.1)

group a vertical column of elements in the periodic table (5.3)

H

habitat loss the destruction of habitats, which usually results from human activities (3.3)

hardness the ability of a substance to be scratched (4.2)

HDPE high-density polyethylene (6.2)

heliocentric model [hee-lee-oh-SEN-trik MAW-duhl] a model of the solar system in which the Sun is in the centre with the planets orbiting it (7.4)

Hertzsprung-Russell (H-R) diagram a graph that compares the properties of stars (8.3)

host an organism in a symbiotic relationship that usually provides nourishment and/or shelter (2.2)

Hubble constant the rate at which the universe is expanding (9.2)

Hubble law the speed of a galaxy is proportional to the galaxy's distance from Earth (9.2)

hydroelectric power generation the production of electricity using a source of moving water (12.3)

hydrosphere all the water found on Earth, including lakes, oceans, and ground water (1.1)

I

incandescence a light emitted from a material because of the high temperature of that material (11.2)

induced charge separation the movement of electrons in a substance, caused by the electric field of a nearby charged object that is not in direct contact with the substance (10.2)

insulator a material in which electrons cannot move easily from one atom to another (10.1)

intensification the creation of high-density residential areas and compact development (2.1)

intermediate load a demand for electricity that is greater than the base load and is met by burning coal and natural gas (12.3)

invasive species a species that can take over the habitat of native species or invade their bodies (3.3)

ion [IH-awn] a positively or negatively charged atom or group of atoms (6.1, 10.3)

ion charge the resulting charge of an atom, positive or negative, after the gain or loss of electrons (5.3)

ionic bond a chemical bond that forms between oppositely charged ions (6.1)

ionic compound a compound made of oppositely charged ions (6.1)

irregular galaxy a galaxy that has an irregular shape (9.1)

isotope one of two or more forms of an element that have the same number of protons but a different number of neutrons (5.2)

J

jagged path the path often followed by lightning as it travels from a cloud to the ground or a tall structure, resulting from air currents and turbulence (10.3)

joule (J) the SI unit of energy; quantities of energy are often expressed in kilojoules (kJ); 1 kJ = 1000 J (12.2)

K

keystone species a species that can greatly affect population numbers and the health of an ecosystem (3.2)

kilowatt (kW) a practical unit of electrical power; 1 kW = 1000 W (12.2)

kilowatt-hour (kW•h) the practical unit of electrical energy (12.2)

L

lander a spacecraft designed to land on a celestial object (8.1)

latitude the location above or below the equator (7.2)

laws of electric charges laws that describe how two objects interact electrically when one or both are charged (10.2)

lightning rod a metal sphere or point that is attached to the highest part of a building and connected to ground (10.3)

light-year the distance that light travels in one year, about 9.5×10^{12} km (7.2)

limiting factor a factor that limits the growth, distribution, or amount of a population in an ecosystem (2.1)

lithosphere the hard part of Earth's surface (1.1)

load a resistor or any other device that transforms electrical energy into heat, motion, sound, or light (11.2)

Local Group the small group of about 40 galaxies that includes the Milky Way (9.1)

luminosity a star's total energy output per second; its power in joules per second (J/s) (8.3)

lunar eclipse the phenomenon in which the full Moon passes into Earth's shadow (7.3)

M

main sequence a narrow band of stars on the H-R diagram that runs diagonally from the upper left (bright, hot stars) to the lower right (dim, cool stars); about 90 percent of stars, including the Sun, are in the main sequence (8.3)

mass number the sum of the number of protons and the number of neutrons in the nucleus of an atom (5.2)

matter anything that has mass and occupies space (4.1)

megawatt (MW) a unit of electrical power; 1MW = 1 000 000 W (12.3)

melting the change of state from solid to liquid (4.2)

melting point the temperature at which a solid turns into a liquid (4.2)

metal typically, an element that is hard, shiny, malleable, and ductile, and is a good conductor of heat and electricity (5.3)

metalloid an element that shares some properties with metals and some properties with non-metals (5.3)

meteor [MEE-tee-uhr] a meteoroid that hits Earth's atmosphere and burns up (7.5)

meteorite [MEE-tee-uhr-iht] a meteoroid that is large enough to pass through Earth's atmosphere and reach the ground, without being totally burned up (7.5)

meteoroid [MEE-tee-uhr-oid] a piece of rock moving through space (7.5)

Milky Way the galaxy that includes the solar system; appears as a hazy white band in the night sky (9.1)

mixture matter that contains more than one kind of particle (4.1)

molecular compound [muh-LEK-yuh-ler KAWM-pound] a compound with particles made up of atoms held together by covalent bonds (6.2)

molecule [MAWL-uh-kyul] the smallest discrete particle of a molecular compound; has one or more shared pairs of electrons in one or more covalent bonds (6.2)

monoxide one oxygen atom (6.2)

multimeter a device that measures several different electrical quantities, including voltage, current, and resistance (11.2)

mutualism a symbiotic relationship between two species in which both species benefit from the relationship (2.2)

N

neutrino [noo-TREE-noh] an uncharged particle that is much smaller than an atom; it passes easily through most kinds of matter and is extremely difficult to detect (5.1)

neutron an uncharged particle that is part of almost every atomic nucleus (5.1)

neutron star a star so dense that only neutrons can exist in its core (8.3)

niche [NEESH] the role and function of an organism or species within an ecosystem (2.4)

non-metal typically, an element that is not shiny, malleable, or ductile, and is a poor conductor of heat and electricity (5.3)

non-ohmic not following Ohm's law (11.4)

non-renewable energy source a source of energy that cannot be replaced as quickly as it is used (12.3)

nuclear fusion [NOO-klee-er FYUSH-uhn] the process of energy production in which hydrogen nuclei combine to form helium nuclei (8.2)

nucleons protons and neutrons, because they both exist in the nucleus of an atom (5.2)

nucleus in chemistry, the positively charged centre of an atom (5.1)

nutrient a chemical that is essential to living things and is cycled through ecosystems (1.1)

O

ohm (Ω) [OHM] the unit for resistance, equivalent to one volt per ampere (V/A) (11.4)

Ohm's law the ratio of potential difference to current is a constant called resistance (11.4)

open circuit a circuit that contains a gap or break (11.2)

open cluster a collection of 50 to 1000 stars; open clusters appear along the main band of the Milky Way (9.1)

orbital radius the average distance between the Sun and an object that is orbiting the Sun (7.4)

orbiters observatories that orbit other celestial objects (8.1)

overexploitation the use or extraction of a resource until it is depleted (3.3)

P

parallel circuit a circuit in which there is more than one path along which electrons can flow (11.3)

parasite an organism whose niche is dependent on a close association with a larger host organism (2.2)

peak load the greatest demand for electricity, which is met by using hydroelectric power and natural gas (12.3)

period a horizontal row of elements in the periodic table (5.3)

periodic table a system for organizing the elements into columns and rows, so that elements with similar properties are in the same column (5.3)

phantom load the electricity that is consumed by an appliance or device when it is turned off (12.2)

phases of the Moon the monthly progression of changes in the appearance of the Moon that result from different portions of the Moon's sunlit side being visible from Earth (7.3)

photosphere the surface layer of the Sun (8.2)

photosynthesis a process that changes solar energy into chemical energy (1.2)

photovoltaic effect the generation of a direct current when certain materials are exposed to light (12.4)

physical property a characteristic of a substance that can be observed and measured without changing the identity of the substance (4.2)

planet an object that orbits one or more stars (and is not a star itself), is spherical, and does not share its orbit with another object (7.4)

pollination a process in which male pollen from one flower fertilizes the female ovary in another flower (2.4)

polymer [PAWL-uh-mer] a compound composed of repeating sub-units linked together by covalent bonds (6.2)

population all the individuals of a species that occupy a particular geographic area at a certain time (2.1)

potential difference (voltage) the difference between the electric potential energy per unit of charge at two points in a circuit (11.2)

predation a relationship between two different species in which one species feeds on another (1.1)

predator an organism that kills and consumes other organisms (2.2)

prey an organism that is eaten as food by a predator (2.2)

primary cell a cell that can be used only once (11.1)

primary producer an organism that can make its own food (1.2)

produce to generate; to create (1.3)

protect to legally guard from harm a species that is listed as endangered, threatened, or of special concern (3.1)

proton [PROH-tawn] a positively charged particle that is part of every atomic nucleus (5.1)

protostar a hot, condensed object at the centre of a nebula (8.2)

pulsar a type of neutron star that sends pulses of radiation toward Earth (8.3)

pure substance matter that contains only one kind of particle (4.1)

Q

qualitative can be described but not measured (4.2)

quantitative can be measured and assigned a particular value (4.2)

quantum a specific amount of energy (5.1)

R

radiation dosimeter [rae-dee-AE-shun doh-SIM-i-tuhr] a small device that detects and measures exposure to radiation (10.3)

radioactive the property of some elements to give off rays of energy as the element breaks down (5.1)

redshift the effect in which objects moving away from an observer have their wavelengths lengthened, toward the red end of the visible spectrum (9.2)

reflecting telescope a telescope that uses a mirror to collect the light from an object (8.1)

reforestation the regrowth of a forest, either through the planting of seeds or trees in an area where a forest was cut down (3.4)

refracting telescope a telescope that uses a lens to collect the light from an object (8.1)

renewable energy source a source of energy that can be replaced in a relatively brief period of time (12.3)

resistor a device used in an electric circuit to decrease the current through a component by a specific amount (11.2)

respiration breathing; the process of inhaling gases from and exhaling gases into the external environment; not to be confused with cellular respiration (1.3)

restoration ecology the renewal of degraded or destroyed ecosystems through active human intervention (3.4)

retrograde motion the movement of an object in the sky, usually a planet, from east to west, rather than its normal motion from west to east; this effect is generally produced when Earth is passing the planet in its orbit (7.4)

revolution the time it takes for an object to orbit another object; Earth's revolution around the Sun is 365.24 days (7.1)

rotation the turning of an object around an imaginary axis running through it; Earth's rotation around its axis is 24 h (7.1)

S

satellite an artificial (human-made) object or vehicle that orbits Earth, the Moon, or other celestial bodies; also, a celestial body that orbits another body of larger size (for example, the Moon is Earth's natural satellite) (8.1)

secondary cell a cell that can be recharged (11.1)

semiconductor a material in which electrons can move fairly well between atoms (10.1)

series circuit a circuit in which there is only one path along which electrons can flow (11.3)

smart meter a meter that records the total electrical energy used hour by hour and sends this information to the utility company automatically (12.2)

solar cell a cell that converts sunlight into electrical energy (11.1)

solar eclipse the phenomenon in which the shadow of the Moon falls on Earth's surface (7.3)

solar energy energy that is directly converted from the energy of the Sun into electricity (12.4)

solar mass a unit of measurement for the mass of stars and galaxies; the Sun is 1 solar mass (8.3)

solar nebula theory the theory that describes how stars and planets form from contracting, spinning disks of gas and dust (8.2)

solar system a group of planets that circle one or more stars (7.4)

solar wind a stream of fast-moving charged particles ejected by the Sun into the solar system (8.2)

solidification the change of state from liquid to solid (4.2)

solubility a measure of the ability of a substance to dissolve in another substance (4.2)

spectral lines certain specific wavelengths within a spectrum characterized by lines; spectral lines identify specific chemical elements (8.3)

spectroscope an optical instrument that produces a spectrum from a narrow beam of light, and usually projects the spectrum onto a photographic plate or a digital detector (8.3)

spiral galaxy a type of galaxy that looks like a pinwheel when viewed from above (9.1)

stability the ability of a substance to remain unchanged (4.3)

standard atomic notation a notation used to represent atoms of elements; it includes the atomic number and mass number of an element (5.2)

star a celestial body made of hot gases, mainly hydrogen and some helium (8.2)

star cluster a collection of stars held together by gravity (9.1)

static charge (static electricity) an electric charge that tends to stay on the surface of an object, rather than flowing away quickly (10.1)

steward someone who manages someone else's property or affairs (3.4)

stewardship the active assumption of responsibility for the welfare of the environment (3.4)

strong force the force of attraction between neutrons and protons (5.2)

subatomic particle a particle that is smaller than the atom (5.1)

sublimation the direct change of state from a solid to a gas (4.2)

succession the series of changes in ecosystems that occurs over time following a disturbance (3.2)

sunspot an area of strong magnetic fields on the photosphere (8.2)

supercluster a gigantic cluster of 4 to 25 clusters of galaxies that is hundreds of millions of light-years in size (9.1)

superconductor a material through which electric charge can flow with no resistance (11.4)

supernova a massive explosion in which the entire outer portion of a star is blown off (8.3)

sustain to endure; to support (1.1)

sustainability use of Earth's resources, including land and water, at levels that can continue forever (2.3)

sustainable ecosystem an ecosystem that is capable of withstanding pressure and giving support to a variety of organisms (1.1)

sustainable use use that does not lead to long-term depletion of a resource or affect the diversity of the ecosystem from which the resource is obtained (2.3)

switch a control device that can complete or break the circuit to which it is connected (11.2)

symbiosis [sim-BIH-oh-sis] interaction between members of two different species that live together in a close association (1.1)

T

tailings waste material left behind after the extraction of minerals (3.4)

terminal a position on a cell that must be connected to other components to form a circuit (11.2)

terrestrial ecosystem an ecosystem that is land-based (1.1)

tides the rising and falling of ocean waters caused by the Moon's and Earth's gravity (7.3)

time of use pricing a system of pricing in which the cost of each kW•h of energy used is different at different times of the day (12.2)

top-down regulation a process in which the abundance of organisms in higher trophic levels affects the abundance of organisms in lower trophic levels (2.2)

toxicity the ability of a substance to cause harmful effects in plants and animals (4.3)

transformer an electrical device that changes the size of the potential difference of an alternating current (12.1)

trans-Neptunian object an object that circles the Sun beyond the orbit of Neptune (7.5)

trophic efficiency a measure of the amount of energy or biomass transferred from one trophic level to the next higher trophic level (1.2)

trophic level a category of organisms that is defined by how the organisms gain their energy (1.2)

U

unsustainable a pattern of activity that leads to a decline in the function of an ecosystem (2.3)

urban sprawl the growth of relatively low-density development on the edges of urban areas (2.1)

V

valence electron an electron in the outermost occupied energy level of an atom (5.4)

Van de Graaff generator a device that accumulates very large charges (10.3)

viscosity the measure of a substance's resistance to flow (4.2)

volt the unit for potential difference; equivalent to one joule (J) per coulomb (C) (11.2)

voltaic cell [vohl-TAE-ik sell] a source of energy that generates an electric current by chemical reactions involving two different metals or metal compounds separated by a conducting solution (11.1)

voltmeter a device for measuring electrical potential difference in volts (11.2)

W

watershed an area of land over which the run-off drains into a body of water (2.4)

watt (W) a unit of electrical power; 1 kilowatt = 1000 W (12.2)

weathering the breaking down of rocks into smaller pieces caused by atmospheric influences (1.1)

wet cell a cell that contains a liquid electrolyte (11.1)

white dwarf a small, dim, hot star (8.3)

wind farm many large wind turbines at one location (12.4)

Index

Bold faced numbers correspond to bold faced terms in the text
f indicates a figure
t indicates a table

A

Aamijwnaang First Nation, 146–147
abiotic, **9**, 13–14
absolute magnitude, **341**, 343
absolute zero, 152
AC source, 457*f*
accuracy, **542**
acetic acid, 143*f*
acid precipitation, 33*f*, 33–35, 34*f*
acidification, 33–35
acids, reactivity, 161*t*
Activities
  alien plant species, 104
  atoms, 180, 185, 189, 191, 246
  ball-and-stick models, 246
  biodiversity, 87, 93
  "black box," 177
  bouncing glue, 219
  cells and batteries, 435, 441
  cereal electroscope, 449
  chemical reactions, 162
  compounds, representing, 244
  constellation creation, 269
  cornstarch plastic, 240
  craters, making, 303
  current, measuring, 459
  Earth's atmosphere, 318
  ecosystem disturbances, 5
  ecotourism, 76
  electric charge, 401, 449
  electric current, generating, 483
  electron movement, 416
  electroscope, 410
  element symbols, 189
  environmental symbol,
    choosing, 11
  flashlights, 435
  galaxies, 359, 365, 366
  hardness, comparing 155
  ice cream, making, 229
  lightning in a glow tube, 401
  limited resources, sharing, 113
  mixtures, 145
  monarch butterflies, 76
  owl pellets, 60
  paper clips, 150
  periodic table, 208
  plant species at risk, 108
  population changes, graphing,
    52
  potential difference, measuring,
    459
  properties, predicting, 195
  recycling in Ontario, 32
  safety in the lab, 141
  series circuit, 459
  solar system, modelling, 293
  static charges, 412, 426
  sunlight, angle of, 285
  switches, 435
  three-dimensional atom, 191
  trip to the Moon, 315

  underwater artifacts, raising,
    137
  viscosity, 151
  voltage, measuring, 459
  wildlife mortality and fences, 47
Adam Beck generating station,
  485, 485*f*
aerial insectivores, 74
aerogel, 136
air, 142
air pollution, 146–147
Alberta Tar Sands, 115, 115*f*
Aldrin, Edwin (Buzz), 317
Alfred Bog, 86, 87, 112
algae, 18*f*, 18–19, 19*f*, 37
alien species, **102**–103, 104, 113,
  114
alkali metals, 205, 205*f*
alkaline cells, 439, 439*f*, 441*t*
alkaline-earth metals, 205, 205*f*
alpha particles, 182*f*, 182–183
alternating current, 483, **486**, 488,
  489
aluminum/aluminium, 143*f*, 150,
  156, 176, 201*f*, 203
American chestnut tree, 96
American eel, 8, 9, 203
americium, 201*f*
ammeter, 450, 457*f*, 458, 459, 470,
  470*f*, 486, 548–549
ammonium, 16, 16*f*
ammonium nitrate, 226
ammonium phosphate, 226
Ampère, André-Marie, 450
amperes, **450**
analogies, 551
analogue meter, **548**
analysis, 529–531
ancient murrelets, 114*f*
Andromeda galaxy, 365, 377–378,
  378*f*, 379
angles, 540–541
Anik 1, 325
anodes, 181
Antares, 344, 344*f*
anti-gravity effect, 380
anti-pesticide by-laws, 19
anti-static sheets, 406
Apollo 1, 330
Apollo 11, 317
apparent magnitude, **278**
aquatic ecosystem, **16**–19, 23
aqueous solution, 153
Arctic cod and DDT, 154
Arctic sea ice, 326
area, calculating, 538
argon, 205*f*
Aristarchus, 274, 275
Armstrong, Neil, 317
arsenic, 203
asterisms, 279
asteroid belt, 298*f*
asteroid impacts, 300
asteroids, **300**, 300*f*, 301, 302, 361
astronauts, 265, 317, 328–330

astronomers, 271–275, **272**
astronomical unit (AU), **293**
Atikaki Provincial Park, 4
Atlantic cod, 104, 104*f*
atmosphere, **13**, 13*f*
  carbon cycle, 14, 15*f*
  carbon dioxide, 30–31, 31*t*
  modelling, 318
  nitrogen cycle, 16, 16*f*
  phosphorus cycle, 17, 17*f*
  water cycle, 14
atom smashers, 418, 418*f*, 424
atomic "black box", 177
atomic mass, **195**, 196
atomic model time line, 185
atomic models, 177, 185, 191
atomic notation, 189, 196
atomic number, **188**, 188–189, 196
atomic theory, 180–185
atoms, 177, **179**–185, 180*f*,
  187–192, 402
  and elements, 194–205,
    207–210
  reactivity, 210
auroras, 338, 338*f*

B

ball-and-stick models, 245–246,
  245*f*
Ballard Power Systems, 443
bar graph, 558–559
Barringer Meteorite Crater, 302,
  302*f*
base load, **501**, 503
base words, 48, 360
batteries, 435, 437, **438**–441, 452,
  452*f*, 457*f*
  in circuits, 457, 457*f*, 459–460,
    548, 549
  in vehicles, 440, 441*f*, 442, 443
beavers, 98, 98*f*
bees, 71, 72–73
Berners-Lee, Tim, 375
bias, **530**
big bang theory, 358, **372**–373, 374,
  375, 380
Big Dipper, 277, 279, 279*f*
binary stars, 343
Bingham Canyon mine, 202
bioaccumulation, **26**, 154, 203
bioaugmentation, **115**
biocontrol, **113**
biodiversity, 86–115, **89**
  in Canada, 87, 91, 92
  crisis, **108**
  documenting, 91, 91*t*
  hotspots, **92**–93, 101
  index, 93
  measuring, 89–93, 90*t*
  threats to, 100–108
biology, meaning of, 6
biomagnification, 26, 154, 203
biomass, **25**
  as alternative energy source, 510

fossil fuel creation, 30
  of living organisms, 25, 25*f*,
    28–29, 96
biomass energy, **510**
bioremediation, **115**
biosphere, **13**, 13*f*
  ecosystem services, **69**–77
  nutrient cycles, 14–18, 14*f*, 15*f*,
    16*f*, 17*f*, 18*f*
  photosynthesis, 21–23
biotic parts of an ecosystem, **9**,
  10, 11
birds, migratory, 8, 8*f*, 74–75
"black box", 177
black hole, 345, 346, 348
black-footed ferret, 97, 97*f*
blackout, 316, 455
blood serum, 153
blueshift, **369**
bog, **57**, 86, 87
bog elfin butterfly, 86, 87*f*
Bohr, Neils, 183–184, 185, 402
Bohr-Rutherford models, 184, 190,
  212, 234, 244, 404, 404*f*
boiling point, 151*t*, **152**
Bolton, Dr. Tom, 348
Bondar, Roberta, 328
boreal forests, 31
bouncing glue, 219
Bowman, Patrick, 204
brainworm, 63, 63*f*
bromine, 205*f*
brown bat, 56, 56*f*
bucket brigade, 146–147
bulb, 457*f*
burying beetles, 72, 73*f*
butterflies, 76, 86, 87*f*, 91
"button" cells, 439

C

calendars, **272**–273
Canadarm/Canadarm2, 328, 329*f*,
  265
Canadian Museum of Nature, 91
Canadian Space Agency (CSA),
  321, 324, 326, 328
Canadian Standards Association,
  494
CANDU reactors, 503*f*
canopy fogging, 90*t*, 91
captive breeding, **97**
carbohydrates in photosynthesis,
  22
carbon atom, 188*f*
carbon cycle, 14, 15*f*
carbon dioxide, 30–31, 30*f*, 31*t*,
  152, 235, 235*f*
  in cellular respiration, 28–29
  in photosynthesis, 22, 22*f*,
    28–29
  in soft drinks, 237, 237*f*
  solid (dry ice), 152, 153*f*
carbon monoxide, 235, 235*f*
carbon sinks, 31*t*

carnivores, 24, 24f, 25, 25f
carnivorous plants 57, 57f
Carolinian Canada, 92, 92f
carrying capacity, **51–54**, 66–67, 69
  and humans, 52, 52f, 66, 66f
  redside dace, 53, 53f
Case Studies
  American eel, 8
  chemical pollution, 146–147
  diamond mining, 202–203
  Dolly Varden (fish), 106–107
  e-waste, 422–423
  electric vehicles, 442–443
  honeybees, disappearing, 72–73
  near-Earth objects (NEOs),
    304–305
  plastic bags, 238–239
  renewable energy sources,
    508–509
  space exploration spinoffs,
    370–371
  space junk, 330–331
Cassiopeia, 278, 278f, 279, 346f
cathodes, 181
cause and effect, 270, 436, 484, 562
cause-and-effect maps, 270, 436,
  484, 567
celestial objects, **270**
cellphones, 73, 187, 187f, 422
cells (energy)
  dry, 435, 439, 439f, 441t
  fuel, 442–443
  primary and secondary, 440,
    441t
  solar, 444, 508–509, 511
  wet, 440, 441t
cellular respiration, 28–29, 29f
Celsius scale, 541
Centen, Corey, 444
cereal electroscope, 449
Ceres, 300
CERN (Conseil Européen pour
  la Recherche Nucléaire), 192,
  375, 466f
CFCs (chlorofluorocarbons), 172
Chadwick, James, 185
charges (electric)
  causes of, 404
  conductors, 406–407, 406f, 420f,
    421, 425
  detecting, 411, 412
  electrostatic, 421–423, 422f,
    423f, 426
  grounding, 407, 407f, 409
  induced, 415–416, 424
  insulators, 406, 407
  laws of, 413–414, 413f, 414f
  lightning, 400, 401, 418, 419f,
    420–421
  static 401, 403–409, 403f, 412,
    426
  transferring, 403–405, 408–409,
    411–416, 418, 419f
charging
  by contact, **412**–413
  by friction, **403**, 403f, 406
  by induction, 415–416, 424
chemical bond, **222**
chemical properties, 160–164
chemical reactions, 162
Chemical Valley, 146–147

chemiluminescence, 160, 160f
chemistry in society and
  environment, 145–147
chlorine, 150, 205f
chlorofluorocarbons (CFCs), 172
chlorophyll, 21, 22, 22f, 23
circuit boards, 434f, 447
circuit breakers, **488**,490t
circuit diagrams, **456**–457, 456f,
  457f, 548
circuits *see* electric circuits
clocks, early, 273, 273f
Clostridium tetani (tetanus), 164,
  164f
coal, electricity from, 30, 501, 501f,
  502, 504, 504f
COBE satellite images, 373, 374
Collins, Michael, 317
colony collapse disorder, 72–73
Columbia space shuttle, 329
combustibility, **163**, 163f
comets, **297**, 297f, 299–300, 299f,
  300f, 301
  Encke, 300t
  Hale-Bopp, 300, 300f, 300t
  Halley, 300t
  Shoemaker-Levy 9, 297, 297f
  Swift-Tuttle, 300t, 301
  Wild 2, 300, 300t
commons (land), 118–119
communications satellites, 325
communities (of organisms),
  95–98
compact fluorescent light bulbs,
  499
comparing and contrasting, 6, 436
competition among organisms, 10f,
  60–61, 60f, 61f
compound words, 316, 562
compounds, 141f, **143**–145
  ball-and-stick models, 245, 245f
  Bohr-Rutherford diagrams,
    243, 243f
  covalent, 233–240, 234f, 235f,
    236f, 245, 245f
  ionic, 222–230
  models of, 242–247, 243f, 244f,
    245f, 247f
comprehension, monitoring, 220
concept map, 566
conclusions, **535**
condensation, 14, 14f, 152, 152f
conducting charges, 406–407, 406f,
  420f, 421, 425
conductivity, 151t, 156, 200t, 227,
  251, 405
conductivity tester, 406, 406f
conductors, **406**, 407
connectivity, **76**, 105, 105f
constellations, 269, **277**–281, 277f,
  335, 363
  Big Dipper, 277f, 278f, 279–280,
    279f, 280f, 281f
  Cassiopeia, 278, 278f, 279
consumers, 24–26, 24f, 25f, 26f
control (of variables), **534**
control device *see* switches
conventional current, 450
Copernicus, Nicolaus, 291
copper, 150, 153,156, 202
corals, 62, 62f

Corelly, Dayna, 240
cornstarch plastic, 240
cosmic microwave background
  (CMB) radiation, **372**–373, 374
cosmology, **368**
cosmonaut, 330
Cottrell, Frederick, 421
coulomb, **449**, 450, 453
covalent bonds, **233**, 233f, 234,
  234f, 236
covalent compounds, **233**–240,
  234f, 235f, 236f, 245, 245f
coyotes, 202
CPRGlove™, 444
Crab Nebula, 347, 347f
cross-pollination, 71, 71f
crystal lattice, 225, 227
Crystal, Michael Lee-Chin, 242
Cullis-Suzuki, Severn, 101
Curie, Marie, 182
current, 436, **448**, 450, 451, 459,
  468–470, 548–550
cyanide, 202
cyanobacteria, 16, 16f
cycle chart, 567
Cygnus X-1, 348

D

Dalton, John, 180, 181
dark energy, **380**
dark matter, 377–379, 377f, **378**,
  378f
data recording and organizing,
  535, 545
David Suzuki Foundation, 101
daylighting, 111
DDT (dichloro-diphenyl-
  trichloroethane), 26, 154, 154f,
  164
de Coulomb, Charles Augustin,
  450
decomposers, 24, 72, 73f
deforestation, **100**–101, 101f
density, 151t, 155, **156**–157
dependent variable, **534**
deposition, 152, 152f
desertification, **70**
Dextre, 329
diagrams, interpreting, 316, 402,
  561
diamond, 155, 155f
Diavik Diamond Mine, 202–203
dichloro-diphenyl-trichloroethane
  (DDT), 26, 154, 154f, 164
digital meters, 548, 549
direct current (DC), **486**, 489
distillation, 144t
DNA, 247, 247f
Dolly Varden (fish), 106–107
dominant species, **96**
Don Valley Brick Works, 111, 111f
Doppler effect, **369**
doubling time, **66**
downy woodpecker populations,
  52
dry cells, 435, **439**, 439f, 441t
dry ice, 152, 153f
ductility, 200t
dwarf planets, 298f, 299

dye-sensitized solar cells (DSSCs),
  511

E

e-waste, 422–423
Earth, 283–289, 291–295, 301–302
  early ideas about, 291
  and Moon, 286, 286f, 287–289,
    287f, 288f, 289f
  orbit, 281f, 283–284, 294t
  properties of, 292t
  shadow of, 275, 275f, 287, 287f
  size, 293, 294t
  and Sun, 284–288, 284f, 286f,
    287f, 288f, 291, 291f, 293
Earth's spheres, 13, 13f
Easter Island, 7, 7f, 11
eastern massasauga rattlesnake, 92f
eclipses
  lunar, 275, 275f, **287**, 287f
  solar, 271, 272f, **288**, 288f
ecliptic path, 308
ecological footprint, **67**, 67f, 82
ecological niches, **56**–57, 61,
  65–67, 69
ecosystem engineers, 98, 98f
ecosystem services, 69–77
ecosystems, **7**
  abiotic characteristics, 9, 12, 12t
  Alfred Bog, 86–87
  biodiversity, threats to, 86, 87,
    101–108
  biotic characteristics, 9, 10, 10t
  carrying capacity, 46, 51, 52–54,
    52f, 54f
  coffee plantations, 75, 75f
  connectivity, 76, 105, 105f
  Earth's spheres, 13, 13f, 21–26
  ecological footprint, **67**, 67f, 82
  environmental impact,
    reducing, 19
  equilibrium, 51–53
  Great Lakes, 8–9, 103, 103f
  human niches, 65–67
  nutrient cycles, 14–18, 14f, 15f,
    16f, 17f, 18f
  parts of, 9–12, 10t, 12t
  services, 46, 69–77
  sustainable, 7–8, 46, 75, 76–77
  symbiosis, 10t, 62–63, 62f, 63f
ecotourism, 76
Edison, Thomas, 437f
efficiency, energy, **497**–499
Einstein X-ray Observatory, 347f
Ekati Diamond Mine, 202, 203
electric charges, 401, 404
electric circuits, **437**
  batteries, 457, 459–460, 548, 549
  blackouts, 455, 455f
  connecting wires, 447
  electric current, 448–450
  electron movement, 448
  loads, 452, 468–469
  measuring current in, 458–459,
    470
  models and analogies, 446
  ohms, 463–465, 466, 478
  open, 447, 468
  potential difference, 452–453,
    458, 459, 470

resistance, 451, 462–466, 465f, 468–470
switches, 447
symbols and diagrams, 456–457, 456f, 457f, 548
see also batteries, cells (energy)
electric current, 436, **448**, 450, 451, 459, 468–470, 548–550
electric fields, **414**, 414f, 415, 450
electric vehicles, 437, 437f, 442–443, 452
electrical energy, 460, **494**
and applicances, 493–494, 493t, 494f, 494t, 497, 498
conserving, 497, 498, 499, 511
cost of, 492, 495
efficiency, 497–499, 511
smart meters, 496, 496f
time of use pricing, 496
units of measurement, 498
electrical power, **493**
electrical resistance, **451**, 462–466, 465f, 468–470
electrical safety, 488, 488f, 490, 490t
electricity, 398, 400, **401**
alternating current (AC), 486, 489
base load, 501
coal, from, 504, 504f
demand for, 501–504
direct current (DC), 486
environment, 482
generating and distributing, 485–490, 506–510, 511
off-peak use, 496, 496f, 501, 504, 511
peak demand, 496, 496f, 504
renewable sources of, 506–510, 511
safety devices, 488, 488f, 490, 490t
static, 401, 403–409, 412, 426
electrodes, **438**, 438f, 439f, 440f
electrolytes, 225, **438**, 438f, 439f, 440, 440f, 452
electromagnetic radiation, **318**, 318f, 320, 320f, 320t, 372
electromagnetic spectrum, 318, 318f, 320, 320f, 320t, 339, 364
electrons, 181, 181f, 183–184, 183f, 188, 400, 404
in covalent bonds, 233, 233f, 234, 234f
free, 448, 448f
in energy levels, 184, 184f, 190, 190f
in static electricity, 403–409, 404f, 405t, 408f
valence, **208**–210, 222, 233, 233f, 234, 234f
electroscope, 402, **411**–416, 411f
electrostatic charges, 421–423, 422f, 423f, 426, 430
electrostatic precipitator, 421–422, 422f
electrostatic series, **405**, 405f
electrostatic spray painting, 421, 421f
elements, 141f, **143**, 145

classifying, 141f, 145, 200
periodic table, **195**–196, 197f, 198–199f, 200, 200f, 205, 207–210, 210f
properties of, 143, 149–158, 568–569
elephants, 49, 49f
ellipse, **283**
elliptical galaxies, 362, 362f
elliptical orbit, 283, 283f
Encke (comet), 300t
endangered wildlife, 97, 97f
EnerGuide label/program, **494**, 494f, 511
energy
from biomass, 25f, 29, 510
from photosynthesis, 21–23, 22f
renewable sources, 21–23, 506–510, 511
solar, 21–23, 21f, 22f, 509, 511
energy levels in atoms, 184, 184f, 190, 190f, 208–210
Energy Star® rating, 494
energy-efficient appliances, 508
entomology, 88
environment
analyzing issues, 529–531
balancing populations, 118–120
chemical pollution, 146–147
and farming practices, 18–19, 37, 145f, 154, 154f, 226
plastics, 238–239
road salt, 230, 230f
space exploration, effects of, 331t
environmental farm plans, 19
ENVISAT (ENVIronmetal SATellite), 326, 326f
equilibrium, **51**
Eratosthenes, 274
Eris, 298f, 299
estimating, **538**
ethics of space exploration, 331t
ethylene, 238
European gypsy moth, 113, 113f
European Space Agency (ESA), 326, 370
eutrophication, **18**, 35
evaporation, 14, 14f, 152
EVARM, 371
Experimental Lakes Area (ELA), 18, 18f, 19, 34
exponential growth, **49**–51, 50f, 51f, 66
exponents of scientific notation, 555
extinction, 97, **106**–108, 107f
exotic species, 102
extrasolar planets, 335, 335f
Exxon Valdez, 156, 156f

F

fair test, **534**
fermentation, **28**, 32–33
fertilizers, 18–19, 37, 145f, 226
filtration, 144t
First Nations, 4, 146–147
flowcharts, 567
fluorescent tubes, 204, 499f

fluoride, 224, 224f
fluorine, 205f
flying squirrels, 51f
food chain, 24–25, 24f, 25f, 95
food pyramid, 25f
forests, 34, 34f, 69–70, 70f, 112, 113
fossil fuels, 30, 30f, 33, 33f, 437
Franklin, Benjamin, 418
friction, 403, 403f, 406
fuel cells, **442**–443
fuel from landfills, 32–33, 32f
fur seals, 51, 51f
fuses, **488**, 490t

G

galaxies, 358, 359, **361**–366, 362f, 363f, 364f
see also Andromeda galaxy, Milky Way
Galilei, Galileo, 318
gamma rays, 318f, 320f, 372, 372f
Gamow, George, 370, 373
gas giants, 292
Jupiter, 290f, 291, 292, 293, 295f, 295f, 299
Neptune, 292, 295f, 295t, 297
Saturn, 292, 295t, 295f, 322, 322f
Uranus, 291, 292, 292t, 295f, 295f, 361
gases, 150
Gassner, Carl, 439
generating plants, 485–487, 485f, 486f
Georgian Bay Biosphere Reserve, 92, 92f
geostationary satellites, 327
geosynchronous satellites, 327
geothermal energy, 510
global positioning system (GPS) satellites, 325
global warming, 30
globular clusters of stars, **363**, 363f, 364f
glow sticks/tubes, 160f, 401
glucose, 21, 22, 28
gold, 143f, 152, 153f, 201f, 202
Golden Horseshoe, 52f, 53, 54
graphic organizers, 270, 360, 484, 562, 566–567
graphs, 484, 557–560, 561
grasses, 25f, 28f
grasshoppers, 58
grassland species, 97, 97f
gravitational force, **289**, 289f, 299, 348
gravitational potential energy, 453f, 460f
gravity, 310, 348, 361, 363
Great Canadian Shoreline Clean Up, 77
great grey owl, 46
great horned owl, 25
Great Lakes Water Quality Agreement, 19
Great Refrigerator Roundup, 511
greenhouse effect, **29**, 29f, 504
greenhouse gases, **29**, 29f, 30, 31t, 442

grey water, 427
ground fault circuit interruptor, 490t
grounding, **407**, 407f, 409
group, **205**
gypsy moths caterpillar, 113, 113f

H

H-R (Hertzsprung-Russell) diagram, **343**–344, 343f, 354
habitat loss, 100
Hadfield, Chris, 328, 328f, 329f
Hale-Bopp comet, 300, 300f, 300t
Halley comet, 300t
halogen lamps, 499f
halogens, 205, 205f
hardness, 151t, 155, 251
Haughton Crater, 302f
helium, 142f, 143, 152, 209, 336
Hera and Heracles, 361
herbivore, 24, 25f
herring gull, 26f
Herschel, William, 361, 363
Hertzsprung, Ejnar, 343–344
Hertzsprung-Russell (H-R) diagram, **343**–344, 343f, 354
Hipparchus, 276
honeybees, 71, 72–73
Hoyle, Sir Fred, 372
Hubble constant, 370, 371f, 382
Hubble Deep Field, 368f
Hubble, Edwin, 368–370
Hubble law, 370
Hubble Space Telescope (HST), 321f, 362f, 366, 368, 369, 370, 375, 379
human niches, 65–67, 66f, 67f
Humason, Milton L., 370
hybrid vehicles, 437
hydroelectric power generation, 485, 485f, 501, 501f, **502**, 501f, 506
hydrogen, 189, 191, 191f, 336
hydrogen fuel cells, 442–443
hydrogen peroxide, 162
hydrogen sulfide, 150
hydrosphere, **13**–14, 13f, 14f, 16–17, 16f, 17f
hypothesis, **533**

I

ice cream making, 229
Ida (asteroid), 300f
incandescent bulbs, 447, 447f, 499, 511
independent variable, **534**
induced charge separation, **415**–416
induction, 415–416, 424
Industrial Revolution, 30, 30f
inferences, making, 177, 220, 484, 561
infrared radiation, 318f, 320, 320f, 322, 322f, 364, 372f
inner planets, 292, 294f, 294t
Mercury, 291f, 291t, 292, 293t, 294f, 294t
Venus, 291, 292, 294t, 294f

see also Earth, Mars
insectivores, 74
insects, 71–74, 76, 90*t*, 91, 96
insulators, **406**, 407
intensification, 48, 54, 54*f*
intermediate load, **504**
International Astronomical Union (IAU), 279, 291
International Space Station, 327–329, 327*f*
introduced species, **102**–103
invasive species, 102–103, 103*f*
Investigation
  age of the universe, 382–383
  algae growth, 37
  Bohr-Rutherford atom model, 212
  CFCs and the ozone layer, 172
  chemical properties, 168–169, 170–171
  common substances, properties of, 170–171, 252
  conductivity, comparing, 429
  covalent compounds, properties of, 250–251, 252
  ecological footprint, 82
  electricity costs, reducing, 516
  electrostatic series, 430
  endangered winter skate, 79
  energy audit, 514
  expanding universe model, 384
  fertilizers and plant growth, 37, 42
  gravity on other planets, 310
  H-R (Hertzsprung-Russell) diagram, 354
  hand drying, environmentally friendly, 515
  ionic compounds, properties of, 250–251, 252
  loads, 474–475, 476–477
  Moon's movement, modelling, 307
  Ohm's law, testing, 478
  ozone layer, 172
  paramecia growth, 80
  photosynthesis, 38–39
  physical properties, 166–167, 170–171, 213
  plant growth, 37, 40–41, 42
  populations, balancing, 118–120
  reactivity trends in periodic table, 214
  rust, causes of, 249
  soil-water acidity, 40–41
  spectral analysis, 352–353
  staircase circuits, designing, 513
  star composition, 352–353
  star observations, 308–309, 350–351
  voltaic cells, constructing, 472–473
  zebra mussels and chlorophyll, 117
iodine, 205*f*
ion, **222**–225, 223*f*, 225*f*, **416**
ion charge, 196
ionic bond, **222**, 225
ionic compounds, **222**–230, 250–251, 252
iron, 203
irregular galaxies, 362, 362*f*

Isle Royale, 59, 59*f*
isotopes, **191**, 191*f*
issues, analyzing, 529–531

J

jackrabbit, 25, 25*f*
James Webb Space Telescope (JWST), 375, 375*f*
Jet Propulsion Laboratory (JPL), 323
joules (J), 453, 498
Jupiter, 290*f*, 291, 292, 293, 295*f*, 295*t*, 299

K

kelp, 96, 96*f*
Kelvin scale, 541
Kepler, Johannes, 291
keystone species, **96**, 96*f*, 97, 97*f*, 110
kilojoule, 498
kilowatt (kW), **493**
kilowatt-hour (kW-h), **494**, 494*t*, 495, 496, 498
Komarov, Vladimir, 330
Kruger National Park, 49, 49*f*
Kuiper Belt, 297, 298*f*, 299
Kuiper, Gerard, 297
Kyoto Protocol, 31*t*

L

Lake Erie, 18, 19, 19*f*
lake trout, 26*f*, 51
Lakeview Generating Station, 501
landers, 323, 324, 324*f*
landfills, 32, 32*f*, 33
Langat, Pinky, 511
Large Hadron Collider (LHC), 192, 192*f*, 375, 466, 466*f*
laser printers, 425
latitude, **281**
laws of electric charges, **413**–414, 413*f*, 414*f*
lead, 201*f*, 203
lead-acid battery, 440, 440*f*, 441*t*, 460, 460*f*
Leitrim Wetland, 92
length, measuring, 538
Leonid meteor shower, 301*f*
Levy, David, 297
Libra, 277*f*
lidar (light detection and ranging), 324
light
  ecosystem requirements, 12*t*
  visible, 318, 318*t*, 320*f*, 421
  speed of, 318, 421
light bulbs
  compact fluorescent (CFLs), 493*f*, 499*f*
  energy efficient, 205*f*, 499*f*
  fluorescent tubes, 204, 499*f*
  Halogen lamps, 499*f*
  incandescent, 447, 447*f*, 499, 511
  light-emitting diodes (LEDs), 499*f*
light pollution, 280
light-emitting diodes, 499*f*

light-years, **277**, 365
lightning, 400, 401, 418, 419*f*, 420–421
lightning rods, **420**–421, 420*f*
limiting factors, **50**, 50*f*, 51
line of best fit, **558**
line graphs, 48, 557–558
liquids, 152, 152*f*, 156
lithium, 222*f*
lithium-ion cells, 440*f*, 441*t*
lithosphere, **13**, 13*f*, 14, 15*f*, 16, 16*f*, 17, 17*f*
load, **452**, 457*f*, 458, 468–469
Local Group (galaxies), **365**
Long Point Bay, 92
long-tailed weasel, 25, 25*f*
low-Earth-orbit satellites, 325
luminosity, **341**, 344*t*
lunar eclipses, 275, 275*f*, **287**, 287*f*
lustre, 150*t*, 155
lynx, 58, 58*f*

M

magnesium, 205*f*, 222, 222*f*
main idea and details, identifying, 88, 402
main idea web, 566
main sequence, **344**
malleability, 150*t*, 200*t*
Marois, Christian, 335
Mars, 13, 291*f*, 292, 294*f*, 294*t*, 300
  landers, 323, 323*f*, 324, 324*f*
  observing, 291, 292, 292*f*
  orbit, 292, 292*f*
  properties of, 294*t*
Mars Climate Orbiter, 323, 323*f*
Mars Polar Lander, 323
mass, measuring, **540**
mass number, **188**, 188*t*, 189
matter, 13, 13*f*, **139**, 141, 142, 152
Mayan civilization, 271, 271*f*
meadow voles, 46
measuring, 538–541
  angles, 540–541
  area, 538
  electrical current, 548, 550
  length, 538
  mass, 540
  temperature, 541
  voltage, 548, 549, 550
  volume, 539–540
megaparsec (light-year measurement), 371*f*, 382
melting point, 151, 151*t*, **152**, 225, 251
melting test, 251
Mendeleev, Dimitri, 195, 196
meniscus, **539**
mercury (metal), 203, 204
Mercury, 291*f*, 291*t*, 292, 293*t*, 294*f*, 294*t*
Mesopotamians, 273
MESSENGER (MErcury Surface Space ENvironment, GEochemistry and Ranging), 323, 323*f*
metal leaf electroscopes, 411, 411*f*
metalloids, **200**, 200*f*
metals, **200**–201, 202, 203, 204, 204*f*, 205*f*
meteorites, **300**

meteoroids, **301**, 302, 302*f*
meteors, **299**, 299*f*
meters, electricity, 488, 488*f*
methane, 30, 32, 32*f*, 33
metric system, 554
microgravity, 328
microscope, 546–547
microwaves, 318, 318*f*, 320, 320*f*, 372, 372*f*
Mielhausen, Shelby, 280
migratory birds, 8, 8*f*, 74–75
Milky Way, **361**–365, 361*f*, 364*f*, 365*f*, 369, 377–378, 379, 384
mining, 202–203
mixtures, 141*f*, **142**, 144, 144*t*, 145
models, **534**, 551
  ball-and-stick, 245–246, 245*f*
  Bohr-Rutherford, 184, 190, 212, 234, 244, 404, 404*f*
  space-filling, 247
  three-dimensional, 244–247
Mohs scale of hardness, 155
molecular compounds, 234
molecules, **234**
Monarch butterflies, 76
Moon
  and Earth, 286, 286*f*, 287–289, 287*f*, 288*f*, 289*f*
  lunar eclipses, 275, 275*f*, **287**, 287*f*
  movement of, 281–287
  phases of, 286, 286*f*
  and tides, 283, 289, 289*f*
moose, 59, 59*f*, 63
moose disease, 63
MOST (Microvariability and Oscillations of STars), 321, 321*f*
mourning dove populations, 52
MSDS sheets (material safety data sheets), 140
multimeter, 457*f*, 458, 549
multiple meaning, 138, 436
mutualism, **62**

N

Nanticoke generating station, 504
NASA, 323, 324, 324*f*
Natural Heritage Information Centre, 91
natural succession, 112, 112*f*
NAVSTAR, 325
near-Earth objects (NEOs), 304–305
nebulas, **333**–335, 334*f*, 347, 347*f*
negative terminal, 439*f*, 447, 447*f*, 456, 456*f*, 548
NEOs (near-Earth objects), 304–305
NEOSSat, 304–305
Neptune, 292, 295*f*, 295*t*, 297
netting, 90, 90*t*
neutrino, 179, 179*f*
neutron star, 346, **347**, 347*f*
neutrons, **185**, 188, 188*t*, 190, 191, 191*f*, 192, 402
niches, **56**
  ecological, 56–57, 61, 65–67, 69
  human, 65–67, 66*f*, 67*f*
nickel-cadmium cell, 440*f*, 441*t*
nickel-metal hydride cell, 440*f*, 441*t*

nitrate, 16
nitric acid, 33, 33f
nitrogen, 16, 16f, 115, 115f
nitrogen cycle, 16, 16f
nitrogen oxide, 33, 35, 35f
noble gases, 205, 205f, 208, 209
non-metals, **200**, 200f, 200t
non-native species, 102
non-ohmic conductors, **466**, 466f
nuclear fusion, 335–**336**
nuclear power generation, 503, 503f
nuclei, 188
nucleons, 188
nucleus, **183**, 184, 184f, 185, 188, 190, 190f
nutrient cycles, 14–18, 14f, 15f, 16f, 17f, 18f
nutrients, 12t, **14**, 18

O

Oak Ridges Moraine, 53, 53f, 54
odour, 150, 150t, 250
Ohm, Georg, 462–463, 465
Ohm's law, **462**–464, 466, 466f, 468–470, 478
ohms, **463**–465
omnivores, 24
Onnes, Heike Kamerlingh, 466
Oort, Jan Hendrik, 299
Oort Cloud, 299
open circuits, **447**, 468
open clusters of stars, **363**, 363f
Öpik, Ernst, 297
optical telescopes, 319, 319f
orbital radius, **293**, 294t
orbiters, 323, 323f
orchid, 89f
Orion, 277, 277f
otters, 10, 10t, 96, 96f
outer planets, 292, 295, 295t
   Jupiter, 290f, 291, 292, 293, 295f, 295t, 299
   Neptune, 292, 295f, 295t, 297
   Saturn, 292, 295t, 295f, 322, 322f
   Uranus, 291, 292, 292t, 295f, 295f, 361
over-harvesting, 8
overexploitation, **104**
overfishing, 8, 104, 105, 106–107
overhunting, 108f
owl pellets, 60
oxygen
   in air, 142, 143f, 234, 234f
   atoms, 234, 234f, 243, 243f
   and biomass, 30
   in cellular respiration, 28, 29, 29f
   in photosynthesis, 22, 22f, 23, 23f, 28–29, 29f
   reactivity, 161t
   sources, 18, 18f, 23
   in water, 18, 18f, 28, 33f, 143, 234, 234f, 245f

P

Palmer, Chris, 512
paper clips, 150
parallel circuits, 436, **456**, 469, 469f, 470, 470f
paramecia growth, 80–81
parasites, **63**, 63f
Parker, Allyson, 77
particle theory of matter, 142
Patel, Nilesh, 444
Payette, Julie, 328, 328f
PCBs (polychlorinated biphenyls), 26, 26f
peak load, **504**
peaksaver® program, 511
Peary caribou, 91, 91f
penumbra, 287, 287f, 288f
Penzias, Arno, 373
peregrine falcons, 26
periodic table, **195**–196, 197f, 198–199f, 200, 200f, 205, 207–210, 210f
periods, **205**, 210
peroxide, 162
Perseid meteor shower, 301
pesticides, 19, 73
pH, 33–34, 34f, 35f
phantom loads, **497**, 497f
phases of the Moon, **286**, 286f
Phoenix Lander, 324, 324f
phosphate, 17, 17f
phosphorus cycle, 17, 17f, 18, 18f
photocopiers, 425, 425f
photosynthesis, 12t, **21**–23, 22f, 23f, 28–29, 29f, 30, 38–39, 339
photovoltaic effect, **508**
physical properties, **149**–158, 166–167, 213, 568–569
   metals and non-metals, 200t
   qualitative, 150, 150f
   quantitative, 151, 151f
   water, 158, 158f
phytoplankton, 23, 23f, 26f, 117, 154, 154f
pie graph, 559–560
Pietrzakowski, Katie, 427
pitcher plant, 57, 57f
pith ball electroscope, 411, 412, 413f, 415, 415f, 416
plagiarism, 553
plains bison, 108f
planetary motion, 292, 292f
planetesimals, 334
planets, **291**
   classification of, 292
   distances between, 293
   inner, 294, 294
   outer, 295, 295
   see also individual planets
plants at risk, 108
plastics, 238, 238f, 239, 239f, 240
Pleiades open star cluster, 363f
Pluto, 298f, 299
polar bears, 51, 154, 154f
Polaris, 280, 280f
pollination, 71, 71f, 72
polychlorinated biphenyls (PCBs), 26, 26f
polyethylenes, 238, 238f

polymers, 238, 240
populations, **49**
   carrying capacity, 51–54, 66–67
   competition, 60–61
   exponential growth, 49–50, 66
   humans, 52, 65–67, 66f, 67f
   limiting factors, 50
   predation regulating, 58–59
   symbiotic relationships, 62–63
positive terminal, 439f, 440f, 447, 447f, 456, 456f, 548
potassium, 190, 190f, 210, 210f, 220
potassium chloride, 226, 243, 243f
potential difference, **452**–453, 458, 459, 470
potential energy, 452
power bars, 490t
power generation, 485–490, 506–510, 511
power ratings, 493
prairie dogs, 97, 97f
precision, **542**
predators, 10f, **58**–59
prediction, **533**
Presqu'ile Provincial Park Waterfowl Festival, 77
previewing text features, 6, 138
prey, **58**, 59
primary cells, **440**, 441t
prior knowledg, making connections to, 270
propane, 163, 163f
properties
   chemical, 160–164
   physical, 149–158
protecting, **89**
proteins, 247
protons, **185**, 188, 188t, 402, 403
protostar, **334**
prototype, **537**
Ptolemy, 291
pulsars, 347, 347f
pure substance, 141f, **142**, 161t
purple loosestrife, 104

Q

quadrat sampling, 90t
qualitative observation, **532**
qualitative physical properties, 150, 150f
quantitative observation, **532**
quantitative physical properties, 151, 151f
quantum, 184
questions, asking, 178

R

rabbits, 25, 58
radiation
   cosmic microwave background (CMB), **372**–373, 374
   electromagnetic, **318**, 318f, 320, 320f, 320t, 372
   gamma rays, 318f, 320f, 372, 372f
   infrared, 318f, 320, 320f, 322, 322f, 364, 372f
   microwaves, 318, 318f, 320f, 372, 372f

   non-visible, 319
   radio waves, 318, 318f, 320f, 322, 322f, 363, 364, 372f
   solar, 288, 339, 339f
   ultraviolet, 318f, 320f, 322, 322f, 372f
   visible light, 318, 318f, 320f, 322, 322f, 372f
   X-rays, 318, 318f, 320, 320f, 372f
radiation dosimeters, **427**, 427f
radio telescope, 319, 319f
radio waves, 318, 318f, 320f, 322, 322f, 363, 372f
radium, 182
reactions, chemical, 162
reactivity, 161, 161t, 208–209, 210, 214
recycling, 11, 31t, 32
red dwarfs, 343f, 345, 345f
red giants 345, 345f
red mulberry, 91, 91f
redshift, **369**, 370
redside dace, 53, 53f
reefs, 62, 62f
reflecting telescope, **319**, 319f
reforestation, **112**
refracting telescope, 316f, **319**, 319f
remote-sensing satellites, 325
renewable energy sources, 506–510, **507**
research projects, 552–553
resistance, **451**, 462–466, 465f, 468–470
resistor, 451, 452, 457f, 458, 462f, 466f, 548
restoration ecology, 110–115, **111**
retrograde motion, 292, 292f
revolution, **273**
ringed seal and DDT, 154, 154f
road salt, 221, 221f, 228–230, 230f
robin moths, 113
rotation, **273**
round gobies, 103, 103f
rounding, 556
Royal Ontario Museum, 91, 242, 242f
ruby-throated hummingbird, 8
ruffed grouse populations, 52
Russell, Henry Norris, 343
rust, 229, 249, 258
Rutherford, Ernest, 182–185, 404

S

safety icons, 140
Saincher, Meghana, 147
salmon, 105, 105f
salt, 153, 153f, 223f
   see also road salt
sampling, 366
Sargasso Sea, 9
satellites, **325**–327, 326f, 327f
Saturn, 292, 295t, 295f, 322, 322f
scale drawing, **544**
scanners, 425
Schiaparelli, Giovanni, 301
scientific drawing, 543–544
scientific inquiry, 532–535
scientific notation, 555
scientific process, 532

sea otters, 96, 96f
sea urchins, 96, 96f
seals and DDT, 154, 154f
seasons, 284, 284f
secondary cells, **440**, 441t
selenium, 425, 425f
self-pollination, 71
semiconductors, **406**
series circuits, 436, **456**, 468, 469f, 470
serum, 153
SETI (Search for Extraterrestrial Intelligence), 319
Shapley, Harlow, 363, 364
shark, 89f
shells (energy levels), 190f, 222f, 233f, 234f
Shelton, Ian, 346
shock (electric), 407–409
Shoemaker, Carolyn, 297
Shoemaker, Eugene, 297
Shoemaker-Levy comet, 297f
"shooting stars", 268, 301
shrews, 58
significant digits, 556
silver-oxide cell, 439, 439f, 441t
Sirius (star), 272
skim, scan, or sturdy, 360
smart meter, 496
Smith, Willoughby, 423
snowshoe hares, 58, 58f
social policy, 19
society in issue analysis, 529–531
sodium, 209f, 210, 210f, 220, 222
sodium chloride, 143f, 153, 223, 223f, 225, 230
SOHO (SOLar Heliospheric Observatory), 321
soil, 12t
soil bacteria, 16, 16f
solar cells, **444**, 508–509, 511
solar eclipse, 271, 272f, **288**, 288f
solar energy, **508**–509, 511
solar flares, 338, 338f
solar mass, 343
solar nebula theory, **333**, 334f
solar radiation, 288, 339, 339f
solar system, **291**
  formation, 333–335
  models of, 291, 293
"solar wall", 482–483
solar wind, **338**
solidification, 152
solubility, 151t, **153**, 154, 225–226, 251
solute, 153
solutions, 141f
solvent, 153
song sparrow, 60, 60f
space exploration, 317–331
space telescopes, 318–320
space-filling models, 247
spectral lines, **342**, 342f, 369f
spectroscope, **342**
spectrum shifting, 369
spider map, 566
spiral galaxies, 362, 362f
spotted turtle, 110f
St. Williams Forestry Station, 70
stability, **164**
standard atomic notation, 189

star clusters, **363**, 363f
star maps, 276, 276f
stars, **333**, 341–348
  see also galaxies, Milky Way
state, 150t
states of matter, 152, 152f
static charge (static electricity), 401, **403**–409, 412, 426
static cling, 403, 406
stewardship, **110**
stickleback fish and competition, 61, 61f
stomata, 22, 22f
Study Toolkit
  asking questions, 178
  base words, 48, 360
  comparing and contrasting, 6, 436, 562
  compound words, 316
  creating a word map, 220, 484
  identifying cause and effect, 270, 436
  identifying main ideas and details, 88, 402
  interpreting diagrams, 316, 402, 561
  interpreting line graphs, 48
  interpreting tables, 88
  making connections to prior knowledge, 270
  making connections to visuals, 48
  making inferences, 220, 484, 561
  making study notes, 316
  monitoring comprehension, 220
  multiple meanings, 138, 436
  previewing text features, 6, 138
  skim, scan, or study, 360
  suffixes, 178
  summarizing, 138
  using graphic organizers, 270, 360, 484
  visualizing, 178
  word families, 6, 270, 402
  word origins, 88
Su, Yvonne, 11
subatomic numbers, calculating, 188
subatomic particles, **181**, 188
sublimation, 152
succession, **98**
Sudbury Neutrino Observatory, 179, 179f
suffixes, 178
sulfur dioxide, 33, 33f, 35, 35f
sulfuric acid, 33, 33f, 440
summarizing, 138
Sun, 333–339, 444
  eclipses,
  energy, **508**–509, 511
  flares, 338, 338f
  nebula theory, **333**, 334f
  radiation, 288, 339, 339f
  solar cells, **444**, 508–509, 511
  spots, 337, 337f
sundials, 273, 273f
sunspots, 337, 337f
superclusters, **366**
superconductor, **466**
supergiants, 343f, 344, 344f, 345f, 346

supernova, **346**, 346f, 347, 380, 380f
surge protector, 490t
sustainability, 7, **67**, 75
sustainable ecosystems, 7–8, 46, 75, 76–77
sustainable use, **65**
Suzuki, Dr. David, 101
Swift, Lewis, 301
Swift-Tuttle comet, 300t, 301
switches, **447**, 457f, 548
symbiosis, 10t, 62–63, 62f, 63f
synthethic elements, 196

T

tables, 88, 545, 561
technological problem solving, **536**–537
telescopes, 317, 318–322, 320f, 321t
temperature, **541**
terrestrial ecosystem, **16**
tetanus toxin, 164, 164f
text features, previewing, 6, 138
texture, 150t
theory, **535**
thermometer, 541
Thirsk, Robert, 328, 328f
Thomson, G. P., 181
Thomson, John Joseph, 181, 182, 404
three-dimensional models, 244–247
tidal energy, 510, 510f
tidal force, 287
tides, **283**, 287, 289, 289f
time of use pricing, **496**
titanium, 201f
titanium oxide, 143f
toxicity, **164**
Trans-Canada Highway, 47
trans-Neptunian objects, 297
transect sampling, 90, 90t
transformers, **486**, 486f, 487, 487f, 488
transmission lines, 487
trophic efficiency, **25**
trophic levels, **24**, 24f, 25, 25f
tungsten, 201f
Tunguska event, 303, 303f
Tuttle, Horace, 301

U

ultraviolet radiation, 318f, 320f, 322, 322f, 372f
umbra, 287, 287f, 288f
underwater artifacts, raising, 137
universal solvent, 158
universe timeline, 374f
unsustainable, **67**
Uranus, 291, 292, 292t, 295f, 295f, 361
urban sprawl, **52**, 53, 54
Ursa Major, 275f, 277

V

valence electrons, **208**–210, 222, 233, 233f, 234, 234f
Van de Graaff generator, **424**, 424f
Varroa destructor mite, 73

variables, 534
velocity, 382–383
Venn diagram, 6, 484, 567
Venus, 291, 292, 294t, 294f
viscosity, **151**, 151t
visible, 318, 318t, 320f, 421
visualizing, 178, 561
visuals, making connnections to, 48
volt, **453**
Volta, Alessandro, 438, 440, 453
voltage, 452, 453, 458, 487, 548–550
voltaic cells, **438**
voltmeter, 453, 453f, 455, 457f, 458, 470, 548, **549**–550
volume, **539**
von Fraunhofer, Joseph, 342

W

water, 12t, 142f, 143, 143f, 158, 161t, 234, 407
water cycle, 14, 14f
water pollution, 26
watershed, **70**
watts (W), **493**
wavelength, 318, 320f
wet cells, **440**, 441t
wetlands, 102, 102f, 112
white dwarf, **345**, 343f
white-tailed deer, 47, 63
WHMIS symbols, 140
Wild 2 comet, 300, 300t
wild turkeys, 50, 50f
wildlife mortality, 47
Williams, Lottie, 330
Wilson, Robert, 373
wind energy, 506f, 507, 509
wind farm, **507**, 506f
wind turbines, 506f, 507
wires, connecting, 447
WMAP satellite images, 373, 373f, 374
wolves, 59
word families, 6, 370, 402, 562
word maps, 138, 220, 484
word origins, 21, 85, 362, 562
word webs, 6
World Biosphere Reserve, 92
World Fire Atlas, 326
World Heritage Site, ecosystems, 4
World Wide Web, 375

X

X-rays, 318, 318f, 320, 320f, 372f

Y

yellow perch, 50, 50f
yellowfin tuna, 104

Z

zebra mussels, 103, 103f, 117
ZENN electric cars, 442–443
zinc-air cell, 439, 439f, 441t
zinc-carbon cell, 439, 439f, 441t
zooplankton, 26f
Zylberberg, Joel, 379

Credits

Photo Credits

COV: (tl) ©medobear/iStockphoto; COV: (c) ©emmgunn/iStockphoto; COV: (cl) ©NASA/Johnson Space Center Collection; COV: (cr) ©Bananastock/Punchstock; COV: (tc) ©Kaz Chiba/Getty Images; COV: (r) ©Alan and Sandy Carey/Getty Images; COV: (tl) ©Peter Griffith/Masterfile; iv-v: (b) ©Francesca Yorke/Getty Images; v: (tr) ©Michael S. Lewis/CORBIS; v: (cr) ©Ethan Meleg/Getty Images; V: (br) ©Francesca Yorke/Getty Images; vi: (tl) ©Roger Ressmeyer/CORBIS; vi: (cl) ©Darrin Klimek/Getty Images; vi: (bl) ©Eric Foltz/iStockphoto; vi-vii: (b) ©NASA-Marshall Space Flight Center; vii: (tr) ©David Nunuk/Photo Researchers, Inc.; vii: (cr) ©NASA Johnson Space Center Collection; vii: (br) ©NASA; viii: (tl) ©Nightlight/zefa/CORBIS; viii: (cl) ©BananaStock/PunchStock; viii: (bl) ©AP Photo/David Duprey; viii-ix: (b) ©Mike Dobel/Masterfile; xiv: (br) ©Michael Thompson/iStockphoto; xv: (tr) ©Stockbyte/Punchstock; xv: (bl) ©John Clines/iStockphoto; xvi: (bl) ©SW Productions/Getty Images; xviii-001: (c) ©Paul A. Souders/CORBIS; 001: (bl) ©Michael S. Lewis/CORBIS; 001: (bc) ©Ethan Meleg/Getty Images; 001: (br) ©Francesca Yorke/Getty Images; 003: (bl) ©Trevor Allen/iStockphoto; 003: (bkgd) ©Oksana Struk/iStockphoto; 003: (br) ©Oksana Struk/iStockphoto; 004-005: (c) ©Michael S. Lewis/CORBIS; 007: (b) ©Bob Krist/Corbis; 008: (tl) ©Scott Leslie/Minden Pictures; 008: (c) ©Rodger Jackman/Jupiterimages; 008: (cr) ©David Wrobel/Getty Images; 010: (tl) ©Ian McAllister/Getty Images; 010: (cl) ©John Cancalosi/Alamy; 010: (bl) ©Andrew Holt/Getty Images; 011: (br) ©Courtesy of Lindsay Bennett; 012: (t) ©Punchstock; 012: (c) ©Dean Turner/iStockphoto; 012: (cl) ©Frank Oberle/Getty Images; 012: (b) ©Designpics/PunchStock; 012: (l) ©Ambulator Photo/Alamy; 013: (b) ©Tom Van Sant/CORBIS; 018: (cl) ©E.DeBruyn/Fisheries and Oceans Canada. Reproduced with the permission of Her Majesty the Queen in Right of Canada, 2009; 019: (cr) ©Jeff Schmaltz, MODIS Rapid Response Team, NASA/GSFC; 021: (r) ©Brand X Pictures/PunchStock; 023: (cr) ©Bill Curtsinger/Getty Images; 028: (b) ©David Coder/iStockphoto; 031: (cr) ©Brigitte Smith/iStockphoto; 031: (tr) ©Lester Lefkowitz/Getty Images; 031: (br) ©Stephanie DeLay/iStockphoto; 034: (bl) ©Oxford Scientific /Photolibrary/Getty Images; 043: (tr) ©Bob Krist/Corbis; 043: (cr) ©Brand X Pictures/PunchStock; 043: (br) ©David Coder/iStockphoto; 046: (c) ©Ethan Meleg/Getty Images; 049: (b) ©Gallo Images-Heinrich van den Berg/Getty Images; 050: (tr) ©Art Wolfe/Getty Images; 050: (b) ©Jukka Rapo/Getty Images; 051: (cr) ©Nicholas Bergkessel, Jr./Photo Researchers, Inc.; 052: (bl) ©NASA, John C. Stennis Space Center; 053: (b) ©Gary Meszaros/Getty Images; 056: (l) ©Jeffrey Lepore/Photo Researchers, Inc.; 057: (bl) ©David Sieren/Getty Images; 057: (br) ©Joel Sartore/Getty Images; 058: (b) ©Creatas/PunchStock; 059: (b) ©D. Robert & Lorri Franz/CORBIS; 062: (cl) ©John Anderson/iStockphoto; 062: (cr) ©Alexis Rosenfeld/Photo Researchers, Inc.; 062: (b) ©M. Chahine, JPL & J. Sussking, Goddard Space Flight Center; 064: (br) ©Klaus Nigge/Getty Images; 069: (b) ©Peter Lilja/Getty Images; 071: (tr) ©Merlin Tuttle / BCI/Photo Researchers, Inc.; 072: (c) ©Gerry Ellis/Getty Images; 072: (b) ©Penn State Univ/Photo Researchers, Inc.; 073: (cr) ©U.S. Department of Agriculture; 075: (br) ©Danita Delimont/Alamy; 075: (bl) ©Ligia Botero/Getty Images; 076: (cr) ©Michael Dykstra/iStockphoto; 076: (bl) ©Cathy Keifer/iStockphoto; 076: (tl) ©James Smedley/Getty Images; 076: (cl) ©JillianNH/iStockphoto; 077: (c) ©Above Lake Superior, c.1922 (oil on canvas) by Lawren Stewart Harris (1885-1970) Art Gallery of Ontario, Toronto, Canada/The Bridgeman Art Library; 077: (br) ©Courtesy of Bruce Parker; 079: (tr) ©Andrew J. Martinez/Photo Researchers, Inc.; 083: (tr) ©Gallo Images-Heinrich van den Berg/Getty Images; 083: (cr) ©John Anderson/iStockphoto; 083: (br) ©Peter Lilja/Getty Images; 086-087: (c) ©Francesca Yorke/Getty Images; 087: (c) ©John T. Fowler; 089: (b) ©David Wrobel/Visuals Unlimited, Inc.; 089: (cr) ©AP Photo/WWF, Leonid Averyanov, HO; 090: (t) ©Nick Upton/Nature Picture Library; 090: (c) ©Nigel Cattlin/Alamy; 090: (cr) ©ArteSub/Alamy; 090: (b) ©AP Photo/The Baxter Bulletin, Kevin Pieper; 091: (tr) ©ilian animal/Alamy; 091: (b) ©Jim Brandenburg/Minden Pictures; 091: (bl) ©Clive Boursnel/Getty Images; 092: (cr) ©Bill Brooks/Alamy; 092: (b) ©LYNN STONE/Animals Animals - Earth Scenes; 093: (tr) ©Roberto Nistri/Alamy; 094: (cr) ©Nick Upton/Nature Picture Library; 095: (b) ©Georgette Douwma/Getty Images; 097: (tr) ©Joseph Van Os/Getty Images; 097: (br) ©Jeff Vanuga/CORBIS; 098: (bl) ©Harry Engels/Photo Researchers, Inc.; 098: (br) ©Ray Bruun; 098: (b) ©Robert Glusic/Getty Images; 099: (b) ©Tony Gallucci; 100: (b) *ROYALTY-FREE* ©Edmond Van Hoorick/Getty Images; 101: (bl) ©AP Photo/Dennis Farrell; 103: (t) ©Visuals Unlimited/Corbis; 103: (br) ©blickwinkel/Alamy; 105: (bl) ©Klaus Nigge/Getty Images; 105: (b) ©Riccardo Savi/Getty Images; 106: (bl) ©Robert E. Barber/Alamy; 108: (tl) ©Kevin Law/Alamy; 109: (c) ©Jacques Croizer/iStockphoto; 110: (b) ©Dr. Jacqueline D. Litzgus, Laurentian University; 111: (bl) ©City of Toronto Archives, Fonds 1128, Series 379, Item 1160;

111: (br) ©Oleksiy Maksymenko/Alamy; 112: (bl) ©NRCS/USDA; 112: (tl) ©Lars Olav/Alamy; 112: (tr) ©Reproduced with permission of the Minister of Natural Resources, Canada 2009; 112: (cl) ©Bob Stefko/Getty Images; 112: (cr) ©Don Johnston/age fotostock; 113: (tr) ©BRUCE COLEMAN INC./Alamy; 114: (b) ©Tim Zurowski/Photolibrary; 115: (tr) ©Micha Pawlitzki/Getty Images; 115: (b) ©Wally Bauman/Alamy; 121: (tr) ©Bill Brooks/Alamy; 121: (c) ©Harry Engels/Photo Researchers, Inc.; 121: (cr) ©Visuals Unlimited/Corbis; 121: (br) ©Bob Stefko/Getty Images; 124: (tl) ©Timothy Morton; 124: (bl) ©luis seco/iStockphoto; 125: (tr) ©CP PHOTO/Toronto Sun/Alex Urosevic; 125: (br) ©Jim Arbogast/Getty Images; 125: (bl) ©Jeff Greenberg/PhotoEdit; 126: (b) ©Trevor Allen/iStockphoto; 127: (tr) ©Oksana Struk/iStockphoto; 128: (br) © Hansjoerg Richter/iStockPhoto; 130: (tr) ©Michael Matthews/Alamy; 132-133: (c) ©Franz-Peter Tschauner/dpa/Corbis; 133: (tl) ©ZZ/Alamy; 133: (bl) ©Roger Ressmeyer/CORBIS; 133: (bc) ©Darrin Klimek/Getty Images; 133: (br) ©Eric Foltz/Getty Images; 135: (bl) ©imagebroker/Alamy; 135: (bkgd) ©Don Johnston/Alamy; 135: (br) ©Don Johnston/Alamy; 136-137: (c) ©Roger Ressmeyer/CORBIS; 137: (c) ©Jeffrey L. Rotman/CORBIS; 139: (REUTERS/Mark Blinch; 139: (cr) ©Rene Johnston/Toronto Star/ZUMA PRess; 142: (bl) ©Jan Stromme/Getty Images; 142: (br) ©Henrik Sorensen/Getty Images; 144: (t) ©Luis Carlos Torres/iStockphoto; 144: (c) ©Andrew Lambert Photography/SPL/Photo Researchers, Inc.; 144: (b) ©Ilene MacDonald/Alamy; 146: (bl) ©Dennis MacDonald/Alamy; 147: (tr) ©Courtesy of Meghana Saincher; 149: (b) ©Alexander McClearn/Alamy; 150: (br) ©Eddie Gerald/Alamy; 153: (tr) ©Robert Kohlhuber/iStockphoto; 153: (tl) ©William D. Bachman/Photo Researchers, Inc.; 155: (tr) ©Lowell Georgia/CORBIS; 156: (bl) ©AP Photo/John Gaps III, File; 159: (br) ©Martyn F. Chillmaid/SPL/Photo Researchers, Inc.; 160: (b) ©Tony Freeman/PhotoEdit; 161: (cr) ©David Young-Wolff/PhotoEdit; 161: (t) ©Dyana/Alamy; 161: (r) ©Oliver Strewe/Getty Images; 161: (br) ©Photodisc/Getty Images; 163: (c) ©Dave Logan/iStockphoto; 164: (b) ©Eye of Science/Photo Researchers, Inc.; 165: (br) ©Davies and Starr/Getty Images; 173: (tr) ©REUTERS/Mark Blinch; 173: (cr) ©Robert Kohlhuber/iStockphoto; 173: (br) ©Tony Freeman/Photo Edit; 174: (br) ©Andrew Lambert Photography/Photo Researchers, Inc.; 176-177: (c) ©Darrin Klimek/Getty Images; 179: (b) ©LBNL/Photo Researchers, Inc.; 181: (c) ©SSPL/The Image Works; 187: (l) ©Karen Mower/iStockphoto; 187: (tr) ©Siede Preis/Getty Images; 187: (br) ©Oleksiy Maksymenko/Alamy; 192: (b) ©CERN; 194: (b) ©Frank Spinelli/Getty Images; 202: (bl) ©Judy Waytiuk/Alamy; 204: (c) ©CP PHOTO/Owen Sound Sun Times-James Masters; 204: (b) ©Courtesy of Patrick Bowman; 205: (bc) ©Andrew Lambert Photograph/Photo Researchers, Inc.; 205: (cr) ©sciencephotos/Alamy; 205: (br) ©Gusto/Photo Researchers, Inc.; 205: (bl) ©Andrew Lambert Photography/Photo Researchers, Inc.; 209: (cr) ©E. R. Degginger/Photo Researchers, Inc.; 210: (bl) ©Charles D. Winters/Photo Researchers, Inc.; 210: (br) ©Charles D. Winters/Photo Researchers, Inc.; 215: (t) ©LBNL/Photo Researchers, Inc.; 215: (c) ©Oleksiy Maksymenko/Alamy; 215: (r) ©Frank Spinelli/Getty Images; 218: (c) ©Eric Foltz/iStockphoto; 221: (b) ©Mark Joseph/Getty Images; 223: (cl) ©Martyn F. Chillmaid / Photo Researchers, Inc.; 223: (c) ©Charles D. Winters / Photo Researchers, Inc.; 223: (cr) ©The McGraw-Hill Companies, Inc./Stephen Frisch, photographer; 224: (br) ©Biophoto Associates/Photo Researchers, Inc.; 224: (bl) ©sciencephotos/Alamy; 225: (cl) ©The McGraw-Hill Companies, Inc./Dennis Strete, photographer; 225: (cr) ©FreezeFrameStudio/iStockphoto; 226: (b) ©Nigel Cattlin / Photo Researchers, Inc.; 228: (b) ©AP Photo/Chris Gardner; 229: (br) ©blphoto / Alamy; 229: (cr) ©Mary Kate Denny/PhotoEdit; 232: (c) ©Peggy Greb/USDA; 232: (bkgd) ©Jennifer Morgan/iStockphoto; 235: (cr) ©Martyn F. Chillmaid/Photo Researchers, Inc.; 236: (tl) ©MH/iStockphoto; 237: (c) ©Charles D. Winters / Photo Researchers, Inc.; 238: (tl) ©Danny Smythe/iStockphoto; 238: (bl) ©Redchopsticks LLC / Alamy; 239: (tl) ©MURRAY, PATTI / Animals Animals - Earth Scenes -- All rights reserved.; 239: (bc) ©Burke/Triolo Productions/Getty Images; 239: (br) ©Roel Smart/iStockphoto; 240: (br) ©Courtesy of Dayna Corelli; 242: (b) ©Ken Straiton/First Light/Getty Images; 242: (c) ©Daniel Libeskind Studio; 244: (bc) ©L. Haarman/Daniel Libeskind Studio; 246: (bl) ©iLexx/iStockphoto; 247: (b) ©The McGraw-Hill Companies, Inc./Jeramia Ory, Ph.D. Figure adapted using coordinates from structure 1A35 in the Protein Data; 252: (tl) ©Courtesy of Canadian Aboriginal Science and Technology Society; 253: (tr) ©Brian Prechtel/USDA; 253: (cr) ©Comstock Images/PictureQuest; 253: (cl) ©Paul Shambroom / Photo Researchers, Inc.; 253: (tr) ©Mark Joseph/Getty Images; 253: (cr) ©Peggy Greb/USDA; 253: (br) ©Ken Straiton/First Light/Getty Images; 253: ©Jennifer Morgan/iStockphoto; 258: (bl) ©imagebroker/Alamy; 259: (b) ©Don Johnston/Alamy; 264-265: (c) ©NASA; 265: (cl) ©The University of Calgary, Faculty of Medicine; 265: (bl) ©David Nunuk/Photo Researchers, Inc.; 265: (bc) ©NASA Johnson Space Center Collection; 265: (br) ©NASA; 267: (bl) ©NASA; 267: (br) ©NASA-Marshall Space Flight

Center; 267: (bkgd) ©NASA-Marshall Space Flight Center; 268-269: (c) ©David Nunuk/Photo Researchers, Inc.; 269: (c) ©John Sanford & David Parker/Photo Researchers, Inc.; 271: (r) ©Cosmo Condina Mexico/Alamy; 271: (cl) ©Deanna Bean/iStockphoto; 272: (b) ©Detlev Van Ravenswaay/SPL/Photo Researchers, Inc.; 273: (br) ©Peter Elvidge/iStockphoto; 276: (br) ©Getty Images/Getty Images; 279: (c) ©Kyle McMahon/iStockphoto; 280: (cr) ©Kaj R. Svensson/Photo Researchers, Inc.; 280: (br) ©Ethan Meleg; 287: (cr) ©Thomas Tuchan/iStockphoto; 288: (tl) ©Manfred Konrad/iStockphoto; 289: (bc) ©Francois Gohier/Photo Researchers, Inc.; 289: (br) ©Francois Gohier/Photo Researchers, Inc.; 297: (b) ©Kauko Helavuo/Getty Images; 300: (tc) ©Roger Ressmeyer/Getty Images; 300: (br) ©NASA; 301: (tc) ©B.A.E. Inc./Alamy; 302: (bl) ©Images provided through NASA's Scientific Data Purchase Project and produced under NASA contract by Earth Satellite Corporation; 302: (br) ©Stephan Hoerold/iStockphoto; 303: (tr) ©AP Photo; 305: (br) ©AP Photo/La Razon, Miguel Carrasco; 310: (tr) ©NASA; 313: (cr) ©Pekka Parviainen/Photo Researchers, Inc.; 314-315: (c) ©NASA Johnson Space Center Collection; 317: (b) NASA Marshall Space Flight Center Collection; 319: (br) ©Peter Warrick; 321: (b) ©The MOST Team, Canadian Space Agency, UBC and the H.R. MacMillan Space Centre; 322: (tl) ©NASA-JPL; 322: (bl) ©NASA-JPL ; 322: (tr) ©J.T. Trauger- JPL and NASA; 322: (br) Image courtesy of NRAO/AUI/NSF; 323: (tr) ©Johns Hopkins University Applied Physics Laboratory/NASA; 324: (bl) ©NASA/JPL/UA/Lockheed Martin; 325: (cl) ©David Young-Wolff/PhotoEdit; 325: (cr) ©Getty Images/Getty Images; 325: (br) ©Ian Logan/Getty Images; 326: (bl) ©ESA; 326: (br) ©ESA; 327: (b) ©NASA; 328: (tl) ©NASA; 328: (cl) ©NASA; 328: (l) ©NASA; 328: (bl) ©CP Photo; 329: (bkgd) ©NASA Marshall Space Flight Center Collection; 329: (tr) ©MDA; 329: (br) ©NASA; 330: (bl) ©Tulsa World; 331: (bl) ©NASA; 332: (br) ESA; 333: (c) ©Ron Watts/Getty Images; 335: (tr) ©C.Marois/National Research Council Canada; 337: (b) ©SOHO (ESA & NASA); 337: (br) ©NASA, ESA, M.J. Jee and H. Ford (Johns Hopkins University); 338: (cl) ©NASA; 338: (cr) ©Cary Anderson/Getty Images; 339: (bl) ©M. Timothy O'K©Paul Edmondson/Getty Imageseefe/Alamy; 339: (br) ©Jim West/Alamy; 339: (bkgd) ©Jim West/Alamy; 340: (b) ©NASA, Solar Physics, Marshall Space Flight Center; 341: (b) ©Jerry Schad/Photo Researchers, Inc.; 344: (t) ©John Chumack/Photo Researchers, Inc.; 346: (tl) ©NASA/CXC/MIT/UMass Amherst/M.D.Stage et al.; 346: (b) ©David Malin, Anglo-Australian Observatory; 347: (cl) ©NASA, ESA, J. Hester and A. Loll,Arizona State University; 347: (cr) ©Smithsonian Institution/Photo Researchers, Inc.; 347: (c) ©Smithsonian Institution/Photo Researchers, Inc.; 355: (tr) ©NASA Marshall Space Flight Center Collection; 355: (cr) ©Ron Watts/Getty Images; 355: (br) ©Jerry Schad/Photo Researchers, Inc.; 358-359: (c) ©NASA; 361: (b) ©Baback Tafreshi/Photo Researchers, Inc.; 362: (tl) ©NASA-JPL; 362: (tr) ©National Optical Astronomy Observatory; 362: (bl) ©NASA, ESA, M. West (ESO, Chile), and CXC/Penn State University/G. Garmire, et al.; 362: (br) ©NASA, ESA, and The Hubble Heritage Team (STScI/AURA); 363: (cl) ©NASA/Antonio Fernandez-Sanchez; 363: (cr) ©NASA, NASA-JPL; 364: (b) ©NASA-JPL; 366: (cr) ©NASA/Robert Williams and the Hubble Deep Field Team (STScI); 367: (tc) ©NASA-JPL; 367: (tr) ©NASA/ESA; 368: (bl) ©NASA/R. Williams (STScI), the HDF-S Team; 370: (b) ©AP Photo/Steve Holland; 371: (cl) ©Pascal Goetgheluck/Photo Researchers, Inc.; 373: (b) ©NASA/WMAP Science Team; 377: (bl) ©NASA, ESA, M.J. Jee and H. Ford (Johns Hopkins University); 378: (bl) ©NASA/Robert Gendler; 379: (tr) ©Courtesy of Joel Zylberberg; 380: (b) ©NASA/HST/High-Z Supernova Search Team; 382: (tl); 382: (b) ©Courtesy of Patrick Ingraham; 383: (bl) ©Canadian Space Agency; 383: (br) ©AP Photo/Victoria Arocho; 383: (tr) ©David Young-Wolff/PhotoEdit Inc.; 385: (tr) ©Baback Tafreshi / Photo Researchers, Inc.; 385: (cr) ©NASA/R. Williams (STScI), the HDF-S Team; 385: (br) ©NASA, ESA, M.J. Jee and H. Ford (Johns Hopkins University); 386: (tl) ©NASA, The Hubble Heritage Team and A. Riess (STScI); 386: (tr) ©NASA, ESA, and The Hubble Heritage Team (STScI/AURA); 386: (bl) ©NASA, Local Group Galaxies Survey Team, NOAO, AURA, NSF; 386: (br) ©NASA-JPL; 390: (bl) ©NASA; 390-391: (b) ©NASA-Marshall Space Flight Center; 391: (bc) ©NASA-Marshall Space Flight Center; 395: (bl) ©NASA; 396-397: () ©Mike Dobel/Masterfile; 397: (cl) ©Scott Barrow/Solus-Veer/Corbis; 397: (bl) ©Nightlight/zefa/CORBIS; 397: (bc) ©BananaStock/PunchStock; 397: (br) ©CNImaging/Newscom; 399: (cr) ©Jim West/Alamy; 399: (bkgd) ©Jim West/Alamy; 399: (bl) ©Paul Edmondson/Getty Images; 400-401: (c) ©Nightlight/zefa/CORBIS; 407: (cr) ©Shawn Lowe/iStockphoto; 408: (b) ©Lester Leftkowitz/Stone/Getty Images; 409: (b) ©Greg Pease/Photographer's Choice/Getty Images; 411: (br) ©Visuals Unlimited/Corbis; 411: (bl) ©Bettmann/cORBIS; 411: (cr) ©Edward R. Degginger/Bruce Coleman Inc.; 418: (tl) ©Robert Deal/iStockphoto; 421: (b) ©Donald Nausbaum/Getty Images; 422-423: (b) ©Owen Price/iStockphoto; 423: (c) ©iStockphotoPaul Morton; 424: (tl) JupiterImages/BrandX/Alamy; 427: (cr) ©Cliff Moore/Photo Researchers, Inc.; 427: (bl) ©Courtesy of Katie Pietrzakowski; 430: (bl) ©Charles D. Winters/Photo Researchers; 431: (cr) ©Visuals Unlimited/Corbis; 431: (br) ©Bettmann/cORBIS; 434-435: (c) ©BananaStock/PunchStock; 437: (b) ©Bettmann/CORBIS; 438: (tl) ©SSPL/The Image Works; 442: (tc) ©BC Transit; 442: (bl) ©Courtesy ZENN Motor Company; 444: (tl) ©Hugh Reilly - Sandia National Laboratories/NREL; 444: (br) ©Courtesy of Corey Centen and Nilesh Patel; 446: (b) ©SSPL/The Image Works; 447: (bl) ©Brand X Pictures/Punchstock; 450: (b) ©sciencephotos / Alamy; 452: (c) ©Achim Prill/iStockphoto; 453: (bl) ©JUPITERIMAGES/ Polka Dot/Alamy; 455: (inset) ©NASA Earth Observatory - Image courtesy Chris Elvidge, U.S. Air Force; 455: (b) ©The Canadian Press/Adrian Wyld; 462: (b) ©Burke/Triolo/Brand X Pictures/Jupiterimages; 462: (bl) ©Gethin Lane/iStockphoto; 466: (cl) ©AP Photo/KEYSTONE/Martial Trezzini; 468: (b) ©Kayte Deioma/PhotoEdit; 479: (tr) ©SSPL/The Image Works; 479: (r) ©SSPL/The Image Works; 479: (c) ©The Canadian Press/Adrian Wyld; 479: (cr) ©Burke/Triolo/Brand X Pictures/Jupiterimages; 479: (br) ©Kayte Deioma/PhotoEdit; 482-483: (c) ©CNImaging/Newscom; 485: (b) ©AP Photo/David Duprey; 485: (c) ©CP Photo/Norm Betts/Rex Features; 487: (l) ©Duncan Walker/iStockphoto; 487: (r) ©Dan Brandenburg/iStockphoto; 487: (c) ©Seth Simonson/iStockphoto; 488: (tl) ©Trevor Fisher/iStockphoto; 488: (cl) ©JUPITERIMAGES/Comstock Images/Alamy; 490: (tr) ©Don Wilkie/iStockphoto; 490: (cr) ©John Clines/iStockphoto; 490: (cl) ©JUPITERIMAGES/Brand X/Alamy; 490: (t) ©JUPITERIMAGES/Comstock Images/Alamy; 490: (b) ©Long Ha/iStockphoto; 490: (br) ©INTERACT/Newscom; 491: (br) ©Debra Wiseberg/iStockphoto; 494: (bl) ©Helene Rogers/Alamy; 496: (cl) ©Trevor Fisher/iStockphoto; 505: (cr) ©CP Photo/Dick Loek; 506: (b) ©Todd Arbini Photography/iStockphoto; 506: (cl) ©Martin Bond/Photo Researchers, Inc.; 508: (bl) ©Jarek Szymanski/iStockphoto; 509: (tr) ©M. Timothy O'Keefe/Alamy; 510: (bl) ©Stephen Saks Photography/Alamy; 511: (bl) ©Courtesy of Pinky Langat and Chris Palmer; 517: (t) ©Duncan Walker/iStockphoto; 517: (cr) ©Helene Rogers/Alamy; 517: (br) ©M. Timothy O'Keefe/Alamy; 520: (b) ©CP Photo/MotorcycleMojo/Rex Features; 520: (t) ©CP Photo/Toronto Star-Keith Beaty; 521: (t) Royalty-Free/CORBIS; 521: (br) ©MAXIMILIAN STOCK LTD/Photolibrary; 521: (bl) Roger Tully/Stone/Getty Images; 522: (bl) ©Paul Edmondson/Getty Images; 523: (bkgd) ©Jim West/Alamy; 563: (cl) ©David Coder/iStockphoto

Illustration Credits

2–3: David Wysotski; 8: Joe LeMonnier; 9: Cynthia Watada, map: Joe LeMonnier; 18: Deborah Crowle; 24: Phil Wilson; 26: Phil Wilson; 29: top: Cynthia Watada; bottom: Argosy Publishing; 32: Deborah Crowle; 33: Deborah Crowle; 44: Neil Stewart; 53: Joe LeMonnier; 54: Tad Majewski; 61: Dave Mazierski; 63: David Wysotski; 65: Dave Mazierski; 75: Phil Wilson; 78: Joe LeMonnier; 92: Joe LeMonnier; 96: Dave Mazierski; 102: Joe LeMonnier; 105: Deborah Crowle; 107: Joe LeMonnier; 134–135: Dave Whamond; 138: Ralph Voltz; 140: Deborah Crowle; 141: Charlene Chua; 143: Deborah Crowle; 145: Cynthia Watada; 149: Dave Whamond; 151: Theresa Sakno; 152: Phil Wilson; 157: Ralph Voltz; 177: Theresa Sakno; 182: Dave Whamond; 193: Dave Mazierski; 201: Joe LeMonnier; 225: Deborah Crowle; 226: Deborah Crowle; 230: Cynthia Watada; 233: Dave Whamond; 234: Deborah Crowle; 235: Deborah Crowle; 245: Deborah Crowle; 263: Deborah Crowle; 266–267: Argosy Publishing; 272: Steve McEntee; 273: Argosy Publishing; 275: Argosy Publishing; 276: Argosy Publishing; 278: Argosy Publishing; 279: Argosy Publishing; 281: Steve McEntee; 282: Deborah Crowle; 284: Argosy Publishing; 285: Argosy Publishing; 287: Argosy Publishing; 288: Steve McEntee; 292-293: Argosy Publishing; 297: Dave Whamond; 298: Argosy Publishing; 300: Argosy Publishing; 302: Argosy Publishing; 305: Argosy Publishing; 307: Argosy Publishing; 311: Dave Whamond; 312: Argosy Publishing; 315: Argosy Publishing; 316: Argosy Publishing; 319: Argosy Publishing; 323: Argosy Publishing; 335: Argosy Publishing; 344: Dave Whamond; 345: Argosy Publishing; 348: Theresa Sakno; 352: Cynthia Watada; 356: Argosy Publishing; 357: Argosy Publishing; 367: Argosy Publishing; 370: Argosy Publishing; 393: Argosy Publishing; 398-399: James Yamasaki; 402: Ralph Voltz; 406: Theresa Sakno; 408: Theresa Sakno; 411: Deborah Crowle; 413: Deborah Crowle; 414: Deborah Crowle; 415: Theresa Sakno; 420: Theresa Sakno; 422: Cynthia Watada; 426: Cynthia Watada; 430: Theresa Sakno; 431: Argosy Publishing; 444: Neil Stewart; 451: Ralph Voltz; 452: Deborah Crowle; 453: Ralph Voltz; 455: Neil Stewart; 457: Ralph Voltz; 460: Neil Stewart; 464: top: Deborah Crowle; bottom: Rob Schuster; 469: Deborah Crowle; 471: Dave Whamond; 477: Deborah Crowle; 488: Deborah Crowle; 489: Dave Whamond; 492: Ralph Voltz; 499: Argosy Publishing; 503: Deborah Crowle; 507: Deborah Crowle; 512: Joe LeMonnier; 513: Deborah Crowle; 527: Deborah Crowle; 542: Dave Whamond; 551: Dave Whamond; 570: Argosy Publishing; 571: Argosy Publishing

Periodic Table of the Elements

Legend:

Atomic Number — Symbol — Name — Atomic Mass
- 22
- Ti
- Titanium
- 47.9
- 4+ 3+ ← Ion charge(s)

- metal
- metalloid
- non-metal
- O natural
- Db synthetic

Based on mass of C-12 at 12.00.

Any value in parentheses is the mass of the most stable or best known isotope for elements that do not occur naturally.

* Temporary names

Main groups

Group	Element	At. No.	Symbol	Name	Atomic Mass	Ion charge(s)
1		1	H	Hydrogen	1.0	1+
1		3	Li	Lithium	6.9	1+
1		11	Na	Sodium	23.0	1+
1		19	K	Potassium	39.1	1+
1		37	Rb	Rubidium	85.5	1+
1		55	Cs	Cesium	132.9	1+
1		87	Fr	Francium	(223)	1+
2		4	Be	Beryllium	9.0	2+
2		12	Mg	Magnesium	24.3	2+
2		20	Ca	Calcium	40.1	2+
2		38	Sr	Strontium	87.6	2+
2		56	Ba	Barium	137.3	2+
2		88	Ra	Radium	(226)	2+
3		21	Sc	Scandium	45.0	3+
3		39	Y	Yttrium	88.9	3+
3		57	La	Lanthanum	138.9	3+
3		89	Ac	Actinium	(227)	3+
4		22	Ti	Titanium	47.9	4+ 3+
4		40	Zr	Zirconium	91.2	4+
4		72	Hf	Hafnium	178.5	4+
4		104	Rf	Rutherfordium	(261)	
5		23	V	Vanadium	50.9	4+ 5+
5		41	Nb	Niobium	92.9	3+ 5+
5		73	Ta	Tantalum	180.9	5+
5		105	Db	Dubnium	(262)	
6		24	Cr	Chromium	52.0	2+ 3+ 6+
6		42	Mo	Molybdenum	96.0	6+
6		74	W	Tungsten	183.8	6+
6		106	Sg	Seaborgium	(263)	
7		25	Mn	Manganese	54.9	2+ 3+ 4+ 7+
7		43	Tc	Technetium	(98)	7+
7		75	Re	Rhenium	186.2	4+ 7+
7		107	Bh	Bohrium	(262)	
8		26	Fe	Iron	55.8	2+ 3+
8		44	Ru	Ruthenium	101.1	3+ 4+
8		76	Os	Osmium	190.2	3+ 4+
8		108	Hs	Hassium	(265)	
9		27	Co	Cobalt	58.9	2+ 3+
9		45	Rh	Rhodium	102.9	3+
9		77	Ir	Iridium	192.2	3+ 4+
9		109	Mt	Meitnerium	(266)	
10		28	Ni	Nickel	58.7	2+ 3+
10		46	Pd	Palladium	106.4	2+ 4+
10		78	Pt	Platinum	195.1	2+ 4+
10		110	Ds	Darmstadtium	(281)	
11		29	Cu	Copper	63.5	1+ 2+
11		47	Ag	Silver	107.9	1+
11		79	Au	Gold	197.0	1+ 3+
11		111	Rg	Roentgenium	(272)	
12		30	Zn	Zinc	65.4	2+
12		48	Cd	Cadmium	112.4	2+
12		80	Hg	Mercury	200.6	1+ 2+
12		112	Uub*	Ununbium	(285)	
13		5	B	Boron	10.8	3+
13		13	Al	Aluminum	27.0	3+
13		31	Ga	Gallium	69.7	3+
13		49	In	Indium	114.8	3+
13		81	Tl	Thallium	204.4	1+ 3+
13		113	Uut*	Ununtrium	(284)	
14		6	C	Carbon	12.0	
14		14	Si	Silicon	28.1	4+
14		32	Ge	Germanium	72.6	4+
14		50	Sn	Tin	118.7	2+ 4+
14		82	Pb	Lead	207.2	2+ 4+
14		114	Uuq*	Ununquadium	(289)	
15		7	N	Nitrogen	14.0	3-
15		15	P	Phosphorus	31.0	3-
15		33	As	Arsenic	74.9	3-
15		51	Sb	Antimony	121.8	3+ 5+
15		83	Bi	Bismuth	209.0	3+ 5+
15		115	Uup*	Ununpentium	(288)	
16		8	O	Oxygen	16.0	2-
16		16	S	Sulfur	32.1	2-
16		34	Se	Selenium	79.0	2-
16		52	Te	Tellurium	127.6	2-
16		84	Po	Polonium	(209)	2+ 4+
16		116	Uuh*	Ununhexium	(292)	
17		9	F	Fluorine	19.0	1-
17		17	Cl	Chlorine	35.5	1-
17		35	Br	Bromine	79.9	1-
17		53	I	Iodine	126.9	1-
17		85	At	Astatine	(210)	1-
18		2	He	Helium	4.0	0
18		10	Ne	Neon	20.2	0
18		18	Ar	Argon	39.9	0
18		36	Kr	Krypton	83.8	0
18		54	Xe	Xenon	131.3	0
18		86	Rn	Radon	(222)	0
18		118	Uuo*	Ununoctium	(294)	

Lanthanides

At. No.	Symbol	Name	Atomic Mass	Ion charge(s)
58	Ce	Cerium	140.1	3+ 4+
59	Pr	Praseodymium	140.9	3+ 4+
60	Nd	Neodymium	144.2	3+
61	Pm	Promethium	(145)	3+
62	Sm	Samarium	150.4	3+
63	Eu	Europium	152.0	2+ 3+
64	Gd	Gadolinium	157.3	3+
65	Tb	Terbium	158.9	3+ 4+
66	Dy	Dysprosium	162.5	3+
67	Ho	Holmium	164.9	3+
68	Er	Erbium	167.3	3+
69	Tm	Thulium	168.9	2+ 3+
70	Yb	Ytterbium	173.0	2+ 3+
71	Lu	Lutetium	175.0	3+

Actinides

At. No.	Symbol	Name	Atomic Mass	Ion charge(s)
90	Th	Thorium	232.0	4+
91	Pa	Protactinium	231.0	5+ 4+
92	U	Uranium	238.0	6+ 4+ 5+
93	Np	Neptunium	(237)	5+ 3+ 4+ 6+
94	Pu	Plutonium	(244)	4+ 6+ 3+ 5+
95	Am	Americium	(243)	3+ 4+ 5+ 6+
96	Cm	Curium	(247)	3+
97	Bk	Berkelium	(247)	3+ 4+
98	Cf	Californium	(251)	3+
99	Es	Einsteinium	(252)	3+
100	Fm	Fermium	(257)	3+
101	Md	Mendelevium	(258)	2+ 3+
102	No	Nobelium	(259)	2+ 3+
103	Lr	Lawrencium	(262)	3+